REA's Test Prep Books Are The Best!

(a sample of the <u>hundreds of letters</u> REA receives each year)

" This book is a really good review and gives you quality questions similar to the AP exam. I got a 5 on the AP U.S. History exam. "
Student, New Orleans, LA

" This is absolutely the best test prep for AP U.S. History! Having read only four chapters of the comprehensive review, I took the test and scored a 4....I believe that if I had not picked up this book I would have scored a 2 or a 3. "
Student, San Andreas, CA

" Your book was such a better value and was so much more complete than anything your competition has produced—and I have them all! "
Teacher, Virginia Beach, VA

" Compared to the other books that my fellow students had, your book was the most helpful in helping me get a great score. "
Student, North Hollywood, CA

" Your book was responsible for my success on the exam, which helped me get into the college of my choice... I will look for REA the next time I need help. "
Student, Chesterfield, MO

" Just a short note to say thanks for the great support your book gave me in helping me pass the test... I'm on my way to a B.S. degree because of you! "
Student, Orlando, FL

(more on next page)

D1290996

(continued from front page)

" I just wanted to thank you for helping me get a great score
on the AP U.S. History exam… Thank you for making great test preps! "
Student, Los Angeles, CA

" Your *Fundamentals of Engineering Exam* book was the absolute best
preparation I could have had for the exam, and it is one of the major
reasons I did so well and passed the FE on my first try. "
Student, Sweetwater, TN

" I used your book to prepare for the test and found that the advice and the
sample tests were highly relevant… Without using any other material, I earned
very high scores and will be going to the graduate school of my choice. "
Student, New Orleans, LA

" What I found in your book was a wealth of information sufficient to shore up
my basic skills in math and verbal… The practice tests were challenging and
the answer explanations most helpful. It certainly is
the *Best Test Prep for the GRE!* "
Student, Pullman, WA

" I really appreciate the help from your excellent book. Please keep up
the great work. "
Student, Albuquerque, NM

" I am writing to thank you for your test preparation… your book helped me
immeasurably and I have nothing but praise for your *GRE* preparation."
Student, Benton Harbor, MI

AP WORLD HISTORY

2nd Edition

TestWare® Edition

Deborah Vess, Ph.D.
Professor of History
and Interdisciplinary Studies
Department of History,
Geography, and Philosophy
Georgia College and State University
Milledgeville, Georgia

Practice Exams by
Lynn Marlowe, M.A.
Lecturer
Los Angeles City College
Los Angeles, California

Research & Education Association
Visit our website at: www.rea.com

Research & Education Association
61 Ethel Road West
Piscataway, New Jersey 08854
E-mail: info@rea.com

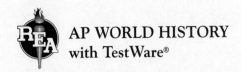 AP WORLD HISTORY
with TestWare®

Printed in the United States of America

Library of Congress Control Number 2009937023

ISBN-13: 978-0-7386-0791-7
ISBN-10: 0-7386-0791-6

J09-0101

CONTENTS

UNIT IV: ASIA AND ITS INTERACTIONS WITH EUROPE FROM 1500 TO WORLD WAR I 307

UNIT V: EARLY MODERN EUROPE 351

ABOUT OUR AUTHOR

Deborah Vess, Ph.D., is Professor of History and Interdisciplinary Studies at Georgia College & State University in Milledgeville, Georgia. She holds a Ph.D. in history from the University of North Texas, with areas of expertise in integrative studies, Church history, medieval monasticism, and gender issues. She co-founded and edited *Magistra: a Journal of Women's Spirituality*, served as Joint Editor for *Vox benedictina: A journal of women's and monastic studies*, and as Internet Review Editor for *The History Computer Review*. Dr. Vess has been active in promoting the use of technology in education, and has received an international exemplary course award from WEBCT for an online U.S. history core course now used in the University System of Georgia.

In 1996, the University System of Georgia Board of Regents named Dr. Vess a Distinguished Professor of Teaching and Learning. In 2001, she received the University System's Board of Regents Research in Undergraduate Education Award. In addition to numerous local awards, she has twice received an Excellence in Teaching Award from the National Institute of Staff and Organizational Development. In 1999, she was named a Carnegie Scholar with the Carnegie Foundation for the Advancement of Teaching. She has published articles in *Inventio, The History Teacher, Teaching History, The American Benedictine Review, Proteus, Mystics Quarterly, Word and Spirit*, and other publications.

ABOUT RESEARCH & EDUCATION ASSOCIATION

Founded in 1959, Research & Education Association is dedicated to publishing the finest and most effective educational materials—including software, study guides, and test preps—for students in middle school, high school, college, graduate school, and beyond. Today, REA's wide-ranging catalog is a leading resource for teachers, students, and professionals. We invite you to visit us at *www.rea.com* to find out how "REA is making the world smarter."

ACKNOWLEDGMENTS

In addition to our author, we would like to thank Larry B. Kling, Vice President, Editorial, for supervising development; Pam Weston, Vice President, Publishing; John Paul Cording, Vice President, Technology, for co-ordinating the design and development of REA's TEST*ware*® software; Diane Goldschmidt, Senior Editor, for coordinating revisions; Heena Patel and Michelle Boykins-Smith, Technology Project Managers, for their testing efforts; Jeff LoBalbo, Senior Graphic Artist, for his graphic arts contributions; Christine Saul, Senior Graphic Artist, for designing our cover; and Aquent Publishing Services for typesetting this edition.

We would also like to thank Cathy G. Locks, former graduate assistant at Georgia College & State University and now an instructional technologist at Wesleyan College, for her help in drafting sections of the 19th- and 20th-century materials.

AP WORLD HISTORY
Independent Study Schedule

The following study schedule allows for thorough preparation for the AP World History Examination. Although it is designed for six weeks, it can be condensed into a three-week course by collapsing each two-week period into a single week. Be sure to set aside at least two hours each day to study. Bear in mind that the more time you spend studying, the more prepared and relaxed you will feel on the day of the exam.

Week	Activity
1	Read and study the Introduction section of this book, which will introduce you to the AP World History Examination. Take TEST*ware*® Practice Test 1 to determine your strengths and weaknesses. You can then determine the areas in which you need to strengthen your skills. Also carefully read and study Unit I, The Ancient Near East and Far East. Study the key terms included in the chapters and answer the review questions at the end of each chapter.
2	Carefully read and study Unit II, The Classical Civilizations of Greece and Rome, and Unit III, The World from 500–1500 C.E., of this book. Familiarize yourself with the key terms at the beginning of each chapter and answer the review questions at the end of each chapter.
3	Carefully read and study Unit IV, Asia and its Interactions with Europe from 1500 to World War I, and Unit V, Early Modern Europe, of this book. Familiarize yourself with the key terms at the beginning of each chapter and answer the review questions at the end of each chapter, referring back to the appropriate section of the World History review.
4	Read and study Unit VI, Europe and the Americas in the Eighteenth and Nineteenth Centuries, and Unit VII, A "Short Century"? The World from World War I through the Collapse of the Soviet Union in 1991. Pay attention to the key terms and review questions within each chapter.

(Continued)

5	Take TEST*ware®* Practice Test 2 and carefully review all incorrect answer explanations. If there are any types of questions or particular subjects that seem difficult to you, review those subjects by referring back to the appropriate section of the World History Course Review.
6	For additional practice you may retake Practice Tests 1 and 2 either in printed form, or using our TEST*ware®*. This will help strengthen the areas where your performance is still lagging and build your overall confidence.

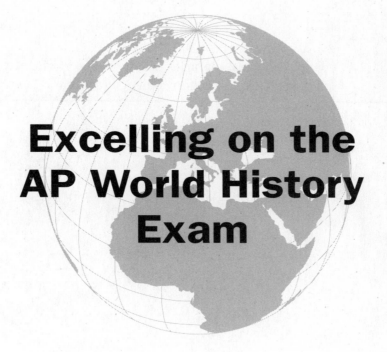

Excelling on the
AP World History
Exam

EXCELLING ON THE AP WORLD HISTORY EXAM

ABOUT THIS BOOK & TEST*ware*®

Featuring a thorough, course-focused review and two full-length practice tests, this book, along with REA's exclusive TEST*ware*® software, provides an accurate and complete representation of the Advanced Placement Examination in World History. Our practice tests are based on the format of the most recently administered AP World History exam. Each model exam lasts three hours (including a 10-minute reading period) and includes every type of question that you can expect to encounter on the real test. Following each of our practice tests is an answer key, complete with detailed explanations designed to clarify the material for you.

The practice tests in this book and software package are included in two formats: in printed form in this book and in TEST*ware*® format on the enclosed CD. **We recommend that you begin your preparation by first taking the practice exams on your computer.** The software provides timed conditions, and instantaneous, accurate scoring that makes it easier to pinpoint your strengths and weaknesses.

By using the course review, completing both practice tests, and studying the explanations that follow, you will pinpoint your strengths and weaknesses and, above all, put yourself in the best possible position to do well on the actual test.

ABOUT THE EXAM

The AP World History exam is offered each May at participating schools and multi-school centers throughout the world.

The Advanced Placement Program is designed to allow high school students to pursue college-level studies while attending high school. The participating colleges, in turn, grant credit and/or advanced placement to students who do well on the examinations.

The AP World History course is designed to be the equivalent of a college introductory World History course, often taken by History majors in their first year of college.

AP WORLD HISTORY EXAM FORMAT AND CONTENT

The AP World History exam is approximately three hours and five minutes long. Each section of the exam is completed separately and each counts for half of the student's score.

The exam is divided into two sections:

Section I: The multiple-choice section of the exam is designed to measure the student's knowledge of World History from the Foundations period (8000 B.C.E. to 600 C.E.) to the present. The approximate breakdown of topics is as follows:

Chronological period	Approximate percentage
Foundations	19–20%
600 C.E.–1450	22%
1450–1750	19–20%
1750–1914	19–20%
1914–the present	19–20%

The section contains 70 questions to be answered in 55 minutes. Each question has five possible answer choices. Each correct answer is worth one point, and 1/4 point is deducted for each incorrect answer.

Section II: This part of the exam is devoted to writing three essays in the allotted 130 minutes. The first question will be a document-based question, the second question will ask the test-taker to write a change-over-time essay, and the third question requires the writing of a comparative essay. All three questions are required to be answered and are weighted equally.

For more information about what to include on the essays, how to manage the time allotted, and how they are scored, please see the AP World History outline provided by the College Board at *www.collegeboard.com*.

You may find the AP World History Exam considerably more difficult than many classroom exams. In order to measure the full range of your ability in World History, the AP exams are designed to produce average scores of approximately 50% of the maximum possible score for the multiple-choice and essay sections. Therefore, you should not expect to attain a perfect or even near-perfect score.

HOW TO USE THIS BOOK

What do I study first?

Read over the course review and the suggestions for test taking. Next, take the first practice test to pinpoint your area(s) of weakness, and then go back and focus your study on those specific problems. Studying the reviews thoroughly will reinforce the basic skills you will need to do well on the exam. Make sure to take the two practice tests to become familiar with the format and procedures involved with taking the actual exam.

To best utilize your study time, follow our Independent Study Schedule, which you will find in the front of this book. The schedule is based on a six-week program, but if necessary it can be condensed to three weeks by combining each two-week program into one week.

SSD accommodations for students with disabilities

Many students qualify for extra time to take the AP exams and our TEST*ware*® can be adapted to accommodate your time extension. This allows you to practice under the same extended time accommodations that you will receive on the actual test day. To customize your TEST*ware*® to suit the most common extensions, visit our Website at *http://www.rea.com/ssd*.

When should I start studying?

It is never too early to start studying for the AP World History Exam. The earlier you begin, the more time you will have to sharpen your skills. Do not procrastinate! Cramming is *not* an effective way to study, since it does not allow you the time needed to learn the test material. The sooner you learn the format of the exam, the more time you will have to familiarize yourself with it.

ABOUT OUR REVIEW SECTION

This book contains an extensive AP World History Course Review that can be used as both a primer and a quick reference as you assess your performance on REA's practice exams. Our course review is designed to complement your AP World History textbook and enhance your classroom discussions. By studying our review along with your text, you will be well prepared for the exam.

SCORING REA's PRACTICE EXAMS

Scoring the Multiple-Choice Sections

For each multiple-choice section, use this formula to calculate your raw score:

$$\underline{\hspace{3cm}} - (\underline{\hspace{3cm}} \times 1/4) = \underline{\hspace{3cm}}$$

Number Correct	Number Wrong	Multiple-Choice
(out of 70)		Score (weighted)

Scoring the Free-Response Sections

For the free-response section, use this formula to calculate your raw score:

Question 1 $\underline{\hspace{3cm}} \times 1\frac{1}{2} = \underline{\hspace{3cm}}$
(out of 10)　　　　　　(weighted)

Question 2 $\underline{\hspace{3cm}} \times 1\frac{1}{2} = \underline{\hspace{3cm}}$
(out of 10)　　　　　　(weighted)

Question 3 $\underline{\hspace{3cm}} \times 1\frac{1}{2} = \underline{\hspace{3cm}}$
(out of 10)　　　　　　(weighted)

$$\underline{\hspace{2cm}} + \underline{\hspace{2cm}} + \underline{\hspace{2cm}} = \underline{\hspace{2cm}}$$

Question 1	Question 2	Question 3	Free-Response
(weighted)	(weighted)	(weighted)	Score (weighted)

The Composite Score

To obtain your composite score for each exam, use the following method.

$$\underline{\hspace{3cm}} + \underline{\hspace{3cm}} = \underline{\hspace{3cm}}$$

Multiple-Choice	Free-Response	Composite Score
Weighted Score	Weighted Score	

Use the following chart to approximate your AP score for each exam:

AP Grade Conversion Chart

*Final Score Range	AP Grade
120–160	5
94–119	4
68–93	3
38–67	2
0–37	1

*Candidates' scores are weighted by a formula determined in advance each year by the Development Committee.

SCORING THE OFFICIAL EXAMS

The College Board creates a formula (which changes slightly every year) to convert raw scores into composite scores grouped into broad AP grade categories. The weights for the multiple-choice sections are determined by the Chief Reader, who uses a process called *equating*. This process compares the current year's exam performance on selected multiple-choice questions to that of a previous year, establishing a level of achievement for the current year's group and a degree of difficulty for the current exam. This data is combined with historical trends and the reader's professional evaluation to determine the weights and tables.

The AP free-response section is graded by teacher volunteers, grouped at scoring tables, and led by a chief faculty consultant. The consultant sets the grading scale that translates the raw score into the composite score. Past grading illustrations are available to teachers from the College Board, and may be ordered using the contact information given on page xxvi. These actual examples of student responses and a grade analysis can be of great assistance to both the student and the teacher as a learning or review tool.

When will I know my score?

In July, a grade report will be sent to you, your high school, and the college you chose to notify. The report will include scores for all the AP exams you have taken up to that point.

Your grade will be used by your college of choice to determine placement in its World History program. This grade will vary in significance from college to college, and is used with other academic information to determine placement. Normally, colleges participating in the Advanced Placement Program will recognize grades of 3 or better. Contact your college admissions office for more information regarding its use of AP grades.

STUDYING FOR YOUR EXAM

It is very important for you to choose the time and place for studying that works best for you. Some students may set aside a certain number of hours every morning, while others may choose to study at night before going to sleep. Other students may study during the day, while waiting in line, or even while eating lunch. Only you can determine when and where your study time will be most effective. Be consistent and use your time wisely. Work out a study routine and stick to it.

When you take the practice tests, create an environment as much like the actual testing environment as possible. Turn your television and radio off, and sit down at a quiet table free from distraction. Make sure to time yourself, breaking the test down by section.

As you complete each practice test, score your test and thoroughly review the explanations to the questions you answered incorrectly; however, do not review too much at one time. Concentrate on one problem area at a time by reviewing the question and explanation, and by studying our review until you are confident that you completely understand the material.

Keep track of your scores and mark them on the Scoring Worksheet. By doing so, you will be able to gauge your progress and discover general weaknesses in particular sections. You should carefully study the reviews that cover areas with which you have difficulty, as this will build your skills in those areas.

TEST-TAKING TIPS

Although you may not be familiar with standardized tests such as the AP World History exam, there are many ways to acquaint yourself with this type of examination and help alleviate any test-taking anxieties. Listed below are ways to help you become accustomed to the AP exams, some of which may be applied to other standardized tests as well.

Become comfortable with the format of the exam. Stay calm and pace yourself. After simulating the test a couple of times, you will boost your chances of doing well and you will be able to sit down for the actual exam with more confidence.

Read all of the possible answers. Just because you think you have found the correct response, do not automatically assume that it is the best answer. Read through each choice to be sure that you are not making a mistake by jumping to conclusions.

Use the process of elimination. Go through each answer to a question and eliminate as many of the answer choices as possible. By eliminating just two answer choices, you give yourself a better chance of getting the item correct, since there will only be three choices left from which to make your guess.

Work quickly and steadily. You will have only 55 minutes to work on 70 questions in the multiple-choice section, so work quickly and steadily to avoid focusing on any one question too long. Taking the practice tests in this book will help you learn to budget your time.

Beware of test vocabulary. For example, words like *generally, usually, sometimes, seldom, rarely,* and *often* indicate there may be exceptions to your answer.

Learn the directions and format for each section of the test. Familiarizing yourself with the directions and format of the exam will save you valuable time on the day of the actual test.

THE DAY OF THE EXAM

Before the exam

On the day of the test, you should wake up early (preferably after a good night's rest) and have a good breakfast. Make sure to dress comfortably, so that you are not distracted by being too hot or too cold while taking the test. Also plan to arrive at the test center early. This will allow you to collect your thoughts and relax before the test, and will also spare you the anxiety that comes with being late.

Before you leave for the test center, make sure that you have your admission form, social security number, and another form of identification, which must contain a recent photograph, your name, and signature (i.e., driver's license, student identification card, or current alien registration card). You will not be allowed to take the test if you do not have proper identification. You will also need to bring your school code. Also, bring several sharpened No. 2 pencils with erasers for the multiple-choice questions and black or blue pens for the free-response questions.

You may wear a watch, but only one without a beep or alarm. No dictionaries, textbooks, notebooks, compasses, correction fluid, highlighters, rulers, computers, cell phones, beepers, PDAs, scratch paper, listening and recording devices, briefcases, or packages will be permitted, and drinking, smoking, and eating are prohibited while taking the test.

During the exam

Once you enter the test center, follow all of the rules and instructions given by the test supervisor. If you do not, you risk being dismissed from the test and having your scores canceled.

After the exam

You may immediately register when taking the exam to have your score sent to the college of your choice. You may also wait and later request to have your AP score reported to the college of your choice.

CONTACTING THE AP PROGRAM

For registration bulletins or more information about the AP World History exam, contact:

AP Services
Educational Testing Service
P.O. Box 6671
Princeton, NJ 08541-6671
Phone: (609) 771-7300 or (888) 225-5427
E-mail: apexams@ets.org
Website: www.collegeboard.com

UNIT I

The Ancient Near East
and Far East

Chapter 1

THE PREHISTORIC ERA

KEY TERMS

Prehistoric

Historic

Neanderthal

Shanidar Cave

Lascaux

Paleolithic Era

Neolithic Era

Agriculture

Civilization

Homo habilis

Homo erectus

Homo sapiens neanderthalensis

Homo sapiens sapiens

Cro-Magnon

Sumer

Ur

Uruk

Gilgamesh

Cuneiform

Rock of Behistun

Ziggurats

Eddubas

Akkad

Sargon I

Babylon

Amorites

The Hanging Gardens of Babylon

Nebuchadrezzar

The Code of Hammurabi

Zoroaster

Zarathustra

Zend Avesta

Ahura Mazda

Ahriman

Darius

Satraps

Cyrus the Great

Medes

Persepolis and Susa

Royal Road

Hattusas

Hittites

Scientists currently estimate that the universe is roughly 13.6 billion years old. The term "prehistoric" refers to the period before approximately 3,000 B.C.E., when written records first appeared in Mesopotamia. The historic era represents a small fraction of the human past, from about 3,000 B.C.E. to the present time. The terms "prehistoric" and "historic" do not so much describe the sort of cultures that existed as they describe the ways that modern historians study them. The historical method emphasizes the use of written primary sources or firsthand accounts of the past. Traditionally, the written record has been considered the most important kind of primary source, whereas in the prehistoric periods, scholars must rely on fossil evidence and artifacts, or objects actually made by human hands. The term "prehistoric," then, simply refers to the vast period before there were written records. The following timeline outlines the major events of the prehistoric era that are important for understanding the human past.

◄—— TIMELINE: COMPARATIVE CHRONOLOGY ——►

2,500,000 B.P. (the abbreviation means "before the present.")	The Paleolithic Era or Old Stone Age
	The rise of the hominids occurs during this period, including *australopithicene, homo habilis, homo erectus*. Stone is the primary medium out of which hominids from *homo habilis* on make tools.
100,000 B.P.	*Homo erectus* migrates from Africa to the Middle East
	Homo erectus has the capacity to make and control fire, which many believe enabled it to leave Africa. By 25,000 years ago, humans had reached the east from Africa.
85,000 years B.P.	Neanderthal (*homo sapiens neanderthalensis*) flourishes
35,000 years B.P.	Cro-Magnon (*homo sapiens sapiens*) first appears in Europe
10,000 B.C.E. (The abbreviation means before the common era.)	The beginning of the Neolithic Era, or New Stone Age
	During the Neolithic era, urban centers develop, such as Jericho and Catul Huyuk. Stone is still the primary medium for making tools and building, but tool making is more sophisticated
8,000 B.C.E.	Agriculture first appears in the Middle East in Jericho
	Agriculture gradually spreads throughout the world, reaching the Americas last.
3,000 B.C.E.	Writing first appears; the beginning of the historic era.
	The earliest writing, cuneiform, appears in Mesopotamia

THE PALEOLITHIC ERA

Human cultures first appeared in the **Paleolithic era**, which means "Old Stone Age." Scholars often characterize the early periods of the human past by the materials used, and stone was the primary medium of tool making in the Paleolithic era. A variety of hominids lived during this vast period of time. Contrary to popular belief, hominids, or early humans, did not live at the same time as dinosaurs, which had become extinct long before the evolution of hominids began. Hominids are a subclass of the primate order, and are characterized by flattened nails and stereoscopic vision. Due to the increased development of their eyes, hominids have smaller noses and a diminished sense of smell as compared to other primates and, consequently, developed a longer, flatter face. Modern humans are classified as hominids of the primate order and the hominid cultures of the prehistoric era were the predecessors of modern human cultures.

"LUCY" AND AUSTRALOPITHECENE

Anthropologists tell us that the single most important event in human history occurred during the prehistoric era, when hominids first learned to walk upright rather than on all fours. The anthropologist Donald Johansson believes that the first hominids to walk upright are represented by the famous fossil skeleton "Lucy," a diminutive australopithecene female about four-and-one-half feet tall. *Australopithecenes* had pelvises adapted to upright walking at least part of the time. Lucy is also famous because she is the only hominid whose remains have been found in such a complete state. By contrast, the first example discovered of australopithicene was the Taung baby, whose skull only was found in South Africa in 1924. Johansson believes that australopithecene is the "missing link" between humans and the great apes. For Johansson, Lucy is the point at which these two lines diverged, her line leading to modern humans, the other to the modern great apes.

Other Hominids

The oldest hominids are found in Africa in the Olduvai Gorge, located on the east coast of Africa in modern Tanzania. *Homo habilis*, or "human with ability," left the most primitive tools on the lowest level of the Gorge. Their crude hand tools, primarily made by chipping flakes off the sides of stones, are known as the Olduwan Industry. *Homo erectus*, or upright human, was first discovered in Trinil, Java, in 1891. Another famous discovery was the Peking man, which was a fragment of a homo erectus cranium found in China in 1929. Based on the charred remains of wood and other materials found at campsites, scientists know that *H. erectus* had the ability to control fire. Many anthropologists speculate that this capacity was what allowed *H. erectus* to leave the continent of Africa and migrate to other parts of the world.

The tools of erectus are called the Acheulian industry, and they have been found close to the charred remains of *H. habilis* campsites, suggesting that these two hominids may have lived side-by-side.

Neanderthal

Homo sapiens, or "knowing human," was another step along the evolutionary path for early humans. Remains of a *Homo sapiens* creature known as **Neanderthal** were first uncovered in 1856 in the Neander Valley, Dusseldorf, Germany. The suffix "thal" means valley. Remains of Neanderthal have also been found in France, Italy, Belgium, Greece, Czechoslovakia, northern Africa, and the Middle East.

Neanderthal lived in glacial periods 85,000 to 35,000 years ago and was adapted to cold weather by its short, stout, muscular body and large nose. The old view of Neanderthal as incompletely erect and walking with bent knees was based on a misconception. The original find was of an arthritic individual who would have indeed walked more like an ape than like a modern human. Neanderthal had a much larger brain than modern humans and its stout bones were adapted for heavy lifting. Neanderthal was a cave dweller who lived in a hunting and gathering culture in small bands of ten to fifteen people. He used tools for hunting.

The Shanidar cave in the Zagros Mountains of modern Iraq is the site of the most famous Neanderthal find. The site is 60,000 years old and contains a gravesite of an individual in a fetal position. Pollen grains, some from plants still used in herbal medicine today, were scattered around the grave in an orderly pattern, suggesting a burial rite and possible belief in an afterlife. The grave was in the cave where the band lived suggesting that they wanted to keep the dead with them and had concern for them. The individual was seriously injured and his injuries had occurred at least twenty years before his death; he was missing part of his arm and half of his face was smashed. Such an individual would have been incapable of surviving on his own, suggesting communal concern for his welfare. This Neanderthal site is the first evidence of a cohesive, caring human community.

Neanderthal, or *Homo sapiens neanderthalensis,* became extinct around 35,000 years B.C.E. Scholars speculate that disease or lack of adaptation to warmer climates might account for the extinction, which occurred roughly at the end of the last great ice age when the glaciers were starting to retreat. Another theory is that Neanderthal was annihilated by newer and more superior species, **Cro-Magnon (*Homo sapiens sapiens*)**, that was beginning to flourish in Europe about this time. Some anthropologists speculate that Neanderthal is not really extinct, as it might have been genetically absorbed into the new group. According to this line of reasoning, Neanderthal was a subspecies of modern humans. Some scholars suggest northern European stock is the product of genetic intermingling of Cro-Magnon and Neanderthal peoples, but others argue that Neanderthal represents a separate hominid line from that of modern humans and that it was too different from Cro-Magnon to have genetically intermingled.

Cro-Magnons

Cro-Magnons were highly skilled at hunting, and there are many sites where thousands of animal carcasses have been discovered. In Torralba, Spain, Cro-Magnon herded animals together, chased them off cliffs, and harvested their flesh. Cro-Magnon humans (*Homo sapiens sapiens*) were first discovered in Europe in 1868 in the Cro-Magnon cave; their remains have also been uncovered in Italy and Great Britain. Remains have been found dating to 35,000–10,000 yrs. ago. Cro-Magnon had a smaller brain than Neanderthal, but a more modern appearance. Cro-Magnon was an expert at making tools and also was the first artist in human history, embellishing tools and the walls of caves with beautiful art. Cro-Magnon tools are known as Aurignacian tools and include such beautiful and functional items as the Laurel leaf flint knife.

Paleolithic Cave Art

Cro-Magnon art reflects the emphasis of early humans on the hunt. One of the most famous examples is the cave of **Lascaux** in France, accidentally discovered by four boys in 1940 when their dog fell into a hole in the ground. The Cro-Magnon artists of Lascaux painted mainly large animals, such as reindeer and bison. Early humans derived their daily sustenance from the hunt, and there are many aspects of the cave art that suggest it had a magical, ritualistic function. The location of the art, for example, is puzzling. The cave of Lascaux is very long, deep, and narrow, and much of the art is painted in very hard to reach places. There are often several layers of paintings, one on top of another. This suggests the actual location of the cave was sacred, as artists tended to return there repeatedly. There are also nick marks on the walls, suggesting that early humans reenacted the hunt there. There are very few images of humans in these caves, and those that exist seem to have animal characteristics as well. In modern hunting and gathering cultures, the shaman is often an important figure. He intercedes with the spiritual world, and often wears a mask made to resemble an animal or pieces of clothing made from animal skins. Since Cro-Magnon believed that the images in these caves were magical, the presence of a shaman would help to ward off evil. These images indicate the close relationship between early humans and the natural world upon which they depended for their daily survival.

Paleolithic Venus Figurines

Other objects commonly found in Paleolithic caves are Venus figures, such as the Laussel Venus and the Venus of Willendorf. These figurines are feminine, and have enlarged body parts associated with fertility. There are no identifiable features on their faces, making them more general symbols of fertility rather than images of individual women. The Laussel Venus symbolizes the unity of the human world and the natural world. She holds what appears at first glance to be a horn. Animals with horns regenerate them periodically and so the horn is a symbol of rebirth or renewal. If so, the horn and her prominent childbearing features suggest fertility. Alternatively, it has been suggested that this object represents the moon; there are markings on it that represent the number of days in the cycles of the moon. The Venus simultaneously holds her stomach, suggesting that the cycles of human life are in harmony with those of the natural universal order. These "mother earth" goddesses represent the dependence of early humans on the earth. Fertility goddesses were very common in the ancient world, and scholars speculate that the earliest human cultures were female-centered. Since almost all ancient cultures had important fertility goddesses, some scholars have suggested there was a universal cult of the Mother Earth, though at present there is not sufficient evidence to support this claim.

Modern Hunters and Gatherers

There continue to be hunting and gathering cultures in the modern world that are similar to that of Cro-Magnon Paleolithic culture. These include the Guanches from Canary Islands, the Australian Aborigines, and the !Kung in Africa. The human race first evolved from hunting and gathering cultures, and some modern humans continue to live that way today.

Human Migration

A major theme of world history is migration. It has long been believed that humans migrated from Africa to the Middle East 100,000 years ago, to Australia by 50,000 years ago, and to the east by 25,000 years ago. This is called the "out of Africa" theory. They migrated 15,000 years ago to North America across the Bering Strait, a strip of land no longer in existence that connected Siberia with the Americas. Humans reached South America by 10,000 B.C.E. Recent finds in other parts of the world, such as China, Australia, and Germany, however are raising questions about the "out of Africa" thesis, as some recent hominid discoveries there appear to be as old as those found in Africa. However, genetic studies show greater diversity within African populations today than between those human populations outside of Africa. These studies support the African origin of human life.

THE NEOLITHIC ERA

The **Neolithic Revolution**, or **New Stone Age**, began somewhere around 10,000 B.C.E. and continued to 3,000 B.C.E. During the New Stone Age, humans developed more refined tools, but more importantly, they developed the beginnings of agriculture and urban centers. Organized cultivation of crops may have arisen by mistake when early humans noticed that dropped seeds resulted in plants. It is also likely that hunters and gatherers sometimes cultivated crops to a certain extent.

New Urban Centers

The development of organized agriculture along with the domestication of animals led to the development of urban centers; as some scholars have remarked, "without agriculture there is no culture." The development of agriculture created a stable supply of food and therefore more leisure time to produce art and other cultural items; the new food supply created a new need for containers to cook, preserve and transport the food. Many beautiful examples of Neolithic art are found on pottery. There were no permanent dwellings in Paleolithic hunting and gathering times, as hunters and gatherers of necessity were constantly on the move. Agriculture enabled humans to stay in one place, giving rise to civilization. The word "civilization" derives from the Latin word "civilis" meaning "political or civic." One of the most important Neolithic cities was Jericho in the Middle East, whose earliest remains date to 8,000 B.C.E. Agriculture first evolved in the Middle East and then spread to other parts of the world. Catul Hayuk, located in modern Turkey, is another famous site. Twelve crops were cultivated here, including nuts, fruits, and three kinds of wheat. Agriculture later arose in the Balkans in 6,500 B.C.E.; in Southeastern Asia rice was cultivated by 5,000 B.C.E.; around the Yellow and Wei Rivers, the centers of early Chinese civilizations, rice was first cultivated around 6,000 B.C.E.; and along the Indus River Valley in India, wheat and barley were cultivated around 6,000 B.C.E. In Mesoamerica, Native Americans developed agriculture between 7,000 and 5,000 B.C.E. Their primary crops were maize, a very hardy form of corn, and beans and squash. Along with agriculture came the domestication of animals, such as dogs.

In the new urban centers, a division of labor arose; some inhabitants performed cooking chores, others were farmers, others hunters, and so on. There was also an economic organization, which grew out of the need to conduct trade. The complexity of trade probably prompted the need for written records. Civilization created the need for more complex governments and written laws. Civilization prompted the development of morality, as family and marriage laws are often related to property concerns.

ANCIENT MESOPOTAMIA

Mesopotamia is known as "the cradle of world civilization." It is the earliest known civilization, and Mesopotamians produced the earliest written records, including the first unified code of law. Mesopotamians also invented the wheel, the calendar, and the clock. Mesopotamian writing is called cuneiform, a word which means "wedge shaped" writing. Cuneiform is written on clay tablets with wedge-shaped instruments called styluses.

Ancient Mesopotamia was located between the **Tigris** and the **Euphrates** rivers; in fact, the word "Mesopotamia" means "the land between two rivers." This region is now the nation of Iraq. The rivers provided an abundant source of water and created very fertile plains, ideal conditions for agriculture. The first settlements in Mesopotamia date back to 4000 B.C.E. Geography played an important role in the creation of the Mesopotamian worldview. The flooding of the Tigris and Euphrates rivers was unpredictable and disastrous; flooding often destroyed city-states in an instant. Many creation stories from the region, such as the *Epic of Gilgamesh*, describe a disastrous flood that wiped out the earth; these stories were likely based on actual events. The constant and unpredictable flooding partially accounts for the very grim view of life evident in the *Epic of Gilgamesh*, in which the first immortal man, Utnapishtim, tells the hero Gilgamesh that the god Enlil sent the flood because humans were too noisy and irritated the gods. When Utnapishtim survives, Enlil is enraged, and rewards him with immortality, a gift Utnapishtim assures Gilgamesh is no favor. Every day, he says, is like every other day, the days continuing on in dreary bleakness without end.

Another contributing factor to the overall pessimism of Mesopotamian culture was the competition for land and water resources. Due to the need for large amounts of land, there were fairly wide separations among settlements. Several independent city-states arose in southern Mesopotamia, such as **Uruk**, where the Sumerian King records the beginning of the reign of Gilgamesh in 2700 B.C.E. and **Ur**, the original home of Abraham, patriarch of the Hebrews and Arabs. Southern Mesopotamia was known as Sumer. Each of these city-states had its own government, customs and deities. Their common customs and culture are referred to as "Sumerian." Empires did not arise in Mesopotamia until Sargon the Great unified the region in the twenty-fourth century B.C.E. The competition for land and water rights led to almost continuous conflict between city-states. In fact, the earliest recorded treaty in world history resolved a conflict over irrigation rights between the Sumerian city-state of Lagash and its neighbors.

The geographical features of Mesopotamia contributed to the lack of stability, as there were no natural barriers to protect the city-states from outside invaders. Throughout Mesopotamian history, there was a constant stream of conquering peoples such as the **Assyrians** and **Amorites**, Combined with the continuous conflict between city-states, Mesopotamians never developed a continuous and long-lived empire. Rather, Mesopotamian history is one of constant invasion and conquest and is the story of successive cultures that borrowed from each other.

The importance of the rivers as well as the ideology of warfare can be seen in Mesopotamian mythology. According to the creation myth of the Mesopotamians, in the beginning Ocean and Chaos began to merge, but Chaos tried to make herself supreme. Marduk, the creator god, killed Chaos by splitting her in half, from which came the heavens and the earth. The tears that flowed down her face from the pain became the Tigris and the Euphrates rivers. Marduk then kneaded the wet earth and created humans. As we have seen, according to the *Epic of Gilgamesh*, eventually the gods grew weary of the noise made by the troublesome humans, and sent a flood to destroy them. The gods sent a heavenly bull to inflict revenge on Gilgamesh for his refusal to marry the goddess Ishtar, but it kills instead his friend Enkidu. On his deathbed, Enkidu had a vision of the underworld, and he told Gilgamesh that there the kings were servants of the gods, and all one can find there is dust and darkness. Enkidu tells Gilgamesh that the gods play with humans like puppets on strings, having a contest to see what misery they can inflict. From the creation myths to the collapse of the Assyrian empire in 612 B.C.E., the devastating flooding of the rivers and the bleak nature of brutal warfare colored Mesopotamian culture. Mesopotamians were not sure they could even turn to the gods for compassion; they were simply at the mercy of a brutal environment whose purpose and plan they did not know.

Although the Mesopotamians were pessimistic about the benevolence of the gods, they continued to worship them devoutly and perform sacrifices to them. In the *Epic of Gilgamesh*, the goddess Siduri tells Gilgamesh to "live for the moment," and to learn to enjoy every minute of life. The Mesopotamians were never sure of what the future held, but they tried to find happiness in the moment and protection by offering whatever sacrifices they could to the gods.

Every city-state had at its center and its highest point a steplike structure called a **ziggurat**, or temple. Religious ceremonies were performed here, but scribes also learned to read and write here in the eddubas or "tablet houses," so-called because Sumerians wrote on clay tablets. At the foot of the ziggurat, there was a marketplace. The king, who was also the chief priest, controlled this important religious and social center. Mesopotamian society was a theocracy, a system of government in which religion and politics were not separate. In Mesopotamia, the chief priest/king was considered to be semidivine. The fact that the ziggurat was the center of education, religion, government, and trade illustrates that the ancient world did not distinguish between history, mythology, religion, or other areas as separate endeavors or areas of knowledge.

The Rise of Empires in Mesopotamia

Several different peoples conquered Mesopotamia and established empires there. The following time line summarizes the main empires of ancient Mesopotamia.

◄──── TIMELINE: COMPARATIVE CHRONOLOGY ────►

2340 B.C.E.	Sargon the Great establishes the Akkadian Empire
2113 B.C.E.	Sargon's empire begins to collapse. Ur-nammu restores it for a brief period.
1500 B.C.E.	Hittites conquer Babylonian Dynasty
1800 B.C.E.	The Amorites conquer Mesopotamia and establish their capitol at Babylon. During this period, Hammurabi compiles the first unified code of law, the Code of Hammurabi.
1000 B.C.E.	The Assyrians conquer Babylon and establish their capitol at Nineveh, where the tablets recording the Epic of Gilgamesh are later found.
612 B.C.E.	The Chaldeans conquer the Assyrian capitol of Nineveh, and establish an empire known as the Neo-Babylonian empire. Its most famous ruler is Nebuchadrezzar.
539 B.C.E.	The Persians under Cyrus the Great conquer the Chaldeans or Neo-Babylonians. The Persians would rule until the expansion of Islam engulfed the region in the seventh century C.E.

The Akkadians

Sargon I (the Great) created the first true empire in Mesopotamia with his capital at **Akkad**. His empire is known as the **Akkadian Empire**. Sargon lived sometime around 2340 B.C.E., and some aspects of his legend are reminiscent of the story of Moses contained in the Hebrew Scriptures. According to legend, his mother launched him on the Euphrates in a reed basket. A farmer found him and raised him. He displayed prodigious abilities, and became the cupbearer to King of Kish. The cupbearer was the king's most trusted servant; he tasted his food and drink to make sure it was not poisoned before the king ate it. Sargon, however, overthrew the king. He then proceeded to conquer important Sumerian city-states such as Uruk, Ur, Lagash, and also the Elamites. Although Sargon created an empire that lasted for two hundred years, his empire finally collapsed in 2100 B.C.E.

The Babylonians or Amorites

In 1800 B.C.E. the Amorites conquered much of Mesopotamia and destroyed whatever of Sargon's empire remained. At that time, the extent of Mesopotamian power increased from an area less than fifty miles in radius to one that extended from the Persian Gulf to beyond Turkey. The Amorite capital was **Babylon**, and the Amorites themselves are better known as Babylonians. Babylon was an economic and cultural crossroads of the ancient world. The Babylonians were notable for creating one of the seven wonders of the ancient world: the beautiful blue-tiled **Gate of Ishtar** that guarded the entrance to the city.

The Babylonians were pioneers in mathematics and created a base 60 number system, which still influences the world today from the division of the hour into minutes and the minute into seconds, to the 360-degree circle. The Babylonians were pioneers in astronomy, and observed and recorded eclipses. They charted the movements of the planets, discovered satellites around Saturn, distinguished stars from planets, and knew that the true length of the solar year was 365 and 1/4 days. Their interest in astronomy was due to their belief that planets had souls and were animate, and that their movements represented the will of the gods and foreshadowed events on earth.

The Babylonians built incredible architectural works, such as their famous ziggurat dedicated to the god Marduk. The ziggurat in Babylon was built in seven layers representing the planets, all colored differently. The ziggurat served as an observatory as well as a religious temple. The height of the great ziggurat of Babylon may have been the basis for the Biblical story of the tower of Babel.

The Hittites

The **Hittites** were one of the most important empires of antiquity to rule Mesopotamia. They were Indo-Europeans who invaded and conquered the Old Babylonian Empire in Mesopotamia in the sixteenth century B.C.E. The homeland of the Hittites was known as Hatti, and was in Central Anatolia. Archaeologists discovered a huge cache of 10,000 Hittite tablets in 1906 in the Hittite capital Hattusas, located near the modern Turkish town of Boghazkoy about 210 kilometers east of Ankara. The Hittites adopted many Mesopotamian customs, and also spread Mesopotamian culture in the near east. Whereas the Code of Hammurabi and later Assyrian codes mandated an "eye for an eye" policy and often the death penalty, Hittite laws were more merciful. The Hittites flourished from 1600–1200 B.C.E., and developed the use of iron. Their iron tools enabled them to become serious threats on the battlefield, and Egypt fought wars with them from 1300–1200 B.C.E. The Hittites, like many other cultures, collapsed in the set of natural disasters that occurred near the end of the second millennium B.C.E. Around the thirteenth century B.C.E., a wave of famines and other natural disasters brought about the collapse of the Hittites as well as other people such as the Mycenaeans.

The Assyrians

Babylon fell to the Assyrians in 1000 B.C.E. The Assyrians were a military society, whose most important god was Ashur, the god of war. The Assyrians used cruel and repressive tactics even at home; they fueled their military machine by encouraging a high birth rate and made abortion punishable by death. The Assyrian empire created one of the first organized and well-trained armies; they were the first truly militaristic society in world history. One reason for their success was the iron weapons they used. Soldiers were rewarded for every severed head. Soldiers were ordered to take no hostages, and often beat in the heads of those they captured, cut off extremities of nobles and those in power, roasted people over slow fire, and deported entire populations. **Ashurbanipal** was the most famous and brutal of Assyrian kings (d. 626 B.C.E.). He was also noteworthy for devotion to learning and created a library of 30,000 volumes. The capital of the Assyrian empire was **Nineveh**, and several tablets with portions of the *Epic of Gilgamesh* were found here dating to the ninth century B.C.E. the *Epic of Gilgamesh*, like almost every ancient text, was told orally for hundreds of years before it was first written down by the Babylonians; the tablets found in Nineveh contain several versions of some of the tales in the epic and it is unclear how they all fit together. Nineveh is also famous for its Biblical connections. According to the Hebrew Scriptures, God ordered the prophet Jonah to preach to the inhabitants of Nineveh; when he refused, a whale swallowed him. In the eighth century B.C.E., the Assyrians destroyed the northern kingdom of the Hebrews, **Israel**. The Assyrian empire collapsed in 612 B.C.E. when the **Chaldeans** captured their capital city of Nineveh.

The Chaldeans or Neo-Babylonians

The Chaldeans restored much of the grandeur of the Babylonian empire and, for that reason, the Chaldean empire is also known as the **Neo-Babylonian Empire**. The **Hanging Gardens of Babylon**, built on top of the king's palace by Nebuchadrezzar II, were known as one of the seven wonders of the ancient world. Nebuchadrezzar built the gardens for his wife, who was a Mede (the predecessors of the Persians); her homeland was a very lush and beautiful region with lots of vegetation. Nebuchadrezzar intended to replicate her homeland, and hydraulic pumps concealed in columns of the palace carried water to the trees on the top. The vegetation was reportedly so lush that the women of the royal harem could walk about unveiled, unseen by the citizens below. Although some scholars now doubt that the gardens were actually located in Babylon, as some famous ancient travelers fail to mention them, they remain one of the most important wonders of the ancient world.

Nebuchadrezzar II and the Hebrew Rebels

Nebuchadrezzar II created an enormous empire by ruthlessly subjugating neighboring peoples, including those of Judea. His subjugation of the Hebrews is documented in the Hebrew Book of Daniel. The Hebrew prophet **Daniel** describes Nebuchadrezzar's court as magnificent and enormously wealthy, attended by astronomers and governmental officials who were all carefully educated. Nebuchadrezzar was an absolute monarch, who could make or break a career with a word. He was given to sharp swings of mood, and had a fierce temper. When threatened by rebellion, he committed atrocious acts. Nebuchadrezzar murdered the Hebrew rebel Zedekiah's sons before his eyes and then put out Zedekiah's eyes. According to Daniel, Nebuchadrezzar had a strange dream, and sought advice from Daniel, who told him that he would be removed from office for seven years as a result of an odd and strange disease. Within a year, Nebuchadrezzar did become ill with what scientists now think was lycanthropy. Lycanthropy results in loss of erect posture, rejection of all human food, and preference for walking on all fours. The King became a maniac. He lived in the open twenty-four hours a day, fed on herbs, rejected clothing, and became covered with a dense coat of hair. Daniel had prophesied that the illness would not be permanent, and after seven years, Nebuchadrezzar was miraculously cured. He ruled until his death in 562 B.C.E., at about the age of 80.

THE PERSIANS

The Neo-Babylonian empire fell to the Persians in 539 B.C.E. The Persians were Indo-Europeans who established a vast, tolerant, and ecumenical empire in the sixth century B.C.E. Persia was known as Elam during Sumerian and Babylonian times; today it is known as Iran. Ancient Persia was bounded by the Indus Valley, the Tigris and Euphrates rivers, and the Caucasus mountains. The empire had a high plateau in its center; in the center of the plateau there were two large deserts. The **Medes**, who united earlier than the Persians, originally ruled Persia. In 550 B.C.E. **Cyrus**, chief of the Persian tribes, defeated the Medes. In 546 B.C.E. Cyrus went on to conquer Anatolia on the coast of Asia Minor. Anatolia gave the Persians access to seaports and so to trade. Eventually, the access to the sea would bring the Persians into conflict with the Greek colonies and the Greeks on the mainland. This series of conflicts is known as the Persian wars. The Persians then turned to Babylon and captured it in 539 B.C.E. These conquests were the beginning of **Achaemenid Empire**, and Cyrus also ended the exile of the Jews in Babylon. Under **Darius I** (522–486 B.C.E.), the Persians achieved peace and prosperity. The stability, peace, and cosmopolitan nature of the government created an era known as the **Pax Archaemenica**.

Darius instituted a uniform system of coinage, standard weights and measures, a postal service, a calendar from Egypt, and a law code. He led expeditions into eastern Europe all the way to the Danube and also into India, where he established the Hindush satrap. He led expeditions from the Indus River to the Red Sea. At one point, Darius even thought of building a canal from the Nile to the Red Sea, which might have made the fifteenth-century C.E expeditions of Portugal around the coast of Africa unnecessary.

The Organization of the Persian Empire

The Persian Empire was organized into provinces or **satrapies**. The land of the Medes was the first province, and at the height of Persian power, there were some twenty such satrapies, each ruled by a provincial governor. Governors could not become too powerful, as in each province there was a military official. The king received tribute from the satraps, as well as recruits for the army. The Persian army was very well trained and at its heart was an elite core of 10,000 soldiers known as the Immortals, so-called because no matter how many died on the battlefield, the next day there were still 10,000 Immortals. The Immortals figured prominently in the Persian wars with the Greeks. Persian kings ruled by "election of the gods" and were just and tolerant of all religions. The Persians were a very eclectic, tolerant, and prosperous culture, who traded with most of western Asia along the **Royal Road**. The Royal Road was a 1600-mile-long stretch of road, the equivalent of a modern-day journey from New York to Dallas, Texas, and connected the capital of Susa to Sardis, a Greek port. In antiquity, this road took the ordinary person three months to traverse. There were 111 stations along the way, and royal couriers using horses could cross it in a week. The Royal Road helped fuse the kingdom together, as did the imposition of an official language, **Aramaic**, the same language spoken by the historic Jesus. There were two capitals of the Persian Empire, **Susa** and **Persepolis**.

Zoroastrianism

The Persians also contributed a religion known as **Zoroastrianism**. The prophet **Zarathustra** (628–551 B.C.E.), referred to more commonly by the English name Zoroaster, founded Zoroastrianism. The main text we have for this tradition dates from the third century C.E and is known as the Zend Avesta. According to this much later text, in his youth, Zoroaster had visions and conversations with divine beings. He became a wandering preacher who urged the Persians to abandon sacrifice to all minor deities, and to be more humane towards animals in sacrifice. He taught a dualist religion, in which good battled evil. Good was symbolized by light while evil was symbolized by darkness. Fire was thought of as divine, since it was a form of light. The god of good was Ahura Mazda, and immortal holy ones or forces of good, such as obedience, truth, law, and immortality, assisted him. His twin, Ahriman, was banished from heaven to hell, where he reigned as the principle of evil. Zoroaster urged the Persians to "turn from the lie (druj) to the Truth (asha)."

Zoroaster taught that people are creations of the good god, and have the free will to turn either towards good or evil. In the end, humans will be judged according to the Book of Life, in which all deeds are recorded. There was a priesthood known as the **Magi**, who absolved sins, and meted out atonement and repentance. Some historians argue that the Zoroastrian concept of good vs. evil influenced Christianity, as did its concept of life after death, the importance of good works, and its cult of Magi, who are mentioned in the Christian gospels as among the first visitors to the infant Jesus.

An important tradition within Zoroastrianism was the cult of **Mithra**. According to legend, Mithra was born on December 25, the date of the winter solstice when the sun returns from south of the equator and is reborn. Mithra was sent by Ahura Mazda to redeem the earth. After the first century of the Common Era, Mithraism was a widespread cult in ancient Rome, where Mithra was called by the Greek version of the name, **Mithras**. In later Roman versions of this myth, Mithras slaughtered a holy bull while on earth. Initiates bathed in the blood of the bull and also ate a sacred meal from its shoulder. The similarity of Christianity to Mithraism was one of the reasons Christianity spread rather slowly through the Roman Empire. Scholars debate the extent to which Roman Mithraism was taken from Persia, as there are several significant differences between the Persian myths and the Roman myths, which often identify Mithras with the sun. Persian versions have no tauroctony, the bull-slaying image so familiar to Romans.

Zoroastrianism became the state religion of the Persian Empire following the conversion of the Persian kings. Darius, for example, was a convert to Zoroastrianism. The Persian Empire collapsed after Muslim invasions in the seventh century C.E.

Review Questions

1. The prehistoric culture that created the paintings at Lascaux was the

    (A) Australopithicene.
    (B) Neanderthal.
    (C) Cro Magnon.
    (D) Homo habilis.

2. The most important invention that distinguished the prehistoric era from the historic era was

    (A) agriculture.
    (B) bronze.
    (C) writing.
    (D) irrigation.

3. All of the following were developments of the Neolithic era EXCEPT

    (A) agriculture.
    (B) pottery.
    (C) urban cities.
    (D) tool making.

4. According to the most commonly accepted theories, agriculture appears to have developed first in

    (A) China.
    (B) the mideast in the region of Jericho.
    (C) the Americas.
    (D) Europe.

5. The first hominid to migrate out of Africa was

    (A) Homo habilis.
    (B) Neanderthal.
    (C) Homo erectus.
    (D) Cro Magnon man.

6. The Shanidar cave site contains fossils from which hominid?

    (A) Cro Magnon

    (B) Homo erectus

    (C) Australopithicene

    (D) Neanderthal

7. All of the following cases involving divorce accurately reflect the principles of the Code of Hammurabi EXCEPT:

    (A) A woman who decided that she did not want her husband, and was not at fault received her dowry back.

    (B) A husband who divorced a wife who was not at fault returned her dowry.

    (C) A woman who was guilty of misdeeds could be divorced by her husband, but she received her dowry in compensation.

    (D) A man who wished to remarry because his wife was ill might take another wife, so long as he continued to provide for his first wife until she died.

8. All of the following scenarios are accurate judgments from the Code of Hammurabi EXCEPT:

    (A) If a house collapses and kills a slave, then the builder is put to death.

    (B) If a house collapses and kills the owner's son, then the son of the builder will be put to death.

    (C) If a house collapses and damages goods of the owner, then goods of equal value belonging to the builder will be forfeited.

    (D) If a surgeon operated on a patient and that patient died, then the surgeon's hands were cut off.

9. The principle "an eye for an eye, a tooth for a tooth" was

    (A) applied equally to all classes in Mesopotamian society.

    (B) applied only to a small subset of crimes.

    (C) applied only to women and children.

    (D) applied in cases where the perpetrator and the victim were both of the same class.

10. The Sumerian civilization was located

    (A) in Northern Mesopotamia.

    (B) in Southern Mesopotamia.

    (C)   on the Tigris river.

    (D)   to the east of the Euphrates river.

11. The general vision of life and death in the *Epic of Gilgamesh* is one of

    (A)   optimism.

    (B)   pessimism.

    (C)   disregard for ethics and human values.

    (D)   firm belief in the involvement in and concern of the gods for human affairs.

12. The first Mesopotamian ruler to create a unified kingdom was

    (A)   Conan.

    (B)   Ramses III.

    (C)   Hammurabi.

    (D)   Sargon the Great.

13. The Assyrian empire was primarily characterized by

    (A)   humane treatment of its subjects.

    (B)   an intense interest in religion.

    (C)   cruel and ruthless conquest.

    (D)   an intense interest in the afterlife.

14. The Code of Hammurabi

    (A)   discriminated against citizens on the basis of race.

    (B)   discriminated against citizens on the basis of social standing and wealth.

    (C)   was applied equally to all members of society.

    (D)   completely exempted the wealthy from any punishments whatsoever.

15. Sumerian writing was called

    (A)   hieroglyphics.

    (B)   cuneiform.

    (C)   petroglyphs.

    (D)   alphabetic.

16. The god of good in Zoroastrianism is

    (A) Ahura Mazda.

    (B) Ahriman.

    (C) Zarathustra.

    (D) The Divine One.

17. The god of evil in Zoroastrianism is

    (A) Ahura Mazda.

    (B) Ahriman.

    (C) Zarathustra.

    (D) The Evil Demon.

18. The famous road that linked various parts of the Persian Empire together was

    (A) the Silk Road.

    (B) the Appian Way.

    (C) the Via Dolorasa.

    (D) the Royal Road.

19. The monarch whose conquests began the Persian Empire was

    (A) Darius I.

    (B) Cyrus the Great.

    (C) Alexander the Great.

    (D) Ashurbanipal.

20. The Persian provinces were called

    (A) provinces.

    (B) ownships.

    (C) calpulli.

    (D) satraps.

21. The elite core of the Persian army was called the

    (A) infantry.

    (B) calvary.

(C) immortals.

(D) Shielded Ones.

22. The religion preached by Zoroaster

    (A) was polytheistic and worshipped natural forces.

    (B) had a pronounced dualism between good and evil.

    (C) believed in the supremacy of moral powers.

    (D) did not believe in an afterlife.

23. Zoroastrianism had a profound impact on both Eastern and Western religious and philosophical thought through all of the following EXCEPT its

    (A) basic dualistic emphasis on good and evil.

    (B) doctrine of life after death.

    (C) development of ethical principles to guide personal lives.

    (D) insistence on the burial and cremation of the dead.

Answers

1. (C)	7. (C)	13. (C)	19. (B)
2. (C)	8. (A)	14. (B)	20. (D)
3. (D)	9. (D)	15. (B)	21. (C)
4. (B)	10. (B)	16. (A)	22. (B)
5. (C)	11. (B)	17. (B)	23. (D)
6. (D)	12. (D)	18. (D)	

Chapter 2

EGYPT: THE GIFT OF THE NILE

KEY TERMS

Nile River

Rosetta Stone

hieroglyphics

Archaic period

First intermediate period

Second intermediate period

Narmer/Menes

Old Kingdom

Pharaoh

Osiris, Isis, and Horus

The Book of the Dead

The Middle Kingdom

Thebes

Hyksos

New Kingdom

Thutmose (Thutmosis) I, II, III

Hatshepsut

Amenhotep IV/Akhenaten

Amarna Revolution

Tel el-Amarna/Akhenaten

Nefertiti

Tutankamun

Ramses II

Hittites

The People of the Sea

Assyrians

Persians

Alexander the Great

GEOGRAPHY OF ANCIENT EGYPT

When the Greek historian Herodotus visited Egypt in the sixth century B.C.E., he called it "the Gift of the Nile." Like Mesopotamia, Egypt was dependent for the rise of its civilization on a river and the fertile soil it deposited. Ancient Egyptian culture was centered on a very small but fertile strip of land only ten to twenty miles wide.

The geography of the **Nile River Valley** created a stable and isolated region in which Egyptian culture could flourish uninterrupted by outside invaders. Consequently, the Egyptians developed a very positive view of life and the afterlife. The Nile River is the longest river in the world. Three rivers meet to create the Nile as it flows through Egypt: The **White Nile**, originating in modern Uganda; the **Blue Nile**, originating in the highlands of modern Ethiopia; and the **Atbara River**. Heavy rains in the Ethiopian Highlands during the summer months produce flooding along the Blue Nile, and this produces the annual period of inundation of the Nile as it passes through Egypt. This annual inundation was regular and predictable and, although records suggest one in five floods were either too high or too low, the floodwaters deposited very fertile soil and agriculture flourished.

The Nile was difficult to navigate due to several cataracts, areas where several small tributaries intersect to create white water rapids. So mysterious was the origin of the Nile that the Greco-Roman geographer Ptolemy believed the source to be the "Mountains of the Moon." In fact, it was not until the nineteenth century that explorer John Speke traced the White Nile back to its source at Lake Victoria. Ancient Egyptians did not progress much further south than the fourth cataract along the Nile.

To the west of the Nile was the world's largest desert, the **Sahara**, which takes its name from the Arabic word for "tan," the color of the sand. North Africa was not very populous in antiquity and presented no threat of invasion. High cliffs protect the eastern side of the Nile. These natural barriers kept invaders out of the Nile River Valley before the arrival of the Hyksos in the Second Intermediate Period.

These features of the Nile allowed the native culture to flourish without interference. Herodotus, who lived in the Golden Age of ancient Greece, was so impressed by the monumental ruins of Egypt that he called it "a land and works beyond expression great." Nevertheless, scholars have argued that Egyptian culture was rather stagnant during the Old Kingdom. During the Old Kingdom, bureaucracy remained unchanged for centuries and so did the basic way of life. Although the Egyptians had a more positive view of life and the afterlife than did the Mesopotamians, they also had a much more rigid social structure in which there was little mobility.

Scholars have more information about ancient Egypt than about ancient Mesopotamia. The hot, dry climate contributed to the preservation of documents written on papyrus, whereas the clay tablets of Mesopotamia dissolved in the flooding of the Tigris and Euphrates. The hot, dry weather also produced the first mummies through a natural process of dehydration in the desert sand. Egyptology first emerged as an area of interest following the late eighteenth-century expedition of Napoleon to Africa. Napoleon and the French scholars who accompanied him had a profound interest in Egyptian culture.

The **Rosetta Stone** recorded a decree in honor of the pharaoh Ptolemy V in Greek, Egyptian hieroglyphic writing (the language used for official and religious documents), and Demotic (the everyday script of Egypt). Since Greek was a well-known language, the nineteenth-century French scholar Jean Francois Champollion deciphered hieroglyphic writing by comparing the Egyptian texts to the Greek text.

CULTURAL CONNECTIONS

Mesopotamian writing is also pictographic in form, and it has been suggested that the Egyptians borrowed from cuneiform in creating hieroglyphics. Scholars who point to the typically Egyptian concepts symbolized by the hieroglyphs commonly reject this suggestion, however.

PERIODS OF EGYPTIAN HISTORY

Modern scholars divide Egyptian history into three main periods based on the stability of the government, with two additional periods before and after. The three main periods of Egyptian history are the Old Kingdom, the Middle Kingdom, and the New Kingdom. The period before the Old Kingdom is the Archaic or protodynastic era, and the period after the New Kingdom is the Late Period.

The Archaic/Protodynastic Era

The Archaic era began in 3100 and lasted until 2700 B.C.E. Herodotus, a Greek writer, and Manetho, an Egyptian priest, claimed that **Menes** founded the first dynasty in 3000 B.C.E. and first united Upper and Lower Egypt. However, the Narmer palette, a decorated stone palette discovered in the nineteenth century designed to hold cosmestics, credits **Narmer** with these deeds, and scholars continue to debate whether these two figures are the same person. Scholars had also debated whether Menes was a mythological figure, but if he is the same person as Narmer, the Narmer palette confirms his historic existence. The name Narmer is associated with the glyph for Menes on some jar labels, but these do not necessarily suggest that these two figures are one and the same person. The name of king **Horus Aha**, first king of the first dynasty, is also often associated with the glyph for Menes. Scholars have suggested that Horus Aha was the son of Narmer, since the Menes glyph follows Narmer's name and Horus Aha seems to have succeeded Narmer. Horus Aha would, therefore, have been the first king to begin his rule over a united Egypt, and Egypt would have been united by his father Narmer. This issue is far from settled in the literature, particularly as the meaning of the glyphs on the labels in question are far from clear, but the discovery of the Narmer palette greatly challenged views of Egyptian history.

At any rate, his wearing of the double crown of Egypt indicates Narmer's role as unifier of Upper and Lower Egypt. The double crown is a combination of the symbols of Upper and Lower Egypt, the lotus and papyrus plants respectively. The palette shows Narmer vanquishing his enemies; the two lions with their necks and heads intertwined symbolize the unity of Upper and Lower Egypt. Upper Egypt was the area southernmost along the Nile Valley, while Lower Egypt was the region nearest the Nile River Valley Delta. The Nile flows from south to north, which accounts for Lower Egypt being to the North of Upper Egypt. Egypt was the most stable when Upper and Lower Egypt were unified, and unification of these two regions helps to determine the dividing points between the various eras of Egyptian history.

The Old Kingdom

The Old Kingdom lasted from 2700–2200 B.C.E. and represents the third through the sixth dynasties. During this period, Egyptian culture was unthreatened by outside invaders and, although goods are found in even prehistoric burial sites from as far away as Afghanistan and Mesopotamia, there was little influence by outside cultures. During the Old Kingdom, Egyptians developed the cult of the pharaoh (a word that means "great house" and technically was not in use before the New Kingdom), established the bureaucracy of Egypt, and built monumental constructions such as the pyramids. Egyptians considered their pharaoh to be fully divine, and thought of him as the living Horus and Osiris of the Underworld.

The myth of **Osiris** created the cult of the pharaoh. Scholars do not know whether Osiris was an actual historic figure, but the ancient Egyptians believed that he was. According to legend, Osiris was a ruler who was very much loved by his people. His brother **Seth** was very jealous of him and designed a special coffin. Guests at a banquet competed to see whom the coffin would fit, and it fit Osiris. Once he had climbed in, however, Seth sealed the coffin with molten lead and threw it in the Nile. It landed in a cedar tree in Byblos, where Seth then dismembered the pieces of his brother. **Isis**, the wife of Osiris, found him and created the first mummy from him. She regenerated him enough to conceive their son **Horus**, the falcon god. Horus then fought with Seth, making Horus ruler of the living and Osiris the ruler of the underworld. Egyptians believed that when Horus finally vanquishes Seth, the personification of evil, Osiris will rule again forever. Just as Osiris was revived, so every pharaoh was revered as the lord of the underworld and as the living Horus while on earth. When Egyptians passed into the underworld, they believed that Osiris himself would judge their deeds. They revered Isis as the goddess of fertility.

As a tribute to the immense power of pharaoh, the Egyptians built enormous pyramids to insure the safe passage of the pharaoh's ka (which can be likened to modern ideas of the "soul") and ba (a mirror image of the person's body and identity) in the afterlife and his unification with the sun god Re.

The third-dynasty ruler Djoser and his architect **Imhotep** first constructed a stone pyramid at Saqqarah. Imhotep designed the stepped pyramid out of several stone mastabas stacked on top of one another, creating the step pyramid. This building was the largest building in the world when it was first created, and Imhotep was revered in Egypt and along the coast of Africa and Saudi Arabia as a god in his own right for his fabulous achievement.

Sneferu, the first ruler of the fourth dynasty, continued to experiment with pyramid building. At least two of his pyramids failed, such as the collapsed pyramid at Medun and the Bent Pyramid at Dashur, but he nonetheless perfected the techniques to eventually create a perfect, though smaller pyramid, the Red Pyramid. His children and grandchildren **Khufu** (called by the Greeks "Cheops"), **Khefre** (called by the Greeks "Chefren"), and **Menkaure** (called by the Greeks "Mycerinus") learned from his experiences and constructed the three **Pyramids of Giza**. The **Great Pyramid at Giza** is one of the Seven Wonders of the Ancient World and was the tallest building in the world until the Eiffel Tower was built. The Great Pyramid has several internal passageways that appear to be aligned with constellations and important stars, leading some to suggest that Egyptians constructed the pyramids to facilitate the union of the pharaoh as Osiris with the sun god Re.

The Egyptians had a very positive view of afterlife, as reflected by the collection of poems known as **The Book of the Dead**. According to one of the texts from this collection, known as "The Negative Confession," the Egyptians valued many of the same virtues as do many modern societies. The Egyptians considered beating one's family or slaves, stealing, and damming up the Nile so as to withhold life-giving water to be evil. The text also makes clear that one should not trespass one's boundaries with the gods. The Egyptians believed that Osiris would reward good deeds with an afterlife that in many ways would be like life itself. The form of the Negative Confessions, which begin with "I have not" and continue with the specific deed to be denied, perhaps influenced the Hebrew Ten Commandments, seven of which are in negative form.

By the fifth dynasty, the priests had become extremely powerful. The last pharaoh of the Old Kingdom, Pepi II of the sixth dynasty, ruled for some ninety years. To balance the rising power of the priesthood with his own power, he gave away pharaonic power and decentralized the government. Although Pepi reigned for almost a century in this precarious state, his successors were unable to hold power. The decline in the pharaoh's power can be seen in the title he took as "Son of Re."

The First Intermediate Period

The First Intermediate Period lasted from 2200–2050 B.C.E. During this period, there was political chaos as four dynasties competed for power. There were two dynasties at **Memphis** and two more at **Herakleopolis**, comprising the seventh, eighth, ninth, and tenth dynasties. An eleventh dynasty developed in **Thebes**, which gradually managed to take control from the other centers of power in the First Intermediate Period. The main god of Thebes was Amun, and during this period the Thebans fused their mythology of Amun with that of the earlier god, Re. **Amun-Re** would be one of the most important deities worshipped throughout the remainder of Egyptian history. Some Egyptologists place the eleventh dynasty in the Middle Kingdom period, while others prefer to include only the twelfth dynasty, which reunited Egypt, in the Middle Kingdom.

The Middle Kingdom

The Middle Kingdom lasted from 2050–1652 B.C.E. and represents restoration of unity and stability after the collapse of the Old Kingdom. **Mentuhotep II** reunited Upper and Lower Egypt. Mentuhotep's dynasty also governed from Thebes and he favored the god Montu, a god of war.

The Second Intermediate Period

The Second Intermediate period lasted from 1567–1085 B.C.E. It began during the thirteenth dynasty, with a series of ineffective rulers. For most of this period, Upper and Lower Egypt were not united and there was civil warfare. The **Hyksos**, a group of people who came from Palestine and perhaps from even further to the east, established a rival dynasty during this period. The Hyksos, or "rulers of foreign lands," were also known as the "shepherd kings" and had actually had a presence in Egypt at Avaris for quite some time. Their settlements show progressive adaptation of Egyptian culture. This was the first time, however, that foreigners controlled Egypt, but the presence of the Hyksos often proved to be beneficial. Later pharaohs would borrow from the Hyskos their technique of fighting in chariots. Egyptians also benefited from Hyksos skill in bronze casting. In addition, the Hyksos preserved a number of papyri from ancient Egypt, including many famous medical texts. Several, less powerful Egyptian dynasties continued to rule during the Hyksos period.

The New Kingdom

The New Kingdom prospered from 1567 B.C.E. until 1085 B.C.E. The New Kingdom began when the eighteenth-dynasty pharaoh Ahmose I defeated the foreign Hyksos and reunited Upper and Lower Egypt. Ahmose was actually the brother of **Kamose**, who had fought the Hyksos in the seventeenth dynasty. Thebes was once again the capital of Egypt. The New Kingdom was a very prosperous period marked by a new kind of pharaoh who excelled on the battlefield.

Thutmose (Thutmosis) I, II, III and Hatshepsut

Thutmose (Thutmosis) I, expanded Egypt to the fourth cataract to the south and to Palestine and Syria in the east. His daughter, **Hatshepsut**, became the most important of six women in Egyptian history to wield power as regent or, as in her case, as pharaoh. Hatshepsut ruled as regent for her stepson **Thutmose (Thutmosis) III**, and then declared herself pharaoh shortly after she took power. While other New Kingdom pharaohs concentrated on conquest, Hatshepsut sent an expedition to Africa and engaged in trade. The tutor of one of her daughters, **Senenmut**, also constructed for her a magnificent mortuary temple near that of Mentuhotep II of the Middle Kingdom in the Valley of the Kings. In the temple is a mural depicting her divine birth from the god Amun. Hatshepsut depicted herself as pharaoh not only in this story of her divine birth, but also in numerous statues where she appears as a sphinx and also wearing the ceremonial regalia of the pharaoh. Thutmose III defaced her monuments several years after he took power and became one of the greatest warriors of the new Kingdom. He led seventeen successful campaigns, including an important victory at the fortress city of Megido, that led to one hundred years of prosperity.

Amenhotep IV (Akhenaten)

One of the more interesting pharaohs of the new kingdom was **Amenhotep IV**, who changed his name to **Akhenaten** in honor of the god he served, **Aten**. Amenhotep was physically deformed and kept from public view in his youth. He had a very elongated neck, face, limbs, toes and fingers and in many statues has rounded hips and other feminine features. Various experts have speculated what malady produced the deformities, and suggestions have ranged from hydrocephaly, to Marfan's syndrome, to Froelich's syndrome, to hermaphrodism, among others. Rather than focusing on the possible physical anomalies of Akhenaten, some scholars insist his portrayals deliberately took on both male and female characteristics to represent the all-encompassing nature of Aten and also perhaps a radical statement about gender equality before Aten. At any rate, his physical problems may account for his emphasis on religious reform rather than on the protection of the frontiers. According to this theory, he did not have the strength to manage both the frontiers and the powerful priests of Amun-Re.

His father, **Amenhotep III**, had strengthened the cult of the sun, Aten, during his reign as a way to counter the growing power of the priesthood of Amun. He very closely identified himself with Aten, something his son, Amenhotep IV would also do. Amenhotep IV began to construct special temples to Aten at the great **Temple of Karnak**, a site devoted to Amun, almost immediately upon becoming pharaoh. **Nerfertiti**, whose name means "the beautiful one has come" (or alternatively, "the perfect one has come"), is prominently featured in these complexes. In fact, her name appears more than that of her husband. After experiencing a direct revelation from Aten, he suddenly announced his intention to move the capitol to a place where the sun rose between two mountains, the very hieroglyph for the sun disk. The name of this place, Akhenaten (now known as Tel el-Amarna), means "the horizon of Aten." He changed his name to Akhenaten, or "he who is beneficial to Aten" and discouraged worship of Amun. His wife name was changed to Nefer-Nefru-aten, or "Beautiful is the Beauty of Aten." The art of Akhenaten was more realistic, and the distorted image of Akhenaten became synonymous with beauty, and artisans distorted even the lovely face of Nefertiti to more closely match that of her husband.

Akhenaten ignored the frontiers and the needs of his people in unprotected places. Even Nefertiti appears to have abandoned him in year 14 of his reign. Here again, there is scholarly controversy. She is not mentioned after year 14, and some scholars assume she died. On the other hand, several scholars point to the existence of inscriptions associated with her children and in other places that would indicate she continued to survive. Some scholars suggest that

Pyramid of Sakkara, one of the Egyptian Pyramids

Akhenaten's successor, **Smenkaure**, who had a reign name very similar to that of Nefertiti, is really Nefertiti posing as a man.

Tutankamun

Tutankaten, later known as Tutankamun, succeeded Smenkaure. Akhenaten apparently took a concubine, Kiya, and some scholars believe she had a son, whom they identify as **Tutankaten**. The birth of this male child might be a reason why Nefertiti disappears, as she had only female children. Tutankaten died while still a young man of nineteen years, but he had managed to quickly overturn the Amarna religion, changing his name to **Tutankamun**. Tutankamun's tomb in the Valley of the Kings, excavated by British archaeologist Howard Carter in 1922, is one of the richest archaeological finds in Egyptian history.

Ramses II

Ramses II (the Great) was another important pharaoh of the New Kingdom. He "defeated" the **Hittites** at the famous battle of **Kadesh**. Although Egyptian records paint this victory as a huge success, Ramses failed to conquer the Hittites as a result of the battle. Nevertheless, he managed to negotiate an important treaty with them and sealed the alliance by his marriage to a Hittite princess. The terms of the treaty actually cede Kadesh forever to the Hittites, suggesting that the Egyptian accounts do not provide us with a completely accurate view of the battle itself.

In 1200 B.C.E., a new group of people of diverse ethnicity, known as the **People of the Sea**, began to enter Egypt. Some of the People of the Sea may have been Mycenaeans who were displaced by the collapse of their empire following the Trojan War around 1250 B.C.E. Some People of the Sea had fought in the armies of Egypt, such as under Ramses II at the battle of Kadesh. Their arrival began the decline of Egypt's traditional power structure that led to the Late Period.

The Late Period

Following the New Kingdom pharaohs, Egypt entered a long period of decline in which it would become part of several other empires. In the seventh century B.C.E., the Assyrians conquered Egypt. In 525 B.C.E., the Persians conquered Egypt; in the fourth century B.C.E., **Alexander the Great** would proclaim himself the "son of Re" and bring Egypt into the Hellenistic world. Under the **Ptolomies**, the successors of Alexander and the last pharaohs, Egypt became part of the **Roman Empire**.

Review Questions

1. The Old Kingdom in Egypt was a period of

   (A) war and conquest.

   (B) prosperity and innovation, as indicated by monumental building projects.

   (C) stagnation and regression.

   (D) cultural and intellectual backwardness.

2. Evidence suggests that Egyptians

   (A) borrowed hieroglyphs from Sumer.

   (B) developed their own unique forms of linguistic expression.

   (C) influenced the culture on Crete.

   (D) (A) and (C).

3. The pharaoh credited by the Egyptian priest Manetho with first uniting upper and lower Egypt was

   (A) Cheops.

   (B) Menes.

   (C) Narmer.

   (D) Zoser.

4. Recent discoveries suggest that Narmer most likely was

   (A) the same person as Menes.

   (B) depicted as a unifier of upper and lower Egypt.

   (C) the father of Menes, or Horus Aha.

   (D) (B) and (C).

5. The Hyksos were important in Egyptian history because they

   (A) defeated the Thebans.

   (B) brought the chariot.

   (C) preserved manuscripts.

   (D) (B) and (C).

6. The basic doctrine of Egyptian religion was a belief in

    (A) nothing but dust and darkness after death regardless of actions.

    (B) the necessity of human sacrifice to appease the gods.

    (C) life after death depending on conduct on earth.

    (D) reincarnation.

7. Akhenaton's reforms can best be described as

    (A) a monotheistic revolution.

    (B) henotheism, or elevation of one cult above many.

    (C) the establishment of a cult of Aten restricted to the royal family and close associates.

    (D) (B) and (C).

Answers

1. (B)	3. (B)	5. (D)	7. (D)
2. (D)	4. (D)	6. (C)	

Chapter 3

THE HEBREWS

KEY TERMS

Abraham
Isaac
Israel
the covenant with Abraham
Palestine
Judah
Philistine
Moses
Hosea
Amos
Isaiah
Elijah
Elisha
Mosaic covenant
Solomon
David
Saul
Temple of Solomon
Wailing or Western wall

Herodian Temple Mount
Kingdom of Israel
Kingdom of Judah
Assyrians
Babylonians
Persians
Babylonian Captivity
Torah
Talmud
Pentateuch
Monotheism
Elohistic
Yahwistic
Deuteronomistic
Ezra
Nehemiah
Joshua
Hebrew

INTRODUCTION

The **Torah** refers to the **Hebrews** as the "fewest of all people." Politically, the Hebrew kingdoms flourished only during the forty-year reign of **Solomon** in the tenth century B.C.E. Nevertheless, "the fewest of all people" have had an immeasurable impact on the development of the world, as their ancient customs gave rise to three of the world's major religions, including Judaism and its offsprings, Christianity and Islam. It is important to remember that the early Christians were all Jews, including the historic Jesus. Ishmael, father of the Arab nations, was the first-born son of Abraham, patriarch of the Hebrews, through his concubine Hagar, making the Jews and Arabs ancient cousins. The Qur'an contains a history of the Hebrew prophets and Abraham and Ishmael, as well as stories of Jesus.

Although the Hebrew Scriptures were never meant to be histories in the modern sense of the word, these texts do contain references that are historically useful. For example, genealogies and references to ancient peoples and kingdoms can be compared to other sources. The Hebrew Scriptures were, however, composed in the same way as many other texts in the ancient period. The life of Abraham, patriarch of the Hebrews, dates to 1850 B.C.E., yet the oldest texts we have of the Hebrew Scriptures date to the ninth century B.C.E. This is approximately the same era in which the Greek epics the Iliad and Odyssey were first recorded in written form. The present form of the biblical texts is not found in written form until the second century C.E.

The **Torah**, or **Pentateuch**, is the foundation of Judaism. The word "Pentateuch" comes from the root "pent," meaning "five." The Torah includes the books of Genesis, Exodus, Leviticus, Deuteronomy, and Numbers. These books are traditionally credited to **Moses**. There is no mention of Moses as author of the Torah in the Torah itself, but the book of Nehemiah, which chronicles the return of the Hebrews from Babylon, tells us that **Ezra** in the fifth century B.C.E. brought out the "book of the law of Moses" (Nehemiah 8:1). Most scholars, however, believe that there were several authors involved in the creation of these texts.

Another issue of great importance is how one defines the group of people referred to as Hebrews. Today, the descendants of the ancient Hebrews are mainly known as "Jews," as they are the survivors of the Hebrew kingdom of **Judah**. It is unclear whether the Hebrews were of a homogenous ethnicity; clearly, they spoke a Semitic language. However, their Scriptures seem to define them by a set of practices contained in the Torah. Chief among these practices was the **bris,** or circumcision of male infants at eight days of age. Modern Jews are also very difficult to categorize; Jews can be found all over the world, and today are not a single ethnicity but a very diverse collection of peoples. Further, many people identify themselves as Jews who do not practice Judaism.

← —— TIMELINE: ANCIENT HEBREW HISTORY —— →

1850–1250 B.C.E.	Abraham and the patriarchs; Abraham migrates from Mesopotamia to Egypt and receives the covenant
	The Code of Hammurabi is compiled in 1750 B.C.E.
Ca. 1250 B.C.E.	Moses and the Exodus; the Mosaic Covenant. Although modern scholars dispute authorship of the Torah, Moses is credited with writing the first five Hebrew scriptures.
	Ramses II rules Egypt in the thirteenth century B.C.E.; in the same century, the People of the Sea begin to ravage Egypt.
1130–1020 B.C.E.	Judges govern the twelve tribes of Israel
1020–930 B.C.E.	Saul first unites the twelve tribes, followed by David. David establishes Jerusalem as the capitol. The Hebrews achieve their greatest period of prosperity under David's son Solomon.
	The Assyrians rule in Mesopotamia from 1000–612 B.C.E.
930–536 B.C.E.	The two kingdoms separate after the death of Solomon. The Assyrians take Israel in 722 B.C.E. and the Babylonians conquer Judah in 865 B.C.E. The Hebrews spend 50 years in captivity in Babylon. Cyrus the Great of Persia liberates them and they rebuild their temple in Jerusalem.

NARRATIVE HISTORY: HEBREW ORIGINS

Hebrew history begins with the life of **Abraham**, who lived in Ur in Mesopotamia around 1850 B.C.E. The era from 1850–1250 B.C.E. in Hebrew history is known as the time of the patriarchs and is recounted in the book of Genesis. Scholars dispute whether Abraham was actually an historic individual or a product of myth. At any rate, Abraham was originally called Abram, and he rejected worship of the traditional deities of Mesopotamia. Abram left Ur and crossed into what is modern-day Israel, and eventually migrated to the Nile delta. The origins of the word "Hebrew" are difficult to trace. After Abraham left Ur, the Hebrews became a nomadic people; the word "abiru," meaning "dusty ones," may be the root of the modern word. Alternatively, Abram crossed the Euphrates, and the word "ibri" in Hebrew means "from the other side."

In Egypt, according to the Bible, the Lord made one of several covenants with Abram promising to reward him with numerous descendants. Abram's name became Abraham, which means "father of a host of nations," and he later had two sons. His first son, **Ishmael**, was born of his concubine **Hagar**. His wife **Sara** had been barren, but in their later years, Sara conceived and gave birth to **Isaac**. According to Genesis, Sara was concerned for Isaac's inheritance and status, and had Abraham expel Hagar and Ishmael. This expulsion is an important story in the Qur'an and the religion of Islam, as it was Ishmael who is credited with being the father of the Arab nations. Isaac, on the other hand, is the beginning of the Hebrew line. The twelve tribes of Israel descended through Isaac's son **Jacob**, renamed "Israel" or "the soldier of God." The covenant also promised that Abraham and his descendants would receive the land of Canaan. The symbol of the covenant was the bris, or circumcision, which physically marked the Hebrews off from other peoples.

The Exodus

In the thirteenth century B.C.E., the books of Exodus, Deuteronomy, Numbers, and Joshua relate the exodus from Egypt under the leadership of Moses and the eventual settlement of the Hebrews in "the promised land." The story of Moses, whom his mother placed in a reed basket and set afloat on the Nile, is very similar to that of Sargon the Great, who founded the Akkadian empire. Moses was discovered by an Egyptian princess, raised as a prince, and later discovered his heritage. Moses became the first prophet in Hebrew history. During the wandering in the desert, Moses went up to Mt. Sinai and brought back the "ten words," or "ten commandments," to the Hebrews. Moses received a new covenant and ordered the construction of the ark of the covenant to house the tablets he had brought down from Sinai. The ark was the physical dwelling place of a transcendental God. Hebrews believed the presence of God to be so powerful that only the holiest priest could see the ark; all others would die immediately.

The covenant between the Hebrew God and Moses found in the book of Exodus is very similar to ancient treaties known as vassal treaties made in the Middle East between a powerful lord and a vassal who does not have the same status. The Mosaic covenant in Exodus follows this form with one exception, in that it contains no list of gods to witness the treaty. Later prophets, such as Jeremiah, reworded the covenant to emphasize that the Hebrews were to be the chosen people of their God.

Hebrew Oral Tradition: The Kabbalah

Moses brought the **Decalogue** or ten commandments down from Sinai, but there is also a belief that he received a great deal of revelation that was never written down. This belief in an oral tradition ultimately grew into the **Kabbalah**, or mystical Judaism. Kabbalists interpret the Torah in part through an oral tradition that they believe began with Moses. Kabbalists argue that the Torah tells one how, whereas Kabbalah tells one why. The main text of the Kabbalah tradition is the Zohar, which dates from the Roman period.

The Wandering in the Desert

According to the Hebrew Scriptures, the Hebrews continued to wander in the desert for forty years. Many modern archaeologists have tried to find evidence of the wanderings of thousands of people, but to date, none has been found. This is one of the puzzling aspects of the Hebrew Scriptures. The Scriptures do not give exact enough references for us to know the path traveled in those years; in fact, there is great debate about exactly where Mt. Sinai is located. The monastery of St. Catherine, on the Sinai peninsula, has long maintained that it is located where the burning bush was located; however, other scholars suggest that Mt. Sinai is located elsewhere on the peninsula.

The Promised Land

The Hebrew texts chronicle the eventual arrival of the Hebrews in "the promised land" or the region known as **Palestine** in Roman times. The word "Palestine" comes from the Roman word to describe the Philistines. Under the leadership of Joshua, the scriptures relate a victory over the Canaanites and the settlement of the Hebrews in the region of modern Israel. There is little archaeological evidence to support this account of a military conquest of the Holy Land. The scriptures interpret what skirmishes did occur as an act in which their God delivered them from bondage and enabled them to found the kingdom of Israel.

The Judges and the Formation of the Hebrew Monarchy

The twelve tribes of Israel were ruled by judges from 1130–1020 B.C.E. The various decisions of the judges and the history of the Hebrews are chronicled in the book of Judges. The judges resisted the idea of a centralized government, as they believed only their god should be regarded as king.

Saul, The First King

The first Hebrew king to unite the twelve tribes was Saul, who reigned from 1020–1000 B.C.E.

David and the Foundation of Jerusalem

Saul's son-in-law **David** reunited the twelve tribes after his father-in-law's death. As a young shepherd boy, we first hear of David in connection with the Philistines; according to the Scriptures, he killed Goliath with his slingshot. David reigned from 1000–970 B.C.E., made **Jerusalem** his capital and built the city to house the ark of the covenant. Jerusalem is the holiest city in the world for Jews and also for Christians. It is also considered holy for Muslims, as they believe it marks the site of **Muhammad's Night Journey** and **Ascension into Heaven** in the seventh century C.E. The presence of the ark there made Jerusalem the center of the Hebrew religion as well as its political center.

The Prosperity Under Solomon

David's son **Solomon** reigned from 970–930 B.C.E. This brief period was the most prosperous period in Hebrew history. Solomon built a magnificent temple for the ark in Jerusalem.

Meggido

The magnificence of Solomon's reign is seen in such ruins as Meggido, where there was a stable large enough for 500 horses. Meggido was located on an important trade route, linking Egypt with the Near East. Moreover, Egypt had been the dominant power in the Middle East and had been for over two thousand years before Abraham. The Persian, Assyrian, and Babylonian Empires balanced the power of Egypt to the east of Israel. The Hebrew Kingdoms became the crossroads where these powers often struggled for supremacy, and Meggido overlooked the site of important battles. The name "meggido" derives from the word Harmageddon; Meggido was so well-known in the ancient world as the center of conflict in the Middle East that the author of the **Book of Revelation**, a Christian text, places the final conflict between good and evil at Armageddon or Meggido. Thutmosis III fought many battles for control of Meggido.

Disintegration of the Hebrew Kingdom of Solomon

Despite the prosperity of Israel under Solomon, the foundations for the destruction of unity were already laid. Solomon heavily taxed the tribes to centralize the government, ignoring tribal loyalties and other issues. His successor, his son Rehoboam, had even less understanding of old tribal issues.

After the death of Solomon, the unity of the twelve tribes disintegrated. Solomon's kingdom was split into two halves, **Israel** in the North and **Judah** in the south. Considerable tension erupted between the tribes during this period, and the Hebrew scriptures are very critical of Rehoboam and other rulers of the northern kingdom as well as the rulers of Judah.

The Northern Kingdom of Israel

The word "Israelite" refers to the inhabitants of the kingdom of Israel, named for Isaac's son Jacob, who was given the name "Israel" or "soldier of God." The capital of the northern kingdom was **Samaria**. The Scriptures are very critical of the northern rulers, and in the period following the collapse of Solomon's empire, many prophets arose, including Elijah, Elisha, Amos, and Hosea.

The prophets argued that the kings of the north had abandoned the covenant, and they urged reform of the state and religion in order to avoid destruction.

The Ten Lost Tribes of Israel

The **Assyrians** conquered Israel in 722 B.C.E. The Hebrew tribes dispersed, giving rise to the search for the "ten lost tribes" of Israel. There are various hypotheses about what happened to these ten tribes. One scholar has suggested that the tribes eventually migrated to the Americas, and, although most scholars do not accept this hypothesis, the Church of Jesus Christ of Latter Day Saints, or the Mormons, is based on this idea. Mormons also believe that Christ made an appearance in the Americas after his resurrection to descendants of the ten lost tribes.

Another thesis maintains that many of the ten tribes migrated to Europe, where they helped to lay the foundation for later European culture. The most credible of all these hypotheses is that the ten lost tribes fled to Judah, whose population doubled shortly after the conquest of Israel by the Assyrians.

The Southern Kingdom of Judah

Judah was the southern kingdom of the Hebrews. Jerusalem was located in Judah. The word "Jew" refers to the inhabitants of Judah. In the period following the collapse of Solomon's empire, prophets arose in both the northern and southern kingdoms. Isaiah was one of the most important prophets, and he served the kings of Judah. In Christian times, Isaiah's words would be interpreted as prophesying the coming of Christ.

The Babylonian Captivity

The Babylonians conquered Judah in 586 B.C.E., and brought many inhabitants to Babylon. This period is known as the Babylonian Captivity, and is chronicled in the second book of Kings, chapters 24–25, and the books of Ezra and Nehemiah, which deal mainly with the later return of the Jews. During this fifty-year period, Jews attempted to preserve their identity. Rabbis, or teachers, taught Hebrew history and religion in the synagogues. This period is also the likely date for the beginnings of the **Talmud**, or rabbinical commentary on the Torah. The Talmud contains explications of such customs as the bar mitzvah, wedding rituals, and Kosher laws for the preparation of food.

The **Persians** liberated the Jews when they conquered Babylon and allowed them to return to Jerusalem. There was a great deal of resentment of those who had remained in Judah; when the Jews returned after the Babylonian Captivity, they refused to allow those who had remained to help rebuild the kingdom. The tensions between these two factions is evident in the Christian scriptures in the references to the Jews and Samaritans.

The Second Temple

When the Persians conquered Babylon, Cyrus the Great allowed the Jews to return to the Holy Land. They built a **second temple** under the leadership of Ezra and Nehemiah. Herod the Great, a Roman ruler, greatly expanded the temple. The Romans razed the temple in 70 C.E. and again in 132 C.E.

The Wailing or Western Wall

The only remaining wall of the second temple is the Western Wall or "Wailing Wall." This is the holiest site in the Jewish world today. Jews go there to pray for the return of their temple and to lament its destruction.

Muslim Structures

Today, the **Dome of the Rock** shrine and the **al-Aqsa mosque** are located on the temple mount. Muslims conquered Jerusalem in the seventh century. Orthodox Jews believe that this sacred ground has been profaned by the presence of these Muslim structures. Jews believe the temple mount is holy; since no one knows the exact location of the ark in the Holy of Holies in the ancient temple, Orthodox Jews will not set foot anywhere on the mount.

Mysteries of the Bible

We know more about the Ark of the Covenant than perhaps any other artifact in history; the Hebrew scriptures are very detailed about its appearance, construction, and even the material out of which it was made. One of the greatest mysteries in Biblical scholarship, however, is the fate of the Ark of the Covenant. Roman reliefs show an object being carried off that might have been the ark. Some scholars suggest that the ark made its way to Ethiopia after the temple was destroyed the second time, where inhabitants still believe it is kept. Others suggest it may have been buried under Jerusalem, but the modern government of Israel refuses to give permission for the extensive excavations needed. Still others believe that the ark is located near **Qum'ran** by the Dead Sea, where the Dead Sea scrolls were discovered.

The Diaspora

The destruction of the temple in Jerusalem also led to a widespread **diaspora** of the Jewish people. Jews live in every nation of the world today, and have suffered many waves of persecution. In the 1890s, **Theodore Herzel** founded the movement known as Zionism, which sought to create a homeland for Jews. Although Zionists did not originally insist that a Jewish state be recreated in the same location as the historic Hebrew kingdoms, Jews did begin to migrate to Israel. Following World War II, Jews began to return in even greater numbers to their ancient homeland, culminating in the controversial creation of the state of Israel in 1949.

THE CULTURAL CONTRIBUTIONS OF THE HEBREWS

The chief tenet of Judaism is a thorough-going monotheistic belief in one god. The development of monotheism was a long process, but culminated in the development of a very abstract concept of God. The Hebrew texts forbade the making of images, a prohibition that also appears in the Qur'an, the main text of Islam. The Hebrew God is limitless and cannot be limited by either images or concrete names. At the burning bush, the deity tells Moses that his "name" is Yahweh. In Hebrew, which has no vowels, the "name" is **YHWH**, the root word for "existence." Therefore, what the deity tells Moses is that it and only it exists. This four-letter word is called the **Tetragrammaton**, and it refers to the unnameable being worshiped by the Hebrews.

We interpolate the vowels in YHWH to get the word "Yahweh"; the word is considered so sacred it cannot be uttered. Later Latin writers transliterated the word from YHWH to JHVH, or Jehovah.

This very abstract concept of God differs greatly from the anthropomorphic concepts of God seen in Egypt and Mesopotamia, where the gods were often represented as half-human and half animal. The Hebrew God was also depicted as loving and compassionate towards its creations, unlike the gods of the *Epic of Gilgamesh*. The Hebrew God is also predictable and offers a rational covenant to his people, promising them prosperity in return for obedience.

The Hebrew story of creation in Genesis captures the rational nature of this deity. Creation occurs over the course of six days, and on the seventh, God rests. The texts tell us that God looked back on what He had done, and said, "behold it is good." This vision of life is in stark contrast to the pessimism of Mesopotamia; for the Hebrews, God created humans in the image of God and were not subject to nature, but given power over it.

The Flood

The Hebrew Scriptures also contain a flood epic that is similar in some ways to that of Gilgamesh but very dissimilar in others. While the flood epic in Gilgamesh is pessimistic in tone, that of the Hebrews is optimistic. The book of Genesis contains a description of the Hebrew version of the flood. In the Hebrew version, the hero is Noah, whom God commands to build an ark and to fill it with creatures so that life will be preserved. The flood is to wipe out the evil that exists; the ark is to preserve what is good. After the flood, the rainbow appears to Noah as a promise that there will be no further destruction.

The story of the great flood recorded in Genesis is a compilation of two different sources, the **Priestly** and the **Yahwistic** traditions. Passages from the Yahwistic source form an important strand of interpretation in the Pentateuch, and tend to use anthropomorphisms in their effort to describe the divine inter-workings of God with his creation. The Yahwistic tradition uses Yahweh as the name for God, and also favors the monarchy. It was likely composed during the late tenth and early ninth centuries in Judah, as Jerusalem was the center of the Hebrew monarchy. The Priestly tradition generally tends to emphasize theology, genealogy, and chronology. It also emphasizes the practices commanded by law and the need to fulfill them in order to preserve the covenant. It likely dates from the period of the Babylonian Captivity in the sixth century B.C.E. The Yahwistic source is generally thought to be the more ancient source, while the Priestly source represents a later, more refined and detailed interpretation of that tradition.

There are two other sources evident in the Pentateuch: the **Deuteronomist** and the **Elohist** sources. The patterns of composition evident in the Hebrew Scriptures are typical of the ancient world, where it is often to tell how many authors worked on a text and over how long a period of time they compiled various traditions.

Review Questions

1. The Ten Commandments were unique in the societies of the ancient world because they

   (A) offered ethical guidelines and moral principles to live by.

   (B) offered a code of social justice.

   (C) were given to a human by a Supreme being.

   (D) were applied equally to all members of society everywhere.

2. The general aim of the social laws spelled out in the Torah was to

   (A) give wealthy Jews an advantage under the law.

   (B) protect individual rights and promote legal, economic and social equality.

   (C) protect private property and business rights.

   (D) help the Jews understand the many other religions that surrounded them.

3. The Talmud is

   (A) the earliest collection of Hebrew writings dating from the exodus in the 13th century B.C.E.

   (B) a detailed examination and explanation of Hebrew theology.

   (C) collection of rabbinical writings and legal judgments written during the Babylonian Captivity and later.

   (D) the first five books of the Old Testament, also called the Pentateuch.

4. The Hebrews enjoyed the most prosperity under the reign of

   (A) David.

   (B) Saul.

   (C) Moses.

   (D) Solomon.

5. The great Hebrew temple in Jerusalem was built during the reign of

   (A) Joshua.

   (B) Solomon.

   (C) Moses.

   (D) Abraham.

6. The Kingdom of Israel was conquered by the

    (A) Hittites.

    (B) Assyrians.

    (C) Babylonians.

    (D) Egyptians.

7. The account of creation in Genesis

    (A) resembles Enkidu's view of the gods in Gilgamesh.

    (B) displays the same attitude toward the worth of man as the Mesopotamians had.

    (C) describes the formation of the earth and animals in the same way as the Egyptians did.

    (D) describes creation as proceeding in an orderly fashion.

8. The Torah is

    (A) the same as the Pentateuch.

    (B) the first five books of the Old Testament and a body of oral tradition.

    (C) the Talmud.

    (D) the Old Testament.

9. The patriarch of the Hebrews was

    (A) Israel.

    (B) Jacob.

    (C) David.

    (D) Abraham.

10. The Torah was composed

    (A) by a single author, Moses.

    (B) over time by a group of scribes who eventually compiled the different variations of the traditions.

    (C) in a unified way, without variations among the traditions.

    (D) by only two groups of scribes.

Answers

1. (D)	4. (D)	7. (D)	10. (B)
2. (B)	5. (B)	8. (B)	
3. (C)	6. (B)	9. (D)	

Chapter 4

INDIAN CIVILIZATION THROUGH THE MAURYAN EMPIRE

KEY TERMS

Indus River Valley
Harappa
Mohenjo Daro
Aryans
Rig Veda
Sanskrit
Bhagavad Gita
Upanishads
Mahabarata
Brahman
Brahma
Vishnu
Shiva
Purusha
castes
Brahmins
kshatriya
vaisya
sudra
Pariahs
Atman
Samsara
Dharma
Karma

Moksha
Buddha
Siddhartha Gautama
Nirvana
Four Noble Truths
Four Great Sights
Night of the Great Renunciation
Queen Maya
Queen Maha-Prajapati
wheel of the law
Middle Path
eightfold path of right conduct
Stupa
Rock pillar edicts
Ashoka
Chandragupta Maurya
Theravada Buddhism
Mahayana Buddhism
Tibetan Buddhism
Greater Vehicle
Lesser Vehicle
Bodhisattvas
Zen Buddhism

◄──── TIMELINE: COMPARATIVE CHRONOLOGY ────►

2500–1900 B.C.E.	Indus River Valley Civilization
	The Old Kingdom in Egypt (2700–2200 B.C.E.)
1800 B.C.E.	Aryans had arrived in India by this time
	Abraham of Ur, patriarch of the Hebrews (1850 B.C.E.); The Code of Hammurabi appears in Mesopotamia, 1750 B.C.E.
1700–500 B.C.E.	The Vedic Period: Hinduism evolves from polytheistic expression to belief in a single, unified reality, Brahman
	The Shang Dynasty (1570–1045 B.C.E.) in China; the Zhou Dynasty (1045–403 B.C.E.; New Kingdom in Egypt (1567–1085 B.C.E.); Kingdoms of David and Solomon, 1010–930 B.C.E.
Sixth Century B.C.E.	Age of the Buddha
	The Axis Age: Zoroaster in Persia; Pre-Socratics in Greece; Confucius and Lao Zi in China; The Hebrews return to the Holy Land from the Babylonian Captivity, after 538 B.C.E.
Fourth Century B.C.E.	Alexander the Great arrives in India; Chandragupta Maurya founds his empire in Alexander's wake
Third Century B.C.E.	Ashoka converts to Buddhism and begins to spread it to other parts of Asia and sends missions to the west as well
	Shi Huangdi conquers the warring states of China in 221 B.C.E.
First century C.E.	Buddhism reaches China during the Han Dynasty
	The Hebrew's Second Temple in Jerusalem is destroyed by Romans

INDUS RIVER VALLEY CIVILIZATION

The Indus River is located in the northernmost reaches of the Indian subcontinent. There were two important centers of civilization here, the twin capitals of **Harappa** and **Mohenjo-Daro**, nearly identical cities located four hundred miles apart. The culture here is commonly called the **Harrapan culture**, as most of the important discoveries came from the city of Harappa. Harappa was first excavated in the 1850's while the British were building a railroad across India; a worker found a small clay brick with an inscription. Scholars still have not learned to decipher the language of Harappa; their language was not related to Sumerian cuneiform, and many believe it was from the Dravidian family of languages. The Harappans recorded texts on tiny clay seals with images of animals. Some of these images are very similar to the Brahman bull that is venerated in India today. Hindus consider the Brahman bull sacred, and they believe it should not be killed even for food although thousands of modern Indians live in poverty and have little to eat. Hindus believe that the Brahman bull was the mount of one of their most important deities, Shiva, and also that the bull was one of the incarnations of Brahma, another important deity.

Artifacts from Harappa date back to 2500 B.C.E., and many aspects of Harappan culture resemble practices of modern Hinduism. Both Harappa and Mohenjo-Daro were very well planned cities, laid out on a grid with streets intersecting each other at right angles. City blocks and buildings were uniform in structure between Harappa and Mohenjo-Daro, suggesting a centralized government. Although this hypothesis has recently been called into question, the similarity of the structures within each city and between the cities also resembles the modern Hindu belief in the unity of all life. The homes of the upper classes, however, are clearly distinguishable from those of the workers; similarly, later Hinduism would distinguish between the Brahmin, or priest caste, and the Sudra, or lowest caste of workers. The cities were also noteworthy for their system of running water and sewers.

Each city had a citadel surrounded by a wall, suggesting that the citadel was a sacred place worthy of special protection. In Mohenjo-Daro, there was a large basin known as the Great Bath, as it was lined with tar, making it watertight and suitable for bathing. It was large enough to accommodate fifteen people, perhaps the number of priests they had.

The Harappan emphasis on cleanliness, evident in their focus on a supply of running water, was unique in the ancient world. Only the Hebrews and Romans could equal it, and these were both later cultures. Their emphasis on cleanliness also reminds one of the modern Hindu water rituals of purification, such as bathing in the Ganges.

In Harappa, very few weapons were found but quite a number of toys, suggesting that the culture had plenty of leisure time and, therefore, few enemies to worry about. Harappa was likely a peaceful society. These aspects of the two cities also resemble many modern Hindu practices and beliefs, as modern Hindus have reverence for all life forms and practice nonviolence.

The earliest Hindu texts date from the later Aryan period, but given the similarity of Harappan practices to those of later Hinduism, scholars speculate on whether the culture who wrote the Hindu texts, the Aryans, borrowed many beliefs and practices from the Indus River Valley culture.

The Decline of the Harappan Civilization

The Harappan civilization began to decline around 1900 B.C.E., when its ports were suddenly abandoned for unknown reasons. Simultaneously, the construction of the homes and buildings was less proficient, and the pottery declined in quality. Scholars offer many possible explanations for the collapse of Harappa, including evidence that the natural resources declined. There is evidence that excessive irrigation of the land led to the buildup of salts and alkalines. Second, the two cities may have declined due to flooding. Archaeological evidence shows that parts of Mohenjo-Daro had to be rebuilt several times after floods destroyed them. Finally, there is some evidence of a violent invasion, as there was a cache of unburied skeletons in Mohenjo-Daro with severe injuries including dismemberment. In fact, we know that by 1800 B.C.E. a new group of Indo-European people, the Aryans had migrated to India. They came from Asia and eventually conquered north India. The most likely explanation for the demise of the Harappan culture is a combination of all three causes.

THE VEDIC PERIOD

The Aryans were part of an extremely widespread and important series of migrations. The Indo-European peoples spread to many parts of the world, including Greece, Iran (a word derived from the Sanskrit word "Arya," for "noble"), Italy, and numerous other locations.

In India, they created the set of traditions known as Hinduism. The period from 1700–500 B.C.E. is known as the **Vedic period**. The word "Veda" means "knowledge." The Aryans wrote the Vedas in **Sanskrit**, and the earliest of the Vedic texts, the Rig Veda, reveals much about their culture.

The **Rig Veda** is the earliest Veda and is a collection of 1028 hymns. Early Hinduism was very polytheistic in nature. In fact, it has been said that there are 330 million gods in Hinduism, though of course, such a large number is meant to convey the fact that Hinduism has a very large pantheon on deities that cannot in the end be counted. Hindu temples are very elaborate structures with literally thousands of carvings of gods and goddesses. Among the deities worshipped are Shiva the destroyer god, Ganesha the elephant god, Krishna, and many others. The Rig Veda also records the formation of the castes from the self-sacrifice of the deity Purusha. The caste system did not exist in India before the arrival of the Aryans, who were in the minority of the population. The caste system evolved in order to subjugate the native population of India. The highest caste was the **brahmin,** or priests; then the **kshatriya,** or warrior, caste; then the **vaisya,** or the herders, farmers, traders, and merchants, and then **sudra,** or the slave and servant class. The class even below the sudra was the **pariahs,** or untouchables, those considered to be outside Indian society.

The Late Vedic or Brahamanic Age

As Hinduism evolved, however, many texts reflect a growing awareness of the unity of all reality. The Hindu concept of Brahman, or the total of all reality, is radically different from the Hebrew concept of God. The Hebrew deity is something apart from its creations; it is transcendent. The Hindu concept of Brahman, however, is of an immanent divine reality, present in the world and actually one with it.

The period from 1000–500 B.C.E. is called the late Vedic or Brahamanic Age. During this period, several classics of Indian literature were produced, including the Mahabharata, the world's longest poem about the power struggle of two clans. A subsection of the Mahabharata is the **Bhagavad Gita**, about a discussion between the warrior Arjuna and the god Krishna. In response to Arjuna's concerns about the possibility of killing members of his own clan, Krishna develops the idea of the atman, or the eternal self, which has always existed and always will exist; it cannot be destroyed. According to the Hindu concept of samsara or reincarnation, the atman lives eternally in innumerable bodies or life forms.

The most abstract account of the unity of all reality is found in the **Upanishads**, the last of the Vedic texts to be written. The Upanishads were written in the eighth century B.C.E. The Upanishads record the dialog between a master and his student; the word "Upanishads" means "teachings received at the foot of the master."

While in any incarnation, the atman has a **dharma**, or duty that it must fulfill. Krishna tells Arjuna, the warrior, that his duty is to fight the righteous battle of good against evil, which is more important than one person's particular family ties or interests. For the Hindu, each caste has its own dharma, and one's duty in life is to fulfill one's dharma to the best of one's ability. In perfectly fulfilling one's dharma, Hinduism teaches that one is freed from all **karma**, or the effects of action. Krishna tells Arjuna that freedom from action is obtained through the path of renunciation. Once one is freed of action or karma, the Hindu attains unity with Brahman, called **moksha**.

According to Hinduism, life is really about growing in self-knowledge. The more one truly understands reality, the more one knows the true self, the atman, and the more one knows that the atman and the Brahman are one. Once one attains such knowledge, there is no longer a self at all, because the self becomes one with all reality. The ultimate goal of the Hindu is to understand the illusory quality of any particular life and any notion of the self as distinguished from all others. The Self, the *Upanishads* tells us, is the atman-Brahman, the unity in moksha with all of reality.

Hinduism has no founder and no body of canonical texts that every Hindu must practice. The concept of Brahman as the totality of reality allows Hindus to accept any tradition as a path to moksha. Hindus believe all are Hindus, that all are on separate paths that will eventually meet in the same place, that reality in which all are one, Brahman. Hindus continue to worship many deities, as they believe Brahman to be limitless, while the human mind in any one lifetime is finite. The 330 million deities are all aspects of that single reality, Brahman, presented in ways the human mind can grasp.

Three Hindu deities tend to be most predominant: **Brahma**, the creator god, **Vishnu** the preserver, and **Shiva** the destroyer. These three deities represent the cyclic nature of all reality. From creation comes preservation, yet ultimately created things are destroyed. From the remnants of destruction, new life often comes, as when the charred remains of a forest fertilizes the ground for new growth. A phallus often symbolizes the god Shiva, for his legends are associated with acts of rape. While rape is a destructive force, it also can bring new life. The Hindu trinity of Brahma, Vishnu, and Shiva symbolizes the continuing cycle of reality of which we are all a part. No one of these deities are separate from the whole, they are rather aspects of it that can be conveniently discussed.

Hinduism is practiced today in many parts of the world, but most predominantly in India and Southeast Asia. Among the many famous Hindu sites in the world is the massive complex at Angkor Wat in Cambodia, the center of the powerful Khmer kingdom abandoned in 1432 C.E.

BUDDHISM

Buddhism is another important world tradition to have emerged in this period. **Prince Siddhartha Gautama** was born into the warrior caste in 563 B.C.E. He died in 485 B.C.E, having become "awake." A number of legends surround the life of the Buddha. For many centuries, scholars were uncertain whether there ever was an historic Buddha, or whether he was simply a legendary figure who exemplified the teachings of Buddhism. In the nineteenth century C.E., however, an inscription was discovered on a stone that decisively proved the historic existence of the Buddha.

According to legend, Queen Maya had a painless birth and the trees bent down to help her deliver her son. He was called "Siddhartha," or "he whose purpose is fulfilled." Immediately after birth, Siddhartha stood up and walked, leaving lotus plants in his footsteps. The Lotus plant is a very beautiful plant that quickly withers, symbolizing the Buddhist belief in the transience of life.

Shortly after the birth, Queen Maya died, another symbol of the passing of one life form into another. Before the birth, Hindu ascetics had prophesied that Queen Maya's son would either be a prince like his father or a Buddha. His father chose for him the former life, and for twenty-nine years, kept his son enclosed within the palace walls. His son was given every luxury imaginable, and had married a beautiful young woman who bore him a son, Rahula. According to legend, he knew nothing of pain or suffering during those years.

Suddenly at the age of twenty-nine, however, Siddhartha began to notice the noise which came from outside the palace walls. He became curious about the world outside, and told his father that he intended to journey outside the palace to discover the world. His father was concerned that he would encounter the nature of the world, its pain, suffering, disease, and misery. To counter that possibility, he sent along a companion, who was to keep Siddhartha from seeing such painful sights.

Life is often unpredictable, and as Siddhartha and the companion journeyed outside the palace, they encountered the "four great" sights. The first great sight was of old people, withered with arthritis and other signs of age. Siddhartha had never known anything like this; he had known only beauty and happiness. He turned to his companion and asked for an explanation; in reply, his companion told him, "That is old age." Siddhartha was puzzled, and as they continued their journey they came across the second great sight: they saw a sick person writhing on the ground in pain. Again, Siddhartha asked for an explanation. In reply, the companion told him, "That is illness." Even more puzzled, Siddhartha continued his journey. He and his companion came upon the third great sight, the funeral procession of a man followed by his weeping daughter and widow. Siddhartha again turned to his companion and asked for an explanation. His companion replied, "That is death." At this point, having seen illness, old age, and death for the first time, Siddhartha was completely puzzled by these mysteries of life. He started to return to the palace, and just as he was almost there, he saw the fourth great sight: an ascetic holding his one possession, the empty bowl which he used to beg for food. The ascetic, however, had a serene smile. At this point, completely mystified, Siddhartha knew the companion could offer no explanations. His previous explanations had explained nothing. At this point, Siddhartha had that deep psychological pain that comes from not knowing the meaning of life or death, of pain or happiness.

When Siddhartha returned to the palace, he vowed to leave and to not return until he had understood those four great sights. On the Night of the Great Renunciation, Siddhartha told his father, wife, and child good-bye, and journeyed with his companion out to some forests where Hindu ascetics lived and meditated. At this point, he told his companion goodbye, for he knew that no one else could answer his questions, but that the answers had to come from within.

He spent several years in the forest with the ascetics, and eventually they looked to him as a master. He endured tremendous deprivation, fasting on a grain of rice and a small drink of muddy water a day. He became emaciated, yet although he had attained the Hindu ideal of renunciation, he had still not attained understanding of the four great sights. He vowed to sit under a Bodhi or Bo tree until enlightenment came, and in a flash of insight, he suddenly understood the Four Noble Truths that became the basis for all of his teachings.

The Four Noble Truths and the Middle Path

According to the four noble truths, understanding begins when one accepts the "first noble truth" that life is full of suffering. All people no matter where or when they live endure suffering. Suffering permeates life, as illustrated by the Buddha's encounter with an old woman who wanted to resurrect her son who had recently died. The Buddha told the old woman to go and find a mustard seed from a house where no one had died. The woman searched for months, and returned empty-handed telling the Buddha that, "The people tell me the living are few but the dead are many." The Buddha then explained the truth about suffering to her.

Had Buddha stopped here, his teachings would have been very pessimistic, yet the "second noble truth" tells us that suffering comes from desire,

Buddha

or attachment to things that are not permanent. The Buddhist teaches that everything is transient. We live; we die. Plants flourish and whither; nothing remains forever. Under the Bodhi tree, the Buddha realized that even the at-man or the self was an illusion. The Hindu demon Mara tempted him with women and other luxuries. When Buddha understood the self as illusory, all temptation vanished, and he placed his hand to the ground calling the earth as his witness. The idea of the self as distinct leads to more and more desire; the self wants to keep not only the self but all things it desires with it. Nothing, however, lasts, and once one realizes this truth, one is able to detach oneself from transient things.

The "third noble truth" teaches that detachment leads to nirvana. Just as the Hindu taught that the cycle of samsara or reincarnation ended with moksha, so too Buddha taught that the cycle of life ends with nirvana. Nirvana, however, is a difficult concept to grasp, as it represents more of a psychological state than the Hindu concept of moksha.

The "fourth noble truth" teaches one how to attain Nirvana. As he meditated with the ascetics, the Buddha came to realize that the severe path of Hindu as-ceticism and renunciation did not bring one to enlightenment; neither had the other extreme, his life of luxury and complete contentment. The Buddha taught the **Middle Path**, a path of moderation and balance accessible to all.

The Eightfold Path of Right Conduct

Buddha also taught the **eight-fold path of right conduct**, which included:
Right Understanding
Right Belief
Right Speech (never to lie or slander anyone)
Right Behavior (never to steal or kill, and never to do anything one might later regret)
Right Occupation (never to choose an occupation that one might consider bad)
Right Effort (always to avoid evil and strive for good)
Right Contemplation (of the Four Noble truths with calmness and detachment)
Right Concentration (the path to peace)

Differences Between Hinduism and Buddhism

The Buddha denied the existence of the atman. He believed that people were not born into castes, but only born with the propensity to do good or evil. He also taught that sacrifice to deities was worthless. When asked by followers whether he was a god, he replied, "I am awake." Buddha forbade his followers from worshipping him as a god. Life in the sixth century B.C.E. in India was very difficult, and the Buddha's doctrine of nirvana appealed to many for whom the thought of endless samsara and infinite numbers of painful lives was hard to bear. Nevertheless, Buddhism spread slowly at first in India; the Buddha's rejection of the caste system conflicted with the mainstream of belief. Further, the Hindu concept of Brahman was able to absorb almost any tradition, and many aspects of Buddhism were reabsorbed into Hinduism. Hindus explain the Buddha as an incarnation of Krishna, just as they explain the historic Jesus and Muhammad as incarnations of Krishna.

The Mauryan Empire

Chandragupta Maurya founded the Mauryan Empire (326–184 B.C.E.) in the wake of the conquests of Alexander the Great. Chandragupta conquered many of the neighboring regions. He was succeeded by his son, Bindusara, and then by the only grandson to survive a series of assassinations, Ashoka. Ashoka's name means "without sorrow," and in his early reign, he instituted a number of harsh punishments for even very small crimes against the state. Following a bloody battle at Kalinga, Ashoka converted to Buddhism and became the first Buddhist ruler of India. Ashoka issued his edicts on many Rock Pillars throughout India, many marking the path to holy sites associated with the Buddha or celebrating events of his life. He also erected many stupa designed to house relics of the Buddha. The round shape of the stupa symbolizes the cosmic consciousness of the Buddha, as do the round protrusions on many statues of the Buddha. During Ashoka's reign, he emphasized the traditional Buddhist ideal of taking "refuge in the dharma, the Sangha, and the Buddha," symbolized by three lions that often adorned the tops of the rock pillars. Ashoka attempted to spread Buddhism through the conquest of righteousness, without force and with tolerance for diversity. Although there is some suspicion that Ashoka used Buddhism in his early days to further his political ends, Ashoka was the greatest ruler in Indian history, and one of the most humane and benevolent monarchs in all of world civilization.

Ironically, the **Muslim conquest** of northern India starting in 1193 C.E. virtually extinguished Buddhism in the land of its birth. Muslims believed that Buddhist images were idolatrous. This was not the first time Buddhist encountered difficulties in their history. Although Buddhism had been protected and fostered by many Hindu monarchs, it had also occasionally suffered from persecutions by Hindus.

The Spread of Buddhism

It was via the Silk Road that Buddhism spread to other areas of Asia. Trade often fostered close working relationships and even alliances, and these relationships were the foundation that made the spread of Buddhism possible. Each area often adapted Buddhism to its own cultural framework. Buddhist temples are found throughout the world, but the greatest concentration of Buddhists is in Southeast Asia, Laos, Thailand, Tibet, China and Japan. The enemies of the Chinese, the Xiong Nu, converted to Buddhism as early as the second century B.C.E. The Han court recorded the arrival of a Buddhist missionary in the first century C.E. The Chinese initially rejected the wandering monks. The Chinese were also puzzled by the notion of reincarnation, but despite the fact that Buddhist teaching conflicted with Chinese values, especially that of filial piety, Buddhism eventually took root. The Chinese translated the Buddhist sutras, and in so doing, fused many of the Buddha's teachings with those of Confucius and other important Chinese thinkers. For example, they translated dharma as Dao (The Way), nirvana as wu wei (inaction), and emphasized those few stories in the existing Buddhist canon that spoke to devotion to parents. Chinese Buddhists eventually created some of the world's greatest Buddhist art, as seen especially in the caves of Magao along the frontiers of China. Here, thousands of caves are adorned with paintings and enormous statues of the Buddha.

In the fourth century C.E., Chinese Buddhist monks, such as Fa Hsien, began to make pilgrimages to India. Fa Hsien learned Sanskrit and made a translation of the *Tripitaka*, the Buddhist canon. The most famous Chinese pilgrim was **Xuan Zang**, who made a sixteen-year pilgrimage to India in the seventh century C.E. in search of Buddhist sutras. These Chinese pilgrim monks largely traveled across the legendary Silk Road. Just as Muslims persecuted Buddhism in the land of its birth, in 845 C.E. the **Chinese Emperor Wu-tsung** ordered the destruction of 4600 Buddhist temples.

Buddhism also spread to Japan, where the Japanese created a unique version of Buddha's teachings, Zen Buddhism. Zen Buddhists are known for the use of rock gardens to meditate. The rocks are often arranged in groups of three to symbolize heaven, earth, and humanity. The formations are also asymmetrical, to symbolize the uneven and imperfect nature of life.

Mahayana and Theraveda Buddhism

Over the centuries, Buddhism evolved into two main traditions: **Mahayana Buddhism** and **Theraveda Buddhism**. These two traditions differed on the issue of how to interpret Buddha's teachings, as reflected in the Tripitaka, or Three Baskets of Wisdom. Mahayana Buddhism is known as the "greater vehicle," and treats the Buddha as a deity. Mahayana Buddhists practice many rituals and emphasize the Buddha's value of compassion. Mahayana Buddhists also believe that salvation is achieved with others, and venerate saints known as Bodhisattvas, those who have achieved nirvana but remain behind to teach.

Theraveda Buddhism, by contrast, is known as the "lesser vehicle" and also as Hinnayana Buddhism. Theraveda Buddhists believe that Buddhism is for monks, and regard the Buddha as a teacher. They avoid rituals, and believe salvation is the concern of the individual. Theraveda Buddhism is primarily practiced in Southeast Asia (Vietnam and Laos).

Despite the remarkable spread of Buddhism, it declined in the regions along the Silk Road following the collapse of the Tang dynasty in 907 C.E. and the invasions of Arabs who had converted to Islam starting in the eighth century C.E.

Tibetan Buddhists

Buddhism took root in Tibet in the fourth century B.C.E. Monasteries such as Drepung Loseling often had as many as 15,000 Buddhist monks, and the Dalai Llama's residence, Poltala Palace, was also the center of Tibetan government. In fact, it was considered a family's sacred duty to give a child to the monastery to be trained. Today, however, the Chinese conquest of Tibet is forcing many Buddhist monks and nuns to make the arduous trek over the Himalayas from Tibet to return to the land of the Buddha's birth. The leader of the modern Tibetan Buddhists is his holiness, the fourteenth **Dalai Llama**, who has returned to India to live in the shadow of the Himalayas, where the Buddha was born. Tibetan Buddhists are a strong force for world peace. Their famous sand mandalas are meant to summon forth the spirits of the deities and to help bring about world peace; yet in typical Buddhist fashion, after days and days of arduous work, the mandalas are scooped into a bag and deposited in a river. This act emphasizes the transience of all life, yet water from the rivers travels to the world's oceans, where it evaporates and eventually returns to the earth as rain. In this way, Tibetan Buddhists hope to spread their prayers for world peace throughout the world, bringing to life the teachings of the ancient "awakened one."

Review Questions

1. The Indian priestly caste was known as the

   (A) Kshatriya.

   (B) Pariah.

   (C) Brahmins.

   (D) Vaisya.

2. The caste known as the sudras

   (A) comprised most of the people of Indian society.

   (B) was the label for Aryan conquerors.

   (C) played a menial role in society, being involved only in manual labor, and having second-class citizenship.

   (D) (A), (B) and (C).

3. All of the following statements are true of the Indus Valley Civilization EXCEPT

   (A) It had a concern for cleanliness, as reflected in its sewage and drainage systems.

   (B) It probably practiced water rituals, as indicated by the Great Bath at Mohenjo-Daro.

   (C) The imagery on the soapstone (clay) seals is similar to later Hindu imagery.

   (D) It fought many battles, as indicated by the war-like artifacts found in the streets.

4. "Moksha" is

   (A) the Buddhist term for the end of the cycle of suffering.

   (B) the Hindu term for the end of the cycle of life.

   (C) the Hindu term for reincarnation.

   (D) the Buddhist term for the Middle Path.

5. "Samsara" is the

   (A) Buddhist term for the end of the cycle of suffering.

   (B) Hindu term for the end of the cycle of life.

   (C) Hindu term for reincarnation.

   (D) Buddhist term for the Middle Path.

6. "Atman" is the

   (A) Hindu term for reincarnation.

   (B) Hindu term for duty or right conduct.

   (C) Buddhist term for suffering.

   (D) Hindu term for the individual soul.

7. "Dharma" is the

   (A) Hindu term for reincarnation.

   (B) Hindu term for duty or right conduct.

   (C) Hindu term for the individual soul.

   (D) Buddhist term for suffering.

8. "Brahman" is the

   (A) Hindu term for reality.

   (B) Hindu term for the soul.

   (C) Hindu term for reincarnation.

   (D) Hindu term for the end of the cycles of life.

9. All of the following are Noble Truths of Buddhism EXCEPT

   (A) Suffering is caused by lack of desire for anything.

   (B) Life is filled with pain and suffering.

   (C) Salvation can be attained through following the Middle Path.

   (D) Suffering will end when one is freed from the chain of existence and achieves nirvana.

10. The language of the Vedas was

    (A) Cuneiform.

    (B) Sanskrit.

    (C) Hindi.

    (D) Mandarin.

11. The Aryan "invasion" affected Indian society by introducing

    (A) massive epidemics that wiped out the Indus River Valley population.

    (B) the caste system.

    (C) animal worship.

    (D) large scale industrial development.

12. The first empire in India was created by

    (A) Ashoka.

    (B) Buddha.

    (C) Zoroaster.

    (D) Chandragupta.

13. The ruler who described his reign as the "conquest of righteousness" was

    (A) Chandragupta.

    (B) Ashoka.

    (C) Zoroaster.

    (D) Buddha.

14. The form of Buddhism which emphasizes the role of Bodhisattvas is

    (A) Therevada Buddhism.

    (B) Arabian Buddhism.

    (C) African Buddhism.

    (D) Mahayana Buddhism.

15. Hinduism differs from Buddhism in all of the following ways EXCEPT

    (A) Hinduism rejects the atman, while Buddhism affirms it.

    (B) Hinduism insists on a pantheon of deities, while Buddhism, as taught by the historic Siddhartha, rejected deities.

    (C) Hinduism preserves an important role for rituals, while Buddhism, as taught by the historic Siddhartha, rejected rituals.

    (D) Hinduism teaches that the end of the cycles of rebirth brings moksha or union with Brahman, while Buddhism emphasizes a psychological awakening called nirvana.

Answers

1. (C)	5. (C)	9. (A)	13. (B)
2. (D)	6. (D)	10. (B)	14. (D)
3. (D)	7. (B)	11. (B)	15. (A)
4. (B)	8. (A)	12. (D)	

Chapter 5

CHINA THROUGH THE HAN DYNASTY

KEY TERMS

Yellow River

Five Heavenly emperors

Shang Dynasty

Anyang

ancestor worship

Zhou (Chou)

eastern Zhou (Chou)

Loyang

Mandate of Heaven

Wei River Valley

Warring States

Daoism

Lao Tzu

Wu-wei

Confucius

Rules of Propriety

filial piety

Qín Shǐ Huángdì (Ch'in Shi Huang-ti)

Qin (Ch'in) Empire

Great Wall

Han Fei

legalism

Han Dynasty

Hàn wǔ dì (Wu-ti),

Ch'ang An period

later Han

Silk Road

Xiong-Nu (Hsiung-Nu)

Ban Chao

Sīmǎ Qin (Ssǔma Ch'ien)

A Note on Chinese Characters and Systems of Transliteration:

There are two systems of transliterating Chinese characters into English: the pinyin and the Wade-Giles system. The Wade-Giles system was developed in the late nineteenth and early twentieth centuries and was the system most commonly used until the Chinese government adopted pinyin as the official system of transliteration in 1979. In the text that follows, the pinyin transliteration is given first, followed by the Wade-Giles in parentheses on the first mention of the term.

GEOGRAPHY, AGRICULTURE, THE FAMILY, AND THE PEASANT

Agriculture evolved as early as 8000 B.C.E. in northern China around fertile river valleys. The Yellow River was one of the most important of these river systems. The Yellow River is often called "China's Sorrow," as throughout history there have been many devastating floods that have killed thousands. The Yellow River is a very turbulent river, which the Chinese crossed by inflating goat skins and creating rafts from them. Chinese culture arose on the small plots in valleys around the Yellow River. The family unit cultivated these plots. The influence of early Chinese agriculture around the Yellow River is still felt in the importance of the family unit in Chinese society. The oldest male was the head of the Chinese family; next in order of importance were the sons, from oldest to youngest; last in importance were the women of the family, from the oldest, the mother, to the youngest daughter.

The chief crop cultivated in ancient and modern China was rice or millet. Rice is a very efficient source of nutrition, but it must be cultivated primarily by hand. Rice sprouts are allowed to grow into shoots and then transplanted by hand into flooded paddies, where they are later harvested by hand. Throughout Chinese history, the special care needed to cultivate rice has meant that the vast majority of Chinese lived in the countryside and worked at manual labor. Women played an important role in the fields, and have for centuries been the most significant group of laborers in China. Just as historical records of the lives of women are scant, so too are records of the lives of the majority of the world's population, the peasants and laborers. Today, as in antiquity, the vast majority of Chinese live in the countryside in impoverished villages. Chinese peasants still live primarily within the family unit in these villages.

THE PREHISTORIC ERA

The Prehistoric era in Chinese history is the era before the **Xia (Hsia) Dynasty** and is primarily dominated by the mythological stories of the **Heavenly Emperors**. Scholars have never been able to authenticate these stories, but for quite some time, they also thought that the Shang and Xia (Hsia) dynasties were mythological in nature.

Whether the stories of the Heavenly Emperors are mythological or not, they represent many elements of traditional Chinese beliefs and practices and also define the ideal emperor and state. The myths of five of these emperors give us the greatest insight into the evolution of Chinese culture. The emperor **Fu Hsi** created the *I Ching*, a text that is made up of long and short lines representing the balance between yin and yang. The Chinese believe that the combination of lines allows one to foretell the future. The emperor **Shan Nung** gave the Chinese the plow and the market place, two quintessential elements of an agricultural community. The emperor **Huang Ti** developed fire. If we look at what these three emperors gave the Chinese and compare these ideas to those of other cultures, we notice that most other cultures credit such developments to the gods, whereas the Chinese credit them to the emperors. The Chinese did not worship deities in the same way as the Mesopotamians, Egyptians, and Hebrews; rather, they worshipped their ancestors and also the emperor. Huang Ti also had twenty-five sons, from whom the feudal families of the **Zhou (Chou)** era traced their heritage. The story of Huang Ti and his twenty-five sons illustrates the idea of China as an extended family. The sixth-century B.C.E. sage Confucius based his entire system of virtue on the family unit.

The emperor **Ti Yao** illustrates the concept of virtue determining the emperor, which was later articulated by Confucius. Ti Yao grew old and needed a successor, but distrusted his own son. He thought his son immoral and shiftless, and so went in search of a worthy successor. He found such a young man, one who was moral, hard working, and learned. However, he did not know his own family origins, as his mother was a prostitute. Nevertheless, Ti Yao ceded the throne this young man, as his ability and inner virtue made him more fit for the throne than those whose genealogy made them candidates for it.

The Chinese creation myth also illustrates some very important Chinese concepts. According to Chinese belief, the universe was created from a giant egg, from which emerged the first cosmic man, **Pan Ku**. Pan Ku labored to construct the universe we know, and as he worked, his breath became the wind, his sweat the rivers, his hair the grass, and the tiny bugs on his body, lice, became humans. For the Chinese, one's identity comes from one's place in the family unit and larger social organizations. The Chinese ideal of humanity is a communal one, where individualism is de-emphasized in favor of the community.

In our discussion of the Xia (Hsia) dynasty, we shall see that the ideal emperor is one who sacrifices his own interests for those of the community. So too, the ideal citizen serves others before himself. In the Daoist tradition, which began in the sixth century B.C.E., humans are a part of the Dào (Tao), which is a cosmic force that determines life. In Daoist art, humans are often seen as tiny specks within vast landscapes, reflecting the same viewpoint of the creation myth as to the place of humans within the grand scheme of things. In many ways, the Chinese have never moved away from the prehistoric era in terms of the traditional values reflected in these stories.

The Xia (Hsia) Dynasty

For many years, scholars thought the **Xia (Hsia) Dynasty** (before 2000 B.C.E. to 1570 B.C.E.) was a mythological dynasty. Its founder was a Heavenly Emperor, **Yu**, who taught the Chinese how to manage the flooding of the Yellow River; Yu left behind his family and walked through China for ten years in order to help his people. At the end of the ten years, he returned a cripple. The emperor Yu illustrates the Confucian notion of the self-sacrificing and virtuous emperor who rules for the good of society. Scholars have recently unearthed artifacts that suggest that the Xia Dynasty was actually an historic dynasty.

The Shang

The first solidly authenticated dynasty in Chinese history is the **Shang Dynasty** (1570–1045 B.C.E.). It was thought that the Shang were another mythological dynasty until the twentieth century. The Shang used tortoise shells for divination and in their cult of ancestor worship. The chief priest was the oldest male in each family, and he would burn the shells and interpret the answers to the questions written on them depending on where the shell cracked. The use of tortoise shells in ancestor worship made literacy a necessity, and the Chinese were the most literate culture on the world for centuries.

The Shang were a warrior people, who moved their capital several times. The walls of the city of Ao, their sixth capital, aptly show their warrior culture, as they were thirty feet thick in places. The Shang buried their warriors with jade, as they believed it had magical properties. Jade is not indigenous to the area dominated by the Shang, and therefore, we know they had established trading networks outside their dominions. The Shang also placed ritual vessels in the tombs, and Chinese skill in bronze casting was unequalled for centuries. The Shang also buried their warriors with live servants, in much the same way as the inhabitants of ancient Ur in Mesopotamia buried their royalty.

The Shang Dynasty was centered around the Yellow River; a slave revolt in the eleventh century B.C.E. overthrew the dynasty.

The Zhou (Chou) (Zhou) Dynasty

The Zhou (Chou) Dynasty (1045–403 B.C.E.) was centered in the Wei River Valley, and the sixth century B.C.E. sage Confucius based his moral and ethical system on the Zhou (Chou) rulers. For Confucius, the best models of virtue were in the distant Chinese past. The Zhou (Chou) had overthrown the Shang during a massive slave revolt, and so had to establish their legitimacy. They argued that the last of the Shang rulers was immoral and that the "mandate of heaven" was withdrawn from him and his dynasty and given to the Zhou (Chou), who were moral. The Zhou (Chou) modeled their idea of the state and the emperor on the heavens, specifically after the polestar or the north star, a fixed point in the northern sky around which other stars revolve. For the Zhou (Chou), the emperor was the polestar, the center of Chinese society. The Classic of History or Shu Jing is a very important collection of documents from seventeen hundred years of Chinese civilization. Although many of these texts were reconstructed during the Han Dynasty, they give us much insight into the Zhou (Chou) system of government and moral value that became the basis for Confucianism.

Under the Zhou (Chou), China was a feudal society in which great and powerful nobles lived on fortified estates and lands and governed their own states. The law of primogeniture was important in this system, as all the possessions of the father passed to his eldest son, thereby preserving the family wealth and power. The legacy of the Zhou (Chou) feudal structure is still seen in China today, where there are only approximately 400 last names despite the ethnic diversity of China. The emperor Qín Shǐ Huángdì (Ch'in Shi Huang-ti) would later unify China, thus limiting the number of family names in China.

The capital of the Zhou (Chou) Dynasty was Xian, which was also the beginning of the famous Silk Road. Xian was an important center for centuries, and was also the location near which the tomb of the first emperor of China, **Qín Shǐ Huángdì** (Ch'in Shi Huang-ti), was constructed.

The Western Zhou (Chou)

The western Zhou (Chou) collapsed in 771 B.C.E.; according to legend, the emperor had a concubine who was quite fond of watching the army assembled with all of its beautifully colored armor and banners. The emperor had routinely summoned them to please her on the pretext that invaders were coming; in 771 B.C.E., there really was a crisis, but when the emperor summoned the troops, no one came!

The Eastern Zhou (Chou)

The Zhou (Chou) also had an eastern capital, Loyang, where they maintained power from 722–481 B.C.E. Unlike many cities that were administrative centers of government, Loyang was a center for religious rites, which betrayed the weakness of the eastern Zhou (Chou). In 403 B.C.E., the eastern Zhou (Chou) collapsed, followed by the period of warring states.

The Warring States

In the period following the collapse of the eastern Zhou (Chou) from 403–221 B.C.E., the feudal lords of China vied for power and the states of China were not united. The chaos of the period of warring states created a desire for order, and the great Chinese schools, such as Confucianism and Daoism, arose in response to the political and social chaos of the Warring States. It was during the Warring States era that the Confucian emphasis on learning led to the rise of the **shih scholars.** The shih scholars dominated the administrative apparatus of China for centuries, as these offices were determined by the Confucian idea of merit.

The Hundred Schools of Chinese Philosophy

During the sixth century B.C.E., a time known as the Axis Age for the important philosophical schools and religious traditions that developed then, the sages **Confucius** and **Lao Zi** (**Lao Tzu** or **Lao Tze**) responded to the chaos surrounding the decline and collapse of the Zhou (Chou) Dynasty by developing philosophies designed to promote order.

CONFUCIUS

Kǒng Fūzǐ (K'ung Fu-tzu) was born in 551 B.C.E. and was a member of the minor noble family Kong. His name means "master Kong" in Chinese and was translated into western languages by the Jesuits as **"Confucius."** Although Confucius rose to a prominent position in the government of his native province Lu, political intrigue forced him from the government and he became a wandering teacher. He wrote no texts himself, but his followers collected his sayings and organized them. The most famous collection of Confucian teachings is the *Analects*. Confucius taught through parables and short aphorisms, which illustrate concepts rather than attempt to prove them. His teachings form the basis of Chinese culture, and were themselves based on earlier traditions going back to the Zhou (Chou) and the Chinese mythology surrounding the Heavenly Emperors. Confucius was not an innovator, but was a respecter of ancient traditions and customs. For Confucius, the most excellent models of virtue were to be found in the past, particularly in the Zhou (Chou) dynasty. Confucius did not consider himself to be a "sage," or extremely wise man; he simply saw himself as one who respected tradition and upheld the ways of the past. Respect for the past would restore balance, harmony, and order to society and to an individual's own life. Confucianism eventually formed the basis for Chinese culture and profoundly influenced Japanese and Korean culture.

The Nature of Confucianism

Although Confucianism is often practiced religiously, it is not a religion. In the Analects, Confucius refused to address questions about the afterlife or the spirit world, as he believed he had no knowledge of such things. Confucianism is not a lofty system of thought on transcendent deities and the afterlife; it is rather a practical system of ethics designed to produce a well-ordered person and state.

The Virtuous Man

Confucius was concerned above all else with virtue and with the virtuous individual. Confucius insisted that he was not an innovator but rather a transmitter of excellent models of the past. He did not regard himself as an especially brilliant thinker or sage. This is an important point, as Confucius insisted that the virtuous life is open to all and can be followed by any ordinary person. For Confucius, filial piety, or the respect of children for their elders, particularly their male elders, was the basis of all morality. In other words, family relationships formed the basis for a strong society.

The Rule of Propriety and the Way or Dào (Tao)

The Rules of Propriety governed Chinese behavior and helped to develop virtuous behavior. One learned to follow these rules and to become virtuous through training. Virtue was not inborn for Confucius, but rather was a learned behavior. Through watching and imitating the virtuous behavior of one's parents and others in society, particularly the emperor, one learns to be virtuous. After years of performing virtuous actions, one becomes virtuous and can always be relied upon in any situation to be virtuous. For the truly virtuous person, rules and their enforcement are no longer necessary. Virtue becomes the essence of that person's character and will always dictate correct action no matter what the circumstances. Outer behavior is not to be identified with virtue. Behavior can help one learn and develop virtue, but inner virtue is something apart from mere actions. When there are no external factors that compel obedience, the truly virtuous person can be trusted to act properly as a result of his own inner being. So important was inner virtue that Confucius taught one to follow the **Way** or **Dào** (Tao) simply for the sake of the Way rather than for the sake of reward or punishment.

These teachings helped to develop a meritocracy in China, or the idea that government should be conducted by those whose virtue and learning merited their positions of authority and respect. In other words, heredity was meaning-less; only ability and inner virtue determined one's advancement.

It was particularly important for government officials to be virtuous. Con-fucius argued that if one governed people well for several decades or centuries, there would no longer be a need for the death penalty or other harsh punish-ments. People will submit to virtuous rulers, whereas they will revolt from dishonest ones. Confucianism was a practical form of action accessible to all which sought to create a virtuous society governed by virtuous rulers, a society in which one knew his place and kept it, in which one had respect for those above him and treated those beneath with benevolence.

LAO ZI (LAO TZU OR LAO TZE) AND DAOISM

Lao Zi's historic existence, unlike that of Confucius, cannot be decisively verified or rejected. The great Han historian Ssu ma Ch'ien wrote the first bi-ography of Lao Zi in the second to the first century B.C.E. According to legend, Lao Zi, known as the wise old dragon, was born in 604 B.C.E. and lived until 517 B.C.E. He was conceived by a shooting star, and carried in his mother's womb for 62 years. When he was born, he had a long mane of white hair. This is an interesting legend, as the dragon is the symbol of the heavens and imperial power, while the Chinese calendar is a sixty-two year calendar. In other words, Lao Zi's wisdom was identified with the wisdom of the heavens themselves. Lao Zi became a shih scholar during the last years of the Zhou (Chou) dynasty and, like Confucius, he became very disenchanted with the collapse of order. According to legends, as he was attempting to leave China, he was detained at the last pass across the frontiers. A guard forced him to record the fruits of his wisdom before being allowed to exit. The result became known as the **Dao De Jing** (**Tào Te Ching**), or The Classic of the Way and of Virtue.

The language of the Dao De Jing, however, is clearly from the Han era; we cannot know how much of this text actually represents the teachings of Lao Zi, much less can we know whether Lao Zi ever actually existed.

According to legend, Confucius once met the "old dragon" Lao Zi, who was the older scholar. Lao Zi was unimpressed with Confucius, and believed him vain and arrogant for attempting to define the Dao (Tao) through his "Rules of Propriety." Lao Zi rejected the Confucian notion that the Rules of Propriety might capture the path to virtue. This was due to his belief that the Dao was not to be equated with filial piety or with any other system of morality or learning, as the Dao itself was limitless and inexpressible. It cannot be named or other-wise described, as any attempt to do so would necessarily limit the Dao. The Dao encompasses everything.

Therefore, the Daoist ideal of the sage was quite different from that of Confucius, who advocated learning and study in order to cultivate virtue. Lao Zi argued that, "When we renounce learning we have no troubles. If we could renounce our sageness and discard our wisdom, it would be better for the people a hundredfold. If we could renounce our benevolence and discard our righteousness, the people would again become filial and kindly. If we could renounce our artful contrivances and discard our scheming for gain, there would be no thieves and robbers."

Daoist Non-action or Wu Wei

The passage above is a direct attack on the Confucian ideal of wisdom and benevolence; what Lao Zi argues is that any system of rules or laws captures only a part of the Dao and therefore necessarily limits a person's innate response. Any system of laws creates disorder, since laws define crimes and criminals. Without laws, there are no crimes nor can there be criminals. Therefore, the Daoist sage and the Daoist emperor best manage affairs through the philosophy of non-action or **wu wei**, which means non-interference with the natural path of things.

The Daoist confidence in human nature is boundless; unlike Confucius, who believed virtue must be learned, Lao Zi believed following the Way would occur naturally if people were left without interference. Lao Zi rejected the idea of meritocracy and sought instead a state where the true sage could become like an uncarved block of marble. Just as a sculptor can take the block and create any form with it, so too, the Daoist sage is able to adapt to any circumstances, as he holds to no rigid school of thought nor any preconceived path of action. Just as water in a river bends and engulfs obstacles in its way, so too, the Daoist sage can adapt to any circumstances.

A common misinterpretation of Daoism is to assume that Daoists advocate no action at all; however, the philosophy of non-action simply means acting in accordance with the Dao and not interfering with the natural path of things. For the Daoist, not interfering with the natural path of humans through artificial laws that can only capture part of the Dao will lead to a harmonious society.

Historically, it has often been said that the Chinese are Confucians in their daily life and Daoists in their private life. Confucianism helped the Chinese in their daily affairs, while Daoism spoke to their more esoteric and private spiritual desires.

THE QIN (CH'IN) EMPIRE

Qín Shǐ Huángdì (Ch'in Shi Huang-ti) was the first emperor in Chinese history. He was known in his youth as Ying Zheng, and was born in the third century B.C.E. His opponents, the Confucians, helped to promote the story that he was not the son of the king of Qin, but rather, the son of the chancellor, Lu Buwei, who had kept his mother as a concubine before giving her to the future king of Qin shortly before Prince Zheng was born. The name Qín Shǐ Huángdì has special meaning. The word "Shi" means "first" and the words "Huangdi" refer to one of the heavenly emperors of Chinese mythology, whose contribution to Chinese culture was the gift of fire and whose twenty-five sons became the basis of the feudal families of Zhou (Chou) Dynasty. Qín Shǐ Huángdì was the first to unite the warring provinces of China.

The Great Wall of China

The Great Wall of China

When Qín Shǐ Huángdì united the warring provinces, he tore down the internal walls that divided them, and erected one wall around his new China. This wall is now known as the **Great Wall of China**. The Wall is the only structure visible with the naked human eye from the surface of the moon, and it is about thirty-five feet high and wide enough for two or three chariots to ride side by side. The Great Wall is not a single wall but rather a series of walls constructed over several centuries of China's history. Most of what can be seen of the Great Wall today was built during the Ming Dynasty, which came to power in the fourteenth century C.E. Most of the wall was constructed primarily through the rammed earth technique, where two walls are filled with earth. Some of the older sections of the wall are only earth, which is still packed so tightly that one can barely chisel it out. The Wall was built on very mountainous terrain and it extends for about 1500 li (approximately 4500 miles) along the northern borders of China.

It is still difficult to imagine how the workers were able to achieve such an enormous engineering feat, and the Chinese have many legends about its construction. According to legend, Qín Sh Huángdì had a magic bludgeon that was able to knock down entire mountains with a single blow. He also had a magic stallion that reared up and pawed the earth at strategic points. Here, the Chinese built watchtowers, where thousands of soldiers once stood guard on the frontiers of China. The towers were built only as far away from one another as a smoke signal could travel. There are also many legends about why the Wall was built. Some scholars say that the Chinese believed that evil spirits could only travel in a straight line, and so the Wall was built to keep out the spirits. Others believe the Chinese constructed the Wall was to keep out the Xiong-Nu (Hsiung-Nu, often identified with the Huns), who terrorized the Chinese frontiers during this period. If that is why the Wall was built, it is one of the most unsuccessful structures in history, as it never succeeded at keeping invaders out. China is the only culture that has attempted to literally wall itself in, and the Great Wall is more of a symbol that divided China from the rest of the world than an effective barrier.

One other hypothesis has been given for the construction of the Wall; it is argued that once Qín Shǐ Huángdì had won his victory over the other Chinese provinces, there was nothing to keep his army busy, and so they were put to work on the Wall. Whatever the historic reasons and legends about the building of the Wall, its construction reflects a monumental feat of engineering, and required massive use of slave labor.

Shǐ Huángdì departed from his predecessors in many ways, not the least of which was the implementation of a new philosophy of virtue and of law, Legalism. Qín Shǐ Huángdì's prime minister, Han Fei, drafted many of the Legalist positions, according to which very harsh punishments for infractions of the law were necessary in order to compel the population to respect the emperor's authority and to obey the law. The Legalists rejected the Confucian notion of inner virtue and did not believe that people would obey the law without some sort of external force present. One of the punishments for breaking laws was to be sent to work on the Great Wall, as the difficult conditions under which the laborers worked was in essence a death sentence. According to legends, when the husband of a young woman was sent to work on the wall, she was worried about his welfare in the cold and harsh conditions. She prepared for him warm clothes and a basket of food and went to visit him. When she arrived, she found him already dead, and wept so profusely that the Wall itself melted away, revealing his bones in the Wall as well as those of many others. According to legend, there are more dead Chinese in the Wall than there are living Chinese. The young woman took the bones of her husband to the coast, where her spirit and that of her husband can still be seen today as boulders off the coast of China.

This story is an extremely important indicator of just how hated Shǐ Huáng-dì was. Traditionally, women in China were subservient to men and had little rights. The fact that a woman's tears could literally bring down the Great Wall, one of the most potent symbols of Shǐ Huángdì's brutal repression, is very telling indeed and foreshadowed his quick demise.

The brutal treatment of workers on the Great Wall is but one of many harsh punishments during the Legalist era. Han Fei was one of the most important Legalists of this era, which included boiling a victim alive in hot water and cutting off limbs or ears.

Anti-Confucianism of Qín Shǐ Huángdì's Reign

The philosophy of Legalism departed radically from Confucianism, which had dominated Chinese thought before the reign of Qín Shǐ Huángdì. One of the most important philosophers who advocated Legalist beliefs was a prince of the Han, Han Fei. Qín Shǐ Huángdì was attracted to the philosophy of Han Fei, but ordered him to commit suicide in 233 B.C.E. out of fear that he would remain loyal to the Han, which he ruthlessly conquered.

Legalist beliefs conflicted with both Confucianism and Daoism. Confucianism was based on the belief that following traditional rites and rituals, respecting elders and the emperor, who served as models, could cultivate inner virtue. This inner virtue would dictate following the Way no matter what external circumstances arose; a virtuous person in Confucius's sense could be counted on to act according to the Way regardless of whether there were external reasons compelling him to act in that manner. Confucius had a very highly evolved notion of humankind and its ability to act virtuously, and it was a notion the Legalists did not share. Legalists did not believe that they could rely on virtue alone to preserve order, but trusted more in the firm rule of law and in harsh punishments and effective rewards. While Confucians believed in following the Way for the sake of the Way, Legalists believed in the need to control people through punishments or to motivate them through external rewards. Confucians refused to accept the Legalist ways of thinking, as they were concerned about whether anyone would obey these harsh laws when there was no coercive force present.

Shǐ Huángdì's policy of moving forward rather than respecting the rites and rituals of tradition also conflicted with Confucianism. He abolished the law of primogeniture, according to which property is passed from the father to the eldest son. This custom had the effect of strengthening the nobility, as nobles were able to amass great estates and pass them intact to their eldest sons. Shǐ Huángdì wanted to break the power of the nobility, and so he forced them to divide their property among all sons. For Confucians, this act weakened the fundamental unit of society, the family. Consequently, Shǐ Huángdì ordered the burning of the Confucian classics, and even had Confucian scholars who refused to give up their books and teachings buried alive.

Standardization of Weights and Measures

Qín Shǐ Huángdì also wanted to unify trade in China, and so found it necessary to standardize the various forms of currency used in China. Before Qín Shǐ Huángdì, the currency was called the Ming Dào, or "imitations of useful tools." The 1/2 ounce Pan Liang coin with the square hole in the center became the standard coin. Its circular shape represents the heavens, while the square hole in the center represents the earth. His ministers also saw to it that writing was standardized. Today, there are five styles of calligraphy, which were first standardized in the reign of Shǐ Huángdì in the third century B.C.E.

The Tomb of Qín Shǐ Huángdì

Qín Shǐ Huángdì was, in many ways, a megalomaniac who sought immortality. He brought diviners, astrologists, and apothecaries to court, who concocted special potions for him. It is believed that some of these potions contained mercury and so contributed to his death in 207 B.C.E. At one point, his advisors told him that his declining health might be due to the fact that the evil spirits could see him. Qín Shǐ Huángdì then built a palace surrounded by walls, so that he could walk through it without being seen. When this failed, his advisors then told him that perhaps the Divine Immortals on the Coast could help him attain immortality; he ordered 3,000 men to go in search of these immortal beings. The 3,000 men never returned, and according to legend, these men then traveled to the islands of Japan and founded Japanese culture. This is surely not historic, as we know that there were indigenous Japanese in Japan, the Ainu, and also other inhabitants migrated from Korea, not from China. Japan borrowed a great deal of cultural ideals from China, but almost certainly that borrowing did not begin in this way.

Although Qín Shǐ Huángdì believed that he would live forever and that he would reign for 10,000 generations, he still built an enormous tomb to celebrate his power on the outskirts of Xi'an, the ancient capital of China. In 1974, some farmers were digging for a well when they discovered he remains of some terra cotta soldiers. This led to the discovery of the actual tumulus of the emperor, which has never been excavated. Partly this is due to the size of the complex uncovered and the difficulty of the excavation project, but it is also due to the accounts of the later Han dynasty, whose historians were renowned in the ancient world for their record keeping. The Han accounts state that the tomb was booby-trapped with poison-tipped arrows, which has at least suggested that modern archaeologists should approach this site with care. The Han historians also state that the tomb had moving rivers of mercury, a map of the heavens on the ceiling, and a map of China on the floor, clearly putting the first emperor not only in the center of China, but also in the center of the universe.

Several massive pits filled with terra cotta soldiers surround the tumulus. Several statues of horses were also found in the pits surrounding the tumulus. The horses are not fully life-size, but anticipate the interest in the horse as an art motif in the Han Dynasty. During the Han Dynasty, the Chinese pushed westward in order to find better horses to combat the Huns, who were expert horsemen.

The excavation project has been difficult, as peasants who revolted upon news of the death of Qín Shǐ Huángdì's brutal rule ransacked the site and burned it to the ground. Some of the buried figures still show burn marks. For centuries, the location of the site was forgotten, peasants built villages over the pits. Much of the site is still in a state of disarray or even rubble. The Great Wall of China and the tomb of its first emperor, Qín Shǐ Huángdì, are clear examples of architecture used to symbolize the power of the emperor. Shǐ Huángdì was a hated despot, but one whom the Chinese have always respected for uniting China and creating a bureaucratic structure that still exists today. Despite the fact that China is the most populous nation on earth, there are not nearly as many Chinese dialects as one would expect given this number of people and ethnicities, and there are only about 400 last names. These are but a few of the ways by which Qín Shǐ Huángdì who took power in 221 B.C.E., helped to mold the China of today.

Terra Cotta Soldiers

THE HAN EMPIRE

The Chinese today are known as the "people of the Han." The Han preserved the administrative structure of the Ch'in Empire but reinstated Confucian ethics. Chinese government for centuries was influenced by the Han fusion of Legalism and Confucianism. The Han buried their rulers in great mounds, which can still be seen in the countryside of China today. The ancient literacy of China flourished in Han record keeping; the Han were the most accurate and astute historians in the world. The Han reconstructed the Shu Jing, or Classic of History, and also compiled several other texts that became known as the Confucian Classics. Sīmǎ Qin (Ssǔma Ch'ien)'s history, the Shih chi or "historical record," went back to before the Shang. The brother and sister of one of the Han's most famous generals wrote a history of Han dynasty, the Han shu. Ban Gu, who served in the imperial court as a poet, began the history, and his sister Ban Zhao finished it. She clearly exceeded the traditional boundaries for women.

The most well known leader of the Han was the emperor **Hàn wǔ dì (Wu ti)**, who reigned from 141–87 B.C.E. Hàn wǔ dì conquered Vietnam, Manchuria, and North Korea. He also battled the **Xiong-Nu (Hsiung-Nu)**, who have often been identified with the Huns. The Chinese described these people as moving "on swift horses, and in their breasts beat the hearts of beasts. They shift from place to place like a flock of birds. Thus it is difficult to corner them and bring them under control." The Han were forced to go in search of allies in their battle against the Xiong-Nu, and the journey of one of Hàn wǔ dì's famous diplomats helped to create the trading relations and routes known as the Silk Road.

Travels Along the Silk Road

The interactions of cultures along the Silk Road is illustrated by the travels of **Zhang Qian**, who first traveled the Silk Road in 138 B.C.E. on the orders of the Han emperor Hàn wǔ dì (Wu-ti). As Hàn wǔ dì struggled against the Xiong-Nu, he sought to create alliances with Yue-chi people of India. The Xiong-Nu, however, captured Zhang Qian and held him for ten years. He eventually escaped and reached the Yue-chi in Northern India only to find them uninterested in an alliance. He did, however, learn about their heavenly horses, which were much larger, stronger, and faster than those of China. Zhang Qian began his return journey, was recaptured by the Xiong-Nu and did not return until 125 B.C.E. By the end of his travels, he had traveled to thirty-six kingdoms of the western regions and brought back knowledge of their customs and trading practices to the Han.

Zhang Qian made a second journey in 119 B.C.E. on a mission to the Wu-sun people, which eventually led to formal trade relations with Persia. During the travels of Zhang Qian, he was surprised to discover many of these lands already importing goods from China over land routes. They most especially prized silk from China, while the Chinese were interested in grapes and wine from other lands, which were then unknown in China, as well as jade, the heavenly horses, and other luxury goods. Although the travels of Zhang Qian failed to gain the hoped for alliances, the new knowledge of the peoples and goods available in the western regions made the Han even more determined to be rid of the Xiong-Nu, who blocked their way to the west.

Zhang Qian died in 113 B.C.E., and Hàn wǔ dì eventually drove the Xiong-Nu out of Mongolia and planted forts along the Silk Road. In his various conquests, Hàn wǔ dì's armies traveled farther from home than the Roman armies ever did, but he neglected affairs at home. The high levels of taxation imposed for his many campaigns led to revolt.

The Ch'ang An Period or Western or Former Han

From 202 B.C.E–9 C.E., the Han maintained power at Ch'ang An. This era is often referred to as the Ch'ang An period or the western or former Han.

The Later Han

From 25 C.E. to 221 C.E., the Han center of power was the old Zhou (Chou) site of Loyang, and this era is known as the later Han. The later Han defeated the Huns in 89 C.E. and extended their power to the Caspian Sea and Persian Gulf by 97 C.E.

THE PERIOD OF SIX DYNASTIES

After the collapse of the Han in 221 C.E., China entered the Period of Six Dynasties (known in China as the Northern and Southern Dynasties), which lasted until 586 C.E., when the Sui dynasty (586–618 C.E.) briefly reunited China. In reality during this Chinese version of the dark ages, there were many more than six dynasties. At the same time, Roman civilization was growing weaker in the areas it dominated along the western boundaries of the trade route. As political power weakened in both China and Rome, trade along the Silk Road also greatly declined. It was far more dangerous to travel the road and because there were now more centers of power, merchants had to pay more and more taxes to transport their goods along the trade routes of the Silk Road. Trade along the Silk Road would be revived again with the conquests of various peoples who converted to Islam after the seventh century C.E. In China itself, however, the collapse of Han society brought about a flourishing of culture. The Chinese were more open to foreign influences, and Buddhist missionaries and merchants traveled the Silk Road even in the absence of the military protection the Han had previously offered. Many literary and other cultural artifacts date from this period, which distinguishes the Chinese dark ages from their counterpart in the medieval west following the collapse of Roman rule in Europe.

Review Questions

1. During the Shang dynasty, religion was centered on

   (A) the heavens.

   (B) the family.

   (C) the gods of the Tao mountain.

   (D) Confucius.

2. The stories of the Five Heavenly Emperors are important in Chinese history because

   (A) they tell us about the historic period before the Shang.

   (B) they tell us about the achievements of the five most important emperors in Chinese history.

   (C) they are informative about the origins of the most important cultural ideals in China.

   (D) they tell us that agriculture came to China late as compared to other cultures.

3. The Shang were overthrown by a slave revolt led by the

   (A) Hsia.

   (B) Chou.

   (C) Fu Hsi.

   (D) Confucians.

4. Confucius taught that

   (A) society should adapt and change as realities change.

   (B) the youngest members of society are the most valuable.

   (C) virtue depends on circumstances.

   (D) virtue is acquired rather than inborn, and the most virtuous person is one who respects the wisdom of the past.

5. The Ch'in emperor was known for all of the following EXCEPT

   (A) building the Great Wall.

   (B) his tomb and the surrounding grounds which contained thousands of life-size figures and horses.

(C) abolishing the law of primogeniture.

(D) bringing the Confucian classics back to China.

6. The school of philosophy according to which the Ch'in emperor ruled was

(A) Legalism.

(B) Confucianism.

(C) Taoism.

(D) Imperialism.

7. According to Legalism, all of the following are true EXCEPT

(A) harsh punishments are necessary to maintain order.

(B) the emperor's word is law.

(C) inner virtue was more important than outer obedience.

(D) emperors should encourage good servants to serve the state, but should firmly insist on complete obedience.

8. The Han Dynasty was known for all of the following EXCEPT

(A) the production of silk.

(B) poor historical writing.

(C) the invention of paper.

(D) the making of porcelain.

9. The Han's most fearsome enemy were the

(A) Romans.

(B) Japanese.

(C) Mongols.

(D) Hsiung Nu (Huns).

10. After the collapse of the Chou in the eighth century B.C.E, the center of the eastern Chou was:

(A) Anyang.

(B) Sian.

(C) Ao.

(D) Loyang.

Answers

1. (B)	4. (D)	7. (C)	10. (D)
2. (C)	5. (D)	8. (B)	
3. (B)	6. (A)	9. (D)	

UNIT II

The Classical Civilizations
of Greece and Rome

Chapter 6

BRONZE AGE GREECE AND THE ORIGINS OF ARCHAIC CULTURE

KEY TERMS

Mycenae	Knossus
Lion Gate	Palace at Knossus
Homer	Snake Goddess
The Iliad	Minoan frescoes
Agamemnon	The Minoans
Achilles	Thalossocracy
Helen	Linear A
Menelaus	Linear B
Trojan War	Martin Bernal
Paris	Black Athena
Priam	Heracles
Troy	Delphi
Arête	Pythia
wanax	Olympics
basileus	Zeus
Hisarlik	Byzantium
Schilemann	Ionian colonies
The hoplite revolution	Dorian Invasion
Arthur Evans	Greek Dark Ages
Crete	

THE MINOANS

The earliest Greek culture was located on **Crete** and dates back to 2800 B.C.E. The Cretans most likely came from Asia Minor, probably as early as 3,000 B.C.E. and originally spoke a non-Indo-European language. The Cretans were literate and they used a style of writing known as **Linear A**. Scholars have never deciphered Linear A, and it does not resemble later Greek. The culture produced by the Cretan civilization is called **Minoan** after the legendary **King** Minos who ruled here. According to legend, Minos had a palace that housed a labyrinth designed by Daedalus. A Minotaur (a half-bull, half-human creature) was in the labyrinth, and every nine years Minos demanded the sacrifice of seven virgins and seven male youths to the beast. One year, the Athenian hero Theseus volunteered to be part of the sacrifice in hopes of freeing Athens from Minoan rule. When Theseus arrived on Crete, he fell in love with Ariadne, the daughter of King Minos, and she with him. Ariadne gave him a golden thread to find his way out. Legend has it that when Theseus killed the Minotaur, Cretan civilization collapsed.

The first to excavate the sites on Crete was the English archaeologist Arthur Evans. Evans took the myth to reveal historic truth, and argued that the Minoans at one time must have dominated the mainland of Greece, including Athens. Hence, in the myth, the Athenians pay tribute to the Minoans in the form of the sacrifice of seven virgins. Although Evans's scholarly views have long since been rejected on this point, the remains of the palace at **Knossus**, the chief center of Minoan culture, do indeed resemble a labyrinth.

There is evidence that the palace was built and rebuilt over the course of many centuries, and it occupies almost an entire hillside. The palace is a self-contained village, with its own olive gardens, presses, and an arsenal. The palace had a system of running water. One of the most interesting sections of the palace is the throne room, the oldest throne room in Europe. Next to the throne room, there is a room with a large basin that probably held water. This water basin was likely used for ritualistic purposes, and its proximity to the throne room suggests that the king was also the chief priest of the civilization. Storage chambers are also very near the throne room. The king stored large vases full of oil and other goods possibly received from other Minoan centers on Crete as tribute. The goods were then redistributed among the king's subjects.

The Snake Goddess

Other interesting artifacts from the ruins of the palace are the snake goddesses, whose bared and exaggerated upper chest calls forth the idea of fertility. Snakes were another symbol of fertility in the ancient world, particularly in Egypt, with which the Minoans had obvious contact. Although many people from the Judeo-Christian tradition often associate snakes with evil, the ancient cultures associated them with fertility, as snakes lose their skins and then regenerate them. The snake goddesses are akin to the mother earth goddesses of the Paleolithic caves. On the basis of the snake goddess figurines, some scholars have suggested that the Minoans were a matriarchal culture, a hypothesis that lacks general support and seems based on scanty evidence. Their chief deity was, however, clearly a female deity, who was worshipped in small shrines on hills.

Minoan Frescoes

Minoan culture was very artistic. The palace itself was originally painted in bright red and other colors. Many columns still have traces of their original paint. Many of the **frescoes** on the palace wall convey the relationship of the Minoans with the sea, such as the beautiful dolphin frescos, which Arthur Evans mistakenly placed on the walls rather than on the floors, where they appear in remains on the mainland. The Minoans had a large seafaring empire, and contact with many other cultures. They exerted tremendous influence over other cultures through trade. Although scholars debate the extent of their power over other areas through seafaring trade, this sort of control of seafaring routes and areas has been called a **thalossocracy**. Archaeologists have found artifacts from Egypt and other cultures in the ruins of the palace. Interestingly, later Greeks on the mainland associated the dolphin with Apollo, and Greek myth credits the Minoans with bringing the cult of Apollo to the famous oracle at Delphi. This myth, along with the story of Theseus, suggested to Evans, wrongly as it turned out, that the Minoans might have controlled the mainland at one point. We now know the Minoans were dominant in the region through trade, but never governed the mainland. Rather, the **Mycenaeans** brought Minoan culture to the mainland.

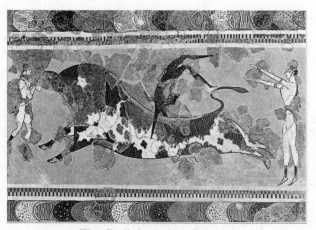

The Bull Jumping Fresco

The House of the Double Ax and the Bull Jumping Ritual

The most famous of all frescoes in the palace is the Bull Jumping fresco. This fresco is renowned for its lifelike portrayal of the popular sport of bull jumping on Crete. The bull itself seems caught in the act of jumping; its back is arched and its legs are not portrayed in a static fashion. The Minoans are shown in the act of jumping. They first grabbed the horns, then flipped over the bull's back, and then landed behind the animal. This ritual took place in the central court of the palace at Knossus, and there are iconic images of bull's horns throughout the location. Scholars are unsure of the exact meaning of the bull cult, but clearly the bull sign was the basis for calling the dynasty at Knossus the House of the Double Ax. Two bull's horns side by side create the double ax image, and the Greek word for ax is labyrinthos, a word that is very similar to "labyrinth."

Another unique feature of the Bull Jumping fresco is that two of the three figures represented are women. The women have lighter skin than the men in the Minoan art, betraying the influence of Egypt, as Egyptians also portrayed women with lighter skin. The importance of women in this fresco, combined with the importance of the snake goddesses, again has suggested to scholars that the Minoans may have been a matriarchy.

The Minoans were slender, dark-skinned people who wore little clothing other than a loincloth. If one has ever been to Greece, one can understand the reasons why the Minoans dressed so lightly, as it is extremely hot especially in the summer months. The style of the frescos is very similar to Egyptian art. While the Bull Jumping fresco is very animated, unlike formalized, static Egyptian art, this and other frescos also show people with their torsos facing frontally but with their legs facing the side. This is the same style as Egyptian art.

The Collapse of the Minoans

The traditional date for the collapse of Minoan culture is somewhere around 1450 B.C.E. Scholars are unsure of the reasons for the collapse, and some have suggested that perhaps there was a cataclysmic natural disaster. The palace shows evidence of rebuilding after tidal waves and also earthquakes; further, there was a huge volcanic eruption on **Santorini** or **Thera** about the time that the Minoan culture collapsed. Recent studies, however, suggest that eruption may date to as early as 1650 B.C.E., in which case we need another hypothesis to account for the decline of Crete in the fifteenth century B.C.E. Perhaps the eruption on Thera (Santorini) weakened various elements of Minoan trade, but this is far from certain. Recent excavations of areas around Santorini show the enormous extent of the eruption, and make the assumption that the eruption had long-term effects on crops and climatic conditions plausible. As an interesting note, some writers have suggested that Santorini and the Minoan world may have been the foundation of the legends of Atlantis, mentioned in the works of Plato. This is a very controversial assertion, however, as not only are there many other possibilities for the location of Atlantis, but some doubt the actual historicity of the references to Atlantis.

It has also been suggested that invaders from the mainland might have conquered the Minoans. The **Mycenaeans** on the mainland date back to 2200 B.C.E., but the period in which they flourished, from the seventeenth to the twelfth centuries B.C.E., coincides with the demise of Cretan culture. The Mycenaeans were a warlike people who dominated the Aegean area, and traces of Minoan culture are found in Mycenaean ruins. Whether this was because the Mycenaeans borrowed from an already declining culture or because they conquered the Minoans is unknown.

THE MYCENAEANS

Our knowledge of the Mycenaean world began in 1870 when **Heinrich Schliemann** excavated Hisarlik, thought to be the site of ancient Troy and now located in modern day Turkey; Schliemann later also excavated Mycenae in an effort to prove the truth of Homer's Iliad.

Before Schliemann, scholars had thought that Greek civilization did not arise until the eighth century B.C.E.; it was Schliemann's expedition that inspired **Arthur Evans,** an Englishman, to search for the existence of the legendary king Minos, a search that eventually led to the excavation of Knossus on Crete.

Linear B

The Mycenaeans were a literate society, who borrowed the script of Linear A for their own Indo-European language, the earliest form of Greek known. Their writing is known as **Linear B**, and numerous Linear B tablets have been discovered in the wreckage of Knossus and numerous other locations on the mainland and even in Hittite records. Evans took this to mean that the Minoans had conquered the mainland, but modern scholars believe the widespread presence of Linear B tablets more properly suggests that the Mycenaeans conquered the Minoans, or at least took over and built upon the ruins of Minoan civilization. The similarity of Linear B to Homer's Greek enabled Michael Ventris to decipher the language. The Mycenaeans migrated to the Greek mainland by about 2000 B.C.E.

Some Hittite writings seem to allude to the Mycenaeans; Mycenaean pottery is found from Naples to Troy to Egypt, which indicates that the Mycenaeans had a vast trading empire.

The Trojan War

The Mycenaeans are most remembered for the war with Troy, a Greek-speaking colony on Asia Minor. One of the main sources of our information on the Trojan War is Homer's *Iliad*, which covers only a ten-day interlude of the war. The Iliad dates to the ninth or eighth century B.C.E., whereas the Trojan War allegedly occurred in the thirteenth century B.C.E. The famous story of the Trojan horse actually comes from a much later work, the Roman poet Virgil's **Aeneid**. Virgil wrote the Aeneid in the first century B.C.E., and it tells the story of **Aeneas**, a participant in the war, who fled Troy and later became one of the founders of Rome.

The Legend of the Trojan War

According to legend, the goddess Aphrodite promised the most beautiful woman in the world to Paris, the son of the Trojan **King Priam**. He was awarded **Helen**, wife of **King Menelaus** of Sparta. Helen was also the sister of **Clytemnestra**, who was married to the older brother of Menelaus, **Agamemnon**. According to legend, Helen was the daughter of Zeus.

During a period in which Menelaus was gone, Paris went to Greece and fell in love with Helen and she with him. They fled together to Troy. Menelaus' brother, King Agamemnon of Mycenae, led an expedition to Troy to "rescue" Helen, and a ten-year long siege began. Among the Greek heroes of the war was **Achilles**, whose goddess-mother had dipped him in the River Styx, making him impervious to harm except on his heel. Achilles got angry with King Agamemnon in the beginning of the epic over his failure to give him the honor that was his fair due; Achilles left his fellow Greeks and fought solely for himself. Achilles's fiercely independent actions to achieve glory and his willingness to sacrifice anything for one moment of eternal glory illustrate the Greek ideal of **arete**, or heroism and nobility of character. The Iliad, however, tells only the story of ten days of the ten-year long siege of Troy, and we must turn to Virgil for an account of the fall of Troy.

According to Virgil, the war ended when the Greeks grew weary of the siege and tricked the Trojans into believing that they had left by hiding in a nearby harbor. They left a beautiful wooden horse outside the gates of Troy, ostensibly as a tribute to the Trojan patron deities and to buy their safe return home. Some of the Trojans were suspicious, among them the prophetess **Cassandara**, who had been cursed to always tell the truth but never be believed, and the priest **Laocoon**, who made an impassioned plea to them not to bring the horse in.

No one listened, and Athena, the patron goddess of the Mycenaeans, was so angered that she sent two huge serpents to engulf Laocoon and his sons. This famous passage from Virgil was later immortalized in sculpture during the Hellenistic era. During the Italian Renaissance centuries later, this famous Hellenistic sculpture was unearthed and influenced Michelangelo.

According to Virgil, Troy fell in a bloody battle. Achilles' son murdered the son of King Priam before his very eyes and then murdered Priam, dragging him through his own son's blood. Priam lived just long enough to see his son and his city destroyed.

Was Helen the Cause of the War?

Thucydides, known as the father of scientific history, disputed Homer's account of the Trojan War, as he believed women were not important enough to have caused a war. The historian Sarah Pomeroy points out, however, that women were often important in marriages and for political alliances, and so perhaps there is more truth in the ancient epic than even the Greek historians believed. On the other hand, **Herodotus**, known as the father of history, doubted the entire account of the origins of the Trojan War. He doubted that Helen was ever in Troy on the basis of the claim made by the sixth century B.C.E. poet Stesichorus that Helen was in fact in Egypt. The Greeks, he says, were duped and were never convinced by the Trojans that Helen was not there. Even the Greeks disagreed on the cause of the Trojan War, making our task that much more difficult.

Other Historic Difficulties

Virgil wrote to glorify the reign of **Augustus**, the first emperor of Rome who claimed descent from Aeneas and the Trojans. Augustus essentially had transformed the Republican form of government of ancient Rome into an imperial one; although he refused to allow the Romans to call him an emperor, he was one in all but name, usurping many of the old Republican offices for himself. Many of the greatest poets of this age tried to make the reign of Augustus appear as the climax of Roman history rather than as the end of Republican Rome. Hence, Virgil's account, written thirteen centuries after the Trojan War, cannot be much trusted as a historic source.

Many elements of Homer, on the other hand, appear factual, such as descriptions of ships. Yet there are also many difficulties with relying on Homer as a historic source.

Homer's Historical Inaccuracies

There are many inaccuracies in Homer's work, which suggest that the story may even have originated before the Trojan War allegedly happened in the thirteenth century B.C.E., and also that Homer or whoever wrote the Iliad modified the story by folding in details of his own age. For example, Homer always describes the shield of the Greek warrior Ajax as like a tower, and shields of this style had already disappeared by the Trojan War, which likely occurred sometime around 1250 B.C.E. In other passages, he describes round shields, which were the style of shield in use in the archaic period, the period in which the epic was written. The epic also depicts a transitional type of warfare, from that of an early period around the time of the Trojan War in which heroes such as Achilles fought their opponents in hand-to-hand individual combat, to that of Homer's time when armies relied on the phalanx, or group of foot soldiers lined up by rank and file. The phalanx was the preferred model of combat during the period in which the Iliad first appeared. Scholars link the so-called **hoplite** or **foot solider revolution** to increased ability of farmers to provide armor, which led to their increased demands for political participation and the growth of democracy. The members of the front lines of the phalanx were relatively wealthy, as compared to the back lines, such as the Locrians in the passage above. Their greater wealth perhaps allowed them to demand more rights in the rising city-states and may have directly contributed to the development of democracy.

Another quirk of the text is that in some passages, iron appears to be rare, as it would have been in the Mycenaean period. Achilles offers iron as a trophy, suggesting its very great value. However, during the **iron age**, the time when the epic was likely written, iron was far more common and less valuable. Notice in one passage a warrior uses an arrowhead made of iron. Since arrowheads are not recovered once used, it would be unlikely that the warriors would have used iron arrowheads in the Mycenaean age. The epic, then, contains some material that seems to capture the Mycenaean era, but other material that is closer to Homer's own time.

The Iliad contains many repetitious phrases known as formularies. In antiquity, epic poems such as the Iliad were passed down orally and embellished by individual bard; the formularies helped the bard remember and organize the epic.

Also, many themes of the Iliad resemble those of other ancient epics, such as the *Epic of Gilgamesh*. For example, Achilles has a goddess for a mother, as did Gilgamesh, and his friend Patroclus is much like Enkidu. Patroculus dies in place of Achilles, and a lament follows his death, just as Enkidu dies for what was Gilgamesh's offense, and a lament also follows his death.

Who was Homer?

There is considerable doubt about whether there ever was a bard named Homer or whether Homer was the name given to a group of bards or the bard who finally wrote down the epic. At any rate, the details of language, construction of shields, and other aspects of the epic suggest that it was told orally for many centuries before it was written. If Homer actually ever lived, he lived in the eighth century B.C.E., making these stories already 500 years old at the time he wrote them down. Further, since many of the details of war seem to describe an age even before the Trojan War, the story must have been told in some form well before the Trojan War occurred. Homer's epics, then, have to be read very critically and cannot be completely trusted as historical sources.

Heinrich Schliemann and the Excavation of Hisarlik

Although many scholars regard the *Iliad* as a literary masterpiece that is of questionable historical value about the period before the hoplite revolution, Heinrich Schliemann, a wealthy German businessman in the nineteenth century C.E. and an avid fan of Homer, was convinced of the truth behind the legend. From the geographic details in the Iliad, he deduced the whereabouts of Troy and was led to a huge tell (a hill or mound of debris) known as **Hisarlik** located in modern Turkey. Schliemann even reenacted the chase of Achilles and Hector around the walls of Troy to see whether the time and distances discussed in Homer matched his own experience.

Schliemann carelessly threw out everything that did not fit the details of Homer's epic poem and dug a deep trench through the middle of the tell. Consequently, many valuable objects were lost, and archaeologists and historians believe that some of these objects might actually have helped to shed light on the Trojan War. Archaeology had not yet been perfected as a science and Schliemann was working under difficult conditions in Turkey. His mistakes helped later archaeologists develop more systematic methods of excavation. They also helped to unearth a part of Greek history that had never been documented.

Hisarlik, the site of ancient Troy, had a very long past. There were nine distinct phases of its history; Phase II of the layers of civilization buried in Hisarlik represented the level Schliemann thought was legendary Troy. It had a ramp outside the gates, much like the one Homer depicted in the fight between Hector and Achilles. Schliemann found a cache of jewelry in this level known as "Priam's Treasure" and secretly removed it from Turkey, where the dig was located and later his young Greek wife appeared in photographs with the jewelry. Schliemann was convinced he had found evidence of Helen of Troy. This level was too old, however, to have been the Troy of Homer.

Wilhelm Dorpfeld's later excavations suggested that Homer's "Troy of the towering gates" was level VI, which had a large square tower and huge city walls fifteen feet thick that sloped, just as Homer said they did. The wall might have indeed protected its inhabitants from a ten-year long siege. An earthquake destroyed level VI sometime around 1260 B.C.E. The god Poseidon was associated with earthquakes, and also with horses. The connection between earthquakes and horses may be the root of the famous legend of the Trojan horse.

Carl Blegen argued that Homer's Troy was level VIIa, which was destroyed by a fire somewhere around the thirteenth century B.C.E. about the time of the legendary fall of Troy. Troy VIIa was built on the ruins of level VI, and its rather shoddy construction showed the impact of a ten-year-long siege. Houses were much smaller and crowded together, as if people were seeking refuge within the city walls. Houses also had double floors, where they could hide supplies in large vases buried in the ground and covered with stone slabs. Some smaller buildings right inside the city gate look suitable for providing refreshments to soldiers returning from battle. Further, this level contains very little Mycenaean pottery, which might be an indication of two cultures at war. Nevertheless, the historian M.I. Finley once wrote that Blegen found nothing to corroborate his claim that level VIIa was Homer's Troy, and even Blegen's associate John Caskey believed that the destruction of level VIIa by fire did not necessarily prove the Mycenaean conquest, as fire that occurred purely by accident often destroyed ancient cities. As Amanda H. Podany put it, "Archaeologists and historians are divided as to whether level VI or level VIIA is more likely to be the Troy of the Trojan War. ... the small houses and poor construction techniques of level VIIA show ... that the city would not have looked like the splendid place described by Homer. The city attacked by the Mycenaeans may have been either that of level VI or level VIIA." [Podany, "Archaeological Evidence from Troy," in *The Origins of Greek Civilization: From the Bronze Age to the Polis ca. 2500–600 B.C.* (National Center for History in the Schools, 1991), p. 51.].

More recently, scholars have uncovered Hittite records that help to clarify the causes of the Trojan War. In antiquity, Troy was known as **Wilusa**, and it was located in an area dominated by the Hittites. Archaeology has uncovered evidence, too, that there was a growing presence of the Mycenaeans in Asia Minor, and they may have been the people the Hittites referred to as the kingdom of **Ahhiyawa**. A letter from the Hittite's King Hattusili III to the king of Ahhiyawa mentions that Wilusa was a point of controversy between the two kingdoms. The fabled Trojan War, then, might have occurred as a result of a long struggle for dominance between the Hittites and the Greeks in Asia Minor.

The Citadel of Mycenae

Having failed to discover Homer's Troy, Schliemann turned to mainland Greece in search of Mycenae, and here he uncovered many important finds. Mycenae was a fortress with a citadel constructed of limestone walls twenty feet thick. The entrance to the citadel is famous for its enormous **Lion Gate**, which is ten feet wide and ten feet high. It is topped by huge lintel weighing twenty tons. Although scholars are unsure of the significance of the lions, they believe it had some sort of heraldic significance and that the lions protected the citadel, like attendants of goddesses of the day.

In the citadel itself, there is only one street that is little more than an alley. The street leads to the palace atop the citadel, and along the street, Schliemann found seven grave shafts in a circle protected by a wall. The fact that a wall surrounds the site suggests that the kings there had some sort of religious significance; the circle itself is eighty-five feet in diameter. In one of the grave shafts, Schliemann found a remarkable gold mask. When he came up from the shaft, he made the famous remark that he had "looked upon the face of Agamemnon." Unfortunately, he had not, as these grave shafts were also from an earlier period of Greek history, likely dating back to at least the sixteenth century B.C.E., making them too old to have been the relics of the Mycenaeans who fought the Trojans. Nevertheless, Schliemann had uncovered a previously unknown civilization, and had proven that Greek history went back to an era well before the Olympics began in the eighth century B.C.E.

Martin Bernal, the author of Black Athena, attempted to tie various artifacts in the tombs to the **Hyksos**, whom he argued colonized Greece from the 18th–17th century B.C.E. However, Egyptian records rarely mention Greeks except as raiders or traders, and make no mention themselves of colonization in the Aegean area. Linear B tablets mention Egyptians occasionally, but not the Hyksos. Most scholars believe that the artifacts in the Mycenaean grave shafts bear no resemblance at all to Hyksos artifacts. A further point suggesting that Bernal's theory is inadequate is that Mycenaean palaces are built around a megaron, or large open area, whereas Egyptian structures are not. Rarely have scholars attacked any scholarly supposition with such vigor as they attack Bernal's work and, although Bernal puts forth a vast array of evidence from diverse fields, most of it is unconvincing to specialists on those areas.

Schliemann's excavation at Mycenae had failed again to find Agamemnon, yet the citadel of Mycenae did prove that the Mycenaean's were a very warlike culture with a thriving kingship. The citadel is located in a very strategic place between mountains, making it difficult to attack, and its huge walls would have defended it well.

The Tholos Beehive Tombs

Other nearby tombs are also remarkable, and are known as the **Tholos** or **beehive tombs**. The culture that produced them is known as the Tholos tomb dynasty. The entrance, or **dromos**, to one of these famous tombs is twenty feet wide and one hundred and twenty feet long; the stone lintel over the so-called **Treasury of Atreus** is estimated to weigh 100 tons. The Tholos Dynasty was also quite definitely an imperial, warlike culture; apparently, they buried their warriors in these tombs. These tombs are a remarkable early western example of the use of the dome.

These tombs date from the fourteenth to the thirteenth century B.C.E., which coincides with the date of the legendary Atreus, after whom the "treasury" is named.

Troy's Later History and the Collapse of Mycenae

Troy was deserted for 400 years after the sack of Troy, and Alexander the Great later visited Troy VIII. Level IX represents Roman Troy, the last of the cities built on the site.

The collapse of Troy VIIa sometime around the thirteenth century B.C.E. also marks the end of the Mycenaean era. Despite the fact that Homer claims victory for the Mycenaeans at Troy, after their victory, Mycenaean cities crumbled and their pottery declined in quality. This is oddly consistent with other disasters of the age. The Hittite empire crumbled, and Egypt endured three serious attacks by the People of the Sea. There was widespread famine throughout the ancient world in the thirteenth century B.C.E., suggesting that whatever happened to the Mycenaeans, their decline was part of an overall decline in all cultures of this era.

THE DORIANS

A group of Indo-European people, the **Dorians**, replaced the Mycenaeans as the dominant power on the Greek mainland. For years, the most common theory is that the Dorians, from north of Mt. Olympus, migrated south, looting and pillaging along the way. Many centers in the Peloponnesus were burned to the ground or otherwise destroyed. Among the evidence for a violent path of destruction is a wall built to protect the Peloponnesus across the Isthmus of Corinth. This migration was known as the **Dorian Invasion** and is mainly confirmed in ancient Greek legend. According to Greek legend, the sons of **Heracles** and his followers were banished from Mycenae and they took possession of the Peloponnesus.

The Dorians spoke the same language as the Mycenaeans. One wonders how they remained isolated for so long. The historian John Fine has suggested that the Dorians were not another group of people at all, but simply another Mycenaean people, long oppressed, who spoke another dialect and who simply outlived the Mycenaeans. If this is true, then perhaps we would be more accurate to speak of a Dorian migration, rather than an invasion. Many historians today believe that a system-wide collapse brought on by famine or other natural disaster, combined with the wanderings of the People of the Sea and internal warfare among Mycenaean chieftains brought the civilization down.

The Greek Dark Ages

The collapse of Mycenae began the Dark Ages in Greek History. Written records disappeared until the eighth century B.C.E.

The Dorians lived in isolated groups by tribe. The Greek mountainous regions hemmed them in. The Dorians were a patriarchical group of people who were ruled by kings and an aristocratic society. Many aspects of Homer's *Iliad* reflect this aristocratic age; for example, Homer has King Agamemnon hold councils with his nobles in the *Iliad* in much the same way as the Dorians held them.

THE AGE OF COLONIZATION

The Greeks began to colonize in the eighth to the sixth centuries B.C.E. In this age, there were too many people for the land to sustain and many people left to colonize other regions.

The Greeks colonized southern Italy, and there battled the Romans during the Pyrrhic Wars. Corinth was another colony that became important during the Christian era as one of the places to whom the apostle Paul wrote. Greeks also established colonies on the northern tip of Africa. The Greek colonies around Egypt helped further the Golden Age of ancient Greece by introducing Egyptian papyrus, geometry and astronomy to the Greeks. Evidence of cultural exchange can also be seen in the Greek statues, whose rigid, formalized poses and wiglike hair is very reminiscent of Egyptian art.

Black Athena?

Martin Bernal, in Black Athena and other works, has argued that the influence of the Egyptians on the culture of ancient Greece has been underestimated and, consequently, the role of Africa in the development of western culture has been overlooked. Bernal's thesis is very controversial, but it does highlight the fact that the Greeks, as remarkable a culture as they developed in the Golden Age, had other cultural models and influences on which to build.

Impact of Colonization on Later Greek History

Ionia, the Greek colonies in Asia Minor, were conquered by **Cyrus the Great** and the Persians in the sixth century B.C.E. These colonies, or Ionia, subsequently went to the mainland Greeks for help against the Persians, beginning the Persian wars.

The Greeks also colonized along the Black Sea. **Byzantium** was a Greek colony that later became the capital of the Roman Empire in the east. Under Constantine the Great, the first Christian emperor, the city was renamed Constantinople. In 1453 C.E., the Seljuk Turks conquered Constantinople and changed its name to Istanbul.

Archaic Culture: The Olympics

Several characteristic expressions of Greek cultural ideals arose during the archaic period. The first **Olympic festival** was held in Olympia in 776 B.C.E.

Before Schliemann's excavations, scholars believed that Greek culture originated with the Olympics. Olympia was dedicated to Zeus, the chief God of the Greeks. The Greeks valued the life of the mind and were known for producing some of the finest philosophical minds in the history of the world, including Socrates, his student Plato, and his student Aristotle. They also valued the health of the body, and held the Olympics as a tribute to the gods through presenting the most highly developed physical bodies possible in grueling competitions. Only free Greeks could participate in the Olympics, and a truce was declared during which no warfare could be conducted.

Olympic athletes competed in brutal sports, such as Greek boxing, in which no holds were barred. Many stories tell of athletes whose teeth were knocked out in fights and who kept fighting despite what must have been agonizing pain. In fact, agon or suffering was a fundamental theme in Greek culture. Through heroic agon, true arete was displayed. Those who emerged victorious at Olympia were given the laurel leaf wreath of Apollo, the god of wisdom.

The Roman **Emperor Theodosius** banned the Olympics as pagan practices. In the nineteenth century, the Olympics were revived, and today, every Olympiad begins with the lighting of the Olympic torch at Olympia in the same place where once it was lit in antiquity.

Delphi

Legend has it that **Delphi** was founded when Zeus wished to find the center of the earth and let two eagles fly from the two ends of the earth. They met at Delphi, which was the "navel" of the earth. Delphi celebrated the god Apollo, and his temple contained an **omphalos** or navel stone, and pilgrims offered objects in the shape of the omphalos. Delphi was one of the most important cultural centers in the ancient world. According to tradition, Delphi was first recognized as a special place when a shepherd's sheep grew intoxicated while grazing near a crevice. Later priestesses, called the Pythia, would sit over this crevice on a tripod and breathe in its fumes. Their seat was placed in the middle of the sacred temple of Apollo. The Pythia would spew out garbled prophecies in monosyllables, and a priest would interpret her words for the pilgrims.

Delphi became prominent during the period of Greek colonization; many colonists consulted the oracle there before selecting their destination, including the founders of the colony of Syracuse. Many colonies called themselves Apollonia, after the patron god of Delphi. The spread of the Greek colonies also spread the fame of Delphi, making it a cosmopolitan center of religion for many cultures. Delphi also exhibits the Greek tradition of paying tribute to the gods through developing both the body and the soul. At Delphi, the Greeks held athletic, theatrical, and other festivities in honor of Apollo.

Delphi began to decline in the Roman period, and Theodosius finally shut it down by the fourth century C.E.

Review Questions

1. The frescoes at Knossus suggest

   (A) the possible influence of Egypt on the Minoans.

   (B) the importance of the cult of the bull, associated with the double ax.

   (C) the lack of status for women in the Minoan culture.

   (D) Both (A) and (B).

2. The main center of Minoan culture was the city of

   (A) Thebes.

   (B) Knossos.

   (C) Sparta.

   (D) Mycenae.

3. The dominant power on <u>mainland</u> Greece during the Bronze Age were the

   (A) Athenians.

   (B) Cretans.

   (C) Trojans.

   (D) Mycenaeans.

4. The most compelling and universally accepted evidence about Hisarlik suggests that

   (A) Level VIIa can be accepted as the probable site of Homer's Troy.

   (B) Level II is the probable site of Homer's Troy.

   (C) Level VI is the probable site of Homer's Troy.

   (D) Homer's Troy was not exactly like any of the levels of Hisarlik.

5. Although Homer's Troy was NOT found by the expeditions in the 19th century, during the course of the search for Troy

   (A) Spartan culture was discovered.

   (B) Athenian democracy was proven to be a fiction.

   (C) the existence of the legendary King Agamemnon was confirmed.

   (D) archaeologists discovered the culture of ancient Mycenae.

6. On the basis of the characteristics of the Mycenaean citadel, Mycenaean culture was

   (A) peaceful.

   (B) artistic.

   (C) warlike.

   (D) intensely interested in philosophy and religion.

7. Following the Trojan War,

   (A) Mycenaean culture collapsed.

   (B) Mycenaean culture dominated the Peloponnesus.

   (C) Mycenaean culture dominated Asia Minor.

   (D) Mycenaean culture began to spread across the Mediterranean.

8. The Dark Ages in Greece were dominated by

   (A) Athens.

   (B) Sparta.

   (C) the Dorians.

   (D) the Delian League.

9. Homer's Iliad presents what picture of warfare?

   (A) An accurate portrayal of warfare during the time of the Trojan War.

   (B) An accurate picture of warfare during his own time.

   (C) A mixed account, including individual combat and use of the phalanx.

   (D) An entirely inaccurate picture of warfare in the thirteenth century B.C.E.

10. Which of the following statements most correctly represents Homer's picture of leadership in *The Iliad*?

    (A) Agamemnon is a wanax.

    (B) Agamemnon is a basileus.

    (C) Agamemnon is a weak leader who cannot control Achilles.

    (D) Agamemnon has some powers equal to a wanax in the time of the Trojan War, but is otherwise limited as a basileus would have been in Homer's time.

Answers

1. (D)	4. (D)	7. (A)	10. (D)
2. (B)	5. (D)	8. (C)	
3. (D)	6. (C)	9. (C)	

Chapter 7

ALEXANDER THE GREAT AND THE HELLENISTIC ERA

KEY TERMS

Alexander

Philip of Macedon

Gaugamela

Granicus River

Issus

Wedding Feast of Susa

Persepolis

Darius III

Babylon

Indus River

proskynēsis

Aechaean League

Aetolian League

Ptolemaic monarchy

Seleucid monarchy

Pergamene

Hellenistic world

Archimedes

Alexandria

Cynicism

Stoicism

Epicureanism

Diogenes the Dog

Zeno

Epicurus

THE AFTERMATH OF THE PELOPONNESIAN WAR

After the Persian wars, the Greeks failed to sustain the unity that had brought them victory. Similarly, they proved unable to keep together the coalition that defeated the Athenian empire in the Peloponnesian war. The Greek love of independence that was the basis of Athenian democracy proved also to be the seed of the dissolution of Greek culture in the wake of the Peloponnesian War. Ironically, it was the Macedonians who took up the task of governing the Greeks and spreading Greek culture throughout the world. The Athenians and other Greeks long had great disdain for the Macedonians; they were primarily farmers who spoke a very rough Greek dialect that the other Greeks regarded as unsophisticated.

Philip of Macedon

The rise of Macedon began in 359 B.C.E., when **Philip** became king. Philip had studied the works of Xenophon, where he had recounted the famous march of 10,000 Greek mercenaries in Persia. From Xenophon, Philip had concluded that the hoplite phalanx supported by cavalry was unbeatable. A phalanx was a square-shaped formation of hoplites, or foot soldiers. Each soldier carried a spear, so that when the phalanx formed, there was a line of spears that projected out several feet in front of the men on four sides. The phalanx was the tank of antiquity; its only weakness was that when it was necessary to turn, the entire formation had to turn at once.

Philip's war tactics proved the phalanx to be the premier battle machine of antiquity. In 349 B.C.E., Philip attacked the Greek town of Olynthus, as he was worried that his two half-brothers might challenge his throne. In 346 B.C.E., he moved further into Greek territories and attacked the home of the oracle, Delphi. Philip urged the Greeks to unite with him on the pretext of attacking the Persians; in so doing, he attempted to appeal to the civic pride of Greeks who had thrown off the Persian threat.

Only **Demosthenes**, an orator in Athens, recognized the threat posed by Philip. Demosthenes walked through the streets of Athens carrying a light, and urging the Athenians to resist in the name of independence. His efforts failed, and by 338 B.C.E., Philip defeated the Greeks.

In 336 B.C.E., Philip was assassinated. He had recently taken a second wife, and some scholars suggest that Philip's first wife Olympias feared for her son's position and his inheritance. Consequently, they suggest that Olympias had her husband assassinated. Philip's son by his first marriage, **Alexander**, did in fact succeed him. To his credit, he pursued the assassin and punished him accordingly.

Alexander the Great

As a young man, Alexander had tamed the horse Buchephalus, whom no one else had been able to tame. Alexander had led many of his father's campaigns

Bust of Alexander the Great

and in 340 B.C.E. had been named regent in Macedonia during his father's absence. Impressed by his son's abilities, Philip had once remarked that he had no kingdom big enough to offer such a talented boy.

Alexander's tutor was the philosopher **Aristotle**, who perhaps introduced him to **Plato's** concept of the Philosopher King, the educated statesman who ruled through reason and education. Alexander had a love of Greek culture and spread it throughout the known world, yet at times his oversized temperament seemed to be ungoverned by reason.

Just as the earlier Greeks sought after arête, a heroic nobility of character exemplified by bravery on the battlefield, and a godlike sense of honor among men, Alexander's career as a crusading Greek hero raised him to the level of the gods in the eyes of many men. In his lifetime, Alexander was revered as a god in many parts of his empire. In later history, his achievements continued to inspire awe even among the most gifted generals. It was said that the Roman Julius Caesar shuddered when he walked past Alexander's statue.

Alexander was twenty when he came to the throne; by the age of thirty-three when he died, he had conquered territories from the Egypt to the Indus River Valley, representing almost all the world known to the Greeks. Few have ever achieved conquests as significant as those of Alexander, yet in his own mind, Alexander believed his goals incomplete at his death, as there was still more to conquer, more to do. Despite the enormity of his achievement, one must also take into account the fact that his empire fell apart immediately after his death.

Rebellion in Thebes

While Alexander had been away securing the northern frontiers, a rumor had spread that he had been killed. The city of **Thebes** revolted. In retaliation, Alexander razed Thebes and burned it to the ground in 335 B.C.E. While he virtually destroyed the city, he left the poet Pindar's house untouched, as well as several Greek temples. The destruction of Thebes was the first demonstration of Alexander's tendency towards ruthless conquest, as well as of his veneration of Greek culture.

The Conquest of Persia

Alexander wanted to realize his father's vision of conquering the east, and formulated one of the most ambitious plans of conquest of all time. Alexander planned to attack Persia, the empire that stood between him and his goal, the conquest of the known world. Alexander's teacher Aristotle had taught him that the ocean at the subcontinent of India marked the boundary of the earth. A century after the Persian Wars ended, the Persians still outnumbered the Greek forces three to one; they were wealthier and also had a powerful navy bolstered by a series of port fortifications. On paper, never had any plan looked as risky as Alexander's plan to conquer the east.

By the time he died, Alexander conquered not only the Persian empire, but also the remnants of the Egyptian and the Babylonian cultures. One reason for his success was his style of leadership; Alexander fought in the front lines with his men; by the time of his death, he had been wounded in battle in nearly every part of his body. When his men were without food, he was without food; when they were without water, he was without water. Alexander's boyish good looks, his charisma and leadership abilities inspired great loyalty not only among his men, but also among his enemies. When he finally defeated the Persian ruler Darius III, he told his men to treat Darius's wife and daughter as the royalty they were. When Alexander died, Darius's wife and daughter grieved for him as if he were their own son and brother.

The Battle of the Granicus River

Crossing the **Hellespont**, the very site where Athens had been defeated in 405 B.C.E., Alexander first met the Persians at the battle of Granicus River in 334 B.C.E. Here, his forces unexpectedly defeated the Persian army. While near Granicus, Alexander visited the site of ancient Troy, and reportedly uttered his famous tribute to Achilles. Alexander wished to be a new Achilles.

The Battle of Issus

Following the battle of Granicus River, Alexander continued to move along the coast line of Asia Minor. He defeated the Persians at the Battle of Issus in 333 B.C.E. Although the Persians caught him off guard by marching on him from behind, Alexander managed to accomplish a stunning victory.

Egypt

Alexander reached Egypt, where he was hailed as a pharaoh at Memphis in 332 B.C.E. After a trip to the oracle in Egypt, his men hailed him as the son of Amon and later also as the son of Zeus. Alexander began to found cities in his name; the famous Hellenistic city of **Alexandria** on the northern tip of Africa became an important center of Hellenistic culture. The lighthouse of Alexandria, the **Pharos**, was one of the Seven Wonders of the World. The lighthouse once guided international traffic from the Nile, Red Sea and the Mediterranean into the harbor. An earthquake later toppled it and today it lies beneath the ocean. The Library of Alexandria contained one-half-million scrolls, but was later destroyed.

The Battle of Arbela/Gaugamela

In 331 B.C.E., Alexander continued his pursuit of the Persian ruler Darius III. At the battle of Arbela/Gaugamela, near the Tigris River, Alexander decisively defeated the Persians at Gaugamela. Darius escaped, leaving behind members of his family. Alexander later married the daughter of Darius, beginning the fusion of Greek and Persian customs. Following his victory at Arbela/Gaugamela, Alexander went to Babylon, whose buildings and possessions he respected. Alexander here sacrificed to the god Marduk, again embracing the customs of another culture. Alexander was not always so tolerant of other customs, however, as would be seen in the Persian capital Persepolis, which met a harsher fate.

The Persian Treasury in Persepolis

Alexander also traveled to Persepolis, the second Persian capital. Here, Alexander took the Persian treasury; the silver coins from Persepolis created wild inflation as Alexander's forces dumped them on the ancient world. In a drunken fit of rage, Alexander also burned the famous Persian capital. Alexander might have been trained in philosophy, but his oversized personality included the full ranges of unrestrained emotion. Alexander often exhibited ferocious fits of temper juxtaposed with the humane treatment of those he conquered. The destruction of Persepolis, however, was in part motivated by a desire for revenge against the Persians, who had earlier burned the Athenian acropolis, but also by the fact that Persepolis was the symbol of the Persian monarchy and the center of many of the rituals surrounding it. The obliteration of Persepolis signaled the end of Persian rule.

The Fate of Darius III

Following the battle of Arbela/Gaugamela, Darius III fled to Bactria. One of his own men, Bessus, the satrap of Bactria, together with other conspirators, succeeded in assassinating Darius in 330 B.C.E. Alexander had pursued Darius to Bactria hoping to capture him, and now had to build alliances with the Persians. Bessus became a pawn in this struggle, and when Bessus's fellow conspirators turned him into Alexander to preserve their own lives, Alexander promptly returned him to his Persian allies to be convicted on charges of regicide and later executed. While in Bactria and Sogdiana, Alexander built further alliances by marrying the daughter of a Sogdian noble, Roxanne, who would later bear him a son. At the same time, Alexander brought many Persians into his army, referring to them as successors and alarming the Macedonians who had followed him from Greece. Many of Alexander's men began to turn against him at this point, wondering to what extent he planned to abandon their own culture and favor the Persians. Here, too, Alexander introduced a new custom for the Greeks, the proskynēsis or ritual prostration formerly made to the Persian monarch.

The Indus River Valley

Alexander reached the Indus River in 326 B.C.E. The impact of the Greeks on India is evident in Indian art of the next several centuries. Alexander's men had been on the march now for almost eight years. Exhausted, for the first time they refused to follow their leader and threatened mutiny. Alexander ordered massive purges in retaliation; it has been estimated that one-third to two-thirds of the men were dismissed or executed. It was at the Indus River that Alexander himself began to deteriorate; having reached the ends of the earth and with a mutiny on his hands, he began to formulate wild plans to conquer Carthage in North Africa and to construct a canal linking Africa with Saudi Arabia. Had his plan worked, the Portuguese would never have explored the coast of Africa in an effort to reach the east during the fifteenth century C.E. or the Age of Exploration; there would have been no need for this as the canal would have made sailing around Africa unnecessary. Alexander also envisioned deporting entire populations to complete the project.

The Wedding Feast of Susa

Alexander left India, returning to the Persian capital of Susa. At the **Wedding Feast of Susa** in 324 B.C.E., Alexander ordered 10,000 of his men to marry Persian women, insisting that all humanity was united through a common creator. Alexander himself married the daughter of Darius and another Persian heiress. The Wedding Feast of Susa symbolized the new world of the Hellenistic empire. The word "Hellenistic" means "Greek-like," and blending of the fiercely independent Greeks with Persians and other peoples changed the Greek world forever. The Hellenistic world was cosmopolitan, a word made up of "cosmos," meaning the universe, and "polis," harking back to the Greek city-state. In Alexander's cosmopolitan empire, the polis became the known world, thus ending forever the ethnocentricity and localization of the old Greek poleis. Alexander allowed conquered areas to keep their laws and customs, and brought many of those customs back into the old Greek world.

Babylon

Alexander left Persia and returned to Babylon in 323 B.C.E. In June he died of a mysterious fever. The origin of his illness is unknown, but some speculate it was more the result of his perceived failure to urge his men farther that caused his final decline. Upon his deathbed, his men asked him whom he wished to rule his empire. Rather than cede his conquests to any of his men, his response was, "Let the best man win." In death as in life, Alexander was a true Achilles, who believed in prowess on the battlefield as the main criterion for leadership. His wife Roxanne and the son she bore Alexander after his death were murdered in 310 B.C.E. The chaos in the wake of his death and that of his son fragmented the Hellenistic world. The tomb of Alexander has never been found, although recent excavations near Alexandria may prove to be his final resting place.

Interpreting Alexander's Personality and Impact

Plutarch, who wrote during the Roman period, emphasized Alexander's virtue of self-restraint and Alexander's learning. He praises Alexander for succeeding where others failed by successfully introducing Greek culture to the non-Greek parts of the world. Plutarch does admit that Alexander was given to boast and loved flattery, which suggests that even the Romans were aware that Alexander has aspects that were less than perfect. In fact, another Roman author, **Cicero**, bluntly condemns Alexander's arrogance and cruelty.

Ancient and modern historians have struggled to balance the positive impact of Greek culture following Alexander's conquests with the less-than-positive aspects of his personality. One should be careful not to idolize Alexander for heroism on the battlefield, without remembering the cruel abuses he often inflicted on his men and those around them and the explosive fits of anger to which he was often subject. The real Alexander was often a man of extremes; despite the Greek love for balance, his own personality may not have always exhibited it.

THE HELLENISTIC EMPIRE

After Alexander's death, his empire was divided into separate kingdoms. For forty years, various figures battled for power.

The Aetolian League

The Aetolian League was centered on the Gulf of Corinth. In the Aetolian league, citizens of the various city-states retained own citizenship but also received citizenship in the Aetolian league. There were two kinds of citizenship offered: **sympolity**, which provided full civil and political rights, and **isopolity**, which provided civil but not political rights. Isopolity was given to citizens in the more distant states linked to the League. The League government could raise armies and collect taxes. The transformation of Greek citizenship in this league symbolized the new cosmopolitan world.

The Aechaean League

The Aechaean League was formed from the city-states of the northern Peloponnesus and was very closely related to the old Peloponnesian League dominated by Sparta. The Aechaean League had a common system of coinage and uniform standards of weights and measurements shared by the city-states. There was also a system of federal courts; unlike the city-states in the Aetolian League, those in the Aechaean League did not exchange citizenship. The League government could raise armies and collect taxes.

The Ptolemaic Monarchy

The Ptolemaic Monarchy was founded by **Ptolemy I**, a Macedonian general in Alexander's army, and became one of the wealthiest centers of the Hellenistic world. It extended over the territory of ancient Egypt. Ptolemy believed that the generals could not hold Alexander's empire together, and proposed its division at a council in Babylon following Alexander's death. Ptolemy enacted a policy of protecting Egypt's borders and also exploiting its economy. He used Macedonian commanders to run daily affairs alongside Egyptians, and there is some evidence that he and his men discriminated against the native Egyptians. He founded only one city, Ptolomais, and introduced coinage, which was unknown in Egypt at that time. He also founded the cult of **Sarapis**, which was a fusion of Greek and Egyptian religions. Ptolemy died in 282 B.C.E. and passed power to his son. The Ptolemies reigned longer than any other monarchy founded on the ruins of Alexander's conquests, and finally succumbed to the Romans in 30 B.C.E. The last Ptolomaic ruler was **Cleopatra VII**, whose union with Julius Caesar and later Mark Anthony threatened to rip the Roman world apart.

The Seleucid Monarchy

Antioch was the capital of the Seleucid monarchy, which extended from Thrace to the subcontinent of India. The Seleucid Empire spanned the outlines of the old Persian Empire. **Seleucus I Nicator**, one of Alexander's generals, became governor of Babylon in 323 B.C.E., two years after the death of Alexander. When Antigonus I, who inherited Alexander's Macedonian throne, expelled him from Babylon, Seleucus allied with Ptolemy against him. In 312 B.C.E., he defeated the Antigonids (the ruling dynasty of Macedonia) and founded the Seluecid monarchy. In the continuing conflict that surrounded the death of Alexander, the son of Ptolemy I later assassinated Selucus. The Seleucid Empire was one of the most important centers of culture in the Hellenistic world, but their favoritism to Greek culture caused many rebellions. In the second century B.C.E., for example, they erected a statue to Zeus in Jerusalem, causing the rebellion documented in the Hebrew book of Maccabees. The Seleucids began a long process of decline when they were first defeated by the Roman Empire in 190 B.C.E. The Romans finally conquered the last remnants of the Seleucid monarchy in 64 B.C.E.

The Pergamene Monarchy

The Pergamene Monarchy covered Asia Minor. The capital city of **Pergamon** was one of the most important cities in the Hellenistic world, with a library second only to that of Alexandria. Pergamon was originally under the control of the Seleucids, but in 263 B.C.E., the Attalid rulers declared independence from the Seleucids. **Attalus I** fought against the Macedonian dynasty of the Antigonids with the help of the Romans in two Macedonian wars. Attalus I was known as a patron of the arts, and the city of Pergamon was also an important city in Roman times, when its population reached 200,000. After the fall of the Western Roman Empire, the Byzantines and then the Ottoman Turks ruled the city of Pergamon.

The Antigonid Monarchy

The Antigonid Monarchy was the ruling house of Macedonia from 306 to 168 B.C.E. The Antigonids rose to power when Demetrius I Poiorcetes ousted the governor of Athens and conquered the island of Cyprus. His father, Antigonus

I Monophthalmus, then conquered all of the Middle East except Babylonia and was proclaimed king in 306 B.C.E. The Antigonids later clashed with the expanding Roman Empire; in 215 B.C.E., the Romans defeated Philip V of Macedon and confined his power to Macedonia. His successor, Perseus, fought for Macedonian freedom against Rome, but was defeated by the Romans at the battle of Pydna in 168 B.C.E.

CHANGE OVER TIME

Alexander's conquests, and the succeeding kingdoms arising from them, created a more unified economy than was previously present. Coinage now had a common standard of value, based on the coinage of Attica, where Athens was located. A more unified coinage made trade easier, and the Seleucids and Ptolemies traded luxury goods via the caravans of eastern peoples with sub-Saharan Africa, India, and Arabia. The Greeks used monsoon winds to navigate sea routes to India. Trade also occurred between China and the Hellenistic world along the Silk Road. The Chinese continued to trade silk, and other goods such as gold, spices, silver, and tea. Greeks exported olive oil, metal weapons, cloth, and wine. Among the more important goods that flowed along the trade routes was grain from the Hellenistic monarchies. This grain enabled many Greek cities, historically unable to provide enough grain for themselves, to survive.

The Hellenistic economy was driven by manual labor, and trade in slaves was one of the most important aspects of the economy. Agricultural production increased due to a plentiful supply of slaves and Hellenistic monarchs who fostered experimentation in agriculture. The Hellenistic botanist Theophrastus represents agricultural innovation. Theophrastus was a student of Artistotle, and understood the process of germination. He also studied the importance of climate and soil, and classified many plants.

The Greek language also helped to unite the Hellenistic world. One particular example of the spread of Greek was the translation of the Hebrew Scriptures into Greek. This translation, which includes a collection of texts called the Deutero-Canonical or Apocryphal books, is known as the **Septuagint**. In fact, during the lifetime of the historic Jesus, Greek was the *lingua franca* of that eastern Mediterranean area then ruled by the Romans, and the language in which Pontius Pilate and Jesus would have communicated.

The Colossus of Rhodes

The **Colossus of Rhodes** was one of the seven wonders of the ancient world. This huge bronze statue illustrated the extent of creativity during the Hellenistic period. It collapsed after only a few decades, as its legs were not large enough to sustain its massive weight. Scholars debate whether the colossus actually straddled the harbor of Rhodes, which would have been almost impossible from a technological point of view, or stood on the shore, the more likely alternative. Although the Colossus is justifiably famous, the technology for it was essentially borrowed from Phidias, and his enormous statue of Zeus in Olympia.

Hellenistic Technology

In general, Hellenistic modes of production, whether in agriculture or other areas such as bronze casting, improved very little. Hellenistic inventors, such as Archimedes, who discovered the principle of displacement and also made great strides in hydrostatics, developed a number of creative machines and other technologies by which the world might have benefited. Unfortunately, just as some have said the Athenians failed to lived up to the standards of their democracy, so too, the Hellenistic world failed to take advantage of its creative minds like Archimedes. Slave labor was plentiful, and many did not see the usefulness of new machines, such as Archimedes's famous screw, which could draw water from the river.

Hellenistic Philosophy

In the wake of Alexander's death, the Greeks experienced what some scholars have called psychological fragmentation. They attempted to search for individual freedom within the chaos of the Hellenistic world. They especially struggled over how to relate to the universe when the symbols of its order, the Greek poleis, had disintegrated and been incorporated into a larger whole. Three main schools of philosophy also arose during this period.

Stoicism was founded by **Zeno** (335–263 B.C.E.). Zeno taught in a painted hall called a Stoa. He urged humans to want only those things a human can control and to submit themselves to a divinely ordered cosmos where reason ruled the universe.

Epicureanism was founded by **Epicurus** (341–270 B.C.E.). Epicurus did not believe in deities, and argued that human lives should and could unfold without fear of reprisal from the gods. Life was controlled by the random movement of particles, meaning that ultimately, we cannot control our lives. Therefore, he taught that one should renounce the world of politics and free oneself from the worries and flux of the world. He believed one should seek only pleasure, which was found through the absence of pain.

Cynicism's most famous teacher was **Diogenes**. The word "cynic" means "dog" in Greek; Diogenes's behavior was often revolting to those around him, as he urinated on banquet tables and pleasured himself in public areas. Diogenes challenged social norms by suggesting that such norms and customs were merely the capricious laws of men. He preached complete freedom of speech and practiced it to the point of rudeness. According to legend, Alexander himself approached Diogenes while he was reading and asked him whether there was anything he might do for him out of respect for his wisdom. The response of Diogenes was merely to say, "get out of my light." For Diogenes, the world should be avoided and life lived at a minimum level of spiritual and material needs. For many in the Hellenistic world, Alexander created a world they no longer fully understood. Greeks intermingled with Persians and those of many other cultures. While many have pointed out that Greek culture was spread to many parts of the world, in many places its influence was only superficial, while other cultures continued to maintain many of their own traditions. Greeks were exposed to and adopted many new traditions, as illustrated by the cult of Serapis in Egypt. The world of the Greek city-states in the Golden Age of Greece was gone forever, yet only the Romans would fully capitalize on the developments of the Hellenistic world.

Review Questions

1. The school of philosophy that defined pleasure as the absence of pain was

   (A) Cynicism.

   (B) Epicureanism.

   (C) Stoicism.

   (D) Hellenism.

2. The school of philosophy that emphasized a divinely ordered cosmos was

   (A) Cynicism.

   (B) Epicureanism.

   (C) Stoicism.

   (D) Hellenism.

3. Cynicism's most famous teacher was

   (A) Zeno.

   (B) Epicurus.

   (C) Plato.

   (D) Diogenes.

4. Which is the following interpretations of Alexander has the most support among ancient and modern scholars?

   (A) He adopted Persian customs to the detriment of Greek culture.

   (B) He believed in his own divinity.

   (C) He adopted customs surrounding the Persian monarchy in order to rule more effectively the Persians he conquered.

   (D) (A) and (B).

5. Which of the following best describes Alexander's legacy?

   (A) Alexander spread a deep layer of Greek culture throughout the known world.

   (B) Alexander spread Greek culture throughout the known world, but in places it was only a thin layer superimposed on indigenous customs.

   (C) Alexander's legacy was primarily positive.

   (D) Alexander's legacy was primarily one of cruel repression and abuse.

6. Which of the following area of Alexander's empire was ruled by the Ptolemies?

(A) Egypt.

(B) Persia.

(C) Macadeonia.

(D) Asia Minor.

7. Which of the following was NOT an impact of Alexander's conquests?

(A) The creation of a more unified economy.

(B) The spread of the Greek language as a common language.

(C) The fragmentation of trade routes.

(D) The increase of slave labor.

Answers

1. (B)	3. (D)	5. (B)	7. (C)
2. (C)	4. (C)	6. (A)	

Chapter 8

THE CIVILIZATION OF ROME THROUGH THE JULIO-CLAUDIANS

KEY TERMS

Etruscans	Tiberius Gracchus
Romulus and Remus	Gaius Gracchus
Aeneas	Marius
Noble Roman Virtues	Sulla
Roman Republic	Julius Caesar
consuls	Pompey
Roman Senate	Vercengetorix
Patricians	Gauls
Plebians	Siege of Alesia
Hortensian Laws	Cleopatra
Sexto-Licinian Laws	Ptolemy
Tribunate	Crassus
Pyrrhic Wars	Octavian, Octavius, Augustus
Pyrrhic Victory	Battle of Actium
Battle of Heraclea	Pax Romana
Punic Wars	Julio/Claudian emperors
Hannibal	Tiberius
Carthage and the Phoenicians	Caligula
Scipio Africanus	Nero
Battle of Zama	Claudius
Battle of Canae	Vespasian
Battle of Lake Tresimene	Virgil
Latifundia	Livy

ROMAN HISTORY THROUGH THE JULIO-CLAUDIANS

Rome began its history as a city on the Palatine Hill, one of seven hills along the Tiber River. According to the historian **Livy**, the legendary foundation of Rome occurred in 753 B.C.E. when **Romulus** defeated his twin brother **Remus** in a cataclysmic battle across the seven hills on the Tiber. Romulus and Remus were the sons of Rhea Silvia and the god Mars. Their uncle had banned their mother from having children due to a family conflict. When they were born, their uncle ordered them placed on the **Tiber River**; they landed on the Palatine Hill, the exact spot where Rome would later be built. A she-wolf found them and raised them to maturity. Remus, however, crossed a wall built by Romulus and the two fought each other to the death. Romulus became the founder of Rome, which was named after him.

Livy further relates that the original inhabitants of Rome were debtors and criminals, and were in desperate need of women. The Romans went to the Sabines and raped several of their women, bringing them home to further their community. The Sabine women became loyal to their Roman husbands and rose to the defense of their husbands when their families tried to rescue them. According to Livy, part of Rome's later greatness was its ability to conquer enemies and then convert them to allies, thereby uniting all of the Italian peninsula and later much of the Mediterranean world. The Romans fought the Sabines in several wars, and several other groups of people, including the Latins. The **Latins** were a group of people named after the volcanic plain on which they lived, the **Latium Plain**, which was bounded on the north by the Tiber River. The Romans eventually made peace with both the Sabines and the Latins. The Latins gave their name to the official language of the Republic and the Empire.

The Etruscans

The Etruscans, a group of Indo-Europeans whose roots were in Central Asia, were another important group of people on the peninsula. Traditionally it has been said that the Etruscans dominated Rome during its first two hundred years of history. However, of the first seven kings of the Romans, only two were Etruscan: **Tarquinius the Elder** and **Tarquinius Superbus** or Tarquin the Proud, who was likely his grandson. The Tarquins did not take Rome by force, but rather by election, and recent historians have reevaluated the extent to which the Etruscans influenced Roman civilization. Several recent historians argue that the Greek colonies on the southern tip of Italy had more influence on the Romans than did the Etruscans.

The Etruscans were a self-governing aristocracy with a military ruling class, and they controlled most of the northern Italian peninsula. The Romans borrowed many customs from the Etruscans, including the Triumph, in which victorious generals were led through the center of Rome. The Romans also copied the Etruscan custom of burying their dead in decorated sarcophagi. The Etruscans wore shoes, an idea the Roman army would borrow and use to great advantage.

The Foundation of the Roman Republic

The Romans, however, eventually threw off the last Etruscan king, Tarquinius Superbus or Tarquin the Proud, in 510 B.C.E. The Roman Republic is traditionally said to have been founded in 509 B.C.E. Some historians believe the foundation of the Republic was actually later, but this traditional date is still the most widely accepted date for the foundation of the Republic.

The Roman Republic was based on the rule of law. The laws of Rome were displayed in Roman forum on twelve bronze tables. This public display of law illustrated the Roman commitment to constitutionalism, which was important in the development of the modern world. The Latin name of the Republic was the **Res Publica**, or the Roman "public thing." Indeed, the public proclamation of law was one of Rome's greatest achievements.

Although the twelve bronze tables have disappeared, we know much about the Roman Republic from the historian **Polybius**. Polybius insisted that the greatest achievement of Rome was the balance of power between the consuls, the senate, and the people. He argued that if one looked at any of these branches of Roman government in isolation, one would have interpreted it as either a despotism, an oligarchy, or a democracy. Rome, however, was a republic, in which all branches were checked and balanced by the others. Yet in many important ways, the Romans never did balance the two competing forces in their society: the patricians or the noble class, and the plebeians, or those considered citizens but without the right to hold office in the early days of the Republic.

At the top of the Roman governmental structure were the two consuls, either of which could veto the decrees of other. Citizens elected the consuls from the patricians for a one-year term and the senate had to approve their election. The consuls were the supreme masters of administration. They were charged to bring matters before the Senate for deliberation, carry out decrees of the majority, make preparations for war and control the military during maneuvers. After the expiration of their terms, they retired to the senate, where they spent the rest of their lives in civic service. Traditionally, one became consul in Rome after having progressively moved through the cursus honorium, or list of offices.

In many ways, the most important governing body in Rome was the Senate, composed of elder statesmen from the patrician class who served for life. The senate oversaw the treasury; in fact, no money was authorized for the state without the decree of the senate. The members of the senate were charged with leading public investigations into treason, conspiracy and murder. They also served as ambassadors to reconcile warring allies. Nowhere were the powers of the senate decisively spelled out, which gave them the ability to establish supreme power in Rome. During the Age of the Reformers in the second and first century B.C.E., tribunes attempted to change laws to benefit the plebeians, and it was the senate that masterminded many of their assassinations.

According to Polybius, the third important body in the Roman Res Publica was the people. The plebeian assembly was the last and final court to decide matters of life and death. The people's assembly met when summoned by the consuls, and later, the office of **tribune** was established to look after the affairs of the people.

The difficulty faced by Rome throughout its history, however, was the tension between the patricians, who came from the ancient noble families and whose name was derived from the Latin word for father, pater, and the plebeians. Both were defined as citizens, but they did not enjoy the same rights. The patricians were the aristocracy and they did not intermarry with the plebeians. They held the highest offices, such as senator and consul. The plebeians, on the other hand, were citizens who paid taxes and served in the army, but were barred from holding office in the early Republic. Although there was no obvious law prohibiting plebeians from holding office, in practice, one had to perform certain religious rites and rituals, which were only open to participation by the patricians.

In effect, the history of the Republic was the history of how the patricians and plebeians resolved these tensions so that they could embark on a wave of conquest which would make them masters of the Mediterranean area; the history of Rome as an empire is the story of how they managed to unite such a disparate group of peoples and cultures under the banner of Rome.

ROME BECOMES MASTER OF THE MEDITERRANEAN

Rome began to address the tensions between the patricians and plebeians with the appointment of the **tribunes** in the fifth century B.C.E. The tribunes were elected by plebian assembly for one year, could convene the assembly, and block measures proposed by the senate by saying "I forbid" or veto in Latin. In 367 B.C.E. Rome passed the **Sexto-Licinian Laws**, according to which plebeians could hold the office of consul and could intermarry with patricians. In 287 B.C.E. Rome passed the **Hortensian Laws**, which mandated that laws passed in the plebian assembly were binding on the Roman senate. These various measures resolved the class tensions long enough to allow Rome to expand beyond the Tiber to the eventual conquest of the Italian peninsula. They did not, however, fully address the issue, because in fact many of the tribunes, were patricians who used the office to climb the ranks of Roman society, and the tribunes almost always sided with patricians out of self-interest. Further, the tribunes rarely fought for any measures which they were not sure would clear the senate. Class tensions, therefore, were never fully resolved in Rome.

Nevertheless, Rome defeated the Greek colonists who still remained at foot of the peninsula during the **Pyrrhic Wars** from 282–272 B.C.E. **Pyrrhus**, King of Epirus, led the Greeks and in the early days of the conflict defeated the Romans at Heraclea. During the battle, Rome lost 7,000 men while the Greeks lost 4,000. While the Romans lost more soldiers, the Greeks could not afford to lose the 4,000 men who died. A "pyrrhic victory" refers to a victory that is too costly for the victor.

The Punic Wars

Rome's expansion to the southern tip of the Italian peninsula was quickly followed by a leap across the water to Sicily. The Punic Wars began when Rome entered Sicily. The Phoencians had a settlement in Sicily, as well as an important outpost at Carthage in North Africa. The Phoencians were not involved in war and conquest so much as they were interested in trade. They marketed purple dye, which was expensive to make. Purple was the symbol of royalty in many cultures. It has been shown that Phoenician ships were capable of crossing the Atlantic. The Latin word for Phoenician was Punicus, and when the Romans entered Sicily, the Carthaginians rose to the defense of the Sicilians. During the **First Punic War** from 264–241 B.C.E., the Romans were forced to fight a sea war. They were ill-equipped for such a conflict, yet they eventually devised a bridge known as a corvus to enable them to board the Carthaginian ships and fight what amounted to a land battle on the decks of the ships. Rome eventually won the conflict, and exacted a large indemnity against the Carthaginians as well as the surrender of territory.

Hannibal and the Second Punic War

During the First Punic War, Rome had taken Carthage's most important province, Sicily, as well as Sardinia and Corsica. To compensate for these losses, the Carthaginians began to expand their holdings on the Iberian Peninsula. The leader of the Iberian forces was the general Hamilcar Barca, who brought with him his ten-year-old son, **Hannibal**. The Romans believed that Hamilcar forced Hannibal to promise eternal hatred for the Romans. When Hamilcar died, Hannibal's brother-in-law, Hasdrubal, was appointed commander in Iberia. In 221 B.C.E., however, Hasdrubal was murdered and Hannibal was made commander. While Hasdrubal had pursued more peaceful tactics in Iberia, such as intermarriage with the Carthaginians, Hannibal returned to his father's more aggressive stance, and laid siege to Saguntum, a Roman ally. At the time, Rome was occupied with the Second Illyrian War, and Saguntum fell after eight months. Enraged, the Romans demanded that Carthage hand over Hannibal for prosecution. Hannibal continued to expand the holdings of Carthage in Iberia, and Rome declared the **Second Punic War** (218–201 B.C.E.).

This time, the Carthaginians decided to attempt to outwit the Romans and force them to fight a defensive battle. Hannibal launched a bold attack directly into the heart of Italy. With a force of 50,000 infantry, 9,000 cavalry and thirty-seven elephants to carry supplies for the troops, he crossed the Pyrenees, and then ferried the elephants across the Rhone River on rafts. Even more remarkably, his forces crossed the Alps in the snow, and by October 218 B.C.E., his remaining forces of approximately 38,000 soldiers and 8,000 knights had reached the plains along the River Po, near the Italian town Turin. Hannibal's achievement was astonishing. The route Hannibal took across the Alps is the subject of much debate.

Our only sources of his route are the Roman historians Livy and Polybius, neither of whose accounts we can completely verify. Hannibal caught the Romans off-guard, and they sent forces to the river Ticinus to meet him. Hannibal defeated them, and the many Gauls who inhabited the region now flocked to his cause. According to legend, Hannibal so mistrusted the Gauls as allies that he continually wore wigs and changed them so as to disguise himself.

Hannibal and his new allies then defeated the Romans again at Trebia. Later, at the Lake of Trasimene, two Roman legions were annihilated. The Romans attempted to stop Hannibal and raised a force of 80,000 men to fight him at Cannae. While Hannibal's army only had about 26,000 Carthaginians, 12,000 Gauls and 7,000 Italians, clever military leadership managed to thwart the Romans again. At the battle of Cannae, Hannibal's troops killed so many senators and patricians that the government was very nearly shut down. Hannibal was thirty years old when he leveled the world's mightiest army. Other Roman provinces revolted, such as Capua, which Hannibal entered triumphantly on his last surviving elephant.

Hannibal's men were exhausted after the campaign, and although Cannae was a tremendous victory, the Romans gradually began to push them further south. Hannibal countered by laying siege to Rome itself, but the Romans launched a counteroffensive in Iberia against Hannibal's brother Hasdrubal (a different person from his brother-in-law Hasdrubal, who was governor before him), whom he had appointed commander. The young Roman **Publius Cornelius Scipio** conquered the Carthaginian capital of Iberia, Cartagena and then proceeded to launch an attack on **Carthage** itself. Scipio forced Hannibal to leave the peninsula to defend his home ground. Rome sent its expedition to Africa under the leadership of **Scipio Africanus**, a young Roman who was not yet twenty-five years of age.

In 202 B.C.E., fourteen years after Hannibal's victory at Cannae, Scipio defeated Hannibal in a stunning maneuver at the **Battle of Zama**. Hannibal's forces were tricked into opening the formidable line of elephants. Hannibal had distinguished himself in the earlier part of the campaign with such brilliance one wonders why he allowed himself to be duped in such a manner.

The peace negotiated between Rome and Carthage forced the Carthaginians to give up their fleet, recognize the Roman conquests in Iberia, and pay an indemnity of 10,000 talents in fifty annual installments. A treaty that resolves one conflict only to create further tension through its terms is referred to as a "Carthaginian peace." Tension between Rome and Carthage continued to escalate.

Despite his loss at Zama, the Carthaginians appointed Hannibal consul. Only a year later, when some of his enemies told the Roman senate that Hannibal planned another attack in conjunction with the Seleucid monarchs, Hannibal fled. When Hannibal advised the Seleucid monarch **Antiochus** to declare war on Greece, the Romans came to their defense. Hannibal fought the Romans, and their allies once again at Rhodes, but was defeated. Hannibal fled again, and later led the Bythnians to victory against Pergamum. Once again, though, Rome intervened, and to avoid extradition, in 183 or 182 B.C.E. Hannibal poisoned himself.

The Third Punic War

The Third Punic War from 149–146 B.C.E. was launched when **Cato the Elder**, a senior statesman of Rome, told the senators that, "Carthago delenda est/ Carthage must be destroyed." The Third Punic War was not a war in the sense the other two conflicts were; it was a minor skirmish that ended quickly. This time, the Romans were determined to wipe Carthage out, and they destroyed the city of Carthage, sold the citizens into slavery, and salted the ground to prevent Carthage from ever being able to grow crops. The Carthaginians were, as Cato urged, utterly destroyed, leaving Rome the master of the Mediterranean.

Later generations would not forget Hannibal. The emperor Septimus Severus erected a monument at the place where Hannibal killed himself, Libyssa, which was still visible in the eleventh century. Throngs of pilgrims came to the site, including many Romans who never forgot the heroic general who led his troops across the Alps. After Hannibal, Roman power was not threatened for 600 years.

Legacy of the Punic Wars

The Romans referred to the **Mediterranean** as mare nostrum, or "our sea." Following the conquest of Carthage, the Mediterranean literally became a Roman lake, and Julius Caesar eventually rebuilt Carthage as a Roman city. The conquest of Carthage made possible the development of an empire that eventually spread to Byzantium in the east and to the British Isles in the north. Livy, a historian of the Silver Age of Culture, the age of Augustus, first emperor of Rome, wrote that, "God has ordained it that Rome should be ruler of the world."

The Punic Wars not only resulted in the destruction of Carthage, but also left their mark on Rome. During Hannibal's siege of Rome in the Second Punic War, he and his troops and elephants destroyed the Roman countryside, forcing many peasants to enter Rome. Rome was forced to accommodate the refugees, but suffered from overcrowding and unemployment. In the wake of the second Punic war, many patricians amassed huge estates known as latifundia and re-treated to lead the shady life, as one Roman historian called it. Preferring life in the countryside to an active life of civic commitment, the patricians forsook public life and therefore, many argue, weakened the fabric of Roman politics. The latifundia also became the basis for the later medieval manorial estates.

As the empire expanded, these problems grew more acute. The provincial governments became corrupt; the distance between Rome and the provinces was often so far Rome had no way of knowing what was adequately overseeing the officials. Tax collectors often collected many times the rate of taxation imposed by Rome and kept the overflow for their own use. The separation between patricians and plebeians grew more acute than at any time since the early days of the Republic.

THE AGE OF THE REFORMERS

The abuses of patrician power led to the career of several tribunes collectively known as the reformers. In 133 B.C.E., **Tiberius Gracchus** initiated a land reform package whereby Rome was to reclaim state land taken by the patricians and redistribute it to the landless plebeians. In order to implement his measures, he by-passed the senate and blocked the vote of the Tribune. Further he tried to have himself illegally reelected to a second term. Tiberius was a good example of what went wrong in Roman politics; he had praiseworthy motives, to help the underprivileged, but the means by which he accomplished his ends were illegal.

Tiberius was clubbed to death by an angry mob led by the senate. The senate, pledged to uphold law and order, now became an angry mob of assassins.

In 123 B.C.E. Tiberius's brother, **Gaius Gracchus**, come into power. The equestrians in the military, an elite class of soldiers, supported Gaius. He passed measures to ensure their support, and for the first time allowed them to become tax collectors. He allowed provincial governors to be tried by equestrians, and generally increased the power of the military. Despite having the support of the military, Gaius too was assassinated, likely at the hands of the senate. His tenure in office had established, however, a dangerous precedent, that of the loyalty of the military to their leader as opposed to Rome.

In 107 B.C.E., this dangerous precedent reached fruition when **Marius**, a powerful general, became consul. The patricians no longer wanted to serve in the military, and Marius needed to increase military recruitment. He offered land for service, and further encouraged loyalty to one man as opposed to Rome. Marius reformed the army, making it a professional corps rather than a volunteer citizen army. He also made it more mobile, and Roman soldiers were often called "Marius's mules."

Marius fought a bitter civil war with **Sulla**, who had been his assistant in the Jugurthine War in Africa. Sulla fought his way up the Italian peninsula and became dictator in 82 B.C.E. After an extended period during which he purged of all his enemies, Sulla doubled the size of the senate by packing it with his own supporters.

Julius Caesar

By the time of Julius Caesar, the republican values of Rome had been significantly weakened. Caesar formed a **triumvirate** with **Pompey**, a powerful general, and **Crassus**, whose name meant "the thick one." Pompey married Caesar's daughter, Julia, to solidify their pact, and Caesar was named governor in Spain and Gaul. The historian Livy called the first triumvirate "a conspiracy against the state by its three leading citizens." Caesar's later actions would permanently bring the Republic to an end.

Caesar's campaigns in Gaul made him wildly popular with the army and the Roman people, to the point where Pompey worried about his motives and growing power. The historian **Suetonius** wrote in his *Life of Caesar* that Caesar was "every man's woman and every woman's man," meaning that he attempted to win over everyone's support through whatever means possible. Further, Plutarch wrote that Caesar was rather uncultured, having a barbaric type of speech. The Romans valued eloquence, and apparently Caesar did not possess that gift of speech. Nevertheless, Plutarch related that his men adored him, as he became one of them in order to win his victories.

Caesar's most famous campaigns were in Gaul. The Romans had control of Cisalpine Gaul, but in 52 C.E. the Celts joined together in a rebellion to free all of Gaul from Roman rule. The tribes to the north of Roman Gaul were the heart of the rebellion, and Caesar's most formidable enemy was **Vercingetorix**. Vercingetorix's father had attempted to make himself king of the Gauls, and had been assassinated, apparently at Roman hands. Vercingetorix knew he could not defeat the Romans in battle, and his strategy was rather to cut off their supply lines. The conflict with Vercingetorix came to a climax at the siege of Alesia. Although Vercingetorix had escaped before the siege began, the Gauls fought the Romans from both within and without the city. After thirty days, their supplies ran out, and the situation was hopeless. Vercingetorix surrendered to Caesar, and was taken prisoner to Rome. He was imprisoned for six years, and after Caesar's final victory over Pompey in 46 B.C.E., he was strangled.

The Crossing of the Rubicon

Caesar's campaign in Gaul was so successful that the senate and Pompey began to worry about Caesar's power over the masses. Further, Caesar's daughter Julia had died, breaking down the alliance with Pompey. In 49 B.C.E., the senate ordered Caesar to hand over his ten legions to a new governor. Caesar, however, refused to hand over power peacefully, and gathered his forces and marched toward Rome. Upon deciding to rebel rather than surrender, Caesar uttered his famous remark that "alea iacta est/the die is cast."

Cleopatra

Pompey fled to Egypt, his greatest mistake. **Ptolemy XIII** and his sister, who was also his wife, **Cleopatra**, then ruled Egypt. Cleopatra and Ptolemy were in the midst of a bitter struggle for power and saw the Romans as possible allies. Ptolemy promptly had Pompey killed in an effort to win the support of Caesar against his sister Cleopatra VII. Cleopatra, however, had other ideas. The historian Plutarch tells us that while she was not terribly attractive from a physical standpoint, she had an inner charisma that drew men to her. Caesar was captivated by her, and took her side against her brother in the Alexandrine War. In 47 B.C.E., Ptolemy XIII was found floating dead in the Nile River. Caesar fathered a son by Cleopatra, **Caesarion**. Cleopatra followed Caesar to Rome, where Caesar openly declared Caesarion his son. His scandalous affair with a foreigner, along with his progressive usurpation of power in Rome, would eventually bring about his downfall.

Caesar as Dictator

In 46 B.C.E. Caesar was proclaimed imperator, or dictator; in 44 B.C.E. he was proclaimed dictator for life. Roman law allowed for the appointment of a dictator in extreme circumstances, but Caesar used the position to transform Rome into a monarchy.

Caesar was elected consul in 48, 46, 45 and 44 B.C.E. Although he shared the consulate in 44 B.C.E., with **Marc Antony**, in 45 B.C.E. he occupied it alone. Caesar transformed the Republic into a monarchy, and while he could not usurp every office, he accepted the powers of several magistratures without occupying the magistratures themselves. Caesar also named a month after himself, **July**; previously, months had only been named for gods.

During his dictatorship, Caesar implemented some important reforms, such as a unified law code, a new calendar based on the Egyptian calendar, and subsidies for farmers. He ordered Carthage rebuilt and offered the impoverished citizens of the Empire a chance to relocate there. Caesar extended some benefits of citizenship to conquered peoples, including some of the Gauls he had defeated.

Caesar also began to bring senators from outside of Italy, and packed the senate with his supporters. According to some historians, such as Ronald Syme in *The Roman Revolution*, Caesar overthrew the corrupt patrician centers of power by using those outside Italy to support his cause.

By 44 B.C.E. many powerful patricians were alarmed. Led by **Caius Cassius** and **Marcus Brutus**, more than sixty men joined in a conspiracy to assassinate Caesar on the Ides of March, March 15, 44 B.C.E., the date the senate was to meet. Caesar almost foiled the plan when he decided to stay home due to illness. Brutus's brother, however, persuaded him to appear at the senate meeting. While preparing to receive requests, Caesar was caught off guard and was stabbed twenty-three times. Contrary to Shakespeare's colorful story, Caesar never uttered a word or sound during the violent attack. He collapsed at the foot of a statue of Pompey. No one dared to come near him, and for several hours, he lay at the statue until three slaves finally carried him back to his home.

Although Caesar wished to be "first among equals," most historians since World War II agree that he established rule by one man. The benefits he brought to the more than sixty million people in the Roman Empire, fully one-third of the world's population, have largely been overshadowed by what many modern historians see as a monarchy reminiscent of the fascist regimes of World War II.

The Civil War and the Rise of Octavian

Although the conspirators hoped Caesar's death would restore the Republic, another civil war ensued. Marc Antony, Caesar's former co-consul, immediately confiscated Caesar's papers and treasury. He gave amnesty to the conspirators, but insisted that Caesar's acts remain law. Antony, however, made use of public opinion against the conspirators. When Caesar's corpse was burned on March 20, Antony publicly announced that Caesar had left his gardens to the city of Rome and had granted every inhabitant money from his own funds. The population was so enraged that the conspirators had to flee Rome.

Unfortunately, Antony's path to complete power was blocked by Caesar's great-nephew, **Octavius**, whom Caesar had also adopted as a son. Caesar had left Octavius two-thirds of his property. Antony had confiscated it with all Caesar's other possessions, and although Octavius was only eighteen at the time, he confronted Antony and demanded its return. Meanwhile, Antony was forced to leave Rome to fight the brother of Brutus. While he was away, the great orator Cicero urged the senate to rid themselves of Antony. Cicero, like many others, did not regard Octavius as a threat, and decided that he must be used as a pawn in the fight against Antony. Cicero remarked that, "We must praise the boy, give him a command and then put him away." In 44 B.C.E. in honor of his adoption by Caesar, Octavius took the name C. Julius Caesar Octavianus, or **Octavian**, and in 43 B.C.E., he turned the tables on Cicero by defeating Antony in two battles and demanding the consulship in return.

Octavian then made peace with Antony in order to pursue and exterminate the conspirators against Caesar. In 42 B.C.E. he and Antony defeated Brutus and Cassius. Octavian formed the **second triumvirate** with Antony and Lepidus, and divided the empire between the three. The triumvirate was sealed through the marriage of Octavian's sister, Octavia, to Antony. Antony, however, was still not pacified. Like Caesar before him, he fell in love with Cleopatra and had four children with her. Cleopatra clearly hoped to gain Caesar's inheritance for her son and, through Antony, to rule Rome. Octavian regarded Antony's affair with Cleopatra and his campaigns in her interests as a violation of Roman interests and a violation of Antony's marriage to Octavian's sister. Sometime between 32–31 B.C.E., Antony divorced Octavia, and put Cleopatra's name and face on Roman denarii that were circulated throughout the Mediterranean area.

These deeds ended the peace between Octavian and Antony, and they met in battle at sea in 31 B.C.E. at **Actium** in Greece, where Octavian defeated Antony. Antony retreated to Egypt, where less than six months later Octavian defeated him again. In 30 B.C.E., Antony committed suicide by falling on his sword. Meanwhile, Cleopatra attempted to negotiate with Octavian, who was not interested in any reconciliation with her or offering any concessions to her. When it became apparent the negotiations were hopeless, Cleopatra allowed herself to be bitten by a poisonous asp. She was thirty-nine years old when she died on August 12, 30 B.C.E. Following her death, Egypt became part of the Roman Empire. Ironically, the last pharaoh of Egypt was a woman, and Egypt had long had very liberal customs regarding women. In defeating Cleopatra, Octavian brought Egyptian women under Roman rule, and never again would they enjoy the autonomy they once enjoyed under the pharaohs.

Following the defeat of Antony and Cleopatra, the way was now clear for Octavian. Octavian would soon become the first emperor of Rome.

The First Emperor of Rome: Augustus

The future emperor had made his first public appearance at his grandmother Julia's funeral, where he gave the eulogy. Julia was the sister of Caesar, likely the connection through which the future emperor came to Caesar's attention. During his career, the young man originally known as Octavius reinvented himself to suit his particular needs, whether it was his assumption of the name Octavian and the formation of the second triumvirate, or his acceptance of the title of Pater Patriae, Father of the Country, in 2 B.C.E. In his guise as Octavian, he knew it was important to at least respect tradition, and his achievement was to transform the government of Rome into a monarchy while maintaining the appearance of the Republic.

On 13 January 27 B.C.E., Octavian ceremoniously walked into the senate and resigned his triumviral powers. Seeing him as the only way to restore order, the senators implored him to assume command of several important provinces, including Gaul, Spain, and parts of Egypt, while they and the people held command over the rest of the Empire. Three days later the senate gave him the title of **"Augustus"** or "revered one," and now he became officially known as Imperator Caesar Augustus.

Augustus was also called "princeps" or first citizen, and held a continuous consulship for many years and also had the powers of tribune as well as numerous other offices. In 23 B.C.E., he was given the right to convene the senate at will, and in 13 or 12 B.C.E., Augustus became "pontifex maximus." Most of the powers granted to Augustus were given only for five or ten years, and thus he avoided Caesar's mistake of naming himself dictator for life. He was known as Rome's "first citizen" or its princeps, and not as imperator or dictator. Further, at every opportunity the senate renewed the powers they granted to him, thus providing the appearance of election through choice. With the senate's blessing, Augustus was able to assume the powers of many offices without actually occupying them, and he became, for all intents and purposes, the first emperor of Rome.

Augustus and the Arts

Augustus was a master of propaganda, and Rome entered its silver age of culture with such authors as Virgil. In the Aeneid, Virgil painted the Trojans as the legendary founders of Rome, and Augustus as the direct heir of Aeneas and Romulus. Livy, a historian, wrote a multi-volume history of Rome in which he glorified the age of Augustus as the highpoint of Roman history. Livy justified the Augustan transition from Republic to empire by arguing that since the time of Romulus, Rome ruled with a mandate from gods.

Augustus also made use of the visual arts to promote his image, such as in his mausoleum modeled after the fourth-century B.C.E. tomb of Mausolus, located at Halicarnassus in Caria in southwestern Asia Minor. The **Tomb at Halicarnassus** was one of the seven wonders of the ancient world. His autobiography, "The Achievements of the Divine Augustus," was inscribed on two bronze tables outside the Mausoleum of Augustus in Rome. Although he denied taking power that was not offered to him freely and repeatedly stressed that he refused the title of emperor, Augustus's presence in the visual arts and in the political arena makes clear that he was an emperor in fact. His autobiography is the only first person narrative of an emperor's career.

Literary Arts in the Silver Age

The flourishing of culture during the age of Augustus is known as the Silver Age of Roman culture. While Greece had a Golden Age, the achievements of Roman culture are symbolized by silver, as many scholars argue that the Romans were but a pale imitation of the Greeks. Many scholars maintain that Roman poets, philosophers, and other scholars were not as creative and original as those of ancient Greece, and that they merely mimicked the achievements of the Greeks. Nevertheless, the Romans made important contributions to poetry, history, philosophy, and preserved many Greek bronze statues by copying them in marble.

Ovid (43 B.C.E.– ca. 17 C.E.)

Publius Ovidius Naso, who was better known as Ovid, was an aristocrat who studied law and rhetoric. He went to Athens, however, and soon developed a greater interest in poetry. His most famous work is The Art of Love. Ovid was banished by Augustus, however, because the work appeared around the time Augustus's daughter Julia was charged with immorality and exiled from Rome.

Horace (65 B.C.E.– 8 C.E.)

Quintus Horatius Flaccus or Horace was the son of a former slave and he studied philosophy in Athens. He served as a tribune under Marcus Brutus, and when Brutus was defeated, found himself without support. He began to write a series of Epistles that addressed social abuses. Horace advocated the need for strong moral qualities in his poetry. Horace entered the court of Augustus and wrote many other famous works, such as the *Odes* and the *Ars Poetica*. One of the most famous Latin phrases, *carpe diem* or "seize the day" was taken from a line in the *Odes*. The *Ars Poetica* influenced poetry during the Middle Ages and the early modern period. Dante, for example, listed Horace as the third poet, following Homer and Virgil. While many works of Roman poets were lost after the Roman Empire collapsed in the West, those of Horace were preserved.

Virgil (70–19 B.C.E.)

Publius Vergilius Maro or Virgil was not a Roman by birth but a Gaul. He was born in Gallia Cisalpina, the region that was governed by Julius Caesar. Virgil wrote the *Eclogues* and *Georgics* about life in the country. The work of the Greek poet Hesiod influenced Virgil. Virgil entered the service of Augustus, and after the victory at Actium, Augustus asked Virgil to write a poem glorifying Rome during the Age of Augustus. The result was an epic poem, the *Aeneid*, which was modeled on the epic poems of Homer. The *Aeneid* was the epic story of the Trojan hero Aeneas and the founding of Rome. Although Virgil never finished the *Aeneid*, the Emperor Augustus published it and it became so famous that the medieval poet Dante chose Virgil as his guide in the Comedia through the Inferno and Purgatorio, but denied him entrance to paradise as Virgil was not a Christian.

Livy (64 or 59 B.C.E.– 17 C.E.)

Titus Livius wrote 142 books of history, only thirty-five of which have been preserved. His history of Rome was unique in that he wrote it in Latin. Earlier historians had written in Greek. Livy, like Horace and Virgil, emphasized the importance of moral qualities in the creation of Rome and thought them necessary for its continued success. Livy was unique in that he was not involved in politics nor was he a member of the senatorial class. Many scholars have found errors in his works and accused him of accepting legend too readily. His lack of involvement in political circles may have deprived him of needed resources, but his *History of Rome* nevertheless stands as one of the greatest works of the age.

Reforms of Augustus

While Augustus was a great patron of the arts and used them to create a grandiose image for himself, he also reformed the military, taking direct command and regulating pay, pensions, and length of service. He mandated that the military's size be permanently fixed at twenty-five legions, and shrunk the borders of the empire to make them more defensible.

Augustus promoted trade, and luxury goods, such as silk and fruits from the east, were brought into the empire. Many famous wall murals, such as the ones at Pompeii, show Roman nobles dressed in silk from Ceres or China, the only word by which they knew China.

During the Principate and the Pax Romana, the Roman Empire enjoyed the longest period of unity, peace, and prosperity of its history. Moreover, it was to be the longest period of peace that Western Europe, the Middle East and the North African seaboard would ever know in their entire recorded history.

Augustus's achievements were remarkable and, although his successors were corrupt, the Rome he recreated would endure for 500 years in the west and for another 1500 years in the east. Augustus, like Caesar before him, named a month in his honor, August, thus giving him divine status. In later centuries, he would be worshipped as the Divine Augustus. Gone was any semblance of the Republic, and Rome would suffer the consequences of this for many generations to come. Many nobles would fight for the restoration of the Republic, but in the end, it was the Augustan Principate that won.

After Augustus

Despite his many successes, the reign of Augustus created a new problem for Rome. When Augustus died in 14 C.E., there were no established procedures to replace someone with his vast powers. The Romans turned to heredity as a solution, and appointed **Tiberius**, the son of Augustus's wife Livia, next emperor. Tiberius, however, grew increasingly corrupt, and the moral depravity at his palace on the Isle of Capri was legendary. During his reign, a Jewish peasant named **Jesus** preached in the Galilee region and his teachings later gave rise to **Christianity**.

Caligula was even more depraved, and had himself proclaimed a god. The Roman army assassinated **Caligula** and proclaimed his uncle **Claudius** emperor. Claudius had physical disabilities and a pronounced stutter, which made him the laughing stock of Rome. Claudius, however, succeeded in conquering Britain and establishing a Roman presence there. He had his wife Messalina murdered for betraying him, and then married his niece, **Agrippina the Younger**, who allegedly poisoned him with a mushroom so that her own son, **Nero**, could succeed her husband as emperor.

Nero focused on the arts, and performed publicly in theatrical events. The Romans were horrified, as theater was a profession dominated by the lower strata of society. Nero often disguised himself and went on binges in public, and even at one point married a young man. Nero had to battle his ambitious mother Agrippina for power, and there were rumors of a sexual liaison between them. He had her murdered. Nero ordered the death of the philosopher **Seneca**, his tutor, and committed suicide himself when it became clear the Romans had turned on him.

The low point of Roman history came when no fewer than four generals vied for power. The winner was **Vespasian**, who first commissioned the Flavian ampitheater, known as the **Coliseum**. Vespasian restored order on the battlefield temporarily, but this was not enough to prevent the further decline of Rome. Vespasian originally served under Nero, who ordered him to conduct a war against the Jews with his son, Titus. Vespasian was one of the least tyrannical emperors, and died a natural death when he was near seventy.

Despite the excesses of Tiberius, Nero, and Caligula, there was some good leadership during the period following the death of Augustus. The emperor **Hadrian**, for example, engaged in several monumental building projects and attempted to shore up the frontiers. **Hadrian's Wall** across northern England still stands, along with the ruins of several Roman forts in England. The wall and the forts attest to the fact that the Romans continued to struggle against other peoples along the frontiers. Eventually, in the fourth century C.E., the Germanic peoples would overrun the empire in the West.

Trajan was another effective ruler, whose monumental column in Rome still stands as a testament to his victory over the Dacians.

Review Questions

1. The Senate assassinated Tiberius and Gaius Gracchus, Caesar defeated Pompey and was later assassinated, Octavius defeated Marc Antony, who then committed suicide, Octavius became supreme and was named Augustus. As a result of the preceding developments, the Republic

   (A) died.

   (B) was restored.

   (C) increased the power of the senators.

   (D) eliminated the monarchy.

2. In his rule as princeps, Augustus

   (A) became the first Roman emperor.

   (B) unified the Empire through a wave of propaganda and by consolidating the frontiers.

   (C) brought continuous warfare to Rome.

   (D) Both (A) and (B).

3. During the early Republic, the plebeians

   (A) could not intermarry with patricians.

   (B) could not be elected to office in the early Republic.

   (C) were more wealthy than the patricians.

   (D) Both (A) and (B).

4. The patricians

   (A) were an aristocratic governing class.

   (B) could not serve as consuls, magistrates, or senators.

   (C) could not use their power to control the plebeians.

   (D) were Etruscans.

5. The devastating legacy of the Punic Wars included all of the following EXCEPT

   (A) the creation of latifundia in the countryside.

   (B) the plebeians and patricians were drawn closer together in a surge of patriotism.

(C) the patricians became progressively corrupt, leading the "shady life."

(D) Rome became overcrowded.

6. Tiberius Gracchus, Gaius Gracchus, and Julius Caesar passed reform packages that benefited the

(A) patricians.

(B) plebeians.

(C) equestrians only.

(D) Senate.

7. Both Gaius Gracchus and Marius implemented reforms to gain the loyalty of the

(A) patricians.

(B) equestrians only.

(C) members of the Roman army.

(D) consuls.

8. Which of the following best describes the differences between the Roman Republic and the Roman Empire?

(A) The Empire was smaller in size than the Republic during the reign of Augustus.

(B) The Empire was governed by a monarchy, while the Republic maintained a series of checks and balances.

(C) The Imperial government was led by rulers who over time, became deified.

(D) Both (B) and (C).

9. All of the following were the result of Hannibal's campaigns in Italy during the Second Punic War EXCEPT

(A) the countryside was devastated.

(B) patricians lost their land to plebeians.

(C) roman consuls and senators were killed and entire legions were destroyed.

(D) some Roman allies abandoned Rome and aligned themselves with the Carthaginians.

10. Which of the following statements best describes the Julio-Claudian line?

(A) They upheld family values both in law and in their private lives.

(B) They were judicious rulers who acted for the good of the Roman people.

(C) They were viciously persecuted by members of the Roman senate.

(D) They were mostly unbalanced rulers who acted for their own good and ambitions over that of Rome.

Answers

1. (A)	4. (A)	7. (C)	10. (D)
2. (D)	5. (B)	8. (D)	
3. (D)	6. (B)	9. (B)	

Chapter 9

ROME FROM THE JULIO-CLAUDIANS THROUGH ITS COLLAPSE IN THE WEST

KEY TERMS

Diocletian
Tetrarchy
Constantine
Battle of Milvian Bridge
Edict of Milan
St. Helena
Donatist heresy
Council of Nicaea
Arian heresy
Nicene Creed
Caesaropapism
Theodosian Code

Barbarian migrations
Visigoths
Vandals
Lombards
Franks
Battle of Adrianople
Ostrogoths
Romulus Augustulus
St. Augustine of Hippo
Edward Gibbon
Henri Pirenne

RELIGION IN THE ROMAN EMPIRE

The Roman Empire incorporated many diverse regions and cultures, including the remnants of Egyptian civilization, Mesopotamian civilization, Hebrew culture along the eastern Mediterranean, and many other cultures. The Pantheon, a temple to all the Roman deities, best exemplifies the plethora of religions in Rome by embracing all the deities of the citizens of Rome.

The Rise of Christianity

The historic **Jesus** was born during the reign of Augustus, sometime around 3 B.C.E. Although the gospel accounts of the life of Jesus relate his birth and some events of his youth, they are silent as to the events of the vast majority of his life. The narratives pick up his life during his last three years. The evangelists describe and interpret his ministry in Galilee, his passion in Jerusalem around 30 C.E., and his resurrection three days later. The gospels paint Jesus as having fulfilled the prophecies in Jewish Scripture, but they also make it clear that Jesus preached a radical new vision of Judaism, one not focused on practice but rather on peace, love, and inner faith as central to spirituality. In the Sermon on the Mount, Jesus preached, "Blessed are the poor in spirit, for they shall see the kingdom of heaven." Jesus ministered to the outcasts of society, but clearly this remark was meant to refer to more than physical poverty. It referred to a kind of inner, spiritual poverty in which the soul was so truly one with the Divine that it was emptied of all other worldly concerns. Many zealots, Jews who opposed Roman rule in Palestine, hoped for a Messiah who would launch a rebellion, but Jesus instead preached a message of peace. Scholars speculate that the disappointment of Judas over Jesus's failure to launch a rebellion led him to betray Jesus to the Romans. In addition, scholars suggest that the fear of Jewish religious leaders that they would be punished for the actions of Jesus and so lead to the downfall of Judaism led them to distance themselves from Jesus and to seek his punishment.

Many scholars argue that the Jesus of history is quite different from the Christ of faith. About the Jesus of history we know little. There are only a few statements in the Scriptures that were known to be statements of Christ. The Christ of faith, however, is the result of centuries of interpretations about what the life of the historic Jesus means. The gospel of John, the last gospel to be composed, is an excellent example of how the life of Jesus was interpreted. John opens his gospel with the following words "In the beginning was the Word, and the Word was with God and the Word was God." Here, Jesus is interpreted as the Word or Logos of God, the ordering principle behind the universe. He is interpreted as having existed for all eternity, and moreover, as having been God himself. The gospel of John is a mystical text that laid the foundation for the teachings of the later **Council of Nicaea** in 325 C.E., where Trinitarian theology was formally put forth.

Following the death of Jesus, his disciples disagreed on how to proceed. The disciples were Jews, who continued to worship in the synagogue. In other words, they did not perceive Christianity to be anything other than a sect of Judaism. They also disagreed whether converts to Christianity had to become Jews first—did they have to be circumcised? Did they have to follow kosher laws of diet? The apostle **Peter** believed Christianity should be for Jews only, while a later convert to Christianity, **Paul**, believed it should be for all. Ultimately, it was the apostle Paul who won, and whose missions throughout Greece and Asia Minor began to attract converts to Christianity.

Nevertheless, Christianity was not legal in the Roman Empire until 313 C.E. Christians were persecuted and often executed. The first persecution of Christians occurred during the reign of Nero. Early Christians met in private homes often owned by women. Phoebe, for example, was one of the most important followers of Paul. They also gathered in the catacombs around Rome. Until the time of **Constantine the Great**, however, they could not openly practice their faith.

The Emperor Diocletian's Persecution of the Christians

Nero's persecution of Christians was one of many, which culminated in the persecution under the emperor **Diocletian** in 303 C.E. As political corruption, problems on the frontiers, and economic instability became progressively more severe for the Romans in the third and fourth centuries C.E., Christians were often blamed for the empire's difficulties. Although Romans practiced many religions, Christianity departed from the common beliefs held by Romans, particularly because Christians placed their God above the Roman Empire and its emperor, and refused to sacrifice in the cult of the emperor. In 303 C.E., the economic instability of Rome and problems on the frontiers led the Emperor Diocletian to hold a traditional sacrificial ritual to determine the cause of Rome's difficulties. According to custom, a pure lamb or other animal was sacrificed, and then the markings on its liver were interpreted as signs of things to come. On this particular occasion, a Christian was present. When the lamb was sacrificed and opened, no markings were apparent. Those present were horrified, and blamed the presence of the Christian. To calm the disturbance, Diocletian ordered that Christians hand over their sacred scriptures and sacrifice in the cult of the emperor. So began the persecution of 303 C.E. It would culminate in one of the most important debates in the early Church during the reign of Constantine: the **Donatist heresy**.

Diocletian Divides the Empire

Beset by trouble on the frontiers and a collapsing economy, Diocletian had previously frozen wages and prices and also divided the empire in 284 C.E. into an eastern half, with its capital at Byzantium on the Bosphorus strait, and a western half with its capital in Rome in order to better administer it. Each half had an emperor and also a Caesar beneath him. Diocletian was the emperor of the east, while **Maximian** served as emperor of the west. It was planned that the emperors would resign in 305 C.E. and hand over power to their Caesars in an orderly way, thereby avoiding the decades of civil war Rome had endured.

Civil War Following Diocletian's Abdication

As planned, Diocletian stepped down in 305 C.E. and was succeeded by **Galerius**; his cohort in the west, Maximian, however, was not similarly inclined, and although he eventually stepped down, he later decided to return to power, waging a civil war before his Caesar, **Constantius**, was proclaimed Augustus. Constantius, the Caesar in the west, eventually was made Augustus and asked that his son, Flavius Valerius Constantinus, later known as **Constantine**, be appointed Caesar under him. When Galerius refused the request on the basis of Constantine's youth, Constantius asked that Constantine at least be allowed to return from the court of Diocletian. Constantine's mother was Helena, a commoner who was apparently a Christian. Evidence suggests that Constantius and Helena were not legally married, but that Helena was a concubine. In any case, when Constantius became Caesar, he put Helena aside and married Theodora, the daughter of Maximian.

Constantine joined his father in Britain, where he fought in the campaign against the Picts. When Constantius died on July 25, 306 C.E., at Eboracum, now known as York, the troops proclaimed Constantine Augustus. One can still visit the location beneath the York Minster where Constantine was proclaimed Caesar. Constantine appealed to Galerius to recognize him as Augustus, but Galerius refused, accepting him only as Caesar and appointing Severus Augustus of the west. Constantine returned to the continent and married Fausta, the daughter of Maximian.

The Battle of Milvian Bridge

However, in that same year, the senate and Praetorian Guard rebelled from the rule of Severus and proclaimed **Maxentius**, the ambitious son of Maximian, Caesar in Rome. In 308 Maxentius claimed to be sole Augustus or emperor, and his supporters eventually executed Severus. The situation was further complicated when Galerius appointed **Licinius** to succeed Severus as Augustus in the west. When Galerius, the Augustus of the east, died in 311 C.E. followed by Maximian's death in 312 C.E., hostilities between the three main contenders, Maxentius, Licinius, and Constantine, erupted into open conflict. Constantine eventually met his enemy Maxentius at the **Battle of Milvian Bridge** in 312 C.E. Accounts differ of what happened prior to the battle. Lactantius later said that during the night before the Battle of the Milvian Bridge Constantine had a dream in which he was commanded to place the sign of Christ on the shields of his soldiers. Lactantius was tutor to Constantine's son and must have been close to Constantine. Twenty-five years later, **Eusebius**, Bishop of Caesarea in the fourth century C.E., wrote an Ecclesiastical History of the Christian Church and the life of Constantine in which he tells us that sometime before the battle Constantine had a vision in the sky in broad daylight of a cross of light and the words "by this sign you shall conquer/in hoc signo vinces." Eusebius also claims that during the next night, Christ appeared to Constantine and told him to place the heavenly sign on the battle standards of his army, which he did. At Milvian Bridge with the sign on their shields, Constantine's army emerged victorious.

Many scholars debate the authenticity of both accounts of Constantine's conversion, since Lactantius's account was not reported until near the end of Constantine's life.

The Edict of Milan

Further, scholars debate the nature of Constantine's conversion. On the one hand, in 313 C.E., shortly after the victory at Milvian Bridge, he and Licinius issued the **Edict of Milan**. The Edict granted legal toleration for the first time to Christians. Some scholars suggest that this edict might have been promulgated to protect his mother Helena, who was Christian. Moreover, the Edict also granted tax-exempt status to the emerging Christian Church, and returned to it all property confiscated in previous persecutions.

On the other hand, Constantine was a devotee of the sun cult, a common cult in Rome, during his youth. The coins he continued to issue still bore the pagan symbol of sol invinctus, the personification of the sun. Why would a Christian emperor mint pagan coins? Practically speaking, it would have been foolish to attempt to change so radically the practices of the Romans.

Constantine also continued to serve as pontifex maximus and to preside over pagan rituals of the empire. These facts, though having a practical explanation, raise issues about the legitimacy of Constantine's reported conversion. In addition, Constantine was not baptized until he was on his deathbed. Although this was common in the early Christian period, it still raises doubts in modern minds about the authenticity of the conversion.

St. Helena

Some of the most important events in early Christianity occurred during Constantine's reign. His mother, Helena, made pilgrimages to the Holy Land and is credited with discovering the location of Golgotha and the fragments of the true cross. She is also credited with founding several churches on holy sites, including a church near the grotto of the nativity in Bethlehem and one on the Mount of the Ascension. Whether Helena became a Christian because of her son's influence or was one before he converted is open to debate. Helena was commemorated in several special coins issued during the reign of Constantine. She made her pilgrimages, however, with the intent of doing penance for some of her son's deeds, which involved killing members of his own family, including his wife Fausta.

The Emperor Constantine: First Christian Emperor of Rome

Constantine continued to battle his enemies for several years following Milvian Bridge. There is no doubt that Constantine viewed Christianity as the key to solidifying his power in the empire. In many letters and other documents, he asserts that the unity of the Church was crucial to maintaining the unity of his empire. For this reason, he was very concerned to stamp out heresy and maintain a united belief system.

The Donatist Heresy

Diocletian's persecution had created issues of great importance for the Christian community. Many Christians had given up their Scriptures as commanded in order to spare their lives; they were known as **traditores**, from the Latin word "to hand over". The English word "tradition" is also derived from the same root word. Others had sacrificed in the cult of the emperor, and were known as **lapsi**, from the Latin word "to fall away." The English word "lapse" comes from the same root word. After the legalization of Christianity, the traditores and the lapsi wanted to reenter the Church, but some also wanted to serve as priests and bishops. Herein lay the problem. How could those who had forsaken their religious beliefs now administer the sacraments to others? If they did, would those sacraments be valid?

A strong faction argued for purity in the priesthood and was led by Donatus. The **Donatists** grew so strong that a competing church arose in North Africa, alarming Constantine. The Donatists argued that lapsi and traditores could not be confirmed as priests or bishops, as the sacraments would not be valid if performed by priests who were traditores or lapsi. When the Donatists refused to accept the consecration of Caecilian as bishop of Carthage, alleging that he was consecrated by one of the traditores, the crisis came to a climax. Constantine summoned a council to Arles in the west. In 314 C.E., the council decided that there was no evidence against Caecilian nor was there evidence of the invalidity of his consecration, and Caecilian was allowed to return to his position. The decision amounted to supporting the view that the validity of the sacraments did not depend upon those administering them. Further, the great theologian **Augustine of Hippo** would later write at great length against the Donatists, and firmly establish the theology of the priesthood when he wrote that it was grace and not human intervention that made the sacraments holy.

The Arian Heresy

Another important heresy of Constantine's reign was the **Arian heresy**. Arius was a priest in Alexandria whose exploration of the Trinity led him to conclude that Christ was not fully divine, which seemed to shake the foundation of Christian views on the redemptive power of the cross. As the followers of Arius grew in numbers, Constantine once again became concerned. He summoned the first ecumenical **Council to Nicaea**, this time in the east. It was the first council to include bishops from both the east and the west. The word "ecumenical" means "a coming together." Constantine presided at the council, while the theologian Athanasius wrote the creed that eventually emerged from the meeting. Today it is called the **Nicene Creed**, and it was later modified at Constantinople in the late third century C.E. Christians throughout the world recite it, as it summarizes the essential beliefs of Christians. Christianity, unlike Judaism and other traditions, is defined by what one believes rather than what one practices.

Constantine's role at Nicaea would seem foreign to many today. Constantine's actions represent a form of government called Caesaropapism, according to which the head of state is also the head of the Church. Throughout the Middle Ages, the Church and state would have to struggle to resolve the tensions created by Constantine's reign.

Impact of Constantine

Although scholars debate the nature of Constantine's conversion, there is no doubt that his legislation to legalize and to protect the Christian Church during his reign forever changed the course of Roman history and western civilization. His son and immediate successor Constantine II was pagan, but his son Constantius was devoted to propagating the Christian religion. Constantius was an Arian Christian, however, and the Arian heresy continued to thrive in the Roman Empire. Most of the Germanic peoples who would infiltrate the empire in the fifth century, such as the Visigoths, were Arian Christians. By the end of the fourth century, however, Orthodox Christianity triumphed within the Roman Empire. The Theodosian Code declared that all Romans must be Christians and that heresy was a crime against the state. Most Romans were still not Christians in the time of Theodosius, and the Code represents a radical transformation of Roman religious beliefs.

Despite the Theodosian Code, it took centuries for Christianity to spread throughout the Roman Empire.

THE DECLINE AND FALL
OF THE ROMAN EMPIRE IN THE WEST

Rome had suffered for centuries from civil war, corruption in politics, economic and other difficulties. By the time the Germanic peoples began to infiltrate the frontiers of Rome in the fourth and fifth centuries, Rome was teetering on the brink of collapse. At first, their arrival was in small groups who came across the frontiers and blended with the Romans. In fact, when the **Visigoths** entered the empire to escape the westward movement of the Huns and revolted against the Romans at the Battle of Adrianople in 378 C.E., the Roman army was itself largely made up of barbarians, a word the Romans used to refer to the Germanic peoples as other than Roman in custom.

The **Battle of Adrianople** sent shock waves throughout the civilized world. The Romans had spread their civilization through the West and maintained order for almost 1,000 years. Suddenly the word's mightiest army had fallen to the barbarian hordes. In 410 C.E. the Visigoths sacked Rome and eventually established a Germanic kingdom in Spain. The onslaught continued as the Vandals made their way into the frontiers and eventually down to North Africa in 429 C.E. North Africa was a hub of trade on the Mediterranean and an important producer of grain in the empire. The Vandal conquest further shook the empire. In 455 C.E. the Vandals crossed the Mediterranean and sacked Rome. Other Germanic tribes, such as the **Franks**, also established their own kingdoms in what once was Roman Gaul.

The old Roman Empire in the west had disintegrated. In many ways, however, Roman civilization did not disappear. Many Germanic Kings, such as **Charlemagne**, would rule with the approval of the eastern emperors in Byzantium and call themselves emperors of Rome in the West. The organization of the Roman Empire was preserved through the structure of the Roman Catholic Church, and Roman law formed the basis for the Church's corpus of canon law. Latin, the language of Rome, influenced the development of the vernacular languages of Western Europe, or the languages spoken by the masses, such as Italian and Spanish.

Nevertheless, while the Byzantine emperor Justinian recaptured parts of what was lost in the sixth century C.E. and the emperor Charlemagne of the Franks later attempted to reform the old boundaries of Rome in the west, the Roman empire in the west was lost and, after Justinian, never again would the east and the west be under one banner. Eventually, the western Christians would turn against their counterparts in the fourth crusade and capture Constantinople. Never again were eastern and western Roman united; never again was Constantine's dream of a united Christendom fully realized.

Review Questions

1. The historian who argued that the Roman Empire fell in the west because it converted to Christianity was

   (A) Augustine of Hippo.

   (B) Tacitus.

   (C) Livy.

   (D) Edward Gibbon.

2. The Edict of Milan

   (A) made Christianity the official religion of the Roman Empire.

   (B) gave the Pope absolute authority over all religious matters.

   (C) launched a new wave of horrible persecutions against Christians.

   (D) legalized Christianity in the Roman Empire.

3. The barbarian tribe that set up a kingdom in northern Africa was the

   (A) Ostrogoths.

   (B) Visigoths.

   (C) Lombards.

   (D) Vandals.

4. The Visigoths first defeated the Roman army at the battle of

   (A) Adrianople.

   (B) White Plains.

   (C) Poitiers.

   (D) Hastings.

5. Christianity was made the official religion of the Roman Empire by

   (A) Constantine.

   (B) Diocletian.

   (C) The Edict of Milan.

   (D) The Theodosian Code.

6. The government founded by Diocletian's division of the empire was called the

    (A) Triumvirate.

    (B) Tetrarchy.

    (C) Rule of many.

    (D) Dual kingship.

7. Constantine changed the course of Roman history by

    (A) adopting Christianity and moving the imperial capital back to Rome.

    (B) outlawing Christianity and moving the imperial capital to Constantinople.

    (C) reuniting the divided empire and defeating the Huns.

    (D) adopting Christianity and moving the imperial capital to Constantinople.

8. According to Rostovtzeff, Rome fell because

    (A) its economy collapsed.

    (B) new peoples entered the frontiers.

    (C) of a combination of factors, none of which alone explain the collapse.

    (D) Rome failed to attract mass participation in politics.

9. According to the Pirenne thesis, the collapse of Roman society

    (A) happened when city life decayed following the conversion of the Empire to Christianity.

    (B) happened when city life decayed following the arrival of Islamic armies, which cut off the Roman world from the Mediterranean.

    (C) happened when city life decayed following the barbarian invasions of the fifth century C.E.

    (D) happened when city life revived following the arrival of the Muslims.

Answers		
1. (D)	4. (A)	7. (D)
2. (D)	5. (D)	8. (C)
3. (D)	6. (B)	9. (B)

UNIT III

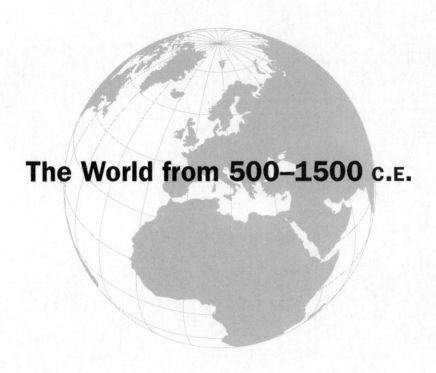

The World from 500–1500 C.E.

Chapter 10

THE RISE OF ISLAM: FROM MUHAMMAD THROUGH THE ABBASID CALIPHATE

KEY TERMS

Muhammad	Land of War (*Dar al-Harb*)
Islam	Umma
Muslim	Fatimid caliphate
Ka'ba	Baghdad
Abraham	Damascus
Ishmael	Tamerlane
hajj	Córdoba
Hegira	Quraishi clan
Five Pillars of Islam	Shari'a
Qur'an	Diwan
Conquest of Mecca	Charles Martel
Medina	Battle of Tours (Poitiers)
Caliphates	Battle of Manzikert
Abbasids	Ibn Rushd
Ummayads	Ibn Sinna
Spanish Umayyads	Mahmud Ghazni
Seljuk Turks	Sultanate of Delhi
Battle of Yarmuk	Shrivijaya Empire
Abode of Submission	Jihad
(*Dar al-Islam*)	

MUHAMMAD AND THE QUR'AN

Muhammad (570–632 C.E.)was born in **Mecca** in 570 C.E. Many legends surround his birth; it is said that a ray of light came out of his mother's breast that was seen for miles away heralding his birth. Muhammad was also said not to have cast a shadow during his lifetime; nevertheless, Islam regards Muhammad as a prophet, and not as a divine figure.

Muhammad was orphaned at the age of six. He was born into a society that was heavily materialistic and polytheistic. He traveled with his uncle in the caravan trade. When he was twenty-five he married an older widow, Khadijah, who involved him more deeply in the caravan trade through Mecca. Mecca was the center of the trade, and it was quite lucrative. There was an annual bazaar and pilgrimage to pay tribute to the gods held in Mecca, which later became the basis of the **hajj** (or pilgrimage). Muhammad became increasingly dissatisfied with the polytheistic, materialistic life of Mecca.

At the age of forty, he went up into the mountains around Mecca into a cave on Mt. Hira. There he stayed in prayer, solitude, and meditation for six weeks. During that time, he was visited by the archangel Gabriel, who conveyed to him in the form of a recitation, revelations from Allah (the Arabic word for "lord"). These recitations, which the angel commanded Muhammad to recite to others, became the **Qur'an**, an Arabic word that literally means "recitation."

The Qur'an contains the fundamental beliefs of Islam, expressed in the Five Pillars. According to tradition, Muhammad did not read or write and dictated the recitation to aides. It is one of the great works of medieval literature, and its style is on a much higher level than comparable poetry found in the West from a similar period. It is written in the Foosha, the official dialect of Arabic shared by all Muslims. Dialects can vary so much from one region of the Arabic world to another that they are barely intelligible to those of different regions, and the Foosha enabled all Arabic-speaking peoples to communicate. Arabic does not contain vowels, and when people read Arabic, they have to know which vowel sounds to insert. For example, the letters "bg" could be read as "big" or "bog" or "bag" in English and one must know from the context which word is being used. The Foosha specifies the vowel sounds so as to leave no doubt as to the proper word. Arabic calligraphy became a highly prized art form, as the language was the language of the Holy Qur'an and the Qur'an forbids the use of images.

The Qur'an contains the Five Pillars, the foundation of Islam.

The first pillar of Islam teaches that there is no God but Allah, and Muhammad is his messenger. This pillar emphasizes the belief in only one God. Muslims are thoroughly monotheistic; to put anything at all on the level of Allah is to worship that thing and to commit the gravest possible sin—shirk.

The Qur'an, like the Hebrew Scriptures, forbids the making of idols and images, as they might be potential objects of worship.

The first pillar also emphasizes the humanity of Muhammad, who is not regarded as a divine being, but as a good human who conveyed the word of Allah. According to Islamic tradition, the revelations to Muhammad were the last time that Allah communicated with humans and the fullest expression of divine revelation. Muslims believe that all the holy prophets in the Hebrew and Christian scriptures imparted some measure of Truth; it was Muhammad, however, who received the most complete version.

The second pillar commands prayer five times per day facing Mecca, the place of Muhammad's birth. Mecca is a significant place in the Islamic tradition for many reasons. Muslims believe in the truth of the Hebrew Scriptures, and Arabs are, in fact, descendants of the Hebrew patriarch Abraham. Abraham's first-born son was Ishmael, whom Abraham's wife Sarah expelled along with his mother Hagar, Abraham's concubine. According to Islamic tradition, when Ishmael was expelled, he and his mother journeyed to what is now Mecca. There he struck the ground in anger and a spring arose.

Muhammad expected Jews to follow his teachings, not only because of the common lineage from Abraham, but also because much of the Qur'an is based on the Hebrew Scriptures. Consequently, Muslims originally prayed toward Jerusalem. When Jews did not embrace his teachings, Muslims separated themselves from the Jewish community, and began to pray toward Mecca.

There are no images in a mosque, as the Qur'an, like the Hebrew Scriptures, forbids the making of idols and the worship of anything but Allah. These beliefs are expressed in the first pillar of Islam. A mosque usually has a square base and a round dome. The square base symbolizes earth, as it has four corners and there are four cardinal directions. The dome, being round, symbolizes heaven. A circle has no beginning or end, and so, too, the afterlife is without a beginning or an end. One enters a mosque without shoes on to symbolize the holiness of the place.

The Islamic prayer ritual symbolizes submission to Allah. The prayer ritual begins with a washing of the hands, feet, and face three times each to symbolize one's cleanliness and ability to come before Allah. Mosques have fountains in front where Muslims wash themselves before prayer. At the beginning of the ritual, Muslims put their hands on either side of their head to symbolize that they are in the hands of Allah during prayer and also in life.

The third pillar of Islam commands almsgiving to other Muslims.

The fourth pillar commands fasting for one month a year. This is the month of Ramadan, in which Muslims neither eat nor drink from sunup until sundown. Ramadan commemorates Muhammad's sojourn on Mt. Hira.

The fifth pillar commands every Muslim to make the hajj or pilgrimage to Mecca at least once in a lifetime. Mecca is the holiest place for Muslims. It is

Islamic Mosque

the site of the Ka'ba, Muhammad's birth, and also the place he conquered in the name of Allah in 630 C.E. Mecca is the heart of the religion of submission.

The "Sixth Pillar": The Jihad

Teachings on the **jihad** have often been referred to as the "sixth pillar" of Islam. The word "jihad" has often been erroneously translated as "holy war." A better translation of the word is to "fight" or "strive" in the path of Allah. In the Qur'an, Muhammad taught believers to "command the right and forbid the wrong" (3:104, 110), and also permitted the jihad when believers were expelled from their homes, not allowed to practice their religion, or in other contexts where self-defense was necessary (22:39). Although the Qur'an also contains more militant verses suggesting that wars of conquest for conversion were a permissable form of jihad (9:5, 29), Muhammad also taught that there was a proper way to fight the jihad. Muslims were not to harm civilians who were not frontline combatants, nor were they to destroy property, such as houses, or the environment. In some of the Hadith, Muhammad also differentiated between the **greater jihad**, the fight of good against evil within the heart, and the **lesser jihad**, the outward fight using words to convert or, in extreme cases, the sword to protect oneself. Sufi mystics typically emphasized the greater jihad, while Muslim legal scholars in the years following the death of Muhammad tended to emphasize the lesser jihad. From the eighth through the eleventh centuries, legal scholars insisted that the duty of all Muslims was to foster the spread of

Islam until the Dar al-Harb or "land of war" was brought within the Dar al-Islam or "land of Islam." This could be done through peaceful conversion or through war, depending on the circumstances. Only those struggles authorized by Islamic leaders were considered acceptable jihads, although Muslims continue to debate what are the lawful authorities and to what extent the jihad is a personal or a communal obligation (or both).

Muslims were required to offer peace first and to provide protected status to those who submitted peacefully, even if they chose not to convert. These people were known as dhimmi within the Islamic world. As Islamic thought evolved, the jihad also encompassed the attempt to preserve an orthodox form of Islam against the development of divergent sects.

The Life and Career of Muhammad

Muhammad's uncle Abu Talib died, and Muhammad had no protection from those who opposed his teachings. The caravan trade was lucrative, and Muhammad's values and teachings conflicted with both the materialism of Meccans, as well as their polytheistic beliefs. In 622 C.E., Muhammad left Mecca and went north to Yathrib, later renamed Medina. This event is known as the Hijra, and marks the first year in the Islamic calendar. The word "Medina" means "city of the prophet," and this is where Muhammad began to collect his first band of followers. The mosque in **Medina** is the second holiest site in the Islamic world.

Muhammad and his followers made a continuous series of raids on Mecca, winning the Battle of Badr in 624 C.E. In 630 C.E. they attempted to make the annual pilgrimage to Mecca. As 3,000 of them approached Mecca, the inhabitants assumed that they were making another attack. They surrendered peacefully to Muhammad in 630 C.E.

Muhammad died in 632 C.E. According to Islamic tradition, he ascended into heaven in Jerusalem from the Dome of the Rock. Inside the shrine is the actual rock from which Muhammad is believed to have ascended into heaven. Muslims believe the rock has the footprints of the archangel Gabriel on it. Muslims believe all souls gather under the rock. This shrine is located on the ancient Hebrew Temple Mount, the most sacred site in the world for Jews and one of the most sacred for Christians. The Dome of the Rock dates from 690 C.E., and it is the third holiest site in the Islamic world after Mecca and Medina. Jews believe that the Ark of the Covenant was once on this very site, and since its exact location is unknown, it is forbidden for Jews to walk on the site. Jewish people also believe that it was on this site that Abraham prepared to sacrifice Isaac, whereas Muslims teach that it was Ishmael whom Abraham prepared to sacrifice and this event occurred at the Ka'ba, not at the Dome of the Rock. For these reasons, Jews regard the Dome of the Rock shrine as a sacrilege, and it is but one reason why there is a continuing conflict between Jews and Muslims today.

After Muhammad's death, there were many successors or caliphs that governed the umma, or ideal community of the faithful. Many caliphs extended the Abode of Submission (Dar al-Islam), or the regions where Islam was practiced. The religion spread west to North Africa, controlled by the Fatimid caliphate, and Spain (controlled by the Spanish Umayyads), and conquered Damascus, Jerusalem, and other cities sacred to Jews and Christians within 100 years. After Muhammad's death in 632 C.E., Abu Bakr, Muhammad's father-in-law, became caliph, or successor. Not all Muslims agreed with this choice, and many supported the claim of Muhammad's cousin and son-in-law, Ali, to be the legitimate successor. Ali would later become the fourth caliph.

Under Abu Bakr's leadership, Islam expanded rapidly. Abu Bakr united the Saudi Arabian Bedouin tribes, and led a series of razzia or raids under the banner of the jihad to expand the religion and domain of the Dar al-Islam. Abu Bakr's Muslims defeated the Byzantines at Yarmuk in 636 C.E., and in 540 C.E. conquered Syria. By 650 C.E., Muslim Arabs had conquered the Sassanid Persian Empire.

Muslim forces also conquered Egypt in North Africa, forming the Fatimid Caliphate. Today, the official language of North African countries is still Arabic.

The Umayyad Caliphate

The fourth caliph, Muhammad's son-in-law Ali, was assassinated in 661 C.E. Mu'awiyah replaced him and made the succession hereditary. His family was a branch of Muhammad's own clan, the Quraishi, and the caliphate ruled by his clan was known as the Umayyad. The Umayyad caliphate (661–750 C.E.) ruled from Damascus. The caliph was responsible for the interpretation of Islamic law, but more often it was a group of legal scholars, known as the ulama, who interpreted the law, which was based on the Qur'an. The body of law that developed was known as the shari'a. The diwan collected taxes and paid soldiers's salaries. Heavily fortified garrison cities were used as outposts for soldiers, and kept the Arab conquerors ethnically and religiously distinct from those they conquered. Arabs were regarded as first-class citizens, while others were of lesser status. Arabs ran the government, and were taxed only in that they paid the required percentage of their income to charity, as commanded in the Qur'an. Conversely, conquered peoples paid a poll tax.

The Umayyads conquered the Berber tribes in the region of North Africa west of Egypt, and in 725 C.E. conquered the Iberian Peninsula. In 750 C.E., one of the Umayyad princes escaped to Spain and established the Spanish Umayyad caliphate. The Spanish Umayyads channeled the game of chess into Europe, as well as Arabic commentaries on Aristotle, whose works had largely been lost in Western Europe.

THE EXPANSION HALTS

Some historians argue that it was Islam rather than the barbarian Germanic tribes that ended Roman civilization in Western Europe. Henri Pirenne, in *Muhammad and Charlemagne*, argues that it was the expansion of Islam that disrupted trade across the Mediterranean and cut off the coastal areas from the heart of Europe, thus bringing an end to Roman civilization in the Western world. In 732 C.E., **Charles Martel** and the Franks defeated the Muslims at Tours. This battle is often also called the **Battle of Tours** or **Poitiers**, because the actual skirmish happened between these two locations in southern France.

The Byzantines also defeated the Muslim forces in 717 C.E. at Constantinople. Muslim forces would not succeed in conquering the city until 1453 C.E.

Shi'ites and Sunnis

During the early period after Muhammad's death, a split arose in the Umma between the **Shi'ites**, or "partisans of Ali," and the **Sunnis**, or "followers of tradition." The Shi'ites believed that the succession to Muhammad should be by bloodline, and Ali was the son-in-law and cousin of the prophet. They believed that Muhammad had given Ali some revelations that he did not write down, and so they insist that only the bloodline succession can preserve the fullness of the revelations. Further, they accept the existence of an oral tradition, which Sunnis do not. They also believe in the coming of the **Mahdi**, or chosen one, who was an imam or prayer leader who disappeared in the ninth century. Shi'ites believe that he will return to guide the faithful through judgment day. Shi'ites insist that only those faithful who accept these teachings in addition to the Qur'an are Muslims, while Sunnis teach that anyone who submits to the Five Pillars is a Muslim.

The split between the supporters of Ali and those of the other successors, already evident in the first years after the death of the prophet, grew more intense during the Ummayad period when Ali's son, Hussein, launched a revolt against the caliph. Hussein, like his father Ali, was assassinated, but the Shi'ite faction of Muslims continues to flourish today in such modern countries as southern Iraq and in Iran. In 973 C.E., Shi'ite Muslims established a caliphate in Egypt known as the Fatimids.

The Abbasid Caliphate

Abu Abbas, a descendant of an uncle of Muhammad, led a revolt against the Umayyads and established the Abbasid caliphate. Its capital was Baghdad, which was first built in 762 C.E. Baghdad served as the capital of the Abbasid caliphate until 1258 C.E. and is today located in Iraq. During this period, the caliphs were known as "caliphs of God," and they adopted many Persian ideals of leadership. The most important Abbasid caliph was Harun al-Rashid, or Harun the Upright (786–809 C.E.). The Abbasids were Sunni Muslims.

The Abbasid caliphs turned to **viziers** to administer their wishes. The caliphs progressively withdrew from leading prayers and other public functions, and left practical administration to the viziers. The position of vizier was borrowed from the Persians.

During the Abbasid caliphate, **Baghdad** was an important cultural center. The philosopher **Ibn Rushd (Averoës)** wrote many commentaries on Aristotle, which were eventually transmitted to Western Europe. Averoës believed in the principle of two-fold truth. He argued that philosophy and religion were different kinds of knowledge, each with its own sphere of truth. Religion was for the unlettered masses, and teaches through signs and symbols. Philosophy, however, represents truth directly. Teachings in the two areas could conflict with one another, and in that case, philosophy should supersede religion. Ibn Rushd's commentaries on Aristotle created a controversy in the Catholic Church, as many of Aristotle's philosophical arguments conflicted with orthodox Christian teaching. In contrast to Ibn Rushd's theory of double truth, the scholastic theologians of medieval Europe, such as Aquinas, sought to harmonize the teachings of religion and philosophy. Ibn Rushd was born in Córdoba in southern Spain, a region known as Andalusia that was controlled by Muslims. While under Muslim control, culture flourished, and monuments such as the Alhambra in Granada and the mosque in Córdoba were among the greatest architectural masterpieces in Europe. Christians recaptured Córdoba in the thirteenth century, and in the fifteenth century, the rulers Ferdinand and Isabella of Aragon and Castille later destroyed the remnants of Muslim culture in their zeal to entrench Roman Catholicism within their domains.

Ibn Sinna, or **Avicenna**, was another important Muslim scholar who was born and worked in Persia. He wrote a medical textbook that was used in medieval universities. Literature also flourished, as seen in the words of **Omar Khayyam**. Although his *1001 Arabian Nights* and *Rubaiyat* have enjoyed limited popularity in the Middle East, they have become classics in the West. In *1001 Arabian Nights*, Scheherazade tells a story a night in order to avoid death. Her tales of "Ali Baba and the Forty Thieves" and "Aladdin and the Magic Lamp" have become favorite tales and have been translated into many languages.

The Fall of the Abbasids

In 1055 C.E. the **Seljuk Turks**, who converted to Islam, conquered Baghdad. They allowed the Abbasids to continue to control religion, but took control over state affairs. The Seljuks were Sunni Muslims who were very intolerant of Shi'ites.

It was the **Mongols**, however, who finally ended the Abbasid rule at Baghdad. **Ghengis Khan** conquered the first Islamic kingdom for Mongols, the Khwarazm Empire. His grandson, Hulego, continued a policy of Mongol expansionism and captured Baghdad in 1258 c.e. The last Abbasid caliph was executed. The Mongols tolerated many religions and made great use of Islamic advisors. In fact, many Mongol rulers converted to Islam, and in the Il-Khanate, Islamic legal structures, religion, and the Arabic language triumphed over Mongol customs. The Mongols were themselves defeated in 1260 c.e. by the Mamluks of Egypt.

In the fourteenth century, **Tamerlane's** hordes sacked Baghdad. Tamerlane founded his empire on the ruins of the Mongol empire begun by Genghis Kahn. He took power in 1369 c.e. in Samarkand, which became the capital of his empire. Alexander the Great had once occupied the great city, and it had also been a Mongol outpost. Tamerlane conquered the region east of the Caspian Sea, Mesopotamia, and Baghdad. Following further conquests in India, he turned to Anatolia, and led his armies to the Bosphorus strait before his death in 1405 c.e. Tamerlane was apparently an intelligent and cultured man, but also a brutal conqueror who massacred thousands of people during his brief reign of terror. Tamerlane was a Turkish Muslim, whose rule did not bring with it benefits, either in trade or in renewed cultural exchanges.

Seljuk Turks Threaten Byzantium

In 1071 the Seljuks defeated the Byzantines at the **Battle of Manzikert**. By 1095, the Byzantine emperor Alexius was alarmed at the threat posed by the Muslim Turks, and called upon the Roman Catholic pope in the West for assistance in delivering his Christian lands from "the infidel." Alexius's call began the **First Crusade**; he could not have known that the Christian knights would come in their own interests and threaten his control over Byzantium. Many scholars attribute the success of the western knights in the First Crusade to the constant quarrels between various Muslim factions. Under **Salah-uh-Din** or **Saladin**, however, Muslims defeated the Europeans and, following his death, by 1291 had defeated the last crusader kingdom at Acre. Europeans borrowed much from Muslims, including their medical knowledge.

The Crusades had a negative impact on Byzantium, and in 1204 during the **Fourth Crusade**, western knights actually sacked the city of Constantinople on the pretense of helping the "legitimate ruler," who was an importer, regain his rightful throne. Though the Byzantines later recovered from this event, in 1453 c.e., Byzantium was dealt a fatal blow when the Ottoman Turks conquered Constantinople, sending a wave of Greek-speaking refugees to Italy, where they helped to fuel the Italian Renaissance.

ISLAMIC EXPANSION AND WORLD TRADE PATTERNS

The Islamic world was master of vast trading networks that helped to increase its wealth and aid its spread to other regions. Muslim domination of trade in the Mediterranean area resulted in the final collapse of the last vestiges of the Roman economy and civilization. Muslims traded with southern Europe, transporting goods across the Mediterranean.

More important than the Mediterranean, though, were routes that began in Cairo and connected the Islamic world with other parts of the world. During the Abbasid caliphate, Muslim traders succeeded in restoring trade routes that declined following the fall of the Roman Empire in the West in the fifth century C.E. and the collapse of the Han Dynasty in China in the third century C.E. The creation of the Abbasid caliphate and the T'ang and Song dynasties of China provided the stability needed to revive the long dormant trade routes that once connected Europe, Africa, and Asia. As trade increased, demand for handicrafts also increased, fueling the growth of urban areas. Egypt became a center for trade in the Islamic world following the collapse of the Abbasid caliphate, as Cairo replaced Baghdad as a center of trade. Merchants traveled from Cairo south to Aswan along the Nile River, where they then formed caravans to transport their goods by camel to the Red Sea. From here, ships carried the goods down to Aden in southern Saudi Arabia and then via ocean routes east to India. Muslim creativity in technology helped to increase trade. Muslims built larger ships than their European counterparts using teak obtained in India.

In fact, the desire to protect trading interests was the pretext for the initial conquest of parts of India during the Umayyad caliphate.

Islam Arrives in South Asia

When pirates from India attacked Arab ships, threatening trade, Muhammad ibn Qasim conquered the Sind in the eighth century C.E. From this point, Muslims increasingly dominated the coastal trade in India, leading to new contacts. The region of the Indus River Valley remained part of the Islamic world for many centuries, but Islam would not spread beyond this region until the invasion of **Mahmud Ghazni**.

The Empire of Mahmud Ghazni and the Sultanate of Delhi

In 962 C.E. Turkish-speaking slaves took power from the Sasanid Persians. In 997 C.E., the founder's son, Mahmud Ghazni, took power and began a series of raids in Indian lands. By the time he died in 1030, he had conquered the upper Indus Valley and areas as far south as the Indian Ocean. By 1200, successors to the Ghazni controlled northern India and had established the Delhi sultanate. Later their power extended over central India as well.

Again, merchants were very instrumental in bringing about conversions to Islam, in both the coastal and inland areas of India and from large cities, such as Bengal in the east, and the Indus River Valley, both of which were important points of entry for many Muslims who came to India. **Sufi mystics** also played an important role in carrying the message of Islam, especially in a time when Buddhism had largely declined. Hindus of lower castes were also attracted to the Sufi mystics, in part because they had an affinity with the ascetic values of Hinduism, but also because Islam brought with it an egalitarian message. Nevertheless, the new Muslim rulers remained largely separated from their Hindu subjects. Hindus worked in administrative and other capacities, but they lived apart from their rulers. Moreover, something of the social prejudice inherent in the caste system infiltrated Islam in India, as Arabs were considered "high caste," followed by Muslims of other ethnicities, followed by Hindu converts, and finally by the lower castes. Muslim rulers also borrowed some of the Hindu mythology associated with rulers, and violated the Qur'an when they proclaimed themselves to be of divine descent. Despite the interchanges between Islam and Indian culture, Islam never successfully infiltrated indigenous Hindu culture to form a cohesive Islamic culture in India nor did it succeed in attracting large numbers of converts. Although the conquests of the Mongols and of Tamerlane in the thirteenth and fourteenth centuries brought a new flood of Muslims seeking safety in India, Islam nevertheless remained less entrenched in the general population here than in other places to which it spread.

Islam Arrives in Southeast Asia Through Trading Ports

As early as the seventh century C.E., Muslim merchants had become active in Southeast Asia. Islam spread to Southeast Asia primarily through port cities, such as Malacca and Denmark (Java), and early converts were those engaged in trade with Muslims. Southeast Asia had important trading links with China and India, and through India, to the Mediterranean world, fueling the further spread of Islam. However, Islam spread slowly at first in Southeast Asia due to the presence of the Shrivijaya empire, which controlled trade in the area and was also strongly Buddhist.

Trade during the 13th–14th centuries: Southeast Asia and Islam

Important changes occurred in the thirteenth and fourteenth centuries that affected trade and the spread of Islam. Islam did not fully take root in Southeast

Asia until the thirteenth century, when the Buddhist empire of **Shrivijaya** collapsed. Shrivijaya dominated the trade that passed through the Strait of Malacca. In 1025, the Dravidian kingdom of Cola defeated it, and Shrivijaya gradually lost its hold over trade in the region. Until the arrival of Chinese merchants and the final collapse of its trading empire in the thirteenth century, the Shrivijaya controlled the Strait of Malacca, located between northern Sumatra and Malaya. Islam, in fact, never made many inroads among the population of Southeast Asia not exposed to the coast. In Java, for instance, there were few converts from the inland areas. Similarly, in other areas that were strongly Buddhist or Hindu, such as Bali, Islam found little success.

The Impact of Arab Conquests in Africa on Trading Patterns

Arab armies first swept across North Africa in the seventh century C.E. Islam spread to West Africa via the trans-Saharan trade, first developed by Berbers around 700–900 C.E. The trans-Saharan trade brought tons of gold to the European markets and also into Egypt, where eventually it was shipped to India in return for spices and silks. The trans-Saharan trade also helped to develop large cities in West Africa, such as Timbuktu.

The thriving gold trade also increased the **slave trade** across the Sahara, due to the need for slaves to work the mines. Further, Muslims took slaves for their armies and also as servants for Muslim households in the north. Many of the African slaves were captured in war. Simultaneously, many African monarchs also bought white slaves.

Slavery was a feature of life in many parts of the Islamic world outside of Africa. As Islam expanded rapidly, it acquired an increasing supply of slaves. Slavery in the Islamic world was not tied to any particular sort of economy, such as a plantation economy. Slaves served many functions in the business world, in the home, and in the armies of the Muslims. Slaves were not of a specific ethnicity or race, and in that respect, slavery in the Islamic world differed from slavery in the American South, for example, before the Civil War. The Qur'an commanded Muslims to treat their slaves fairly, and although it encouraged masters to free their slaves, slavery continued to grow in the Islamic world in proportion to its expansion.

Similarly, Islam also spread from Egypt south along the Nile and then west into Darfur and Wadia. Islam spread along the east coast of Africa again via trade routes. From Saudi Arabi, Islam spread across the Red Sea to the Horn of Africa, and then south along the coast. Persian and Arab Muslim merchants established large port and trading cities, such as Mogadishu. Gold from the Great Zimbabwe region also flowed into the Muslim cities along the east coast and, in fact, the history of the Great Zimbabwe is tied to the rise and fall of the eastern Muslim port cities.

The eastern cities also strengthened sea routes in the fourteenth century. These cities connected southern Africa to the Indian Ocean and to Middle Eastern trade routes. Trade along land routes to China through Persian and Central Asia and to the Persian Gulf declined in this period.

These vast trading routes brought many goods and inventions to the Islamic world. From China, Muslims learned how to make paper, and many Islamic centers, such as Córdoba in Spain, held hundreds of thousands of books. Europeans, by contrast, still produced their books using vellum, and books were consequently much rarer. Muslims traded glass, copper, gold, silver, and textiles for Chinese silk, porcelain, spices, and various other herbal items.

Besides the numerous goods exchanged, Arabic traveled as a language of communication along the trade routes. While Muslims did not require those in conquered regions to convert, they did require them to speak in Arabic. The language served as a unifying factor throughout the vast expanse of territory dominated by Muslim rulers, and helped increase trade.

Review Questions

1. The term "jihad" in Islam refers to

    (A) a holy striving of word and deed against nonbelievers and against evil in the individual soul.

    (B) the practice of a man having several wives legally.

    (C) the body of laws derived form the Koran.

    (D) special religious courts to handle violations of Islamic law.

2. The faction of Muslims that follows orthodox traditions is known as the

    (A) Shi'ite.

    (B) Sunni.

    (C) Sufi.

    (D) Umayyad.

3. The Ka'ba is the rock where

    (A) Muhammad ascended into heaven.

    (B) the Archangel Gabriel revealed God's message to Muhammad.

    (C) Abraham prepared to sacrifice his son Ishmael.

    (D) Muhammad recaptured Medina.

4. The Hegira refers to

    (A) the capture of Mecca.

    (B) Muhammad's journey to Medina.

    (C) Muhammad's ascent into heaven.

    (D) Muhammad's conquest of Istanbul.

5. The hajj is

    (A) fasting.

    (B) almsgiving.

    (C) ritual walking toward the Ka'ba.

    (D) the pilgrimage to Mecca.

6. Shi'ite Muslims are

    (A) followers of tradition.

    (B) partisans of Ali.

(C) followers of Umma.

(D) followers of Gabriel.

7. The first date of the official calendar of Islam is

(A) 610.

(B) when Muhammad and his supporters went to Medina.

(C) when the Hegira occurred.

(D) Both (B) and (C).

8. Which of the following is NOT one of the pillars of Islam?

(A) Belief in Allah and Muhammad as his prophet

(B) Observation of the holy month of Ramadan with fasting from dawn to sunset

(C) Standard prayer once a day and public prayer at noon on Sundays

(D) Giving alms to the poor and unfortunate

9. Under the Abbasid caliphate, the capital of the Islamic empire was

(A) Damascus.

(B) Beirut.

(C) Alexandria.

(D) Baghdad.

10. Which of the following statements is NOT true of slavery in the Islamic world?

(A) It was based on ethnicity.

(B) The gold trade across the Sahara increased the need for slaves.

(C) Slaves fulfilled many functions in households and other positions.

(D) Slavery was not dependent on plantation economies.

Answers

1. (A)	4. (B)	7. (D)	10. (A)
2. (B)	5. (D)	8. (C)	
3. (C)	6. (B)	9. (D)	

Chapter 11

AFRICAN CIVILIZATION FROM ITS ORIGINS THROUGH THE EVE OF THE AGE OF EXPLORATION

KEY TERMS

Bantu
Iron making
Nile
Sahara desert
Kalahari
Zambezi River
Great Zimbabwe
Meröe
Napata
Transhumant lifestyle
Phoenecians
Nok

Ethiopia
Adulis
Axum
Ghana
Kumbi Saleh
Soninke people
Mali
Sundiata Mali
Mansa Musa
Timbuktu
Benin
Congo

OVERVIEW

Although the ancient Greeks had contact with Africa, and the Romans had extensively colonized the northern part of Africa, Europeans in the medieval period had little knowledge of African geography. Africa is the world's second largest continent. It covers nearly twenty percent of the earth's surface and is three times the size of Europe. Myths were widely circulated in Europe about the boiling waters near the equator and the seaweed that might swallow entire ships. European woodcuts portrayed Africans as strange creatures; sometimes they were depicted with huge feet that they used to cover themselves from the boiling sun, while others portrayed them as Cyclops with one eye.

Europeans knew Africa as "the Dark Continent," not only because of the lack of knowledge about it, but also because of the difficulty of exploring its treacherous terrain and rivers. The rivers of Africa are very difficult to navigate and contribute to the isolation of one region of Africa from another. The Nile is an excellent example of why Africa is known as "The Dark Continent." It was not until the twentieth century that the British explorer Livingston discovered the source of the Nile River in Lake Victoria. African cultures are also separated by vast deserts, such as the Sahara, located across Africa and forming an often difficult to traverse barrier between north Africa and the grasslands south of the Sahara. A much smaller desert, the Kalahari, is located on the southern tip of Africa. Cultures here were separated from those in the north by the rain forests and the Sahara desert.

The geography of Africa isolated the many cultures of the continent from one another and created one of the most diverse arrays of cultures in the world. The languages of Africa reflect its geographical diversity as well as the impact of the expansion of Islam. Arabic is the language of northern Africa. In addition to Arabic, many other languages are spoken that also reflect the history of the continent. During the Age of Exploration, beginning in the fifteenth century, the Portuguese established many outposts along the coastal areas of Africa. Portuguese is still the language of trade in many regions of Africa. In the nineteenth century, the Age of European Imperialism also influenced the development of African cultures. Modern Africans speak English and French in addition to Arabic, Portuguese, and hundreds of African Bantu languages. The Bantu are a large family of Negroid tribal peoples who inhabit Africa south of the Sahara.

THE DEVELOPMENT OF CIVILIZATION IN AFRICA

The **Olduvai Gorge** is a prominent feature on the eastern coast of sub-Saharan Africa. As noted in the chapter on prehistory, the earliest known hominid fossils come from the Olduvai Gorge.

The world's largest desert, the **Sahara**, covers 3.5 million square miles across the center of the African continent. The word "Sahara" comes from the Arabic word for "tan," the color of the sand. Some traditions suggest it comes from the sound a thirsty man makes when in need of water. There is evidence that the Sahara was not always a desert. Fossil finds indicate the presence of water in the desert 5,000 years ago; a recent controversial theory suggests that the erosion patterns on the Sphinx at Giza are those of water, making the Sphinx much older than originally thought. The ancestors of the **Bantu** people, who live south of the Sahara, and the **Berbers**, who live north of the Sahara, once inhabited this parched land. The Sahara continues to grow today, and the desertification of this region is one of the world's major ecological issues. Although the vast expanse of the desert is a formidable barrier, the Arabs and Berber traders, for example, established thriving trade routes across the Sahara. These trade routes connected markets south of the Sahara to those north of it, and the west of Africa to the east and even to markets beyond Africa, such as the Mediterranean and Indian Ocean trades.

When the Sahara dried up, the people living there were pushed south. The region south of the Sahara, known as the **Sudan**, is covered by dense rain forests on the west coast, while flat grasslands or savannah cover the central part of the continent and the east coast. Rainfall here is very heavy. African rain forests are very dense and difficult to penetrate; the insect life also presents many health hazards, even in the modern era.

CONTACTS BETWEEN AFRICA AND WEST ASIA: AGRICULTURE AND IRON MAKING

Agriculture likely arose in Africa as a result of contact with the Near East. Egypt had such contact, but so too did the region where modern Ethiopia is located. Livestock, such as cattle, goats, and sheep, also originated outside of Africa, likely from Asia. The **Hyksos**, who established a dynasty in Egypt, brought horses to Africa and their use spread west to the Sudan. The camel also arrived from Asia, sometime around the first century c.e. and made trade across the Sahara easier. Africans developed a **transhumant** lifestyle, which means they moved from place to place according to the season.

The knowledge of iron making likely also came to Africa from Asia. One scholarly theory maintains that the Phoenicians brought iron making to their colonies in North Africa by the eighth century b.c.e. As we have seen in the case of various religious traditions, trade routes play an important role in the spread of ideas and cultures. Iron making then spread along trade routes to Phoenician ports along the coast of present-day Morocco or south through the Sahara along the trade routes. It then spread along the coast or south across the Sahara during the first millennium B.C.E.

The first known makers of iron in West Africa were the **Nok** culture. The Nok culture dates from 800 B.C.E. to 200 C.E. The culture takes its name after the town of Nok where archaeologists discovered one of the first objects produced by the culture. Scholars do not know what the people who produced this art called themselves. The Nok are also known for their sophisticated sculpture in the form of unique and realistic terra-cotta heads that portray the individuality of the subject. Most artifacts are of fired clay or terra-cotta sculptures. Some are small like pendants, while others are life-sized figures. Some scholars believe there is a similarity between Nok sculptures and those of the Yoruba people, suggesting that there may be as yet unknown connections between Nok culture and Yoruba peoples in West Africa, particularly those of Benin, who produced bronze heads and other works in bronze.

Another theory suggests that iron making spread from **Meröe**, a successor state to Egypt, and then to the west, but since most of Africa had acquired this technique by around 250 B.C.E. and Meröe did not become the preeminent iron-smelting center until the first century C.E., those who support the Phoenician origin of iron making seem to have the better case. Whether or not Meröe originated iron making, one path of its later transmission was southwards along the Nile to Meröe and then eventually all the way to the south of the continent.

Africa was unusual in that most of the people known for iron making appear to have skipped the bronze stage. Although the artisans of Benin were renowned for their bronze heads, most of Africa seems to have progressed directly from the stone age to the iron age. The migrations of the **Bantu** people were crucial in the spread of iron making across the continent and to the making of African civilizations.

THE SPREAD OF IRON MAKING: THE BANTU MIGRATIONS

The Bantu, a black-skinned people, live in the area south of the Sahara and speak over 800 languages. Most of them lived in illiterate societies that preserved their heritage through strong oral traditions. The Greeks described the Bantu people along the east coast as Ethiopians, which translates as "people with burnt faces." We still use the word "Ethiopia" today for the East African nation. The Arab description of the area as the Bilad-al-Sudan, or "land of the blacks," also survives in the name of the modern West African nation of the Sudan.

The Bantu people are enormously important in the history of Africa, as they were the first to introduce the smelting of iron and use of iron tools. While the iron age may have started in Africa as early as the first millennium B.C.E., iron making did not spread across Africa until after the first century C.E. The Bantu people originated near the area where modern Nigeria is located in West Africa. Starting in the second millennium B.C.E., they moved into the rain forest zones south and to the east, and then to the Savannah regions straddling the **Congo River**. The Congo and other rivers were an important path of migration. It took another 1500 years for the Bantu to migrate throughout the Savannah region. During this period they began to adopt agriculture, and possibly the growth in their populations led to a series of other migrations. During the first 1500 years C.E., they migrated to eastern and southern Africa. Agriculture prompted the series of migrations, as successful cultivation of crops like bananas created more and larger villages and the need for more territory. The **Zambezi River** was an important path for the Bantu as they moved to the south. The Bantu migrations resulted in not only the spread of iron making but also agriculture.

The Pygmies, short brown-skinned people, inhabited central Africa, and were among the last purely hunting societies remaining after the Bantu migrations.

ANCIENT AFRICA FROM THE EGYPTIANS TO THE ARRIVAL OF ISLAM

Kush

The **Kushites** were located to the south of ancient Egypt and were the heirs of Egyptian culture. There are more pyramids standing today in Kush than in Egypt. These pyramids are not as large as those of Egypt, but archaeologists often rely on them to help unravel the mysteries of the great pyramids of Egypt. The capital of Kush was Kerma, and Egyptian influences reached Kush, centered on the third cataract of the Nile, through Nubia, a land centered on the first cataract and conquered by the Egyptians in the New Kingdom. The Egyptians conquered Kush during the New Kingdom, but when Egypt collapsed in 1000 B.C.E., Kush then declared independence and conquered Nubia. At this time they moved their capital to Napata, and assumed Egyptian royal titles. They conquered Egypt itself and became the twenty-eighth pharaonic dynasty of Egypt.

Meröe

The arrival of the Assyrians in Egypt in the seventh century B.C. eventually forced the Kushites to move south. When their capital Napata was conquered in 591 B.C.E., the Kushites moved their capital to Meröe. For several centuries, Meröe was the path through which trade went to North Africa, and on to the Middle East and Europe. The king was elected from the royal family through the maternal line, and there were several female monarchs. Meröe eventually lost its supremacy in trade to Axum in east Africa. Meröe was also the preeminent iron-smelting center by the first century B.C.E. and, as mentioned above, was one leg of the route via which iron making was carried to the rest of the continent of Africa.

Axum and Adulis

Axum is today known as Ethiopia. Its main port city of Adulis was a major center of trade in the Mediterranean and a gateway to trade with the east. Slaves, ivory and salt from Axum were shipped via Indian Ocean routes. During its history, Axum traded with Alexandria in Egypt, the Roman world, Byzantium, and India. During the period following Muhammad's career, many Muslims fled to Adulis. In the first century C.E., Axum began to replace Meröe as an important trading center, and in the third century C.E., Axum defeated Meröe.

The king of Axum, **Ezana**, converted to Christianity in 250 C.E. and eventually converted his people. Axum maintained strong ties with Byzantium, and was influential in the conversion of other east African peoples before the expansion of Islam took over the trade in the Mediterranean region. Axum adopted the Coptic or Egyptian form of Christianity, according to which Christ had only a single, divine nature, as opposed to the Orthodox view that he had both a human and a divine nature.

Islam in Africa

By the seventh century C.E., followers of Muhammad were spreading their faith and their control west across the northern shores of Africa and south along the eastern regions of the continent. Egypt, which had previously been a Byzantine province, quickly became an Arab state in 641 C.E. For many of the commoners, life improved, and partially as a result, many Egyptians willingly converted to the new faith of Islam. The Arab conquerors established a new capital at Cairo and used it as a base for further expansion into Africa.

By the early eighth century, much of western north Africa, called the **Maghrib**, meaning "west," was also under Arab control. From here, they spread across the Mediterranean into Spain and southwards into Africa across the Sahara. The end result was that Axum remained one of the few non-Muslim states in northern and eastern Africa. Axum provided shelter and refuge for many Muslims during the early history of Islam, when Muslims were driven out of Mecca. Out of respect for this help, Muslims never attempted to conquer Axum. Muslims did later control the trade routes, which weakened the kingdom, and despite the cosmopolitan and eclectic nature of Axumite society, the Axumites never converted to Islam. Despite later crises over the succession, and later colonization efforts by Europeans, Axum continues to be largely Christian today and is known as the nation of Ethiopia.

A key result of the Islamic conquest of large portions of Africa was the establishment of a vast trading network. As we saw in the chapter on Islam, port cities arose along the east coast and facilitated contact with the Arabian peninsula and even settlements near the Indian Ocean. Ghana and later Mali in western Africa eventually became linked with this trading network, becoming influential partners through their lucrative gold trade. Moreover, many societies along the trade routes had mostly oral rather than written traditions. The introduction of the written Arabic language, as well as Arabic laws, allowed local rulers greater authority and improved administration over their subjects.

Ghana

The kingdoms of West Africa began to grow as a result of their role as intermediaries in the trans-Sahara trade. Kingdoms located in the savannah region traded salt to the forest settlements in exchange for gold, which they then traded with Africa north of the Sahara. **Ghana**, which flourished from 900–1100 C.E., was a military kingdom of the **Soninke** people directly on the trans-Saharan trade routes. It conquered a region approximately the size of Texas in what is today Mali. The name "Ghana" comes from the Soninke name for "war chief," which is what they called their leader. Muslim traders transferred the name to the whole area, at least by the eighth century C.E. Gold from Ghana was the basis of the Mediterranean trade with the East, and its king was known as the "king of gold," or Kaya-Maghan. According to Al-Bakri, an Arab chronicler, Ghana had an army of 200,000 warriors, and 40,000 of them carried bows and arrows. The king maintained a standing royal guard of 1,000 men. The kingship was hereditary, through the matrilineal line. Income from conquered areas helped to support the extensive administrative apparatus of Ghana. Taxes were also levied on imported goods such as salt, the largest import. Traders from the south, who brought gold, also paid taxes.

Social rank in Ghana was based on heredity and on service to the king. The Muslim administrators of Ghana were the highest rank on the social ladder; merchants ranked directly beneath them. Slaves were the lowest class.

The rulers of Ghana were forcibly converted to Islam by the Almoravids. In West Africa, Islam was often used to strengthen the native royal cults. The main city of Kumbi Saleh was divided into two cities, one for the king and administrators, and another for merchants and Islamic scholars. Kumbi Saleh housed twelve Islamic mosques, an indication of its size and prosperity.

Ironically, the growth of other Islamic movements weakened Ghana. The **Almoravids**, a group of people among the **Berbers** to the north, instituted a movement to purify Islam in the eleventh century, and began to move across the Western Sahara and eventually went north into Spain. They also eventually gained control of the gold trade across the Sahara and gradually moved toward Ghana, which they conquered in 1076. Ghana was considerably weakened by the thirteenth century and several other successor states arose in West Africa.

Mali

One of the successor states to break away from Ghana was **Mali**, founded by the **Mandike** people. The Mandike were primarily farmers, but also benefited from the gold trade. Under the leadership of Sundiata Mali (thirteenth century), a cripple whose exploits are immortalized in the Epic of Sundiata, and his descendent **Mansa Musa** (fourteenth century), Mali conquered the warring peoples and established an empire larger in size than that of Ghana. Sundiata divided the kingdom into clans, and assigned to groups of clans certain functions and responsibilities. Mansa Musa strengthened his control over his empire by appointing relatives as provincial governors. Mansa Musa made an historic pilgrimage or hajj to Mecca; his entourage carried so much gold with them that the economy of Egypt suffered from inflation for generations and the currency was devalued. Mansa Musa's travels brought many scholars and artists to Africa, and **Timbuktu**, a city on the Niger River, became a renowned center of Islamic learning and trade. The pilgrimage also opened trade with other Muslim areas, and fostered intermarriage between Muslims and African women.

The Songhay Kingdom

By the eleventh century, the rulers of the **Songhay** had converted to Islam. Their capital was at Gao, and under Sunni Ali in the fifteenth century, the Songhay conquered Timbuktu and Jenne in Ghana and further expanded their territories. Sunni Ali insisted on total obedience, even from the Islamic scholars of Timbuktu, but the Songhay kingdom actually became a mixture of Islamic and native, pagan elements. For example, men and women intermingled in the market places, which often deeply disturbed Muslim travelers. Muslims from Morocco conquered Songhay in the sixteenth century.

OTHER WEST AFRICAN KINGDOMS

Benin

The **Yoruba** people of West Africa did not speak one of the Bantu languages and may have been linked somehow to the earlier Nok culture. **Benin** was a strong, centralized city-state in West Africa with significant military and economic power. Kings called "Obas", who claimed divine ancestry, ruled Benin; they controlled trade so effectively that the Europeans could never manage to dominate Benin. Today, members of this family still rule in Benin. The Obas ruled the land by dividing it into fiefs held by officials, who were appointed by the Oba himself. The Oba in many ways was the absolute ruler of spiritual affairs as well as temporal ones. For example, he could speak with the voices of ancient ancestors of the people. Bronze casting reached a high point in Benin in the fifteenth century, in part fueled by the bronze and copper brought by Portuguese sailors. Nonetheless, the power of the Oba was so strong that the Portuguese were unable to dominate Benin as they would do in a number of other African states.

KINGDOMS OF CENTRAL AND SOUTH AFRICA

The Congo

The kingdom of the **Congo** arose around the thirteenth century and flourished in the fifteenth century. Its kingship was hereditary and its people were farmers. The Congo fell to the Portuguese when they succeeded in converting its leaders to Christianity and remaking its main city in the image of Lisbon.

The Great Zimbabwe

The massive walls of the **Great Zimbabwe** are the most important monuments in Africa south of the Nile Valley. The Bantu people were responsible for the great ruins, which were built between the eleventh and fifteenth centuries from local materials and covered more than sixty acres. There are two complexes, a fortress, and the "temple," which is an elliptically-shaped enclosure. A massive wall surrounds the entire complex. The buildings were highly decorated with ornaments and carvings, including ceramics from Asia. The massive ruins convey the strength of the economy of the Great Zimbabwe, which was based upon the gold trade. They also convey the power of the Great Zimbabwe as the center of a vast empire. The most well-known walls of the complex date to around the fourteenth and fifteenth centuries C.E., but the site was occupied by Bantu as early as the third century C.E. Great Zimbabwe was the center of a vast trading network, which controlled the export of gold to the coastal cities of East Africa. The gold trade reached its high point from 1400–1500 C.E., and scholars have discovered remains of objects imported from Persia, China, and the Near East in the ruins of the Great Zimbabwe. Great Zimbabwe arose at about the time Arab trade was developing on the East African coast, and declined at around the same time that Arab trade on the East Coast declined. This suggests a direct relationship between the gold trade and the prosperity of Zimbabwe. The gold trade declined in the fifteenth century due to falling world prices and the depletion of natural resources, and at the same time, the Great Zimbabwe was abandoned. Other scholars suggest that there were additional factors that brought about the decline of the Great Zimbabwe. In the fifteenth century, drought and failing agriculture damaged the pastoral economy of the Great Zimbabwe, and some scholars suggest that the Great Zimbabwe may have derived as much of its wealth from cattle as from gold.

Review Questions

1. Africa is called the "Dark Continent" for all of the following reasons EXCEPT
   - (A) its rivers are difficult to navigate.
   - (B) its deserts isolate one section of the continent from another.
   - (C) its rain forests are difficult to traverse.
   - (D) the lush forestry makes the nights longer and darker.

2. The African people who conquered the Egyptians in the eighth century B.C.E. and ruled as the 28th pharaonic dynasty were the
   - (A) people of Meröe.
   - (B) Kushites.
   - (C) Nok.
   - (D) Pygmies.

3. The people who speak languages of the Bantu family primarily inhabit
   - (A) the Sahara.
   - (B) the Kalahari.
   - (C) Africa south of the Sahara.
   - (D) Algiers.

4. The capital of the Kushites after the arrival of the Assyrians was
   - (A) Axum.
   - (B) Timbuktu.
   - (C) Meröe
   - (D) Napata.

5. The first Christian state in Africa was
   - (A) Meröe.
   - (B) Kush.
   - (C) Ghana.
   - (D) Axum.

6. The African culture that produced beautiful terra-cotta masks was
   - (A) Kush.
   - (B) Nok.

(C) Meröe.

(D) Axum.

7. The world's largest desert is the

(A) Kalahari.

(B) Gobi.

(C) Sahara.

(D) Nigev.

8. Of the continents of the world, Africa is the

(A) largest.

(B) third largest.

(C) fourth largest.

(D) second largest.

9. The African monarch who made a pilgrimage to Mecca, carrying with him much gold, was

(A) Sundiata Mali.

(B) Bantu Kubungu.

(C) Griot Mabunga.

(D) Mansa Musa.

10. The African civilization whose fate and fortune were linked to the gold trade with Muslim centers on the eastern coast of Africa was

(A) Kush.

(B) Great Zimbabwe.

(C) Meröe.

(D) Axum.

11. Which is true of the Bantu people?

(A) They originated in South Africa.

(B) They originated in the region of modern Nigeria.

(C) They spread iron-making in the course of their migrations.

(D) Both (B) and (C).

12. Which is true of iron making?

(A) The evidence is strongest for an indigenous origin of iron making in Africa.

(B) The evidence is strongest for the Phoenician introduction of iron making in Africa.

(C) The evidence more clearly suggests that iron making originated in Meröe.

(D) The Bantu played no role in the transmission of iron making.

13. Which of the following originated in Africa?

(A) Horses

(B) Sheep

(C) Camel

(D) Pyramid building

Answers

1. (D)	4. (C)	7. (C)	10. (B)	13. (D)
2. (B)	5. (D)	8. (D)	11. (D)	
3. (C)	6. (B)	9. (D)	12. (B)	

Chapter 12

THE AMERICAS BEFORE COLUMBUS

KEY TERMS

Bering Strait	Tenochtitlan
Anasazi	Calpulli
Olmec	Aztecs
San Lorenzo	Tequiua
Monte Alban	Tecuhtli
Teotihuacán	Maceualtin
Maya	Tlalmaitl
Palenque	Berdaches
Chichan Itza	Inca
Pacal	Ayllu
Quetzalcoatl	Curacas
Milpa	Mitima
Uxmal	Machu Picchu
Toltec Confederation	Mound Builders

MIGRATION TO THE AMERICAS

The native population of the Americas began coming from Asia across a land bridge that once covered the Bering Strait between 50,000 and 20,000 years ago. Over the course of thousands of years, people trickled down to the southern tip of South America.

There were several strong kingdoms and civilizations in the Americas that flourished and collapsed before the arrival of the Europeans in the fifteenth and sixteenth centuries C.E. Although the European explorers who "discovered" the Americas described them as a "New World," clearly there were advanced civilizations here that dated back thousands of years before the arrival of the Spanish.

Native cultures included the Olmec, the Maya, the Aztecs, the Incas, the Mound Builders of the Mississippi region, and the Anasazi of the American Southwest. Some of these cultures, such as the Anasazi and the Maya, had already collapsed prior to the arrival of the Europeans; others, such as the Aztecs and Incas, would collapse as a result of contact with the Europeans. Historians differ over the size of the native population of the Americas in 1500 C.E. The American historian John Tindall, for example, estimates that there were 50 million Native Americans when the Europeans arrived, while other historians claim the figure was closer to 19 million. There can be no certainty about this issue, as official censuses were rare. Further, many Native American cultures were nonliterate and relied upon oral traditions.

THE NATIVE AMERICAN CULTURES OF MESOAMERICA

The Olmec

The **Olmec** originated around 1500 B.C.E. at **San Lorenzo**, south of present-day Veracruz, Mexico. Although they were originally an egalitarian society, by 1500 B.C.E. a small class of hereditary ruler/nobles had evolved. The Olmec were farmers who cultivated maize, squash, beans, and other crops and who also hunted wild game. The Olmec were literate, and their symbolic system influenced the Mayas. There were several Olmec centers scattered over a very large region, and the Olmec were not a unified people. They created enormous stone portraits of their leaders weighing tons and managed to move them into place, even though they did not have the use of the wheel. The stone heads also suggest the possibility that the Olmec had contact with cultures across the Atlantic, as some of the stone heads have Negroid features. However, such features are also found in works from other parts of the world, so this fact alone does not prove trans-Atlantic contact.

San Lorenzo fell in 900 B.C.E., and **La Venta** then arose as a prominent Olmec center. La Venta is known for its 110-feet-high Great Pyramid. La Venta collapsed in 300 B.C.E. **Tres Zapotes** became prominent after the fall of La Venta, and was the last great Olmec site. Olmec centers had large open ball courts, a feature later found in Maya centers. The Olmec also practiced ritual sacrifice of humans, another practice also found among the Maya. The Olmec were the foundation of the later cultures in the classic period from 300–900 C.E. in Mesoamerica.

Trade in the Olmec World

The Olmec were very successful traders, ferrying their goods to central and western Mexico and to the Pacific Coast. They imported obsidian, from which they made weapons, iron ore, shells, and perishable goods. They exported pottery, rubber, cacao, and jaguar pelts.

The Classic Period

Following the decline of the Olmec, several other cultures arose in **Mesoamerica** from around 150–900 C.E. This period is known as the classic period.

Teotihuacán

Teotihuacán arose as a major center of Mesoamerican civilization around 300 B.C.E. and flourished until 700–800 C.E. It was located about thirty miles northeast of modern-day Mexico City and had a population of about 150,000 people. Teotihuacán had stratified social classes, with the elite living in a special precinct and the working classes in barrios on the edge of the city. Agricultural laborers lived outside of the city's boundaries. Teotihuacán contained more than 5,000 ceremonial structures and was laid out on a north-south and east-west axis. The **Pyramids of the Sun and Moon** dominated the city. The Pyramid of the Sun had four levels and was over 200 feet high. Each side is 700 feet long. There are many images of the god **Quetzalcoatl** on the ruins. Teotihuacán's early structures are primarily religious in nature, whereas its later structures are primarily secular. Since many of the later structures are palaces, some scholars think that the control of Teotihuacán shifted from religious leaders to civil authorities. Around 650 C.E., invaders from the southwest burned Teotihuacán. Like the Olmec, Teotihuacán influenced other cultures of Mesoamerica. The collapse of Teotihuacán perhaps contributed to Maya warfare in the south, as the Maya may have sought control over some of the trade routes formerly dominated by Teotihuacán.

Monte Alban

Sometime around 500 B.C.E., the **Zapotec** people began to build much larger cities and monumental structures at Monte Alban. The structures at **Monte Alban** are built on a stone terrace on a 1,200 foot high mountain overlooking modern Oaxaca. Approximately 20,000 people lived here on terraces for farming carved into the mountainsides. Monte Alban fell to invaders somewhere around

Pyramid of the Sun

Pyramid of the Moon

700 c.e., having flourished for over 1200 years in Mesoamerica. Teotihuacán was clearly the most powerful influence on the architecture and culture of Monte Alban. Monte Alban fell shortly after invaders destroyed Teotihuacán.

The Maya

The **Maya** of Mesoamerica were the heirs of Olmec culture. While Teotihuacán dominated the central plateau of Mexico, the Maya dominated what is today southern Mexico and Central America. There may once have been 14 million inhabitants in the Maya cities on the Yucatan peninsula. The largest city was **Tikal**, which may have had a population of 100,000. The Maya had an elaborate system of writing as well as time keeping. Their civilization reached such a degree of sophistication that it is often referred to as the "Greece of the New World."

Trade and Agriculture

The Mayan civilization flourished on the Yucatan peninsula and was based on agriculture. The Maya grew maize, chili peppers, beans, squash, and a variety of fruit. They used raised plots of land and also **milpa,** created by the burning of forests. The Maya dug holes in the ash and planted maize. After two years, the milpa had to be abandoned for four to seven years to replenish the soil. The textile arts were an important part of Mayan trade, and their cotton was exported throughout the region. Mayan cities were largely for ceremonial purposes, and trade fairs were a vital part of religious celebrations. In addition to textiles, they traded cacao, jade, obsidian, and shells. Trade occurred between various Mayan centers and also with Teotihuacán and the Oaxaca Valley, but goods had to be transported either along the rivers and waterways or on the roads that linked the Mayan centers. As in other cultures, travel overland was more difficult than via waterways, but this was particularly true in the Mayan world. Goods had to be transported over land using only human labor and without heavy pack animals, as these did not exist before the arrival of the Spaniards.

Mayan Centers

Palenque

Palenque is an important city of the Maya, associated with the ruler Pacal. There are fifteen structures on the palace platform. The Temple of the Inscriptions is the highest temple in the complex at 75 feet above ground level. It was built to house the tomb of **Pacal**, the ruler responsible for many of the buildings at Palenque. His sarcophagus weighs five tons, and several sacrificial victims were placed outside of it. Many of the sculptures and images here celebrate the victories of Pacal. As Mayan centers starting in the eighth century, Mayan centers in the Yucatan peninsula began to expand. People from central Mexico began to influence Mayan cities such as Chichan Itza and Uxmal.

Chichan Itza

Chichan Itza was one of the last Mayan centers to be abandoned. Even after Tikal and Palenque had been deserted and overgrown by the jungle, Chichan Itza continued to flourish. One reason Chichan Itza is so well-preserved is that it became a Toltec center after the decline of the Maya. Images of the Maya god Kukulcan or the "feathered serpent" are omnipresent in Chichan Itza and other Mayan sites; the Toltec identified the "feathered serpent" here with the god **Quetzalcoatl**, worshipped at Teotihuacán. According to tradition, the Toltec Quetzalcoatl came here after being ousted by the Toltec god Tezcatlipoca. Chichan Itza, then, appealed to the Toltec as a ceremonial center. The name "Chichan Itza" means "mouth of the Itzas' well" or "at the edge of the well of the water sorcerers." The **Itzas** were the group of Maya who settled here. In this part of the Yucatan, there is little rainfall and no sources of water on the surface; cenotes, or places where the limestone has collapsed exposing underground water, were very important. Consequently, the cult of **Chaac**, god of rain and waters, was important here.

The Maya built their cities around a central ceremonial pyramid and other buildings, with a sacred ball court nearby. The Pyramid of Kukulcan or El Castillo is a famous ruin at Chichan Itza. It is a nine-story structure symbolizing the planes of the underworld with a temple on top and another pyramid on the inside of the structure. At 3:00 P.M. on the spring and fall equinoxes (March 20 and September 21), the sun forms a design on the north staircase that looks like an undulating serpent; this design symbolizes the descent of the god Kukulcan to earth and hence, the beginning of the agricultural cycle.

There is also a ball court that is one of the largest courts of the Maya. The game played on the ball court near the pyramid had deep religious significance for the Maya. Although the ritual practiced here is not fully understood, the players bounced a large ball back and forth using their hips. The game was dangerous, and the balls were thrown with such force that players had to wear protective padding. The court had metal rings on the walls through which the combatants attempted to drive the ball. Scholars believe the ball court represented the cosmos, while the ball represented the sun. The game symbolized the conflict between light and darkness. Maya sacrificed the losers to the gods after the games.

El Caracol is another famous ruin, and the Maya and later the Toltec used it for astronomical purposes. It was built between 900–1000 C.E. The movements of the heavens were very important for the Maya and later the Toltec. The Maya developed their sophisticated solar calendar of 365 days through observing the heavens at structures such as this. Maya divided the solar calendar into 18 months with 20 days each, with five additional empty days. There was also a ritual calendar that governed the lives of humans and deities. The Maya made very sophisticated observations and calculations of the solar, lunar, and Venusian cycles, eclipses of the sun, and the movements of constellations.

The cylindrical observatory tower known as "the snail of El Caracol" has a small room from which the Maya observed the heavens.

The Nunnery Complex at Chichan Itza is the largest structure at Chichan Itza dating from the classic period. It has many small rooms and was used by **priestesses** in Mayan rituals. For these reasons, Spanish explorers gave it its modern name.

Uxmal

"Uxmal" means "thrice occupied." Its most famous ruin is the Nunnery Quadrangle, and it also contains the Governor's Palace, the Great Pyramid, and the Pyramid of the Magician. Like other Mayan cities, it had a ball court.

The Decline of the Maya

The Maya reached their peak from 500–800 C.E. but began to abandon their cities between 800–1000 C.E. The reasons for this are unknown, but scholars have suggested that foreign invasions, civil unrest due to disease, overpopulation, crop failures, administrative problems caused by an overly large empire, or natural disaster might have prompted the decline of the Maya. Although the Maya developed a very sophisticated society, they also fought numerous and bloody wars to expand their territory. These wars devastated the surrounding region, perhaps further contributing to the agricultural problems that developed in the Mayan world. Some scholars suggest these wars may have been motivated by the desire to gain control over the trade routes once dominated by

Mayan Ruins

Teotihuacán. Although the civilization of the Maya collapsed, over two million Maya continue to survive today in the Yucatan peninsula.

Toltec Confederation

Under the leadership of **Toliptzin** (980–1000 C.E.), the **Toltecs** rose in the central plateau of modern-day Mexico in the vacuum left by the fall of Teotihuacán. Following the fall of the Maya, they established themselves as masters of Mesoamerica. Their capital was **Tula**. The Toltecs intermarried with the remnants of the population of Teotihuacán. Toliptzin even took the name "Quetzalcoatl" to symbolize his position as high priest of the cult of the plumed serpent god worshipped in Teotihuacán. According to later Aztec legend, the Toltec god Tezcatlipoca had a struggle with Toliptzin-Quetzalcoatl and drove Quetzalcoatl into exile. Coincidentally, the year that Quetzalcoatl promised to return was the same year in which Hernando Cortes arrived in Mesoamerica. After the collapse of the Mayan centers, Toltec influence spread south. The Toltec influence may also have spread north to the Anasazi in the southwest of North America. The Toltec empire collapsed in 1200 C.E.

The Aztecs (Mexico)

The **Aztecs** wandered for 150 years before settling on the swampy islands of **Lake Texcoco**, the modern-day location of Mexico City. They worshipped their god **Huitzilopochtili** in the city there. In 1428, the Aztecs began a policy of expansion. Although the Toltecs had once looked upon them as barbarians, the Aztecs quickly assimilated the cultural legacy of the Toltecs, and by 1519, the Aztec confederation occupied virtually all of Mesoamerica. In **Tenochtitlan**, there were 60,000 households, and the total population was somewhere around 500,000. Tenochtitlan was larger than any European city of its time. The population in the Aztec empire was over 5,000,000. The Aztecs built this empire through warfare. Aztec kings summoned warriors to duty through the calpulli, an organization based on households and kinship. These units rotated service, the length of which was determined by the king. The lack of pack animals here, as in the Maya world, meant that human porters carried the supplies the army needed. Warfare might have strengthened the empire on one level, but over the long run it weakened it. Conquered areas paid tribute to the Aztec king, but they were also centers of rebellion. When an area rebelled, the Aztecs would conquer it again with more brutal methods, rule it until it rebelled again, and then conquer it again. This cycle depleted the empire of its manpower and energy.

Much of the Aztec's success can be attributed to the cult of their chief god Huitzilopochtili, the god of the sun. The Aztecs believed that this god had to be kept moving so as not to be overtaken by darkness. They believed that he had to be fed human blood, and they practiced ritual sacrifice, sometimes on a mass level. There are many theories as to why the Aztecs practiced sacrifice; some argue that sacrifice was a check on population growth. Others say that it served as an instrument of state terror and controlled nearby populations; some historians and anthropologists have even suggested that ordinary people fed on the bodies of the sacrificial victims as a form of protein. The Emperor **Montezuma II** lived in splendor greater than any European monarch of the day; at his coronation, 5,100 people were sacrificed. This religious ritual, for whatever reasons it was practiced, strengthened the Aztec state on one level. On another level, however, it also weakened the Aztec empire, as the thousands of people sacrificed might otherwise have been productive members of society.

Aztec Social Structure

As was the case with Olmec society, Aztec social structure changed over time from an egalitarian society to a hierarchical society for unknown reasons. After the king, who was elected by important nobles, priests were also of very high status in Aztec society. Regions paid tribute to sustain some of the famous Aztec temples. The next highest ranking members of Aztec society were the tecuhtli, a group of nobles who had won distinction as warriors. They served as judges, governors of provinces, or as generals. Just as samurai were the only Japanese to have last names and carry swords, Aztec tecuhtli were the only ones who could wear jewelry and cloaks with embroidery. Warriors who captured four prisoners or killed four enemies became part of the tequiua, nobles who were given a portion of the plunder of war. A warrior who failed in such a task was relegated to the class of workers, or maceualtin. In the Aztec capital the maceualtin had land that they held for life. They also paid taxes and were required to work on imperial projects. A landless class of workers were the tlalmaitl, who were also required to perform military service. Aztecs also had slaves. Like slaves in Mesopotamia, they could intermarry with free people and their children would be free. Aztec slaves could also own goods and land. As in Mesopotamia, they could purchase their freedom. Unlike Mesopotamia, however, an escaped slave would earn his freedom should he manage to reach the emperor's palace.

GENDER ISSUES

Women

Women were confined to the household in Aztec society, though some served as priestesses. The need for women to grind maize and other grains by hand made their labor essential to the household. Lack of more efficient technology to produce basic foodstuffs essentially limited women's roles. A couple's parents arranged marriages.

Third and Fourth Genders

Aztecs, as well as other Native American groups, also developed a "third" gender. Male children born into families that already had several other male children were often made to dress like females and to assume the gender roles of females. Other men had sex with them. These transvestites were known as **berdaches**, and they performed women's work. Nobles often had several of them, and often gave them to other nobles in return for some good or service. In some Native American societies, there were also female berdaches, creating yet a fourth gender. Berdaches formed sexual relationships with members of their own sex, essentially creating an institutionalized system of homosexuality in Native American cultures. Some Native Americans today prefer the term "two-spirit," as the word "berdache" had its origins in Asian culture, from where it was imported into European usage. The word had various and subtly different meanings, depending on the culture to which it was applied.

NATIVE AMERICAN CULTURES OF SOUTH AMERICA: THE INCA

Recent archaeological finds suggest that urban civilization first arose on a large scale in **Caral**, located in modern Peru. The site has 17 temple complexes across 35 square miles in the Supe Valley. If radiocarbon dating is correct, this center dates back to the twenty-seventh century B.C.E., over 1,000 years before scholars originally thought urban life and agriculture evolved in the New World.

The Inca

In the 1980s archaeologists discovered evidence of great civilizations along the west coast of Peru going back 5,000 years. These civilizations were older than those of the Mayas or Aztecs. These civilizations built step pyramids and other large monuments. For reasons unknown to us, these people moved into the Andes highlands, the highest mountain range in the Western Hemisphere. They became known as the **Inca**, a name taken from a ruling family in Cuzco, and then applied to all Native Americans living in the Cuzco basin. The Inca became militaristic during the reign of **Pachacuti Inca** (1438–1471) and conquered surrounding groups. They controlled their population through strong government; they unified the language and the religion of their subjects.

The Inca were organized in clans or ayllu who worked plots of land in return for tribute paid to a provincial governor and for their service on state building projects. A rotation system known as a mita determined when state duties were required. Members of an ayllu intermarried. Members of a clan also owed their allegiance to a curacas, but under Pachacuti Inca, allegiance was transferred to the Inca ruler rather than to the curacas. Under Pachacuti, a system of colonization called the mitima deported the populations of newly conquered regions and replaced them with a more servile and docile group of people previously conquered. A well-organized system of roads facilitated the movement of Inca armies and peoples.

The Inca settled primarily in the valleys of Huaylas, Cuzco, and Titicaca where they constructed terraces along the slopes of the steep mountains. How or why they made the transition from dependence on the sea for food in the early period to settled agriculture between 600–1000 C.E. is still a mystery. They grew corn and potatoes and learned to preserve the potatoes through freeze-drying. In 1911, Hiram Bingham discovered the most famous Inca site, **Machu Picchu**.

NATIVE AMERICAN CULTURES OF NORTH AMERICA

The Mississippian Culture or the Mound Builders

The **Mississippian culture** arose along the Mississippi River and flourished from 900–1350 C.E. The culture spread along the rivers to many parts of what is now the central and eastern United States. The Mississippians were farmers who grew corn, squash, beans, pumpkins, and tobacco. Among the most important centers of Mississippian culture were **Cahokia**, Illinois, the largest settlement north of Mexico; **Moundville**, Alabama; and **Ocmulgee**, Georgia. The Mississippians are also known as the **Mound Builders** due to the enormous flat-topped temple mounds they constructed in the centers of their large, well-organized cities.

Cahokia, eight miles east of modern St. Louis, reached the high point of its development between 1050–1150 C.E., and the city covered nearly six square miles. There were 120 mounds at Cahokia, the largest of which is Monks Mound, covering 15 acres on its base and soaring 100 feet high. Scholars estimate that the complex had a population of between 10,000–40,000, although 20,000 is the most likely number. Inhabitants built a circle of wooden posts, now called Woodhenge, and used it as a calendar. A ten-foot high stockade surrounded a large part of the complex. Cahokia began its decline around 1200 C.E. and was completely deserted by 1400 C.E.

Ocmulgee takes its name from the river upon which the Mississippians settled here. The name "Ocmulgee" means "boiling water," and the river water literally seems to boil and bubble as one stands near the shore. At one time, Ocmulgee had a population of as many as 1,000 people. Ocmulgee is primarily known for the remains of several mounds. There are at least seven mounds still remaining on the site, including the largest mound, the Great Temple Mound. The Great Temple Mound is approximately 45 feet high. Its base is 300 feet by 270 feet long. At one time, there were rectangular wooden structures on top of

Cahokia Mounds, the site of the largest pre-Columbian Indian city north of Mexico. This painting, by L. K. Townsend, shows central Cahokia circa 1150 to 1200 B.C.E. Courtesy Cahokia Mounds Historic Site.

the mound, whose purpose is uncertain. There is also an Earthlodge at Ocmulgee, and the doorway was aligned so that once a year on the winter solstice, sunlight poured through the entrance and flooded the platform. Rituals here may have commemorated the beginning of the spring and harvest seasons.

Scholars know very little about how the Mississippian mounds were used, except that they were built for public ceremonies. Some scholars have suggested connections between the Mound Builders and the Mesoamerican pyramid builders, primarily because of the large ceremonial structures built in both areas, but no artifacts from Mesoamerica have been discovered to verify such a hypothesis.

The Southwestern Native Americans: The Anasazi

Spanish explorers first encountered the southwestern Native American tribes in the 1540s. There were three major Native American cultures in the southwest: the **Hohokam**, who were an agricultural group located in the river valleys of the desert, the **Mogollon**, who were hunters and gatherers, and the **Anasazi** (**Hisatsinom**), who were cliff dwellers.

The Anasazi (Hisatsinom) were likely the descendants of an Archaic Desert culture in the southwest from 6,000 B.C.E. known as the **Basketmaker I culture**, or from the Mogollon. They first appeared in the Four Corners region (the intersection of New Mexico, Arizona, Utah, and Colorado) around the time of the historic Christ. The ruins of the Anasazi (Hisatsinom) culture are the best-preserved ruins in North America. The word "Anasazi" is a later Navajo word that means "ancient people who are not us" or "ancient enemies." The **Hopi** consider themselves to be descendants of the Anasazi (Hisatsinom), and prefer that their ancestors be called the Hisatsinom, which means "people of long ago." The Anasazi (Hisatsinom) did not build cliff dwellings for the first 1,000 years of their history, but rather lived in open communities or in caves. They lived near fields where they grew corn, squash, and beans. They also gathered nuts and other wild foods and hunted game. Given the very open nature of their lifestyle, archaeologists argue that the Anasazi (Hisatsinom) had few enemies in their early history.

Sometime between 900–1100 C.E. (called the **Pueblo II period**), the Anasazi (Hisatsinom) began to build kivas, or communal rooms for ceremonial purposes, in their villages. Their population increased, and during this period small Anasazi villages began to spread throughout the southwest.

Starting from 1100–1300 C.E. (called the **Pueblo III period**), the Anasazi (Hisatsinom) began to build the cliff dwellings for which they are most well-known. Many buildings in these villages under the cliffs were several stories tall. These villages were in places that were easily defensible, suggesting that the Anasazi (Hisatsinom) had perhaps acquired enemies they did not have in earlier periods. For unknown reasons, near the end of this period the western Anasazi (Hisatsinom) sites were completely abandoned, while the eastern sites continued to flourish and expand.

From 1300 until 1598 C.E. (called the **Pueblo IV period**) the Anasazi (Hisatsinom) moved further south near the homes of the Hopis and Zunis. Many Anasazi (Hisatsinom) cliff dwellings, or pueblos, became much larger, often housing thousands of people and being several stories high.

Chaco Canyon

The ruins of the Anasazi (Hisatsinom) were first discovered in the nineteenth century, and many have since been designated national monuments and World Heritage Centers. The earliest Anasazi (Hisatsinom) site to enter the Pueblo stage of development was **Chaco** in northwest New Mexico. Chaco Canyon was the center of Anasazi (Hisatsinom) civilization by 900 C.E., and may have had a population that numbered in the thousands. There were three major building styles perfected here: great towns with enormous room blocks with up to five levels; great houses with plazas and kivas; and outlying villages probably designed for family groups. The Anasazi (Hisatsinom) here were known for their turquoise jewelry, and traded with other Anasazi (Hisatsinom) groups. They reached the height of their development around 1130 C.E. Some twenty years later, following a long period of drought, the Chacoans abandoned this region. In 1980 Chaco became a national monument. Pueblo Bonito is one of the Great Houses in Chaco Canyon; each pueblo here typically has around 216 rooms.

Mesa Verde in southwestern Colorado was another very important center of Anasazi (Hisatsinom) culture. Anasazi (Hisatsinom) of the Basketmaker III period lived here, perhaps as far back as 575 C.E. The Anasazi (Hisatsinom) began to construct villages on top of the mesas here as early as 800 C.E. By the 1300s the Anasazi (Hisatsinom) were building much more elaborate cliff dwellings protected by caves. Mesa Verde contains more than 4,000 prehistoric sites.

The Anasazi made the shift from the mesa top to the cliff dwellings below sometime in the 1200s. The inhabitants of **Sun Point Pueblo** on the mesa top actually dismantled their stone and wooden structures and carried the materials to the shelter of the caves below. Given the tremendous amount of labor involved, scholars have suggested that there must have been a serious threat to their safety above.

Mesa Verde contains some of the best-preserved cliff dwellings in the southwest. Cliff Palace is the largest cliff dwelling in North America. It has 217 rooms and 23 kivas, and probably had a population of 200–250 people. The kivas here were sunk into the ground, and one entered them by climbing down a ladder.

Other large dwellings include Spruce Tree House, which has 144 rooms and eight kivas. There are over 600 cliff dwellings in Mesa Verde and, although there are other large villages such as this in Mesa Verde, 75 percent contain only one to five rooms. Balcony House is another famous dwelling in Mesa Verde, and is located high on the cliffs 600 feet above the canyon floor. Through tree-ring dating, its first timbers have been dated to 1190 C.E., and its latest timbers to 1290 C.E.

Decline of Mesa Verde

The Anasazi (Hisatsinom) abandoned most cliff dwellings in Mesa Verde around 1270 C.E. The reasons why the Anasazi (Hisatsinom) left this site are uncertain, but drought, climatic change, or depletion of natural resources are the most likely explanations. Most scholars believe that the inhabitants of the villages in Mesa Verde moved south to join the Hopi or many other tribes in the area. The ruins of the villages were not discovered until December 18, 1888, when a Colorado rancher named Richard Wetherhill happened to spot them from the mesa top. In 1906 the site became a national park, was later excavated by the Smithsonian, and was made a World Heritage Center in 1978.

Native American culture would change greatly with the arrival of the Europeans in the fifteenth century.

Review Questions

1. The greatest of all prehistoric New World civilizations, often referred to as the "Greece of the New World," was the

    (A) Teotihuacán culture.

    (B) Olmec.

    (C) Aztec.

    (D) Mayan.

2. The Mayan complex at Tikal appears to have served primarily as

    (A) a main political and administrative center.

    (B) a major commercial and manufacturing center.

    (C) the permanent residence of the Mayan ruling elite.

    (D) a religious ceremonial center.

3. According to the most recent finds, the first great urban civilization in the New World was developed by

    (A) the Mayans.

    (B) Teotihuacán.

    (C) the Olmec.

    (D) the Peruvians (Inca) at Caral.

4. The first major civilization of the Americas was the

    (A) Aztec.

    (B) Olmec.

    (C) Teotihuacán.

    (D) Mayan.

5. The Mayans were noteworthy for all of the following EXCEPT

    (A) a system of hieroglyphic writing.

    (B) a complex calendar.

    (C) self-mutilation and human sacrifice.

    (D) peaceful coexistence with their neighbors.

6. The Aztecs organized households into administrative units called

   (A) states.

   (B) provinces.

   (C) calpulli.

   (D) audiencas.

7. Enemies of the Aztecs who were captured in battle were

   (A) executed promptly on the spot.

   (B) saved for later sacrifice in religious ceremonies.

   (C) released as a humane gesture to their neighbors.

   (D) forced to crawl back to their camps after their legs were cut off.

8. Gender roles in the Native American cultures were

   (A) limited to male and female roles.

   (B) varied, including a male (and female) member of a third (and fourth) gender known as berdaches.

   (C) limited by lack of technology.

   (D) Both (B) and (C).

Answers

1. (D)	4. (B)	7. (B)
2. (D)	5. (D)	8. (D)
3. (D)	6. (C)	

Chapter 13

TRENDS IN SOUTH ASIA, SOUTHEAST ASIA, AND EAST ASIA FROM 500 C.E. TO 1400 C.E.

KEY TERMS

Gupta dynasty
White Huns
Kingdom of Chola
Sri Lanka
Srivijaya
Mahmud Ghazni
Delhi Sultanate
Tamerlane
Funan
Vietnam
Thailand
Burma
Pagan dynasty
Angkor Wat
Khmer Kingdom
Sumatra
Palembang
Jurchen people
Sui dynasty
Sui Yangdi
T'ang dynasty
Song dynasty

Civil service examination system
Lungmen Buddhist caves
The Silk Road
Foot binding
Ghengis Khan
Ogedai
Karakorum
Chaghadai Khanate
Samarkand
Khanate of Persia
Baghdad
Khanate of Kipchak or the
    Golden Horde
Koryo Dynasty
Prince Shotoku Taishi
Kamajura Shogunate
Minamoto Yoritomo
Ashikaga Shogunate
Shoen
Bakufu tent system
Kamikaze
Daimio

OVERVIEW

Many conquerors established powerful and important empires in Asia during this period. After the fall of the Roman Empire in the West, Europe entered the Middle Ages and Germanic peoples began the establishment of the European monarchies. While Europe struggled to reassert itself following the collapse of Rome, some of the most important and vibrant Asian empires flourished, including the various Mongol Khanates and the Mongol dynasty in China, the Yuan. The Mongols contributed to the further development of Islam, though their initial effect on the Islamic world was negative. Islam spread to Southeast Asia in this period.

TRENDS IN SOUTH ASIA

The Gupta Empire in India

Early in the fourth century c.e., the **Gupta state** emerged around the Ganges River in eastern India. Samugragupta was the most important ruler in the development of the state, which was never as large as the Mauryan Empire nor as centralized, but nevertheless modeled on it.

The Gupta were tolerant of many religions, though they were themselves Hindus. During the Gupta period, the Chinese Buddhist monk **Faxian** traveled to India and wrote about its Buddhist monasteries (see Chapter 20 on China for further information on Faxian), and also artisans codified ways of portraying the Buddha. The arts flourished during the Gupta period.

The Gupta controlled the trade on salt and metals, and also the trade between India, the Middle East, and China. Goods such as cotton, sugar, cinnamon, and pepper flowed out of India in exchange for other goods. The Gupta controlled their realm by a tax of one-quarter of the agricultural produce and by requiring labor on state projects. However, rulers in areas not close to the administrative center had considerable power and some of these positions were hereditary. The Gupta Empire collapsed in the fifth century c.e. following a disastrous invasion by the White Huns.

Great Migrations: The Huns

The **Huns** were from Central Asia and their movements had disastrous affects on much of Asia and Europe. In our chapter on Rome, we discussed the westward movement of the Huns, and the subsequent movement of the Visigoths further west. The Visigoths later defeated the Romans at Adrianople in 378 c.e.; the Huns continued their westward movement and eventually threatened Rome under **Attila**. A group of Huns known as the **White Huns** entered India in 450 c.e. Although the Gupta managed to defend India, the effort required eventually brought about the collapse of the Gupta.

India After the Collapse of the Gupta: The Kingdom of Chola

Following the decline of the Gupta, there were several centers of power. **Chola** controlled the southern tip of the subcontinent and first rose to prominence in the south during the ninth century. In the tenth century, Cholas succeeded in gaining control over other existing kingdoms in the region. Under Rajaraja the Great or Rajaraja I, the Chola conquered Sri Lanka. Chola often clashed with the Delhi Sultanate, once it was established in the north.

Chola dominated trade in the eastern Indian Ocean until the twelfth century. Chola's control over trade was further strengthened when its King Rajendra I defeated **Srivijaya** in Southeast Asia in 1025 C.E. Srivijaya continued to exist, but its control over the Indian Ocean trade was diminished. Chola weakened in the thirteenth century and was greatly affected by the Muslim invasions of the fourteenth century.

The Empire of Mahmud Ghazni

In 962 C.E. Turkish-speaking slaves took power from the Sasanid Persians. In 997 C.E. the founder's son, **Mahmud Ghazni**, took power and began a series of raids in Indian lands. By the time he died in 1030 C.E., he had conquered the upper Indus Valley and areas as far south as the Indian Ocean. By 1200 C.E. successors to the Ghazni controlled northern India and had established the **Delhi Sultanate**. Under the Delhi Sultanate, Islam spread firmly throughout northern India, and Muslim rulers frowned upon the use of Hindu and Buddhist statues. They destroyed many such religious statues, and were especially intolerant of Buddhism. Nevertheless, Hinduism continued to flourish, and during this period, the caste system was fully defined. People married only within their castes and ate meals with caste members; each caste had a proper function. Muslim rulers essentially remained separate from their Hindu subjects.

Trade During the Delhi Sultanate

Indian merchants continued to trade via the Indian Ocean routes and established new port cities in Southeast Asia, further spreading Indian influence to that region. The textile industry was more fully developed during this period and Indian textiles were prized commodities.

Changes in Gender Roles During the Delhi Sultanate

Muslim rulers adopted many Hindu practices that weakened the status of women in the Islamic world. During this period, Hindu practices contributed to the loss of status for women. Girls were married before the onset of their menstrual periods to protect their virginity, and many Muslims adopted this practice. Further, women could no longer own or inherit property, in contrast to earlier practices in the Vedic age. Women were confined to their households and when widowed, only their children saw them. Hindus expected women to live very ascetic lives, wearing plain clothes, rarely eating, sleeping on the hard ground, and often shaving their heads. While the **Qur'an** taught greater equality for women, Muslim conquerors were profoundly affected by these Hindu customs. The status of women declined in this period both for Hindus and their Muslim conquerors.

Mass Migrations Threaten India

Mongols led by **Ghengis Khan** entered the Indus River Valley in the north in 1221. The Great Khan left troops there, and in 1229, they launched an attack on the Delhi Sultanate. The Mongols were unsuccessful at conquering India, and the defeat of the Mongols is one of the great achievements of the Delhi Sultanate.

Unfortunately, in the fourteenth century, a new wave of invasions occurred, as the Turk **Tamerlane**, who was of Mongol descent but not from Genghis Khan, led his troops into India after conquering the region east of the Caspian Sea, Mesopotamia, and Baghdad. He entered northern India, where he massacred 100,000 Hindu prisoners before entering Delhi. The sultan there surrendered. Tamerlane's rule was brief and brutal.

Trends in Southeast Asia

Indian influence was profoundly important in the development of Southeast Asia. Merchants and wandering Buddhist monks and Hindu priests traveled the trade routes and encountered many cultures. Of the kingdoms in Southeast Asia, only what is today Vietnam remained immune from Indian influence from around the second through the tenth century C.E., as the Chinese controlled this region for most of this period until it won its independence in 939 C.E. Even after it won independence, Vietnam continued to make use of Chinese bureaucratic structures and a Chinese-style civil service examination system.

Southeast Asian willingly embraced Indian influences, and Ashoka's dream of the "conquest of righteousness" found its fulfillment in the spread of Buddhism, but also of Hinduism and other Indian influences through peaceful trade and wandering monks and priests.

Indian travelers traded with the state of **Funan**, whose capital was in what is today Vietnam. Funan was the first state to arise in this area, and it controlled parts of the Malay Peninsula and Indochina. Indian religious figures often served in administrative capacities here or as advisors to rulers. Indian merchants succeeded in ferrying goods from ports to points further inland.

Thailand

Thai tribes united in the eighth century. The T'ang Chinese checked their growth northwards until the Mongols took Thailand in 1253.

Burma/Pagan Dynasty

Burma, now known as **Myanmar**, also arose in the eighth century from the migrations of tribes who moved westward to settle there. At Pagan they built a complex city ruled by the Pagan dynasty starting in the eleventh century. Again, influences from India were strong, and the Pagan rulers were **Theraveda Buddhists**. At Pagan, there are magnificent temples. In the thirteenth century, Mongols toppled the Pagan dynasty.

Angkor

Cambodian peasants reported to French colonial powers during the nineteenth century that they had found remnants of "temples built by gods or by giants." No one took them seriously until 1860, when Henri Mahout discovered the ruins of the **Angkor Kingdom**. The temples are spread out over some 40 miles, and are located about 192 miles from present-day Phnom Penh, at the magnificent city of **Angkor Thom**. The **Khmer** kingdom of Angkor arose in the ninth century and was the most powerful kingdom in Southeast Asia before the sixteenth century. The Khmer people, unlike the Burmese, were indigenous to the area. The capital city, Angkor Thom, covered an area of more than four square miles. The temple of **Angkor Wat** was a Hindu site, with as many as 3,000 priests at its apex. It was built between 1113 c.e. and 1150 c.e. and has a moat 570 feet wide and four miles long. Its thousands of sculptures portray Hindu mythology from the Mahabarata and Ramayana. Another famous temple is the Buddhist shrine Bayon. The Temple of Bayon was built between 1181 c.e. and 1220 c.e. and has 172 giant heads representing the Bodhisattva of Mercy. Buddhists venerate Bodhisattvas as those who have attained nirvana, but remained behind to teach others the path to salvation. The architectural style of the Temple of Bayon is a mix between Hindu and Buddhist elements and was influenced by the conversion of Jayavarman from Hinduism to Buddhism.

The Khmer were in constant conflict with the Vietnamese. They reached their high point in the thirteenth century. The Thai destroyed the capital city in 1432 c.e.

Srivijaya

Srivijaya developed in the eighth century and was a trading society whose primary commodity was spices. Centered on the island of **Sumatra**, recently the epicenter of the disastrous earthquake and subsequent tsunami of December 26, 2004, the Srivijaya controlled the trade waters around Borneo, Java, and later dominated the southern part of the Malay Peninsula. Their deepwater port and capital Palembang provided refuge from the monsoons. Srivijaya dominated the trade that passed through the **Strait of Malacca**. The Srivijayans embraced Indian influences, from the use of Sanskrit for official documents to the propagation of Indian religions and mythology. This influence is clearly seen in architecture, as at Borobudur, an incredible Buddhist complex built in the eighth century. While Therevada Buddhism triumphed on land in Southeast Asia, in Srivijaya, **Mahayana Buddhism** was the preferred form of practice. In 1025 C.E., the southern Indian kingdom of Chola defeated it, and it gradually lost its hold over trade in the region. Merchants from China arrived in the thirteenth century, further weakening the Srivijaya hold over trade.

Majapahit

After the defeat of Srivijaya, **Majapahit** on Java rose to prominence in the thirteenth century. In the mid-fourteenth century, it had united the archipelago of islands and part of mainland Southeast Asia.

TRENDS IN CENTRAL AND EAST ASIA

China

After the final collapse of the Han dynasty in the third century C.E., northern and southern China were not united and the north often was invaded by Asian nomadic peoples. Buddhism also began to infiltrate China, though the first recorded arrival of a Buddhist dates back to the Han dynasty. During the chaos of this period, Buddhism displaced Confucian influences, and the Chinese worried about foreign influences, especially in the face of increasing invasions by foreign nomadic peoples.

Yang Jian founded the **Sui dynasty** in 581 C.E. and reunited China. He also drove out the nomadic invaders. The Sui capital was Chang-an. Yang Jian patronized both Buddhism and Taoism and founded many monasteries. Yang Jian and his son and successor, **Sui Yangdi**, built a 1,400 mile long **Grand Canal** that linked the Yellow and Yangtze Rivers. Yangdi was a tyrannical ruler, who assassinated his own father to gain power.

Impact of the Grand Canal on Trade and Migration Patterns

Most of the Chinese lived in the south, where they produced rice. Those living in the north produced millet. Rivers were the easiest way to transport goods, but they ran from west to east. As in other parts of the world, it was difficult, time consuming, and costly to transport goods over land. The Grand Canal linked the north with the south, and when the south quickly grew to be the most productive in crops, the Grand Canal became essential to move the goods between regions. During the T'ang dynasty, trade in silkworms and tea flourished as a result of easier access to regions made possible by the Grand Canal. Tea eventually spread to Japan during the ninth century and also to Korea. During the late T'ang and later Song dynasties, migration continued to flow southwards in search of new lands to cultivate.

Yangdi's Excesses

Yangdi conscripted thousands of peasants to work on lavish palace projects. Rebellions arose after a series of disastrous attempts to subjugate Korea. **Li Yuan** eventually assassinated the hated Yangdi and founded the T'ang dynasty.

The T'ang Dynasty

Li Yuan was of mixed Chinese and nomadic heritage, and allowed many Turkish nomads to enter the service of China and its armies, especially on the frontiers, where the T'ang rebuilt and strengthened the Great Wall. The T'ang held power in China for over three centuries until it collapsed in 907 c.e. China expanded greatly under the T'ang, conquered Tibet and forced the Koreans to pay tribute. The empire of the T'ang was even larger than that of the Han dynasty. The T'ang continued the efforts of the second Sui ruler Yangdi to revive Confucianism, and the **civil service examination system** grew more important. More officials entered government positions through this means than in the Han period. Nevertheless, hereditary connections were still important in the T'ang bureaucracy. Although the T'ang revived Confucianism, they continued to patronize Buddhists, who had continued to grow in influence. The notorious seventh/eighth-century **Empress Wu** was one of the most noteworthy patrons of Buddhists. The **Lungmen Buddhist caves** were milestones of T'ang artistry, and successfully introduced the Chinese to the art of sculpture. However, in the ninth century, the Chinese began to restrict the influence of Buddhism through a wave of persecutions. The influence of Buddhism gradually waned following this period, though it never ceased to exist.

During the T'ang dynasty, culture flourished in China. One of the favorite art forms of T'ang China reflected the revived trade along the Silk Road. The T'ang's success at conquering regions in central Asia led to the revival of trade along the ancient trading route. During the period of chaos and nomadic raids following the decline of the Han, trade had dwindled along the Silk Road. Now the T'ang transported their silks, paper, and porcelain to Islamic centers along the various routes of the Silk Road. Persian rugs and horses were among the commodities imported from the Islamic world.

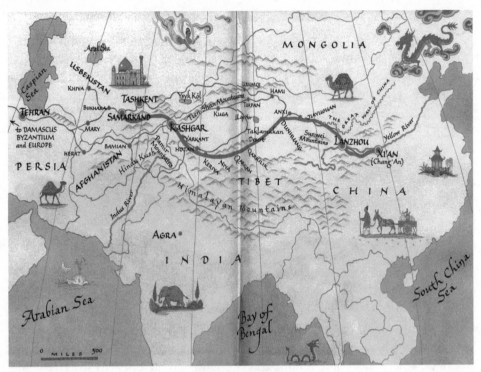

Silk Road Map

T'ang artisans produced beautiful blue, yellow, and gold ceramic horses and camels that are still highly valued by collectors today.

The T'ang also increased trade via sea routes, and imported spices and woods from Southeast Asia, while exporting manufactured goods. The Chinese junk made it possible for the Chinese to eventually dominate trade in the East Asian waters. Market centers arose in T'ang towns and paper money was first issued in the form of credit vouchers that merchants could carry from one location to another. More people in China lived in urban centers that arose than in any other area of the world. Largely, trade was responsible for this surge in urban life. **Changan** was the largest city in the world during this period.

The arts also flourished as seen in the poetry of Li Po, an important poet during the T'ang period who wrote about the beauty of nature.

The Song Dynasty

The **Kirhgiz** people overthrew the T'ang, and a new dynasty took their place. The **Song dynasty** ruled China from 960–1279 c.e. The Song were never as successful at uniting China as the T'ang had been, but they did continue to strengthen Confucianism and the civil service examination system at the expense of aristocratic families. The Grand Canal had encouraged further trade in

Chinese Junk Boat

tea and other goods during the Sui and T'ang dynasties. Tea had become such an important crop that the Song established a government monopoly on the tea trade and traded tea for horses from outlying regions, such as Mongolia and Tibet, where tea could not be easily cultivated.

Migration Patterns and the Song Dynasty

Nomadic migrations continued to pose a threat to the Chinese. The Khitan peoples from Manchuria formed the **Liao dynasty** in the tenth century in the north, which exacted tribute from the Song. In the eleventh century a new wave of nomadic peoples, the **Jurchen**, overthrew the Liao, established the **Jin Kingdom**, and again demanded tribute. The Song moved south and established a new capital at **Hangzhou**, where it survived until the thirteenth century as the Southern Song. Culture flourished during this period, but again, waves of nomadic conquerors, this time in the form of the Mongols, ultimately defeated the Song.

Gender Issues: Changes in the Status of Women

During the late T'ang dynasty, foot binding was introduced in China and became common practice during the Song dynasty. Foot binding was a painful process that involved breaking the bones of the feet and then binding the feet to ensure that they did not grow to normal adult proportions. Foot binding restricted the ability of a woman to walk or to work, and so led her to greater confinement to the household, especially for upper-class women. The lower classes, who had to work to survive, did not embrace foot binding as quickly. For the higher classes, having feet in the "lotus petal" shape was considered beautiful and became a condition without which a successful marriage could not be negotiated.

Central Asia and the Rise of the Mongols

Central Asia is largely made up of grasslands that are not easily cultivated. The peoples that arose there were nomadic and forced to trade with agricultural societies for what they needed or to simply take what they wanted through raids. Several groups of Turks dominated Central Asia and had been engaged in massive migration movements for centuries. We have already seen, for example, the success of the Afghan-based Turks under Mahmud Ghazni. Other groups of nomads developed mixed cultures that built cities after contact with China, such as the **Jurchens** and **Khitans**.

Another important group of people in the Central Asian grasslands were the **Mongols**, who moved their animals from place to place in search of pastures while carrying their yurts, or tents, with them. The Mongols lived in tribes and clans and marriage could not occur within the same clan. Competition for resources was a constant threat to peace. Mongols learned to become excellent warriors on horseback, often riding for days without stopping. They also learned to use the compound bow.

Two factors contributed to the rise of the Mongols. First, their pastureland began to disappear following a drop in the annual temperature in the twelfth century. Second, Temujin finally united the Mongols.

Temujin was born in the 1160s. He was destined to become one of the world's greatest conquerors. Although he spent a portion of his childhood as a refugee in the wilderness following his father's assassination, he won a number of victories against rival Mongol chieftains and in 1206 he was elected Genghis Khan or "universal ruler" of the Mongol tribes at a kuriltai, or meeting of all of the Mongol chieftains. Genghis borrowed the written script of the Uighur Turks and the Mongol language was first written down and used to record laws. Ghengis forced the Jurchens to pay tribute, and then moved on to China in 1212–1213. Again, he sought tribute and quickly moved on to this next conquest, the Islamic Khwarazm Empire of Persia. In 1226, Ghenghis returned to demolish the Tangut state of the Xia, in what is northwest China today.

Genghis Khan's army was not overwhelmingly large, but he and his forces unleashed terror in the hearts of those who fought them. Mongol warriors wore silk shirts, so that arrows entering their bodies could be easily removed without further tearing of the flesh. They traveled easily because their portable, round felt tents, or yurts, could quickly be disassembled and assembled. They were expert military tacticians.

Conquests Under Ogedai

After the death of Genghis Khan, his principal wife divided his empire amongst his sons in accordance with the Khan's wishes. Various khanates were carved from his territory and ruled by the sons of Genghis Khan, including the **Chaghadai Khanate in Central Asia**, whose capital was **Samarkand**; the **Khanate of Persia** with its capital at **Baghdad**; **Khanate of Kipchak**, or the **Golden Horde**, which, under one of Genghis's grandsons, dominated Russia.

Ogedai, Temujin's third son, was elected universal Khan, but was not as able a leader as his father had been. The capital of the Mongol empire under Genghis Khan and his son Ogedai was **Karakorum**; today it is located in Outer Mongolia. Under Ogedai, the Mongol Hordes conquered Moscow and Kievan Russia and went deeper into Europe to threaten cities in Poland and Hungary. Following Ogedai's death, his son led the assault on the Islamic world, culminating in the defeat of the Abbasids in Baghdad in 1258 c.e. Mongols also conquered Korea, but stopped short of China. Meanwhile, the Delhi Sultanate and the Mamluks had stopped Mongol advances on India and Egypt, respectively.

Kublai Khan, the grandson of Genghis Khan, continued the wave of conquests by attacking the Song dynasty in China beginning in the 1260s. Kublai captured surrounding regions, such as Vietnam, in an effort to cut off the Song, but found it necessary to attack their river cities to finally topple them. The Mongols massacred virtually the entire population of Changzhou, and finally defeated them in 1276 c.e. Kublai twice attempted to invade Japan, and twice failed. In China, however, the story was very different.

The Yuan Dynasty

Kublai Khan established the **Yuan dynasty**. His capital was **Khanbaliq**, the city of the Khan. This city would later be known as **Beijing** or **Peking**, the northern capital. Kublai Khan extended the Grand Canal of the Sui to the capital city Khanbaliq, which was twenty-four miles in diameter. The Italian wanderer Marco Polo lived there during his visit to Asia, and wrote of its magnificence. Although his account has been subjected to doubt in many respects, his tales of the grandeur of China under Kublai Khan earned him the nickname "il millione," as Italians believed his stories were too remarkable to be true and were, therefore, just a million tall tales.

The Yuan dynasty treated the Chinese with contempt and relegated them to lower status than Mongols and other non-Chinese foreigners. Although the Mongol rulers brought in artisans from throughout the Mongol realm, their contempt for the Chinese had the effect of diminishing Chinese interest in other cultures. While Kublai did employ some Confucian scholars, he did not make use of the civil service examination system for selecting his officials, which ultimately decreased the influence of Confucians.

Gender Issues

Mongol women were kept strictly separate from the Chinese, and Mongol women also often fought on horseback. Not surprisingly, Mongol women had rights to their property and control within their own households. Mongols also did not adopt the practice of foot binding, which so limited the roles of Chinese women. The wife of Kublai Khan had tremendous influence and power; on two separate occasions Empress Dowagers ruled the Mongol empire during interims between the death of the Great Khan and the time when the next Great Khan was selected. Mongol women were often seen in public. Muslim travelers, such as Ibn Battuta, were often alarmed at the status of women in the Mongol world.

The Collapse of the Yuan

Yuan rule collapsed in the 1340s when a poor peasant named **Zhu Yuanxhang** led a rebellion that toppled the fabulous Mongol dynasty. Zhu's dynasty would be called the **Ming**, or the "brilliant" dynasty, and it ruled China from 1369–1644.

Cultural Exchange and the Mongols

The Mongols conquered so many regions one would naturally expect a great deal of cultural exchange. Mongols often employed the very people they had captured as they assaulted new targets, and often adopted their military tactics. For example, they made use of Chinese catapults until they discovered that the Turks in Afghanistan made better machines. Mongols also borrowed from China projectiles with gunpowder and exploding arrows. Yuan China benefited greatly from the presence of Muslim doctors and also from Persian astronomers. Mongols under Kublai Khan employed many Uighur Turks as translators and officials. The Mongols were profoundly interested in other religions, but the religion that benefited the most from Mongol rule was Islam, which made great progress in Chinese Central Asia, for example, which had previously been Buddhist. The rulers of the Il-Khanate also converted to Islam.

Trade and the Mongols

The Mongols had both a positive and negative impact on trade. Trade was important to them and Mongol rulers tended to protect trading routes in their realms. It became safer for merchants to travel land routes, and there were routes from the Mediterranean to China. One of the beneficiaries of the increased safety of travel was Marco Polo. On the other hand, the khanates often were at war with one another, which could just as often disrupt trade. One aspect of trade that was not much affected by the Mongol conquests was the thriving Indian Ocean trade, which was extensively developed during the Islamic period. As we have seen in earlier chapters, trade via sea was much more practical than over land, and the sea trade was much more voluminous that anything that went over land. Mongol conquests did not threaten this trade nor change it in any appreciable way.

During the Age of Exploration, there was a tremendous exchange of biological materials. The Mongols may have unwittingly transmitted the Black Plague. As they rode through desert areas like the Gobi Desert, they came into contact with rodents, which carried the fleas that also carried the plague. When Mongols laid siege to the Black Sea port of Kaffa and threw infected bodies over the walls with their catapults, the Genoese sailors there fled, and then took the plague with them to Sicily, from whence it spread throughout Europe. The Black Death devastated the population of Europe.

Mongol Impact on Conquered Areas

The Mongols succeeded in reuniting China and in expanding its frontiers. Since the Yuan dynasty, China has never been fragmented as it was following the decline of the Han.

Russians, on the other hand, have always seen the long-term impact of the Mongol conquest in very negative terms, often blaming the backwardness of Russian society on the Mongols. However, Moscow was not an important center of civilization prior to the arrival of the Mongols, and it quickly rose to prominence.

The conquest of Persia, or modern Iran, also had long-term implications. The essential outlines of Mongol Persia were the same of those of modern Iran, and Persian became the dominant language, replacing Arabic.

Tamerlane's Empire

The fourteenth-century ruler **Tamerlane**, a Turk of Mongol descent, founded his empire on the ruins of the Mongol empire begun by Genghis Khan. He took power in 1369 C.E. in Samarkand, which became the capital of his empire. Alexander the Great had once occupied the great city, and it had also been a Mongol outpost. Tamerlane conquered the region east of the Caspian Sea, Mesopotamia, and Baghdad. He entered northern India, where he massacred 100,000 Hindu prisoners before entering Delhi. He then turned to Anatolia, and led his armies to the Bosphorus strait before his death in 1405 C.E. While Tamerlane used the brutal methods of the Mongols and massacred those who resisted him, the impact of his conquests was brief. While the Mongol conquest left a lasting influence on those regions they conquered, the same cannot be said of Tamerlane.

EAST ASIA

Korea

The **Koryo** dynasty arose in the tenth century C.E. and the name of the dynasty is the origin of the modern word "Korea." In earlier times, previous rulers were strongly tied to T'ang China and, although the Koryo were more independently minded than their predecessors, they still copied the Chinese system of civil service examinations and bureaucratic structures. Zen and Tendai Buddhism were important influences here, as they were in China and also in Japan. Slavery was an important and noticeable aspect of this society, and in this way, the Koryo departed from their Chinese models. A person could serve in the government only if for eight generations there was no evidence of slavery or lowborn status in their family. The Mongol conquest of the Koryo left long-term effects, as the kings were taken in captivity to Yuan China and intermarried with Mongols. When Mongol rule declined in China, it also weakened in the Koryo realm. When the Ming in China overthrew the Mongol, a general took advantage of the instability and overthrew the Koryo and established the **Yi dynasty**.

Japan

Prince **Shotoku Taishi** (572–622 C.E.) sent a mission to Chang-an in China to learn more about Tang-style administration. Shotoku then launched a series of reforms designed to limit the power of the hereditary nobility. In the seventeen article constitution, he designed a merit system for promotion in the government and created a centralized government around the person of the ruler. After his death, more reforms were passed, including the famous **Taika** or "great change" reforms of the seventh century C.E. The Taika reforms established a Grand Council of State and divided Japan into administrative districts.

The **Fujiwara clan** rose to prominence after the death of Prince Shotoku. Their position was primarily due to intermarriage with the royal family; while the Yamato emperor ruled in name, the Fujiwara often ruled in fact. In 710 C.E. the Japanese built Nara, a capital modeled on the Chinese city Chang-an. In 794 C.E. the emperor moved the capital to **Heian**, where modern **Kyoto** is located. The Fujiwara continued to control affairs during the Heian period. One of the most famous chronicles of court life during the Heian period was Lady Murasaki's *The Tale of Genji*. Ironically, women had few rights in Heian Japan, but a woman who served in the imperial court wrote the most famous record of its culture and customs. Genji illustrates the norms for men and women. Courtship was often conducted through exchange of sophisticated poetry; the more beautiful the poetry written, the more attractive the suitor. Women were confined to their households, and their suitors often did not so much as look upon them until they were in their bedchambers.

Japanese culture was very influenced by its native religion, **Shinto**, and Buddhism, which arrived in Japan from China in the sixth century C.E. The two most important sects of Buddhism in Japan were Pure Land and Zen Buddhism.

In the twelfth century C.E., **Minamoto Yoritomo** defeated several rivals and established the **Kamakura Shogunate**. He created the bakufu or "tent" system of government led by a shogun, who was the most powerful military leader. Although the emperor continued to have authority in name, the shogun had actual authority. In 1266 the Yuan emperor Kubilai Khan demanded tribute from Japan. The Japanese refused, and the Khan sent a force of 30,000 to invade the islands. The Yuan invasion was thwarted by bad weather, but in 1281 C.E. they returned with a force of 150,000. The Japanese fought them for two months, but eventually a "divine wind" or kamikaze destroyed the invading fleet. The event had a profound effect on Japanese national memory, and the term kamikaze would be used for the suicide bombers in World War II. No foreign invader would threaten Japan again until World War II, when the Americans dropped the atomic bombs on Hiroshima and Nagasaki in 1945. The Kamakura Shogunate spent large amounts of money to defend Japan from the invaders and, although it did not collapse, it was seriously weakened by the invasions. On a more positive note, however, scholars often cite the defense of Japan as one of the first instances of national unity.

In 1333 the **Ashikaga** overthrew the Kamakura and established a shogun in Kyoto. The unity of Japan was seriously threatened during the Onin War from 1467–1477; this period parallels the period of Warring States in ancient China. During this period, the samurai played an important role on the battlefield. According to their code of Bushido, loyalty was important above all else. During the reign of Hideoshi in the sixteenth century, only the samurai were allowed to carry weapons and have last names. The fighting skill of the samurai was strengthened by the meditative techniques of Zen Buddhism, while their notion of their sword as their soul was influenced by the Shinto veneration of nature.

Review Questions

1. In Southeast Asia, which area was NOT affected by Indian influence?

   (A) Funan

   (B) North Vietnam

   (C) Thailand

   (D) Burma

2. Of the following powers in India, which were the most tolerant of religious diversity?

   (A) The Delhi Sultanate

   (B) The Gupta Dynasty

   (C) Tamerlane

   (D) The Chola Kingdom

3. Which of the following areas was NOT influenced by China?

   (A) Koryo

   (B) Thailand

   (C) North Vietnam

   (D) Funan

4. Which of the following is NOT a true statement about comparisons between Western European Imperialism in the nineteenth century and Mongol expansion in this period?

   (A) Mongol civilization did not seem to be "superior" to those regions it conquered in the twelfth century.

   (B) The Mongols were engaged in capitalistic enterprise, as were the western Europeans.

   (C) The Mongol civilization was vastly superior to those areas it conquered, such as China and the Abbasid caliphate.

   (D) Both (B) and (C).

5. Which of the following is a difference between the feudal society of Japan and that of medieval western Europe?

   (A) The samurai were paid in rice while European knights received grants of land.

   (B) Samurai fought in groups while knights fought in single combat.

   (C) Daiymo often did not live on their *shoen*, while European knights generally resided on their manorial estates.

   (D) Both (A) and (C).

6. Which is true of the Mongol impact on trade?

   (A) Their conquests did not disrupt the trade via the Indian Ocean.

   (B) Conflicts between the khanates disrupted trade routes.

   (C) The Mongols failed to protect trade routes, as they were more interested in nomadic wanderings.

   (D) Both (A) and (B).

7. In general, under which rulers/period did women have greater privileges?

   (A) The Delhi Sultanate

   (B) The Mongols in Yuan China

   (C) The Heian period in Japan

   (D) Mahmud Ghazni

8. Foot binding was first introduced during the

   (A) Yuan Dynasty

   (B) Song Dynasty

   (C) Sui Dynasty

   (D) T'ang Dynasty

9. The transportation of crops and goods between south China and north China was facilitated by the

   (A) journey of Marco Polo.

   (B) collapse of the Abbasid caliphate.

   (C) construction of the Grand Canal.

   (D) Japanese kamikaze.

10. Which is the most correct description of the impact of the Mongols?

   (A) Their conquests exceeded the impact of the Voyages of Exploration in terms of cultural and biological exchange.

   (B) Their conquests resulted in cultural and limited biological exchanges, but not on the scale of the Columbian Exchange following the European Voyages of Exploration.

(C) Their failure to penetrate western Europe may have allowed it to develop.

(D) Both (B) and (C).

Answers

1. (B)	4. (D)	7. (B)	10. (D)
2. (B)	5. (D)	8. (D)	
3. (D)	6. (D)	9. (C)	

Chapter 14

THE WESTERN MIDDLE AGES

KEY TERMS

Monasticism
Eremitical monasticism
Cenobitic monasticism
St. Benedict of Nursia
Justinian
Battle of Manzikert
Merovingian dynasty
Pepin the Short
Battle of Poitiers (Tours)
Charlemagne
Carolingian Renaissance
Feudal society
Manorialism
Treaty of Verdun
Battle of Hastings
Magna Carta
Henry II
Thomas à Becket
Philip II Augustus
Ottonians
Investiture Controversy
Gregory VII

Concordat of Worms
Investiture Controversy
Cluny
Citêaux and the Cistercians
Twelfth-Century Renaissance
Peter Abelard
Thomas Aquinas
Hanseatic League
Hildegard of Bingen
Heloise
Urban II
Saladin
Battle of Hattin
Conquest of Jerusalem
People's Crusade
First Crusade
Third Crusade
Fourth Crusade
Richard the Lionheart
Scholasticism
Gothic style
Norsemen

DATING THE MIDDLE AGES

The Middle Ages span over one thousand years of European history. Although different scholars cite different dates for the beginning and the end of the Middle Ages, the most commonly accepted date for the beginning of the medieval period is **476** C.E., the date the last Roman emperor of the West, Romulus Augustulus, was deposed. From this point of view, the medieval period is characterized by the disappearance of Roman city life until its revival in the eleventh century, and the development of a localized economy on vast manorial estates. Further, the level of literacy and educational achievements dropped in the wake of the collapse of the Roman Empire in the West. During the medieval period, the Church preserved literacy, especially in monastic communities where monks devoted a third of their day to studying and copying the Scriptures and other writings of the Church fathers.

Another commonly cited date for the beginning of the Middle Ages is **529** C.E., the date of the foundation of St. Benedict's monastery of Monte Casino, about 80 miles south of Rome. In the medieval period, Monte Casino was the center of Benedictine monasticism and continues to be so today. The emphasis of the Benedictine monks and nuns on "Ora et labora," or "Prayer and Work" preserved the legacy of Greco-Roman culture and transformed the economy of Europe. In the same year as Benedict founded Monte Casino, the Byzantine emperor Justinian closed the last of the pagan schools. The events in the year 529 C.E. symbolize the beginning of the Christian era in Europe, and for this reason, the Middle Ages are commonly also known as "The Age of Faith." The medieval mind focused on the sacred as opposed to the profane.

The date given as the end of the Middle Ages is also a matter of great debate among historians. The year **1453** C.E. is the most commonly accepted date, as this was the year that the Islamic Seljuk Turks conquered Constantinople, the capital of the eastern Roman Empire. In 1453 the last vestiges of Roman Imperial power collapsed. Under Muslim rule, the beautiful Hagia Sophia basilica, for centuries a symbol of Greek Orthodox Christianity, became an Islamic mosque. Many historians argue, however, that the transition from the medieval period to the early modern era cannot be pinned to a decisive date or event. Interpretations of the differences between the medieval and early modern era vary widely.

THE HISTORIOGRAPHY OF THE MEDIEVAL PERIOD

Not only are the dates of the medieval period a matter of great debate, but interpretations of the period are also varied. In the fourteenth century, the

Renaissance humanist **Francesco Petrarca (Petrarch)** referred to the Middle Ages as "the Dark Ages." Petrarch, as did many humanists, valued the inner life of the individual; he found awareness of individual growth to be lacking in several respects in the writings of the medievals. The later humanist **Erasmus of Rotterdam**, who poked fun at the convoluted logic of scholastic thought, further developed Petrarch's description of the medieval period as intellectually dark. Erasmus believed that the medieval scholastic theology failed to speak to the individual in terms that would impact his or her growth. The Renaissance humanists saw their own era as a new beginning, and as a radically different era from the medieval period before. Many scholars, including the nineteenth-century scholar Jacob Burckhardt, argue that the Renaissance was the first modern period, while the medieval period was a time of vast intellectual stupor.

THE BYZANTINE EMPIRE DURING THE EARLY MIDDLE AGES

While the western Roman world collapsed in the fifth century C.E., the eastern Roman world remained intact. The eastern Roman world was known as Byzantium, after the original name of a Greek colony that became the eastern capital of the Roman Empire. Constantine, the first Christian emperor of Rome, later renamed the city Constantinople. Constantinople was one of the most important cities in the world and in the tenth century C.E. it was the greatest city in the Christian world. Constantinople was the center of a vast network of international trading routes. Despite the importance of trade, however, merchants did not have high social status in the Byzantine world. Most merchants engaged in trade were Muslim, Jewish, or Italian, while the highest ranking members of Byzantine society were aristocrats whose basis of wealth was land.

During the sixth century C.E., the emperor **Justinian** attempted to reconquer the western Roman world. His general **Belisarius** defeated the Vandals in North Africa, and soon thereafter defeated the **Ostrogoths**, who had taken the Italian peninsula. By 552 C.E., Justinian had reconquered Spain, North Africa, and parts of Italy. General Belisarius took Ravenna in 540 C.E., and a church was built there commemorating Justinian's achievements. At Ravenna he is shown with a halo, suggesting his role as the supreme protector of the Church. Justinian married a former actress, **Theodora**, who played an important role in the creation of laws. At that time, being an actress was considered a despicable profession akin to prostitution, but Theodora managed to wield considerable power. In fact, most of Justinian's accomplishments as a ruler occurred during her lifetime. At Ravenna, Theodora is also depicted in an important position.

Justinian never managed to fully recapture the old outlines of Rome in the west, and his conquests were lost shortly after his death. One of Justinian's major achievements was the revision of Roman law in the Corpus Iuris Civilis or Body of Civil Law. Justinian also codified the Digest, a collection of imperial decrees. His codification of Roman law was the basis for law in the Byzantine Empire until its collapse in 1453 C.E. Justinian also built the Hagia Sophia or the Church of the Holy Wisdom. This church reflects the importance of religion for the Byzantines. Icons played a powerful role in the Greek Orthodox religion, and this image of Christ Pantocrator from the interior of the main dome was one of the most famous images of the Christ.

In general, the Byzantines did not tolerate divergent views of Christianity, and persecuted heretical sects such as the Monophosites, who believed in a single divine nature of Christ, and the Nestorians, who questioned whether the mother of Jesus, Mary, should be referred to as the Mother of God rather than simply as the mother of the human Jesus. Byzantines also persecuted Jews, especially during the reign of Emperor Heraclius, who insisted on forcible conversions to Christianity.

After Justinian's death, the Byzantines had to fight off the Persians and the Slavs; neither of these threats was as serious as that posed by the converts to Islam, who defeated the Byzantines at Yarmuk in 636 C.E. The Muslims took Syria and Palestine from Byzantium. As the Muslims threatened the frontiers of Byzantium, a controversy over the use of images or icons broke out. Muslims forbade the use of images in religious art, and many people began to wonder whether the use of images in art had led to the defeat of the Byzantines. During the **Iconoclastic controversy**, the Byzantine emperor attempted to abolish all images; the Byzantine people reacted violently, and eventually the emperor was forced to recant and once again allow the production of icons. The Iconoclastic controversy, however, separated the Greek Orthodox world from the Roman Catholic world and some scholars argue it laid the groundwork for the alliance of the Bishop of Rome with the Franks. Rome no longer trusted the Eastern Patriarch and the Eastern Church. While Byzantine influence waned in Italy, for example, and in Western Europe, Byzantine missionaries helped to convert Russia and other Slavic areas.

Medieval Russia and Byzantine Influence

Russian Queen **Olga** visited Constantinople around 957 C.E. and was converted to Christianity. Although she requested missionaries from the German ruler Otto I, most of Russia remained rooted in its pagan traditions. Her brutal grandson **Vladimir**, however, adopted Christianity largely out of political motives. Basil II, ruler of Byzantium from 976–1025 C.E., was having difficulty managing various rebellions, and he appealed for help to the Russian King Vladimir. Although Vladimir already had several wives and at least eight hundred concubines, he demanded the hand of the emperor's sister, Anna, and also agreed to convert to Christianity. He later repudiated his pagan wives, and set upon abolishing paganism from Russia. Vladimir ordered the chief deity of the pagans, Perun, thrown in the River Dnieper; upon his command, thousands of Russians were baptized in the same river.

Eastern Europe

The native people, the **Slavs**, of Eastern Europe suffered from the migrations of Asiatic nomads, such as the Huns, Bulgars, Avars, and Magyars. The Slavs were once a single group of people, but they later settled in western, southern, and eastern Europe forming three distinct groups of people. The western Slavs became the Polish and Bohemian kingdoms. By the tenth century C.E., missionaries from Germany had converted both groups to Christianity. This group of Slavs adopted Roman Catholic Christianity. The southern Slavs, on the other hand, were more influenced by Greek Orthodox Christianity. Cyril and Methodius, two Byzantine missionaries who were brothers, converted the Moravians in the ninth century C.E. The Serbs converted to Greek Orthodox Christianity, as did the Bulgarians, who later conquered the Balkan peninsula. The Croats, on the other hand, converted to Roman Catholicism. The eastern Slavs settled in the region where the modern Ukraine and Russia are located. The Vikings called the eastern Slavs "the Rus," and this is the origin of the modern name of Russia. Hungary was not a Slavic nation, but it adopted Christianity after the tenth century C.E.

WESTERN EUROPE IN THE EARLY MIDDLE AGES

Christian Monasticism

When the Roman Empire in the West collapsed, it was the Church that filled the vacuum. The early Church in Europe had been organized along the same lines as the Roman Empire. The dioceses and archdioceses of the Church had been modeled after the same structures in the empire. Christianity was often spread by wandering monks and nuns. Monasticism flourished in the age following Constantine's legalization of Christianity, and many foundations arose around the Nile River Valley in Egypt. Monasticism then gradually spread throughout Europe.

The Desert Hermits and Eremitical Monasticism

Monasticism was an important social, economic, and religious force in the Middle Ages. The word "monasticism" is derived from the Greek word "monos," meaning single or alone. The earliest form of the monastic life was in the desert around the Nile River in Egypt, and was inspired by the meditative life of Christ himself in the desert. As Christ had no wife or permanent dwelling, so early desert hermits gave up the world of men in favor of the life of prayer. St. Anthony the Great spent twenty years in a cave along the Nile battling his inner demons, and so influenced his age that it was said the desert literally became a city teeming with monks. The lifestyle lived by Anthony is called **"eremitical,"** from the Greek word "eremos," meaning "empty or desolate," which was in turn the basis of the noun "eremia," meaning "desert." The desert lifestyle was a very disciplined lifestyle of prayer and fasting, and this discipline of the body and spirit is known as asceticism. John Cassian, a monk who spent several years in the great desert foundation of Scete along the Nile and who traveled widely through the great foundations of the East, transmitted the wisdom of the desert hermits to Europe. His conversations with the desert monks were preserved and spread throughout Europe in his conferences.

Cenobitic Monasticism

St. Basil of Caesarea in the East was the first to question the isolation of the eremitical life and its consistency with the Christian belief in love of one's neighbor. Basil advocated a form of monasticism called the **cenobitic lifestyle**. It is based on the "rule" of community, and the idea of progressing in holiness through one's relationship with others. Another famous founder of cenobitic communities was Pachomius, whose monastery in Thebes along the Nile had over 1,300 men. Although the eremitical lifestyle was the most influential form of monasticism along the Nile after the legalization of Christianity, in medieval Europe cenobitic monasticism was more common.

Benedict of Nursia

The cenobitic monastic life in Europe was largely modeled on the Rule of **St. Benedict of Nursia**. Benedict was born in 480 C.E. in Nursia, Italy, in the midst of the collapse of the western Roman empire. He studied in Rome and found it decadent. As a result, he sought out a spiritual teacher and later became a hermit at Subiaco whose holiness attracted followers. Benedict eventually founded the monastery of **Monte Casino** in 529 C.E., and it became a symbol of the Christian era.

The success of Monte Casino was largely due to Benedict's genius as expressed in his Rule for monastic life. Although much of it is not original and resembles an earlier document known as the Rule of the Master, Benedict tempered the master's harshness and adapted the regulations found in it to individual circumstances. **Benedictine monks** take vows of obedience, stability, and conversion to the monastic way. The Benedictine day involved work, study, and prayer. The ethos of work, study, and prayer colored all of medieval European culture. Through work Benedictines practiced stewardship of the earth, and they were instrumental in reclaiming vast amounts of wasteland in Europe as well as in developing new crops. Through study, the Benedictines preserved many ancient Greek and Roman manuscripts as they copied texts for one-third of their day.

According to tradition, Benedict's twin sister **Scholastica** lived at the foot of Monte Casino. Scholastica is the patroness of modern Benedictine nuns. Gregory the Great's biography of Benedict painted him as a new hero for a new age. Many Benedictines helped to convert Europe, including the monk Boniface and the nun Leoba and several of her nuns, who came from England and converted the Germans. These Benedictines and many others like them carried on the legacy of Benedict and Scholastica.

Celtic Monks

In Europe before the reign of Charlemagne, monasteries often mixed parts of the Rule of St. Benedict with that of **Columbanus**, an Irish monk whose travels established many of the most famous houses in Europe such as Bobbio. Irish monks, who lived a very ascetic lifestyle not based on the Rule of St. Benedict, traveled widely and were very instrumental in the spread of monasticism and in Christianizing the pagan world. Irish monks from Iona Christianized Northumbria in England. Lindisfarne is a famous monastery in Northumbria founded by Irish monks, and these monks produced the Lindisfarne Gospels.

THE DEVELOPMENT OF THE MEDIEVAL WESTERN EUROPEAN KINGDOMS

Anglo-Saxon England

The Romans withdrew from Britain in the fifth century C.E.; in the chaos that surrounded the Roman withdrawal, a hero emerged who in later times was known as **King Arthur**. Many sources do not even refer to this hero as Arthur, but rather as **Ambrosius Aurelianus**. It is doubtful whether anyone ever lived who did all the things legend credits to Arthur, but he become the symbol of the English monarchy in later centuries.

During the time of "Arthur," **Saxons** began to arrive in Britain, and to settle in Kent, Wessex, and other kingdoms, and to merge their culture with that of the native population, the Britons. Another group of people, the **Picts**, lived in the region now known as Scotland. Roman influences were felt once again in the sixth century C.E., when **Pope Gregory the Great** decided to send a mission to

Christianize the "barbarians" in Britain. Roman Catholicism arrived in Britain in 596 C.E. when Augustine of Canterbury landed in Kent and later converted its royal family. Roman Christianity spread to Northumbria, where the missionary Paulinus converted King Edwin. English monks and nuns helped to spread Christianity to the continent. The missionary Boniface traveled to Germany, where he was aided by the nun Leoba and countless other women.

Women had considerable power in the Anglo-Saxon Church, and they very often presided as heads of double monasteries for men and women. The nun Hild led the double monastery at Whitby and was one of many powerful women in this era. Among the important monastic foundations of Anglo-Saxon England were Jarrow and Monkwearmoth, where the **Venerable Bede** spent his life. Bede was the first historian to use the Anno Domini (AD) system of dating, and in the eighth century C.E. wrote a monumental *History of the English Church and Peoples*. His history chronicled the conflict between Roman and Celtic customs, particularly over the issue of dating Easter, and its eventual resolution at the Synod of Whitby. Before the Synod of Whitby, Celtic Christianity flourished in the northern regions of the island at Lindisfarne and on Iona, off the coast of Scotland.

The greatest Anglo-Saxon ruler was **Alfred the Great**. In the ninth century C.E., King Alfred defended Wessex and England from the Viking attacks. He had a number of important works translated from Latin into the Anglo-Saxon language.

The Franks

Germanic peoples in Europe who migrated into the old Roman Empire largely lived according to tribal and customary law. **Franks** decided legal matters through such customs as the ordeal. Powerful chieftains such as **Clovis** gained the loyalty of Frankish nobles. Franks often fought vicious blood feuds in their early history that weakened their kingdom. Later, they instituted the custom of paying the wergeld, a fine for damages based on the notion that a person has monetary worth. The wergeld was intended to put an end to the blood feuds, which often extended to the ninth degree of kinship. Another factor that helped the Frankish state to evolve was its conversion to Roman Catholicism.

The Franks and the Church

Despite the rapid progress of Christianity in the fourth century from a persecuted religion to the official state religion of Rome, in the following centuries the new religion spread slowly throughout the Western world. Many Romans remained pagani for decades and centuries after the Theodosian Code. After the fall of Roman power in the West, the barbarian kings, such as Clovis of the Franks, along with scores of Christian monks and nuns continued the conversion of

Europe. In 500 C.E. Clovis, founder of the **Merovingian dynasty** of the Franks, became the first barbarian to convert to Catholic Christianity. Other barbarian tribes, such as the Visigoths, had adopted Christianity, but followed the Arian heresy. Clovis's conversion, which was sealed through his marriage to the Christian princess Clotilda, was the beginning of an alliance between the Franks and the other strong power in Europe, the papacy.

Under the leadership of **Charles Martel**, mayor of the palace, the Franks defeated the Muslims at the **Battle of Tours (Poitiers)** in 732 C.E. This monumental victory was a turning point in European history; had Martel not defeated the Muslims, all of Europe might have been conquered. Many scholars have suggested that the need to fight the Muslims was one of the factors that prompted the creation of feudal society.

Martel's son, **Pepin the Short**, was later able to transform his role as mayor of the Palace into that of King of the Franks on the basis of his father's victory. While the barbarian **Lombards** besieged Rome, the pope turned to the Franks for military aid. In return for such aid, Pepin was anointed the king of the Franks by a papal legate. Pepin was not of royal blood, but even before Charles Martel, the Frankish kings had been inept, leaving the daily affairs of the kingdom to the mayor of the palace. When the papal legate anointed Pepin king through the approval of the pope, the suggestion was clearly made that papal approval could create a king even where there was no legitimate claim through blood. In return for this favor, Pepin carved out a tract of land across central Italy for the pope known as the **Donation of Pepin**. These estates would later be known as the **Papal States**, and would play a central role in Renaissance politics. Pepin forged a new dynasty known as the **Carolingian dynasty** after his son, Charlemagne.

Charlemagne and the Carolingian Renaissance

Charlemagne's Latin name was Carolus magnus, or Charles the Great, and by the time he died, he came close to reestablishing the frontiers of the Roman Empire in the West. The emperor Charlemagne continued to support the Church, through reform of the educational system for priests, Benedict of Aniane's reform of the monastic life which mandated the Rule of Benedict for all monasteries, and the forcible conversion of the Saxons in the ninth century. Charlemagne brought the monk Alcuin from Northumbria in England to help him in the reform of the clergy. Alcuin established a school at Aachen that revived the education of the priesthood and so addressed several issues of corruption in the Church. Alcuin and his assistants developed a new style of writing, Carolingian miniscule, that helped to preserve the writings of the Greeks and Romans. Many manuscripts were in such a poor state that they were virtually illegible and Alcuin's monks helped to restore many texts that otherwise would have been lost. The revival of learning during Charlemagne's era was known as the **Carolingian Renaissance**. Einhard wrote a biography of Charlemagne that describes him as a man with a boisterous personality, a great love of meat and wine, a great love of his "doves" or daughters, but above all else, a devotion to reforming the Church. His court at Aachen was a center of education and church reform.

Charlemagne united his realm through the use of the missi dominici, who were messengers sent to proclaim his laws and report back to him on events throughout the realm. Through his capitularies, Charlemagne enforced military obligations, the missi dominici system, and the reform of the Church.

The Campaigns Against the Basques and the "Song of Roland"

In 778 C.E. Charlemagne led an attack against the **Basques**, who were Christians, in northern Spain. During the campaign, his rear guard fell behind and was ambushed by the Basques. The leader of the rear guard was Count Roland, and the "Song of Roland," which was written several hundred years later, commemorates the defeat of these troops. Charlemagne would later successfully conquer the Spanish March, a strip of land that he used as a buffer zone between the Kingdom of the Franks and Muslim Spain.

The Saxons

Charlemagne led several campaigns against the pagan Saxons. The Franks found the Saxon custom of leaving their dead out on funeral pyres offensive, as Christianity taught that the body would be resurrected. Since animals often ate the dead Saxon bodies, they believed this practice was an affront to Christian teachings. Over a thirty-year period, Charlemagne tried forcibly to convert the Saxons, and after each assault, the Saxons reverted to paganism as soon as his men withdrew. When the Saxons destroyed one of Charlemagne's forces in 782 C.E., he ordered his men to behead 4,500 Saxons. In 785 C.E. the Saxon leader **Widukind** surrendered and converted to Christianity, and thereafter, Charlemagne made the relapse into paganism a crime against the state. He fortified his conquests by constructing a series of forts, endowing monasteries in Saxony, and deporting Saxons to Frankish areas while replacing them with Frankish nobles.

Conquest of Italy

Pepin had won control over large parts of Italy, but his conquests were already beginning to fall back into Lombard hands. Although Charlemagne had married one of Lombard King Desiderius's daughters, he repudiated her, causing tension between the two kingdoms. The Lombard king began to support rebellious Frankish nobles against Charlemagne, leading him to attack the Lombards in 773 C.E. Charlemagne shuffled Desiderius off to a monastery, and proclaimed his own son king of Italy. Charlemagne, however, was for all intents and purposes the ruler of Italy. Charlemagne won the allegiance of the Roman Catholic pope in Rome for his victory; when in 799 C.E. the pope was attacked in the streets, Charlemagne once again sent a contingent of forces to the rescue.

Coronation in 800 C.E.

In 800 C.E., while attending Christmas mass in Rome, the pope approached Charlemagne from behind and crowned him emperor of Rome in the West. Although the act did not have Charlemagne's approval, nevertheless it supported the tradition begun with Pepin that the pope anointed the emperor and so created his right to rule. Charlemagne sought to overturn this precedent by ceding his power to his son Louis the Pious before his death, but Louis would later ask the pope to crown him officially and thus further solidified the fusion between the medieval Church and state.

The Viking Raids and the Collapse of the Carolingian Empire

Strong monarchs like Clovis and Charlemagne, who conquered large areas of land, had their empires dissolved as their sons quarreled and divided their father's holdings. Although Charlemagne had wanted to recreate the Roman Empire in the West, the **Treaty of Verdun** in 843 C.E. divided his empire between his three grandsons.

While his grandsons vied with each other for power, invaders ravaged Europe. Muslims invaded Sicily in 827 C.E. and controlled it for over a century. The Magyars traveled up the Danube River and plundered Bulgaria in 890 C.E. and in 906 C.E. ravaged Saxony. They raided Germany and other regions, and in 937 C.E. traveled as far inland as Rheims in France. The Scandinavians led by far the most threatening of these invasions from Norway, Denmark, and Sweden. One often hears these warriors referred to collectively as "**Vikings**," but in fact, they each had their own characteristics. Europeans called them the Norsemen, or Northmen. The Swedish Vikings ravaged Russia and established outposts at Novgorod, a medieval Russian capital, and at Kiev, another capital during the Middle Ages. The Swedish Vikings were called the Varangians in Russia, and their center at Kiev was the first true Russian state.

In 787 C.E. the Norwegian and Danish Vikings reached England, and later sacked and burned the monasteries of Lindisfarne and Jarrow. In 841 C.E. Vikings traveled up the Seine in France and ravaged Rouen. In 843 C.E. they went up the River Loire and destroyed Nantes and slaughtered all the inhabitants. By 857 C.E. they had plundered Bordeux, Tours, Orleans, Poitiers, and Paris. In 885 C.E. the Vikings returned to Paris and laid siege to the city for two years.

In England the situation was even worse. The Vikings captured East Anglia in 870 C.E. and in 876 C.E. occupied a good bit of Northumbria and then moved into Mercia in 877 C.E. Although King Alfred the Great successfully battled the Danes in Wessex, most of East Anglia, eastern Merica, and modern-day Lincolnshire and Yorkshire were controlled by the Vikings and became part of the Danelaw. Viking warriors reached Ireland in the ninth century C.E., and eventually attacked the famous monastery of Clonmacnois. The Vikings controlled the Isle of Man and the Scottish Isles until the mid-thirteenth century C.E.

In 874 C.E., the Vikings settled on Iceland, and then went on to Greenland. The king of Denmark ruled Iceland until 1944, and Greenland continues to be ruled by Denmark.

Feudal Society

During the reign of Charlemagne, a system of landholding and obligations began to develop in Europe that is often referred to as **feudalism**. Historians prefer the term **feudal society** to describe the complex social, economic, and political relationships that characterized Europe from the ninth century through the French Revolution, which began in 1789. Historians now avoid the term "feudalism," because it implies that there was a single set of features shared by all western European medieval cultures. This is anything but the case, as life in feudal France differed greatly from that of the feudal Germanies or other locations.

Feudal society developed out of a need for the king and other powerful figures to have the support of an army. Feudalism developed to provide a system of armed retainers for those who would have power.

Feudal society was based upon private contracts, and the historian Joseph Strayer has described medieval feudal society as having three main characteristics:

- public power was held in private hands
- fragmentation of power
- armed forces were used to obtain and keep power

In order to understand these three characteristics, one must first understand the system of **fief holding** and **investiture** during medieval times. Land was the basis of the feudal economy; with enough land, one could support oneself, a household, and retainers to protect one's holdings. Though there were coins and other forms of currency minted during the Middle Ages, the medieval economy was not based primarily on monetary exchange but rather on barter.

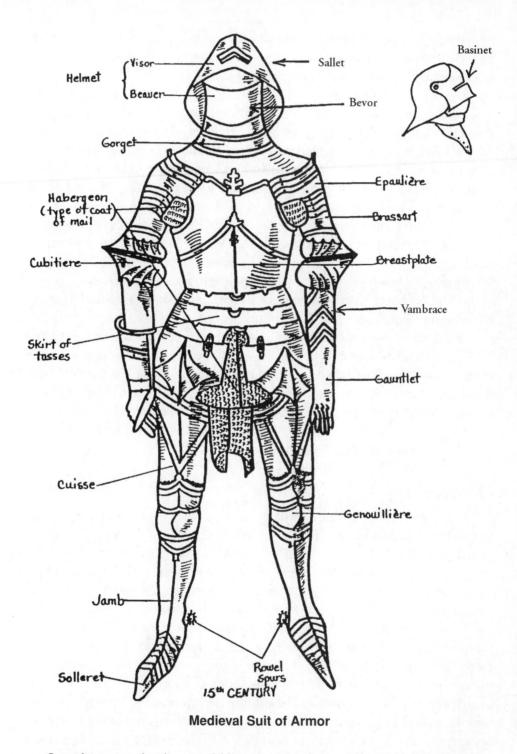

Helmet {
  Visor — Sallet
  Beaver — Bevor

Basinet

Gorget

Epaulière

Habergeon (type of coat) of mail

Brassart

Cubitiere

Breastplate

Vambrace

Skirt of tasses

Gauntlet

Cuisse

Genouillère

Jamb

Rowel Spurs

Solleret

15th CENTURY

Medieval Suit of Armor

In order to survive in a world based on warfare, a king or lord needed **vassals** or knights. In order to be a knight, one had to be wealthy. The training of a knight was lengthy and costly, and the suit of armor he wore was also very costly. A knight's suit of armor could take up to two years to make; it was made by hand and each link was riveted to other links. Further, the battle horse was a costly animal to acquire and to feed and train.

In order to obtain a vassal, then, a lord had to supply the vassal with the means to maintain his profession; in medieval times, that was only possible through the gift of a plot of land known as a fief. A knight or vassal was "invested" with his fief, in return for which he pledged **homage** (from the French word "l'homme" for man) to his lord. A vassal was required to fight when his lord demanded it and to ransom his lord if captured on the battlefield. The length of service varied, but by the twelfth century C.E. in many parts of Europe, a knight only had to serve his overlord for 40 days a year. Because vassals became powerful in their own right, a vassal had to seek the permission of the lord before his daughters could marry or before he himself could enter into such a contract. Marriage was often used as a tool to gain political, social, and economic power in the Middle Ages; hence, the right marriage could propel a vassal to greater status than his lord if allowed to occur unchecked.

The agreement between lord and vassal was of a personal nature, and often resulted in conflicts within the feudal system. For example, a knight might have more than one lord and those two lords might wage war on one another, both demanding the services of the knight. Such situations eventually created **liege homage**, where the vassal pledged homage to a particular lord above all others. A vassal of a lord might also divide the fief received and so create his own vassals. This process was called **subinfeudation**.

Manorialism

The way that these landed estates or fiefs were worked and governed is known as **manorialism**. Land was cultivated on vast manorial estates, which were divided into the lord's **demesne**, or area of land reserved for the lord, and tracts reserved for peasants. This system of dividing land into two or three units is known as the open field system. The open field system was modified to include three fields rather than two by the ninth century C.E. Whereas 50 percent of the land in earlier times went uncultivated, now much of that land became productive again. Crops were rotated on the cultivated land, and one-third of the land lay fallow every year to allow the land to recover needed nutrients. Also in the ninth century C.E. the introduction of a better iron plow known as the **moldboard** improved farming, as it allowed for deeper cultivation of fields. Agricultural yields increased markedly between the ninth and thirteenth centuries C.E. The diet of the Middle Ages was based primarily on bread and vegetables; peasants consumed very little meat. Crop yields were not high compared to modern standards, and there were often famines.

The **free peasants**, who were not bound to the land, and **serfs**, peasants who were bound to the land for life, worked the lord's demesne in return for their small tract of land. Peasants and serfs owed the lord a certain number of days of work per month on the land. They were required to return to the lord a percentage of the harvest on their lands. Peasants could take crops to the village mill for a fee to the lord. They had to seek the permission of the lord to marry their daughters. Peasants and serfs could not move up the social ladder easily during the Middle Ages. The social hierarchy was generally rigid and based upon status determined by birth. Peasants labored in return for the lord's protection. The system of agriculture and serfdom on the manorial estates created a very localized economy in the Middle Ages. Whereas the Roman Empire thrived on the city, the heart of medieval Europe was the manorial estate. By around 800 C.E., the age of Charlemagne, over one-half the population of Europe were serfs.

Women ran the households in medieval Europe and were active as laborers on the manorial estates. Further, many manorial estates were managed by aristocratic women whose husbands were off fighting campaigns.

THE CENTRAL MIDDLE AGES

Economic Changes of the Central Middle Ages

The Central Middle Ages were a period of revitalization of medieval Europe, from the economy, to town life, to trade, to intense religious reform movements. The invasions of the ninth century had destroyed much of the coastal areas of Europe and had disrupted government. The Carolingian Empire then disintegrated and was eventually divided among Charlemagne's heirs. By the eleventh century, though, an agricultural revolution had occurred, leading to increased production. The use of the horse collar, which was padded, contributed to more efficient agriculture, as horses could pull more weight than oxen. The use of horses in farming became more widespread after the twelfth century, and by the thirteenth century, horses were used to take goods to markets. Combined with the open field system of agriculture, production levels rose dramatically.

Increase in agricultural production contributed to a rise in population, and eventually city life was revived. Many of the first new cities had at one point been important Roman towns. A new class of **artisans** arose in the towns, mainly from peasant stock. Peasants who migrated to towns and lived there for one year and one day could earn their freedom from feudal restrictions. By the twelfth century, artisans organized themselves into **guilds**, which regulated their activities. Trade between areas also was revived, and cities such as Venice, located on the sea, played an important role. Venetian goods went to Constantinople and many other areas. Italian merchants traded in North Africa in places such as Cairo, in Damascus, and even went as far away as India and China. Flanders was an important outlet for English wool, an economic alliance that played a role in the Hundred Years' War. There was a thriving trade between Italian cities and Flanders, and fairs were set up in places along the way from one region to the other, such as France, to sell goods. Leagues of cities were formed, such as the **Hanseatic League** in the north, granting exemptions from tolls and other privileges. Hanseatic member cities had areas in other countries that served as trading bases known as factories. These changes that began in the eleventh century C.E. were an extremely important commercial revolution that saw the rise of a **money economy** and the creation of a system of credit and capitalistic enterprise in Europe. The economic changes also elevated the status of many peasants who otherwise would have been doomed to life on a manorial estate. Women also benefited from this shift, as many women engaged in business enterprises. The changes also began a shift away from the landed aristocracy of early medieval Europe towards a commercial class. This would peak in the Italian Renaissance.

THE EMERGENCE OF THE MEDIEVAL MONARCHIES

France and England

The medieval monarchies emerged during this chaotic period, and many grew out of the settlement of the Treaty of Verdun. The western section of Charlemagne's old territories became the kingdom of France. In 987 C.E., the last Carolingian ruler died, and the Frankish nobles selected Hugh Capet as king. The **Capetians**, however, never had the power of Charlemagne; although they were overlords of Normandy, Brittany, Burgundy, and Aquitaine, in reality they only controlled the small area of land around Paris known as the Ile-de-France. When William, Duke of Normandy, defeated Harold II of England at the **Battle of Hastings** and became King of England in 1066 C.E., the French king was literally overshadowed by his vassal who was now a king in his own right. William's successors, most notably **Henry II** of England, gained control of much of the territories surrounding the Ile-de-France; these regions were known as the **Angevin Kingdom**. However, his heirs were less successful in maintaining the empire. His son, **Richard I, the "Lionheart,"** spent more time away on crusade than he spent at home. Upon his death, his brother **John** lost the Angevin territories to the French **King Philip II Augustus** (1180–1223 C.E.). During John's foreign war with Philip, the English barons drew up a list of grievances that formed the basis of the **Magna Carta** (1215 C.E.), an agreement limiting the power of the English monarch and placing him under the rule of law. Several late rulers confirmed the Magna Carta but with modifications, and the document has played an important role in England's constitutional history. **Philip IV "The Fair"** (1285–1314 C.E.) fought **Pope Boniface VIII** for control over the French church. In the fourteenth century, the tensions between France and England erupted in the **Hundred Years' War**. Such tensions within feudal society make it all the more remarkable that vestiges of feudal society survived in France until the French revolution in 1789.

Germany in the Central Middle Ages

The eastern section of Charlemagne's territories became the basis for Germany, which would not exist in its modern form until the age of Bismarck in the nineteenth century. The German monarchs, like the Frankish monarchs before them, forged strong alliances with the papacy. **Otto I** was crowned Emperor of Rome in 962 C.E. by a pope he had selected himself, **Sylvester II**. German emperors appointed many bishops and archbishops and exerted strong control over the Church. In the eleventh century, the Church's desire to rid itself of imperial control erupted in the **Investiture Conflict**. The reforming pope **Gregory VII** issued a decree in 1075 C.E. against lay investiture, or the practice of the German emperor, his princes, and nobles of investing clergy with their offices. The Church insisted on the right to control selection of its bishops and archbishops. The German emperor Henry IV ignored the decree and continued to invest churchmen. Gregory VII excommunicated Henry; Henry, in turn, eventually appointed his own pope. The struggle waged on until the German nobles began to turn on Henry; in desperation, Henry went to Canossa where Gregory was in hiding and begged forgiveness while standing barefoot in the snow. The crisis was eventually resolved in 1122 by the **Concordat of Worms**, according to which the empire might still invest the cleric with his temporal benefice, while the Church alone might invest them with the symbols of their spiritual office. A similar crisis occurred in England in the twelfth century when **Thomas á Becket** collided with **Henry II** over control of Church affairs. Becket was martyred while at prayer in Canterbury Cathedral.

Later German emperors would experience some of the same difficulties with the Church. The Hohenstaufen ruler **Frederick I Barbarosa** (1152–1190 C.E.) attempted to build a holy empire by conquering northern Italy, but the Italian city-states defeated him in 1176 C.E. His idea of a "holy empire" was the origin of the description of the German empire as the Holy Roman Empire. As the witty Voltaire in the eighteenth century pointed out, the Holy Roman Empire was "neither holy, nor Roman, nor an empire." In fact, it was in many ways the papacy in Italy that conquered the Germans. **Innocent III**, the most powerful of all medieval popes, agreed to protect the four-year-old **King Frederick II** from rebellious Norman barons in Sicily. He guarded him for nine years and then continued to guide him as monarch in later life. Frederick II also tried to conquer northern Italy but was defeated. The German nobles developed considerable power over their own duchies, leaving the Holy Roman Emperor with little power of his own. The Protestant Reformation would further undermine the political structure of the Holy Roman Empire in the sixteenth century; in 1555 C.E. the **Peace of Augsburg** gave the German princes the power to choose either Catholicism or Lutheranism.

The Twelfth-Century Renaissance

In the eleventh century, the Pope Gregory VII began to centralize the Church, culminating in the Investiture Crisis, and scholars such as Gratian and Ivo of Chartres worked to reform canon law. Other scholars applied logic to theology, creating the movement known as **Scholasticism**. **St. Anselm** of the monastery of Bec in Normandy believed that reason (in the form of logic) and faith could be harmonized, and formulated one of the most famous proofs for the existence of God, which Kant later called the Ontological argument. Anselm also believed in the sola ratione method, according to which some truths of the faith might be proven solely through reason without reference to Scripture. However, Anselm continued to insist that faith provided a corrective context for reason and that applications of logic without reference to faith were unreliable. Those things proven through the sola ratione methodology must also be consistent with the faith in order to be reliable. Anselm's general approach has been called one of "faith seeking understanding;" that is, faith comes prior to reason and occupies a superior position in Anselm's system.

Peter Abelard first made his reputation as a logician who challenged powerful teachers of his era. In *Sic et Non* ("Yes and No"), he argued that contradictions within the Scriptures could be reconciled through the use of logic. Abelard worked in hermeneutics, or the exploration of language and its meanings, and many scholars regard him as a less profound theologian than St. Anselm. However, he generated tremendous controversy, as when he made the daring claim in his *Christian Theology,* that even God was constrained by logic. In his famous *Ethica* or *Know Thyself,* he argued that sin could only come from consent to what is against the will of God. Therefore, there could be no original sin, and those who crucified Christ were not guilty of sin. Abelard believed the Greeks and Hebrews had foreshadowed Trinitarian belief. Many of these teachings were considered heretical and Abelard was twice condemned for heresy, once at Soissons and again in 1140 at Sens.

Abelard also became controversial when his affair with **Heloise** became public. Heloise was renowned even in her youth as one of the most learned women of her time. Abelard was her tutor, and they eventually had a child together, Astrolabe. When Abelard married her but attempted to keep the marriage a secret, Heloise's uncle had Abelard castrated in revenge. Abelard and Heloise both entered monasteries, and Abelard wandered from monastery to monastery, frequently surrounded by controversy. He later founded the Paraclesis, a monastery that he later donated to Heloise and her sisters from the monastery of Argenteuil. Heloise was one of the most learned women of her time and became the most famous abbess of the Central Middle Ages. She and Abelard exchanged a famous series of letters that are known for their reliance on Greco-Roman pagan works as well as for what they illuminate about the inner feelings of the parties. Heloise's letters, in particular, are renowned for their polished rhetorical style. The letters are examples of what scholars have referred to as medieval humanism, and Abelard's story of his life is the first autobiography since Augustine of Hippo wrote the *Confessions*. Abelard was condemned for heresy for the second time at the council of Sens in 1140, two years before he died. He spent the last two years of his life in a Cluniac daughter house as a penitent monk. He remains today a symbol of the questioning intellect.

Abelard is representative of the new schools of the Central Middle Ages, which were not in monasteries, but in cathedrals. The **schoolmen**, or **scholastics**, were those who taught in such schools. Although Abelard was a controversial figure, his methods were also used by **Thomas Aquinas**, the most important scholastic theologian. Aquinas wrote the *Summa Theologia*, which contains his famous five ways of proving God's existence. In the early thirteenth century, the works of Aristotle had begun to be available in Europe. Although Abelard, for example, knew of a few of Aristotle's works, many were unknown to Europeans before Islamic scholars transmitted them to the West. These works created great controversy, as many of Aristotle's ideas conflicted with those of Christian teaching. Aquinas sought to harmonize the teachings of "The Philosopher," as Aristotle was known, with Christianity. As scholasticism evolved, it increasingly became associated with Aristotelian logic, and in the Italian Renaissance, many humanists moved away from scholasticism and its emphasis on dialectic and back towards an emphasis on rhetoric.

In the later Middle Ages, another educational revolution occurred as **universities** arose in Europe. This started around the thirteenth century C.E. and the University of Paris was among the most important. Although Abelard has no direct connection with the much later institution, many scholars credit Abelard with having laid the foundation for the University of Paris by attracting large numbers of students to Paris.

During the Central Middle Ages, the **Gothic style** of architecture first appeared at the abbey of St. Denis in France, the monastery Abelard entered after his affair with Heloise. The abbot Suger first developed the soaring ceilings, stained glass, and flying buttresses of the Gothic style to express his theology of light, the idea that light symbolized the divine presence. Gothic cathedrals such as Chartres and Notre Dame in France are designed to allow as much light in as possible, and their stained glass windows are justifiably famous throughout the world.

The Central Middle Ages were a period of tremendous intellectual vitality. While early scholastics such as Abelard developed new theological views, visionaries such as **Hildegard of Bingen** wrote prolifically. Hildegard was a Benedictine nun who founded the monastery of Eibingen. She claimed to experience visions since a young age, but only began to write about them in her forties. She wrote in many areas, including theology, music, and medicine. Her chant is some of the most beautiful ever written, and it requires a tremendous vocal range difficult for performers to achieve today. Hildegard's theology has often been described as evocative of a "feminine" sense of the divine. While other figures, such as Bernard of Clairvaux, also wrote of "Jesus as mother" and the maternal qualities of the godhead, Hildegard's illuminations and visions stand as an exceptionally fine statement of ideas that characterized her age. Hildegard was an outspoken critic of the papacy and a promoter of reform and was widely respected in Europe as the "sibyl of the Rhine."

The Cistercians

The spirit of reform also spread to monastic life. An early sign of monastic reform was the foundation in the tenth century C.E. of the Benedictine house of Cluny. In order to free the community from the increasing entanglements and obligations of feudal society, Cluny was subject only to the pope. The Cluniac life was largely devoted to liturgy, and the Cluniac Order, which grew to huge proportions, became fabulously wealthy through donations of nobles.

In fact the increasing wealth of the Cluniacs, as well as their emphasis on prayer to the exclusion of Benedict's insistence on manual labor, inspired other kinds of reforms. **Robert of Molesme**, a monk of St. Benedict, wanted to return to the pristine origins of the Benedictine Rule and left his position as abbot of Molesme for a wilderness retreat far from civilization. There he founded a new monastery, the novum monasterium, at Cîteaux. Eventually his followers expanded and formed a new order of monks who lived strictly according to the Rule of St. Benedict, the **Cistercians**. The Cistercians interpreted the Rule literally and revived the manual labor component of monastic life and forbade the use of gold and silver items in their churches. Their monks wore clothes made of harsh white wool to avoid the distraction of color and comfortable clothes, and so they became known as the "white monks," while Benedictines who were not Cistercians were known as the "black monks." So austere was Cistercian life that they avoided color in their stained glass windows, using only monochromatic shades of gray. As the Cistercians expanded, they admitted lay brothers or conversi to work their fields. The Rule forbade travel further than one could return in a day, and as their estates grew, they needed workers to manage them so that the monks could continue to pray the liturgy of the word. These lay brethren were able to share in the prayer life of the monastery even if they were not able to be choir monks. Vocations in the Cistercian Order were becoming so wildly popular that in the minds of some historians, "all Europe become Citêaux." Yet the ideals of the Cistercians, too, evolved over time, and many of their daughter houses gravitated away from the austerities of their early years.

The Impact of Church Reform in the West on the Roman and Greek Churches

By the eleventh century C.E., the popes such as Gregory VII centralized the Church, western popes pushed their insistence that the pope in Rome had supremacy over the other patriarchs. This increasing insistence on papal supremacy eventually led the Greek Orthodox Church and the Patriarch of Constantinople to separate from the Roman Catholic Church. In addition to the issue of papal supremacy, various other theological issues were at stake. The Greeks rejected the "filoque" clause from the Nicene Creed, which says that the Holy Spirit proceeds "from the father and the son." The Byzantines maintained the Holy Spirit proceeds only from the Father. In 1054 C.E. the bishop of Rome and the patriarch of Constantinople excommunicated each other over theological differences.

The Crusades

The Byzantines had been defeated by the Muslims in the seventh century C.E., and the onslaught of the Islamic Turks continued when in 1071 C.E. they defeated the Byzantines at Manzikert. In 1095, the Byzantine Emperor **Alexius Comnenus** called upon **Pope Urban II** to send assistance. Urban offered an indulgence to all those who would go on crusade. Before the Western powers could even gather their official forces, a **People's Crusade** led by **Peter the Hermit** left for the Holy Land, sacking and pillaging towns in their way. A casualty of crusading religious fervor were European Jews, who were massacred by the thousands for what Christians believed to be their role in the crucifixion of Christ. The People's Crusade was a spontaneous and uncontrolled event that brought tragedy to the lives of many European Jews.

Eventually, an official force of western knights gathered their supplies and forces, made plans for the running of their estates in their absence, and followed the call of Pope Urban II for an official first crusade. Although the immediate pretext for a crusade was to support the Byzantine cause, the various accounts of Pope Urban's speech at Clermont redirected the effort towards freeing the Holy Land and Jerusalem itself. Many of these knights were the lesser sons of aristocrats, however, who were denied a heritage at home and were seeking new lands elsewhere. Their goals often seemed at odds with those of the papacy, and the crusading knights from Western Europe caused greater disruptions within the Byzantine world as they attempted to carve out kingdoms for themselves. Alexius's daughter, Anna Comnena, left an account of the First Crusade and the arrival of the western knights. She found their behavior barbaric, as did many of the Muslims with whom they battled. Despite frequent disagreements even amongst themselves, the western knights successfully laid siege to Nicaea, which was then taken from Muslims by Byzantines, conquered Antioch, and then finally reached Jerusalem, which they conquered in 1099 c.e. In Jerusalem and also at Antioch, they brutally massacred many of its Muslim and Jewish inhabitants, including women and children. The Knight Baldwin, who separated from the main group of knights, managed to install himself as leader of Edessa, which became one of four crusader states created from the spoils of victory.

Many historians attribute the success of the First Crusade to the disunity and infighting in the Islamic world, as Sunnis fought against Shit'ites. Nevertheless, the Muslims eventually fought back against the Crusaders, whom they regarded as invaders. Zengi managed to unite a coalition long enough to successfully take the Latin Crusader state of Edessa in 1144 c.e., prompting the Cistercian monk **Bernard of Clairvaux** to preach the Second Crusade. Many modern monks have criticized Bernard for his active involvement in politics, but his words fueled another crusade. This crusade was an endeavor of kings. The pious King Louis VII of France led this crusade, but it was ultimately unsuccessful.

In 1187 the Muslims under the leadership of the Kurd **Saladin**, who had managed to take Egypt and enforce Sunni practices there over previous Shi'ite practices, recaptured Jerusalem from the Christian knights following the famous battle at the **Horns of Hattin**. The loss of Jerusalem inspired the Third Crusade. Richard the Lionheart, son of Henry II of England, left on the Crusade along with Frederick Barbarosa of Germany and Philip II Augustus of France. Barbarosa, or "red beard," had a dream that he would die at sea and so decided to cross by land; ironically, he drowned while crossing a river and never arrived at his destination. Richard the Lionheart fought bravely during the Third Crusade, especially at Jaffa and Acre, but was not successful in his quest to conquer Jerusalem. He did, however, negotiate a settlement allowing Christian access to Jerusalem with Saladin, who had captured the city in 1187 c.e.

Saladin died in 1193 c.e., and the powerful pope **Innocent III** called the Fourth Crusade. During the Fourth Crusade in 1205 c.e., the western knights sacked the Christian city of Constantinople. The Byzantines did not recapture their city until 1261 c.e. If Alexius had known what he initiated in 1095 c.e., he might never have asked Urban II for help. In the end, the Muslims pressed on, and the Latin knights left the Holy Land. Several other unsuccessful crusades followed, but in 1453, the Islamic Turks conquered the once mighty city of

Constantinople, and converted Justinian's Hagia Sophia into an Islamic mosque. Today the city is known as Istanbul.

The Crusades created ill will between Christians and Muslims, and their lasting negative effect can still be seen today in the Middle East. Crusader castles still dot the landscape of the Middle East, a vivid reminder to modern Muslims of their mistreatment at the hands of the Christian knights. Many new kinds of religious orders were founded for knights, such as the **Templars** and the **Knights of St. John** or the **Hospitalers**. The Templars were founded to protect pilgrims to the Holy Land following the First Crusade, while the Hospitalers were founded to care for sick pilgrims. However, both evolved into fighting knights with the help of Bernard of Clairvaux, who preached that to extinguish evil in the form of a Muslim combatant was malecide rather than homicide. This new kind of warrior knight lived like a monk but fought like a knight, and their orders amassed great fortunes during the Crusades. The Templars owned vast estates in Europe, including some of the most famous vineyards, but were eventually dissolved by the French monarch Philip IV, who desired to acquire their vast holdings. The Hospitalers relocated Rhodes, but a defeat by Sulieman the Magnificent forced them to move to Malta, where Sulieman again laid siege to them. Though they repelled the Muslims at Malta, Napoleon expelled them from Malta and they moved to Rome, where they continue to have a presence today. On a more positive note, there was a tremendous amount of cultural exchange during this period between Europeans and Muslims. Europeans learned much about medicine, for example, from Muslims in the Holy Land.

The Central Middle Ages were a period of reform, change, and vast movement of peoples from west to east in the Crusades. The cultural exchanges between the European, Byzantine, and Islamic worlds continue to have an impact on today's cultures.

Review Questions

1. Belief in the need for community to enable a person's spiritual growth is most consistent with the teachings of

   (A) Pachomius.

   (B) Basil.

   (C) the desert hermits.

   (D) Benedict.

2. Which of the following statements best describes the Kingdom of the Franks?

   (A) Its boundaries were stable.

   (B) Warrior kings like Clovis controlled their territories through sheer force.

   (C) Clovis and others amassed territories and passed them to their eldest sons, creating a larger and larger kingdom.

   (D) Its wealth was distributed among the people.

3. The investiture controversy was a conflict over the issue of

   (A) whether priests could marry.

   (B) whether priests could own land.

   (C) whether priests could occupy government offices.

   (D) whether the kings or princes could grant a fief and the symbols of office to the ecclesiastical rulers.

4. Which statement does NOT accurately describe Charlemagne's coronation on Christmas day 800 C.E.?

   (A) Charlemagne planned the event with the pope prior to its occurrence.

   (B) A foundation had been laid for the papal claim to supremacy over secular rulers.

   (C) The coronation symbolized that Charlemagne had recovered the full extent of the boundaries of the old Western Roman Empire.

   (D) It occurred immediately after the surrender of Widukind and the Saxons.

5. The Crusades

   (A) successfully captured and retained control of the Holy Land.

   (B) created distrust between Christians, Muslims, and Jews.

   (C) unified Western Europe and Byzantium.

   (D) unified Europe.

6. Which is the most correct statement about the Frankish engagement of the Muslims at Poitiers (Tours)?

   (A) The use of horses by the Muslims inspired the use of cavalry by the Franks and the creation of feudal social and economic structures.

   (B) The arrival of the stirrup from China enabled the Franks to defeat the Muslims.

   (C) Muslim armies did not have cavalry or horsemen in significant numbers at the time of the Battle of Poitiers (Tours) and cannot account for the creation of feudal social and economic structures.

   (D) Muslim armies defeated Charles Martel and the Franks but returned to Spain without further penetration of Europe.

7. The heart of the feudal system of governing was the bond between

   (A) citizen and state.

   (B) independent states and a joint confederation.

   (C) independent states and an international organization.

   (D) individual persons.

8. The total political effect of European feudalism was to

   (A) centralize and strengthen the power of kings and to weaken that of the nobles.

   (B) revive a rich, powerful Roman Empire in the West.

   (C) create powerful, unified nation-states along modern lines.

   (D) decentralize and weaken the power of kings and strengthen that of nobles.

9. The principal change that the Norman Conquest brought to England was the

   (A) complete elimination of Anglo-Saxon laws and institutions.

   (B) imposition of a centralized feudal system based on a Norman aristocracy.

   (C) end of English influence and territorial claims in France.

   (D) end to the English colonial empire.

10. The real significance of the Magna Carta was its embodiment of the principle that

   (A) basic human and civil rights belonged to every English citizen.

   (B) the feudal system, with all its many provisions, was dead in England.

   (C) England would voluntarily give up its territorial claims in France.

   (D) monarchs are subject to the law and can be restrained if they violate it.

11. The reforms of the Central Middle Ages included all of the following EXCEPT

(A) monastic reform, as evidenced by the foundation of Cîteaux and Cluny.

(B) reform of canon law.

(C) centralization of the papacy.

(D) increasing control of local bishops as opposed to the pope.

Answers			
1. (D)	4. (B)	7. (D)	10. (D)
2. (B)	5. (B)	8. (D)	11. (D)
3. (D)	6. (C)	9. (B)	

Chapter 15

THE LATE MIDDLE AGES

KEY TERMS

Black Death
Bubonic plague
Mongols
Yersinia pestis
Flagellants
Revolt of the Jacquerie
Peasants' Revolt
Philip IV
Boniface VIII
Unam Sanctam
Babylonian Captivity

The Great Schism
Marsilius of Padua
Execrabilis
The Hundred Years' War
Battle of Crécy
Battle of Agincourt
Salic Law
Edward III
Henry V
Charles VII
Joan of Arc

THE CALAMITOUS FOURTEENTH CENTURY: THE BLACK DEATH

Origins of the Plague

Rumors of a great pestilence that started in China and spread to India, Persia, Syria, Mesopotamia, and Egypt had reached Western Europe by 1346. The traditional view was that the **plague** originated in the Gobi desert in China in the 1320s and that the migrations of the Mongol Hordes brought the long-dormant bacterium from the remote desert into contact with various centers of civilization. From here it spread from the East to the West via trade routes. Scholars have suggested that when the Mongols catapulted dead bodies infected with plague into the Genoese stronghold at the port of Caffa, the fleeing Genoese sailors carried the plague with them to Europe as they fled the Mongol attack and landed at Messina on the island of Sicily, where the plague then spread to Europe.

Recently, some scholars have suggested that reports of the great pestilence in China were not necessarily reports of the bubonic plague, but rather reports of death and disease from famine, drought, and other causes now thought to have begun in the 1330s. Since the plague appeared in India in 1346, some scholars think the events in China in the 1330s were too early to have been the cause.

Cause of the Plague

The cause of the plague was the bacterium ***Yersinia pestis***, which is transmitted by fleas carried by rats. The rat was very plentiful in medieval Europe. Every household was infested with brown rats; rats inhabited the beams of houses and especially the family hearth. Medieval families lived with their animals; a typical house had an area for the animals and another for the family. Sanitation in the towns was also problematic, as families disposed of their waste by throwing it into the narrow streets. All of these customs attracted a sizeable rat population. Black rats were present on every ship and often survived even when the crew did not. When a ship docked, the rats would scurry down the ropes that tied the ship to the dock, go into the town, and then into the homes of the population.

It was not the rats that actually caused the Black Death, but rather the fleas they carried. Fleas ingested the bacilli, bit human hosts, and then vomited the bacilli into the human blood stream. The sizeable population of rats brought an even more sizeable population of fleas into Europe.

The word "bubonic" comes from the Greek word for groin, "boubon." One of the first signs that someone had been infected with the plague was a blackish purple pustule at the site of a flea bite, which would swell and become very tender. It could grow as large as an egg. Subcutaneous hemorrhaging caused the skin to appear black. The victim's nervous system began to collapse, causing dreadful pain and neurological disorders.

There were three forms of the plague: **bubonic plague**, in which an infected flea bites a person or when materials contaminated with Yersinia pestis enter through a break in a person's skin; **pneumonic plague**, in which the bacillus invades the lungs; and **septicemic plague**, in which the bacillus enters the bloodstream.

Controversy Over the Plague Today

Some modern scholars have suggested that the disease that spread throughout Europe in the fourteenth century was not plague, but rather the ebola or some other hemorrhagic virus. Others have suggested it was anthrax. By far the most convincing thesis remains that the plague was caused by Yersinia pestis, as recent excavations of graves in Europe show the bacilli in the pulp of teeth. However, in some parts of Europe, as in Iceland, no rat bones are found in appropriate layers, suggesting that there may have been more than one disease at work in the fourteenth century.

The Transmission of the Plague in Europe

The plague spread primarily along the major trade routes of Europe. Modern historians estimate that somewhere around twenty-five million out of approximately forty-four million people, representing anywhere from one-third to as many as fifty percent of the population of Europe, died of the plague in the fourteenth century. Since the medieval world had no accurate census, it is very difficult to state with accuracy the number of victims.

Although the plague itself was deadly, its impact was made worse by the fact that the climate had become progressively colder in the fourteenth century, causing disastrous results for crops. The population had also increased by 2.5 times. When the plague erupted in Europe, the population was at its highest point in many decades, while the food supply was at its lowest point. The population was weakened by famine, then, when the plague struck, its affects increased dramatically. The population of Europe would not reach its pre-plague levels again until the beginning of the sixteenth century.

One can only imagine the horror of life in medieval Europe from 1347–1350. Most historians argue that the plague first erupted in Europe at Messina, a town on the island of Sicily. A ship docked there with the disease, and although it was quarantined, the rats with their fleas nevertheless managed to escape onto the island. Within two months, half of the population of Messina was dead. Another Genoese ship was reported to have carried the disease to Marseilles in 1348. By 1350, the plague had traveled through France, England, Scotland,

and Ireland to the northernmost parts of Europe, including Sweden, Denmark, Norway, Prussia, Iceland, and Greenland. When Norwegian sailors returned to Greenland again in the early fifteenth century, they found only wild cattle roaming through the deserted villages.

Reactions to the Plague and Popular Remedies

The plague affected people in more ways than the mere physical. So many people died that disposal of the bodies became a problem. In Italy, a group of people known as the becchini hired themselves out to carry away the dead; they terrorized the population, and were known to extort them on the threat of carrying them away with the piles of dead bodies.

In Milan, Italy, citizens walled up all the occupants of a house in which there was a victim and left them to die. Boccaccio tells us in the *Decameron* that people abandoned their families in order to survive, fleeing to the countryside to escape the plague. Medical knowledge in the fourteenth century was scant. No one understood that it was a bacterium that caused the plague, much less that rats and fleas transmitted it.

The medievals still practiced medicine according to Galen's theories of disease, which stated that disease spread by miasmas, or poisonous vapors that corrupted the air. The Faculty of the University of Paris, who argued that the plague was the result of the conjunction of the planets Saturn, Mars, and Jupiter in the fortieth degree of Aquarius at 1 P.M. on March 20, 1435, gave the most "scientific" view of the day. This conjunction of planets had corrupted the atmosphere. People attempted not to breathe the air, either by breathing in noxious fumes, or in some cases, by holding their noses and carrying flowers to avoid breathing atmospheric air.

Flagellants

Many Europeans believed that the plague came because of human sinfulness. In Germany, a penitential movement began in 1348 known as the Brethren of the Cross or the Brotherhood of the Flagellants. The flagellants paraded throughout Germany and other parts of Europe in groups from 200–300 to as large as 1,000 in some cases. The penitents beat themselves with leather thongs tipped with metal studs as atonement for sins. They continued the rituals for thirty-three days and eight hours, one day for every year of the life of Christ. Without the use of antibiotics, many must have died before the end of their thirty-three-day pilgrimage. The flagellants might have been partly responsible for the further transmission of the plague.

The most interesting aspect of the movement was its anti-clericalism. The flagellants in Germany denounced the Catholic Church hierarchy, and refused to take the Eucharist. They interrupted masses, drove priests from churches, and even looted Church property. The anti-clerical behavior of the Brethren indicated a strong foundation of resentment toward the Church well before Luther began his work in the sixteenth century.

The flagellant movement spread from Germany through Hungary, Poland, Flanders, and the Low Countries. Inevitably, the anti-clericalism of the movement turned the Church against it. In 1349 Pope Clement VI issued a papal bull condemning the group for their contempt of Church practices.

Persecution of Jews

Among other things, the denunciation in 1349 also condemned the flagellants for persecuting Jews. The treatment of Jews and other minorities during the Black Death was one of the many tragedies associated with the era. While Arabs, lepers, and other minorities were accused of bringing on the plague, it was by far the Jews who suffered the most. In Germany, in particular, the Jews were the money-lending class. They had attained this status primarily because they had been ousted from civil and military functions and prohibited from owning land or working as artisans. Many Jews had large numbers of people indebted to them. This created tension. The Church prohibited usury, or the loaning of money to others with interest. Further, since the Jews were associated with those who persecuted the historic Christ, Jews were often blamed for every ill in society. People argued that Jews poisoned their wells, and that brought about the plague. In point of fact, the Jews had a greater understanding of hygiene, and so avoided the polluted public wells. Their dietary and cooking practices also helped spare them from the transmission of the plague; they appeared to die in far fewer numbers than did the rest of the population. All of these facts created a sense of near hysteria against the Jews.

Whether the Jews survived in greater numbers or not, prejudice against the Jews created a wave of persecutions, which would not again be equaled until the twentieth-century. At Speyer in Germany, bodies of murdered Jews were put in wine casks and floated down the Rhine River. Some chronicles suggest that as many as 16,000 Jews died in Strasbourg. A total of 350 massacres took place. Over sixty large Jewish communities were exterminated, and 150 smaller communities were also depopulated. The Jewish population shifted in Europe.

Impact of the Plague on Art, Society, Economy, and Politics

In the wake of the Black Death, the shortage of workers created a demand for higher wages and prices. Peasants' revolts occurred throughout Europe, the most famous being the **Peasants' Revolt** in England in 1381 and the **Revolt of the Jacquerie** in 1356. In England, Wat Tyler and John Ball led the peasants against nobles and the Church. The leaders of these revolts were yeoman farmers, more wealthy than the typical peasant but not of noble lineage. Many historians maintain that the plague weakened the feudal system by creating a shortage of labor.

Corruption also increased in the Church, as priests, bishops, and other officials died in great numbers. Many who had no particular vocation or calling to the priesthood entered the ranks of the Church. The Dominican order, for example, prided itself on learning, but was forced to admit many uneducated brothers into the order. The decline of learning in the Church perhaps contributed to the rise of superstition and heresy prior to the Reformation; it helped to create the conditions that led Martin Luther and other reformers of the sixteenth century to attempt to reform and later to separate from the Catholic Church.

Art reflected the omnipresence of death in medieval Europe in the fourteenth and fifteenth centuries. Art became more stilted, less naturalistic, and more focused on death. The art of Sienna, Italy, in particular, is very dark and gloomy.

The **Danse macabre** also became an important cultural phenomena in Europe following the Black Death. Macabre describes the interaction of the dead or death with the living. The dance of death first originated as a set of frescoes at the Cimetière des Innocents in Paris in 1424 and other examples are later found on cemeteries, family vaults, and churches throughout Europe. Death appears as a skeleton chastising sinners for wanton sexual practice, excessive riches, and other sins. Kings and emperors were chastised no less than ordinary people. Even the leaders of the Church were not exempt.

Death reigned triumphant in European art and culture in the wake of the Black Death. In 1490 Hieronymous Bosch painted *Death and the Miser*, an allegory about life and death in which the miser must make a choice between the crucifix and a purse full of riches given to him by a devil. In *The Four Knights of the Apocalypse* (1498) Albrecht Dürer portrayed four riders that represent, from left to right, Death, Famine, Discord, and War. An angel watches while the last three figures tread on men and women from all social classes. Death rides a skeletal horse and throws a bishop in the mouth of a dragon emerging from the bowels of the Earth.

Many scholars argue that the Black Death has been with humans for centuries prior to the outbreak in the fourteenth century. Plague struck Pelusium, Egypt, in 540 C.E. and reached Constantinople in 542 C.E. Procopius of Caesarea described that plague that ravaged Byzantium in 542 C.E. During the next ten years, the disease, then called "the plague of Justinian," spread into Europe and Asia. Some historians think the disease that killed the ancient Athenians while they were under siege by Spartans in the Peloponnesian War was plague. Some even maintain that many instances of "plagues" in the Bible might have been the Black Death. Just as historians and scientists hotly debate the exact cause of the reported deaths and symptoms of the fourteenth century, so too, they debate the identification of these other historic events with Yersinia pestis.

The medievals regarded the Black Death as a mysterious visitor; in many ways, the modern world continues to regard the historic instances of outbreak as mysteries that science and history have yet completely to resolve.

THE DECLINE OF THE CHURCH IN THE LATE MIDDLE AGES

Philip IV and Boniface VIII

The fourteenth century was also a time of crisis for the Church. One of the most notorious of all medieval popes was **Boniface VIII**, whose papacy was affected by preparations for the Hundred Years' War. King Philip IV (The Fair) of France and King Edward of England were preparing for war and were forced to raise money by taxing the clergy. In 1296, Boniface VIII issued a papal bull in protest of the taxation of the clergy, *Clericis Laicos*. *Clericis Laicos* forbade clergy in any state to pay taxes to a prince or monarch without the consent of the pope. Boniface was attempting to assert the Church's independence from the state and its right to govern itself.

Unfortunately, he chose the wrong monarch with whom to wrestle. In response to the bull, Philip IV banned exports of gold and silver from France, cutting off the flow of money to Rome. Boniface recanted the bull, but Philip continued to interfere in Church politics, charging a French bishop with heresy. Heresy was an issue that the Church should determine.

Pope Boniface believed that the independence of clergy was again at stake, and promptly reissued the basic doctrine behind the bull *Clericis Laicos*. King Philip IV summoned the Estates General, who declared Boniface a heretic. In response, Boniface excommunicated Philip and then issued another bull in 1302, **Unam Sanctam**. *Unam Sanctam* rejected the famous "theory of two swords," which maintained that there were two separate spheres of power, the Church and the State. Boniface, in contrast, argued that while there may be two swords, they were both to be put in the same sheath. That sheath was the Church.

In one of history's most memorable remarks, Philip told Boniface that "your weapons are theory, mine are fact." He then kidnapped Boniface at Anagni, tortured him and then released him. Although Boniface was apparently not seriously hurt, he died soon afterwards. Some would maintain that he died more of the shame of defeat rather than the torture itself.

The Babylonian Captivity

With Boniface out of the way, the French elected their own pope, **Clement V**, who moved with his curia to Avignon. The papacy at Avignon was clearly a pawn of the French monarch. During the Hundred Years' War, the English refused to pay the Peter's Pence, an annual tithe directly to the papacy. To have done so would have been to further fuel the power of the French to resist their campaigns. Over ninety percent of the cardinals elected during the time the pope resided in Avignon were French. The popes lived in lavish luxury here, constructing an enormous palace. The papacy remained at Avignon until 1378, a period of seventy-three years, known as an image the phrase "Babylonian Captivity," associated with the period during which the ancient Hebrews were in captivity in Babylon. Just as the Hebrews were literally held captive, so Martin Luther and other later Protestant reformers would argue the Roman Catholic Church was held captive during the Avignonese papacy.

The Great Schism

In 1377 **Pope Gregory XI** moved the curia back to Rome and died shortly thereafter in 1378. To counter French control of the papacy, the cardinals elected an Italian to replace him, **Pope Urban VI**. However, the French cardinals later challenged the election and voted **Clement VII** the new pope. Clement VII resided in Avignon, while Urban continued to reside in Rome. So began the **Great Schism**. As the Hundred Years' War raged on, the states of Europe were divided in their papal loyalties largely based upon which side they supported, the English or the French.

Popular resentment of the Church grew during the Avignonese papacy and the later Great Schism. In 1324 Marsilius of Padua wrote the *Defensor Pacis* and published it anonymously. According to Marsilius of Padua, all power resides in the people. The people delegate authority to a legislator, or king. The state has complete authority, and delegates power over spiritual matters to the Church. Within the Church, Marsilius argued that the Councils had supreme authority, and that the pope's claim to coercive power over the state disrupted Christendom. The pope consequently had spiritual authority only, and that only on the authority of the state. According to Marsilius, ultimate authority rests with the state.

John Wycliffe, an Englishman, argued that all Christians were equal. He also stated that monarchs should be able to tax the Church, as these were temporal affairs. He insisted that practices be based solely on the Bible as a standard and insisted that the Church should return to its simple teachings. His insistence on biblical authority was certainly an outgrowth of the uncertainty surrounding papal status and the obvious corruption of the Avignonese papacy and the Schism; it was also very similar to the later Protestant insistence on sola scriptura, or the Bible alone as authoritative versus the traditions of the Church. Wycliffe criticized the doctrine of the real presence in the Eucharist and challenged the efficacy of confession. He attacked the Church itself as corrupt, arguing that "Dominion is founded in grace," and that those who sin lose the dominion given to them by God. This included the Church as well as the temporal overlords. Wycliffe issued these doctrines immediately before the Peasant's Revolt in 1381; in the wild outbreak of passion following the revolt, the Church was even more alarmed about his teaching. The Church regarded many of his teachings as heretical and condemned his doctrines in 1382. His career in many ways foreshadowed the Protestant Reformation of the sixteenth century.

The Conciliar Movement

The conflict culminated in a debate over the nature of power within the Church. The Conciliar Movement was based on the idea that power resided in the hands of the people rather than the pope, and that this power was best represented by the general council of the Church. A Church Council met at Constance from 1414–1418 C.E. The Council of Constance deposed the competing popes and elected Martin V. The declarations of the council were contained in *Haec Sancta*.

The Papal Response

While the Conciliar Movement held much promise for the governance of the Church, in 1459, the pope issued the bull *Execrabilis*, in which he firmly declared that ultimate authority in Church affairs rested with the pope. This decree negated one of the most important platforms of the Conciliarists, that appeals could be made to the Church Councils.

THE HUNDRED YEARS' WAR

The **Hundred Years' War** was a very significant series of battles from the mid-fourteenth through the mid-fifteenth centuries that resulted in the alteration of many political institutions in France and England. The war contributed to the collapse of the feudal society and ushered in the beginnings of the nation-state and more modern ways of waging war.

Origins of the Conflict

The origin of the Hundred Years' War can be found in the conflicts within feudal society. The feudal conflicts between France and England began in the eleventh century. The French were still a very loose confederation of duchies or provinces united under the leadership of a single monarch. One of these provinces, Normandy, was under the control of a group of people who became known as adventurers and crusaders. In 1066 **William of Normandy**, on the pretext that he was the true heir to the throne of England, crossed the English Channel and, at the **Battle of Hastings**, defeated Harold II, the English monarch. In addition to being Duke of Normandy, vassal of the French king, William now became the King of England. In effect, the French monarch now had another king as a vassal. This proved to be a difficult situation. As vassal to the French monarch, William was obligated to support him. As king of the English, he was obligated, and of course had a natural desire, to protect his own interests. Thus, the Norman Conquest of 1066 initiated the friction that would later erupt into one hundred years of war.

During the reign of **Henry II**, one of the descendants of William, this friction and tension became even stronger. Henry II acquired much territory in France, in particular, the wealthy duchy of Aquitaine through marriage to **Eleanor of Aquitaine**. The English king now controlled an enormous expanse of land now called the Angevin Kingdom, and was actually more powerful than his overlord, the French king.

The English and French attempted to resolve these tensions by the marriage in 1303 of the English King Edward II and Isabella, the daughter of the French King Philip IV or Philip the Fair. This was to prove a crucial event that would ultimately provide the pretext for formal hostilities. Edward II and Isabella had an uneasy marriage, but did produce a son, Edward III. Philip IV died, and so did his three sons soon afterwards, leaving only Isabella and her son, then **King Edward III** of England. Philip of Valois, a nephew of Philip IV, claimed the throne. Edward III, the only other male descendant, could make a claim only through his mother's line, a succession forbidden by the Salic Law. Although the French rarely followed this law, they used it now to bypass the claim of Edward III to the throne. Philip of Valois was eighteen years older than Edward, was French, and had lived in France all his life. Edward, on the other hand, although a more direct descendant of Philip IV, had not been raised in France and was accustomed to English styles of government. The Normans had learned to manage very well the English nobles, and the French feared the tight restrictions Edward might make on their powers.

Although Edward gave Philip liege homage in the early part of his reign, hostilities started in 1337, when Philip of Valois, now king of France, confiscated Aquitaine, accusing Edward of acts of rebellion. Among the points of dispute were the English support of a candidate for leadership of the duchy of Brittany against a French candidate, and French concern over the connection between Flanders, near France, and the English wool trade.

The First Battles of the Hundred Years' War

In 1346 Edward III finally launched his attack, basically to aid his candidate in Brittany. He landed in Normandy, swung to Paris, and was headed out again when the French caught up with him. Edward's men were tired from the long march, and chose a strong defensive location near Crécy on a hill. The Englishmen were armed with longbows that were very powerful and were shooting downhill. They totally disrupted the unorganized charges of the French, who attacked seventeen times. Although the French army outnumbered the English army by at least three to one, the English had superior leadership and military skill. The longbow had a greater range than the crossbow, the French weapon of choice, and the longbow could penetrate a suit of plate armor at 200 yards. The English experience fighting the Welsh had perfected their use of the longbow. Philip violated the rules of chivalry when he fled the battle.

The following year after Crécy, the English laid siege to Calais, thus capturing a stronghold on the French coast. That year as well, the English captured the King of the Scots as well as the French candidate for the kingdom of Brittany.

Poitiers

Recovering from the eruption of the plague in the 1340s, England began a three-pronged attack on France, meeting the French at Poitiers in 1356. The son of Edward III, known as the **Black Prince**, defeated the French and captured the French king, sending him to the Tower of London. Again, the English were numerically inferior to the French but won by superior tactics and arms. The French never ransomed their king. The French in Aquitaine protested the rule of the Black Prince, eventually causing the French monarch to confiscate the duchy once again, renewing hostilities. The war continued into the fifteenth century.

Agincourt

During the fifteenth century, the French monarchy again faced a huge problem. The king at this time was **Charles VI**. He was mentally incompetent and degenerating more each day. He had become king while still a child, and his uncles ruled as regent for him. Of these, the most important were Philip, the Duke of Burgundy, and his brother, Louis of Orléans. The rivalry between these two became intense when Philip died, and his son John the Fearless became Duke of Burgundy. John had his uncle Louis of Orléans assassinated in 1407, and Louis' relatives, known as the **Armagnacs**, became bitter enemies of the **Burgundians**.

The English took advantage of the civil war raging in France. The king of England at this time was **Henry V**, who decided to end the conflict in a decisive series of attacks. Henry V made an alliance with the Burgundians and proceeded to invade France in 1415. He landed with 2,000 men at arms and 6,000 archers. The English besieged Harfleur, which fell after about six weeks in September. The English were considerably weakened by an epidemic of dysentery. Despite the physical weakness of Henry's men and the shortage of supplies after the siege, he decided to march to Calais. The French army, led by the Armagnacs or the supporters of the Duke of Orléans, caught up with the English at **Agincourt**. Henry's men were too tired to flee, and they prepared for battle. It had been raining for three says prior to the battle. The French once again tried to march against the English archers; the archers broke up the first assault, and the arrows quickly killed the French horses. The French dismounted knights then advanced, but by the fifteenth century, armor had become so heavy that the knights sunk down quickly in the mud.

When the battle was over, the French had lost 1,500 nobles and 3,000 men at arms and the Duke of Orléans was captured. The English lost less than one hundred men. Agincourt is perhaps the best example of the poor military leadership of the French; they never mastered the art of fighting against the English longbowmen.

Following Agincourt, the Duke of Burgundy made another alliance with Henry V, and this led to the **Treaty of Troyes** in 1420. This was a most important treaty, for the English and the Burgundians agreed to disinherit the dauphin, the son and heir of Charles VI. His mother agreed to claim that he was not the legitimate son of Charles VI, and upon the death of the mad king Charles, Henry V was to become king of France as well as king of England. To seal the deal, Henry married the French king's daughter Catherine. The Duke of Burgundy acquired full sovereignty in his own lands.

In 1422, both Charles VI and Henry V died, and the throne of both countries passed to the young **Henry VI** of England. Since Henry was a child, the English nobles seemed more concerned with obtaining more power at home, and were not very concerned with their monarch's French holdings. The disinherited **French dauphin (Charles VII)**, meanwhile, had a stronghold of support in the south of France with the Armagnacs. He was unable to effectively muster this support, however, since unscrupulous nobles who consistently stole his revenue also dominated him.

Orléans

In 1429 the English decided to wipe out resistance in the south of France and besieged Orléans. The situation looked grim for the French, until a young woman from the small village of Domremy, **Jeanne d'Arc** or **Joan of Arc**, appeared in the camp of the dauphin claiming to have had visions that directed her to free Orléans and escort the dauphin to Rheims. French monarchs were traditionally crowned in Rheims. Joan's voices told her that the English were evil usurpers and that the dauphin Charles was the legitimate monarch. Although the medievals venerated visionaries, Charles' men were suspicious of this young village girl. After having her questioned and examined for witchcraft, they escorted her to the dauphin. When Joan entered his chambers, he was in the company of several other men and disguised to test her visions; although she had never seen Charles, she immediately recognized him in the crowd. Charles told her she was mistaken, but again, she insisted he was the true monarch. Charles was intrigued, and told her that if she could tell him a secret he had never confided to anyone, he would recognize her. Joan told him such a secret; unfortunately, the sources do not reveal the secret. After having her once again questioned about witchcraft, Charles too began to listen to her story.

The French followed Joan to Orléans and successfully defeated the English. The victory at Orléans made Joan a legend. According to the earlier medieval prophecies of Merlin, a maid of Lorraine was to save the French in just such a situation. Joan was identified with this legend. Although she likely did not actually lead the French army but only served as a moral incentive, she was hailed throughout France as a hero.

Rheims

After the battle of Orléans, Joan of Arc led the dauphin to Rheims, the traditional site of French coronations, and he was crowned King of France as Charles VII. Although the English Henry VI had also been crowned king of France, he had been crowned in Paris. This point was not lost on the French. Joan had appealed to their patriotism, and now the French were determined to defeat the English. Charles VII, however, was not far-sighted enough to continue the fight. Having been crowned, he thought his struggle was over and quickly dismissed the Maid of Orléans.

Compiègne

Joan of Arc continued to fight to oust the English after her success at Orléans in 1429. She was eventually captured by the Burgundians and English outside of Compiègne and held prisoner and tried on charges of witchcraft. Charles did nothing for her, even though the Burgundians appeared to be willing to sell her to her friends; Charles also had the military might at that time to rescue her. He did nothing, however, appearing to forget the Maid of Orléans as soon as he had achieved his goal. Joan was convicted, and burned at the stake for heresy. Charles later seemed to have second thoughts about owing his coronation to a convicted heretic and, in 1429, her case was reopened with the help of her family and she was cleared of all charges. In the twentieth century, Joan of Arc was canonized.

Impact of the Hundred Years' War

Although Charles seemed to forget Joan, the French did not. By 1453, the English had lost all their possessions on the continent except Calais. For all practical purposes, English power on the continent was ended. Although English kings up through George III, king during the American Revolution, would continue to proclaim themselves kings of France, it was an empty title. Despite their poor military record during the Hundred Years' War, the French had succeeded in resolving disputes amongst the various dukes and creating a new and more centralized government which was well on its way to becoming a unified nation-state.

The Hundred Years' War was important in many ways. It helped resolve the complex feudal relationship between France and England and within France itself. It also had many other momentous results. Both France and England had to develop new ways of assembling an army. The old feudal ways did not work well. First of all, many nobles were not really very skilled on the battlefield and could not always provide enough men. Both the French and the English resorted to the use of private soldiers who were paid for their services. They came to recognize that leadership did not depend on birth but on ability. The power of the medieval nobility was thus compromised, another hallmark of modernity. This was the beginning of a professional military. Many English and French saw the need to keep a standing army ready at all times; and the English, in particular, argued that there was a real need to develop a navy that could respond to attacks on the English coastline. The English did in fact develop a navy, which was, for a very long while, to be the most powerful naval force in the world.

During the conflict, the English monarch was forced to consult Parliament. He had to transport men and supplies while fighting an aggressive war overseas. Parliament's power rose, and it acquired the structure it has today. During the war, the English monarch agreed that he could not levy taxes without the permission of Parliament.

In France, the French monarch was able to muster the support of the Estates General and the nobles. To raise finances, the French monarch acquired a monopoly over the salt tax, and became more and more master of the Estates General. This chain of events laid the groundwork for the French Revolution in 1789, when nobles would protest taxation.

The Hundred Years' War destroyed the French countryside. The English found it difficult to besiege well-protected towns. Medieval towns, however, depended on the countryside for food, and the English discovered that destroying the countryside also eventually weakened the resistance of the towns. The new professional soldiers roamed the countryside in search of plunder during interludes of peace. The peasants suffered most in all this. The suffering of the peasants awakened social consciousness and debates on the nature of war and its limits. Many tracts argued that war should be fought only between armed combatants, and the population should be spared. Also, many argued that wars ought to be fought only for the good of the state rather than for personal gain.

During the Hundred Years' War, nationalism began to emerge. The strengthening of the French monarchy and the English parliamentary system helped to pave the way for the later nation-state. The medieval worldview was definitely on the decline, and the humanists of the Renaissance would only further separate themselves from the medieval outlook.

Review Questions

1. The crop failures and famines that occurred in Europe in the fourteenth century were the result of

   (A) slow population growth, which limited the available workers.

   (B) a drop in the overall temperature, creating drastic unfavorable changes in the weather patterns.

   (C) a persistent decline in crop prices.

   (D) unwise agricultural policies.

2. Social revolts in England and France in the fourteenth century were sparked by government attempts to restrict economic advancement of peasants, and also by

   (A) Scottish spies who whipped up the masses into a revolutionary frenzy.

   (B) fears stirred up by French agents.

   (C) heavy additional taxes to support military efforts in the Hundred Years' War.

   (D) attempts by nobles to induct the peasants into the army.

3. All of the following were factors that caused the Peasants' Revolt of 1381 and the Revolt of the Jacquerie in 1358 EXCEPT

   (A) the general lowering of the temperature in the fourteenth century caused crop failures.

   (B) the Hundred Years' War was fought primarily in the countryside, which caused great hardship for the peasantry.

   (C) the Black Death created a shortage of labor, causing peasants to demand higher wages, while the government insisted on freezing wages to combat inflation.

   (D) the French monarch was forcing the peasants to fight in the war, due to their superior skill with the longbow.

4. The Hundred Years' War profoundly affected France politically by

   (A) forcing kings to gain approval from the Estates General before imposing taxes.

   (B) forcing the kings to look for allies in the Middle East.

   (C) giving nobles veto power over kings.

   (D) allowing the kings to impose taxes and enact laws without the prior consent of the Estates General.

5. The economic sectors that suffered the most damage in the Hundred Years'
   War, particularly in France, were the

   (A) industrial centers.

   (B) urban centers.

   (C) rural, country areas.

   (D) banking and finance institutions.

6. Despite being outmanned and having less wealth at its disposal, England won
   major victories in the Hundred Years' War primarily due to its

   (A) superior naval forces.

   (B) superior longbow archers.

   (C) mobile cavalry.

   (D) more intelligent and better trained infantry.

7. The Hundred Years' War profoundly affected England politically by

   (A) forcing kings to gain the approval of Parliament before imposing taxes.

   (B) forcing kings to look to eastern Europe and Italy for allies.

   (C) freeing kings from the control of nobles.

   (D) allowing kings to impose taxes and laws without the approval of
   Parliament.

8. In Church history, the term "Babylonian Captivity" refers to the period when

   (A) the Hebrews were held captive in Babylon.

   (B) the crusaders captured Babylon from the Asiatic hordes.

   (C) Babylonian armies captured Vienna from Christian forces.

   (D) the papacy was located in Avignon.

9. Marsilius of Padua's *Defensor Pacis* argued that

   (A) the state should control the church.

   (B) the church should control the state.

   (C) *Unam Sanctam* was the true doctrine of the Apostles.

   (D) power in the church should be delegated to the representative body of the
   people, the Councils.

10. In *Haec Sancta*

(A) Boniface VIII declared that the temporal sword was in the power of the spiritual sword.

(B) the council of Constance declared that Councils were superior to popes.

(C) Pope Gregory the Great defended the right to excommunicate kings.

(D) Boniface VIII refused to pay taxes to France and England.

Answers

1. (B)	4. (D)	7. (A)	10. (B)
2. (C)	5. (C)	8. (D)	
3. (D)	6. (B)	9. (D)	

Chapter 16

THE RENAISSANCE

KEY TERMS

Renaissance

studia humanitatis

uomo universale

Gutenberg printing press

Fugers

Neoplatonic Academy

Michelangelo

Revolt of the Ciompi

Battle of Lepanto

Three Crowns of the Holy Roman
    Empire

Wars of the Roses

Slavery

Vernacular languages

Dante

Petrarch

Hans Baron

Jacob Burckhardt

Civic humanism

Humanism

Gonzagas

Borgia

Sforza

Medici

Duomo in Florence

OVERVIEW

Many scholars have hailed the Renaissance, or "rebirth," as the beginning of the modern era. The Renaissance began in Italy, in part due to its unique economic position throughout the Middle Ages. After the collapse of the Roman Empire in the West, urban life virtually ceased to exist in Western Europe. The Italian city-states, however, survived, and had developed apart from many of the restrictions of feudal society. Many merchant and banking families not of the hereditary nobility amassed great wealth, and this wealth helped to fuel the artistic Renaissance. Of these, the **Medici** family in Florence and the **Fugers** in the north were prime examples of a new class of people known as the popolo grossi, or fat people. The Medicis came to power after the Revolt of the Ciompi in 1378, one of many peasant revolts in the wake of the Black Death. They were the bankers for the papacy, and they received deposits from England, France, and Flanders. They also had banking branches in Lyon, London, and Antwerp. The Medicis lent money at exorbitant interest rates for wars or other endeavors to various European heads of state. With the revenues, they bought English wool, had it shipped to Florence, and exported the fabrics created with a large profit. The Florentine gold florin became the monetary standard for much of Europe. While the medieval Church taught that usury, or the making of a profit from interest, was a sin, the Renaissance redefined the role of money and profitable business. The patron saint of Florence was John the Baptist, and in many paintings, he appears in his loin cloths surrounded by gold florins. Surely, money was not a part of John the Baptist's historic mission, but in the hands of the Renaissance families such as the Medicis, even an ascetic figure such as John the Baptist was associated with the wealth of Florence.

Cosimo de Medici, known as the pater patriae or "Father of the country" of Florence, was a great patron of the arts. He founded the Neoplatonic academy and commissioned many works. His son **Lorenzo the Magnificent** was also a patron of the arts and a poet. The Medicis were patrons of Michelangelo, Donatello, Botticelli, and many other artists, and they financed the construction of the famous Duomo for the cathedral on Florence designed by Brunelleschi. Patronage is one of the most important factors leading to the rise of artists such as Michelangelo, who was the first wealthy artist in history. During the Renaissance, the artist came to be valued as a "genius" rather than a mere craftsman in the service of church or state. The explosion of artistic genius during the Renaissance must partly have been due to the fact that for the first time, the artist was supported by wealthy patrons and now had the time and financial resources to devote themselves to their art. Many artists had their own workshops and developed their own unique styles of art.

Another factor in Italy's economic development was that many of the Italian city-states had maintained a thriving trade with Constantinople and other areas during the Middle Ages. This was particularly true of Venice, and when Constantinople fell to the Seljuk Turks in 1453, many Greek scholars fled along with their texts to Venice. The Italian Renaissance was in large part characterized by its fascination with the culture of Greco-Roman antiquity. Many Greek churchmen and scholars had attended the Council of Ferrara from 1438–1445; although the Council failed in its goal to reunite the Greek Orthodox and Roman Catholic Churches, many of the attendees, such as Manuel Chrysoloros, stayed in Italy and helped to spread their knowledge of Greek philosophy and culture. Many Italian humanists, such as Pogio and Boccaccio, were avid hunters of long forgotten Greco-Roman manuscripts and artworks, and this mania for antiquity infused Italian art and literature with a new character that continued to build on the achievements of the medieval world.

The rediscovery of many works of Greco-Roman art, with their sheer technical mastery and startling realism which departed from that of the medieval artisan, prompted an explosion of new artistic creativity. The rediscovery of many ancient Greco-Roman scholarly manuscripts opened a new world to the humanists, as many ideas contained in them departed from those of the medieval Church. While the medieval Church taught that pagan works were not particularly relevant to the Christian world and in many cases, should be avoided, the humanists found inspiration in the Greco-Roman interest in the human condition and in their belief in the power of human reason. The Renaissance zeal for Greco-Roman antiquity was one source of the humanist interest in individual achievement.

The changes that marked the advent of Renaissance art can be seen in the proto-Renaissance art of **Giotto,** who for the first time painted religious scenes where individual faces and expressions displayed the powerful emotions that must have been felt by those who witnessed the events surrounding the life of Christ. One achievement of the Renaissance artists was to portray the Holy Family as fully human, and to have explored the human experience and feelings of the historic Christ. The Renaissance artists portrayed the same events as the medieval iconographers, yet they had more awareness of these events as happening in human time and being experienced by human followers. While the humanists of the Renaissance found the hand of God in the beauty of the world and the human form, the medieval Church had taught that worldly interests were evil and the body sinful. The artist **Michelangelo,** who was influenced by the philosophy of Neoplatonism, depicted the nude human body in the famous S curve, a symbol for the tension between the soul and the body. For Michelangelo, however, the body was an image of the soul, and the more beautiful the soul, the more beautiful the body. **Leonardo da Vinci** studied human anatomy through dissecting cadavers, thought to be a mortal sin, but his emphasis on realism resulted in several fine self-portraits. During the Middle Ages, the

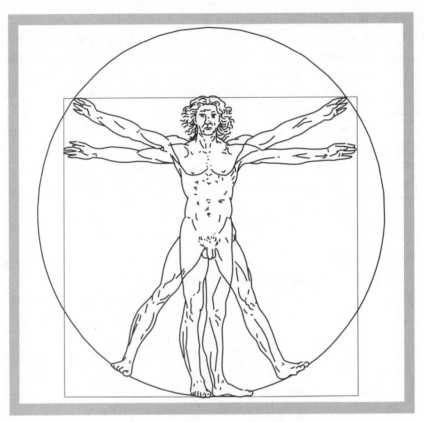

Da Vinci's Human Anatomy Drawing

self-portraits would have been considered profane and vain, but da Vinci, like other humanists, valued the uniqueness of each individual.

Michelangelo also incorporated Greco-Roman figures in the Sistine Chapel ceiling, and painted the ceiling with a Neoplatonic agenda. This was also true of the art of Sandro Botticelli and other Neoplatonists. Botticelli's *Birth of Venus*, for example, depicts a pagan myth but its iconography is Christian. Botticelli intended Venus, the pagan goddess of love, to be a symbol of Christian love; her birth from the sea to be an allegory of baptism; the pagan gods of wind in the corner to be an allegory of the Holy Spirit. Similarly, **Titian** also painted a number of allegorical works using pagan imagery to convey Christian ideals. The humanist **Pico della Mirandola's** *Oration on the Dignity of Man* suggested that pagan and Christian works might be fully harmonized. Further, the humanist fixation on the individual, as well as on the secular and profane as opposed to the sacred, distinguished Renaissance culture from medieval culture.

The advent of the **Gutenberg movable type printing press** in 1446 also made books more widely available. During the Middle Ages, the Bible and other texts had to be hand copied and manuscripts were rare and, for the most part, housed within monasteries. The more widespread availability of books coupled with the wealth of families, such as the Medicis, promoted an intense flourishing of the arts. During the Renaissance, the literary, visual, and architectural arts would flourish, and politics would take a decisive turn away from the attitudes and values of the medieval Church and more towards the secular orientation of modern politics.

HUMANISM

The term often used to describe Renaissance culture, **humanism**, was not in use in the Renaissance. However, the word "humanist" was used in the Renaissance. The term "umanista," or "humanist," technically referred to a professional teacher whose subject matter was the *studia humanitatis*. The *studia humanitatis* consisted of all those educational disciplines outside of theology and natural science, two important areas of medieval learning. While the most important aspect of the trivium in the Middle Ages was dialectic or logic, the Renaissance humanists focused on another area of the trivium, rhetoric, and highly valued eloquence of speech. In their view, if one could not interest an audience sufficiently for them to learn, all the logic in the world was wasted. If one could not move an audience toward ethical action, natural theology was useless. The humanists found Scholastic theology dry and so abstract that it had little bearing on the ways to live a good Christian life. The humanists were not so interested in the medieval Scholastic's abstract, logical explorations of theology as they were in teaching one how to become a better person. While the medieval Scholastic focused on dialectic, theology and natural science, the humanists focused on grammar, rhetoric, history, literary studies, and moral philosophy.

Baldesar Castiglione's *Book of the Courtier* (1516) reflected the interest of the humanists in developing personal skills and virtue to a high point. Castiglione was a count and a diplomat who described the ideal man as a *uomo universale*, more commonly known as a "Renaissance man" or "universal man." Castiglione's *uomo universale* was master of a wide variety of knowledge and skills. His model of the well-rounded individual has become the emblem of the Renaissance.

Education in the Renaissance

The humanists insisted that education was an important foundation of the virtuous man. Peter Paul Vergerio promoted the study of the liberal arts, but especially history, ethics, and rhetoric. History, he said, was valuable for its illustrations of past models of virtue, ethics for its exploration of the virtuous person in society, and rhetoric for its emphasis on how to teach, please, and move people.

In his *Oration on the Dignity of Man*, Pico della Mirandola described humans as able to reach any heights they desired. Humans alone, he argued, were created without natures that limited what they might achieve. Humans alone, then, might transform themselves into whatever they desired to be.

The humanists insisted on the value of education, and Erasmus, a northern European humanist, wrote that education should be made available to even the ploughboy in the field, who might then transform himself. Despite such lofty sentiments, humanist education was an elitist endeavor. Humanists promoted the study of languages, in particular, Latin and Greek, so that one might gain a better understanding of Greco-Roman texts. Erasmus, for example, thought the Scriptures would be better understood through knowledge of their original languages. He published a new translation of the New Testament with the Greek text alongside his new Latin translation. He also included notes on the Hebrew. Luther's reading of the *Novum Instrumentum* or *Testamentum* helped to fuel the Reformation.

Another example of the importance of linguistic studies in the Renaissance was Lorenzo Valla. Valla was a Renaissance philologist who studied the origins and use of language. His study of the *Donation of Constantine* created a shockwave throughout Europe. The *Donation of Constantine* was allegedly written during the reign of the first Christian emperor, Constantine. Upon the death of Constantine, it purported to give the pope in Rome both temporal and spiritual power over the domain of Constantine. Valla proved, however, that the document used language not in existence before the ninth century. For example, it used terminology related to feudal society, and that terminology was not in use prior to the reign of Charlemagne. If so, Valla had proven that the document was a medieval forgery and not written during the age of Constantine. His discovery encouraged further criticisms of the Church.

The Vernacular Languages

Other humanists, such as Dante, began writing in the vernacular languages, or languages actually spoken. **Dante** was the first to write in vernacular Italian, and although his ***Comedia*** contained many medieval ideas, the use of the Italian opened new frontiers. During the Reformation, Luther translated the Bible into his native German, thereby allowing Germans to actually read the Scriptures in a language they spoke.

Humanist Awareness of Their Own Uniqueness

The humanist interest in language reflected their awareness that words could change meaning from age to age and from culture to culture. It reflected as well their awareness of their own age as distinct from that of other ages. The fourteenth-century humanist **Petrarch** is credited with being the Father of Humanism. In many texts, Petrarch argued that his own age was vastly different from the culture of the Middle Ages. In fact, he argued that the medieval period was dark culturally, that it was lacking in literary and artistic masterpieces, and that it reflected no awareness of the potential of the human spirit. Petrarch coined the term "Dark Ages" to refer to the medieval period, and that appellation and its negative overtones has plagued the historiography of the Middle Ages ever since.

The humanists saw their own era as vastly different from earlier eras. The humanists may have exaggerated their own uniqueness, as some scholars have seen more continuity between the Middle Ages and the Renaissance than Petrarch admitted. Dante, for example, structured the *Comedia* around the mystical Christian number three; there are three large parts to the *Comedia*, the Inferno, the Purgatorio, and the Paradisio. The *Comedia* also makes numerous uses of the number 10 in its structure, the perfect Christian number. The numerology of the *Comedia* is entirely medieval. Dante's view of sin in the Inferno was also very medieval; Dante based the punishments given to sinners on the medieval notion of retributive justice, or to each according to what he or she deserves. Beatrice is symbolic of Divine Love and the desire of all Christians to unite with the Godhead. Nevertheless, his use of the vernacular Latin as well as the pagan poet Virgil as his guide marked new attitudes.

Gender Issues in the Renaissance

Given the lofty ideals of the humanists, scholars have often questioned to what extent these ideals revolutionized the lives of women. While more women were educated in the Renaissance than before, in general, the ideals of humanism did not transform the lives of women to the extent that it transformed the culture of Italy. **Christine de Pizan** worked in the court of the French monarch Charles V and wrote the *Book of the City of Ladies* as well as other works, which defended the virtues of women and argued for greater access to education. Nevertheless, Christine was not advocating a social revolution and the overthrow of marriage or other traditional structures for women. Some scholars, such as Joan Kelly-Gadol, argue that the rediscovery of ancient Greek and Roman writings helped to confirm and strengthen the ideals of the medieval period concerning women. They were to be chaste, be restricted to the household, and in the Renaissance to continue to be the bearer of children in a male-centered environment.

One area in which women's lives did change was marriage. By the fifteenth century, women were not marrying until their twenties, in contrast to Asian cultures, as for example Hindus in India, where women married much earlier. Later marriage ages were linked to property ownership. The structure of families was changing as well, from the extended families of the medieval period to the nuclear families more typical of the modern era. Family size was more limited, and the relationship between a woman and her husband became closer. Women might help their husbands in their businesses, but the cultural ideals of the Renaissance held that women who worked outside the home were more suspect than those who remained in the home.

Slavery in the Renaissance

Humanistic veneration of the individual also did not have an impact on slavery in European societies. Slavery existed in Europe throughout the Middle Ages. Many slaves in the medieval period came from Eastern Europe and were captured during war; many were of Slavic descent. Venice was an important port through which many of these Slavic and Eastern Europeans entered Europe as slaves.

The voyages of the Age of Exploration, which began during the Renaissance in the fifteenth century, brought many black slaves to Europe. Although most were concentrated in Spain and Portugal, Italians also owned black slaves, and Genoa was an important port through which Portuguese traders often brought their African slaves. Despite the condemnation of the papacy of the African slave trade and the lofty ideals of the humanists, Europeans had no apparent aversion to slavery in this period.

THE ITALIAN CITY-STATES AND CIVIC HUMANISM

The cultural flourishing of the Italian Renaissance was accompanied by tremendous changes in culture and political structures throughout Europe. Italy was not united as a nation state until the nineteenth century, and Renaissance Italy was a collection of Republics and duchies that were often at war with one another. Often the warring parties called on other powers, as the Milanese did when they invited the French to invade in the 1490s. Italy became a stomping ground for France and Spain as they fought for control over the city-states and as city-states themselves vied for power.

Milan: Milan was one of the richest city-states in Italy. Many mercenaries used in the Hundred Years' War came from Italy. Francesco Sforza came from a condottiere, or mercenary family, and in 1447 he took control of Milan. The Sforzas were well-known patrons of the arts. Leonardo da Vinci worked for the Sforzas for a portion of his career and designed a number of military devices and fortifications for them.

Republic of Venice: Venice maintained a thriving trade with Constantinople through the Middle Ages. In the Fourth Crusade, the Venetians helped to support a false claimant to the Byzantine throne, and eventually led the western knights in their conquest of Constantinople. Venice was governed by a small oligarchy of elite merchants, and led by the **Doge**. The Doge's palace in Venice is a masterpiece of Gothic architecture. It contains a number of Renaissance works of art, including a painting of the **Battle of Lepanto** in 1571, when an alliance of Europeans, including the Venetians, defeated the Ottoman Turks at the Gulf of Patros. The important military victory in 1571 stopped the advance of the Ottomans, whose various conquests threatened to turn the Mediterranean into a Muslim sea. Another famous location in Venice is **St. Mark's Cathedral**, which was designed on the plan of a Greek cross. The Venetians maintained a thriving trade with Constantinople and the influence of Greek culture is seen in the cathedral.

Republic of Florence: Florence was located in Tuscany and it was an important center of the arts during the Renaissance. Michelangelo was born near Florence and worked here; Leonardo da Vinci also worked in Florence. The Revolt of the Ciompi brought Cosimo de Medici to power in 1434. Although Florence was a republic, the Medici ruled it as despots. The Medici ousted **Machiavelli** and he wrote *The Prince*, which may have been intended to satirize their political practices. Machiavelli advocated the separation of politics from ethics and/or theology in *The Prince*, and many consider him to be the founder of modern politics. Machiavelli was also an advocate for a unified Italy, which he argued could only be achieved by a man such as he described in *The Prince*. The Medicis were important patrons of the arts, and their palace is famous for its use of several different styles of architecture. Lorenzo de Medici was a poet who patronized the artist Michelangelo. Hans Baron, a modern scholar, argues that the political conflicts of the Medicis and others helped to prompt the shift from medieval to Renaissance thought. He argues that civic humanism, an interest in leading an active, public life, originated in large part from the political crisis in early modern Florence. Civic humanism and interest in public life led to the creation of open, public spaces, and to such architectural masterpieces as the Duomo in Florence. The Duomo was a masterpiece of engineering that could be seen from miles away. It came to be the symbol of the Renaissance itself.

Urbino: The Montefeltro dynasty ruled Urbino. Federigo da Montefeltro was a condottiere or mercenary, but was also a benevolent and classically educated ruler.

Ferrara: The most famous person to emerge from Ferrara was Isabella d'Este, daughter of the Duke of Ferrara. She was known as the "first lady of the world" for her learning and patronage of the arts. She married Francesco, Duke of Mantua, and after his death ruled Mantua alone. Isabella is an excellent example of an educated woman who managed to function in a man's world and in a man's role.

Mantua: Francesco Gonzaga, marquis of Mantua, ruled Mantua and was the husband of Isabella d'Este, daughter of the Duke of Ferrara.

Siena: The art of Siena was much darker than other Renaissance art, particularly in the wake of the Black Death.

Papal States: The Frankish ruler Pepin donated the tract of land known as the Papal States. Revenue from the Papal States helped the medieval and Renaissance popes centralize the Church and develop vast political power.

During the Renaissance, the **Borgia** family largely controlled the Papal States. **Rodrigo Borgia,** the family patriarch, was born in Spain in 1431. His favorite son was **Cesare**, who was accused of murdering his own brother Juan. In 1502 he pillaged the Dukedom of Urbino and took four large cartloads of art treasures, which contained tapestries, silver, and paintings; these treasures were worth an estimated 150,000 ducats. Cesare tried to establish a hereditary monarchy in central Italy and Machiavelli praised him as the ideal prince. He also used his sister, **Lucrezia**, as a pawn in the marriage game to increase his power. When she was only thirteen, Cesare married her to Giovanni Sforza, but later had the marriage annulled when a more suitable partner appeared, Alfonso of Aragon. Cesare later murdered Alfonso and Lucrezia married the Duke of Ferra. Cesare died in battle in 1507.

The Borgia family produced two popes, **Pope Callistus III** and **Pope Alexander VI**, father of Lucrezia and Cesare. Pope Alexander was openly devoted to his many children, and procured for his sons powerful positions in the Church. He appointed Cesare a cardinal in the Church. Alexander VI was the epitome of the corruption of the Renaissance papacy. Alexander was also a patron of the arts and learning, and as pope issued a bull dividing the new world between Spain and Portugal. He also imposed a tithe for crusades against the Turks.

THE NORTHERN RENAISSANCE

The Renaissance of the north had a considerably different character than the Italian Renaissance. The northern humanists wanted to reform Christianity so as to promote a deeper awareness of spirituality, and the art of the northern Renaissance in Germany had a decidedly fierce overtone. The art of **Dürer**, for example, focused on God as a judge who wrought vengeance on sinners.

Erasmus, Prince of the Humanists, lived and worked in Rotterdam. Erasmus corresponded with many important humanists and leaders of Renaissance Europe, including Thomas More. Erasmus emphasized the value of education, which he wanted made available to even the ploughboy in the field. Erasmus published a new translation of the Bible known as the *Novum Testamentum*, based on his study of the original languages.

POLITICAL DEVELOPMENTS DURING THE RENAISSANCE

Spain: The marriage of **Ferdinand and Isabella** in 1469 united Aragon and Castille and created a new Spain. Spain would profit greatly when Isabella convinced Ferdinand to finance the first voyage of Christopher Columbus in 1492. The wealth generated from the Spanish colonization of the Americas not only strengthened the Spanish monarchy, but caused a price revolution in Europe.

The power of Spain also propelled it to leadership of the Catholic world during the Reformation era. Ferdinand and Isabella had permission from the Church to select the most important churchmen in Spain. To deal with issues surrounding the conversion of significant Jewish minorities in Spain, they also requested the pope to start the **Inquisition** in 1478. In 1492, Ferdinand and Isabella conquered Muslim Granada and expelled all professed Jews from Spain; in 1502, all professed Muslims were also expelled.

The intense orthodox Catholicism of the Spanish monarchs also attracted the attention of the Catholic **Queen Mary of England**. Mary was a staunch opponent of her father Henry VIII's reformation. She married Philip to restore Catholicism to England. When she died, Philip launched the **Armada**, the largest naval fleet ever assembled, against her Protestant half-sister Elizabeth. In 1588, the legendary "Protestant Wind" grounded the Armada before it could attack, thus assuring the success of the Protestant reformation in England.

England: The victory of **Henry VII**, a member of the **Tudor** family, over the infamous **Richard III** in 1485 at Bosworth Field brought an end to the **Wars of the Roses** and ushered in a new era in England. Henry VII enacted various policies to curtail the power of the English nobles, thus ending their constant squabbles in the Wars of the Roses. Henry planned for his eldest son, Arthur, to succeed him. Unfortunately, Arthur died, and Henry's second son became king as **Henry VIII**. Henry VIII separated the English Church from the Roman Catholic Church and began the Reformation in England.

The English humanist **Thomas More** objected to Henry's actions and refused to sign the Act of Supremacy. For that crime against the state, he was beheaded. More's *Utopia* was one of the most famous works of English Humanism. The Utopians were a pre-Christian society whose monastic-style practices made those of his own Christian England seem immoral by contrast. More exemplifies a style of writing common to many humanists. While the Scholastics wrote argumentative treatises, the humanists wrote humorous works designed to suggest ideas rather than to prove them.

Henry VIII's daughter **Elizabeth** later succeeded her half-sister Mary as queen. She was known as the "Virgin Queen." Although she never married, she used the possibility of marriage as an effective diplomatic tool. During her reign, English culture enjoyed a Renaissance. Shakespeare worked during the reign of Elizabeth.

France: France developed a strong monarch as a result of the Hundred Years' War. **King Louis XI** won control of the taille, an annual tax on land and property. He used the funds from this tax to strengthen his control over troublesome provinces such as Maine, Anjou, and Provence.

Flanders: Flanders supported the English during the Hundred Years' War. Artists here during the Renaissance developed the use of perspective. **Jan van Eyck**, for example, literally played with his technical virtuosity in such paintings as *Giovanni Arnolfini and His Bride*.

Holy Roman Empire: The **Hapsburgs** first became rulers of Austria in 1278 and, despite the turmoil of the Reformation and succeeding eras, they managed to rule Austria until WW I. Austria was the center of the Holy Roman Empire in the early modern period.

Frederick Barbarossa first described his empire as the "Holy Roman Empire," but the term itself dates from 1254. In the Middle Ages, the German duchies were never firmly united, and neither was the Holy Roman Empire during the early modern period under Austrian rule. The Austrian Hapsburgs ruled over a tremendously diverse group of people, making it very difficult to achieve any kind of unity. At its height the empire contained most of the territory of modern Germany, Austria, Slovenia, Switzerland, Belgium, the Netherlands, Luxembourg, and the Czech Republic. It also contained parts of eastern France, northern Italy, and western Poland. Therefore, many of the movements of the early modern and modern world, in particular the rise of nationalism, rocked the empire as various groups fought for their own self-interests.

During the Renaissance and Reformation Eras, the Holy Roman Empire was increasingly fragmented. There were some 300 states in the Holy Roman Empire capable of independent action. There were nine electors who chose the Holy Roman emperor, and among them was the Duke of Brandenburg, who became King of Prussia according to the Treaty of Utrecht in 1713. The King of Prussia was one of Europe's most powerful monarchs during the Age of Absolutism, further illustrating the difficulty the Hapsburgs had in unifying their domains.

The Hapsburgs had no great trading markets, in contrast to the Netherlands and France, another factor impeding its development of a centralized state. While other states such as France and Prussia later developed absolutist monarchies, the Holy Roman Empire remained too fragmented to achieve comparable success at centralizing the government.

The Austrian Hapsburgs controlled three separate regions, and their power in these areas was known as the **Three Crowns of the Holy Roman Empire**. There was little unity in terms of culture or religion within the Holy Roman Empire.

The Crown of St. Stephen represented Hungary, Transylvania, and Croatia. Hungary became the most important state in Eastern Europe during the Renaissance era. King Matthias Corvinus (1458–1490) managed to control the wealthy nobles and create a centralized government. In 1526 the Ottoman Turks defeated the Hungarians at the Battle of Mohács. The Turks also conquered the cities of Buda and Pest. Pest fell to the Turks in 1526 and Buda fell fifteen years later. The Turks also laid siege to Vienna, but failed to take it, and tried again in 1683. The Hapsburgs defeated the Ottomans in 1699 and reconquered Hungary.

The Crown of St. Wencelas represented Bohemia, Moravia, and Silesia. The attempt to impose Catholicism on Bohemia led to the Thirty Years War, covered more fully in Chapter 18. Citizens of Prague threw the emperor's governors out the window in the second "defenestration of Prague." After the war ended, the Hapsburgs imposed Catholicism on Bohemia and were seen as very repressive.

Austria was a hereditary holding of the Hapsburgs and was the third crown held by the Holy Roman emperors. After 1806, the imperial title was recognized only within Austria. The Protestant Reformation dealt a fatal blow to the empire; both the Peace of Augsburg and the Peace of Westphalia weakened the emperor's power. We will review these events in more detail in Chapter 18.

Poland: Powerful nobles who controlled the Sejm or national diet thwarted the attempts of the Polish kings to centralize the government. By 1511 the nobles reduced the peasantry to serfdom and established their right to elect their kings.

Russia: Russia was converted to Christianity during the Middle Ages, but it was conquered by the Mongol hordes in the thirteenth century. Moscow gradually rose to prominence under Ivan III. Ivan III annexed other Russian principalities and defeated the Mongols in 1480.

Byzantium: The Byzantine Empire declined during the early modern period. In the thirteenth century, the Byzantines had to deal with a new threat, the Ottoman Turks. In 1453, the Turks conquered Constantinople, the mighty bastion of Roman culture in the East. The Hagia Sophia, one of the greatest Christian churches from the reign of Justinian, was converted to an Islamic mosque. Many Christian scholars fled Byzantium and went to Venice, with whom the East had a thriving trade. Their presence helped to fuel the Italian Renaissance.

SUMMARY

The Renaissance was a time of tremendous change, and these changes created a willingness to question, which helped to usher in the Reformation. It was an explosion of artistic creativity, and a period that saw the rise of powerful families such as the Medicis in Florence, yet the Protestant Reformation rocked the stability of Europe. The fracturing of the Church also further fragmented the Holy Roman Empire, and led to the Wars of Religion, which affected many areas of Europe.

Review Questions

1. Which of the following is not consistent with statements made by Machiavelli in *The Prince*?

    (A) It is better for leaders to be feared than loved.

    (B) Politics is based on eternal laws of morality.

    (C) It is better to cultivate the appearance of virtue or whatever the public demands than to exemplify such virtues in reality.

    (D) Expediency should determine the course of conduct.

2. Which of the following artists was NOT influenced by NeoPlatonism?

    (A) Michelangelo

    (B) Botticelli

    (C) Jan van Eyck

    (D) Titian

3. A humanist in the Italian Renaissance was

    (A) someone who left sacred studies and worked only in secular areas.

    (B) a professional teacher of the *studia humanitatis*.

    (C) someone who advocated against slavery.

    (D) someone who advocated for women's rights.

4. Humanism

    (A) transformed the rights of women.

    (B) had a significant impact on the slave trade, causing it to decline.

    (C) did not significantly impact the lives of women.

    (D) helped to resolve the constant wars between city-states.

5. During the Renaissance, the lives of women

    (A) changed significantly as they entered the workforce and were accepted in different social roles.

    (B) changed as the average age for marriage increased.

    (C) reflected a change in family structure as the extended family declined and the nuclear family became a more prominent feature in society.

    (D) Both (B) and (C).

6. European slaves were concentrated in

   (A) northern Europe.
   (B) Spain and Portugal.
   (C) Central Europe.
   (D) France.

7. According to Hans Baron, civic humanism can be traced to crises in which Italian city-state?

   (A) Milan
   (B) Naples
   (C) Rome
   (D) Florence

8. Which Italian family was brought to power as a result of the Revolt of the Ciompi?

   (A) Gonzaga
   (B) Medici
   (C) Sforza
   (D) Borgia

9. What did Luther's Bible and Dante's *Comedia* have in common?

   (A) They were both written in Latin.
   (B) They were both written in German.
   (C) They were both rejected by the people.
   (D) They were both written in the vernacular languages of their people.

10. Which of the following statements is NOT a correct description of Humanism?

    (A) Pivotal works such as Dante's *Comedia* might reflect a very medieval foundation and perspective.
    (B) The humanists, such as Petrarch, saw themselves as very distinct from their medieval counterparts.
    (C) Humanism was a total break from the medieval past.
    (D) Many humanists incorporated elements of pagan and Christian thought in their works.

Answers

1. (B)	4. (C)	7. (D)	10. (C)
2. (C)	5. (D)	8. (B)	
3. (A)	6. (B)	9. (D)	

Chapter 17

THE AGE OF EXPLORATION

KEY TERMS

Columbus	Black Legend
Ferdinand and Isabella	Encomienda system
New monarchs	The Inca
Lateen sail	The Aztecs
Caravel	The Colombian Exchange
Prince Henry the Navigator	The Price Revolution
Magellan	Zheng He
Cabot	Mestizo
Diaz	Mulatto
da Gama	Castas
Cartier	*Peninsulares*
Treaty of Tordesillas	Creoles
Conquistadores	Gun and Slave Cycle

OVERVIEW

The Europeans of the fifteenth and sixteenth centuries are often credited with the "discovery" of the "New World," not because they "discovered" something previously unknown but because they exploited what they found. The so-called "New World" was already known to the Native American inhabitants, and had already been visited by Europeans as early as the ninth century. The exploration of the Americas by Europeans, however, created a new global economy and forever transformed Europe, Africa, and the Americas. In this sense, the European experience of the Americas in the fifteenth and sixteenth centuries was far different from earlier "discoveries" or explorations of the continent.

The first European to land on the North American continent was **Leif Erikson**, who sailed from Scandinavia in the late ninth century. His voyage, however, occurred at a time when Europe was still in the throes of illiteracy, superstition, and localism, and his voyage went almost unnoticed; there were no attempts to follow up on his experience for hundreds of years.

Between the tenth and fifteenth centuries, however, several concurrent movements began that would lead Europeans into the Age of Exploration. During the Crusader era, beginning in the eleventh century Europeans were introduced to desirable products from East Asia: spices such as pepper, cinnamon, ginger, nutmeg, and cloves; tropical foods such as figs, rice, and oranges; and luxury goods including perfumes, silk, cotton, dyes, and precious stones. The complicated trade routes involved tariffs at many ports of entry as products went overland to Constantinople, through the Mediterranean on Venetian sailing vessels, and ultimately to Western European ports. This trade was costly not only because of the number of handlers, but also because every petty tyrant whose land Arab caravans crossed exacted a tax on the goods. Scholars have estimated that the price of pepper in Europe was fifteen times more expensive than in the East Indies. The balance of trade was unfavorable from the standpoint of the European countries; the necessity to cut out the middlemen was crucial.

The fifteenth century was also a time of economic, political, and intellectual recovery as the Renaissance introduced new ideas and encouraged new ways of thinking. During the fourteenth century, Europeans suffered from famine and died in great numbers from the Black Death. As the plague subsided, Europeans developed new ideas that emphasized individualism, secularism, and humanism. A desire to challenge old ways and old ideas swept Europe and, at the same time, strong rulers emerged. Called the "new" monarchs, these kings unified their countries, sought ways to expand their economies, and competed with each other at every turn.

A number of technological tools of both European and Asian origin were important in the fifteenth-century explorations. By 1350 the Europeans had perfected the cannon, capable of firing iron or stone balls which, when mounted on a seagoing vessel, created a formidable force. A new sailing vessel, the **caravel**, replaced the old galleys that had relied on rowers for motion. Although slower than the galleys, the caravel relied on wind power and was designed to carry larger cargoes. The lateen sail, which now supplemented the ancient square sail widely used in the Mediterranean region during earlier periods, made it possible for ships to sail into the wind through a movement known as tacking. When combined with square-rigged sails in the Renaissance, the caravel now had increased maneuverability on the seas. Earlier inventions used in navigation included the compass, perfected by the Chinese many centuries before, and the astrolabe, a tool developed by the Arabs. The astrolabe allowed sailors to determine the altitude of the sun and thereby to plot latitude. Improvements in cartography gave navigators more exact information on distances, sea depth, and geography.

THE VOYAGES OF EXPLORATION

The Portuguese were the first Europeans to become involved in the voyages of exploration. Following the lead of their king, **Prince Henry the "Navigator,"** they set sail down the west coast of Africa in search of a sea route to the "Spice Islands" of the East Indies. In 1487 **Bartholomew Diaz** reached the tip of South Africa, and in a second Portuguese effort from 1497–1499 **Vasco da Gama** rounded the southern tip of Africa and sailed east to reach India. The Portuguese had limited success in their conquest of Africa, however, due to the difficulty of penetrating the continent's harsh terrain and also because of the strength of the African monarchies.

King Manuel I of Portugal was impressed by the samples brought from India by Vasco da Gama and sent an expedition the following year, 1500, under the leadership of **Pedro Cabral**, to set up trading posts in India. Following what he thought was da Gama's path, he headed for India. The fleet was blown off course, however, and on April 22, 1500, sighted Brazil and claimed it for the Portuguese crown. After spending a few days on the east coast of South America, Cabral and his crew continued on to India, arriving in 1501. From that point on, ships were sent from Lisbon each March headed for India and the Spice Islands. Lisbon harbor became the entry point for goods from the East.

While the Portuguese were attempting to reach the East by sailing around the tip of Africa, the Spanish turned to another route suggested by **Christopher Columbus**. Columbus was an Italian from Genoa who had studied the ancient maps of Ptolemy, a second-century geographer whose works were still highly regarded in the Renaissance. Ptolemy's map of the ancient Mediterranean area was very accurate, and scholars had always assumed, without proof, that his other geographical works were equally accurate. Ptolemy, however, overestimated the landmass from Europe to Asia and extended Asia much farther to the east than it actually is; on the other hand, he underestimated the amount of water on the planet. According to his map, the measurements of the known world were about 4,580 miles from north to south and 8,250 miles from east to west. All of these factors led Columbus to conclude he could more easily reach the East by sailing west across the seemingly limited expanse of ocean that separated Asia from the western coast of Europe than the Portuguese could reach it by sailing around the enormous continent of Africa. Of course, Columbus had no idea that the Americas separated Europe from Asia.

Christopher Columbus

Columbus first approached John II of Portugal with his plan of sailing west to reach the East. In 1485, Christopher Columbus approached Ferdinand and Isabella of Spain; at the same time his brother Bartholomew tried to sell the idea to Henry VII of England. Although the Spanish were at first disinterested in Columbus's ideas, Spain was newly unified and eager to counter the rising power of the Portuguese resulting from their initial voyages around Africa. It was Queen Isabella who was converted first to the plan of Columbus, and in 1492, shortly after the fall of Granada to the crown, she promised Columbus everything he had asked for and in 1492 Christopher Columbus set off on his first voyage. In October of that year he reached the Caribbean, convinced that he had in fact attained his goal of sailing west to reach the East.

Columbus made four journeys in all to the islands of the Caribbean, embarking in 1492, 1493, 1498, and 1502. Although Columbus was convinced that he had reached the East Indies and called the natives he encountered "Indians," he failed as governor of Hispaniola, and in 1500 spent time imprisoned in Hispaniola and Spain. His last voyage in 1502, during which he was marooned for a year in Jamaica, was his most adventuresome. He returned to Spain in 1504, however, arthritic and poor. He died in 1506.

OTHER VOYAGES TO THE AMERICAS

In 1499 and 1500 **Amerigo Vespucci** took part in an expedition led by the Spanish explorer **Alonso de Ojeda**. In the course of this trip, Vespucci wrote at length about the "New World" reached by the Europeans. Because of his descriptions and his realization that indeed the Europeans had not reached the Indies, but continents previously unknown, the German mapmaker Martin Waldseemuller suggested that the new land be named for Vespucci. Columbus never received even this recognition for having charted new lands.

Other nations also financed voyages. **John Cabot**, a native of Italy, and born Giovanni Caboto, sailed under the English crown in 1497, the first Englishman to reach North America. He, like Columbus, da Gama, and Cabral, was interested in a shorter route to India and chose a more northern one. Embarking in May 1487,

Portrait of Magellan

he reached land, probably either Newfoundland or Cape Breton, in June. Cabot made a second voyage in 1498. His voyages gave England claim to the North American mainland; they would lead to future English colonization. The next English expedition did not take place until the late sixteenth century.

Magellan, a student of astronomy and navigation, further developed some of Columbus's pioneering ideas. He believed that a shorter route to India was possible, if, instead of sailing around the tip of Africa, ships sailed west and rounded the tip of South America. The Portuguese king would not support his request for ships, men, and money so Magellan turned to the Spanish King, Charles I. Magellan set sail in 1519 and became the first European to circumnavigate the globe. Magellan's route took him from Europe, around the tip of South America, through the Pacific Ocean, the Philippines, the Indian Ocean, around the Cape of Good Hope, and back to Spain. He set out with a fleet of five ships and returned home three years later with one ship and only seventeen of the original crew.

One of the surviving crewmembers was an Italian, Antonio Pigafetta, who painstakingly recorded the events of the trip. Although Magellan failed to find a shorter route to India, his voyage contributed to the geographical knowledge of the world.

In 1535 **Jacques Cartier** sailed under the French flag toward the "New World," and was the first European to explore the St. Lawrence River. The following year the French attempted their first colony in Canada.

DIVIDING THE CONQUESTS

The early success of both the Portuguese and the Spanish in exploration led to many disputes. On May 4, 1493, the Pope, **Alexander VI**, attempted to adjudicate the controversy. Essentially, he established an imaginary line running north and south through the mid-Atlantic, 100 leagues (480 km) from the Cape Verde Islands. Spain would have possession of any unclaimed territories to the west of the line and Portugal would have possession of any unclaimed territory to the east of the line. In 1494, the **Treaty of Tordesillas** redrew the line at 370 leagues (1,770 km) west of the Cape Verde Islands. Portugal came up the big loser in the Americas, as it received only Brazil. The Spanish became the beneficiaries of the vast wealth of the Americas.

THE SPANISH IN THE "NEW WORLD"

Just as technological advances spurred exploration, they also aided the Spanish in their conquest of the natives of Mesoamerica and South America. Many Spaniards sought fame as **conquistadores**, but their abuse of the Native Americans have made their names live on in infamy.

Juan Ponce de Leon might have begun his career as a conquistador on the second voyage of Columbus. By 1502 he was serving as a captain under the governor of Hispaniola. After he suppressed an Indian uprising, he was made governor of eastern Hispaniola. In 1508–1509 he explored Puerto Rico, as he had heard reports of gold there. He founded the oldest settlement there, the city of Caparra. Although he was named governor of Puerto Rico, he lost the position due to political rivalries. Hearing reports of a fountain on an island called Bimini whose waters could rejuvenate humans, he set out from Puerto Rico in 1513, the same year Balboa first sighted the Pacific Ocean. He landed on the coast of Florida near modern St. Augustine. Like Columbus, he did not realize he had reached the mainland, and thought he was on an island that he named "Florida," or Pascua in Spanish, referring to the fact he had reached it at Easter. He explored the Florida Keys and then returned to Puerto Rico. Somewhat later he returned to Spain, where he was made governor of Bimini and Florida. In 1521 he again sailed to Florida, but upon his landing, he was attacked by Seminoles and wounded by one of their arrows. He was taken back to Cuba, where he died. One of the largest cities in Puerto Rico is named "Ponce" in his honor.

Conquistadores

Balboa

Vasco Núñez de Balboa was the first European to see the Pacific Ocean and was the leader of the first stable colony in South America. In 1500 Balboa sailed along the coast of modern Colombia with Rodrigo de Bastidas, and later lived in Hispaniola. He was a poor farmer, however, and when his creditors threatened to take him, he became a stowaway on an expedition to a colony in Colombia. When the expedition arrived, they found the colonists, but on Balboa's suggestion moved to the Isthmus of Panama where they founded the town of Santa Maria de la Antigua, which was the first stable European settlement in South America. In 1511 King Ferdinand made Balboa governor of the colony. In September 1513, Balboa went in search of the fabled riches to the south, which may have been a reference to the Inca Empire. On September 25 or 27, 1513, he sighted the Pacific Ocean. A few days later he reached the Gulf of San Miguel and took the South Sea in the name of the king. He and his men carried ships in pieces over the mountains to the Pacific, and from 1517–1518 he explored the Gulf of San Miguel.

Cortes

The Aztecs of Central America and the Incas of Peru had well-established nations by the end of the fifteenth century. Nevertheless, in less than two years, **Hernando Cortes** destroyed the monarchy, took possession of Tenochtitlan, and defeated most of the Aztecs.

Cortes was a notary and farmer on Hispaniola in the early years of the Spanish discovery of the Americas. Here he contracted syphilis, but had recovered sufficiently by 1511 to accompany Diego Velazquez in his conquest of Cuba. Cortes later became clerk under Velazquez. For his service, Cortes received a repartimiento or gift of land and native slaves. He also received the first house in Santiago. Cortes was imprisoned and was involved in other scandalous incidents here when he came into conflict with Velazquez, but was twice the mayor of Santiago. In 1518 Cortes was put in charge of an expedition to establish a colony on the mainland. He sailed for the Yucatan coast on February 18, 1519, with eleven ships, 508 soldiers, and sixteen horses. Cortes captured an Indian slave, Malinche, who spoke both Mayan and the Aztec language, Nahuatl. She was known as the "tongue" of Cortes, and was eventually baptized as Doña Marina. Doña Marina was likely one of the reasons Cortes was initially able to charm Montezuma. Through his interpreter Doña Marina, Cortes learned of unrest among the subjects of the Aztecs. He swayed over 20,000 of the Aztec subjects to his side, and marched to Tenochtitlan. Montezuma at first welcomed Cortes, as he identified him with Quetzalcoatl, the legendary god of the Aztecs who had, by coincidence, promised to return in this very year. Although Cortes enjoyed momentary success in Tenochtitlan, his troubles with the Spanish had not subsided. After Cortes founded Vera Cruz, the explorer Narvaez attacked him in 1520. While Narvaez distracted Cortes, the Aztecs, who had become increasingly resentful of the Spaniard's lust for gold and loathsome of Cortes's noxious deputy, finally revolted and attacked the Spaniards. On the *noche triste* or "sad night" of June 30, 1520, the Aztecs drove Cortes and his men down the causeway of Tenochtitlan. Cortes laid siege to the city, which finally surrendered on August 15, 1521. Meanwhile, Cortes was still under attack from the Spanish. His old enemy Velazquez began to attack him in Spain, which prompted Cortes to write five letters to King Charles V.

In 1524 Cortes led an expedition to Honduras. His health deteriorated during the two-year trek, and those he left in charge of the empire he had conquered confiscated his property and abused the natives. These events prompted his famous fifth letter to Charles V, and in 1528 he returned to Spain to defend himself. In 1530 he returned to the Spanish empire in the New World, now known as New Spain, and found it in a state of anarchy. His subjects accused him of murdering his first wife and, in 1540, Cortes returned to Spain. He died, in his own words, "old, poor, and in debt." Towards the end of his life, he had intended to return to New Spain, but died before he could even reach Seville in Spain.

Pizarro

The Incas met a similar fate in 1532 at the hands of 175 Spanish troops led by **Francisco Pizarro**. Francisco Pizarro first traveled to the New World in 1510 on an expedition led by Alonso de Ojeda to what is modern Colombia. In 1513 he accompanied Balboa on the expedition that first sighted the Pacific. From 1519–1523 he served as mayor of Panama. In 1523, at the age of forty-eight, Pizarro left on the expedition that would discover the empire of the Incas. From 1524–1527 he journeyed to the south, and his men endured many hardships. Upon finding traces of civilization, Pizarro sent for reinforcements from Panama. The governor told him to return, whereupon Pizarro drew a line across the ground asking those who desired wealth and glory to cross it. Thirteen men crossed the line, and Pizarro continued south. He named the land "Peru," which he derived from the name of the river Viru. In 1528 Pizarro traveled to Spain to ask for further help; at the same time Hernando Cortes had returned from the New World. In 1529 Charles V gave Pizarro a coat of arms, and made him governor of the region now called New Castille, which extended 600 miles south from Panama along the coast. In January 1530 he and four of his brothers set sail with 180 men for Peru, and in April they made their first contact with Atahualpa. Pizarro attempted to convert the Inca king, who threw the Bible to the ground. Pizarro attacked and quickly defeated the Incas. Pizarro ordered Atahualpa to be put to death by strangulation on August 29, 1533. In November Pizarro then took Cuzco, the Inca capital, without a struggle. Pizarro founded Lima, Peru, in 1535. During the last years of his life, his rival Almagro attacked him. On June 26, 1541, Almagro attacked Pizarro's palace in Lima. Pizarro was killed in the attack, and as he lay dying, drew a cross on the ground with his own blood.

Cabeza da Vaca

Álvar Núñes Cabeza de Vaca was treasurer for the expedition of Narvaez to Tampa Bay, Florida, in 1528. By the time the expedition reached Galveston, Texas, only about sixty men were left. By the next spring, only fifteen men were still alive and, eventually, only Núñes and three others were left to explore the remaining way into northern Mexico. His accounts of the **Seven Golden Cities** or **El Dorado** inspired the expeditions of de Soto and Coronado. He was appointed governor of Rio de la Plata, and from 1541 to 1542, he explored the region from Brazil to Paraguay. He later wrote a valuable work on the geography of the region. He was eventually deported to Spain for misconduct in office and sentenced to work in Africa.

Coronado

Francisco Vásquez de Coronado explored the North American southwest and discovered the Grand Canyon. He and his men were the first Europeans to see the enormous herds of bison in the southwest. Coronado earned a reputation for pacifying the Native Americans and was made governor of Nueva Galicia in 1538. Other explorers had returned with tales of the Seven Golden Cities of Cibola, which we now know were the Zuni Pueblos. In 1540 Coronado was put in charge of the main force sent to look for what the Spanish believed were cities of gold. He moved up the west coast of Mexico to Culiacan, and sent a smaller force that captured the Pueblos of Zuni. He and his men spent that winter along the Rio Grande River, where they were attacked several times by natives. In 1541 Coronado discovered the Palo Duro Canyon in Texas, and then proceeded with a smaller contingent to Kansas. Coronado was indicted in the residencia or investigation of his expedition for misconduct, but was later exonerated. He was also indicted and condemned after his governorship.

De Soto

Hernando de Soto accompanied Pedrarias Davila to the New World on his explorations along the coast from 1516–1520. De Soto participated in the conquest of what is now Nicaragua and became the military commander there. In 1531, he joined the expedition of Pizarro, and he was Pizarro's ambassador to the Inca King Atahualpa. De Soto became friends with Atahaulpa, and when Pizarro executed the king, de Soto returned to Spain. De Soto sailed again for the New World in 1538 as leader of an expedition with 10 ships, 600 to 1,000 men, and 300 horses. He landed in Florida, just south of Tampa Bay, in 1539. He encountered the small village of the Apalachee Native Americans. The next year he forged on to Alabama near modern Mobile; there he fought with the local chief. He traveled on through Tennessee to the Mississippi River, which they first saw on May 21, 1540. The name "Mississippi" means "Father of the Water." His forces made their way into Arkansas and Oklahoma, where they encountered hostile natives on many occasions. Later that same month, he turned back to the Mississippi River, where he died a few days later. De Soto brutally mistreated the Native Americans by chaining them together with iron collars and using vicious dogs to keep them in line. He was so hated by the natives that his companions interred him in the Mississippi River for fear the natives would desecrate the corpse.

Reasons for the Success of the Spanish Conquest

The superstitious conviction of many natives that the Spanish were somehow either divine or extraterrestrial combined with European technology contributed to the defeat of the Native American populations. Aztec and Inca warfare was no match for the well-trained Spanish troops, the strange men in "floating houses," and their cannon.

Frightened and then defeated by European technology, the Mesoamerican and South American Indians fell prey to the Spanish conquistadores. The scenario that followed has been described as a New World "holocaust," which resulted from the policies of the Spanish overlords and the devastation caused by European disease. Falling victim to the **encomienda** system of forced labor in mines and sugar cane fields and exposed to such European diseases as smallpox, the Indians died in droves. Although there is dispute among historians as to the exact number of Indians who died, some believe that in Peru the population of Native Americans fell from 1.3 million in 1570 to 600,000 in 1620. In Central America, of the 25.3 million Indians living there at the time of the arrival of Cortes in 1519, only 1.3 million remained by 1620.

The Spanish treatment of the Native Americans gave rise to the "black legend," first discussed by **Bartolome de las Casas** in 1552. De las Casas was the Dominican Bishop of Chiapas, who participated in a debate in 1550 concerning the treatment of the Native Americans. He argued that the Spanish abused and exploited the Native Americans, whom he portrayed as innocent, noble beings. The Spanish, he said, did not realize the achievements of Native Americans nor what the natives shared in common with the Europeans. **Sepulveda**, a Spanish Bishop, challenged his arguments, and presented what was the more common European view of the Native Americans. De las Casas wrote nine essays, eight of which were published in 1552 and the ninth in 1553.

THE CREATION OF A GLOBAL ECONOMY

The European Voyages of Exploration also created a global economy through sea trade. The Portuguese reached India and then went on to Japan and China. They brought back spices to Lisbon and often paid for these goods with textiles from India and gold and ivory from East Africa. From the Portuguese outpost at Macao, they took Chinese silk to Japan and the Philippines. There, they traded silk for Spanish silver. Spanish silver from the New World had a dramatic effect on the Chinese economy; the Single Whip Reform united the taxation system of China through a single tax payable in silver. The Portuguese also brought horses to India from Mesopotamia and copper from Arabia, and carried hawks and peacocks from India to China and Japan. The Portuguese also traded in African slaves; African slave labor produced the sugar on their plantations in Brazil, which produced the bulk of Europe's sugar supply in the sixteenth and seventeenth centuries. Portuguese became the language of trade in East Africa and in the Asian trade. The legacy of the Portuguese trading empire continued until the late twentieth century; Macao was ceded back to the Chinese in 1999. The Portuguese are also planning to relinquish control of other areas conquered during the Age of Exploration.

The Spanish also established a large maritime empire in the Age of Exploration. Miguel Lopez de Pegazpi established Spanish control over the Philippine Islands. Manila linked Spanish trade in the Americas with the eastern trade. The Portuguese brought silk to the Philippines, and the Spanish carried it to the New World where it was exported to Spain. The silk trade transmitted huge amounts of bouillon from the New World to Manila; in 1597, 12 million pesos made the journey across the Atlantic to fuel the silk trade. This was almost the total value of the entire transatlantic trade.

The Dutch also established a large trading empire based on spices. In 1599 a Dutch fleet brought over 600,000 pounds of pepper and large quantities of other spices, such as cloves and nutmeg, to Amsterdam, and made over a 100 percent profit. The Age of Exploration brought Europe into contact with not only the Americas, but with the Asian trade market. It forever changed the worldview of the Europeans, and created the first global economy. Nevertheless, many parts of the world were not fully a part of the new global economy or they played an unequal role in it. Russia, for example, was largely left out of the new economy. Other areas continued to focus on their own internal developments, and although they did trade in certain areas with Westerners, their economies were not transformed. These areas included the Ottoman, Safavid, and Mughal empires. Other areas, such as China and Japan, sought to limit trade and contact with the West.

Changes in World Trading Patterns in the Age of Exploration

European explorations did not entirely obliterate the old trading networks. Prior to the European Age of Exploration, the Islamic world dominated the trade networks west of India, linking Africa, the Middle East, and parts of Asia to the Indian Ocean trade. On the eastern side of India, China dominated trade, linking

India, Southeast Asia, and Central and Eastern Asia over the vast network of land routes known as the Silk Road. China also controlled sea routes after the thirteenth century and the decline of Srivijaya, which started in the eleventh century. India was the central link between these various powers and their sea/land routes. The arrival of the Europeans did not obliterate the old trade routes nor make it impossible for Arab and Asian merchants to continue trade. For example, Asian merchants continued to dominate trade in the seas connecting China to India, while Arabs continued to trade between the east coast of Africa and other parts of the Islamic world. However, Europeans gradually began to dominate shipping via sea routes.

When the first Portuguese traders and explorers arrived in Calicut under Da Gama, they brought little to trade beyond crude European iron pots, textiles, or coral beads. Merchants in the Indian markets were not interested in these goods, but rather in the exotic silks of China, their porcelain, or paper. Indians, for example, were not particularly interested in European cloths, as India excelled in the production of cotton cloth. The one commodity that Europeans brought that did interest merchants in Calicut was silver bullion, which originated in the newly developing Spanish empire in the New World.

Aside from the silver and gold they brought, Europeans were also helped by the fact that in the areas where these trading routes converged, such as the Straits of Malacca, in Southeast Asia, or the Persian Gulf and Red Sea in the Islamic world, there was little in the way of centralized control over trade. Further, Muslims, for example, were deeply divided politically. The rise of competing sects within the Islamic world, even in the early years following the death of Muhammad, contributed to deep political divisions.

Lack of interest in European products by those in the East and European unwillingness to sacrifice all their supply of bullion on trade for highly desired items made Europeans willing to use force to obtain the desired end. The Portuguese, for example, attacked ports along the African and Indian coasts, eventually controlling trade from places like Ormiz and Malacca. Their ships were more heavily armed and larger than the ships of other traders, except for the Chinese. The Portuguese attempted to establish a trading monopoly in regions they conquered, and later, so too did the Dutch East India and other private companies.

Europeans had less success as they attempted to move away from the port cities and further inland. Although in some cases they were able to subjugate native peoples and establish a tributary system, in general, their primary success was in the coastal regions. In places such as China and Japan, isolationism kept European merchants from making great strides inland, and in both cases, Europeans had special places to reside, from which they could trade, such as Nagasaki, Japan, where Dutch merchants lived in a special section. Lack of interest in European goods in China, for example, also kept trade from progressing further. China really had no need of imported goods, but as we have seen above, did find trade for silver beneficial.

Impact of the New Economy on European Countries

Increased revenue from colonies in the Americas flooded European markets with silver and other wealth, which increased manufacturing in some parts of Europe. In Portugal, however, increased bullion was traded to other European nations, such as England, for goods, and in fact, ultimately discouraged manufacturing production in Portugal. Although the flow of silver into Spain from the New World was vital to the Spanish economy, it also had a negative effect, as the Spanish kept borrowing more and more money to fund their wars on the basis of expected silver shipments. By the eighteenth century, Spain's revenues from the New World could no longer keep up with escalating debt, and other powers, such as England, rose to take its place.

The Slave Trade

In Africa, Europeans often traded for slaves. Sub-Saharan African economies were transformed by this trade and entered the new global economy. Trade with Europeans brought a new focus on trans-Atlantic trade routes as opposed to earlier focus on the trans-Saharan trade. However, Arabs continued to dominate the slave trade across the Sahara and along the eastern coast of Africa and then to the Red Sea. The trans-Atlantic slave trade just accounted for the largest volume in slave trading.

The development of colonies in the Americas fueled the demand for slaves, especially after Native Americans died in large numbers from the diseases Europeans brought. Brazil, for example, developed the first plantation colony through its cultivation of sugar cane. By the end of the seventeenth century, slaves made up fully one-half of Brazil's population, and most of these slaves came from Africa. The areas that supplied the greatest number of slaves in Africa tended to shift over time. In the sixteenth century, the slave trade was concentrated along the west coast of Africa, in the region of the Senegambian states. Later, in the seventeenth century, it shifted to west central Africa. Later, regions such as Dahomey and Benin, in areas of Southern West Africa known as the Gold Coast and the Slave Coast, were important suppliers of slaves. While Benin never allowed the slave trade to become its primary focus, Dahomey did, and Dahomey continued to trade in slaves into the nineteenth century. Dahomey expanded its control over neighboring regions with the aid of firearms, which Europeans brought to Africa. Desire to control the slave trade led to wars among the Africans. The Ashante, in fact, rose to prominence as a result of the slave trade, especially after acquiring firearms. The link between firearms and increased trading in slaves, leading to further acquisition of firearms and the renewal of the cycle has been called the "gun and slave" cycle. Many African kingdoms also themselves had institutionalized slavery, even prior to the arrival of the Europeans.

The impact of the slave trade on African societies was profound. Scholars estimate that the population of west and central Africa in the nineteenth century was only half of what it would have been had not the slave trade succeeded in taking large numbers of people across the Atlanta. In part, the increasing number of slaves transported over the centuries was due to their huge mortality rate, both from the horrors of the Middle Passage and the difficult working conditions at their destinations. Further, since more men than women were transported, the proportion of women to men was inflated in Africa itself. Interestingly, the trans-Atlantic trade did bring one benefit to those areas depopulated through the slave trade—new crops like maize provided a new food supply.

Race and Ethnicity

In colonized areas, race ethnic structure changed radically as Europeans intermarried with natives. In the Spanish colonies in the Americas, for example, Europeans were considered to be of the highest status in the social structure, while slaves from Africa and Native Americans had the lowest status. In between, a whole new class of people arose who were of mixed ancestry, and these people primarily became farmers and shopkeepers. There were various designations for those of mixed European and Native American ancestry (**mestizo**) and those of mixed European and African ancestry (**mulatto**). This group of mixed people made up of both the mestizo and the mulatto people was called the *castas*. Those Europeans, too, who were originally from the continent (*peninsulares*) and not born in the New World had higher status than those of European heritage who were born in the New World (Creoles).

Review Questions

1. The nation that was the first to finance the early Voyages of Discovery was

   (A) Spain.
   (B) England.
   (C) the Netherlands.
   (D) Portugal.

2. The first explorer to reach the Cape of Good Hope was

   (A) Vasco da Gama.
   (B) Bartholomew Diaz.
   (C) Balboa.
   (D) Magellan.

3. Magellan discovered a passageway around South America called the

   (A) Cape of Good Hope.
   (B) Straits of Magellan.
   (C) Malabar Coast.
   (D) Panama Canal.

4. The first expedition that circumnavigated the globe was led by

   (A) Balboa.
   (B) Columbus.
   (C) da Gama.
   (D) Magellan.

5. Columbus's voyage in 1492 was financed by

   (A) Portugal.
   (B) Italy.
   (C) Spain.
   (D) England.

6. Columbus got his idea that the East could be reached by sailing west from the work of

   (A) da Gama.
   (B) Aristotle.

(C) Ptolemy.

(D) Plato.

7. All of the following crops and animals were brought from the Old World to the New World EXCEPT

   (A) potatoes.

   (B) horses.

   (C) cattle.

   (D) pigs.

8. All of the following crops and animals were brought from the New World to the Old World EXCEPT

   (A) tobacco.

   (B) potatoes.

   (C) horses.

   (D) beans.

9. The disease that was brought back to the Old World from the New World was

   (A) measles.

   (B) smallpox.

   (C) syphilis.

   (D) influenza.

10. All of the following diseases brought by the Spaniards devastated the Native Americans EXCEPT

    (A) measles.

    (B) smallpox.

    (C) syphilis.

    (D) None of the above.

Answers

1. (D)	4. (D)	7. (A)	10. (C)
2. (B)	5. (C)	8. (C)	
3. (B)	6. (C)	9. (C)	

Chapter 18

THE REFORMATION

KEY TERMS

Justification by Faith
Council of Trent
Peace of Augsburg
Martin Luther
Protestantism
95 Theses
Diet of Worms
Schmalkald League
Exsurge domine
Zwingli
Calvin
Marburg Colloquy
Weber Thesis

Presbyteries
Geneva
Transubstantiation
Consubstantiation
St. Bartholomew's Day Massacre
Edict of Nantes
Act of Supremacy
Henry VIII
Thomas More
Index of Prohibited Books
Peace of Westphalia
Thirty Years' War
Witchcraft

OVERVIEW

The Reformation was, in many ways, an outgrowth of the Renaissance. It was also an outgrowth of centuries of general problems in the Church, dating back to the Babylonian Captivity of the fourteenth century and the Great Schism that followed. The corruption evident in the Church during these periods had sparked a great deal of dissent and literature of protest. Other problems included absent bishops, or those who held appointments by virtue of family standing or wealth but who were rarely present in their bishoprics and, therefore, did not meet the needs of the people. The Renaissance helped to create more criticism of the papacy and of the Church in general.

The Renaissance humanists had opened up a new era in which existing authorities were subject to thorough critique. Lorenzo Valla, for example, had shown through a sophisticated study of language that the so-called Donation of Constantine was a forgery and dated well after the time of Constantine. This document had purported to cede the temporal or earthly power of the emperor Constantine to the pope in Rome, thus giving him power over secular and sacred affairs. This document was a fundamental plank of arguments in support of papal power over secular affairs in the Middle Ages, yet Valla had shown that it could not date to a period before that of Charlemagne in the ninth century, during which some of its language, relating to feudal society, first came into being.

Erasmus of Rotterdam was another good example of the links between humanist critique and the desire for reform in the Church. He published the *Novum testamentum* or *Instrumentum*, a new critical edition of the New Testament based on the study of its original languages. It was this edition of the New Testament that helped Luther to frame his revolutionary idea of justification by faith, but the approaches of Erasmus and Luther to reform were radically different.

Erasmus was very dissatisfied with the attitudes and methodology of the medieval scholastic theologian. He argued that scholastics tried to systematize everything, even the most remote mysteries of the faith. In so doing, their ideas often became unintelligible to the ordinary man and so could not contribute to one's spiritual growth. In the *Praise of Folly*, he pointed out that even the Apostles could not have understood the scholastics, and in his Paraclesis, the preface to the *Novum Instrumentum*, he argued that the Scriptures ought to be made accessible to the plowboy in the field. Erasmus urged Christians to go back to the basics as contained in the Scriptures. In the Praise of Folly and other works, Erasmus criticized the corruption of the clergy and of monks and nuns, whom he felt focused on outer manifestations of piety without any true inner piety. For this reason, he was very critical of the practice of selling indulgences, whereby one might earn remission of the penalty for sin by being in the presence of the bones or other relics of saints or, as Tetzel argued, by donating money to the Church. Erasmus argued that one's inner state was more important for forgiveness than the mere act of donating money, which one could do while still not repenting inwardly.

Martin Luther

Martin Luther

Many, including the young German monk **Martin Luther**, shared Erasmus's desire for reform. Luther's parents were very harsh and authoritarian, which may have contributed to his obsession with his own faults and sins. As a young man, Luther was caught in a storm while out walking one day; he was terrified and prayed to St. Anne that if she rescued him, he would dedicate his life to religion and become a monk. So he did and joined the Augustinian order. As a monk, Luther was obsessed with his sinfulness, and spent hours beating his back in penance. He went so much to his confessor Staupitz that he was finally told not to come back unless he had something really important to confess. Staupitz tried to free Luther of his overwhelming sense of guilt, but did not succeed.

Luther was troubled by the sinfulness of man, but he carried his worries to an extreme. While the Italian humanists glorified man and his achievements, Luther focused on man's sinfulness, as well as his own. When Luther celebrated his first mass, he trembled at the altar out of fear of the Almighty and of God as a Transcendent Judge.

Luther was respected in the Augustinian Order for his austerities and penances, and they selected him to make a trip to Rome, the heart of the Roman Catholic Church. His trip to Rome began to enlighten him on areas of corruption and the need for reform, and on the impossibility, in his view, of achieving true forgiveness and purity through acts of penance.

Luther was incensed by the sale of indulgences, but whereas Erasmus used humor to make a point, as in the *Praise of Folly*, Luther's language was one of hellfire and brimstone, and downright crude at times.

Luther had never resolved his intense inner struggle with sin and repentance. It was a passage from Erasmus's new translation of the Bible that prompted a flash of insight that would forever change not only Luther's life, but the life of many Christians then and now. In this new translation, Luther read in the Pauline Epistles the words "be penitent" where the Latin Vulgate had read "do penance." The emphasis on inner spirituality rather than outward piety distinguished the thought of Erasmus, and his new translation of the Bible reinforced Luther's disgust with indulgences and helped to explain his theological struggle with penance. All the outer penance in the world cannot affect inner repentance, and this can only come as a gift of grace, not as an act of the human will because humans can never do enough good to earn salvation.

Luther was troubled by indulgences because he was troubled by the relationship of good deeds to salvation. If God really is a just God, then man could never be saved. Man could never do enough good to merit salvation in the eyes of God, and this is what had driven Luther virtually mad as a monk. No amount of penance was satisfactory in his view; every bad deed must immediately be confessed. If one lived in such a manner, one could never attain peace, much less salvation.

In 1517, Luther posted his **95 Theses** on the door of the Church at Wittenberg. Though we have no definitive proof Luther actually posted his theses as opposed to simply calling for debate, it was a common practice to post on the Church door. Luther chose October 31, or the Eve of All Saints' Day, on which to make his statement. He asked the Church to consider 95 points of dispute, among them, the claim that the pope had any power at all to forgive sins. Luther believed only God had this power.

The outcry over Luther's 95 Theses led to the Leipzig Disputation, in which the Church attempted to refute Luther's ideas, and eventually, when they failed to silence him, led to his being summoned to appear in Rome during the Diet of Augsburg. Luther refused to go to Rome, but met the papal legate Cajetan at Augsburg in October 1518. Luther refused to recant, and returned to Wittenberg on the anniversary of his posting of the 95 Theses.

Revolts and Social Unrest

Luther's writings also initiated a massive social rebellion that Luther had not anticipated. Although Luther condemned these revolts and upheld the power of the state, nevertheless, he had started a mass movement that would ultimately fragment the Holy Roman Empire. Many historians debate whether the Reformation would have happened or unfolded with the viciousness it did without the complicated set of social, political, and economic conditions that existed in Luther's age. For what it is worth, Luther's protest was motivated by theological concerns, but spoke to the social, political, and economic interests of the Germans.

In his treatise, Luther also denied the value of Holy Orders or the validity of the priesthood. Luther argued that all Christians are able to be their own priests and to interpret the Scriptures for themselves. Similarly, he insisted that the monastic life was not a special state of life, and that every person's work is God's work. Luther urged the dissolution of monasteries and himself married an ex-nun, Catherine von Bora, with whom he had six daughters. He rejected the idea that clergy should be celibate, and insisted on the family as the center of Christian life. In Lutheran households, women gained new respect as those primarily responsible for teaching the word of God.

Luther died in 1546, and with his last breath wished for the end of the Roman Church. In 1537, he had allegedly wished for his epitaph to read: "Pestis eram vivus, moriens ero mors tua, Papa/living I was a pest to thee, O Pope, dying I will be thy death." Luther did succeed in unleashing a movement that the Roman Church could not contain: the Protestant Reformation. In 1555, the **Peace of Augsburg** finally addressed the differences between the Lutherans and Catholics.

The Impact of the Reformation on the Holy Roman Empire

The Emperor Charles V had numerous problems during his reign over and above Martin Luther's protest movement, including the invasion of the Ottoman Turks into Hungary and the siege of Vienna. One year after the Peace of Augsburg, Charles V abdicated (1556). Consequently, the Hapsburg holdings were divided between an Austrian and a Spanish line. To his brother Ferdinand in Austria, Charles ceded the Holy Roman Empire, while to his son Philip, he ceded his personal kingdom of Spain. Philip is better known as Philip II of Spain, an important leader of the Catholic Counter Reformation and the husband of Queen Mary of England. In the period after the Peace of Augsburg, many wars of religion rippled throughout Europe. Luther had opened the floodgates, and the tide could never be turned back.

Calvin in Geneva

In 1536, **John Calvin** published the *Institutes of Christian Religion*, considered by many to be the definitive work of Protestantism. At the Marburg Colloquy, differences between Luther and Calvin were already apparent. Both denied the Catholic doctrine of transubstantiation, whereby the bread and wine become the body and blood of Christ in the Mass. According to this doctrine, the substance of the bread and wine is changed while the appearance remains the same. Luther argued for consubstantiation, the idea that if one's faith was great enough Christ was spiritually present along with the bread and wine.

Calvin, on the other hand, argued that the host and wine were a symbol rather than the reality of Christ himself. Calvin continued to view the sacrament as primarily symbolic.

Calvin also believed that the religious community, or the church, should control the state. He believed, like Luther, that the laity should control church affairs. Calvinist churches were led by elders and were called presbyteries. Calvin advocated the idea of the calling, the notion of doing God's work as a holy endeavor.

The Huguenots in France

France was one of the areas most affected by the wars of religion. The **Huguenots** were French Protestants who followed the teachings of Calvin. These Protestants refer to themselves as "réformees" (reformers) rather than "Huguenots." The origin of the name "Huguenot" is uncertain, but appears to date from approximately 1550 when it was used in court cases against heretics. The absolute monarchy of France refused to tolerate any dissent, especially that of such Protestant groups as the Huguenots. Luther's teachings had ripped apart the Holy Roman Empire, and the French were deeply suspicious of Protestantism. The Wars of Religion erupted in France when 1,200 Huguenots were massacred at Vassy on March 1, 1562. The St. Bartholomew's Day Massacre, during the nights of August 23–24, 1572, was the most infamous event of these wars. More than 8,000 Huguenots were murdered in Paris. The massacre occurred during the wedding of Henry of Navarre, a Huguenot, to Marguerite de Valois, the daughter of Catherine de Medici. Many Huguenots were in Paris for the wedding. Catherine de Medici had persuaded her son Charles IX to order the massacre, which lasted three days and eventually spread to the countryside. On the morning of August 24, 1572, a Sunday, she personally walked through the streets of Paris to inspect the carnage. Even the pope rejoiced at the massacre and the victory of Catholicism over the heretics. Catherine and Charles spared Henry's life when he pretended to support Roman Catholicism. In 1593 he renounced Protestantism, and within five years he became King Henry IV, known as le bon Henri, the good Henry, of France. On April 13, 1598, Henry eventually signed the **Edict of Nantes**, which allowed the Huguenots to practice their faith openly in twenty selected French cities, now known as "free cities." Unfortunately, later figures such as Cardinal Richelieu and Louis XIV were not as tolerant of the Huguenots and continued to persecute them. Many fled to the Americas and other parts of the world to practice their faith.

Zwingli

Ulrich Zwingli was another important leader of the reformation and, like Luther, was first ordained a Catholic priest, serving at the Great Minster Church in Zurich. Zwingli preached powerful sermons straight from the New Testament rather than from the lectionary and so launched the reformation in Switzerland. While Luther believed that "the Word worked" and relied only on the Scriptures rather than the traditions of the Roman Church, Luther also believed that what the Bible did not prohibit was acceptable. Zwingli, on the other hand, believed that everything not specifically mentioned in the Bible should be prohibited. Like Luther, he emphasized the ability of the people to interpret the Bible for themselves. Following Zwingli's teachings, the Swiss in Zurich rejected the prohibition of meat during Lent and ate sausages right before Easter in protest of Roman policies. Zwingli met with Luther and Calvin at the Marburg Colloquy, and rejected transubstantiation in favor of the view of the Lord's Supper as a memorial. He also rejected Luther's view of consubstantiation as a form of cannibalism, while Luther rejected his view of the Lord's Supper as empty. Like many reformers, Zwingli urged the return to the Apostolic Church as described in the New Testament. Just as Luther married an ex-nun, Zwingli secretly married Anna Reinhart, a widow with three children, while still a priest. They had four more children together. Zwingli fought for the Swiss against the Holy Roman Emperor Charles V, organizing a defensive force and being wounded at the Battle of Capel. He later died of the plague in 1531, a hero of the Swiss Reformation.

THE ENGLISH REFORMATION

King Henry VIII (1509–1547) was originally a defender of the Roman Catholic faith, having written the *Defense of the Seven Sacraments* against the teachings of Luther. However, his marriage to his brother Arthur's widow and Hapsburg heiress, Catherine of Aragon, had produced only a daughter, Mary. Out of a desire for a son, Henry sought permission from Pope Clement VII, who was the cousin of Leo X, to obtain a divorce. The Holy Roman Emperor Charles V meanwhile invaded Italy in order to prevent the pope from annulling the marriage of the Hapsburg Catherine of Aragon. Ultimately, Clement VII would not give permission for the divorce. Partly, too, this was because the papacy had earlier granted permission for Henry to marry his brother's widow, itself a controversial move. To then annul the marriage after so much legal work would have seemed inconsistent as well as foolish.

Consequently, Henry separated the English Church from Rome in order to marry **Anne Boleyn**, who bore him a daughter, Elizabeth, later to be known as Elizabeth the Great. Anne's failure to produce a son resulted in the loss of her head and in a traumatic childhood for her daughter **Elizabeth**, who became a Protestant, while her half-sister Mary remained a staunch Catholic.

In 1534 Henry passed the **Act of Supremacy** whereby he became the head of the Church of England. His Lord Chancellor Thomas More refused to support the act and consequently was beheaded. More was a friend of Erasmus and wrote the famous work *Utopia*.

Henry confiscated Church property, dissolved the Roman Catholic monasteries and took their land and other possessions, but everything else about religion remained the same.

In 1539, the Six Articles articulated the structure of the Church of England, and they retained bishops, archbishops, and essentially the rest of the structure of the Roman Church without the pope.

The Six Articles affirmed the Catholic doctrines of transubstantiation and of the celibacy of clergy, but did insist on the mass in English, a protestant plank.

Henry finally did produce his long awaited son, Edward, by his third wife, **Jane Seymour**. He would marry three more times; he divorced his fourth wife and beheaded his fifth wife. Only his last wife, Katherine Parr, survived marriage to Henry without being divorced or beheaded.

As for Edward VI, he, like his mother, was sickly and frail and died at an early age, leaving only his half-sisters to rule. Under Edward, the **Book of Common Prayer** more clearly defined the Protestantism of the Church of England, or the **Anglican Church**.

Henry's daughter Mary by Catherine of Aragon was staunchly Catholic, and through her vicious persecution of Protestants became known as Bloody Mary. To further the Catholic cause, she married Philip of Spain, son of the Holy Roman Emperor Charles V, who had fought Luther and was the strongest Catholic monarch on the continent. Philip was also a relative of Mary's mother, Catherine.

Philip despised Mary, but allied with her to defend Catholicism from the rising tide of Protestantism. Partly as a result of its newfound wealth from the New World, Spain became the leader of the Counter-Reformation, and the Spanish Inquisition was one of the most brutal and intolerant episodes in history.

When Mary died childless in 1558, her half-sister Elizabeth came to the throne. During the reign of Elizabeth the Great, the Church of England rejected saints and allowed the clergy to marry, all Protestant ideals. Elizabeth never married, thus earning her the nickname of the Virgin Queen, but she used the possibility of marriage to make many alliances. As a woman monarch in a man's world, she managed to rule for sixty years. Many scholars argue that her rule was not an especially great one, but it was against the backdrop of the Renaissance in England and the careers of such notables as William Shakespeare.

Elizabeth was under constant threat of rebellion led by supporters of her Catholic cousin, Mary Queen of Scots. After Elizabeth ordered the execution of

Mary, Philip of Spain decided to launch an invasion in the name of Catholicism. Philip of Spain summoned the largest armada ever collected to invade England and rid it of the Protestant Elizabeth, but in 1588, before the fleet could reach England, a massive wind, called the Protestant wind, blew the fleet around the island and wrecked it. England did not become Catholic, and Protestantism would rule the Church there. The victory over the armada also made it possible for England to later rule the seas.

THE COUNTER REFORMATION

The Roman Church fought the growing threat of Protestantism in a movement known as the **Counter Reformation**. **Ignatius of Loyola** founded the **Jesuits** or **Society of Jesus** as an imitation of Christ, and he insisted on complete submission in matters of faith. According to Loyola, if the Church says that white is black, then white is black. The immense learning of the Jesuits was for the purpose of refuting Protestant doctrines and teaching the Catholic faith. The Jesuits would carry the faith to the Far East, and also make numerous contributions to science.

The **Council of Trent** met sporadically from 1545–1563. There would not be another Church Council until 1870. The Council, like the Jesuits, reaffirmed the basic tenets of Catholicism. It rejected the Protestant justification by faith and argued that good works were necessary for salvation. The council affirmed that priesthood was a special vocation, the doctrine of transubstantiation, and insisted on the Latin Vulgate as the only authoritative translation of the Bible. This was perhaps unfortunate, as we now know the Vulgate was not a particularly good translation.

The Council also issued a list of banned books, the Index of Prohibited Books. They regulated art, affecting Michelangelo's painting in the Sistine Chapel. The Council rejected the Conciliar Movement and kept the papacy as the authoritative center of the Church. The Council insisted on the unity of the Church, and rejected those doctrines of the Protestants that resulted in the plethora of sects seen today. The Church rejected Luther's notion that any Christian could interpret the Bible as well as any other in favor of the consensus of the faithful and the need for the Church as a mediating authority.

The Council also affirmed the seven sacraments in the face of Luther's criticisms. Many scholars have suggested that their rigidity on theological points of debate with the Protestants kept the Roman Church from reconciliation with the Protestants. On the other hand, the Council also implemented many reforms of the priesthood. The Council reformed the controversial sale of indulgences, forced bishops to reside in the region they presided over, and forbade the practice of simony, or the buying and selling of church offices. It reformed the education of the clergy.

The Thirty Years' War

The rising tide of Protestantism within the Holy Roman Empire resulted in the **Thirty Years' War**, beginning in 1618. When the Catholic king of Bohemia attempted to close Protestant churches, Protestants threw his representatives out an upper story window in an event known as the "defenestration of Prague." Protestantism was squashed in Bohemia, but the conflict continued and entered its "Danish Phase" when the king of Denmark, Christian IV, entered to defend the Protestants. He was no more successful than earlier Protestants had been against the Catholic Hapsburg rulers, but the Swedish King Gustavus Adolphus turned the war around for Protestants in its "Swedish phase." When the French entered on behalf of the Protestants, the war entered its "international phase." The **Peace of Westphalia** in 1648 concluded the Thirty Years' War, and finally included Calvinists and gave them the freedom of religion offered to Lutherans in the Peace of Augsburg. However, the Peace of Westphalia gave independent authority to the German princes, once again fracturing the Holy Roman Empire.

Humanism and the Reformation

The Reformation grew out of developments of the Renaissance, in particular new techniques for the critical analysis of texts. Luther used such techniques when he studied Erasmus's *Novum Instrumentum*, and also when he made his translation of the Bible into German. Calvin, too, had been trained in humanist techniques, and so had others active in the Reformation. However, many of the reformers' ideas conflicted with those of the humanists. Luther, for example, denied that humans had free will, in complete contrast to Pico della Mirandola's view that humans alone of all creatures were not constrained by their nature. Even Erasmus debated Luther on the issue of free will. Luther as well as Calvin taught that humans were governed by predestination, whereas humanists such as Pico believed in the infinite power of humans to create their own destinies. While the Reformers were often masters of humanist critical techniques and reflect the desire of many humanists to go back to the original sources of their texts and even to the origins of Christianity in the way the religion was practiced, many of their deeply held beliefs about human nature were not compatible with humanism. Luther once remarked that humans were "worms in the bowels of God," in total contrast to the lofty view of humanity presented by humanists of the Italian Renaissance.

The Reformation and Gender Issues: The Witchcraft Scare

The zeal of many Protestant reformers perhaps created a climate where people were more willing to believe in the presence and active intervention in human lives of the devil. Thousands of cases of witchcraft were prosecuted in Europe, and many people were burned at the stake. The majority of these victims were women, and many of those women stood apart from traditional social structures, as they were unattached to men. Many of these women were widowed or single and most were older women over fifty. Most were of lower social status. There are many hypotheses about the cause of the witchcraft craze. Some scholars believe because the women were noncomformists, they were singled out for persecution. Others maintain that because the witches were accused of having intercourse with the devil, witchcraft was a way to release pent-up sexual urges repressed through Christian values regarding sex, on the part of both the Reformers and Catholics. Whatever the reasons for the events that resulted in perhaps as many as 100,000 women being burned at the stake, the hysteria represented continuing negative beliefs about women and their mysterious, alluring power to corrupt men. Though women made gains in the Renaissance and Reformation in terms of their roles within the family and entering marriage at later ages, nevertheless, the witchcraft craze illustrates that women had still not broken from the molds cast in earlier ages. Since early Christianity, the story of Eve had been used to identify women with evil; in Reformation Europe, judges in witchcraft cases were still inclined to believe women had a greater propensity for evil.

Review Questions

1. His studies and observations convinced Luther that human salvation could only come from

   (A) charity and good works.

   (B) grace and faith.

   (C) pilgrimages to Rome and the Holy Land.

   (D) special blessings from the pope or his agents.

2. The Peace of Augsburg placed the choice of which religion would be followed in Germany in the hands of

   (A) individual worshipers.

   (B) councils of believers in each land.

   (C) the Holy Roman emperor.

   (D) the German territorial princes.

3. Calvinism influenced the growth of a capitalistic economy due to Calvin's doctrines of

   (A) democratically elected ministers and elders to run the church.

   (B) work as a Christian duty and the acceptability of profits as a sign of good work.

   (C) each individual's sole responsibility to oneself and to his business.

   (D) complete equality of women in both worship services and work.

4. The governing body of a Calvinist church is called the

   (A) synod.

   (B) episcopalian diocese.

   (C) parish.

   (D) presbytery.

5. The English Reformation was fundamentally

   (A) the work of a dominant religious leader.

   (B) Calvinist in tone and form.

   (C) an act of state.

   (D) Lutheran in tone and form.

6. After its formal break with Rome, in terms of doctrine the Church of England under Henry VIII followed lines that were basically

   (A) Lutheran.

   (B) Catholic.

   (C) Calvinist.

   (D) Anabaptist.

7. In matters of theology, the Council of Trent

   (A) accepted some Protestant doctrines while rejecting others.

   (B) firmly reaffirmed all doctrines challenged by Protestants.

   (C) accepted virtually all Protestant doctrines.

   (D) marked the triumph of the Catholic humanists over the scholastics.

8. The ruler who brought England firmly and permanently into the Protestant camp was

   (A) Henry VII.

   (B) Mary I.

   (C) James II.

   (D) Elizabeth the Great.

9. All of the following were characteristic of the new Protestant churches EXCEPT

   (A) the use of candles in services.

   (B) abolishing the priesthood as a special "estate."

   (C) rejecting the cult of saints.

   (D) services in the language of the people (English, German).

10. The Council of Trent accomplished all of the following EXCEPT

   (A) reformed education for the clergy.

   (B) accepted justification by faith as a basis for Catholic theology.

   (C) published the Index of Prohibited Books.

   (D) regulated art.

Answers

1. (B)	4. (D)	7. (B)	10. (B)
2. (D)	5. (C)	8. (D)	
3. (B)	6. (B)	9. (A)	

UNIT IV

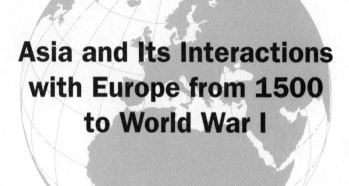

Asia and Its Interactions with Europe from 1500 to World War I

Chapter 19

JAPAN FROM THE WARRING STATES THROUGH THE MEIJI RESTORATION

KEY TERMS

Warring States
Ashikaga Shogunate
Oda Nobunaga
Hideyoshi
Shogun
Edo
Kyoto
Ieyasu Tokugawa
Battle of Sekigahara
Samurai
Ronin
Daimyo
Inns of the Shogun
Seppuku
Bushido

Nagasaki
Dutch traders
Kokugaku
Haiku
Bunraku
Ukiyo-e woodblock prints
Hokusai
Ihara Saikaku
Commodore Matthew Perry
The Meiji Restoration
Sat-Cho Alliance
Meiji Constitution
Ministry of Industry
"Revolution from above"
"Incomplete revolution"

THE WARRING STATES

By 1467, during the **Ashikaga Shogunate** (1338–1567), there were almost 260 feudal houses or daimyo. Each daimyo was independent and maintained its own separate army, making Japan in reality 260 separate countries. Since the Ashikaga had no powerful central administration, there were constant armed conflicts between the daimyo. During the **Onin War** (1467–1477), Japan was literally in the "sengoku jidai," meaning "the age of the country at war." This age is commonly called **Warring States Japan**. Powerful warlords arose, such as Nobunaga, who tried to remedy this situation by taking strong control of the daimyo.

Oda Nobunaga (1534–1582)

Nobunaga made the first attempt to unify Japan at the end of the Warring States period; he attempted to bring all of Japan "under a single sword" (*tenka-fubu*). He destroyed the Buddhist monastery on Mt. Hiei, as the monks there had often been involved in Japan's political and military struggles. To further thwart the influence of Buddhism, Nobunaga encouraged Christianity and was especially interested in the teachings of the Jesuits. He also embraced the use of Western firearms and retrained his army to accommodate new weapons, including the pike, built stone forts, and became the first Japanese leader to clad his ships in iron. Nobunaga, however, never managed to eradicate the warring lords, and he was assassinated by two of his generals.

Toyotomi Hideyoshi (1536–1598)

Hideyoshi was the son of a peasant who became the complete master of Japan by 1590. Hideyoshi had no last name when he began to serve Oda Nobunaga; by the end of his life, he had assumed the family name, Toyotomi, or "Abundant Provider." Hideyoshi, like the Hong Wu emperor of Ming China, was concerned about the ability of people, such as himself, from lower classes to rise to power. Consequently, he froze the social classes, making class status permanent for people and their children. In 1586 he ordered farmers to stay on their land. Hideyoshi gave the samurai, who had helped to create the chaos of the warring states and who were the professional soldiers of Japan, special status. In 1587 Hideyoshi decreed that only the samurai could carry their famous long sword or katana or wear armor, and only the samurai had "last names"; others in Japan were simply known by their functions.

Hideyoshi invaded Korea in 1592 and 1597 in order to prepare for an eventual invasion of China. He died without accomplishing his goal. His ambitions abroad perhaps account for his failure to completely unite Japan. While Nobunaga had used force in his attempts to pacify the daimyo and rebellious Buddhist monks, Hideyoshi relied on personal loyalties. When he died, those loyalties died as well. Although the emperor had refused to give Hideyoshi the title of shogun due to his poor lineage, the Japanese named him a Shinto deity shortly after his death and gave him the title "Hokoku" or "Wealth of the Nation."

TOKUGAWA JAPAN 1600–1867

Ieyasu Tokugawa (1542–1616)

In 1600 **Ieyasu Tokugawa** won the Battle of Sekigahara and began a process that would eventually create a centralized government and unite Japan. The Tokugawa ruled Japan until 1867, and created the longest period of peace in Japanese history. The Tokugawa period is also known as the Edo period, after the place of residence of the shogun.

The emperor gave Ieyasu the title of shogun, or chief military leader. The Tokugawa Shogunate relied upon the bakufu domain system, and the shogun became the most important leader in Japan. Under the Tokugawa shoguns, the emperor lived in Kyoto, while the shoguns resided in Edo, a city that later was known as Tokyo. The emperor became a mere figurehead, and the daimyo became mere vassals of the shogun.

Various methods of controlling the daimyo were developed, such as the requirement to march to the shogun's court in Edo every year. At the court, they were forbidden to draw weapons, and along the way, daimyo stopped at Inns of the Shoguns, thus generating revenue for the shogunate and keeping the daimyo under control as they marched. Their absence from their territories further contributed to their inability to wage wars with one another or revolts against the shogun, and the shoguns held their families hostage during the period when the daimyo were not in Edo.

Lord Asano and the 47 Ronin

The samurai lived by the **Code of Bushido**. There were about two million samurai during the Tokugawa period, out of the thirty million in the total population. One of the most famous stories of the period, which continues to be told and retold in the Japanese cinema and in books, stories, and other forms, is the story of Lord Asano and his forty-seven samurai. **Lord Asano** was angered by **Lord Kira** while at the shogun's court and drew his sword against him. He was ordered to commit seppuku (also known by the slang term hara kiri, or "belly slashing"). According to the samurai code of honor, this was the only way to restore one's honor when one disagrees with and then morally protests an order of the shogun. Seppuku was a ritual in which one disemboweled oneself while still alive, as the Japanese believed the seat of all life or the life force was to be found in the abdomen.

Asano's samurai believed he had been treated unjustly by Kira and by the shogun, and so plotted their revenge. For two years, they gave the appearance of accepting the verdict and watched Asano's estate dismembered. They lived as **Ronin**, or unemployed samurai. In the middle of winter two years later, they stormed Kira's palace, killed him, and put his head on a pike and took it back to Asano's gravesite, where they displayed it in triumph. Because they had violated the shogun's codes here, they too committed seppuku. They are the greatest heroes of Japanese literature, but they also illustrate the many contradictions of Japanese life during this period. One was forced to display loyalty to the shogun in one's outer life, no matter what the contradictions might be in one's inner life.

Japan and the West

During the Tokugawa period, Dutch traders appeared in Japan. They were restricted to the port of Dejima in Nagasaki. Jesuits also were in Japan, but while Hideyoshi allowed them to teach to thwart the influence of Buddhism, Ieyasu ordered them expelled in 1616. Those who failed to leave were killed and converts to the faith were executed or forced to recant. The shogunate adopted an increasingly isolationist strategy, and expelled all Westerners after 1638. The Tokugawa forbade Japanese to travel abroad. Contact with the West would not occur again until Commodore Matthew Perry's expedition in 1853.

Japanese isolationism resulted in the development of an interest in Japanese culture. A branch of scholarship called kokugaku, which means "Native Studies" or "Nativism" became prominent in this period. Since the Japanese had imported much from China, it was always difficult for them to separate out their native traditions, such as Shinto.

Motoori Norinaga (1730–1801) concentrated on the recovery of the Japanese language, and he argued that the use of the Chinese writing system interfered with the understanding of Japanese itself. He studied the Kojiki, or the oldest history of Japan. Although the work was written in Chinese, he discovered that it was meant to be read in Japanese. He also explored the first collection of Japanese poems, the Manyoshu. These studies led him to develop his theory of the sensitivity to things or the "mono no aware," according to which one experienced the world and was touched by it, and used Japanese to directly express it.

Haiku

His studies led to the popularity of haiku, a three-line form of seventeen syllables, in which one captured, through attention to a single moment in nature, the deepest aspects of life. The most famous haiku poet of the time was Basho.

Commodore Perry

In 1853 **Commodore Matthew Perry** arrived in Japan with a fleet of warships and a letter to the shogun from American President Millard Filmore requesting that trade be established between Japan and the United States. A few months later, when Perry returned to Japan, the shogun agreed to a treaty. Rebellions erupted in the southern regions of Japan, particularly in Satsuma and Choshu. After Western ships fired on the rebels in Choshu, the rebels strengthened their forces and their opposition to the Western presence as a result, leading to the demise of the Tokugawa Shogunate.

The Meiji Restoration

In 1866 Saigo Takamori, the leader of the Satsuma domain, and Kido Takayoshi, the leader of the Choshu domain, formed the **Sat-Cho Alliance**. Its purpose was the overthrow of the Tokugawa in order to restore the emperor to power.

On November 9, 1867, the fifteenth Tokugawa shogun, Tokugawa Yoshinobu, resigned, and imperial rule was restored. This event is known as the Taisei Houkan or "restoration."

In January 1868 the Boshin War or the War of the Year of the Dragon started with the Battle of Toba Fushimi. The armies of Choshu and Satsuma defeated the Tokugawa army at the siege of Hakodate on the second largest island of Japan, Hokkaido, in 1869.

The fourteen-year-old heir to the imperial throne, **Mutsuhito**, became emperor and took the title **Meiji**, meaning "enlightened rule." Shortly thereafter, he signed the **Five Charter Oath** (1868), according to which the feudal order was abolished, the Tokugawa freezing of classes abandoned, the isolationism of Japan ended, and the formation of a deliberate assembly promised. In 1871 the daimyo were stripped of their hereditary titles to their land. Similarly, samurai were forbidden to wear the symbols of their hereditary status, their swords. An imperial army was formed to replace the old feudal structures.

Important positions in the new government were given to the genro, elder samurai from the Sat-Cho alliance. The **Meiji Constitution** (1890) created a parliament with an upper house that was appointed and a lower house that was elected called the **Diet**. The Diet could pass laws provided both houses agreed, but in the end, it served merely in an advisory capacity. Only five percent of Japanese males owned enough property to elect representatives to the Diet. The Diet also was subordinate to the executive branch, which directly controlled the military and handpicked its cabinet.

Historians debate the extent to which the Meiji Restoration changed the old social order of Japan. Some historians maintain that the only real political change of the Meiji period was that the Tokugawa were removed in favor of the powerful daimyos that overthrew them.

Industrialization in the Meiji Era

Economic changes during the Meiji period were more profound. First, the Meiji fought against the growing impact of Western Imperialism in Asia by purchasing Western interests in businesses and discouraging foreign investments in Japan. Trade rules favored exportation, rather than imports. Foreign loans were repaid and no more were taken. The Meiji raised revenue through a new agricultural tax of three percent. Formerly private domains were ceded to those who worked the land. The new tax raised needed revenue, but often proved disastrous to the farmers.

Much of this revenue was channeled into industrial development, and government banks provided capital to promote industries, such as shipbuilding, sake, and weaponry. The government implemented improvements in transportation and communication and subsidized industries with financial grants. A system of state education was developed to provide training in areas beneficial to industry, such as science. Exports of tea and silk generated tremendous revenue. Some samuarai went into industry, such as Iwasaki Yataro, who founded the Mitsubishi company. Mitsubishi received many government contracts, just as did other companies.

Western models were often imitated, especially in the educational system. Japanese students traveled and were educated abroad and brought back Western ideas. Other aspects of Western culture, such as art and architecture, also influenced the Japanese during this period. Tensions erupted in Japanese society over new Western influences, but the government retained control of the industrialization process through the Ministry of Industry, created in 1870, and channeled other tensions into nationalistic pride.

Farmers who lost their lands due to inability to pay the new agricultural taxes migrated to urban areas, where they provided a source of cheap labor. Conditions in Japanese factories were as bad if not worse than many of those in Europe during the Industrial Revolution. Workers who attempted to escape their miserable plight were often shot in Japan.

While Europeans industrialized over the course of more than a century, the Meiji had industrialized Japan in less than 40 years. Some historians point out that Japan adapted more readily than China to Western models because Japan had been accustomed to borrowing from other cultures, such as it had from China.

Gender Issues

In the Tokugawa period, Japanese women had been kept confined to the house and followed Confucian expectations about obedience to their fathers, husbands, and sons. Women could not inherit property and could not obtain a divorce, whereas men could do both. Marriages were arranged.

However, the industrialization of the Meiji era opened up to them new opportunities for education, and women started to work in the new factories. Despite some gains in this area, the constitution of 1890 did not grant women eligibility to vote, and in later years, their rights were defined within the traditional context of the family. Even by 1900, the Meiji were still prohibiting women from joining political organizations. Women contributed to industrialization, especially through labor in the textile industries, but they did not receive political rewards. The inequities that continued under the Meiji for women, farmers, and other members of the lower classes have been often referred to as "an incomplete revolution." Although the Meiji leaders achieved much in the way of economic and industrial transformation, they did not succeed in changing the unequal distribution of wealth so characteristic of the Tokugawa and earlier eras.

Interpreting the Meiji

The Meiji Restoration was accomplished without violence, and so was not a revolution in the typical sense of the word, but it wrought many changes in Japanese society and these changes were revolutionary. It accomplished these changes, however, entirely in a top-down, dictatorial manner. For this reason it has been called a "revolution from above." While a centralized group of elite people restructured Japan but managed to leave their former power intact, they also combined their efforts with those of a new order, such as people with capitalistic interests formerly not highly placed in the government. The sheer despotism of the Meiji leadership arose out of the feudal precedents of the Tokugawa period, yet they combined these tactics with capitalistic enterprise. Some historians have referred to the Meiji as a form of "Asian fascism," and argue that this unique combination of despotism and capitalistic interests drove the Japanese to fixate on national power and wealth. What followed was a wave of imperialist expansion on the part of Japan, which was only stopped by World War II.

Review Questions

1. The leader who attempted to thwart the influence of Buddhist monks and warring daimyos through bringing in Western religions and firearms was

    (A) Ieyasu Tokugawa.

    (B) Hideyoshi.

    (C) Oda Nobunaga.

    (D) Takamori.

2. The code of honor that governed the life of the samurai warrior was

    (A) bunraku.

    (B) kabuki.

    (C) haiku.

    (D) bushido.

3. The self-inflicted honorable death of the samurai is

    (A) bunraku.

    (B) seppuko.

    (C) kabuki.

    (D) bushido.

4. Hideyoshi's reforms included all of the following EXCEPT

    (A) stripping the peasantry of weapons.

    (B) the census.

    (C) allowing all people to bear last names.

    (D) standardizing weights and measures.

5. The first Tokugawa shogun was

    (A) Hideyoshi.

    (B) Ieyasu.

    (C) Chikamatsu.

    (D) Ihara Saikaku.

6. During which period was Japan the most isolated from Western influences?

    (A) The reign of Hideyoshi

    (B) The reign of Oda Nobunaga

    (C) The Meiji period

    (D) The Tokugawa shogunate

7. All of the following are true of the Meiji Restoration EXCEPT

    (A) the social classes were no longer frozen.

    (B) isolationism ended.

    (C) a parliamentarian system was created.

    (D) the Five Charter Oath promised the abolition of the feudal order.

Answers

1. (C)	3. (B)	5. (B)	7. (C)
2. (D)	4. (C)	6. (D)	

Chapter 20

CHINA FROM THE MING TO THE QING DYNASTY

KEY TERMS

The Ming or Brilliant Dynasty
Hongwu Emperor
Yongle Emperor
Guards with Brocade Uniforms
Eight-legged essays
Forbidden City
Zheng he
Champa rice
li-chia
Ta-Ming lü
Single Whip Reform
Ming porcelain
Jesuits
Wouko
Eunuchs
Mongols
Beijing
Great Canon of the Yongle Emperor
Matteo Ricci
Yen Sung
Chongzhen (Ch'ung-chen)
Jurchen tribe
Aixinjueluo Nurhachi

Taiji or Abahai
Qing or Pure Dynasty
Li Zicheng (Li Tzu-ch'eng)
Shunzhi emperor
Revolt of the Three Feudatories
Kangzi Emperor
Qianlong Emperor
White Lotus Rebellion
Taiping rebellion
Hong Xiuquan
Kingdom of Heavenly Peace
Tianjin or Tientsin
Boxer Rebellion
Treaty of Nanjing
Treaty of Tientsin
Society of Harmonious Fists
Dowager Empress Cixi
Open Door Policy
John Hay
Pu Yi
Double Ten Incident
Sun Yat Sen
National Army

THE MING DYNASTY (1368–1644)

The Yuan dynasty of the Mongols may have been successful in many areas, but there were still many patriotic rebellions on the part of the Chinese against Mongols, whom they saw as invading conquerors. Among other issues was the fact that the Mongols tended to hand all-important positions to Mongols, employing Chinese bureaucrats in non-Chinese areas of their empire.

According to Chinese historians, in 1351 a group of laborers digging along the Yellow River found a statue with only one eye and an inscription indicating a coming rebellion. There had been a number of natural disasters, such as floods and landslides, and the Chinese took these signs as an omen that the Mongols had lost the Mandate of Heaven. In the 109 years of Mongol rule, only the emperor Kublai Khan had any kind of success as an emperor, while the short reigns of the other monarchs had allowed the eunuchs to rise in power. The Mongol rulers supported their lavish lifestyle through heavy taxes, and the peasants bore most of the burden. Toward the end of the Mongol rule, very high inflation was common throughout China.

Zhu Yuanzhang (Chu Yuan Chang): The Hongwu Emperor

The rebels were mostly peasants who were affected by the flooding of the Yellow River, which brought about serious famine. One of the most important of these rebels was a Han Chinese peasant, **Zhu Yuanzhang**, whose father was an itinerant agricultural worker. He served as general for one of many rebellious warlords, Kuo Tzu-hsing. Zhu Yuanzhang successfully defeated the Mongols, and became one of only two peasants to have founded a dynasty. By 1368, he had conquered southern China and by 1369 had driven the Mongols out. Zhu Yuanzhang took the reign name of **Hongwu**, which means "great military power." He reigned from 1368–1398, and most scholars see him as one of the greatest emperors in Chinese history. So began the **Ming dynasty**, whose name means the "brilliant dynasty." The Ming leaders did create a period of brilliance in culture and in their care for their people. They were also the last native dynasty to rule China. Under the Ming, China experienced its greatest social and economic revolution prior to the twentieth century. The Ming were also the first dynasty to interact with Europeans on a large scale.

The Reconstruction of the Economy and Changes in Agriculture

The Mongol conquest had, in fact, left the border areas of China virtual deserts. Even today, much of this region remains desolate. In order to reclaim useless land, the Ming transferred a segment of their population to deserted regions. Irrigation pumps allowed peasants to introduce fish into the rice paddies. The fish fertilized the paddies and also removed mosquitoes, which often brought disease. The Chinese learned to cultivate Champa rice, which was able to resist the effects of drought and could be harvested more quickly than traditional rice. Agricultural output rose dramatically, and from around 1550, so did the population of China. Unfortunately, greater output of crops did not mean higher income for the people. In fact, it was greater use of peasants for labor that helped to fuel the increased production. The increase in population increased the number of market towns, as people clustered in towns. Greater population density in towns led to greater demand for goods. Consequently, trade and industrial development increased, even despite the general disdain that the Confucian scholars had for merchants. Nanjing, for example, became an important center for textile production and there were several other urban manufacturing centers that evolved during the Ming dynasty.

The government also planted over one billion trees in an effort to reforest China. Fifty million trees were planted in Nanjing alone in 1391, and these became the material that built the ships used in the maritime expeditions of the Yongle (Yung-lo or Yung-le) emperor, the third Ming ruler. These trees also created the basis of the Chinese merchant marine; during the sixteenth century, this merchant marine was one of the most successful in the world, as China entered the new global trade created in the wake of the European Age of Discovery.

Governmental Reforms

The **Hongwu emperor** instituted an absolute monarchy, comparable to that established by Louis XIV. He was very conscious of his peasant origins, and so distrusted the nobles, eunuchs, and scholars. He moved the capital to Nanjing, which means "southern capital," and he forced nobles to live at his court there and to participate in many elaborate rituals designed to establish the court as divine.

The Hongwu emperor publicly beat any officials who criticized him or dissented in any way. This involved having 100 men beat the offender on the buttocks, and most offenders did not survive. The emperor demanded complete submission, as opposed to the Confucian ideal that the superior man should not be beaten or subjected to punishment. The emperor at one point tried one of his comrades on suspicion of cooperating with Mongols and the Japanese; over 15,000 people were involved in the trial.

To take complete control of the government, the Hongwu emperor abolished the Imperial Secretariat, the main central administrative body under previous dynasties. Six ministries of the government were under the Hongwu emperor's direct supervision. The emperor now ran the government, in great contrast to earlier dynasties. The Hongwu emperor had to hold court three times a day to manage the government, a task Ming emperors were able to maintain for the first three reigns, but not thereafter. The emperor forbade eunuchs to read to lessen their power and reduce their numbers. Later, dissatisfaction with the repressive government would result in their resurgence.

The emperor also took control of the army and developed the Guards with the Brocade Uniforms, a secret police that spied on political officials. The Guards with the Brocade Uniforms originated in Hongwu's personal entourage. In an effort to create stability and peace along the frontiers, Hongwu also enrolled many Mongols into the Chinese army, and they supported themselves by raising their own food along the frontiers.

Civil Service Exams

The Hongwu emperor revived the civil service system of exams, and created a three-part exam that was held at the district, provincial, and imperial levels. He created an extensive system of examinations that were very difficult to pass. One had to write answers in eight parts, and to explain portions of sentences according to various interpretations. Under the Ming, one had to use the interpretation fostered by the state. These essays were known as the "eight legged essays," and one had to make use of no more than 700 characters. Only about ninety scholars a year passed these exams. The exams supported the Confucian ideal that advancement should be on the basis of competence as opposed to high social standing. They also emphasized the importance of an orderly hierarchy of authority, with respect due to one's superiors. The Hongwu ruler did not tolerate dissent, and only those who abided by Ming philosophies passed. Even within such a system, however, poor people could rise to positions of prominence.

The Confucian Scholars and China's Failure to Industrialize

Those who acquired wealth used it to educate themselves so as to acquire the status of a Confucian scholar. This class of scholars was known as the gentry. The importance of the gentry, in fact, was a contributing factor to China's failure to industrialize. Although the Chinese were a highly inventive people, they focused their efforts during the Ming period on the Confucian literary classics, as opposed to the sciences. Further, the wealthy used their resources for education, rather than investing in business and manufacturing interests. According to Confucianism, merchants were parasites who did not produce anything useful for society. Confucians generally distrusted trade because it encouraged change. Although China had the beginnings of industrialization in the Ming dynasty due to the development of trade and handicraft industries, the pattern in China did not follow that of the West, for reasons that will be discussed further below. The Hongwu emperor generally preferred an agricultural economy, and many have traced this to his own peasant origins.

Functional Division of the Population

The emperor had risen from the peasantry to the imperial house and, as a result, he greatly feared social mobility. He ordered a functional division of population, whereby anyone born a peasant, soldier, or craftsman remained in this station throughout life. The system of taxation led to the need for a census, and they divided the population into li-chia, or groups of ten families responsible for levying taxes equitably among their members and for maintaining order. The poor of China often became dependent on the gentry. Taxes were paid in rice. Unlike the absolutist governments of Europe, though, the Hongwu emperor failed to establish a central ministry responsible for taxation and lack of centralization in this respect weakened the Ming government.

The Hongwu emperor's greatest achievement was the creation of the Ta-Ming lü, a code of laws. These laws were considered the lü, or "unchanging laws." The emperor also developed a set of laws to address changing situations, and these laws were known as the li. Later Ming emperors abused the li, and the constant changes in the set of laws resulted in their losing the trust of the people.

Expansion Under Later Emperors: The Maritime Expeditions of the Yongle Emperor

The **Yongle (Yung-lo** or **Yung-le)** emperor (1403–1424), the third emperor of the dynasty, began a series of naval expeditions in 1405. The Hongxi (Hung-hsi) emperor (1425) and the Xuande (Hsüan-te) emperor (1426–1435) continued the expeditions. The Yongle emperor liked exotic goods and also wanted to expand trade, and he sent seven expeditions led by the eunuch **Zheng He (Cheng Ho)**, a Muslim from Yunnan, to such places as Ceylon, Calcutta, South Vietnam, and Africa. Zheng He commanded 60 vessels with 500 troops. His ships were 400 feet long and weighed 500 tons, far bigger and faster than those of the Portuguese. The expeditions brought back zebras, ostriches, and tribute from other kings. Zheng He left steles (stone monuments with inscriptions) proclaiming that these areas were vassals of the Ming and inhabitants of some of these areas still revere him as a god. In Southeast Asia, for example, he is revered as the god **San-Pao**. In 1391 over fifty million trees had been planted in Nanjing to prepare for maritime exploration, and during this period, the Ming had the most powerful sea empire in the world. The Yongle emperor's empire was bigger than all of Europe in size, and his expeditions were far larger.

The maritime expeditions led to great commercial success, and those involved became very wealthy. The full economic impact of the voyages was not evident until the sixteenth century. Plants from the New World led to agricultural reform in China, as maize and the sweet potato became staples of the Chinese diet. These products could flourish in poorly irrigated areas. Silver mined in the New World also made its way across the globe, and about one-half of it ended up in China. Goods from China's various craft industries, such as silk and lacquerware, were in great demand in other parts of the world, and China received a disproportionate share of New World silver. Merchants from Europe began to appear in Macao and Canton. The influx of silver from the Americas made it possible for the Ming to take 30 or 40 taxes and reduce them to one payable in silver. This was known as the **Single Whip Reform**. So much silver came into China, however, that by 1620, its value had dropped by over two-thirds. Previously, the Hongwu emperor's practice of issuing more and more paper money had lowered its value to one-fortieth of its previous worth and caused economic inflation. The country's financial base was seriously weakened.

By the time many of these events occurred, the expeditions had long since ceased. The voyages started by the Yongle emperor ended in 1435, after astrologers convinced the Ming rulers that the exotic goods imported would bring about the downfall of the dynasty. Ironically, it was in part the European presence in China during the nineteenth century that contributed to the downfall of the following dynasty, the Qing. The voyages of Zheng He generated tremendous wealth for those involved. Jealousy on the part of the Confucian scholarly gentry likely led to the renewed emphasis on agriculture, in keeping with the Hongwu emperor's style of government. The Yongle emperor had moved the capital back to Beijing (the "northern capital") before the expeditions had ceased; this move brought about renewed focus on the Yellow River Valley, which was the agricultural heartland of China, as opposed to the south.

China and the West: Comparative Patterns of Development

The reasons for different development patterns between China and the West have been much disputed. First, China did not have access to coal and other resources that were near manufacturing centers, as was the case in Britain. In 1700, China and Europe were relatively equal in terms of technological and economic development. Britain, for example, forged ahead in industry due to the natural resources available. Later, industrialization spread to other countries in Europe. Central to this spread was the development of absolutist monarchies in Europe that protected industry and commerce and actually used it to generate revenue for the state. In China, Hongwu developed an agricultural economy, and generally did not foster trade and commerce, due to his Confucian belief that merchants were nonproductive members of society.

Another factor in the growth of industry in Europe was capitalism. Again, absolutism in Europe promoted capitalism, as the wealth of merchants could be channeled into the state. In China, however, there was also a money economy. Hongwu issued paper money and the influx of silver from the New World created a true coin economy. Chinese merchants developed new ways of producing goods, such as porcelain, in response to demand from outside China and to the new supply of silver. However, Hongwu's use of paper currency was not prudent, and the value of the currency was debased. The same thing happened later with the overflow of silver. The Chinese, then, did not effectively manage the opportunities currency provided, and this may go back to Hongwu's preference for an agricultural economy.

China had the beginnings of mercantilism and overseas trade with the voyages of Zheng He. Many historians argue that when China cut off these voyages and turned inward rather than outward, the Ming effectively also stifled industrialization and the further development of the economy. Other historians, such as Jonathon Spence, point out that China continued to have a vast trading empire in southeast Asia, so that China never completely turned as inward as some historians maintain. Nevertheless, many historians maintain that China simply did not capitalize on its opportunities for industrial expansion. These historians also link the arrival of European capitalism to the decline of the Ming. Europeans began to arrive in Macao and Canton in the sixteenth century, creating a foundation for later nineteenth-century European imperialism. The decline of the Ming also led to its eventual conquest by the Manchus. These events effectively stopped any trend towards industrialization or a vibrant economy.

Artistic and Cultural Accomplishments of the Ming

During the Ming period, there was a cultural renaissance, in part fostered by success with trade. The Ming was famous for their style of porcelain, featuring blue on white. Much of this porcelain was sent out on the merchant fleets to Europe, whose merchants coveted the secret of making the delicate white China. The Dutch imported tea from China, which became a very popular drink in Europe. Success at trade made China one of the leading manufacturing centers in the world.

China encountered Europeans through trade, but also through the work of Catholic missionaries, who followed Portuguese to the East. In the sixteenth century, the Jesuit Matteo Ricci came to China to convert them to Christianity. The Jesuits helped to bring about a resurgence of long-forgotten Chinese mathematical and astronomical skills. Christianity, however, was too foreign an influence to take hold in China. The Chinese were not acquainted with the ideal of a transcendent being. Confucianism was a practical system of ethics not involving the worship of deities; the Chinese were more prone to worshipping ancestors than deities. Although the Jesuits respected the ethical values of Confucianism and used stories and parables to teach in hopes of reaching the Chinese, they forbade their cult of ancestor worship. The Chinese experience with the Jesuits eventually led to great mistrust of foreigners.

An Example of Ming Porcelain

The Decline of The Ming

Ming emperors spent too much money supporting the aristocracy with maintenance payments. Some had as many as 94 heirs and relatives. Many expeditions against the Mongols, including five under the Yongle emperor, had forced the Ming to levy higher and higher taxes. They built lavish tombs while the peasantry suffered. After the Yongle emperor, later Ming rulers did not handle the demands of the Hongwu emperor's bureaucracy well. By the time of the Jiajing (Chia-ching) emperor (ruled 1522–1566), the emperor had become a figurehead who retreated into his private world while the eunuchs ran China. During the Jiajing (Chia-ching) emperor's rule, the Grand Secretary, Yen Sung (1480–1568), brought China to its knees with an abusive style of leadership. By the seventeenth century, the corruption of the eunuchs was so intense that the Chongzhen (Ch'ung-chen) emperor (1628–1644) attempted to oust them from power by running the government alone. This proved an impossible task and contributed to the downfall of the Ming.

Though the Ming emperors had all they could handle with the eunuchs at home, they had to contend with pirate raids along the coast from the Japanese, whom they referred to as the Woukou, from the word "wo," meaning "dwarf."

Further Mongol attacks from 1438–1449 caused the Ming to build a second line of defense, a set of inner walls that were double or triple in some places and 5,000 kilometers long. In fact, the Ming built most of the remaining sections of the Great Wall.

THE QING (CH'ING) DYNASTY (1644–1911)

By far the greatest threat to the Ming were the **Manzus** (**Manchus**), members of the Jurchen tribe who lived in Manchuria. Their dynasty, founded in the twelfth century, was the **Jin** (**Chin**) or "Gold" dynasty. Their leader **Aixinjueluo Nurhachi** (**Aisin Gioro Nurgachi**, 1559–1626) forged them into a tightly unified single political unit by 1616, and the Mongols so respected him that they gave him the title Kundulen Han, or "Respected Emperor." The Jin were controlled by the Mongol Yuan dynasty until the Yuan were overthrown by the Ming; during the Ming dynasty, the Jin gradually regained their independence.

Hong Taiji (Abahai)

Nurachi's second son, Hong Taiji or Abahai, succeeded him, and he launched an attack on Korea and then marched on China. Abahai looted Beijing and then set up a civil administration. A Manchurian prince administered each ministry or board. Each prince had five assistants, including at least one Mongol and one Chinese. Abahai called his people the **Manchu** and renamed the dynasty the **"Qing (Ch'ing)"** or the "Pure" to avoid the negative associations with the third century B.C.E. Qin (Ch'in) Empire. Given the presence of Manchurians and Mongols in the bureacracy, it was anything but "pure" from the Chinese point of view.

Devastating famine and plague created mass unrest in the countryside. A peasant named Li Zicheng (Li Tzu-ch'eng) led an armed uprising and entered Beijing on April 25, 1644. Consequently, the Ming emperor, Chongzhen (Ch'ung-chen), committed suicide by hanging himself and ended the "brilliant" dynasty.

Fulin and Dorgan

At the time Li was in Beijing, Abahai's son, Fulin (Fu-lin), who was only six years old, led the Manchurians. Two regents, Jirgalang and Dorgan, controlled the government. Dorgan moved on Li in Beijing and buried the Ming emperor. He eventually succeeded in finding the rebel Li and having him killed in 1645. Dorgan then placed the child Fulin on the throne, inaugurating the Qing rule in China. Fulin ruled as the **Shunzhi** emperor. The Qing were the last imperial dynasty to rule China. Rebellion in support of the Ming continued in southern China for 20 years into the Qing period. Three generals ruled for the Qing in southern China and, although two of these generals and the son of the third revolted, the Qing eventually won control of the south. This was known as the Revolt of the Three Feudatories.

The Kangzi and Qianlong Emperors

The learning of the Jesuits influenced the Qing, and they became great patrons of the arts. The most famous Qing ruler was Kangxi (K'ang-hsi, 1622–1723), the third son of the Sunzhi emperor, Fulin. The emperors Yong Zheng (Yung Cheng, 1723–1736) and **Qianlong (Ch'ien-lung**, 1736–1796) were two other important rulers. Qianlong's reign was one of the longest in history, and during his reign China controlled the largest expanse of territory in its history, including Mongolia, Tibet, Nepal, Taiwan, and portions of Central Asia. Qianlong also sponsored a compilation of the Confucian Classics called the Five Classics, a standard of Chinese learning. His mother was a Manchurian and he was a grandson of Kangxi. He retired after 60 years so as not to exceed the reign of his grandfather.

During the reigns of Kangzi and Qianlong, the history of the Ming was published, as well as catalog of paintings and calligraphy, a dictionary, and a 5,000-volume encyclopedia. Gu Yanwu (Ku Yen-wu) published an important work in the area of philology, the study of languages, relating to textual and historical criticism. Dai Zhen (Tai Chen) pioneered the use of scientific reasoning, seeking proofs as opposed to mere hypotheses. Zhang Xuecheng (Chang Hsueh Ch'eng) wrote a philosophy of history, arguing that history had the same value as the classics.

Literature flourished during the Qing period, including China's greatest novel, *The Dream of the Red Chamber*, which is also sometimes known as *A Dream of Red Mansions,* or *The Story of the Stone*. The Qing interest in learning earned the loyalty of the literati, who had opposed the Ming as repressive.

Prosperity

During the Qing, the population exploded, increasing by two or three times what it had been under the Ming. China became the most populous region in the world, reaching a population of 450 million by 1850. The need to feed such a large population led to innovations in agriculture and the development of two rice crops per year. Due to the lack of land, the Chinese learned to terrace, or create fields from mountainsides.

Gender Issues

The status of women in China declined during the Ming and Qing periods. The Hongwu emperor had emphasized Confucian ideals, according to which women were subservient to men. During the Ming and Qing dynasties, women were to be married as virgins. They could not seek a divorce from their husbands, but their husbands could divorce them for failure to produce sons. Female children were not highly valued, as they were not as strong and also the family would have to provide a dowry for the eventual marriage of the child.

Women entered the households of their husbands' families, and men often had concubines. Their husbands' relatives often forced widows to remarry, because the in-laws could then retain their dowries. Marriages were arranged and were not dependent on love. In fact, because the couple lived within the larger family unit, love matches were often seen as problematic, for they put too much emphasis on the couple's relationship as opposed to their duties within the larger group. Despite the growing emphasis on the Confucian scholar gentry, only one to two percent of women were literate during the Ming and Qing periods.

The White Lotus Rebellion

The Qing had numerous problems during their reign, including **The White Lotus Rebellion**, a rebellion in Nien in 1853 led by an offshoot of the White Lotus Sect, Muslim rebellions in the southwest from 1855–1873, and the **Taiping Rebellion**. The White Lotus Sect had beliefs that combined aspects of Buddhism, Taoism, and other schools, but their most central belief was in the impending reincarnation of the Buddha as Maitreya. The return of the Buddha would bring a new government and a new era of peace and prosperity. The Qianlong emperor banned the sect in 1775, but it reappeared under the leadership of Liu Chi-she in 1796. He claimed to have found the Buddha-Maitreya in the son of his own master Liu-Sung. Further, he attempted to drum up support for a surviving member of the Ming dynasty as the legitimate emperor. The Qing reacted strongly, intending to exterminate the White Lotus Sect. The government used very harsh methods to attack White Lotus strongholds, resulting in more splinter groups joining the movement. These groups protested Qing taxation. Unfortunately, the Qing entrusted leadership to Heshen (Ho-shen), who stole money for himself and misreported his activities in the countryside. In 1799 the new Emperor Chia Qing removed Heshen, who committed suicide, and thereafter their fights against the White Lotus were more successful. The Qing resettled large portions of the population in areas of rebellion and gave amnesty to White Lotus deserters. The Qing finally crushed the rebellion in 1804, but it resurfaced in the Nien and Boxer Rebellions.

The Taiping Rebellion

Hong Xiuquan (Hung Hsiu-ch'üan), the son of a poor farmer near Canton, led the **Taiping Rebellion**. He had failed the civil service examinations twice, and had a nervous breakdown, after which he began having visions that he believed were God the Father and Jesus, his Elder brother, speaking to him. He believed himself to be the Younger Brother, sent to earth to wipe out demon worship. Seven years later he studied with a Baptist minister, Issachar J. Roberts, and then formed a new Christian sect, the God Worshipers. He believed that the overthrow of the Manchu (Qing) dynasty would bring about the Kingdom of Heaven. Many Western scholars argue that the famines of the

1840s contributed to revolts such as this one, as peasants looked for new ways and groups to provide for them. In the 1840s the organization began to amass weapons and develop a military structure, and in the 1850s, the government saw them as a big enough threat to attack them. Hong Xiuquan followers successfully repulsed the attack, and in 1851, Hong declared that the Kingdom of Heavenly Peace had been founded, and humans were now in the era of Taiping, or peace, with Hung as the Heavenly King. Taiping was to be a classless society with all wealth distributed equally. Women were equal to men. The generals of the movement claimed to receive visions from God and the Heavenly King himself tolerated no dissent. The movement failed to maintain authority in the areas it conquered, and Hong withdrew from public life and immersed himself in a wanton life in the large harem he had accumulated. In 1864, faced by the desertion of his most important general, Hung committed suicide. The Chinese found his body in a sewer wrapped in imperial yellow. The twenty-year long rebellion was over.

The Opium Wars

The Qing also had to manage issues related to an increased European presence in Asia. The Qing initially only allowed the Europeans into Canton. In 1793 the Europeans asked for more privileges, but the Chinese were not interested and had forbidden the importation of opium in 1800, a drug more and more commonly used for recreational purposes. By the 1830s, the Chinese were no longer masters of the trade market; rather, Europeans had the advantage and they wanted fewer taxes on their goods and the right to trade opium. By the 1830s, more than 30,000 chests of opium, each of which held about 150 pounds of the extract, were coming into China a year. Some scholars have suggested that the loss of Chinese supremacy in trade was the result of the **opium trade**. By 1839, the Chinese were desperate to stop the trade, as it was damaging the health of their citizens and bringing in unwanted foreign intrusions. They burned several tons of opium in Canton. The British reacted by surrounding Canton, and in 1842, the British defeated the Chinese. In the **Treaty of Nanjing**, the Chinese lost Hong Kong to the British, who held it until the late twentieth century, when it reverted back to China. The treaty forced the Chinese to open other ports to the British, and by 1844, the French and Americans had a trading presence in China as well. The French allied with the British to fight a second opium war, which led once again to the defeat of China in 1856. The **Treaty of Tientsin** (Tianjin, 1858) opened new ports to trading and allowed foreigners with passports to travel in the interior of China. The Chinese granted Christians the right to spread their faith and to own property, and in separate treaties, the United States and Russia received similar privileges.

The Boxer Rebellion

The defeat of China in the Opium Wars led to mass outpouring of antiforeign sentiment. This culminated in the **Boxer Rebellion**, led by the Society of Harmonious Fists, which first arose in Shandong province. The name of the rebellion came from the fact that members of the society practiced shadow boxing, which they believed made them impervious to bullets. In 1900 the Boxers invaded Beijing, with the complete support of the **Dowager Empress Cixi (Tz'u Hsi)**. The Dowager controlled the country through her son **Guang Xu (Kuang-hsu)**, whom she in effect kept under house arrest. She was a strong opponent of reform, and so supported the Boxers. In Beijing, the Boxers attacked foreign embassies, including those of Britain, Germany, Japan, Russia, and the United States, while Chinese troops watched the events. The foreign ambassadors survived the assaults for two months before an international relief force came, known as the Eight Power Allied Forces. They occupied Beijing and put down the rebellion, and the American Foreign Secretary John Hay formulated the Open Door Policy, allowing all nations access to the China market.

Confucianism and the West

The increasing presence of Europeans in China also led to the decline of the Confucian scholar-bureaucrats. By 1906, when the government abolished the civil service system, most bureaucrats had purchased their degrees rather than earning them through traditional means. The Qing attempted to create a system of public schools modeled on those of Europe. The structure of Chinese society had changed drastically during the nineteenth century.

The Fall of the Qing

In 1908 the captive Emperor Guang Xu died, followed quickly by his mother, the Empress Dowager Cixi. As successor, she had chosen her two-year-old nephew, Pu Yi. The conservative Prince Chun ruled as regent. In 1911 the harvest failed and revolts began. On October 10, 1911, soldiers from the Wuchang armory, led by Yuan Shikai (Yuan Shih-k'ai), joined in a rebellion. On February 12, 1912, Pu Yi abdicated, ending 270 years of Ch'ing rule.

Sun Yat-sen

The leaders of the rebellion formed a republic, with **Sun Yixian (Sun Yat-sen)** as provisional president.

The new government allowed Pu Yi to continue living in the Forbidden City until 1924, but forced him to live in the inner court of the complex. In November

1924, the National Army gained control of China and, on November 5, they abolished all of Pu Yi's titles and ousted him from the Forbidden City. He ended his life as a humble gardener in the streets of Beijing; his ashes were moved to the western Ch'ing tombs in 1995. Despite Pu Yi's personal tragedy, the Chinese were ready to end 5,000 years of imperial rule. Unfortunately, the twentieth century would bring many more upheavals.

Review Questions

1. During the Opium Wars, the British defeated and earned trading rights from the

   (A) Ming Chinese.

   (B) Qing Chinese.

   (C) People's Republic of China.

   (D) Koreans.

2. The expeditions of Zheng He began during the reign of the

   (A) Hongxi (Hung-hsi) emperor (1425).

   (B) Xuande (Hsüan-te) emperor.

   (C) Yongle emperor.

   (D) Hongwu emperor.

3. Confucianism

   (A) weakened the agricultural lifestyle of the Chinese.

   (B) emphasized education.

   (C) was suspicious of trade or change.

   (D) Both (B) and (C).

4. Which of the following emperors most promoted agriculture as a focus of Chinese civilization?

   (A) The Yongle emperor

   (B) The Hongxi emperor

   (C) The Hongwu emperor

   (D) The Xuande emperor

5. The European Age of Exploration

   (A) created less demand for Chinese products such as porcelain.

   (B) resulted in an influx of silver into China, leading to the development of a true coin currency and the Single Whip Reform.

   (C) brought European merchants into Macao and other regions.

   (D) Both (B) and (C).

6. Which of the following is NOT a correct statement about women in the Ming and Qing periods?

   (A) Women were mostly literate due to the influence of Confucianism before the Opium Wars.

   (B) Women were forced into arranged marriages.

   (C) Women could not get divorces.

   (D) The Opium Wars brought about a decline in Confucian values, and women began to be educated.

7. Which of the following statements does NOT accurately describe the reasons why China failed to industrialize along European lines?

   (A) Europe had absolute monarchies that protected trade, while Chinese emperors generally fostered agriculture and Confucian values.

   (B) China did not have a money economy and had neither paper money nor coinage, while European capitalism based on paper and coinage allowed Europe to advance.

   (C) Although China continued to sponsor trade in Southeast Asia, it progressively turned inward following the voyages of Zheng He.

   (D) Confucianism discouraged change, which was associated with trade, while European philosophies encouraged trade, expansion, and profit.

8. Which of the following factors does NOT account for the decline of the Ming?

   (A) Their currency was debased due to improper management starting with the Hongwu emperor.

   (B) Raids by the Japanese caused instability.

   (C) Difficulties with the Mongols created instability.

   (D) The eunuchs were unable to protect the Chinese from the corruption of Confucian scholars.

9. Which of the following rebellions were inspired by Buddhist beliefs?

   (A) The Taiping Rebellion

   (B) The Double Ten Incident

   (C) The White Lotus Rebellions

   (D) Both (A) and (B).

10. China controlled the largest expanse of territory in its history in the reign of the

   (A) Yongle emperor.

   (B) Hongwu emperor.

   (C) Qianglong emperor.

   (D) Kangxi emperor.

Answers

1. (B)	4. (C)	7. (B)	10. (C)
2. (C)	5. (D)	8. (D)	
3. (D)	6. (A)	9. (C)	

Chapter 21

THE ISLAMIC WORLD FROM THE OTTOMANS THROUGH THE EARLY TWENTIETH CENTURY

KEY TERMS

Ottomans	Safavids
Istanbul	Mughals
Phanariots	Purda
Gunpowder Empires	Sati
Caliph	Akbar
Battle of Mohács	Peacock throne
Sulieman	Taj Mahal
Devshirme	Battle of Plassey
Sipahis	Robert Clive
Beys	British East India Tea Company
Tanzimat Reforms	Sepoy Mutiny
Ataturk	Sikhs
Isfahan	British Raj
Abbas II	Indian National Congress

THE OTTOMAN EMPIRE

Mehmed the Conqueror (1451–1481)

The **Ottomans** were a Turkish dynasty that rose to prominence when **Mehmed**, Turkish for Mohammad, conquered Constantinople in 1453. After 1930, the city was officially known as **Istanbul**, from the Greek words "stan poli," meaning "at the City" or "City of the Cities." The city had been the capital of the eastern Roman Empire and of Byzantium, and would also be the capital of the Ottoman Turks. The Hagia Sophia, the great basilica of Justinian, became a mosque.

Mehmed's success was largely due to huge cannons, developed for his forces by a Hungarian engineer. One cannon was twenty-six feet long and eight inches in diameter and could fire a 1,200-pound ball as far as one mile. Mehmed attacked the walls of the great city from the west, the only part of the city not protected by water. His army arrived on Easter Monday, April 2, 1453, and fired cannon volleys at the Byzantines for seven weeks. The Byzantines had protected the waterways across the Golden Horn with a large chain, and so he built a road of logs across the north side of the Golden Horn. He then rolled his ships across and attacked on May 29, 1453. The Ottomans entered the city through the Kerkoporta gate in the Blachernae section, which had been left unlocked, and looted it for three days.

Many Greek scholars fled and sought refuge in Italy, particularly in Venice, where they helped to fuel the Italian Renaissance. Some remained behind and served as advisors to the sultans. These Greeks were called Phanariots.

The fall of Constantinople marked the end of Roman rule in the East, and many scholars date the end of the Middle Ages from 1453. Even today the Greeks still speak of reconquering Constantinople, but it remains one of the most important cities in the Islamic world.

Selim

Under the next two sultans, the Ottomans became an Asian as well as a European power. **Selim** conquered the Egyptian Mamluks, North Africa, and Syria-Palestine, and brought Mecca and Medina under Ottoman rule. After conquering Mecca and Medina, he took the title of caliph, or successor of Muhammad. This title had not been used since the Mongols captured the capital of the Abbasid caliphate, Baghdad, in the thirteenth century.

Suleiman the Magnificent (1520–1566)

Suleiman extended the Ottoman Empire to Mesopotamia (modern Iraq), Kurdistan, and Georgia. He captured Belgrade in 1521, and in 1526 the Ottoman Turks defeated the Hungarians at the battle of Mohács. The Turks also conquered the cities of Buda and Pest. Pest fell to the Turks in 1526 and

Buda fell fifteen years later. Sulieman besieged Vienna from 1526–1529, and lost only because of torrential rains that caused his heavy carts to bog down. Sulieman's presence as a European monarch contributed to the ferocity of the Wars of Religion, as he aided Protestant nations in an effort to destabilize Europe. Many scholars believe the Reformation succeeded in part because of Sulieman's financial support. During his reign he also took the island of Rhodes from the Knights of St. John or Hospitalers, and laid siege to their new stronghold at Malta.

Sulieman's conquests earned him the title of the "protector of the sacred places," which were Mecca and Medina, and also the title of padishah, or emperor. The Ottomans became the new heirs to the Abbasid caliphs.

Sulieman built magnificent walls around Jerusalem, which still surround the Old City today. Under Sulieman, the Ottoman Empire reached its high points, and ruled an empire from Hungary to Yemen on the Saudi Arabian Peninsula, to Persia to Oran. Sulieman's empire encompassed six of the ancient Seven Wonders of the World.

Sulieman restructured the Ottoman legal system and Muslims referred to him as the Kanuni or the Lawmaker. He codified the kanun, a system of laws dealing with cases not covered by the Shari'ah. Mehmed had begun to compile the kanun and in the early sixteenth century, it was added on to; but after Sulieman, it was never changed again.

He created a military state, where the ulema, or school of study of Islamic law, was a part of the government. He controlled the aristocracy by creating the devshirme, a system of conscripting Christian boys from the provinces, raising them as Muslims, and using them as soldiers. Although many improved their lot in life through the **Devshirme** and families often competed for the honor, these boys were in essence conscripted slave soldiers. As the system evolved, it became highly selective.

The Janissaries

Conscripted slave soldiers made up the elite force of infantry soldiers known as the **Janissaries**. Members of the Janissaries could not wear beards, as free Muslims did, and could not marry until 1566 in the reign of Selim II. Their chief loyalty was to the empire, and they were taught to consider the sultan their father. Since the empire controlled their property, there were no claims based on heredity from members of their families. One of the most famous boys who began their career through the devshirme was the architect Sinan, who built more than 400 structures, including the Suleymaniye Mosque.

In 1683, the Janissaries had become so successful that the sultan **Mehmed IV** abolished the devshirme, allowing Turkish boys to enter the elite ranks. Starting in 1449, the Janissaries led revolts and demanded higher wages and other rewards. Through palace coups, they even succeeded in controlling the sultanate.

Suleiman's relationship with a captured Russian slave girl, **Roxelana**, hastened the decline of the empire. Roxelana convinced Sulieman to marry her, something unheard of for sultans, and she increased the power of the harem. She was suspicious of Sulieman's boyhood friend and chief assistant in his rise to power, Ibrahim, and had Sulieman arrange for his death. Roxelana feared the sultana and her son, Mustafa, and fought for the succession of her own son, Selim. Although Sulieman loved Mustafa, he ordered him killed and Selim became his successor.

Sulieman also advanced his personal favorites and progressively retreated into isolation in the Topkapi palace.

Ottoman Government

The position of **sultan** arose from the role of the Turkish bey, a word meaning "knight." The beys were provincial governors who collected taxes from the tribal chiefs and who had both administrative and military control. Muslim laws were not as important as tribal laws were. When the Ottomans conquered Byzantium, they adapted their leadership to Byzantine customs. The sultan became more powerful at the expense of tribal leaders, and the position was a hereditary one. The administration was centralized and the Topkapi palace was not only the residence of the sultan and his harem, but also an administrative center. The Ottomans practiced brutal customs, and as each leader rose to power as sultan, he killed all of his male relatives except one brother to prevent rebellions. He also killed his brother's children and wives.

The sultan's orders were channeled through an imperial court, chaired by his chief minister, the **vizier**. From behind a screen, the sultan conveyed his orders to the vizier. Often the vizier had risen to power through the devshirme system. Many bureaucrats under the vizier were also drawn from the devshirme. Merit played an important role in one's advancement.

Provinces and districts continued to be run in much the same way as when the old tribal leaders controlled things. The sultan granted land as a fief to the most important leaders in the provinces, who were often descendents of the tribal beys. They collected taxes and provided military support. These leaders in turn divided their lands among their military leaders, known as sipahis. The salaries of the sipahis came from taxes collected from peasants.

Gender Issues

Women were generally well-treated under Islamic law and could own and inherit property. They could not be forced into marriage. Further, in the sultan's harem, women close to the sultan might gain tremendous influence. Many women in the harem were slave girls and while Christian slave boys might rise through the devshirme and service in the Janissaries, girls might rise through admission to the harem. Slaves were drawn from the non-Muslim population, as Islamic law forbade the enslavement of Muslims. Some girls of the harem were permitted to leave to marry officials, while the Queen Mother, the mother of the sultan, often arranged the marriages of her daughters to important figures and even engaged in diplomatic relations with other countries.

Diversity in the Ottoman World

As the Ottomans conquered regions in Europe and other areas of the world, they incorporated people from many religious traditions into the empire. The various religious groups were known as millets (meaning "nations" or communities") and each had a patriarch that reported to the sultan. Each millet administered its own form of law and collected taxes for the government.

The Fall of the Ottoman Empire

The Ottoman Empire was never again as great as it had been under Suleiman, and they were defeated at Vienna in 1683. In response to military difficulties, the sultan **Selim III** attempted to reform the Janissaries along European lines, but the Janissaries revolted and Selim was executed. Napoleon invaded Egypt in 1798, thus severing this portion of the empire, and the Ottoman governor of Egypt, Muhammad Ali, moved against the Ottoman sultan and occupied Syria. Only the intervention of Europeans on the side of the sultan eventually defeated Muhammad Ali. Later, however, Europeans would actually take Egypt, when the British put down a revolt at the request of Muhammad Ali's successors, the khedives, and then effectively ruled Egypt. For further coverage of these events, consult the chapter on Imperialism.

A series of reforms called the **Tanzimat** attempted to Westernize the Ottoman world through granting equality to non-Muslims and allowances for the importation of foreign goods. Western education, especially in mathematics and the sciences, and other Western customs were also adopted. The Ottoman reformers built railroads and created a state postal system. Miltary officers and bureaucrats became increasingly Westernized.

The Tanzimat, however, did not succeed at stopping the decline of the Ottomans. Granting equality to non-Muslims contributed to growing nationalism and created further tensions within the conservative elements of Ottoman society. Further, massive importation of goods, especially from Britain, threatened the livelihood of the Ottoman artisans. Removal of the tariffs and other trading barriers also removed the protections that the Ottoman merchants had from competition with the West.

A continuing string of defeats on the battlefield also contributed to the decline. The Ottomans fought for the **Crimea** against Russia starting in 1854 and lost it. Another factor that contributed to Ottoman decline was financial instability.

In 1875 the Ottomans declared a state of near-bankruptcy and European creditors gained a strong foothold on Ottoman finances.

The sultan **Abdul Hamid** realized the threat that Western influences posed to his bureaucracy and military. Westernized officers increasingly saw the sultan himself as the biggest barrier to reform, and Abdul Hamid attempted to thwart their influence by restricting freedom of the press and other civil liberties and eventually by nullifying the constitution. Nevertheless, he continued to Westernize the military and to promote the foundation of Western-style educational institutions. In 1908 Abdul Hamid was removed as sultan in a coup engineered by the Young Turks, who wished to see the Tanzimat reforms restored. World War I undercut their efforts and brought the final collapse of the empire, which officially ended in 1922 when Turkey became a Republic under the leadership of Mustafa Kemal or Ataturk (see Chapter 31 on World War I for further information).

THE SAFAVID SHI'ITES IN IRAN

The **Safavid** rulers of Persia were descendants of Sufi mystics. According to their own histories, which they rewrote to suit their purposes, their founder was Sheikh Safi al-Din (d.1334) from Ardebil, leader of an order of Sufi mystics in Persia. His tomb became the headquarters of the Safavids, who took their name for their founder. In 1501 the fourteen-year-old Shah Ismail I (1501–1524) defeated the Turkoman ruler of Iran at Sharur and occupied Tabriz. The population had originally been Sunni, but the new shah rigidly enforced Shi'ite traditions and laws. They believed that there had been twelve infallible *imams* since Muhammad. Imams are prayer leaders and rulers that claim descent from Muhammad. The twelfth imam had gone into hiding, but would one day return. In some accounts, Ismail was presented as the hidden imam. His followers wore red hats with twelve points in memory of this tradition. The shah lost considerable territory to the Ottomans, who defeated him in 1514 at Chaldiran.

The leaders of the Safavids were known as shaykhs or shahs. The Shi'ites rejected the first three caliphs and the Sunni kingdoms. The Shah Abbas I (1588–1629) defeated the Ottomans in Iraq and Azerbaijan, largely with the help of British mercenaries.

Under Abbas I, the capital of the empire was Isfahan, still a renowned center of Islamic architecture. Many of its buildings were built during the reign of his great-grandson, Abbas II. Many of these rulers feared members of their own family, and were known for killing their brothers and even their own mothers to prevent revolt. The severity of the rule of Hussein, the grandson of Abbas II, led to revolt among Sunni Afghans, who forced the abdication of the shah in 1722. After a brief period of Afghani rule, Tahmasp II recovered the empire for the Safavids. Under Tahmasp's son, Abbas III, the general Nadir Khouli (1736–1747) recovered much territory that had earlier been lost to the Ottomans. Nadir eventually became shah and abandoned Shi'ism as the official religion of the empire.

Persian became the common language in Safavid lands. The art of the Safavid kingdom reflected Chinese and other Asian influences.

The Mughals in India

The word "mughal" is the Persianate form of "mongol." The **Mughals** were descendents of the Mongols from Turkestan, and they brought Persian influences to India, especially that of Sufi mysticism. The Mughals were not the first Muslim power in India, as Arabas had invaded in the seventh century C.E. and Rajput, in southeastern India, was ruled by the Delhi sultanate, whose ruler was an Islamic Turk.

Babur the Tiger

Babur the Tiger was a descendant of Genghis Khan on his mother's side and of Timur on his father's side. Coming to power in 1483, he conquered Afghanistan and captured Kabul in 1504, the Delhi sultanate, and Hindustan. His success may be attributed in part to the arrival of the Portuguese in 1510, who weakened the Delhi sultanate enough for Babur later to conquer it. Although his army was small, their firearms more than balanced their numbers. Babur was the first Islamic leader to use firearms and created what many scholars call the first gunpowder empire.

Humayun (1556)

Babur's son **Humayun** lost much of his father's territory between 1530–1540, but by 1555 he had managed to regroup his army while in exile in Persia. They succeeded in reconquering significant amounts of lost territory, but Humayun fell down a flight of stairs and broke his neck. Humayun, however, encouraged the appreciation of Persian culture, especially in his son Akbar, who became the most famous Mughal ruler.

Akbar (1556–1605)

Akbar was only thirteen when he came to power, but he continued the wave of conquests started by Babur. By the time he died, he had conquered most of northern India and Afghanistan. His empire was larger than Babur's and he believed that any empire not expanding must be in decline. Akbar's empire, like that of Babur's, is often referred to as a "gunpowder empire," as many historians credit his success to his use of heavy artillery. Other historians say that negotiations and other military tactics contributed to his success, as well as skill at leadership. The religious zeal of various Mughal leaders has also been pointed to as a factor in their success.

Akbar's bureaucracy was very efficient, and he put military governors, or mansabars, in charge of each region. Each governor was responsible for the military of the province. Akbar severely punished abuses of power and mistreatment of the poor or weak, sometimes with death.

Akbar's rule was benevolent, as he canceled the poll tax on non-Muslims and offered tolerance to all faiths. He stopped the pilgrimage tax on Hindus, and so earned their support. Many Hindus served in his bureaucracy, and he even married a Hindu, who was his favorite wife and mother of his son, Jahangir. He had over 5,000 wives, many of them daughters of the various kings of his regions. He allowed Hindus to be governed by their own law, the Dharmashastra, as opposed to the Shari'ah or Muslim code of law.

Akbar's political theorist was Abu'l Faz'l, who, like Akbar, was influenced by Shi'ite thought, especially the doctrine that the Divine Light was passed to the world through the Imam. Abu'l Faz'l believed that the Imam in the world was the just ruler, and this ruler was to guide humanity. Akbar adopted this idea and developed a new religion that he called the Din-i Ilahi, or "The Religion of God," based on the belief that all religions contained a grain of truth about the single unifying principle of reality, God. In 1578, Akbar completed the construction of a new city designed to symbolize his new religion, Fatehpur Sikri.

Akbar was opposed by the Islamic ulema or elite body of learned Muslim spiritual leaders, who were threatened by the suggestion that the Imam in the world, or the just ruler, was above the Shari'ah. Akbar also supported the notion of the divine kingship, equally disturbing to them.

Trade During the Reign of Akbar

By the reign of Akbar, India had developed a commercial economy based on capitalist enterprise. Manufacturing industries were present and these were supported through a money economy. The chief export of India was cotton cloth made by artisans who worked at home, known as India's cottage industry. Through the sillim, brokers provided materials and money to the artisans in return for finished cloth products. In fact, the "putting out" system used in England during the early Industrial Revolution was borrowed from India. The cotton industry grew to such proportions under Akbar that new road systems were necessary. Cloth was exported through Guharat, across the Indian Ocean to east Africa and from there across land to west Africa, across the Red Sea to the Mediterranean, up the Volga to Russian cities, through the Persian Gulf to Persia; and to China, Japan, and many other areas. The Indian trade, in fact, extended over a wider area of territory than did trade, for example, conducted by the Medici family in Renaissance Italy.

Goods were so much in demand from India that in 1695, English merchants wanted their government to stop the importation of Indian cloth. The success of the Indian cloth industry created an imbalance of trade between India and the West, still reflected in some of our modern names for cloth, such as calico (derived from the name of the port city of Calicut) and muslin. In general, Asians were not interested in European goods.

Affluence helped many merchants to transcend earlier caste restrictions and to distribute wealth to groups outside of the traditional elite.

Gender Issues

Women contributed to the success of India's cloth industry and wove the cloth in their homes. Women from mercantile families also often played an important role in business transactions. Greater visibility and involvement of women in business was made possible by Akbar's creation of market days for women, which was intended to free them from the restrictions of purdah. Purdah evolved from Islamic laws about women that resulted in their being kept cloistered at home. Many Hindus had adopted this practice.

Hindus also continued to follow the custom of sati, the practice of placing a woman on her deceased husband's funeral pyre. Hindus also arranged marriages for their female children at a young age. Akbar attempted to discourage both practices as well as the Hindu custom of prohibiting the remarriage of widows. Nevertheless, the plight of women continued to be somewhat dismal as Hindus sometimes forcibly married Muslim women or stripped those Hindu women who converted to Islam of their inheritance.

Akbar also provided education to the women of his court and even established a school for girls in Fatehpur Sikri. Akbar was not entirely successful in abolishing various religious practices that subordinated women, but his reign was remarkable for its attention to women's issues.

Although there were notable and powerful women in the courts of later Mughal rulers, such as Jahangir's wife Nur Jahan and Shah Jahan's wife Mumtaz Mahal, the plight of women continued to decline following the reign of Akbar.

Jahangir (1605–1628)

Although **Jahangir** added Bengal to his father's domains, Jahangir focused on patronage of the arts. His reign is known as the "age of Mughal splendor." In 1627, Jahangir gave the **British East India Company** permission to build a fortified factory at Surat, the most important Mughal port. Within ten years, they were headquartered at Bombay. The British would eventually control India.

Shah Jahan (1628–1658)

Shah Jahan continued Akbar's wave of conquests. Shah Jahan conquered parts of the Deccan Plateau in southern India and turned back the Portuguese intrusion at Bengal. He moved the capital from Agra to Delhi and built a magnificent palace for himself within the famous Red Fort. His famous Peacock throne symbolized the success of the Mughals, and some estimate that it cost as much as $5 million in today's money. In 1739, the Afghans, who conquered the Safavids, entered India and took the Peacock throne back to Iran, where it remains today.

Shah Jahan's most famous project was the **Taj Mahal**, built to commemorate the memory of his favorite wife, Mumtaz Mahal, who died following the birth of her fourteenth child. The monument took more than 20,000 people to build and is intended to be representative of paradise. Shah Jahan's military conquests and the expense of the lavish tomb, however, caused him to raise taxes from the one-third of the crop value paid under Akbar to over one-half of the crop value. The heavy tax was a burden for poor Hindus.

The Taj Mahal

Aurangzeb (1658–1707)

Late in his reign, Shah Jahan's two sons fought over the succession. His son **Aurangzeb** viciously took power, had his father imprisoned, and gouged out his eyes so that he could no longer see the Taj Mahal. Aurangzeb also had his brother executed. He continued the wave of conquests, but was also a very pious Muslim who insisted that the Shari'ah be followed. No laws that were not found in the Shari'ah could be enacted, and Aurangzeb overturned years of tolerance for Hindus and other non-Muslims when he reenacted the jizya, or poll tax for non-Muslims. He also abolished the practice of sati, a practice in some areas of India, such as Rajasthan, among the Hindu warrior caste where widows threw themselves on their husband's funeral pyres.

Hindu resistance increased to Aurangzeb. Aurangzeb had conquered the Marathas of the Deccan Plateau, and by 1740, the Marathas controlled more territory than the Mughals.

The Sikhs

The **Sikhs** were also a threat to Aurangzeb. The word "Sikh" means disciple, and in this case, they were disciplines of the Gurus. The religion dates back to the reign of Babur, and teaches that God is one and present in all creation. They believed that God can be directly apprehended by the human mind and there is no need for churches, rites, or other practices. Since all humans have God within them, there are no castes. The Guru, leader of the movement, reveals to his followers the Name of God, through which one can experience unity, and the Word of God, which provides the acceptable methods of achieving union. Under Aurangzeb, the most influential Guru was Gobind Singh, who transformed the Sikhs into a radical brotherhood or khalsa. Aurangzeb regarded them as heretics, but by the eighteenth century, the Sikhs had a separate kingdom within Mughal territory and were allies of the British as they incorporated India into their empire in the 1850s. The Sikhs continued to be a revolutionary force, as it was the Sikh bodyguards who assassinated Indira Ghandi in the twentieth century.

The British in India

The progressive intrusions of the **British East India Tea Company**, which sought to control the economy of India, further complicated the situation. Britain's lead in the Industrial Revolution created a need for raw materials and for outlets for manufactured goods, leading them to seek colonies for their support. Further, their rivalry with the French throughout the eighteenth century also contributed to the expansion of their frontiers. After the British established factories at Bombay, Madras, and Calcutta, the East India Tea Company expanded to the interior of India and bit by bit won rights to govern areas there. Following the Sepoy Mutiny, the Mughals were finished as rulers of India and the British controlled India through World War II. For further discussion of British Imperialism in India, see Chapter 29.

Review Questions

1. The Safavid Persians were

    (A) Sunni Muslims.

    (B) Hindus.

    (C) Shi'ite Muslims.

    (D) Sikhs.

2. Who led the forces that conquered Constantinople in 1453?

    (A) Sulieman the Magnificent

    (B) Selim II

    (C) Ibrahim

    (D) Mehmed the Conqueror

3. The elite corps of the Ottoman troops were the

    (A) Junkers.

    (B) Junta.

    (C) Janissaries.

    (D) Mujahideen.

4. According to Noel Barber, his sixteenth-century "empire stretched from the gates of Vienna to Yemen and Aden, from Persia to Oran, and he ruled over the Six Wonders of the World." Whose reign was the author describing?

    (A) Charles V of the Holy Roman Empire

    (B) Ismail of the Safavids

    (C) Mehmed I of the Ottomans

    (D) Sulieman the Magnificent

5. Which of the following does NOT describe the policies of the Ottomans towards Christians within their frontiers or Christians in Europe?

    (A) Christian boys could rise to power through the devshirme.

    (B) Sulieman helped fuel the Protestant Reformation by creating tensions through his invasions of Europe.

    (C) European powers helped the Ottomans retain control when the governor of Egypt, Muhammad Ali, invaded Syria.

    (D) Christian girls could not be part of the sultan's harem.

6. Which of the following is NOT an example of the concept of a gunpowder empire?

    (A) Mehmet's conquest of Constantinople

    (B) The conquests of Babur

    (C) The conquest of Akbar

    (D) Constantine's rise to power in the Roman World.

7. An important factor in the conquest of Constantinople by Mehmet was heavy canons. This is an example of the

    (A) weakness of Byzantine walls.

    (B) poor planning of the Byzantines.

    (C) concept of the gunpowder empire.

    (D) ruthlessness of the Ottomans.

8. Which of the following is NOT a correct description of changes in India during the reign of Akbar?

    (A) The plight of women improved through the creation of market days.

    (B) Exportation of cloth decreased.

    (C) He attempted to stop the practice of early and arranged marriages and the prohibition against widows remarrying.

    (D) He provided schools for girls.

Answers

1. (C)	3. (C)	5. (D)	7. (C)
2. (D)	4. (D)	6. (D)	8. (B)

UNIT V

Early Modern Europe

Chapter 22

THE AGE OF ABSOLUTISM

KEY TERMS

Versailles
Absolutism
Thomas Hobbes
The Five Great Farms
Enlightened Despotism
War of the League of Augsburg
War of the Spanish Succession
Great Northern War
St. Petersburg
Peter the Great
Frederick II
Old Believers
Slavophiles
Revolt of the Streltsy
Frederick William I

Enlightened Despotism
Inductive Reasoning
Bacon
Deductive Reasoning
Descartes
Philosophes
Encyclopédiae
The Scientific Revolution
Geocentric universe
Heliocentric universe
Ptolemy
Copernicus
Galileo
Classicism

ABSOLUTISM

Absolutism was a method of controlling the government through the central power of the king. Frederick the Great once remarked that, "The fundamental rule of governments is the principle of extending their territories." The Thirty Years' War had greatly increased the size of the armies in European countries. Large armies could only effectively be maintained by a strong king who had the wealth and power to recruit and control them. The rise of absolutism in Europe was intimately connected with warfare and the need to protect the state from other powerful states. Further, the more powerful absolute monarchs such as Louis XIV grew, the more they desired to expand their territories, leading to the need for greater revenue through taxation. This in turn led to the need for greater centralized control over one's kingdom. Of the great powers in Europe, only the English monarchs failed to establish absolute control over their kingdoms.

ABSOLUTISM IN FRANCE: LOUIS XIV

Louis XIV developed an absolute monarchy in France. His complete power was summed up by his famous motto, *l'etat c'est moi*, or "the state is me." Events during Louis XIV's childhood had convinced him of the need to forge a strong monarchy, one able to curb the power of nobles and the church. **Cardinal Richelieu** had dominated his father's reign, while **Cardinal Mazarin** dominated his mother's reign after the death of his father. During the **Revolt of the Fronde** in 1648, the nobility and the French *parlements* asserted territorial privileges. The nobles had even called on Spanish forces to help them. At one point, a group of rebels had burst into the young Louis' room, an event he never forgot.

Louis was known as the Sun King and his reign as the "age of *gloire*." His Palace at **Versailles** was an apt symbol of his power; just as rays of sun spread across the earth, so too the symbolic rays of the Sun King spread throughout France and, later, Louis attempted to spread them throughout Europe.

The location of the Palace of Versailles, on the outskirts of Paris and away from population, was perhaps due to the events during the revolt of the Fronde. The grandeur of Versailles accompanied the grandeur of culture during the Age of Louis. All life here centered around Louis and, in the process, Louis reduced the nobility of France to his own personal valets. Elaborate etiquette existed for all areas of life and behavior. Louis controlled the nobility by giving them duties in the court rituals, and one's status depended on one's proximity to the king. Nobles left their estates in order to maintain a costly life at the palace. In effect, Louis reduced the nobles to servants, and some scholars have suggested that while the nobility was absorbed in the rules of etiquette, they neglected the most important aspect of status, which was power.

Thomas Hobbes

The **Bishop Bossuet** first articulated the philosophy behind Louis's reign that the King is God. The English philosopher **Thomas Hobbes** also articulated the philosophy of absolutism in his 1651 work, *The Leviathan*. The government of France under Louis XIV implemented the philosophy of *The Leviathan*. The Leviathan was a mythical creature of enormous proportions mentioned in the biblical books of Enoch, Job, Psalms, and Isaiah as living in the deep realms of the ocean. According to Hobbes, humans are wicked creatures who cannot be trusted. The only way to protect oneself was to give all power to a central monarch, who then implemented laws to protect the people from each other and other nations and to create a state of peace. Even a people's assembly, such as the French *parlements*, could not be trusted, as they would act in their own self-interest. Although the sovereign's power derived from the people, the people were bound by complete submission to its power. The sovereign was the new Leviathan of the early modern era, a power that dominated every aspect of life.

Colbert and Economic Reform

Louis developed a vast, centralized bureaucracy, supported by the economic reforms of **Jean Baptiste Colbert**, the comptroller of finance. Colbert's economic policies were likely motivated by the need to finance Louis XIV's grandiose lifestyle and foreign policy. By 1661, the treasury was broke. The nobles and clergy were exempt from the taxes in existence at this time, which included the *aides, douanes, gabelle*, and *taille*. The *aides* and *douanes* were customs taxes, the *gabelle* was a salt tax, and the *taille* was a land tax. Colbert first attempted to reform the system of taxation. The old way was corrupt, as the nobility purchased offices and then would make a profit from them, developing an independent source of wealth. Only one-third of the funds generated were channeled into the treasury. Colbert allowed no tax exemptions for the nobility and taxed them for the first time.

Colbert's greatest achievement was the encouragement of **mercantilism**. He wanted the flow of bullion to come into France, rather than out of it. He encouraged production at home, and focused on commerce rather than on agriculture, following the examples of the Dutch East India Company and the Spanish in the New World. He developed new industries and allowed for the formation of new monopolies to increase revenue. These monopolies drove the price of necessities up, and the peasantry bore most of the burden through the payment of the *taille* and *gabelle*. He charged heavy tariffs on imported products, but no tariffs on internally produced goods. In France, there was a free market known as the **Five Great Farms**, the largest tariff-free area in Europe. To further increase trade, he developed a navy, leading to the creation of the French East India Company.

The Centralized Bureaucracy

Louis also centralized the management of the government, as opposed to the independent regions that existed before his reign. The Council of State oversaw foreign policy, while the Council of Dispatches was responsible for internal affairs. The Council of Finances addressed the economic needs of the realm, and the Privy Council served as the court of the king's justice and the final court of appeal in the land.

To maintain order, Louis developed a strong and centralized army. Before Louis XIV, colonels had been responsible for their own units and were very independent and not accountable to the crown. Louis established a chain of command, recruiting rather than buying and selling positions. He commissioned officers, and the government was responsible for equipping troops and providing uniforms. The army of Louis was four times larger than it had been previously.

Control of the Three Estates

The three estates of France were the clergy, nobility, and the commoners. The commoners made up the vast majority of the population of France. In order to curb the power of the nobility, Louis ennobled those who were not hereditary nobility, making them grateful to Louis and also enlarging the court treasury. Louis controlled the Church through emphasizing unity in religion, which he believed was supportive of and necessary to achieve unity in the political sphere. The French Church had always had a strong identity, as illustrated by the battles of Philip IV to control the Church over the will of Pope Boniface VIII and the French control of the papacy at Avignon during the Babylonian Captivity.

Louis wished to control the Church in France, and although he professed Catholicism, he wished to be in control of its resources in France. In 1682, Louis passed a decree that the councils were to be considered superior to the pope. The French Church was once again in service to the state.

Louis viewed Protestant movements, such as the Huguenots, and conservative Catholic movements, such as the Jansenists, as threats to the royal authority. In war, he feared that the French Protestants might side with other Protestant nations. He suppressed movements like the Jansenists, an austere ascetic sect who believed in predestination and removal from the secular world, because he feared their dedication to religion over the state and thought they were too fanatical. He razed the Jansenist convent at Port Royal in 1661, while he "encouraged" the Huguenots to convert by quartering the army in their homes, holding guns up to their heads, and offering them money to convert. In 1685, believing that most Huguenots were gone, Louis revoked the Edict of Nantes. Many Protestants fled; since the Huguenots were often successful in business, Louis may have unwittingly thwarted the efforts of Colbert.

Nec Pluribus Impar (None His Equal): Louis's Foreign Wars

Louis wished to have more power and glory than any other leader, and expanding French rule on the continent was one of his most important goals. In part, Louis's wars were motivated by the need to create more secure boundaries for France, which was surrounded by Hapsburg domains.

The War of Devolution (1667–1668)

In 1667 Louis started the **War of Devolution**. "Devolution" is a term invented by his aides, and referred to the idea that property in certain areas of the Netherlands to which France had some shaky claims arising out of a 1659 settlement with Spain could only be passed to children of a king's first marriage. The Spanish King Charles II was weak and mentally incompetent. Moreover, Charles had no children, and was himself the child of his father's second marriage. Louis had married one of his sisters, who was the child of her father's first marriage. On this basis, Louis claimed that this property should "devolve" to France.

The war brought France into conflict with the Dutch, as the Spanish Netherlands had previously been a buffer for them against France. The Dutch were at the height of their imperial and cultural prosperity. The Dutch had established a vast trading empire in the New World with the Dutch East India Company. They had also captured the Cape of Good Hope on the southern tip of Africa from Portugal in 1652. The Bank of Amsterdam, founded in 1609, was then the financial center of Europe. It had established a universal system of coinage, whereby the population of Europe often exchanged their native coins, which fluctuated in value, for those of the Dutch.

The Dutch were a distinct threat to France, which was trying to establish an overseas trade of its own. The French, on the other hand, were a threat to the Dutch, as they had an absolutist form of government, while the Dutch had a republican form of government. Further, the Dutch were Calvinists, an immediate conflict with the policies of Louis XIV. The Dutch intensely disliked the pomp and circumstance of Versailles, as well as the lack of freedom for Protestants in France.

The Dutch immediately allied with the Swedish and English. In 1668, the Treaty of Aix-la-Chapelle forced the French to surrender their initial gain in the War of the Franche-Comte, but the French managed to keep eleven towns in Flanders.

The Franco-Dutch War (1672–1678)

In 1672, Louis made another attempt at conquest, leading to the **Franco-Dutch War**. This time Louis bribed Sweden and obtained the support of the

English King Charles II through a treaty. The French were so successful this time on the battlefield that they were referred to as Huns. The Dutch, for their part, opened their dikes and flooded their land in an effort to halt the progress of Louis. Eventually, the Dutch elected **William III of Orange** as their leader, who would become Louis's most important enemy and the leader of the Protestant opposition to the Catholic Louis. William went to the Austrian and Spanish Habsburgs, who stood to lose the most to the consolidation of Louis's absolutism in France and its expansion in Europe, for help.

In 1678 the Treaty of Nijmegen ended the war, allowing Louis to take the Franche-Comte, but in 1679 Louis invaded the Holy Roman Empire. Vienna was under siege from the Ottoman Turks, distracting the Holy Roman Emperor. Moreover, Louis had considerable support from important principalities in the Holy Roman Empire, such as Brandenburg, and the Church states of Cologne and Trier. In 1681, he succeeded in taking Strassburg, and set up the infamous *chambres de reunion*, courts that had no authority in the Holy Roman Empire, but to which Louis delegated the responsibility of deciding territorial questions in his favor.

War of the League of Augsburg (War of the Grand Alliance, 1688–1697)

Louis's flagrant violation of the Holy Roman Empire and his frightening wave of expansion galvanized the Protestant world behind the Dutch leader William of Orange. The Catholic world united against Louis under the Holy Roman Emperor Leopold. The combined Protestant forces created the **League of Augsburg**. Among their leaders were the Holy Roman Emperor, the kings of Spain and Sweden, the Holy Roman prince electors of Bavaria, Saxony, and the Palatinate, and the leaders of the Dutch republics and England in 1689.

From 1688–1697, Louis fought this impressive force in the **War of the League of Augsburg**. The combined fleet of Dutch and English was simply too large for him to defeat. The war had created a near state of bankruptcy for Louis, forcing him to conclude it with terms unfavorable to France. In 1697, the war ended with the Peace of Ryswick, which established a system of trade with the Dutch. Moreover, the treaty forced Louis to recognize William of Orange as leader of the Dutch and as King of England, a position he obtained in the Glorious Revolution of 1689.

The War of the Spanish Succession (1701–1714)

The **War of the Spanish Succession** was the second war that engulfed Europe, but it was one that was also a global conflict. In North America, the war was called **Queen Anne's War**. The War of the League of Augsburg had barely ended when the conflict over the Spanish Succession broke out. Exhaustion on the part of all parties contributed to their decision-making process.

The war arose as a result of the ill health and mental incompetence of the Spanish King Charles II. Charles never produced heirs, but his half-sister, the child of her father's first marriage, was married to Louis XIV and had produced an heir. Louis, of course, earnestly wished for his son to obtain the Spanish crown, as then France would control Spain's vast wealth in the New World. Since France was already threatening to take over much of Europe, this choice was problematic for other rulers.

The other choices were Emperor Charles VI and Prince Joseph Ferdinand of Bavaria, an elector of the Holy Roman Empire. The former frightened many with the possibility of resurrecting the Spanish-Austrian Habsburg Empire of the sixteenth century. Consequently, England and the Netherlands favored Prince Joseph Ferdinand. Continuous warfare had exhausted the parties involved, and England and France quickly negotiated the First Partition Treaty, giving the crown to Joseph Ferdinand, while Louis's son and the Archduke Charles received territory in Italy.

The next year, Joseph Ferdinand suddenly died, and the parties negotiated the Second Partition Treaty. According to this treaty, Charles was now heir to the crown, but the Italian territories awarded in the First Partition Treaty were now to go in their entirety to France. While France, the Netherlands, and England happily accepted these new terms, Austria did not and now attempted to gain the entire Spanish inheritance. At this point, Charles II unexpectedly named Louis's grandson, the Duke of Anjou, as his heir, thus preventing Louis from having direct control over France. Louis refused to honor the treaty, but the Spanish crowned his grandson king as Philip V.

The situation grew more intense when Louis recognized **James Stuart**, the son of the exiled Catholic King of England James II, as the legitimate king of England, Scotland, and Ireland. The English were furious and determined to defeat Louis XIV. During the war, the British captured Gibraltar in Spain, which they continue to hold today. The Austrian and English forces defeated the French at the Battle of Malplaquet, but at a tremendous cost.

The war ended with the **Peace of Utrecht** in 1714. Louis's grandson Philip became the Spanish king, but was forbidden to be in line for the French throne. Austria received the Spanish Netherlands, Naples, and Milan, and Savoy received Spanish Sardinia. More importantly, the treaty gave Britain the exclusive right to trade slaves in Spanish America and to maintain control of Gibraltar as well as Minorca, both former territories of Spain. The British also gained several French colonial possessions, making them by far the greatest beneficiaries of the treaty.

Historical Evaluations of Louis's Reign

Louis's foreign wars were costly, and detracted from Colbert's success in the economic sphere. On the other hand, the author Voltaire credited Louis with the excellence of French culture during this period, as Louis was a great patron of the arts. Louis made Paris the beautiful city that it is today, with paved streets and streetlights. He had a system of hospitals that performed charitable work, highways, and a thriving commerce. There are, however, more negative evaluations of Louis. The Duke of Saint Simon called Louis the "King Bee" and argued that Louis chose his advisors for their ignorance rather than for their knowledge. According to him, Louis had an "intellect beneath mediocrity." Contemporary historians argue that while Louis deified himself and flaunted morality, he divided the labor of government to maintain power, and thus began the age of bureaucracy. While Louis's centralization of the French government might be praised from this point of view, Louis also brought the French one step closer to the massive uprising of the population in 1789 against the abuses of absolute monarchy.

ABSOLUTISM IN RUSSIA: PETER THE GREAT (1682–1725) AND THE WESTERNIZATION OF RUSSIA

The Russian Monarchy

Russia had a history of autocracy even before Peter the Great. **Ivan the Terrible** had created a domain under his complete control called the *oprichnina;* the tsar used the *oprichnina's* secret police, the *oprichniki*, to terrorize his subjects. Although Ivan the Terrible conquered the Tartars and established a kingdom that went all the way east to the Urals and west to Poland and Sweden, following his death, there was chaos during the "time of troubles," which lasted from 1604 to 1613. The nobles became more powerful and elected **Michael Romanov** as tsar, since he was not a member of any faction. His descendants ruled Russia until 1917.

Romanov was fanatically pious, attending church four or five times a day. Michael's death created a controversy, as he had two wives. By his first wife, there were several daughters and two sons; by his second wife, there was one son, who became **Peter the Great**. Michael's eldest son died and the other by his first wife was a weak candidate. The Russian nobles or boyars wanted Peter to rule with his mother as regent. One of his stepsisters, Sophia, stirred up the *streltsy* or Russian army against Peter, and they invaded the Kremlin and killed Peter's grandfather before his very eyes, killed his mother's brothers, and forced the *boyars* (aristocrats) to accept his half-brother Ivan as tsar with his half-sister Sophia as regent.

Peter never forgot these atrocities, so he was determined to create for himself a strong position where nobles, church, or family could not threaten him. In 1869, one of Peter's many supporters among the boyars sent a false message to him that Sophia planned to have him arrested; he and the boyars then deposed Sophia as regent and exiled her to a convent. His half-brother Ivan yielded his power to Peter, and Peter became the new tsar.

Peter was a striking figure at seven feet tall. He was larger than life in both stature and power, yet had very crude manners. He and his companions were known for trashing hotel rooms in Europe and he was also known for his brutality. Peter wanted to make Russia a powerful nation with a powerful monarch who could control serfs, nobles, and the Church. He wanted to make Russia a major power that could fight off Turks, Poles, and Swedes, who surrounded Russia.

Peter's Search for a Warm Water Seaport

The Swedes held the key to warm water ports, so Peter in 1696 captured the port of Azov, giving Russia access to the sea. But without a navy this gain was meaningless. Peter also tried to capture more of the Black Sea coast, but he could not hold it and he quickly learned the inferiority of the Russian army against European forces.

In his youth, Peter was exposed to Western scholars. His half-sister Sophia pioneered Western ideas, such as freedom for women. In 1697 Peter visited Europe, traveling incognito. Russia was so backwards that his subjects might have revolted had they known of his journey and goals. While traveling in Europe, Peter became enchanted with the arts of shipbuilding and navigation. He brought 1,000 Western experts to Russia to bring it into line with Western technological advances.

The Revolt of the Army

While he was away, however, events at home further convinced him of the inadequacy of the army and the need to modernize Russia. In 1698, the army revolted. Peter viciously put down the revolt, ordering the execution of over 1,200 rebels, whom he had put on public display. Peter personally executed many of the rebels.

The Great Northern War

Peter's continued quest for an adequate seaport led to the **Great Northern War** (1700–1721). When the Swedes crowned Charles XII as king at the young age of fifteen, Peter thought this the perfect opportunity to attack. At the Battle of Narva in 1700, however, Charles defeated Peter's force of 40,000 with a force of only 8,000. This failure once again highlighted to Peter the weaknesses of the Russian army and convinced him to rebuild the army after Western models. Peter implemented the use of European officers and Western uniforms, and drew soldiers from each territory. He armed the regiments with Western weapons, so that by 1703, Peter, disguised as Pyotr Mikhailov, led his forces to victory at the mouth of the River Neva. Following the victory, Peter founded the city of **St. Petersburg**. In 1704 Peter's forces retook Narva.

In 1709 Peter successfully drew the Swedes into the Russian winter and defeated them at the Battle of Poltava. The Treaty of Nystadt awarded Russia the much sought after warm water port.

The Modernization of Russia

St. Petersburg was known as the "window to the West" and it symbolized a revolution. It was a new city facing Europe, and Peter gave very favorable terms to foreign merchants. St. Petersburg was built on piles in swampy ground. Thousands of people died while constructing it. Many Swedish prisoners of war died here, but so did many Russians. The toll taken by the project is symbolic of the hardships Russians suffered as Peter the Great stopped at nothing to drag Russia into the modern era. Peter himself said that "Russia must be coerced" to enter the modern era. Peter Westernized Russia over the protests of Slavophiles and others who resisted Westernized customs.

The new European-style city symbolized a complete revolution in society and the Westernization of Russian belief systems. Peter ordered the long Asiatic style beards of boyars trimmed. This was controversial because Russians believed that the beards were necessary for salvation, as the Apostles and Prophets wore them. Some Russians saved their beards after they had been shaved and had them placed in their graves.

Dress changed to more a Western style, and women appeared in public. Peter imported printing presses from Europe and printed Russian newspapers, and a book of Western etiquette. Peter reformed the alphabet and the Russian calendar to bring it more in line with the Julian calendar.

Peter secularized the Russian Orthodox Church by abolishing the office of Patriarch; after 1721, there was not another put in place. He created the Holy Synod, headed by the Procurator, who was a government official and directly controlled by Peter. He taxed the Old Believers heavily for continuing to wear beards and holding on to the old ways. Many were burned to death, tortured, or imprisoned for life. Many went to their deaths holding their fingers in the characteristic two-finger gesture with which they crossed themselves.

Peter tolerated many faiths and allowed Calvinist and Lutheran churches to be built on the Nevsky Prospect, which became known as the Prospect of Toleration.

Repression of the Boyars

The Russian boyars, or aristocrats, still sought too much power, so Peter created a Table of Ranks, according to which rank was independent of one's noble status. One's rank in society was now equated with one's rank in Peter's bureaucracy and Peter required service to the state. This reform was perhaps one reason his package of reforms endured. The new government was organized into ten territorial governments. There were no heads of departments, but rather committees to run affairs of state.

Peter supported his new Westernized state with taxes on just about everything, from the right to marry, to wear a beard, or to be an Old Believer. Peter instituted a tax on each head, which Russians pejoratively referred to as the soul tax. Previously, taxation had been by household, and it was possible for many to cheat the government out of money. Peter had no toleration for those who cheated the government, and even executed boyars who stole tax money.

Peter brought new industries to Russia, which had been primarily a backward agricultural land and used peasants as conscripted labor. His reforms succeeded in further distancing the aristocracy from the rest of the population. The boyars now spoke Western languages, while the peasants spoke Russian. The condition of the serfs was worse than ever before, and Peter regarded them as brutes for their lack of the new Western culture. He simply exploited them as a supply of cheap labor.

Peter the Great was one of the most hated rulers during his time in world history. Even his own son wanted him dead. In retaliation, Peter ordered his son put to death. The Russian Orthodox Church hated his reforms and saw him as the anti-Christ. Those dedicated to Russian culture, known as Slavophiles, were in open revolt. Peter's reforms may have Westernized the boyars, but this only further separated them from the masses. Nevertheless, Peter is justifiably credited for dragging Russia "kicking and screaming" into the modern age.

ABSOLUTISM IN PRUSSIA

The origins of Prussia go back to **Brandenburg**, one of the German states of the Holy Roman Empire. In 1415, the Emperor Sigismund granted the margravate of Brandenburg to the house of **Hohenzollern**, who would rule Brandenburg until the end of World War I. The margrave of Brandenburg was an elector of the Holy Roman Empire until the Empire collapsed in 1806. Brandenburg converted to Protestantism during the Reformation. In 1614, the Hohenzollern annexed Cleves, which had a mixed population that was one-half German and one-half Polish. Its population was also divided by religion, as it was one-half Lutheran and one-half Catholic. The Hohenzollern dynasty was limited as a European power by its lack of seaports, poor mineral resources, and lack of natural frontiers to protect it from invasion. Its domains were disconnected and widely scattered.

In 1618 the Hohenzollern acquired the **Duchy of Prussia**, which gave them access to the sea. In 1701, **Frederick III** assumed the title of "King of Prussia."

Prussia was outside of the legal boundaries of the Holy Roman Empire, but the Holy Roman emperors did not agree to his use of the title until 1713, when the Treaty of Utrecht officially named the Elector of Brandenburg the King of Prussia. Brandenburg remained the heart of the kingdom, but it increasingly became identified with Prussia.

Frederick William, The Great Elector (1640–1688)

Frederick William was a dedicated Calvinist. He created a standing army, which he funded through the resources of the crown domain and taxes. The officers of the army collected the very taxes that supported their existence. Frederick created a hereditary class of officers through the landed aristocracy, called Junkers. They were forbidden to sell their land to non-nobles, and their service was based on duty, obedience, and service to the king.

Frederick William I (1713–1740)

Frederick William I devoted his reign to the improvement of the army. He spent little money on his own coronation, and cut three-fourths of the royal household from state expenses. He channeled the money saved into the military. He rearranged the order of court by elevating the officers of the army and relegating civilians to lower ranks. His army appeared in uniform. Its might was symbolized by the height of many soldiers, who were often six to seven feet tall. He doubled the size of the army through a system of recruitment from the cantons. His militaristic attitude was manifested in his discipline of the citizens with a walking stick on his regular strolls. His militaristic bearing prompted one biographer to call him the "Potsdam Führer." Frederick worked constantly and developed the bureaucracy necessary for further development.

CONSTITUTIONALISM IN ENGLAND: THE GLORIOUS REVOLUTION

The Glorious Revolution in England occurred during the Age of Absolutism, in which the power of European monarchs was reaching an all-time high. England, by contrast, had a long tradition of representative government going back to 1215, when English barons made King John sign the Magna Carta. The Magna Carta established the idea that the king, just like everyone else in society, was subject to the law. During the Hundred Years' War, the power of the parliament increased, while that of the monarch decreased.

In 1603, Elizabeth the Great died childless, leaving her cousin Mary Stuart's son James VI of Scotland as her heir. He became **James I** of England and established the Stuart line in England. The Stuart monarchs did not subscribe to the

English Parliamentary tradition and behaved as autocrats. James wrote the *True Law of Free Monarchy*, in which he asserted that there should be no parliamentary power. He argued that the king got his authority from God, and so should be responsible to God alone. During the English Civil War, the conflict between the Stuarts and Parliament was resolved in favor of the Parliament.

The Puritans

The Parliament at that time was composed of **Puritans** who were landed gentry (wealthy) and who were composed of at least three different factions who, to varying degrees, supported presbyterianism. The Puritans fought for religious freedom and wanted to abolish the rites and rituals of the Anglican Church as well as the structure of the clergy and to establish a presbyterian structure for the Church. Some of the more radical Puritans were known as Separatists, for their desire to separate from the Church of England. The Pilgrims who went to the Americas were **Separatists**.

The Catholicism of the Stuarts

King James was Catholic and relaxed many of the prohibitions against Catholics instituted since the reign of Elizabeth the Great. He also reaffirmed the use of Anglican rites in the face of the Puritan desire for simplicity.

Absolutist Policies of the Stuarts

Both James I and his son Charles attempted to raise funds without the consent of Parliament. Charles attempted to use these funds to keep the navy armed in a time of peace. In 1628 Parliament passed the Right of Petition, according to which Charles could not billet soldiers in private homes, arbitrarily tax without the consent of Parliament, or randomly imprison anyone. In response, Charles dissolved the Parliament in 1629 and did not recall it until 1640.

Under Charles, the Archbishop of Canterbury, William Laud, bitterly repressed the Puritans, many of whom went to the New World. He believed in the total uniformity of the Anglican Church and expelled clergy who failed to conform, censored the press, and allowed no religious meetings outside of the Anglican Church. He also persecuted the Presbyterians, followers of Calvin in Scotland. Charles further outraged the Puritan and Protestant world when he married the Catholic sister of Louis XIII.

The Long Parliament

Problems with the Presbyterian rebellions in Scotland starting in 1637 forced Charles to summon the Parliament in 1640. This session was known as the **Long Parliament**, and they sent Archbishop Laud to the Tower of London and attempted to limit the King's power through regular meetings of Parliament.

The Long Parliament also abolished the Court of the Star Chamber and passed legislation so that the king could not levy taxes without the consent of Parliament. Many of the members of the Parliament wanted to go further and completely transfer all authority from the king. Charles ultimately sent troops into Parliament to contain the situation, but they passed the militia ordinance giving Parliament control over the army.

The English Civil War

By 1642, England was in a state of civil war between the **Roundheads**, who were Puritans and got their names because of their round haircuts, and the Royalists, known as the **Cavaliers**. **Oliver Cromwell**, a staunch opponent of the Anglican Church, rose to prominence as the leader of the Roundheads and created a New Model Army that defeated the forces of the king in 1645.

The Rump Parliament

In 1648, Cromwell's extreme Puritan supporters purged Parliament of moderates and other foes in an event known as Pride's Purge, named after the colonel who led the soldiers. The resulting Parliament was known as the **Rump Parliament**, and Cromwell and his supporters abolished the House of Lords.

The End of Monarchy and the Establishment of the Protectorate

The Rump Parliament was responsible for the trial and execution of King Charles I as a public criminal. Following this event, they established a Puritan commonwealth that ruled England from 1649–1653. In 1653 Cromwell dismissed the Rump Parliament and established the Protectorate, with himself as Lord Protector. Cromwell viciously crushed Ireland, where the Catholics there favored the Stuarts. He was intolerant of Anglicans, and vigorously enforced Puritan morality in England.

The money needed to maintain his army caused grave financial difficulties, and these were compounded by the wars with Spain and the Dutch. Rising opposition forced Cromwell to resort to military rule. When he died in 1658, many Englishmen were ready to go back to the old monarchy. Cromwell was initially buried in Westminster Abbey, the traditional burial place of England's monarch, but a few years after his death, angry crowds removed him from his coffin, dragged his body through the streets to Tyburn, where criminals and traitors were often executed. Cromwell's body was hanged there with his head placed on a spike and was displayed for twenty-four hours. Later his remains were thrown on a dunghill. Cromwell's dictatorial methods seem to contradict his desire for religious freedom, especially from intrusion by the monarch and a state church. He set up exactly the sort of system he worked to defeat.

THE RESTORATION

The Stuarts were restored to power when **Charles II**, the son of the executed King Charles I, was crowned in 1660. He ruled until 1685. Upon the restoration of the monarchy, Charles agreed to limit his power, not to pass taxes without the consent of Parliament, and to make no religious changes. However, Charles II very much admired Louis XIV, a fellow Catholic and one who shared the Stuart belief in absolute monarchy. They negotiated in secret the **Treaty of Dover** in 1670. According to the treaty, England would join in Louis's war with the Dutch, and in return, money would flow from France to England.

The Declaration of Indulgence

Charles II's Catholic sympathies also led him to enact the **Declaration of Indulgence** in 1672, whereby there was toleration for those who dissented from the Church of England.

The Titus Oates Plot

Meanwhile, James, Charles's brother, publicly announced his conversion to Catholicism, creating further ill-will for the Stuarts. The Titus Oates Plot, a conspiracy to place James on the throne, made fears of a Catholic monarchy more intense. Although Charles II ordered the conspirators put to death, the damage was done.

The Cavalier Parliament

The Cavalier Parliament, a royalist Parliament that met through 1679, enacted several laws in reaction to Cromwell's Puritanism. It attempted to diffuse Puritan influence by reinstating the Anglican Church. Through the **Conventicle Act** of 1664, they forbade dissenting religious assemblies of more than five people; through the Act of Uniformity, they required the use of all rites and rituals in the Book of Common Prayer in church services; through the Five Mile Act they forbade dissenters from living in incorporated and chartered towns. Since the king was the head of the Church in England, the church and king worked to support one another.

Two parties dominated the Cavalier Parliament: the **Whigs** and the **Tories**. The Whigs supported the Act of Exclusion proposed in 1678 and again in 1681 to bar James, a Catholic and the brother of Charles, from the throne; they wanted a Protestant monarch. The Tories supported the traditional succession and monarchy. In 1679 the Cavalier Parliament was dissolved, but in 1681, Charles did not summon the new Parliament, renewing old fears about the monarchy.

The Rye House Plot

In 1683, Charles's Catholic leanings led Whig leaders to conspire to assassinate Charles in the **Rye House Plot**. Charles ordered the execution of the Whig leaders.

James II

In 1685 **James II** became king and would rule until 1688, when he would be deposed in favor of Protestant monarchs.

James's reign began on a negative note, when in the **Bloody Assizes** he put a thousand Protestant rebels to death. He then suspended the Test Act, which barred Catholics and other dissenters from holding office, and issued two Declarations of Indulgence that provided tolerance for Catholics and other dissenters.

William and Mary

When James's second wife, Mary of Modena, bore him a male heir, the Parliament worried that their desire to see his Protestant daughter Mary (from his first wife) on the throne would be thwarted. The Parliament invited Mary and her husband William of Orange, the most important leader of the Protestant forces in Europe, to take the throne. On November 5, 1688, **William and Mary** landed in England and became the new rulers of England in a bloodless revolution known as the **Glorious Revolution**.

The Penal Codes

James fled to Catholic Ireland and later to France, where he spent the rest of his life. The English never forgave the Irish for harboring James, and bitterly punished them. Penal codes were enacted according to which, among other things, Catholics did not have the freedom to worship, receive an education, enter a profession, hold public office, engage in trade or commerce, live in a corporate town or within five miles thereof, own a horse of greater value than five pounds, purchase or lease land, bear arms, or vote.

Legislation After the Glorious Revolution

In 1698 Parliament passed the **Bill of Rights**, giving Parliament the right to levy taxes, make new laws, and raise a standing army. The bill guaranteed free elections, trial by jury, freedom of speech and the right of citizens to petition, and keep arms. In that same year, the Act of Toleration granted freedom of worship to Puritans, but did not revoke the Test Act. Puritans still did not have full civil and political equality. The Act of Settlement, passed in 1701, restricted the succession to Protestants. After William died, James's daughter **Anne**, whose mother was a Protestant, became queen, and during her reign, the Parliament passed the **Act of Union** in 1707. The Act of Union created Great Britain by finally fully uniting England and Scotland. Ireland, repressed by the **penal codes**, did not join the Union until 1801.

John Locke and the Right of Rebellion

John Locke wrote the political rationale behind the Glorious Revolution in the *Second Treatise on Government*. Despite the fact the revolution was bloodless, the English had overthrown a legitimate monarch. Locke argued that people were born with natural rights, including life, liberty, and possessions, and when the government deprived them of these rights, they had a natural right of rebellion. Much to Britain's chagrin, Locke's ideas became the basis for the American Revolution in 1776.

CULTURAL CHANGES IN THE AGE OF ABSOLUTISM: THE SCIENTIFIC REVOLUTION AND THE ENLIGHTENMENT

The Scientific Revolution, like the Renaissance, helped to end the old medieval ways of thinking and to usher the world into the modern era. During the Scientific Revolution a new, scientific attitude toward the study of the world emerged, one whose conclusions often clashed with the teachings of established religions. During the subsequent movement known as the **Enlightenment**, the philosophes would ultimately reject the religion of past eras as superstition in favor of the use of reason. While the medieval work relied upon authorities, such as the Bible and the Church, the figures of the Scientific Revolution helped to establish the attitude that one should not believe anything unless one could empirically verify it or prove it mathematically.

The seventeenth century was an age of genius, in which such figures as Galileo, Kepler, Bacon, and Descartes flourished. All of these men believed that the universe is a rationally ordered, harmonious whole, and that humans have the ability to penetrate and to understand its structure.

For the figures of the seventeenth-century Scientific Revolution, nature was no longer a manifestation of some transcendent entity, but an "it" to be understood and manipulated for human benefit. Humans could understand nature through empirical observation. The new thinkers of the seventeenth century in large part insisted on the use of experience rather than on revelation, and sought to correlate experience with the truths and principles of mathematics.

Nicholas Copernicus (1473–1543)

Copernicus was from Poland and in 1543 published *On the Revolutions of the Heavenly Orbs*, in which he articulated the theory that the universe was heliocentric, or sun-centered. He argued that the earth and planets revolved around the sun in circular orbits. The most common theory of the time was that of the ancient Greco-Roman geographer Ptolemy, who taught that the universe was made up of a series of concentric spheres that revolved around each other. According to this theory, the earth was in one glass sphere, while the other planets were in others. The universe was geocentric, Earth-centered, according to this model.

Tycho Brahe (1546–1601) developed many instruments for astronomical observations and made detailed observations over a long period. These observations highlighted anomalies on the orbits of the planets, and he hired **Johann Kepler** to help calculate the orbits. Brahe's observations proved that Copernicus's remarks on the circular orbits of planets were not correct and, therefore, not many adopted Copernicus's theory. Most preferred to maintain the Ptolemaic conception, as it also supported various passages in the Scriptures that suggest that the Earth stands still while the heavens move around it.

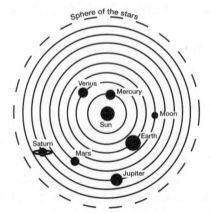

Copernicus's Concept of the Universe

Johann Kepler (1571–1630)

Kepler was the first to make detailed observations and to plot the elliptical orbits of the planets. Kepler also noted that the closer a planet is to the sun, the faster it moves. Its length of orbit also varies according to its distance from the sun.

Galileo (1564–1642)

Galileo's observations rocked the world when he proved that Copernicus was right about the sun-centered structure of the solar system. Galileo observed four of Jupiter's moons, and thereby decisively proved that the Ptolemaic concept of the universe was inaccurate. He also proved that the planets were not just luminous objects, as taught by the ancients, but that they had mass and that the laws of mathematics applied to them as to everything else. Further, he observed spots on the sun and proved that the sun rotated, thereby again contradicting Ptolemy. The Church condemned Galileo, who argued that Scripture was meant to be read figuratively. The Church ordered Galileo's works to be burned and forbade him to teach; according to tradition, when the sentence was given, Galileo uttered under his breath, "It still moves."

Isaac Newton (1642–1727)

Newton's achievement was to synthesize all previous systems by asking the simple question, "Why?" Other figures, such as Galileo and Kepler, had observed and described, but Newton wanted to know why the universe behaved as it did. Why, for example, the planets did not fly off in a straight line as they rounded the sun?

In 1687 Newton published perhaps the most important work ever published, the *Principia Mathematica*. It had been written while students were in exile from Cambridge due to the outbreak of the plague in the seventeenth century, and it had sat in his desk for many years as a collection of notes he thought unimportant. In these notes was perhaps the most important discovery ever put

Portrait of Isaac Newton

forth, that of universal gravitation. Newton had discovered three laws of motion that applied to all bodies, no matter what they are.

Newton believed that his mathematics allowed him to look directly into the mind of God. Although the philosophes of the Enlightenment that followed in the eighteenth century would become agnostics or even atheists, Newton remained profoundly religious. He believed, if anything, that the mathematical nature of the universe proved the existence of God, and like the medieval scholastics, he believed that God had made it possible for the human mind to penetrate many of the mysteries of the universe and so come that much closer to an awareness of its maker.

PHILOSOPHY DURING THE SCIENTIFIC REVOLUTION

Blaise Pascal (1623–1662)

Similarly, the brilliant mathematician **Blaise Pascal** believed that a wagering person must believe in God. Pascal became a profound mystic and, in his famous *Pensées*, Pascal pointed out that it is more reasonable to have faith than to not. If one supposes the teachings of orthodox Christianity to be false and they are false, then one has not lost much except the false promise of an afterlife. If one believes the teachings of orthodox Christianity to be true and they are true, then one's faith is aptly rewarded. If one believes these teachings to be true and they are not true, then one has lost nothing. However, if one believes the teachings of orthodox Christianity to be false and they turn out to be true, then one has lost more than one can imagine. Therefore, the odds suggest faith is more productive than lack thereof. Pascal used reason to prove the reasonableness of having faith, whereas many of his colleagues rejected religion altogether.

Francis Bacon (1561–1626)

Francis Bacon's *New Organon* criticized old forms of knowledge and ways of attaining it. Bacon criticized medieval scholastic learning, as he thought it was based on idle speculations rather than on direct experience.

Bacon argued that old knowledge served to perpetuate errors rather than to uncover truth. For example, Aristotle argued that some principles could not be proven, but rather must be accepted. Bacon rejected such logic, and argued that the world needed a new form of knowledge that tells us what is actually there; he argued that we needed to obtain knowledge from experience, rather than from predetermined principles. Bacon suggested that one needs to move from the ground up, to build the pyramid of knowledge from the blocks, rather than to take the blocks from a preconstructed pyramid. Bacon's method is known as the **inductive method**, and is the method according to which most scientific hypotheses are formulated today.

David Hume (1711–1776), a Scottish philospher, raised some questions, however, about the integrity of the inductive method. Like Bacon, Hume believed in the primacy of human experience in the knowledge process. In other words, both Hume and Bacon were **empiricists**. Hume argued that to validate induction, however, we have to make an induction, and that this departs from our actual experience. For example, how do we know that since we have seen 999,999 white swans that the 1,000,000th swan will be white? We can only say that in the past such inductions appear to be reliable, but if the question is where the process is valid, then to use induction itself to prove its validity is to make a circular argument. Hume's questions here are now known as "the problem of induction."

Rene Descartes (1596–1650)

Descartes, unlike Bacon, was a **rationalist**. Like the scientific figures of his age and even Bacon, he was interested in obtaining true knowledge as opposed to the reliance on authority of past eras. Descartes argued that this was only possible if one proceeded by foundations that were known for certain to be true. Many things we think are true are just opinions, so one must discover the foundations that are certainties. Just as a building cannot be built on a weak foundation, so knowledge cannot be built on mere opinions. In the *Discourse on Method*, Descartes argued that one should not accept anything as true unless it is certain, and to proceed from the simple to the more complex. His methods were deductive, whereas Bacon's were inductive.

In the *Meditations,* Descartes introduced the method of radical skepticism when he supposed that there might be an evil demon deceiving us all along the way in everything we think we know or experience. In such a case, Descartes argued that almost everything we think we know must be rejected, as it was susceptible to even this wild supposition. The only thing we cannot doubt, however, is the contents of our own minds, particularly, the notion that if "I think, therefore I am" or the famous *cogito ergo sum*. Descartes argued that the absolutely clear knowledge we have of the contents of our own minds was the certain foundation for all knowledge for which he was looking. Descartes said that the contents of the mind were "clear and distinct," and this became his new criteria for knowledge. Descartes's method was entirely based on the use of reason; one could come to his conclusions without ever leaving one's armchair, and therefore, Descartes differed from the empiricist methods of Bacon, Hume, and also John Locke, who believed that all knowledge came from experience.

The Cartesian view fundamentally separated mind from body, and the Cartesian idea that the mind was transparent would not be challenged until Sigmund Freud argued that there were areas of our psyches that were opaque to us.

Baruch Spinoza (1632–1677)

Spinoza was a Jewish philosopher who argued that science had demonstrated that the only thing we need to understand nature was nature itself. Therefore, Spinoza equated God with nature; that is, he believed in pantheism, the idea that God does not exist apart from the world.

Critique of the Bible

The emphasis of the seventeenth century on observation led to a new interest in the historical scholarship and critique of the Bible. In a *Critical History of the Old Testament*, Richard Simon attempted to unravel some of the mysteries of the Bible. Simon raised doubts about the integrity of the Hebrew texts, explored the question of the authorship of the Books of Moses, and other questions. Since the Protestant world, for example, recognized the Bible as its infallible source, his book shook the religious world, although it presented little that was new in the world of biblical scholarship.

John Locke (1632–1704)

Locke was an English philosopher who pushed the Newtonian worldview to its logical conclusions. In *Two Treatises of Government* Locke developed a **natural rights theory of government**, according to which the laws of government and of society were embedded in nature itself. Newton had proven the universe to be mechanical, and now Locke insisted that according to nature itself, humans had the rights of life, liberty, and property, and that these rights were to be respected and protected by their governments. He pushed to its logical conclusion Newton's third law of motion relating to cause and effect by arguing that there should be checks and balances in an efficient and acceptable system of government. Locke wrote that when the government did not respect the natural rights of man, that people had a right and even a duty to rebel. Locke's theories justified the Glorious Revolution in England against the Stuart monarchy.

Classicism

The Scientific Revolution and Enlightenment profoundly influenced music and other art forms. Musicians translated Newton's third law of motion, that for every action there was an equal and opposite reaction, into love of perfectly ordered form, balanced phrases of the same length, and rhythmic emphasis on the beat as opposed to off the beat, creating a sense of stability. Various rhythmic formulas became standard, such as the Alberti bass, as did various melodic motifs, such as the Mannheim rocket, a short motif based on rapidly ascending triadic harmony. The sonata-allegro form became the standard form for many works, and it represented a balanced exploration of two or more themes within a standardized harmonic framework. At the end of a piece in sonata-allegro form, one came back to the starting point, both tonally and thematically. No matter how much the composer varied the themes in the middle, development section, the themes reappeared in their original key in the recapitulation, or final section, of the piece. A gifted composer such as **Beethoven** or **Mozart** might considerably develop these themes in the development section, but Beethoven's use of motivic development almost treated the themes as if they were made of atoms, breaking them into their natural, component segments and exploring the ways in which they could be combined. Another important composer of the classical era was **Haydn**. Musical sonata-allegro form paralleled the Enlightened view in the laws of nature as stable and as guiding the unfolding of the universe.

There was also a revival of interest in classical architecture. In many ways, the Greek love of balance, order, and harmony complimented the enlightened emphasis on the laws of nature. Greek-like temples dotted the landscapes of many estates, and landscape architecture also forced nature to comply with the "laws" of nature. Unruly vegetation was sculpted into ordered designs. Landscape gardens, such as the famous gardens of Versailles in France or Hampton Court in England, defied the unruliness often inherent in nature to present a fabricated sense of order in nature itself.

THE EIGHTEENTH-CENTURY ENLIGHTENMENT

The Enlightenment was an eighteenth-century outgrowth of the Scientific Revolution. Although it was primarily centered in France, examples of enlightenment thought were also found in Germany and other parts of Europe. The most basic feature of Enlightenment thought was reliance on reason above all else. The German philosopher **Immanuel Kant** wrote a work on "What is Enlightenment?" in which he stated it was the move from immaturity to maturity, a progression in critical thought in which one is not reliant on the "guardians of truth" or authorities to inform one about the nature of reality. Kant and others of the Enlightenment insisted on the public use of reason, meaning that past authorities made assertions without proof, and merely expected others to follow. All thought now was to be subjected to public scrutiny, and there would be no repositories of mysterious wisdom, such as the Church.

An important consequence of this rationalizing attitude was Deism, a movement in which God was seen as a watchmaker who set world in motion and then left it to run alone. David Hume, for example, suggested that the existence of a creator God might be inferred from the presence of an orderly universe. An orderly machine must have a builder, he argued. The Deist God did not interfere in the world, but rather, the laws of nature continue to govern the unfolding of the universe. The God of the Deists was not the compassionate and involved God of the past, but a secular God identified with nature. Many French philosophes carried this idea further. While Deists were willing to believe in the existence of a watchmaker God, some philosophes saw no need for one.

Francois Marie Arouet (1694–1778): Voltaire

Arouet was more commonly known as **Voltaire**, and he was born in Paris. He produced many satiric plays, for which he was imprisoned in the Bastille for eleven months. He then spent three years in England, and learned to like the freedom there following the Glorious Revolution, when the absolute Stuart monarchs had been overthrown. Voltaire even wrote a work on Newtonian physics before he retired to Switzerland. Here he communicated often with Frederick the Great, wrote 30 letters a day, and was a prolific writer with many friends and visitors. Voltaire's ideas were typical of the period. In the *Philosophical Dictionary* (1764) he attacked religion as fanaticism and superstition.

In *Candide* (1759) he attacked the rationalist argument put forth by the philosopher Leibnitz that this is "the best of all possible worlds." Every misfortune possible befalls Candide; he is beaten, sees death and destruction on the battlefield and in the earthquake at Lisbon, and eventually comes to believe that the best possible thing to do is to cultivate one's own garden. In *Candide*, Voltaire advocated reform close to home as an appropriate beginning place, and suggested that is the only thing one might be able to control. In this statement, he differed from some of his colleagues, whose idealism about human nature and the possibilities of reform he came to doubt by the end of his life. Although Voltaire criticized the Church, he received last rites on his deathbed, and so while he found much to doubt about religion, still the possibility of its truth lingered with him.

Montesquieu (1689–1755)

The Baron de **Montesquieu**, Charles de Secondat, applied the scientific methodology of the seventeenth century to the idea of natural law. In *The Spirit of the Laws*, Montesquieu dissected various kinds of government, and in particular, focused on the parliamentary system of England and its checks and balances. Montesquieu believed that England's government created the greatest amount of freedom, and his theories had a profound impact in the United States, where they influenced the drafting of the Constitution.

Thomas Paine (1731–1814)

Similarly, **Thomas Paine** rejected institutionalized religion. In the *Age of Reason*, Paine wrote that since even Jews who witnessed the life of Christ did not believe in his teachings and his own Apostle Thomas rejected him, then why should anyone believe? Paine was also well known as a revolutionary, and migrated from England to America, where his pamphlet *Common Sense* made the case for independence. Later, he went to France and wrote in support of the French Revolution.

Denis Diderot (1713–1784)

Diderot's compilation of the writings of various authors, the *Encyclopédie*, was an important work that critiqued many aspects of life. This work contained an article by Diderot in which he wrote about the fictitious voyage of Bouganville. His main character comes to a place where Christian morality is foreign, and even evil and strange. There, very different morals were tolerated. Diderot wrote in favor of greater sexual liberties and toleration of moral systems outside of Christianity, as did many other authors, such as Thomas Paine.

Edward Gibbon (1737–1794)

Gibbon's masterpiece was the massive work the *Decline and Fall of the Roman Empire*. In this work, he argued that Rome fell because of the pernicious influence of Christianity. Gibbon's thesis has since been strongly challenged, but his condemnation of Christianity reflects the opinions of his age. Gibbon also suggested that the Romans suffered from lead poisoning, due to their system of plumbing.

Marie Jean Antoine Nicolas de Caritat Condorcet (1745–1794)

The **Marquis de Condorcet** is best known for his belief in the *infinite* perfectibility of humankind. Like Pico in the Renaissance, Condorcet believed humans were capable of any achievement they so desired.

Other Enlightened Thinkers

Condorcet's belief was reflective of the Enlightenment emphasis on progress. For example, **Cardinal Beccaria** led a movement for penal reform, and advocated abolishing cruel and unusual punishments. Enlightened thinkers criticized the slave trade, leading to emancipation and abolition movements on the continent and in the Americas. Many principles of the Enlightened thinkers also resulted in the women's rights movement. **Mary Wollstonecraft** wrote the *Vindication of the Rights of Woman*, arguing for rights for women that had been denied to them, especially the right to equal education. Enlightened thinkers also argued for freedom of the press, believing that humans could teach themselves and also formulate their own opinions. **Jean Jacques Rousseau** argued in his famous *Emile* that education should be left to nature, that when one returned to nature, one could truly learn.

These ideas resulted in the strong critique of the absolute monarchy in France and other places, and would profoundly influence the course of both the French and the American Revolutions.

THE ENLIGHTENED DESPOTS

The enlightened despots had much in common with the absolute monarchs, but they were influenced by the ideals of the Enlightenment and enacted reforms in education and other areas.

Russia and Catherine the Great

Catherine the Great was a German princess. Her birth name was Princess Sophia August Frederika. With the help of a lover, Catherine deposed her husband, Peter III, and became the sole ruler of Russia in 1762. Catherine followed the Westernization program of Peter the Great, and continued to subjugate the serfs. Rebellions followed, including the Pugachev Rebellion, an effort in 1773–1774 to abolish serfdom led by a Cossack chief. Catherine crushed the rebellion and executed Pugachev. She continued to whittle away the power and possessions of the Russian Orthodox Church. Despite her growing autocratic tendencies, Catherine had an interest in enlightened ideals and imported many scholars from the West. She continued to construct Western-style buildings in St. Petersburg. Like Peter the Great, however, her Westernization efforts were solely for the purpose of strengthening the central government. Catherine did not tolerate dissent any more than Peter had, and she banned the writings of those with radical ideas, such as the noble Radishev, who advocated for the abolition of serfdom based on ideals of the French Revolution.

The Austrian Hapsburgs and Maria Theresa

Charles VI (1711–1740) had no male heirs, and so forged a treaty known as the **Pragmatic Sanction** (1713). The Pragmatic Sanction made Hapsburg territory indivisible, and mandated one line of heirs through his daughter, **Maria Theresa** (1740–1780). It was unusual to have a woman heir, and Maria Theresa consolidated holdings by bringing government to Vienna. She centralized the government, reformed the army and the economy, and introduced a public system of education. Maria Theresa was an "enlightened despot," who ruled with a firm hand but nevertheless implemented reforms based on enlightenment thought. Along with Frederick the Great, Maria Theresa was one of the most well known enlightened rulers of her time. During her reign and those of her successors, Vienna became a renowned center of culture, a city where Haydn, Mozart, and Beethoven created some of their finest compositions.

Joseph II (1741–1790)

Joseph II, the son of Maria Theresa, abolished serfdom and enacted laws that provided for religious toleration. He abolished torture and the death penalty, and cared for his people through the creation of hospitals and other public welfare programs. Nevertheless, Joseph was able to achieve these goals through absolutist methods. He had complete control over the government and, although he achieved many noteworthy enlightened reforms, his methods were entirely those of the absolute monarchs who preceded him.

Prussia: Frederick II (The Great)

The reforms of Frederick William I made it possible for **Frederick II**, known as **Frederick the Great** (1740–1786) to maintain an army of 200,000. Prussia was very small, and ranked thirteenth in Europe in terms of the size of its population. Nevertheless, it maintained the third largest army.

Frederick wanted to expand Prussia, and violated the Pragmatic Sanction by annexing Silesia, an Austrian territory, beginning the **War of the Austrian Succession (1740–1748)**. Britain and Austria fought with France and Prussia in this war, which extended to Asia and North America. Frederick continued to strengthen Prussia in the **Seven Years' War** (1757–1763), which was a global war.

Despite his military actions, Frederick was an enlightened despot who encouraged education and provided for his subjects. He supported freedom of the press and religious toleration. Frederick abolished the use of torture and the death penalty could only be given on his authorization. He instituted the first law code and improved the plight of the people through education and the construction of roads. While it is tempting to romanticize Frederick as an enlightened ruler, one must also remember that he firmly believed in nobles as the basis for a strong state, and insisted that they all serve as soldiers. Serfs and peasants were simply for work. Frederick did little to overturn the old class structure.

Like many philosophes of the Enlightenment, Frederick rejected religion; like Thomas Hobbes, he believed that it was necessary to relegate power to a judicious monarch. Nevertheless, he claimed to be the "first servant of the state."

Frederick made Prussia one of the strongest nations in Europe, and in the nineteenth century, Bismarck would further transform it through the unification of Germany into one of the most powerful empires in the world.

The Age of Absolutism and the Enlightenment was an era of great change in Europe. Powerful monarchs centralized their governments, often at the expense of the lower classes. Nevertheless, many of these rulers enacted humane reforms that benefited their people.

Review Questions

1. The heliocentric theory of the solar system was first established by

   (A) Galileo.

   (B) Kepler.

   (C) Brahe.

   (D) Copernicus.

2. Galileo's observation of moons around Jupiter demonstrated that

   (A) Jupiter was at the center of the universe.

   (B) Jupiter rotated while the earth did not.

   (C) the universe was not geocentric.

   (D) the earth rotated around Jupiter.

3. The figure during the Age of Reason who emphasized induction as a valid method of reasoning was

   (A) Descartes.

   (B) Hume.

   (C) Voltaire.

   (D) Bacon.

4. The most important intellectual consequence of the Scientific Revolution was

   (A) the addition of required science courses in the curricula of all major universities.

   (B) a weakening of faith in the traditional Christian God of salvation and the Bible as an infallible source of truth.

   (C) the appearance of new publishing houses to print the new scientific works.

   (D) the belief that the universe is basically incomprehensible.

5. All of the following are examples of enlightenment ideals EXCEPT

   (A) freedom of the press.

   (B) penal reform.

   (C) man is basically evil and depraved.

   (D) toleration for all beliefs.

6. Which of the following most correctly describes the enlightened philosophes?

   (A) They adhered to old values, especially the teachings of the Roman Catholic Church.

   (B) They rejected institutionalized religion as superstition.

   (C) They advocated for reform of government based on "natural laws."

   (D) Both (B) and (C).

7. "L'etat c'est moi." This statement is representative of what style of government?

   (A) Constitutional monarchy

   (B) Absolutism

   (C) Republicanism

   (D) Socialism

8. The Glorious Revolution

   (A) installed William and Mary on the throne.

   (B) confirmed the reign of the Stuart James II.

   (C) freed Ireland from English domination.

   (D) established Catholicism as the religion of England.

9. What method did NOT enable Louis XIV and his ministers to centralize the state?

   (A) Mercantilism

   (B) Religious toleration

   (C) Control of the Parlements

   (D) Lit de justice

10. Which of the following statements most correctly describes absolute monarchies?

    (A) The demands of constant war created a need for absolute control of the state.

    (B) Lower taxes led people to overlook the creation of absolute monarchies.

    (C) The desire to instill deeper religious piety and to move away from secularity was a factor in the development of absolutism.

    (D) The monarchs who developed absolutist governments had very secure childhoods.

Answers

1. (D)	4. (B)	7. (B)	10. (A)
2. (C)	5. (C)	8. (A)	
3. (D)	6. (D)	9. (B)	

Chapter 23

THE BRITISH COLONIES IN THE AMERICAS AND THE AMERICAN REVOLUTION

KEY TERMS

Plantation colonies	Congregationalists
Trading colonies	Salem Witch Trials
Settlement colonies	Maryland
Triangular trade	Maryland Toleration Act
Middle Passage	Rhode Island
Dutch colonization	Mercantilism
French colonization	New Colonial Policy
Seven Years' War	Internal taxation
Plymouth	External taxation
Jamestown	Declaration of Independence
Massachusetts Bay Colony	Articles of Confederation
Wampanoag	Constitution of 1789
Algonquin	Bill of Rights
Puritans	

THE EUROPEAN COLONIES IN THE AMERICAS

While the Spanish dominated the colonization of the New World in the sixteenth century, the French and English dominated the colonization efforts in the seventeenth century. The Spanish had primarily been concerned with taking wealth and riches from the New World and converting the heathen natives. The French and English, on the other hand, saw the benefits of developing a self-sustaining economy in the New World, and focused on trade with the natives and the cultivation of crops. The various European powers established three types of colonies in the seventeenth century: plantation colonies, trading colonies, and settlement colonies.

Plantation Colonies

Plantation colonies were based on the cultivation of crops for profit. Sugar was one of the first crops cultivated on the plantation colonies of the Spanish, French, and English in the Caribbean; the cultivation of sugar led to the use of African slaves in the eighteenth century and the development of the **triangular trade**. One leg of the triangular trade involved transporting food staples, such as meat and flour, to the West Indies. The plantation economies of the West Indies relied upon the production of sugar, and so these imports were necessary. Colonists from New England traded their food stuff for sugar, which they then took to England in return for manufactured goods. The effect of this leg of the triangular trade was to strengthen slavery in the plantation areas. In another leg of the triangular trade, merchants from New England brought their manufactured goods to the west coast of Africa, where they exchanged them for slaves. They then took the slaves to the West Indies via the notorious **Middle Passage**. Those slaves that survived the ordeal were exchanged for molasses and rum. American colonists then carried these goods to the Americas and sold them, where the cycle began again. This aspect of the triangular trade also strengthened slavery.

While the cultivation of sugar was central to plantation colonies in the Caribbean, tobacco and rice also became important crops in North America. Planters from Barbados, who developed trade in Indian slaves, dominated South Carolina and grew rice there. Colonists used slave labor to cultivate and harvest these crops as well. In fact, the more profit from the crops, the more colonists resorted to the use of African slaves, as they had greater resistance to disease.

Trading Colonies and the French Colonization of the Americas

In contrast to the plantation and settlement colonies that competed and often conflicted with the Native American population, the **trading colonies** were dependent on the goodwill of the native population. The French had begun to explore the Americas in 1524 when Giovanni da Verrazano had sailed along the North American coastline from the Carolinas to perhaps as far north as Maine. Colonization began ten years later, but the French were preoccupied with the wars of religion that raged across Europe and resulted in a civil war in France. French colonization of the Americas began again in the seventeenth century. **Jacques Cartier** explored the Gulf of St. Lawrence and traveled up the St. Lawrence River to what is modern Montreal. In 1542 he founded Quebec. It did not survive for long, and **Samuel de Champlain** reestablished Quebec in the seventeenth century. The French concentrated on trade in beaver furs in Canada and in the west of North America, and cultivated their relationships with the Native Americans, as did many of the Dutch traders at New Amsterdam. In the **French and Indian War**, known as the **Seven Years' War** in Europe (1756–1763), the British defeated the French and pushed them off the continent, except for two small islands off the coast of Newfoundland. Britain acquired all French possessions, including Canada, in the **Treaty of Paris** (1763). The British presence in Canada forced many French to migrate south to Louisiana, forming the Cajun population that is still a strong presence there.

Dutch Colonization: New Netherland (New York)

New York was once known as New Netherland and was founded by **Henry Hudson**. In 1602 Hudson sailed for the Dutch East India Company in search of a northern passage to China. Hudson discovered Delaware Bay in 1609, and sailed up the Hudson River to Albany, where he made a friendly pact with the Iroquois. In 1614 the Dutch founded fur-trading posts on Manhattan Island and at Fort Orange. In 1626 **Governor Peter Minuit** purchased Manhattan from the Indians, and founded **New Amsterdam** as the capital of New Netherland. Although the Dutch were primarily interested in the fur trade, the Dutch West India Company made provisions for stockholders to obtain estates if they stocked them with at least 50 people. In 1664 the English led by James, Duke of York and later King James II, took New Netherland from the Dutch governor **Peter Stuyvesant** in a bloodless coup d'etat. The English changed the name of New Amsterdam to New York, and Fort Orange to Albany.

Settlement Colonies and English Colonization of the New World

Settlement colonies, such as the New England colonies, were based on farming for subsistence. Both plantation and settlement colonies resulted in significant conflicts with the Native American population, as both required large tracts of land to cultivate. The European colonists believed in the ownership of land, while the Native Americans believed land belonged to all in common. When the native populations refused to vacate land Europeans desired for cultivation, conflicts often erupted.

Roanoke

In 1584 **Sir Walter Raleigh** first discovered **Roanoke Island** off the outer banks of North Carolina, and in 1597 the first settlers arrived. The first English child born in the New World was Virginia Dare, the granddaughter of the colony's governor, John White. White left one month after their arrival, and did not return until 1590. By the time he returned, the colonists had disappeared, leaving behind only the word "Croatoan" inscribed on two trees. The fate of the lost colony of Roanoke is still a mystery today. The historian Karen Ordahl Kupperman has called Roanoke the "twice-lost colony," as not only were its original inhabitants lost, but also history has long emphasized the importance of Jamestown while failing to credit Roanoke's significance as the first English colony.

Jamestown, Virginia

Jamestown, the first successful English colony in the Americas, was founded by the Virginia Company, chartered by James I, the heir and successor of Elizabeth the Great of England. The Virginia Company was a joint stock company, in which stockholders hoped to make a profit from their investment. The London branch of the Virginia Company planted the first permanent colony in Virginia, which was named after Elizabeth, the Virgin Queen. On May 6, 1607, three ships landed on the Chesapeake Bay. They settled on the River James, as they thought it might provide a northwest passage to Asia. The colonists were not adept at farming, and so forged trading alliances with a confederation of 30 Algonquin tribes under **Powhatan** (Wahunsonacock).

Captain John Smith

Captain John Smith was the leader of the colonists and managed to keep them alive by forcing them to work. He was captured by Powhatan, and according to unsubstantiated legends, was freed through the intervention of Pocahontas. After Smith returned to England in 1609, the colonists endured a time of famine known as the "starving time," and disintegrated into anarchy. By 1610 there were only about 60 settlers left in the colony.

John Rolfe and Pocahontas

A turning point occurred in 1612 when **John Rolfe** took charge, married Powhatan's daughter Pocahontas, and began the cultivation of tobacco in Virginia. After Sir Francis Drake brought tobacco to England in 1586 from the

Caribbean Islands, tobacco had grown in popularity. After Virginia began to cultivate it and export it, the English smoked more tobacco per capita than any other European nation. The cultivation of tobacco is labor intensive, which eventually resulted in the need to import labor. In the seventeenth century, labor came in the form of indentured servants, whose price of passage was paid in return for a specified number of years of service. Although indentured servants had rights, two of five died from the difficult working conditions in the hot, moist climate of the Chesapeake. In the eighteenth century, the colonists would turn to slaves from Africa in order to meet their labor needs.

The cultivation of tobacco also had consequences for the colonists' relations with Native Americans. Tobacco depletes the soil, forcing planters to continually search for new lands. Three crops of tobacco can be grown before a field must lie fallow for several years. This need for new land brought about new conflicts with the Algonquin, who were no longer led by Powhatan but by his brother Opechancanough. In 1622 the Algonquin killed John Rolfe along with 350 colonists in an attempt to keep the colonists from further expansion. After this event, the English deliberately embarked on a policy of extermination, and in 1623 Captain William Tucker killed 200 Indians with poison-laced wine under the pretense of negotiating a treaty. In 1644 the Algonquins attacked again, but were firmly routed by the English. Thereafter, the English promoted a view of the Indians as savages whose destruction was warranted in order for civilization to advance.

Plymouth

Plymouth was founded by **Separatists** who had fled to Holland after having been persecuted under James I in England. While Puritans criticized the Church of England for various practices, Separatists did not believe in the validity of the Church and wished to separate from it. Although the Dutch were sympathetic to the Separatists, they had discriminated against them. In 1620 **William Bradford** secured a land patent from the Virginia Company, and 101 Separatists left Leyden aboard the *Mayflower* for the journey to the New World. Less than one-third of the passengers were among the "elect," or those believed to be predestined for salvation. After a stormy voyage, the Separatists arrived in Cape Cod and eventually settled at Plymouth. They signed the **Mayflower Compact** on November 21, 1620. Although revisionist historians now challenge the intended scope of the document, many traditional historians see the Mayflower Compact as the predecessor to the Constitution, as it established the ideal of consensual government.

The Pilgrims at Plymouth endured much hardship and famine, but were aided by **Wampanoag** Indians, especially Squanto, who taught the settlers to grow maize. In 1621, they produced a bountiful crop and celebrated with a feast now known as Thanksgiving. The colony was absorbed by the larger Puritan colony of Massachusetts Bay in 1691.

Pilgrims on Plymouth Rock

Massachusetts Bay

Puritans who, unlike the Separatists at Plymouth, hoped to reform the Church of England, founded **Massachusetts Bay**. They were known as non-separating Congregationalists. In 1629 Charles I granted the Massachusetts Bay Colony a charter for the area north of Plymouth. Their leader, **John Winthrop**, was a lawyer who wanted to establish a Christian utopia in the New World. In 1630 the Puritans left on the *Arbella* and six other ships. Winthrop delivered his famous speech "A Model of Christian Charity" during the voyage. Boston became the capital of the colony, and soon a Great Migration of some 80,000 more people followed. Only official churchmen could be stockholders, later known as freemen, in the Massachusetts Bay Company. The Massachusetts Bay Company eventually became the governing body of the colony, and status as a "visible saint" as indicated by membership in the Puritan church became the criteria for voting. The colony had a General Court, a representative body with two houses. Massachusetts Bay was intolerant of dissent, and banished **Roger Williams** and others whose views conflicted with those of the freemen. The tensions caused by rigid adherence to norms erupted in the Salem Witch Trials in 1692.

Puritans (and Dissenters) Found Other Colonies

Roger Williams founded **Providence** in 1636, after being banished from the Massachusetts Bay Colony for his advocacy of the separation of church and state. In 1640 the dissenters who had come to the area formed a confederation, and in 1643 received their first charter. **Rhode Island** was the smallest colony in America, and was also the first colony to legislate freedom of religion.

Other dissenters from Massachusetts Bay founded **Connecticut**, under the leadership of **Thomas Hooker**, but the "Fundamental Orders of Connecticut" allowed those who were not members of the Puritan church to vote. John Davenport and a group of Puritans founded New Haven on Long Island Sound in 1638 as a very rigid Puritan colony. It was absorbed into Connecticut in 1662. Dissenting Puritans from New Haven founded Newark in East Jersey.

Religious Freedom in the Colonies

While Massachusetts Bay was governed only according to Puritan beliefs, other colonies provided more religious freedoms. **Sir George Calvert**, **Lord Baltimore**, converted to Catholicism in 1625 and sought a charter to found **Maryland** as a refuge for Catholics. His son, Cecilius Calvert, founded Maryland in 1634 at a place known as St. Mary's on a stream of the Potomac. Maryland was the first **proprietary colony** granted to an individual as opposed to a joint stock company. Its primary crop was tobacco. Maryland's Toleration Act granted equality and freedom of religion to all Christians. While Maryland tolerated all Christians, the "Fundamental Constitutions of Carolina" of South Carolina was unique in the degree of religious toleration it granted to Jews and non-Christians.

Religious liberty was also an issue that led **William Penn** to found **Pennsylvania**, which was a proprietary colony founded by Quakers. The Quakers were almost in direct contrast to the Puritans, as they believed in individual inspiration or the "inner light." They rejected formal sacraments and ministries, called everyone by the familiar "thee" and "thou," refused to accept hierarchical authority, and were pacifists. Penn's Frame of Government was based on the idea of a Quaker state that supported freedom of individual conscience and there was no established church in Pennsylvania.

BRITISH COLONIAL RULE

British colonial rule in the Americas was based on the economic philosophy of **mercantilism**, a theory articulated in detail by the Scottish economist Adam Smith in his 1776 *Wealth of Nations*. According to mercantilism, colonies supply raw materials for the mother country. This philosophy led to the many of the taxes levied on the colonies and to other policies protested by the colonists.

The British colonists who went to the Americas, however, often went with very different assumptions. First, they went on the assumption of having full rights of a British subject. These rights included all the assumptions of the Glorious Revolution, which occurred in 1688. Many colonies had representative houses, such as the Virginia House of Burgesses, and in colonies such as Massachusetts Bay, an extraordinarily large percentage of the population was able to vote. For many years, the British had allowed the colonists to live virtually unaffected by taxation, and when taxation became an issue following the Seven Years' War, the American colonists demanded the right to participate in the decision-making process.

Debt from the Seven Years' War

The **Seven Years' War** (1756–1763) drastically affected England's financial situation. The British were in debt and needed to raise revenue. Moreover, the British now needed to defend new territories won in the war. The American colonies posed a special problem for the British, as the colonists represented one-quarter of the population of the empire, yet they paid only 1/100 of the cost to maintain the colonies. The American colonists only paid some 2,000 pounds a year in taxes, yet it cost 8,000 pounds a year to collect them. The perception that the colonists were not contributing to the cost of protecting them led the British to institute new policies.

The New Colonial Policy

In 1763, the crown enacted the **New Colonial Policy**, which was an attempt by the British to collect what was rightfully their due. Their first attempts to collect taxes were actually very mild. There was already a tax on molasses in 1733, for example, yet no one paid it, and the New Colonial Policy was in some ways only an attempt to actually collect taxes that had gone unpaid. In other ways, it attempted to bring the colonists up to what the British regarded as a reasonable level of taxation.

The Sugar Act (1764)

The New Colonial Policy resulted in the **Sugar Act**, which increased duties on imported sugar and other items such as textiles, coffee, wines, and indigo. It doubled the duties on foreign goods reshipped from England to the colonies and also forbade the import of foreign rum and French wines.

The Currency Act (1764)

In this same year, the British prohibited the colonists from issuing paper money in the **Currency Act**. Colonists feared the act would destabilize the colonial economy. James Otis responded to the new taxation with "The Rights of the British Colonists Asserted and Proved," in which he argued that governments should not take the property of citizens without their consent. He also advocated the natural law theory of government, although his version of natural law was God's law. Meanwhile, Boston merchants responded by boycotting British luxury goods.

The Stamp Act (1765)

The British were undisturbed by colonial protests and implemented the **Stamp Act** in 1765, the first direct tax on the colonists. The act levied a tax on newspapers, cards, legal documents, and other items, such as dice and playing cards, enraging colonists. Those who united against the tax were those most affected, such as lawyers, merchants, and landowners. While the Stamp Act would have essentially doubled the amount of taxes American colonists paid to 2 shillings a year, most British living at home paid 26 shillings a year. From the British point of view the tax was an entirely reasonable one to demand of a citizen of the British Empire.

In response to Otis's points and those of other colonists, the British asserted that colonists were "virtually" represented by the Parliament at home. The colonists, for their part, insisted that the interests of the Parliament and of the English at home were far different than those of the colonists in the Americas. This was true, especially from the point of view that most American colonists were landholders engaged in independent farming. There was no hereditary nobility in the colonies, either.

Virginia Resolutions

In May, **Patrick Henry** presented seven Virginia Resolutions to the **Virginia House of Burgesses**. The Virginia House of Burgesses was the first democratic assembly in the colonies, and Virginia was the most populous colony. Henry argued that only the House of Burgesses could legally tax Virginia residents.

The Stamp Act Congress (1765)

In October, representatives from nine colonies met in New York and drafted a petition to King George III, asserting that only the colonial legislatures could tax the colonists. On the date when the tax was implemented, November 1, 1765, people appeared in public wearing black armbands and carrying coffins down the street. Almost all daily business ground to a halt as colonists refused to use the stamps.

The debate over the Stamp Act continued to rage even in England, and a distinction arose between external taxation on colonial imports and internal taxation on products already in the colonies. During the debate Benjamin Franklin appeared before Parliament, and many thought he implied that external taxes were permissible while internal taxes could only be passed with the consent of those taxed.

In 1766, the British gave in and repealed the Stamp Act, but they also passed the **Declaratory Act**, which asserted their right to tax the colonists and their power to pass laws to govern them. Continued rebellions occurred over the **Quartering Act**, as British General Thomas Gage, commander of all English military forces in America, attempted to force the New York Assembly to house and supply his troops.

The Sons of Liberty

Rebellion increased and in July, the **Sons of Liberty** were formed. The Sons of Liberty was an underground organization opposed to the Stamp Act whose members used violence and intimidation against British stamp agents and against American colonial merchants who ordered British goods.

In 1767 England's continuing economic difficulties forced them to take a stronger stance towards the colonists, and the British appointed four admiralty courts to judge cases. This was the equivalent of martial law in the opinion of the colonists. In that same year, the **Townshend Revenue Acts** imposed a new series of taxes on the colonists. Imports such as paper, tea, glass, lead, and paint were now taxed.

Even moderates, such as John Dickinson, began to protest. Dickinson wrote *Letters from a Farmer in Pennsylvania, to the Inhabitants of the British Colonies*, rejecting the distinction between internal and external taxes and insisting that all taxes must be self-legislated. Similarly, the Virginia Resolves expressed opposition to taxation without representation.

The Boston Massacre (1770)

In 1770, as a mob was angrily harassing British soldiers in Boston, the soldiers fired on the crowd, killing three colonists. The **Boston Massacre** was a breaking point, after which the colonists could no longer see the British as friends or protectors, but as an armed enemy.

Repeal of the Townsend Duties

In 1770, the British repealed the Townsend Duties. American colonists had learned the power of collective action. The British had given up on taxation, but there was a general feeling that the colonists had been unreasonable. Perhaps they were, since they did not pay a comparable share of the taxes for their maintenance, yet they wanted the full protection and benefits of the British government.

Tea Act (1773)

The British passed the **Tea Act**, enforcing a tax on tea already in existence, but allowing the **British East India Company** to sell directly to colonial agents, thus creating a virtual monopoly on the tea trade and undercutting colonial merchants. The first tea ships affected by the act arrived on November 28, 1773.

Boston Tea Party

The Boston Tea Party occurred on December 16 when colonists disguised as Mohawk Indians dumped several tons of tea into the harbor rather than pay taxes.

Coercive Acts or Intolerable Acts (1774)

In 1774 the British shut down the port of Boston and forced Bostonians to reimburse the British East India Company for lost goods. The Bostonians were also forced to pay taxes on the tea. There were several other provisions of these acts, which represented an attempt by the British to gain further control over the colonies. In March 1775, Patrick Henry summed up the attitudes of many colonists when he said, "Give me liberty or give me death!" to the delegates of the Virginia House of Burgesses.

In April 1775, the first shots were fired in what would become known as the American War for Independence. In 1775 it was not yet clear, however, that all the colonists or even most of them wanted independence. In April the British General Gage attempted to suppress rebellion and marched with the intent of destroying the colonists' arms there. **Paul Revere** rode to Lexington to warn the colonists, and the first skirmish of the war occurred on the Lexington common. The first shot fired is known as the "shot heard around the world." The British killed eight colonists and wounded ten others, and then marched on to Concord, where the British again skirmished with a colonial militia.

In June 17, 1775, the first major battle between British and American troops occurred in Boston at Breed's Hill. The battle is known as the **Battle of Bunker Hill**.

The Olive Branch Petition

During the first year, colonists continued to hope the British would address their grievances. In July 1775 the **Continental Congress** drafted the Olive Branch Petition, which attempted to reconcile the colonists to the monarchy. It was addressed directly to King George III and asked for his help. The king refused to look at the petition and, instead, declared the colonists to be in a state of rebellion.

The Declaration on the Causes and Necessity of Taking Up Arms

By this time, **George Washington** had assumed command of the Continental Army, and the Congress drafted the Declaration on the Causes and Necessity of Taking Up Arms explaining their reasons for continuing to fight and "die as free men" rather than to live "as slaves." King George III then closed the colonies to trade.

The Declaration of Independence

Thomas Paine had first raised the issue of independence in his 1775 pamphlet *Common Sense,* but it was not until 1776 that independence was formally declared. The **Second Continental Congress**, representing the colonial governments, adopted the **Declaration of Independence** in July 1776. **Thomas Jefferson** drafted the document, but the declaration was influenced greatly by John Locke's *Two Treatises on Government.* The Declaration opened with a statement of principles and concluded with a list of the "injuries and usurpations" of the British monarch. Since many of the ideas articulated by Jefferson had, in fact, been the basis of the Glorious Revolution, the document presented a reasonable argument for independence. Jefferson had a flair for writing, and while Locke had said that the rights of life, liberty, and property were inalienable, Jefferson changed "property" to the "pursuit of happiness."

The war for independence had begun. The colonies, now states, had no central system of government, inadequate military forces, and no European ally. What they did have, however, was a common experience as colonials and a common determination to escape from the system of "tyranny" imposed on them by the British. As many as one-half of the colonists in the Americas remained loyal to Britain. Many of these loyalists, who were mostly wealthy landowners with moderate political beliefs, left during the Revolutionary War.

The first year of the war, from the spring of 1775 to summer 1776, saw inconclusive action as the British tried to figure out whether, indeed, they were engaged in warfare, or simply caught up in the irritating plots of a group of spoiled colonists. At first, the war was a struggle localized in and around the

Signing of the Declaration of Independence

city of Boston. Following the Declaration of Independence, the conflict spread. In the fall of 1776, the largest British fleet ever sent abroad arrived in New York harbor. On Christmas night, 1776, the Americans won their first victories at Trenton and then at Princeton, New Jersey.

The campaigns of 1777 brought mixed success to the British. Under such capable leaders as William and Richard Lord Howe and John Burgoyne, they devised a plan to divide the United States into two sections. This plan failed and the American victory at Saragota brought an end to their New York campaign.

Saratoga resulted in more than just a defeat for the British in New York; it convinced the French, and their new King Louis XVI, that the new American states might actually win the conflict, and in February 1778, the French government extended official recognition to the United States. A military alliance and military aid were forthcoming. The French were also driven by bitterness of their loss in the Seven Years' War.

The final phase of the war took place in the South. With the surrender of **Cornwallis at Yorktown**, the war for independence ended. The American Revolution, however, had just begun.

The Second Continental Congress

At the time independence was declared, and until the fighting had ended, the central "government" consisted only of the Second Continental Congress, a body of men charged originally with considering the redress of grievances submitted to the mother country in 1774. The Congress had no authority from the old colonies, or the new states, to conduct a war or to make laws.

The Articles of Confederation

In November 1777, the Continental Congress proposed the **Articles of Confederation**, which created a national system so weak that it barely had more power than the Congress itself. The conflict between those who wanted to emphasize the rights of the states as opposed to the rights of the whole (the **Federalists**) dominated American history until the Civil War. The thirteen states ratified the Articles of Confederation in 1781. They were in effect until 1789. Under the Articles of Confederation, the first "national" laws were passed, and these laws addressed the issue of lands west of the Appalachian Mountains.

The Constitution of 1789

Delegates to a constitutional convention met in 1789 to address the weaknesses of the Articles of Confederation. They expected to revise the Articles of Confederation, but instead created a radically new kind of government for the new nation based on the ideas of the French philosopher Montesquieu. Montesquieu had discussed the need for a strong central government comprised of branches empowered to check each other. **James Madison** proposed that the government's powers be divided among three branches, the **legislative**, **judicial**, and **executive**. The legislative branch was to be **bicameral**, following the model of the British Parliament. There were **checks and balances** established to prevent any one branch from controlling the government.

The Great Compromise, credited to Roger Sherman of Connecticut, resolved disputes between large and small states about representation by having representation in the lower house in proportion to population and equal for every state in the upper house. In 1791, the **Bill of Rights** was added to the Constitution guaranteeing individual rights. The Bill of Rights represents the first ten amendments to the constitution.

Review Questions

1. Which of the following is the most correct description of the American Revolution?

   (A) It was a radical revolution that departed from previous English ideals, such as were articulated in the Glorious Revolution.

   (B) It succeeded in creating a democracy immediately after the defeat of the British.

   (C) The colonists abolished slavery in many areas following the Revolution.

   (D) It was influenced by the Enlightenment, but this did not result in the end of slavery or an increase in women's rights.

2. Which of the following statements is NOT true of the New Colonial Policy?

   (A) The British expected colonists to pay more than it cost to maintain the colonies.

   (B) The colonists had not been paying taxes that already existed.

   (C) The need to defend new territories gained in the Seven Years' War had created a financial crisis in Britain.

   (D) The British believed the colonists were "virtually" represented.

3. Which colony was founded by a dissenter from the Massachusetts Bay Colony?

   (A) Pennsylvania

   (B) Connecticut

   (C) Maryland

   (D) Georgia

4. Sugar was primarily cultivated in

   (A) Georgia.

   (B) North Carolina.

   (C) the Caribbean plantation colonies.

   (D) Africa.

5. In the triangular trade, slaves were exchanged for molasses and rum in

   (A) Africa.

   (B) New England.

(C) the southern colonies.

(D) the West Indies.

6. Which is true of the French efforts to colonize North America?

    (A) They established large plantation colonies.

    (B) They established trading colonies.

    (C) They were interested in settling the New World.

    (D) They succeeded in maintaining a lasting colonial presence in the New World.

7. Which is the most correct statement about the colonial reaction to the issue of taxation?

    (A) The colonists generally accepted internal taxes on their goods.

    (B) The colonists generally accepted external taxation on their imports.

    (C) As protest evolved, colonists like James Otis rejected the distinction between external and internal taxation.

    (D) The colonists accepted their duty to pay taxes, but rejected the Stamp Act.

8. The repeal of the Stamp Act was immediately followed by

    (A) the Coercive Acts.

    (B) the Declaratory Act of 1766.

    (C) the Intolerable Acts.

    (D) the battles at Lexington and Concord.

9. When Thomas Paine published "Common Sense," most American colonists

    (A) were in favor of Independence.

    (B) rejected the authority of King George.

    (C) rejected the attempt to tax the colonists.

    (D) rejected the authority of the various assemblies, such as the Viginia House of Burgesses, to protest taxation.

10. Which is the most correct statement about the French involvement in the American Revolution?

    (A) They provided direct support only after it became clear that the colonists might achieve success following the Battle of Saratoga.

(B) They provided direct support only after it became clear that the colonists might achieve success following the Battle of Yorktown.

(C) They were motivated by a desire for revenge against the British for the losses inflicted during the Seven Years' War.

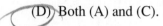 (D) Both (A) and (C).

Answers

1. (D)	4. (C)	7. (C)	10. (D)
2. (A)	5. (D)	8. (C)	
3. (B)	6. (B)	9. (C)	

Chapter 24

THE FRENCH REVOLUTION

KEY TERMS

Revolt Noblesse
Third Estate
Estates General
Tennis Court Oath
National Assembly
Declaration of the Rights of Man
Civil Constitution of the Clergy
Active and passive citizens
Girondists
Jacobins
sans-culottes
Declaration of Pillnitz
The Reign of Terror

The Emergency Republic
Thermidorian Reaction
Napoleon
The Consulate
Second and Third Coalitions
The Berlin Decrees and the
    Confederation of the Rhine
Waterloo
Holy Alliance
Congress of Vienna
The Quadruple Alliance and
    the Concert of Europe

THE REVOLT NOBLESSE

Discontent with the absolutist government created by Louis XIV boiled over in the eighteenth century. The financial crisis following the Seven Years' War (1757–1763) contributed to the rise of revolutionary sentiment. Fully half of the royal budget went towards interest payments on the royal debt, and although the nobility had great wealth, they found numerous ways to escape the payment of mandated taxes. Louis's ministers Turgot and Necker both attempted to stabilize French finances, but to no avail. When the government attempted to reform the tax system so that the nobility paid the taxes they were intended to pay, the Parlement of Paris resisted and revolted, followed by other Parlements throughout France. The Parlements then demanded that the Estates General be summoned, something that had not been done since 1614. This initial stage of the revolution is known as the **Revolt Noblesse**, or the Revolt of the Parlements.

Summoning of the Estates General

Although there was great hope among the masses surrounding the first meeting of the Estates General in 1789, that hope was quickly dashed. The Estates General voted by body, that is, one vote per estate. The three estates were the clergy, the nobility, and the commoners. The first two could and did always outvote the Third Estate, which represented the majority of the French population. The famous pamphlet by the Abbe Sieyes, "What is the Third Estate?" pointed out the folly of this process, when he argued that the answer to the title question was, "everything." The Third Estate performed most of the work in France and paid most of the taxes, and, therefore, was entitled to more rights. When the Estates met for the first time after the Revolt Noblesse, the first two estates marched in by body sitting in their traditional locations and dressed in their finery. The Third Estate soon realized that nothing would change for them through this process.

The National Assembly

On June 1, 1789, the Third Estate left the assembly and then invited the clergy and the nobles to join them. By June 17, they had declared themselves the **National Assembly**. On June 20, they took the famous **Tennis Court Oath**, promising not to disband until the Assembly had created a new constitution. The majority of the clergy and a large number of nobles joined with them.

The French Revolution is considered the first movement in which the masses participated. The role of the people became intense about the time the National Assembly began its work. In 1788, there was a Great Famine, leading to bread riots in 1789. The royal family had little or no understanding of the needs of the masses. Although **Marie Antoinette**, the German queen of

Louis XVI, never made the infamous remark, "Let them eat cake," the remark symbolized the distance between the royal family, who led a life of great pomp at Versailles, and the masses, who led lives of misery. While Marie Antoinette frolicked in a country village constructed on the grounds of Versailles for her amusement, the masses did not even have bread to eat. Rarely had royals been so distant from those they governed.

The Storming of the Bastille

The bread riots alarmed the monarchy, and it already had many troops in Paris due to the revolutionary activities of the Third Estate. The masses became further agitated when Louis dismissed his minister, Necker, whom the people saw as their champion against the aristocracy. This volatile situation erupted on July 14, 1789, and culminated in the storming of the **Bastille**, a fortress prison where the monarchy traditionally kept dissenters. The rioters killed troops and released seven prisoners and formed a new municipal government, **the commune**. In response, the government created a militia in Paris, which became the National Guard. Its emblem was a cockade made up of the two colors of the city of Paris, blue and red. Louis XVI gave command of the Guard to General Lafayette, despite his involvement in the American Revolution, of which the monarchy had disapproved.

The Great Fear

The situation became progressively more volatile as the Great Fear swept through France in 1789. Fear of an aristocratic conspiracy to overthrow the Third Estate in the National Assembly, desperate needs in time of famine, and long-standing anger over feudal dues brought about violent protest against ancient manorial privileges. Peasants still paid fees for the use of village mills and other privileges known as banalities. They paid rent for land.

Abolition of Feudal Obligations

On the night of August 4, 1789, while the nobility was absent, the National Assembly abolished feudal society in France. The assembly outlawed banalities, tithes to the Church, and mandated that jobs be made open to all. Peasants, however, still had to buy their land to legally own it, which for most of them amounted to the same thing as the old rent payments.

The Declaration of the Rights of Man

On August 27, 1789, the Assembly issued the **Declaration of the Rights of Man**, by which everyone in France was considered born free and equal in rights, especially those of life, liberty, property, security, and of resistance to oppression. Although the document contained many lofty sentiments, including freedom of the press, the delegates' use of the word "man" clearly left "women" out of the equation. Mary Wollstonecraft would later write a rebuttal of the assumptions that women were not equal to men in her "Vindication of the Rights of Women." The ideals of the Declaration of the Rights of Man and Citizen, however, later led to a wave of abolitionism throughout Europe.

The Civil Constitution of the Clergy

In July 1790 the Assembly passed the **Civil Constitution of the Clergy**, whereby they secularized the French Catholic Church. They confiscated church lands, especially those owned by monasteries, and dissolved the monasteries. The Assembly used these lands as the basis for selling bonds called assignats. The clergy was now to be paid a salary by the state and elected by the appropriate parishes. Such clergy would feel no real allegiance to the Roman pope, but rather would be loyal to the new Republic. The Assembly forced the clergy to take an oath to uphold the Civil Constitution. The Roman Catholic pope repudiated the Civil Constitution in 1791, but it reflected centuries of seething resentment toward the Church.

Active and Passive Citizens

The term of the National Assembly expired in September 1791, and their achievement was a new constitution. The constitution distinguished between **active and passive citizens**, on the basis of the amount of taxes paid. Active citizens could fully participate in the government, while passive citizens were more limited. Only males were considered citizens. Passive citizens had to have had French parents or to have been born in France. In order to become active citizens, one had to take a civic oath, be 25 years of age, and pay a tax equivalent to three days' wages. The revolutionary leader **Jean Paul Marat**, one of the most radical revolutionaries who advocated universal male suffrage, was horrified by this distinction and cried out in a famous pamphlet, "The Worst Has Happened."

The Legislative Assembly

After the National Assembly was dissolved, the **Legislative Assembly** took its place. Girondists, Feuillants, and Jacobins dominated the Assembly. The **Girondists** were primarily deputies of the department of the Gironde, and supported the idea of a foreign war in the belief that war would unite France and help to spread the revolution to other countries. They were also interested in a constitutional government. The **Feuillants** were a group that supported a constitutional monarchy, but since they opposed a foreign war, many associated them with the royalist factions. The **Jacobins** opposed all counter-revolution, but wished to limit the power of the king and to institute a republic.

The Storming of Versailles

Meanwhile, the Revolution was beginning to fragment as the revolutionaries disagreed, and European monarchs began mustering forces to oppose them. Peasant revolts had erupted all over Europe in response to the French revolutionary motto of "liberty, equality, and fraternity." European monarchs rightly believed that the Revolution threatened their own monarchies, and this was further confirmed when an angry Parisian crowd stormed Versailles on October 5, 1789, and brought the king and queen, whom they mockingly called "the baker and the baker's wife," to the Tuileries Palace in Paris.

Portrait of King Louis XVI

Louis XVI and the Flight to Varennes

Louis XVI's wife, Marie, was the sister of the Holy Roman Emperor. Louis believed they could expect help from the Emperor, as well as other monarchs, and so attempted to leave France. Revolutionaries got wind of his desperate flight on June 20 and 21, 1791, and halted him at Varennes. The king and queen were escorted back in humiliation and Louis was eventually forced to accept the new constitution.

Declaration of War Against Austria in 1792

As the Revolution gained in momentum, the Feuillants fell. In August 1791, the Holy Roman Emperor and King of Prussia met at Pillnitz, and issued an ultimatum to the French in the **Declaration of Pillnitz**. That ultimatum demanded the protection of Louis XVI on the threat of war. The Girondists hoped that the declaration would be interpreted as a declaration of war and on April 20, 1792, the second revolution began when the Legislative Assembly declared war on Austria.

In addition to Marie Antoinette's brother, the Holy Roman Emperor, among the foreign leaders that now aligned themselves against France were the King of Sweden, the Russian Tsarina Catherine the Great, the King of Prussia, and even Alexander Hamilton of the United States.

The National Convention and the September Massacres

The war went very unfavorably, and the masses began to turn against the king and queen as they feared a royal conspiracy. In August, they stormed the Tuileries, where the king had been kept since his flight, and imprisoned him. The rebels set up an insurrectionary commune that replaced the legally elected one of the early revolution. They rejected the constitution of the National Assembly, and demanded new elections by universal manhood suffrage for a National Convention, whose task would be to draw up a new constitution. There were mass arrests of royalists and in September, a wave of massacres in which approximately 2,000 prisoners died.

The *sans-culottes*

Radical revolutionaries dominated the National Convention, especially members of the *sans-culottes*, or "those without fancy breeches." Although often portrayed as frenzied commoners, the *sans-culottes* were lawyers, clerks, tradesmen, and the working people of France. Among their leaders were the most radical revolutionaries, such as Georges Jacques Danton, Jean Paul Marat, and Camille Desmoulins.

Abolition of the Monarchy

The convention met for the first time on September 21, 1792, and immediately abolished the monarchy. It proclaimed Year One of the French Republic. Not only were the years to be dated from this event, but also new names were to be used for the months and weeks were to have ten days. The convention then accused the king of treason and on January 21, 1793, executed Citizen Capet, as Louis was then known. Mass citizen uprisings in areas of strong support for the royalist cause occurred in the Vendée. The opposition of foreign monarchs became more intense and civil strife in France increased.

The Convention created a democratic constitution that was approved by 1.8 million voters in a plebiscite, but it was never implemented.

THE REIGN OF TERROR

From 1792–1795, the **Emergency Republic** ruled France, dominated by the **Committee of Public Safety**, created in April 1793. The committee was essentially a dictatorship, whose tasks were to manage the war abroad and the growing chaos at home. Wages and prices were frozen, and the French ordered the use of the worthless assignats as money. The most important leaders were **Georges Danton** and **Maximillian Robespierre**, who vigorously argued in defense of any measures to ensure the survival of the "Republic of Virtue." Robespierre instituted a **Reign of Terror** starting in 1793. Robespierre supported such lofty ideas as universal suffrage, but the society he created was anything but utopian. He turned against any and all whom he believed did not support the revolution and who might see its reforms turned back. The Girondists, for example, were now enemies of the spread of the revolution. In 1793 **Charlotte Corday**, whose brother had been denounced and condemned by the Committee of Public Safety, assassinated Marat while he was soaking in his bathtub. Robespierre condemned many of his own friends, such as Danton, to the guillotine.

Fall of Robespierre

By July 27, 1794, however, many feared that Robespierre would turn against them, and they shouted him down in the assembly. Robespierre fell victim to his own extremities and was executed on July 28, known as the ninth of Thermidor in the revolutionary calendar.

Thermidorian Reaction

The conservative reaction that followed is known as the **Thermidorian Reaction**. A new constitution created a **directory** and a two-chamber legislature. There were five directors, but unfortunately, they and their colleagues were corrupt.

Napoleon

Many feared the return of the royalists, but at the same time, many royalists were able to reassert their ideas. The Abbé Sieyès, once a leader of the Third Estate, now called for direction from above and supported the efforts of a French war hero, **Napoleon Bonaparte**, to restore order. Napoleon had recently crushed the Austrian armies and the First Coalition (Spain, Holland, Austria, Prussia, England, and Sardinia). The Treaty of Campo Formio in October 1797 ended the first phase of the Napoleonic wars.

Napoleon Bonaparte

The Battle of the Nile

The Directors feared Bonaparte, and so in May 1798, they sent him out of France to capture Egypt. The possibility of his success greatly worried the British, for if the French dominated the Middle East, they would control the land route to India. In August 1798 at the **Battle of the Nile** (or Aboukir Bay), Lord Nelson wiped out the French fleet while it was anchored in shallow water, leaving 38,000 French soldiers stranded.

The Second Coalition

Now a **Second Coalition** formed against the French to take advantage of their defeat on the Nile. From 1799–1801 the Second Coalition, made up of Turkey, England, Austria, and Russia, fought France. In 1799, Austria drove the

French back across the Rhine, a Russo-Austrian army defeated the French and drove them out of Italy, and Britain pushed the French out of Holland. A three-pronged attack was planned on France by Britain, Austria, and Russia.

The Consulate

Meanwhile, Napoleon returned to France and on the nineteenth of Brumaire, or November 10, 1799, Napoleon established the **consulate** and named himself as first consul. In 1801, Napoleon shocked many revolutionaries by making peace with the Roman Catholic pope. He argued that since Roman Catholicism was the religion of people, peace was good, but at the same time, he kept all the Church lands previously confiscated. Napoleon continued to insist that the clergy swear an oath of loyalty to the state, and submitted a new constitution to the public for ratification according to universal male suffrage.

The Napoleonic Code

He also instituted the **Napoleonic Code**, which tended to favor employers over their employees, and males over females within the family. Prior to the code, France did not have a single set of laws. The code was also the first code established in a country where there was a civil law system, and it followed Roman law in dividing civil law into personal status, property, and acquisition of property.

Napoleon becomes Emperor in 1804

In 1802, Napoleon made peace with Britain, thus ending the threat of the Second Coalition. Napoleon alienated many of his supporters, however, in 1804 when he declared himself emperor. The ceremony occurred in the Cathedral of Notre Dame, and at the point when the pope had blessed the regalia, Napoleon took the crown and placed it on himself.

The Third Coalition

The **Third Coalition** of Britain, Russia, and Austria formed against France, and on October 21, 1805, **Admiral Horatio Nelson** defeated the French at the **Battle of Trafalgar**. The British now had control of the sea. On land, the story was different. Napoleon occupied Vienna and in December 1805, he defeated Austria and Russia at Austerlitz. Austria retreated from Italy, leaving Napoleon in control of everything north of Italy. Napoleon proclaimed himself the king of Italy and annexed Genoa. Napoleon appointed his relatives in control of his new territories. In 1808 Napoleon made his brother Joseph the king of Spain after obtaining the abdication of Charles IV and his son Ferdinand VII.

Napoleon also defeated the Prussians at Jena in 1806. As a result of the Treaty of Tilsit in 1807, Prussia lost half its territory, and Russia recognized the French gains and eventually lent support to Napoleon in his defeat of the Swedes.

The Berlin Decrees and the Confederation of the Rhine

Europe was now virtually unrecognizable from the prerevolutionary period. The Holy Roman Empire was essentially dissolved in 1806, and Napoleon now controlled most of the West German princes through the Confederation of the Rhine. Napoleon made kings of the Electors of Bavaria, Württemberg, and Saxony; created the kingdoms of Holland and Westphalia; and made his brothers Louis and Jérôme Bonaparte their kings. In 1806, the Berlin decrees forbade his allies to import British goods. Napoleon instituted the Continental System and imposed his codes all over Europe.

Napoleon Marries Marie Louise

The Austria Hapsburgs were so weakened by this time that the Holy Roman Emperor was now calling himself the "emperor of Austria." In 1810, after Napoleon had his marriage to Josephine annulled, he married Marie Louise, the daughter of the Austrian emperor Francis I, formerly the Holy Roman Emperor Francis II. Together they had a son, the "king of Rome," later known as the Duke of Reichstadt or Napoleon II.

Revolts

Many Europeans as well as Napoleon's allies were beginning to revolt from his heavy-handed policies. The Continental System ruined the economies of many of Napoleon's allies. There were revolts in Spain, and in 1810 Russia withdrew from the Continental System.

Napoleon Invades Russia in 1812

In 1812 Napoleon collected the largest army ever seen and invaded Russia. The Russians tried to slow them by following a scorched earth policy, but both sides lost huge numbers of casualties at the Battle of Borodino on September 7. The French lost 30,000 men and the Russians twice as many. Napoleon reached Moscow on September 14, only to find that the Russians had burned the city. The French army now was caught in the Russian winter and began a disastrous retreat on October 19, 1812. Those who did not die of exposure died of sheer hunger. Napoleon left with 600,000 men and returned with only 100,000.

Capture of Paris in 1814

Nevertheless, upon his return to France, Napoleon was once again planning war. Many former allies now turned against him. Prussia allied with Russia in 1813, soon followed by Britain and Sweden, and finally, by Austria. At the **Battle of the Nations** at Leipzig in October 1813, they defeated Napoleon. The allies now offered peace if Napoleon would stay within French borders, but he refused, and the allies then took Paris on March 31, 1814.

Napoleon Abdicates and then Returns for the 100 Days

Napoleon abdicated in 1814 and went into exile on the island of **Elba**. The Bourbon monarchy was restored, and **King Louis XVIII** took power. While the allies debated the future of Europe at the **Congress of Vienna** (1814–1815), Napoleon made a return, landing at Cannes on March 1, 1815. Many French were still suspicious of the Bourbons and remained loyal to their former emperor. Napoleon entered Paris on March 20, 1815, and for 100 days ruled again.

Defeat of Napoleon at Waterloo

The Continental Congress declared Napoleon an outlaw and sent the **Duke of Wellington** to defeat him. At **Waterloo**, in what is now Belgium, on June 18, 1815, Napoleon was finally defeated. Napoleon abdicated and was sent into exile on the remote and tiny island of **Saint Helena** in the Atlantic off the coast of Africa, where he died of stomach cancer in 1821. In 1840, Louis Philippe ordered the return of Napoleon's remains, and they remain enshrined today in the Invalides in Paris.

German Nationalism

Napoleon's return made the attitudes of the allies toward France more harsh and spurred on an intensely conservative reaction. Napoleon's attempt to dominate the German principalities spurred on a wave of German nationalism. Later figures, such as Herder, would write about the Volksgeist, or special spirit, of the German people. Napoleon succeeded in inspiring a wave of nationalistic sympathies that would culminate in the unification of Germany and Italy in the nineteenth century.

The Congress of Vienna

The **Congress of Vienna** created a balance of power in Europe that would dominate Europe for the next century. The allies agreed that no single nation should dominate Europe, and that the Bourbon monarchy should be restored to prevent France from becoming a threat again. The Congress erected a series of powerful border states to contain French expansion, such as the Netherlands and Prussia, but they failed to revive the once mighty Holy Roman Empire, leaving in its place the German Confederation.

The Holy Alliance

The Holy Alliance of Russia, Austria, and Prussia was founded to uphold the Congress and to preserve Christian ideals.

The Quadruple Alliance and the Concert of Europe

The **Quadruple Alliance** of Great Britain, Austria, Prussia, and Russia, which had successfully defeated Napoleon, later evolved into the **Concert of Europe** and included France, making a Quintuple Alliance, in 1818. The Concert of Europe was founded in order to preserve peace through diplomacy. In the wake of Napoleon's attempt to conquer Europe, peace and the balance of power were desired at all costs. The Ottoman rulers, as Muslims, were left out of both alliances, one of the weakest decisions of the aftermath of Napoleon.

Review Questions

1. Which of the following statements accurately depicts the developments of the French Revolution prior to September 1792?

   (A) The National Assembly created a basic declaration of liberties and a new constitution to establish a limited monarchy.

   (B) Louis XVI supported the National assembly.

   (C) Warfare broke out between France and Austria, which was endeavoring to restore the French monarchy.

   (D) Both (A) and (C).

2. The French Reign of Terror

   (A) was an effort to eliminate all domestic threats to the authority of the Committee of Public Safety.

   (B) permitted some cities to continue to protest without interference.

   (C) resulted in the execution of Robespierre, which led to the Thermidorian reaction.

   (D) Both (A) and (C).

3. Which of the following was an achievement of Napoleon?

   (A) He continued to suppress the Catholic Church in France.

   (B) He codified the laws of France in his famous Civil Code.

   (C) He created a powerful, centralized bureaucracy in France.

   (D) Both (B) and (C).

4. Napoleon intended to use his Continental System to

   (A) create a European trade community.

   (B) diminish British power by depriving it of wealth from European trade.

   (C) force the Russians to ally with Britain.

   (D) Both (A) and (B).

5. Napoleon was ultimately defeated because of

   (A) the triumph of the Continental System.

   (B) Britain's ability to sustain its power and ultimately defeat him.

(C) nationalism's growing strength throughout Europe.

(D) Both (B) and (C).

6. The First, Second and Third Estates represented which groups of society, respectively?

(A) Clergy; peasantry, middle class and artisans; nobility

(B) Nobility; peasantry, middle class, and artisans; clergy

(C) Clergy; nobility; peasantry, middle class, and artisans

(D) Peasantry, middle class, and artisans; clergy; nobility

7. The Civil Constitution of the Clergy (1790)

(A) destroyed the Catholic Church's financial independence and made it a state agency.

(B) extended all civil rights enjoyed by laymen to the Catholic clergy.

(C) reaffirmed the administrative and financial independence of the Catholic Church.

(D) reserved a percentage of state jobs for Catholic clergy.

8. The National Assembly accomplished all of the following EXCEPT

(A) the abolition of the feudal system.

(B) the complete equalization of society.

(C) the abolition of the church as a religious and political power.

(D) the abolition of all titles.

9. The Constitution developed by the National Assembly

(A) fully implemented the revolutionary demand for liberty, equality, and fraternity.

(B) applied to women as well as to men.

(C) kept the Roman Catholic Church as a privileged institution.

(D) distinguished between active and passive citizens.

10. Which of the following statements most correctly describes interpretations of the French Revolution?

(A) All historians agree that it originated out of a class conflict, and that Marxist analyses are adequate.

(B) Some historians point out that the leaders of the Revolution had much in common with the aristocracy, casting doubt on the Marxist interpretation of the Revolution.

(C) Historians agree that the events of the French Revolution was a unified series of events with a common goal.

(D) Historians agree that the Reign of Terror was an aberration of the French Revolution.

Answers

1. (D)	4. (B)	7. (A)	10. (B)
2. (D)	5. (D)	8. (B)	
3. (D)	6. (C)	9. (D)	

Chapter 25

THE AMERICAN AND FRENCH REVOLUTIONS SPARK OTHER MOVEMENTS FOR INDEPENDENCE

KEY TERMS

Hispaniola
Saint-Domingue
gens de Couleur
Boukman
Maroons
Francois Dominique Toussaint
  "Louverture"
Haiti
Creole
Miguel de Hidalgo
Augustin de Iturbide
Benito Juarez
La Reforma
Emiliano Zapata

Francisco Villa (Pancho Villa)
terra y libertad
Mexican Constitution of 1917
Gran Columbia
Simón Bolivar
Emperor Pedro I
caudillo
Juan Manuel de Rosas
Coffee
Panama Canal
Theodore Roosevelt
Argentina
Porfirio Diaz

THE HAITIAN REVOLUTION

On the island of **Hispaniola** in the Caribbean, the ideas of the French and American revolutions did not fall on deaf ears. There were both French and Spanish colonies on the island, and the French colony of Saint-Domingue was one of the most productive colonies of all European colonies in the Caribbean. During the American Revolution, French support had meant that many *gens de couleur*, or free people of color, had been sent to aid the American colonists. The white colonists in Saint-Domingue took advantage of the opportunity created by the French Revolution to establish their own government, but had not conceded rights to the *gens de couleur* nor to any of the large slave population.

In 1791 Boukman, a Voudoo priest, led a slave revolt that ignited the struggle into a full-scale civil war. Many former or escaped slaves, known as maroons, joined in the revolt. Boukman died, but his revolt did not. **Francois Dominique Toussaint** now rose to lead the slave revolt, calling himself "Louverture," meaning "the opening." By 1797 he controlled most of the island, and by 1801 he had created a constitution that granted equality and citizenship to all residents of the colony. Although Toussaint did not declare independence from France, in 1803 his successors did. On January 1, 1804, the new nation of **Haiti** became the second independent republic in the Western Hemisphere. As for Toussaint, invading French forces took him in 1802, and he died in a French jail in 1803. Nevertheless, his name is synonymous with slave revolts, and with the fight for human rights among repressed peoples everywhere.

Latin America

A struggle for independence in Latin American countries also followed in the wake of the French Revolution. When Napoleon invaded Spain and Portugal in 1807, he weakened their power and inspired revolution in their colonies. Revolutionary activity would not succeed, however, in changing the face of Latin America until after World War II. The revolutions of the early nineteenth century succeeded in strengthening the white, Creole elite, as well as their European traditions of Roman Catholicism and slavery.

Mexico

In Mexico, **Miguel de Hidalgo** led a rebellion against the Spanish. The white inhabitants of European ancestry there were called Creoles, and they executed Hidalgo. Later, a Creole general, **Augustin de Iturbide**, conquered the capital and named himself emperor. Although he declared Mexico's independence, other Creoles deposed him later and declared a republic. Shortly thereafter, the southern regions of the Spanish empire in Mexico declared independence and formed the Central American Federation. In 1838, the Federation split into Guatemala, El Salvador, Honduras, Nicaragua, and Costa Rica.

Benito Juárez attempted to curtail the influence of the Church and of the military. In the Constitution of 1857, Juárez limited the privileges of priests and other elite members of society. Church properties were confiscated, and Mexicans received such civil liberties as freedom of speech and universal manhood suffrage. Juárez was a native Mexican and not a Creole, and he intended his La Reforma to benefit the native peoples. Not surprisingly, Creoles bought much of the confiscated Church lands.

Zapata and Villa

Over 95 percent of Mexican peasants remained landless until the **Mexican Revolution** of 1911–1920. **Emiliano Zapata** and **Francisco Villa (Pancho Villa)** fought for *terra y libertad* or "land and liberty." U.S. support of the Mexican government led Villa to attack U.S. citizens. Zapata seized land and redistributed it to peasants. The **Mexican Constitution of 1917** allowed for land redistribution and restrictions on foreign ownership of Mexican land and resources. Other provisions mandated minimum wage levels, limits on hours that could be worked, and a state system of education. Zapata and Villa continued their fight, however, and were both assassinated.

Gran Colombia

In South America, the Creole **Simón Bolivar** worked to create an independent and unified Latin America. Venezuela, Colombia, and Ecuador formed a republic called **Gran Colombia**. By 1830, however, differences between these three had broken Gran Colombia apart.

Brazil

Meanwhile, Napoleon's invasion of Portugal in 1807 had driven the royal family into exile in Rio de Janiero. During the time King Dom João VI lived in Brazil, Brazil became the center of royal power. Although the king returned to Portugal in 1821 following the defeat of Napoleon, his son Pedro stayed behind as regent. Revolution erupted only one year later. Pedro disobeyed his father's command to return home and eventually revolutionaries established him as **Emperor Pedro I**. Of the Latin American countries Brazil alone remained under the control of a monarchy.

Argentina

Creole leaders continued to abuse native populations, however, in places such as Argentina, where the **caudillo** (regional military leader) **Juan Manuel** de Rosas (1835–1852) put down rebellions through brutal means. Rosas ruled as a despot, but did succeed in establishing a centralized government.

ECONOMY AND TRADE

In the years following the independence of the Latin American countries, their economies stagnated. Britain quickly stepped into the vacuum left when the Latin American countries gained their independence from Spain and Portugal. Britain became the dominant economic power through the sale of manufactured goods to the Latin Americans, especially in Brazil. Latin American countries grew more and more dependent on foreign imports until around 1850 when their economies revived, due to increased demand from Europeans for goods such as coffee from Brazil. From 1880–1920 especially, the economy grew as the Industrial Revolution in Europe and the United States resulted in demand for more and more raw materials.

The economic growth of Latin America, combined with a United States victory in the **Spanish American War** leading to an American presence in Cuba and Puerto Rico, eventually resulted in U.S. interest in the area. **President Theodore Roosevelt** backed a revolt in Panama and then negotiated a treaty granting rights to the **Panama Canal**, which opened in 1908.

The economic vitality in Latin America after 1850 had negative consequences for the poor. In Brazil, for example, great landowners increased their holdings to meet the demands for increased exports, dispossessing poor farmers from lands.

Migration

Immigrants from Portugal and also from Italy came in great numbers to Brazil. These new workers gradually eliminated the need for slavery, and it was eventually abolished in 1888. When slavery was abolished, the link between the monarchy in Brazil and the planter aristocracy was broken, and the monarchy was deposed in 1889.

Argentina also had an influx of labor as industrialization created the means for them to export greater quantities of beef, for example. Tensions between workers and their employers resulted in a series of strikes and eventually led the government to clamp down. Immigrant workers brought many aspects of European culture to Argentina.

Mexico also industrialized during this period, primarily as a result of the policies of **Porfirio Diaz**, who was elected president in 1876. Diaz encouraged foreign investment, which helped to build railroads and other transportation systems. The workforce in Mexico was primarily made up of native Mexicans, whose repression erupted in a bitter series of strikes. Diaz maintained control until the tensions resulted in the Mexican Revolution and toppled his regime.

Review Questions

1. Which of the following is not a correct description of the changes in Latin America in the nineteenth century?

    (A) Britain became the dominant economic power in Latin America through sale of its manufactured goods.

    (B) The economy increased as a result of the demand for raw materials by Europeans following the Industrial Revolution.

    (C) The demand for more Latin American exports such as coffee benefited the poor.

    (D) More women entered the workforce.

2. Which is the most correct statement about immigration to Latin America following the Industrial Revolution in Europe?

    (A) Renewed demand for exports brought new jobs for the poor in Argentina.

    (B) Renewed demand for exports brought a wave of immigrants from Europe, transforming Latin American culture.

    (C) Renewed demand for exports broke up large landed estates in Argentina.

    (D) Renewed demand for exports and a revitalized economy eventually increased demand for slaves in Brazil.

3. What was the role of Creoles in Latin America in the nineteenth century?

    (A) They were a minority who lost power in the early part of the century.

    (B) They gave native populations many civil rights.

    (C) They supported continuing control by old European regimes.

    (D) They maintained their power base in countries such as Argentina and in Mexico maintained control of large landed estates.

4. Which figure(s) attempted to implement reforms to benefit the native peoples?

    (A) Benito Juárez

    (B) Juan Manuel de Rosas

    (C) Emiliano Zapata

    (D) Both (A) and (C).

5. Whose leadership inspired the formation of Gran Colombia?

    (A) Hidalgo

    (B) Zapata

(C) Rosas

(D) Bolivar

6. Which leader attempted distributing Church property to the poor and establishing basic human rights in Mexico?

(A) Hidalgo

(B) Rosas

(C) Juárez

(D) Bolivar

Answers

1. (C)	3. (D)	5. (D)
2. (B)	4. (A)	6. (C)

UNIT VI

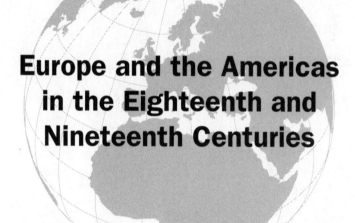

**Europe and the Americas
in the Eighteenth and
Nineteenth Centuries**

Chapter 26

THE INDUSTRIAL REVOLUTIONS OF THE EIGHTEENTH AND NINETEENTH CENTURIES

KEY TERMS

Spinning jenny
Fly shuttle
Richard Arkwright
Steam engine
Cotton gin
Dual Revolution
Liberalism
Nationalism

Socialism
Romanticism
Revolutions of 1848
Garibaldi
Mazzini
Schleswig and Holstein
Second Industrial Revolution

FIRST INDUSTRIAL REVOLUTION

Conditions in Britain

The **Industrial Revolution** began in the late eighteenth century in Britain. There were reasons why this revolution occurred in Britain: It had good natural resources, such as a good water supply for mills and steam power, waterways for transportation of goods, and a budding colonial empire with which to trade these goods. The geographic location of Britain, for the most part, protected them from invasion, so they enjoyed peace and liberty in this era. The Glorious Revolution, engineered by the Puritan landed gentry, created freedom from the constraints of an absolute monarchy and encouraged development of capitalistic enterprises.

Changes in Population and Agriculture

During the eighteenth century, the population of Europe grew dramatically. In 1700, the population of Europe was around 120 million; by 1800, it was 200 million. By 1850, the population had reached 266 million. The population explosion created a ready supply of labor for the Industrial Revolution. A contributing factor to the population growth was increased immunity to the plague and other diseases that had cycled throughout Europe since the Middle Ages. Further, crops from the Americas, such as the potato and maize, combined with new agricultural techniques increased the food supply. Continuous rotation of crops replaced the open-field system that had dominated European agriculture since the Middle Ages. With the open-field system, some fields were allowed to lie fallow while others were cultivated and there was land reserved for common use. Under the new system, common rights were lost as wealthy landowners enclosed common fields and a variety of crops were then cultivated on a continuous basis. **Enclosure** was already under way in England before the eighteenth century, but the enforcement of **enclosure laws** by Parliament in the last half of the eighteenth century consolidated the gains the landowning classes made during the Glorious Revolution. The enclosure movement displaced many peasants from the countryside, and they flocked to the developing cities providing a good, cheap supply of labor.

Wars of the Eighteenth Century and the Origins of the Industrial Revolution

England was the dominant power in maritime trade in the eighteenth century. After a series of wars with the Dutch, Great Britain went on to win a series of victories against the French in the War of the Spanish Succession and the Seven Years' War. The success of Britain in these wars helped to create a vast network for trade. Britain's colonies provided yet another outlet for trade. The stage was thus set for the Industrial Revolution.

The Textile Industry

The Revolution began in the area of **textile manufacturing**, Britain's chief industry. They were always in search of cheaper and newer ways to make cotton. In 1733, John Kay invented the **fly shuttle**, a machine that was able to weave thread together better than a one-person loom. It performed the work of two weavers and increased the speed of weavings, as the shuttle was passed mechanically across the warp threads. Prior to this invention, one could not weave a piece of cloth wider than the human body, as the shuttle had to be passed from hand to hand. The device cut in half the cost of labor, and in 1753, weavers sacked Kay's house in protest.

The Spinning Jenny

In 1760, James Hargreaves invented the **spinning jenny**, a device named for his wife. The jenny could spin eight spindles of thread at once and later was expanded to a sixteen-spindle device. This was the first machine to improve on the spinning wheel. In 1769, **Richard Arkwright** became the father of the industrial revolution when he produced the first power-driven spinning mill, the **water frame**. It took six spinners to keep a weaver busy, and although the spinning jenny helped that situation, it had to be operated by highly skilled laborers. Arkwright's invention eliminated that difficulty and also produced stronger warp thread. It also enabled the rise of the **factory system**. The first factories were very small in comparison to modern factories. In the early eighteenth century, most manufacturing was done in homes in the countryside around the turn of the eighteenth century. The system of sending out raw materials and farming out manufacturing work to country homes was known as the cottage industry. The invention of the spinning jenny and other devices made work in cottage industries more efficient and eventually other inventions, such as Edmund Cartwright's **power loom** and Eli Whitney's **cotton gin** (1793), helped to fuel the growth of factories. The cotton gin mechanically removed the seeds from the cotton, a very laborious process by hand; therefore, the demand for and supply of cotton increased dramatically, thus contributing to the use of slavery in the Americas. The manufacture of cotton in England increased five-fold after 1793. By 1820 cotton made up one-half of all exports.

The Steam Engine

During the 1700s there was a severe wood shortage in England that led to the search for other sources of fuel, such as coal. Coal, however, was deep in the ground and demanded new techniques to get it out of deep shafts and to pump out the water that inevitably filled the shafts. **Thomas Newcomen** invented the first steam engine in 1702 and **James Watt** further perfected the steam engine in 1763. The steam engine transformed the iron industry in Britain, and production of coke rose dramatically.

The steam engine created a revolution in transportation when **Robert Fulton** used the steam engine in his riverboats in 1807, and in 1829, **George Stephenson** first pioneered the **Rocket**, which used the steam engine in a locomotive. The Rocket traveled at 16 mph from Liverpool to Manchester. The steam engine on boats and locomotives made communication possible between various parts of England, and later the world, increased trade, and contributed to the expansion of the economy.

Robert Fulton

The Industrial Revolution Spreads

The Industrial Revolution spread to other parts of Europe, such as France, Belgium, and Germany, and eventually to North America to the United States.

Nevertheless, not all areas industrialized at the same speed or in the same way. In fact, by 1815 the gap between Britain and continental Europe was even wider than it had been in the early phases of the industrial revolution. Unstable political conditions in Europe and the expense and skill required to implement Britain's increasingly complex technology made it difficult for Europe to keep up with advances in Britain. This was true in areas outside of Europe as well. European colonies were generally not as industrialized as their mother lands; Britain, for example, exported manufactured goods to India and attempted to confine the Indian economy to the production of raw materials for export to Britain.

IMPACT OF THE INDUSTRIAL REVOLUTION

Urban Life

City life increased dramatically as a result of the Industrial Revolution. Cities such as Manchester, England, increased their population from 25,000 in 1772 to 455,000 in 1851. By the mid-nineteenth century, half of the English population lived in cities, whereas before the Industrial Revolution most lived in the country. A similar trend occurred in the late nineteenth century in North America; following the Second Industrial Revolution, the population began to move from the rural areas to the urban areas, to the point where today the majority of Americans reside in urban areas. Such a rapid rate of expansion naturally led to problems in urban areas with sanitation and overcrowding. Slums developed in the factory cities, and whole families lived in single rooms or on the streets.

Urban planning became important, especially after 1850. In Paris, for example, urban planners such as Georges Haussmann built wider streets and tore down many of the slums. Better housing districts arose complete with city parks. Paris also gained an improved water supply. During the second phase of the industrial revolution, other urban centers began to implement similar renewal projects.

Public health in urban areas also improved, as discoveries were made that explained the transmission of disease. Beginning with **Edwin Chadwick's** report in 1842 on the connection between unclean water and the transmission of disease, Britain worked to develop a sewer system to carry off impurities. **Louis Pasteur** developed the germ theory of disease by 1870, and proved that the **pasteurization** process, whereby liquids are heated to kill germs, could prevent epidemics.

Working Conditions

Despite such improvements, working conditions in the early factories were squalid. Because workers in the cottage industry were often unwilling to work in the conditions of the new factories, many workers were paupers and abandoned children. Even after Britain banned the use of pauper children as apprentices in factories in 1802, child labor and long hours were common. Workers had little or no rights in the early factories and received no worker's compensation for injuries, which were frequent, no minimum wage, no breaks, or other rights enjoyed by modern workers in America, for example. Although working conditions were hard, modern scholars point out that the buying power of the worker increased by 50 percent from 1770 to 1850.

Gender Issues in the Industrial Revolution

Britain first restricted the hours children could work in 1833, and this may have helped create a new division of labor not previously present in European society. The cottage industry was run by families, and families went together to the new factories. When children could no longer completely share the parents' work schedule, it became difficult for women to work at the same jobs as men. Factory life was regulated in a way that life in the country was not, and it was often much more difficult for a woman to work in a factory and raise a child. While there is no agreement about how this division of labor arose in the Industrial Revolution, certain jobs were open to women and others not. Men were paid more than women, and those women who did work outside the home generally came from the lowest classes. In general, women could not make enough to support themselves. By 1850 in Britain, the roles of women had changed dramatically from what they were in the early modern period.

Prostitution and illegitimacy also exploded in the wake of the Industrial Revolution. From 1750–1850, one birth in three was illegitimate.

Ideologies of the Nineteenth Century

Liberalism was based on the ideals of liberty and equality. Liberalism advocated representative government, equality before the law, freedom of speech, assembly, the press, and freedom from arbitrary arrest. Liberalism also promoted free enterprise and lack of governmental control of the economy, also known as laissez-faire or classical liberalism. After 1815, advocates of liberalism were largely from the middle class. Their interests collided with those of the lower classes, and often they wished to limit the right to vote, for example, to those with property.

Nationalism was based on the belief in cultural unity based on a common language, history, territory, and ethnicity. The nationalists sought to create nations based on cultural unity.

Socialism first emerged in France. One of the most influential early advocates of socialism was **Count Henri de Saint-Simon**. Saint-Simon welcomed industrialization, but advocated government control of the economy with the "doers" or industrialists in charge. Socialists like Saint-Simon advocated help for the poor, government control to ensure economic equality between the rich and poor, and regulation or abolition of private property. **Marxist socialism**, which arose following the publication of *The Communist Manifesto* in 1848, rejected the emphasis of Saint-Simon on the emerging middle class and instead advocated the interests of the working class, or **proletariat**. The proletariat would rise against the industrialists who controlled the "means of production," and establish a "dictatorship of the proletariat." Eventually, the need for a state would wither away, leading to true **communism**. Marx's view of history is known as **historical materialism**, and it relied upon the notion that class conflicts over economic issues moved history.

Romanticism

In addition to nationalism, liberalism, communism, and socialism, **romanticism** was another force that dominated European culture in the late nineteenth century. Waves of change in the arts ran parallel to the reactionary forces that led to the revolutions of 1848. Musicians reacted to the formalized music of the eighteenth century. According to the canons of classicism, phrases were uniform in length, rhythm was also in tight, tidy little balanced units, and the form of the entire composition was also balanced and codified. Romanticists broke those boundaries, creating phrases of vast, sweeping length that often covered a tremendous range from low to high notes; rhythm was more syncopated, and Romantic composers preferred the minor mode for its pathos to the major mode. **Ludwig van Beethoven** was one of the first composers to break the classical mold, when he exploded sonata-allegro form by lengthening it and creating long codas. Beethoven's late piano sonatas, such as the Opus 111, also broke tonal boundaries to the point where contemporary audiences attributed the dissonance they heard to the composer's tragic deafness.

Composers such as **Franz Liszt** dazzled the world with sheer virtuosity and pyrotechnic etudes such as the Transcendental Etudes; the Polish composer **Frederic Chopin** wrote melodious nocturnes that made use of rhubato, a technique for bending the rhythm in the melodic line over a stable base to create a more emotional affect; and **Franz Schubert** wrote melodious and beautiful pieces that often threatened to flow on without end.

Music also took on a nationalistic tone as in **Peter Tchaikovsky's** "1812 Overture," a tribute to the Russian victory over Napoleon in 1812 and which contained Russian melodies. **Bedrich Smetana** wrote "Má vlast" about his native Czechoslovakia; **Antonin Dvorak** wrote "The New World Symphony," a tribute to his newfound home in America that combined the musical styles and influences of African-American spirituals and other American and even European influences; Chopin wrote many polonaises for piano, a form used in his native Poland; Liszt wrote a number of Hungarian rhapsodies, and **Bela Bartok** in the twentieth century continued to explore Hungarian music in his Hungarian dances.

Visual artists developed a love for the exotic, non-European, and mythological subjects. **Delacroix,** for example, painted *The Death of Sardanapalus* and *Arabs Skirmishing in the Mountains.* The English **J.M.W. Turner's** swirling, misty paintings created amorphous, mysterious impressions of his subjects that defied the classical belief in the ordered universe.

Poets also broke form. **Samuel Taylor Coleridge's** *Kublai Khan* captured the exotic world of the East; he claimed the poem came to him in a dream while he was intoxicated with opium. Many Romanticists tried to portray the supernatural as real. The American poet **Walt Whitman**, on the other hand, tried to portray reality itself as remarkable and out of the ordinary. His *Song of Myself* made use of long, unbroken lines that poured forth inner emotion and rejected formalized use of stanzas, lines, meters, and other poetic techniques. Whitman's boundless lines paralleled the American belief in its Manifest Destiny, by which it was sweeping across the continent to occupy both east and west. Just as America was literally breaking through its old geographical boundaries, so too Whitman broke the boundaries of formal poetry.

The Revolutions of 1848

In 1848, the fires of revolution once again spread across Europe, and they were fanned by economic hardships caused by rapid industrialization. Factory workers protested working conditions, women demanded greater rights, and workers skilled in traditional crafts worried about loss of the market for their labor. Social movements such as nationalism, liberalism, and socialism brought diverse groups together, all striving to better their society. Revolutionaries were primarily **bourgeoisie**, a Marxist term for wealthy members of society who controlled the means of production. The bourgeoisie protested the conservative, reactionary governments created in the wake of the Napoleonic Wars. Romanticism encouraged further innovative thinking, as literati and artists broke out of the cultural confines of classicism.

Revolts occurred throughout Europe that affected France, Italian and German States, and the Austrian Empire. Only England and Russia were spared. By the end of 1849, the revolutions had failed, but the idea of revolutionary social change would live on.

Revolt in Paris and the Abdication of Louis Philippe

The people of Paris revolted in February, forcing **Louis Philippe** to abdicate. He had abdicated in favor of his grandson, but the people would not accept another king. A provisional republic was declared and the **Second Republic** was born. This French revolution was interested in social reform and reform of the government and working conditions. It freed colonial slaves, abolished the death penalty, and recognized rights for the working classes.

Louis Napoleon

While liberal socialism dominated Paris, political moderates dominated the rest of France. Free elections brought a majority of moderates to the Constituent Assembly. By June this clash of ideologies resulted in more violent uprisings in the streets of Paris. The army put the uprisings down at a cost of thousands of lives. The elections of December brought Louis Napoleon to power.

Revolt of Hungary from Austria

The revolution in France inspired liberal uprisings throughout Europe. Hungarian revolutionaries demanded freedom from Austria. When the Austrian government did not respond positively, protestors filled the streets of Vienna and were active in the countryside as well. Emperor Ferdinand I freed the serfs and gave in to the protestors' demands. But the various revolutionary groups that had united to bring about change in the Austrian government had differing goals and so could not remain united for long.

The revolutionaries that wanted an independent Hungary for Hungarians could not cope effectively with the other ethnic groups that would be half of an independent Hungary's population. Croats, Serbs, and Rumanians as well as Hungarians lived in the territory that would be Hungary. Each of these groups wanted its own independent country. They did not want to exchange being a minority in the Austrian Empire for being a minority in Hungary.

The monarchy and its supporters, which regrouped around a new emperor, Francis Joseph, after the abdication of Ferdinand I, exploited these ethnic divisions. The Austrian army was brought in to end the revolts. With the aid of the Russian military, the Hungarian revolution was crushed and Hungary was occupied to deter further uprisings.

Revolt in Prussia

In March 1848, revolution reached Prussia. Working and middle class protestors joined together in Berlin to rally against the monarchy. **Frederick William IV** of Prussia responded with a promise of a liberal constitution and was willing to allow Prussia to be a part of a new united Germany.

A threat to German unification arose in the matter of **Schleswig** and **Holstein**. Schleswig and Holstein were two Germanic provinces. Holstein was also a member of the German Confederation and Germans were the primary inhabitants of both. The King of Denmark, however, controlled both. When Frederick VII of Denmark attempted to solidify his control over these two provinces, he sparked a revolt among their German residents.

The German National Assembly called on Prussia, as the largest of the German states, to deal with Denmark. Frederick William IV sent his Prussian army forth to settle the matter. Meanwhile, the National Assembly finished the constitution and elected Frederick William IV of Prussia as the new emperor of Germany. Frederick William IV refused, not wishing to be bound to the liberal constitution.

In Prussia, he terminated the Prussian constitutional assembly and instead issued a conservative constitution. He then attempted to have himself elected emperor of Germany on his own terms. Austria blocked him and, since Austria was backed by Russia, it was strong enough to force Frederick William to back down. The liberals had failed, and those wishing for German unification had failed also.

The Italian States

Italians wanted liberal government and the expulsion of Austria from the Piedmont region. In the 1830s **Joseph Mazzini** organized a secret society called Young Italy. In 1847 the hated Austrians took the town of Ferrara in the Papal States, but were forced out. When the Milanese threatened in January 1848 to quit using goods that contributed to the Austrian financial machine, such as tobacco, Austrian soldiers shot and killed 61 Italians. The Austrians laid siege to Milan, but were repulsed by armed citizens. Mazzini, who had been in hiding in South America, returned in June 1848. Most inhabitants of Milan still supported the Austrians, and many potential allies, such as the Kingdom of Naples, abandoned the revolutionary cause. Only Lombardy and the Piedmont provided aid.

Field Marshal Radetzky, who defeated the Italians at Custozza in the end of July, commanded the Austrians. The Italians retreated to Milan and, when the Austrians gave permission for those who wished to leave to do so, Milan promptly lost half its population and fell on August 7. The Kingdom of Piedmont alone continued to fight, and the rebellion ended at Novarra on March 23, 1849.

On November 15, 1848, the prime minister of the Papal States was assassinated in Rome, and the pope fled to Geata in the south. Mazzini then took charge, and improved the plight of the poor. He distributed some of the Church's land to the poor, reformed prisons and insane asylums, granted freedom of the press, and provided secular education.

The French invaded on April 20, 1849, and eventually the pope returned. **Giuseppe Garibaldi**, who had helped to delay the French arrival, escaped to the United States. In the 1850s he would return to fight for Italian unification. Mazzini fled to England.

Venice continued to fight on, and the Austrians blockaded the city during the winter of 1848–1849. Venice surrendered at the end of August.

The Revolution in Italy of 1848 had failed to achieve a united Italy.

The Aftermath of the Revolutions

The Hungarians won more self-determination from the Hapsburgs by 1867. Prussia eliminated feudalism by 1850.

A group of the German liberals who failed in the revolution of 1848 migrated to the United States. There they were called the "Forty-Eighters," and almost 177,000 of them fought for the Union against slavery and other issues of interest to their radical mindset. Whereas they failed to unify Germany in 1848, by 1871 Otto van Bismarck had succeeded in so doing.

The **Italian Risorgimento** eventually succeeded in uniting Italy in 1860, with Rome and the Papal States coming into the union in 1870.

The failure of the revolutions of 1848 was a reflection of the new social order created by the Industrial Revolution. The old aristocratic elite and their intricate system of alliances had been displaced by the sheer power of money, and this was controlled now not through birth but by those whose ingenuity made them successful in the business world. The failure of the revolutions of 1848 also pointed to the need for more gradual reform. Liberals and conservatives alike became more willing to compromise.

THE SECOND INDUSTRIAL REVOLUTION

The end of the revolutions of 1848 brought renewed stability to Europe, and another wave of industrialization began in 1870. The development of more efficient ways to produce iron with the steam engine in the First Industrial Revolution fueled this **Second Industrial Revolution**. Greater availability of iron encouraged the building of railroads. In the nineteenth century, railroads expanded virtually across the world. Although they brought many benefits, they also contributed to the decline of Native American lifestyle in the American West, and of tribal cultures of Africa, and also negatively impacted the indigenous, cottage industries of India. Steel made possible the production of lighter and smaller machinery, and the Industrial Revolution of the nineteenth century was centered on the production of steel to produce railroad tracks. New industries, such as the electrical industry, arose to meet demands for new sources of power. Hydo-electric power industrialized Italy, which had never had adequate supplies of coal to compete with Britain in the early phases of the Industrial Revolution. The development of the **internal combustion engine** led to the rise of the automobile industry in the early twentieth century and also to the development of the airline industry.

During the second phase of the Industrial Revolution, Germany overtook Britain as the industrial leader of Europe. The United States was another leading manufacturer, particularly in the steel industry. The gaps between industrialized nations and the areas where technology had not yet reached became even larger during the second phase of the Industrial Revolution. Southern and Eastern Europe remained well behind Britain, Germany, Belgium, the Netherlands, and northern Italy. Places such as Russia, Spain, Portugal, the Balkans, and most of the Austro-Hungarian Empire continued to have an agricultural economy, and they served to produce the raw materials and basic food supply for the industrialized nations. Russia started to industrialize under Sergei Witte in the 1890s (see Chapter 31), while Japan also began an industrial movement in the late nineteenth century (see Unit IV).

Social Changes During the Second Industrial Revolution

The class structure of Europe and other industrialized areas, such as the United States, became more complex in the nineteenth century. While the average level of income increased in the Industrial Revolution, the gap between the rich and the poor segments of society persisted. The working classes, which included agricultural laborers, accounted for as much as 80 percent of the population, collectively earned less than the wealthy elite and the middle classes together. The Industrial Revolutions created a new group of people in the middle classes, and this group was extremely diverse. New industries created a demand for new, highly skilled workers, and each of these groups were separated from others by competing interests and lifestyles. A new upper middle class was created out of the most successful industrial business families. After the revolutions of 1848 failed, many of these people had moved away from their radical leanings of earlier years and more towards the aristocracy. Gradually, they developed a lifestyle similar to the old aristocracy. Below them were less successful merchants without the great wealth of the industrialists, but nevertheless, successful and secure. This group included professionals in law, medicine, or other areas. Small business owners formed another very diverse subclass of the middle class, and as industrialization created demands for new products, a vaster array of these businesses continued to develop. Those working in areas that demanded specialization, such as engineering, were another subclass. Very highly skilled workers became almost a new kind of aristocracy within the working classes. A new class of "white collar" workers emerged in these businesses and distinguished themselves from those who worked with their hands.

Gender Roles in the Late Nineteenth Century

Whereas the First Industrial Revolution disrupted gender roles and family life, the Second Industrial Revolution provided a more stable context. During the second half of the nineteenth century, more births occurred within the context of marriage, as compared to the **illegitimacy explosion** of 1750–1850.

The distinction between gender roles for women and men continued to grow larger in the late nineteenth century. When women's work was more restricted to the home, women gained a great deal of autonomy over the running of their homes and rearing of their children. There was more attachment between children and their mothers. Women also chose to have fewer children, and the birth rate dropped. It was not until 1882 in England, though, that women gained property rights in marriage, and women's groups agitated for the right to vote and for rights of working class women. Around the turn of the twentieth century, the fight for women's rights created a new ideal, that of the "new woman" who broke with tradition and worked outside of the home in a profession.

Industrialization also created new opportunities for leisure activities, as subways and streetcars enabled people to travel for recreation. Organized team sports became popular. Mass events like fairs also became a significant aspect of life in urban areas.

Finally, industrialization created a greater need for educated workers. **Compulsory education** became common in the West. The drive for voter's rights also contributed to the need for education. Daily life changed greatly in the eighteenth and nineteenth centuries, because industrialization resulted in dramatic changes in gender roles, the structure of the family, and working conditions.

The Industrial Revolution and Global Inequality

In 1750, the standard of living in Europe was roughly the same as in other parts of the world. By 1970, however, income for an average person in the wealthy, industrialized countries was 25 times the income in the poorest countries. While the first and second industrial revolutions brought about significant gains in income for the average person in Europe and in the United States, similar growth in income did not occur in underdeveloped countries, such as many of those of Africa and Asia. Global inequities continue to be a pressing problem in the modern world.

Review Questions

1. The origins of the Industrial Revolution lay in the search for improved methods of producing

   (A) wood and stone.
   (B) cotton cloth and coal.
   (C) oil and steel.
   (D) better crops.

2. The Industrial Revolution of the eighteenth century began in

   (A) China.
   (B) France.
   (C) Britain.
   (D) Germany.

3. In the eighteenth century, the essential products of the Industrial Revolution were

   (A) iron and steel.
   (B) coal and iron.
   (C) agricultural products.
   (D) cotton textiles.

4. The spinning jenny was able to

   (A) weave cloth more efficiently and rapidly.
   (B) weave several pieces of cloth at once.
   (C) separate cotton from the seeds.
   (D) spin several spindles of thread at once.

5. All of the following were results of the Industrial Revolution EXCEPT

   (A) lowering of the child mortality rates.
   (B) urbanization of Western society.
   (C) disintegration of the family.
   (D) increased availability of cotton cloth.

6. Which of the following statements is true of the Industrial Revolution of the eighteenth century?

    (A) Economic consequences for the lower classes helped bring about the Revolutions of 1848.

    (B) It opened to women the same opportunities as men.

    (C) It spread from Britain throughout Europe and benefited all countries equally.

    (D) Urban life was not affected by the Industrial Revolution, but rural life was.

7. In the Second Industrial Revolution, which nation took the lead?

    (A) Britain

    (B) France

    (C) Russia

    (D) Germany

8. Which statement best describes the impact of the Second Industrial Revolution?

    (A) Women's roles continued to be confined to the home, and the birth rate rose dramatically.

    (B) A new upper middle class evolved of educated and highly skilled professionals.

    (C) Global inequities were diminished as the Second Industrial Revolution spread to Russia and southeast Europe.

    (D) Industrialization meant less time for leisure activities.

9. The Revolutions of 1848

    (A) were successful in some countries but failed in others.

    (B) were led by social conservatives.

    (C) dampened enthusiasm for liberalism.

    (D) established socialist governments in many parts of Europe.

10. Which of the following is NOT true of the Hungarian revolution of 1848?

    (A) Ethnic tensions resulted in the ultimate failure of the revolution.

    (B) Ferdinand I refused to free the serfs.

    (C) Franz Joseph I used the Austrian army to end the revolts.

    (D) Hungarians wanted freedom from Austria.

11. The Revolution of 1848 failed in Italy due to

   (A) Austrian intervention.

   (B) lack of French intervention.

   (C) the failure of Naples and other potential allies to support the cause.

   (D) Both (A) and (C).

Answers

1. (B)	4. (D)	7. (D)	10. (B)
2. (C)	5. (A)	8. (B)	11. (D)
3. (D)	6. (A)	9. (C)	

Chapter 27

THE UNIFICATION OF ITALY AND GERMANY

KEY TERMS

Dual Revolution	Victor Emmanuel
Congress of Vienna	Zollverein
Sardinia	Bismarck
Sicily	Schleswig-Holstein
Papal States	William I
Naples	German Confederation
Lombardy	Franco-Prussian War
Kingdom of the Two Sicilies	Austro-Prussian War
Mazzini	German Empire
Garibaldi	Nationalism
Cavour	

ITALY

Italy entered the nineteenth century not as one single country, but rather as a collection of small kingdoms that had evolved from the city-states of the Middle Ages. The relations of these kingdoms with each other varied from cooperation to competition, sometimes hostile, sometimes friendly, but always independent of each other.

The Congress of Vienna in 1815 confirmed the disunity of Italy. Lombardy and Venetia were handed over to Austria. An Italian king of the house of Savoy ruled Sardinia and the Piedmont, while a Bourbon king ruled in Sicily and Naples (formerly the kingdom of the Two Sicilies), and the pope controlled the Papal States in central Italy. Other small kingdoms filled in the rest of northern Italy.

The move towards unification began following the Congress of Vienna. There were three distinctive early movements. The first, led by **Giuseppe Mazzini**, called for the formation of an Italian democratic state with universal suffrage. The second, led by the priest **Vincenzo Gioberti**, called for the formation of a federation of Italian states with the pope as president, an idea that was too impractical. The third group wanted to form a united Italy with Sardinia-Piedmont as the central power.

Italy had been touched by the revolutions of 1848, just as most of the rest of Europe had been. In Italy, as elsewhere, the revolutions of 1848 failed. Revolts in support of Mazzini's efforts had occurred in the provinces controlled by Austria. The revolts were crushed by the Austrians and Mazzini's support faded.

Victor Emmanuel of Sardinia had responded to the uprisings in 1848 by granting a liberal constitution. This constitution had the unexpected effect of making Sardinia appealing to the Italian middle class, and so Sardinia became the natural center of unification goals.

Cavour

Count Camillo Benso di Cavour was the leading figure in Sardinian politics from 1850–1861. Cavour was the chief minister of Victor Emmanuel. Cavour's original aim was to unite northern and some of central Italy into a state dominated by Sardinia. Cavour worked on strengthening the infrastructure of Sardinia, supporting civil liberties, and opposing the privileged status of the Church. He also built highways and railroads, which brought benefits to northern Italy and increased support for Sardinian rule. Increased revenues also made it possible for Cavour to assemble and train army.

To unify northern Italy, Cavour realized that he had to free Lombardy and Venetia from Austria. To this end he negotiated secretly with Napoleon III of France for military support against Austria. In July 1858, Austria reacted to Cavour's provocative actions by attacking Sardinia. To its surprise, Austria was defeated by the combined forces of Sardinia and France.

Sardinia expected to be able to claim Lombardy and Venetia at last. Instead, Napoleon III suddenly changed his position. He had no stomach for war. Since Pope Pius IX had declared the Sardinian policies relating to Church and state to be contradictory to Church teachings, Napoleon III could not risk alienating French Catholics by aiding Sardinia. As a result, Sardinia did not obtain the territorial gains it sought. Instead it received only Lombardy. Deeply angered by this turn of events, Cavour resigned.

In other parts of Italy, particularly in central Italy, nationalists rose in successful revolt and called for a united Italy, demanding that their particular regions be joined to Sardinia. Cavour returned in 1860 to control most of Italy in the name of Sardinia.

Garibaldi

Giuseppe Garibaldi had been active in the fight for Italian unity and in the fight to liberate parts of Italy from foreign control since the 1830s. His followers, guerrilla fighters, were known as the **"Red Shirts."** In 1860, Garibaldi turned his attention to the Kingdom of the Two Sicilies. Cavour supported Garibaldi, but only in secret. While Garibaldi's goals might seem to match well with Cavour's, Cavour recognized that Garibaldi's appeal to the common people could make him a dangerous enemy. Cavour wanted to use Garibaldi to further Sardinia's cause, but at the same time, he wanted to remove Garibaldi as a potential threat.

Garibaldi liberated Sicily and Naples in 1860, claiming them in the name of Victor Emmanuel of Sardinia Following this victory, he intended to march on Rome. Cavour blocked Garibaldi, realizing that an attack on Rome, which meant an attack on the pope, would almost certainly mean war with France.

A Unified Italy

Cavour organized elections in Sicily and Naples that resulted in a vote to join Sardinia as Cavour had expected. Garibaldi and Victor Emmanuel met and rode through the streets in triumph. Italy was united, with the exception of the Papal States and Venetia. Venetia was brought into the newly united Italy in 1866. Rome was the only part of Italy not a part of the unified country. As a result of the Franco-Prussian War of 1870–1871, the French lost control of the Papal States, and the new Italy took Rome. In 1870, Rome became capital of a united Italy.

In reality, the unified Italy was not the liberal state that so many of Sardinia's supporters had believed it would be. It was a state governed by a monarch and a parliament that allowed limited voting rights for Italian males. There was a gap between the landed upper class and the rest of the population. While

Cavour's efforts had made it possible for northern Italy to rapidly industrialize, southern Italy remained a rural, mainly agricultural society.

GERMANY

Prussia and Austria were the two strongest Germanic states. Each wished to dominate a unified Germany, and each feared the results if the other succeeded. In 1848, Frederick William of Prussia almost succeeded in becoming the ruler of a united Germany. He was thwarted at the eleventh hour by Austria, backed by its occasional ally Russia. In this case, the need to stop the growing power of Prussia drew Austria and Russia into an alliance.

By 1853, the economy had become a factor in German unity. A customs union, the **Zollverein**, had been established in 1834. The Zollverein was intended to increase trade and thereby generate revenue for its membership. The Zollverein, led by Prussia, worked out quite well and soon every German state, with the exception of Austria, was a member.

The revolts in Italy in 1859 had caused Austria numerous problems, and Prussia had learned important lessons. Prussia was now under the rule of **William I**, who was well aware of the potential for war and greatly concerned that Prussia was not prepared as well as it should be. The energetic and militaristic William I set about military reform. His goal was to restructure the Prussian army and double its size. To do this, William I needed a larger defense budget, which meant higher taxes.

William I was, however, not an absolute monarch. He could not simply raise taxes, no matter how just the reason. The **Prussian Assembly** had been formed in 1848 and had some power. The liberal members of the Assembly, mostly wealthy and middle class, wanted to increase their power and to make the Assembly more powerful than the king. There was no enthusiastic support for increasing the military, since Prussians did not want to live in a military state and there was no obvious, undeniable military threat to Prussia's borders to sway the people to William I's position. The Assembly rejected William I's proposed military budget in 1862.

Otto von Bismarck

William I reacted decisively. He created a new ministry and appointed **Otto von Bismarck** as its head. Bismarck, an aristocrat, was devoted to Prussia and its king, and to Prussian supremacy in Germany. His career began in the Prussian Assembly in 1848, where other members considered him to be a conservative. He served as the Prussian Ambassador to the German Confederation from 1851–1859, working for Prussia and against Austria. He then served as Prussian Ambassador to Russia and France, gaining valuable experience in dealing with the other powers in Europe.

In 1862 Bismarck took control. He ignored the Prussian Assembly, which declared it alone had the right to authorize taxes. Bismarck ordered taxes collected even though the Assembly refused to approve the budget. Bismarck then set about reorganizing the army according to the wishes of William I. Meanwhile, the people of Prussia continued to elect liberal representatives who were absolutely opposed to Bismarck's policies and methods. Bismarck refused to give in to the lack of popular approval and continued to do his duty as he saw it. He remarked that only "blood and iron" could decide the great questions of his day.

Schleswig-Holstein

In 1864, Bismarck found an opportunity to raise Prussia's standing and possibly convince some of the people that his methods and aims were justified. The Danish king again tried to add **Schleswig-Holstein** to Denmark. The people of Schleswig-Holstein, a Germanic province and member of the German Confederation that was ruled by the king of Denmark, did not want to be part of a larger Denmark. They were Germans, no matter who their king happened to be. Austria joined Prussia in this nationalistic cause, fighting for the rights of oppressed Germans, and they succeeded in defending Schleswig-Holstein.

The situation was delicate, but Bismarck had laid his plans carefully. To begin with, he neutralized Austria's casual alliance with Russia by supporting **Alexander II** of Russia in 1863 when he had put down an uprising among the Poles. If war came between Prussia and Austria, Russia would remain neutral. France was the other major question mark. Bismarck used diplomacy to bring Napoleon III of France to a neutral stance. With Russia and France committed to neutrality, Bismarck had only to be concerned about angering other German states when declaring war on Austria.

Austro-Prussian War

The **Austro-Prussian War** (1866) was a short, contained war. The careful reorganization of the Prussian army paid off, and Prussia defeated Austria at the **Battle of Sadowa**. The war lasted seven weeks. Bismarck wanted Austria out of German affairs, but Bismarck also did not want to create a permanent enmity between Prussian-led Germany and Austria. The terms of the truce were generous, not punitive, but Austria would no longer interfere in German affairs. The German Confederation, in which Austria had played a leading role, was ended.

North German Confederation

Bismarck formed a new **North German Confederation** from the Protestant German states north of the Main River. Prussia, as the largest state, dominated the group. The Catholic southern German states became independent allies of Prussia. Bismarck constructed the new constitution for the Confederation, which gave each state an independent government, but the king of Prussia became the central authority governing the Confederation as its president. There was now to be a **Chancellor of the Confederation** who answered only to the president. Bismarck became the first chancellor and together with the president directly controlled the military and the foreign relations of the Confederation.

The constitution established a legislature with two houses, each of which could make laws. One house consisted of representatives appointed by the different states; the other consisted of representatives elected by the all-male voting population. This move by Bismarck created a way for the common man to actively participate in the government of the Confederation. It gave the people a sense of empowerment they had not previously had while not really giving them any power. Bismarck and his king retained the real power.

Although occupied with the formation of the new government of the Confederation, Bismarck did not neglect Prussia. He knew that he had offended many with his rough tactics of ignoring the Assembly. He also knew, however, that everyone loves a winner and Bismarck had made Austrians winners too. Bismarck asked the Assembly to approve the taxes he had already collected to fight the war he had already won. The Assembly did so and the middle-class liberals fell in line.

Still, the dream of German unity was not truly realized. The southern states remained independent allies, not actually part of Bismarck's confederation. Bismarck realized that if he could but find a way to appeal to their nationalistic passions, he could bring about the unity he so devotedly sought. A well-planned war would serve his purposes. France conveniently appeared as the enemy.

Franco-Prussian War

The official reason for the conflict was a potential heir to the Spanish throne, who was related to the king of Prussia. In reality, France was alarmed by the growing power of the militaristic Prussian-led Confederation so near its own border. War broke out in 1870. The southern German states supported the North German Confederation, just as Bismarck had planned. Austria, having been well treated by Bismarck after its own war with Prussia, now repaid its debt by not involving itself in this war. Russia too, stayed out. On September 1, 1870, the Prussians defeated the French at the **Battle of Sedan**. The blow was too much for the government of Napoleon III, and it fell three days later. The French formed the **Third Republic of France** and attempted to carry on the war, but abandoned the effort five months later.

Bismarck was not as kind to France as he had been to Austria. He had no need to be. While there had been great sympathy and loyalty to Austria among the other German states, no such feelings existed among the Germans for France. Bismarck demanded huge indemnities from France and acquired **Alsace-Lorraine** for Prussia. The latter, particularly, sparked great resentment among the French.

The New German Empire

The southern German states now joined with the North German Confederation to form the new German Empire with King William I of Prussia as Emperor William of Germany. The emperor, his chancellor, his army, and his people were united and in less than ten years, Bismarck had transformed Prussia into the main power of Central Europe.

Review Questions

1. An obstacle to the unification of Italy was

   (A) Austrian control of Lombardy and Venetia.

   (B) Papal condemnation of Sardinia.

   (C) French desire to increase the power of Sardinia.

   (D) Both (A) and (B).

2. The leader who focused his unification efforts on the Kingdom of the Two Sicilies was

   (A) Cavour.

   (B) Garibaldi.

   (C) Mazzini.

   (D) the pope.

3. The only part of Italy that did not initially join the newly united Italian states was

   (A) Venice.

   (B) the Kingdom of the Two Sicilies.

   (C) Rome.

   (D) Naples.

4. Which of the following Germanic areas was more closely aligned with Protestantism?

   (A) Prussia

   (B) Austria

   (C) Schleswig-Holstein

   (D) Both (A) and (C).

5. Bismarck's victory in which war first paved the way for complete Prussian domination of the Germanic states?

   (A) The Austro-Prussian War

   (B) The Franco-Prussian War

   (C) The conflict over Schleswig-Holstein

   (D) Russia's fight against the Poles

Answers

1. (D)	3. (C)	5. (A)
2. (B)	4. (D)	

Chapter 28

THE UNITED STATES IN THE NINETEENTH CENTURY

KEY TERMS

Manifest Destiny

Louisiana Purchase

Frontier Thesis

Trail of Tears

Battle of Little Bighorn

Wounded Knee

Emancipation Proclamation

Nationalism also played an important role in the development of the United States in the nineteenth century. The United States expanded rapidly in the years following its Revolutionary War. Britain ceded to the United States the area west of the Appalachian Mountains to the Mississippi River, almost doubling the size of the territory occupied by the thirteen original colonies. In 1803, Napoleon knew he could not defend French territories from the Mississippi to the Rocky Mountains, and so chose instead to gain the revenue from their sale. The **Louisiana Purchase** again doubled the size of the U.S. Meriwether Lewis and William Clark then mapped the new territory from 1804–1806. In 1845, Texas entered the union, forcing a war between Mexico and America from 1845–1848. The U.S. paid Mexico $15 million for Texas, California, and New Mexico according to the **Treaty of Hidalgo**.

The nineteenth century became the era of **Manifest Destiny** for Americans. Landscape paintings reflected endless boundaries and no visible horizons. Americans believed it was their manifest destiny to control all of North America, and some even talked of an American presence in Canada, Cuba, Latin America, and South America. Manifest Destiny assumed that the democratic experiment in America was a superior form of civilization, and that the white man who brought it westward was superior to those people and cultures they replaced.

THE "FRONTIER THESIS"

Frederick Jackson Turner put forth his famous **"frontier thesis"** three years after the U.S. Census Bureau announced the closing of the American frontiers. Turner argued that the American character was formed by its continuing engagement of changing frontiers, and that these frontiers were "the meeting point between savagery and civilization." Americans had to continually reenact the advances of industrialization in the late nineteenth century along successive frontiers, which he described as "free land." Turner saw westward expansion as synonymous with progress. The continuing need to civilize the frontiers formed the distinctively rugged, individualistic, and practical American character. The frontier also functioned as a safety valve of sorts, in that it provided a way to diffuse discontent in the urban areas.

Though many historians dispute Turner's main ideas, the "frontier thesis" has become one of the most significant theses about the American character and the formation of American democratic institutions as a distinctive form of government. Many historians challenge Turner's idea that all frontiers encountered by Americans had something in common, as the frontiers experienced in the colonial period were vastly different from those in the late nineteenth century.

Further, Turner saw the West as a free frontier that offered unlimited freedom and opportunity. The conflicts that arose between Native Americans and those who traveled west suggest that the frontiers were not as free as Turner thought they were, and more modern historians tend to prefer to talk about the violence and depravity that occurred as Anglo-Saxon settlers displaced Native Americans. Further, many ethnic peoples, such as Asians, experienced repression in the West, which belies Turner's description of the frontier as offering limitless opportunity for all. Other historians point to the need for greater complexity in one's analysis of American history, and refer to the role of technology and other elements in the development of American ideals and characteristic institutions. Finally, Turner saw the closing of the frontier as the end of the first chapter of American history. In so doing, he ignored the significance of the national debate over slavery.

American Expansion and Native Americans

As America expanded west, conflicts arose as settlers encountered many native peoples. In 1830, the **Indian Removal Act** forced Native Americans east of the Mississippi into reservations in what would later become Oklahoma. Among those who suffered the most were the Seminoles in Florida and the Cherokee, whose **Trail of Tears** (1838–1839) serves as a symbol of the suffering of Native Americans throughout this period. Conflict between the American settlers and natives culminated in the **Battle of Little Big Horn** in 1876, where thousands of Lakota Sioux wiped out an army under George Armstrong Custer. Conflict continued, and in 1890 American soldiers slaughtered more than 200 Sioux at **Wounded Knee**, where Sioux were engaged in the Ghost Dance. As the Ghost Dance involved beliefs in a world free of whites, the government felt threatened by it. Many Native American cultures were virtually wiped out by westward expansion. As Anglo-Saxon settlers came west, hundreds of diverse cultures disappeared.

Native Americans were not the only population to suffer as the United States expanded. Slavery continued to grow in the southern states, where the plantation economies were in stark contrast to the industrialized cities of the North.

THE CIVIL WAR

The northern states bitterly disagreed with the southern states over slavery. The issue of state's rights as opposed to the power of the central government was also hotly debated. During the **American Civil War** from 1861–1865, the northern and southern states fought one another over many issues, some

Abraham Lincoln

economic and some political. The attempt to forge a union out of many competing interests began with the Articles of Confederation, and the Civil War illustrates the extent to which Americans had unsuccessfully resolved their underlying ideological differences.

Emancipation of Slaves

Scholars often debate whether the issue of slavery alone might have provoked a civil war, but almost all scholars believe that slavery was the one issue without which Americans might not have gone to war. During the Civil War, President Abraham Lincoln issued the **Emancipation Proclamation** of 1863, which applied to areas under rebellion.

Leaders of the reconstructed union would have to decide upon civil rights for the freed slaves of the South. Although former slaves became citizens and earned the right to vote during reconstruction, discrimination continued in the form of the **Jim Crow laws**, and finally erupted in the Civil Rights movements of the 1960s.

The development of American nationalism as expressed in Manifest Destiny and waged in the Civil War created conflicts between various elements of its population at home. In the late nineteenth century, the United States would expand on the notion of Manifest Destiny and emulate many European powers in a wave of imperialist expansion, creating conflict abroad.

Review Questions

1. Which of the following statements best describes the Frontier Thesis?

   (A) The debate over slavery played an important role in forming the national identity.

   (B) The frontiers were places that Americans civilized and the need to do so created the individualistic character of Americans.

   (C) Each frontier was vastly different in character.

   (D) The frontiers were rigid boundaries that kept Americans constrained.

2. Which of the following points was NOT a reason that the Frontier Thesis has been criticized?

   (A) Turner did not take sufficient note of the role played by slavery.

   (B) Each frontier encountered in different eras was different from every other.

   (C) There were no defenders of the frontiers, making the expansion an effortless one.

   (D) The frontiers did not offer limitless opportunity for all groups.

3. Which of the following best describes Manifest Destiny?

   (A) It was manifest to all that American frontiers should be limited to the original outlines of the thirteen colonies.

   (B) It was manifest that America should occupy the Louisiana Purchase, but stop its expansion.

   (C) The Louisiana Purchase and Treaty of Hidalgo stopped the expansion westward.

   (D) Some American expansionists advocated dominating the entirety of North and South America as well as Cuba.

Answers

1. (B)　　　2. (C)　　　3. (D)

Chapter 29

IMPERIALISM IN THE NINETEENTH CENTURY

KEY TERMS

Imperialism

Mission civilisatrice

"Imperialism the Highest Stage of
    Capitalism"

Social Darwinism

Panama Canal

Suez Canal

Tropical dependencies

Settlement colonies

Scramble for Africa

French Equatorial Africa

Belgian Congo

Khedives

Mahdi

Battle of Omdurman

Dutch East India Company

Afrikaners

Boer War

Great Trek

Republic of Natal

Orange Free State

South African Republic

German Southwest Africa

German East Africa

German East Africa Company

Italian East African Empire

Italian Benadir Company

Liberia

Abyssinia

Captain James Cook

Aboriginals

Maori

Hawaii

Queen Lili'uokalani

Monroe Doctrine

Manifest Destiny

Big Stick Policy

Spanish-American War

Sakhalin Island

Manchuria

Russo-Japanese War

Johnson-Reed Act

OVERVIEW

Europeans had established colonies in other parts of the world since the Age of Exploration. In the late nineteenth century there was really nothing new about Europe extending its control and power over other parts of the earth. Europeans first used word **"imperialism,"** however, in the mid-nineteenth century to describe the web of colonial empires built between 1870 and 1914. The word refers to the European domination of other nations and cultures, such as those in Africa and eastern Asia, the only parts of the world not already dominated by Europeans. However, others nations besides those in Europe also became imperialistic in the late nineteenth century. In Asia, Japan also developed into an imperialistic power and expanded its holdings; in North America, the United States developed an expansionist philosophy and acquired new territories.

In this era the word "colonization" took on a new meaning, and referred to the political, economic, and social structures created by Europeans in foreign lands that supported their efforts to dominate native cultures. Many political leaders viewed imperialism as the only way to preserve national security, and also saw new colonies as a possible outlet for the population explosion. Further, industrialization had created a need for raw materials to support European manufacturing. Colonies provided a means to get raw materials, as well as an outlet for manufactured goods. Another contributing factor was population growth brought on by the advances of the Industrial Revolution. Parts of Europe were now greatly overpopulated, and one motivation for imperialist expansion was to create opportunities for Europeans elsewhere.

J. A. Hobson

The British economist J. A. Hobson, however, attributed the wave of European imperialist expansion in the late nineteenth century to special new economic forces arising out of the industrialized nations of western and central Europe. Although the British author **Rudyard Kipling** wrote about the **"white man's burden,"** the duty of the Europeans to civilize the barbarous native peoples of other lands, and the French spoke about the mission civilisatrice, or civilizing mission, of the Europeans, Hobson argued that their true motives were based on capitalistic greed for cheap raw materials, advantageous markets, good investments, and fresh fields of exploitation. **Cecil Rhodes** is one of the best examples of Hobson's point of view, since he had made a fortune in the Kimberly diamond fields of South Africa. Ninety percent of the world's diamonds came from these fields, and Rhodes vigorously supported British imperialism in order to preserve his business enterprises. In 1889 Rhodes founded the South Africa Chartered Company to develop the Zambezi valley.

Hobson argued that the "economic taproot of imperialism" was "excessive capital in search of investment," and that this excessive capital was, in essence, the result of unequal distribution of wealth.

Lenin on Imperialism

In his 1916 pamphlet, "Imperialism the Highest Stage of Capitalism," **V. I. Lenin** also suggested that capitalism gave rise to imperialism, and that World War I was the ultimate result of European attempts to dominate world markets. Lenin argued that while the standard of living increased for workers in imperialist countries, Europeans were now exploiting a new kind of proletariat in the colonies.

Interpretive Problems

The main problems with the theses of both Hobson and Lenin were that France led the way in the race towards empire, doubling her colonial holdings between 1815 and 1870 and establishing outposts in Senegal, Indochina, and Algeria. France was, in fact, the least industrialized of all Western nations. Lenin's argument, too, about the quality of life in imperialist countries could not be easily demonstrated, as the standard of living in France, for example, was relatively low for workers as compared to Denmark or Sweden, who had no colonies in the late nineteenth century.

Joseph de Gobineau and Herbert Spencer

Contributing to the European belief in their civilizing mission were new, allegedly "scientific," views, such as those developed by **Count Joseph Arthur de Gobineau**, a French noble who divided humanity into four basic races. Each race had unique characteristics. In his four volume *Essay on the Inequality of the Human Races*, Gobineau argued that Europeans were superior to the other races. Modern sociologists argue that race is a social construct, and biologists argue that there is no such thing as a "pure" race. Gobineau's views, however, combined with Charles Darwin's thesis concerning the survival of the fittest became **"Social Darwinism."** Herbert Spencer argued that stronger and more able individuals competed better and so became more successful. Therefore, European domination of less well-developed cultures was a natural and just situation.

Many modern scholars now reject social Darwinism or the idea of a civilizing mission for Europe. While modern academics are making a strong effort to recover the indigenous history and cultural contributions of those areas of the

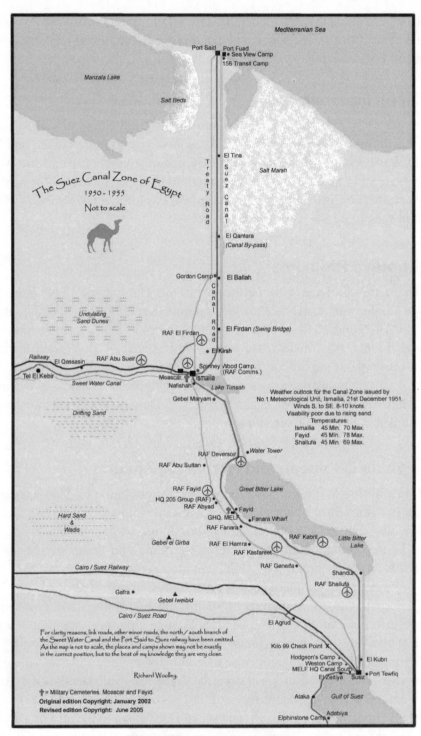

Map of the Suez Canal Area

world colonized by European and American powers, it is difficult to counter the legacy of ill-will created by European beliefs in their cultural supremacy, especially in those areas whose cultures were so denigrated. Further, imperialism created a wider gulf between industrialized nations and those that were not, which still remains today.

New Developments in Technology

The European powers were aided in their efforts to create new empires by the development of military vessels powered by the steam engine. The Opium War was brought to a conclusion in part by an expedition up the Yangtze in 1842 by the British gunboat *Nemesis*. Steam-powered military boats made the most inaccessible regions more accessible.

New canals enabled these new ships to travel to remote parts of the world more quickly. The **Suez Canal** (1859–1869) and the **Panama Canal** (1904–1914) linked oceans and seas and made trade between the imperialist powers and their colonies more profitable. Steamships could now travel between Britain and India via the Suez Canal in less than two weeks. Steam power also made it easier to import goods into Britain from her colonies. Communication was also revolutionized by the development of undersea telegraph cables, which were capable of transmitting messages from Britain to India in about five hours.

Railroads also contributed to the ease of travel and trade, and to the demise of native cultures.

Perhaps the most frightening tools of the imperialist age were the more accurate rifles and machine guns. The power of these weapons is illustrated by events in 1898 near Khartoum, when a British force with only 20 machine guns killed a force of 11,000 Sudanese at Omdurman. The British were fighting for their lives against the Mahdi, who led a massive insurrection against Turkish rule in Egypt, but the Sudanese were no match for the machine gun. The British were one of many European powers involved in a mad "scramble for Africa." They eventually established a regime in the Sudan, but not before the Mahdi defeated British General Gordon Pasha in a shocking victory at Khartoum in January 1885. The Mahdi died shortly thereafter, with shock waves still emanating through the British Empire. Four years later, the British **Lord Kitchner** led a combined force of British and Egyptians to Khartoum and recaptured it. In 1889, they did eventually succeed in controlling the Sudan. The British remained there until the Sudanese won their independence in 1956.

European Explorations of Africa

European explorers helped to chart remote places of Africa. **David Livingstone**, a Scottish minister, explored central and southern Africa in search of suitable locations for missions. The American journalist **Henry Morton Stanley** traveled throughout Africa in search of Livingstone to report on his activities. **Richard Burton** and **John Speke**, both English, explored east Africa in search of the origin of the Nile River. **Serpa Pinto** explored the headwaters of the Cuanza River in Angola and followed the course of the Zambezi River to Victoria Falls in present-day Zimbabwe. Similar events would be recorded in India and other places where the British ruled.

The Scramble for Africa

The "scramble for Africa" officially began when Henry Stanley claimed the Congo River Valley for Belgium. King Leopold II of Belgium, in essence, created a personal colony there, using forced labor on rubber plantations. He essentially thrust out the Portuguese, who had established a colony in the Congo in the fifteenth century. He declared the Congo a free trade area, but his legacy of repressive rule there eventually forced the government of Belgium to take control of the colony in 1908. It then became the **Belgian Congo**.

EUROPEAN IMPERIALISM IN AFRICA

Egypt and the Ottomans

Britain's presence in Egypt grew out of events following the revolt of **Muhammad Ali** (1769–1849), who was pasha of Egypt under the Ottomans. He fought for the Ottomans in the Balkan Wars against Greece until he revolted against his overlords for failure to establish him as governor of Syria. Only the failure of his European allies to support him kept him from toppling the Ottomans. He never successfully established Egypt as a power that could withstand European pressures. Although he attempted to implement Westernized reforms in Egypt, competition from Western goods ultimately brought about the failure of his attempts to industrialize Egypt. Muhammad Ali had insisted that Egypt attempt to increase its production of goods such as cotton for export, leaving it vulnerable in the area of food production and dependent on its cotton exports for survival.

After the construction of the **Suez Canal** transformed Egypt into a strategic location, competition among European powers for influence in Egypt became intense. In 1882 the British occupied Egypt to ensure their access to the Suez Canal, which they virtually stole from the French by becoming the major stockholders.

To the south, in the Sudan, rebellions emerged against both the corrupt Egyptian rulers and their British allies. The most significant of these was led by **Muhammad Achmad**, who in 1881 called himself the **Mahdi**, or "deliverer." He claimed to be appointed by Allah to lead the rebellion against the British intruders and the corrupt Egyptian version of Islam. Although the Mahdi died, it was not until a decade later that the British put down the revolt, continued by his follower

Khalifa Abdallahi. Following the British victory over the Mahdists at the **Battle of Omdurman** in 1898, the way was clear for British domination of Africa.

The French in West Africa

As early as 1659, the French established a trade port on the West African coast at St. Louis in present-day Senegal. Unlike other European powers following the Age of Discovery, France never played a major role in the slave trade and was primarily interested in Africa for trade. During the wave of imperialist expansion in the nineteenth century, the French at first began to move eastward into the savanna regions. Military men such as General Louis Faidherbe primarily led their expansion. By the twentieth century, France controlled much of present-day Senegal, Mali, Burkina Faso, Benin, Guinea, Ivory Coast, and Niger. France also controlled Algeria, Morocco, and Dahomey (part of present-day Benin) in Africa. Out of various territories in West Africa, France created **French West Africa**. Their base remained St. Louis in Senegal, and only there did they allow the native populations any voice in the government created. The French attempted to rule nine million West Africans with a force of only 3,600 men.

France also conquered the region on the north bank of the Congo and created **French Equatorial Africa**. On the east coast France claimed part of Somaliland. By 1896 France had also conquered the island of Madagascar. The leader of Germany, Bismarck, cooperated with the French to counter British influence.

The Berlin West Africa Conference, 1884–1885

Fourteen European nations and the United States determined that any European nation could found a colony in unclaimed territory if it notified the other nations of its intentions. Effective occupation of an area was to take the place of historic precedent, and Portugal was officially thrust out of the Congo. The Conference awarded Mozambique, Angola, and Guinea to Portugal. Not one African attended the conference.

South Africa

The British also established a presence in South Africa well before their occupation of Egypt in 1882. In 1652 the Dutch East India Company had founded Cape Town as a supply station on the route to Asia. Company employees settled there as well as other Europeans and were known as **Boers**. Later, they were called **Afrikaners**, from the Dutch word for "African."

In 1806, the British took over the Cape of Good Hope and drove the Afrikaners further inland. The British abolished one of the key features of Afrikaner life, slavery, prompting the **Great Trek**, or movement northwards, of Afrikaners. Another group moved to the east, and this eastward movement led to conflict between the Afrikaners and the native populations. The voortrekkers, the Afrikaan's word for "pioneers," eventually defeated the Zulu and other groups and created the **Republic of Natal**, the **Orange Free State**, and the **South African Republic**.

The Boer War (1899–1902)

The discovery of diamonds and gold in 1866 and 1867 in Afrikaner territory and subsequent competition for resources eventually led to the **South African** or **Boer War** between the British and Afrikaners. The British defeated the Afrikaners in the war, and by 1920 had carved Afrikaner territory up and created the **Union of South Africa**. As the British sought to reconcile Afrikaner interests with British interests, they often discriminated against black Africans. In fact, black Africans fought on both sides of the Boer War, but the British treatment of them was foreshadowed by their imprisonment of over 100,000 black Africans.

The British method of colonization involved what Frederick Lugard, the British colonial administrator, called **indirect rule**, or relying on indigenous, tribal authorities and local populations to manage the colonies. Other powers, such as the French, practiced more **direct rule**, whereby they appointed officials to rule for them.

Other British Colonies in Africa

By the end of the nineteenth century, the British also took Bechuanaland (1885), Rhodesia (1889), and Nyasaland (1893).

Other Powers in Africa

Germany established German Southwest Africa and German East Africa. The **German East Africa Company** developed this region. By 1914, Germany had acquired new territories of one million square miles and as many as thirteen million people.

Italy formed the **Italian East African Empire** in Eritrea by 1885, and appropriated Asmara and the southern coastal strip of Somaliland in 1889. The **Italian Benadir Company** developed Somaliland. Italy attempted to form a protectorate in the African kingdom of Abyssinia, but the Abyssinians defeated them at Adowa in 1896.

Governments granted monopoly rights to the various companies formed to develop the regions. The Royal Niger Company, for example, colonized Nigeria.

Impact of European Colonization on Africa

In 1875 Europe had colonized less than one-tenth of Africa. By 1895, Europe dominated nine-tenths of the world's second largest continent. Between 1870 and 1900 Britain added 4.25 million square miles and 66 million people to her empire; France added 3.5 million square miles and 26 million people.

At the turn of the century the only independent states south of the Sahara were **Liberia** and **Abyssinia**.

Belgium added new territory to its empire of 900,000 square miles and 8.5 million inhabitants. The colonial empires of Portugal and the Netherlands established during the Age of Exploration became increasingly powerful in this era. Portugal, for example, controlled much of the western coast of Africa and Mozambique.

The languages of modern Africa reflect the colonial period. Portuguese is still the language of trade in Mozambique and areas along the west coast. French and English, for example, continue to be spoken in areas colonized by the Europeans during the nineteenth century.

EUROPEAN IMPERIALISM IN ASIA

The British in Asia

By the 1850s, the British had established rule in India. Britain had taken the lead in the Industrial Revolution of the eighteenth century. Their continuing need for raw materials and outlets for their manufactured goods as a result of the Industrial Revolution prompted further expansionistic tendencies. Intense rivalry with France in the eighteenth century also played a role in British expansion. Britain fought five global wars with the French during the reign of Louis XIV. British imperialism was motivated by a desire to protect her national security and possible outlets for her goods, especially after the loss of her North American colonies as a result of the American Revolution. Following these events, her colony in India took on special significance.

After the British established factories at Bombay, Madras, and Calcutta in the seventeenth century during the Mughal period, the **East India Tea Company** expanded to the interior of India and bit by bit won rights to govern areas there. **Robert Clive** defeated the army of Siraj-ud-daulah, the Nawab of Bengal, at the **Battle of Plassey** in 1757. He bribed the Nawab's soldiers and his chief rival, and so began the British Raj domination of India and the transformation of the East India Tea Company from traders to the rulers of Bengal and eventually to all of India.

In 1760 the British defeated their French rivals for India at Wandiwash and in 1761 at Pondicherry, thus paving the way for complete domination. In 1765, the East India Tea Company acquired the right of the diwani of Bengal, or the right to collect revenue in the name of the Mughal emperors in the Bengal region. British rule in India would last nearly two hundred years.

In 1803, the British **General Wellesley**, who was governor general of British India, continued to expand British control when he defeated the Maratha chieftains. He began to build an empire in India through conquest of several native rulers or making treaties with them.

The Sepoy Mutiny

The British controlled their conquests with British forces, supplemented by larger numbers of Indian troops called sepoys. Rebellions against the British culminated in the 1857 **Sepoy Mutiny**. The chief cause of this revolt was the refusal of the Hindu troops to use animal grease on the cartridges of their Enfield rifles. Soldiers had to bite off the end of the cartridges to load the rifles, which violated both Islamic and Hindu beliefs. Muslims worried that the fat might be from pigs, prohibited animals under their dietary laws, while Hindus feared it was from cows, prohibited by their beliefs.

By June, nearly 90,000, about 70 percent of the Bengal army's Sepoy force, were involved in the mutiny. The Sepoy defeated the British at the Kanpur garrison and Lucknow, but the British army, helped by their Sikh and Gurkha forces, eventually stopped the rebellion. This marked the final defeat of the Mughal Empire.

The British Parliament then replaced the East India Tea Company with a **Secretary of State for India**, who was directly responsible to the British Cabinet. In November 1858, Queen Victoria gave the governor-general of India the title of **viceroy**.

British Contributions to Indian Society

The British built railroads and telegraph lines in India and developed a postal system, all of which improved communication. They cleared large areas of forest and planted coffee, tea, and opium crops for trade in their growing imperial world. From China, the British brought tea to Ceylon and India, where they cleared forests to plant tea plantations. Native women were used in the labor force, and tea was then exported to Europe. The approximate monetary value of tea exported from south Asia rose from 309,000 pounds sterling in 1866 to 6.1 million pounds sterling in 1900. Similarly, British rule in other parts of Asia transformed economic production, such as in Malaysia and Sumatra, where the British planted rubber trees in the1870s and began to export these commodities to the rest of the world.

The American Civil War prompted the British to search for a new source of cotton in India, and Indian cotton began to be produced for export rather than internal use. Export of cotton increased from 10 million rupees in 1849 to 410 million rupees in 1913. Simultaneously, the British imported textiles, and these imports undermined the native Indian market for finished cloth. India was once the principal producer of cotton cloth, but was now transformed into a consumer of British imports and their chief supplier of raw cotton.

English goods produced by machine, however, weakened the market for the traditional Indian village artisan. Poverty increased and Indian agriculture collapsed. A serious drought in the 1870s created widespread famine throughout India.

The British united all of India, including present-day Pakistan and Bangladesh, as well as Sri Lanka or Ceylon under a single government. The British hoped to consolidate their presence by transforming India through Western education. Many of those so educated became officials in the British government, and served as lawyers, businessmen, and teachers. The newly educated Indians, however, became the backbone of strong opposition groups to the British. Although the British had hoped to eradicate many native traditions through education, if anything, education provided a force for strengthening opposition by exposing the Hindus to such ideals as freedom, justice, and equality. Despite the activities of the Indian National Congress, Britain would rule India until 1949.

The Late Nineteenth Century

In the late nineteenth century, Germany was beginning to take the lead in the Second Industrial Revolution. As other European powers rushed to colonize various parts of the world, Britain worried that her European rivals would close foreign markets and also, consequently, take away possible sources of raw materials. Germany's rapid progress in the Second Industrial Revolution and her move to colonize Africa, coupled with French imperialism in Asia, posed a threat to Britain's position among European nations.

The British in China

British trade in opium eventually negated Chinese supremacy in trade and eventually resulted in the downfall of the Qing dynasty. Although the Chinese prohibited its use in 1800, by the 1830s more than 30,000 chests of opium, each of which held about 150 pounds of the extract, were entering China each year. In 1839 the Chinese were desperate enough to burn several tons of opium in Canton. The British surrounded Canton, and in 1842, they defeated the Chinese in the First Opium War. According to the **Treaty of Nanjing**, the Chinese lost **Hong Kong** to the British, who held it until the late twentieth century, when it reverted back to China. The treaty forced the Chinese to open other ports to the British, and by 1844, the French and Americans had a trading presence in China as well. The French allied with the British to fight a **Second Opium War**, which led once again to the defeat of China in 1856. The **Treaty of Tientsin** (Tianjin, 1858) opened new ports to trading and allowed foreigners with passports to travel in the interior of China. The Chinese granted Christians the right to spread their faith and to own property, and in separate treaties, the United States and Russia received similar privileges.

Following the victories in the Opium Wars, China experienced a wave of antiforeign sentiment in the Boxer and other rebellions. The British helped to put this and other rebellions down and established a power base in China. For more coverage of the aftermath of the Opium Wars, consult Chapter 20.

The French in Asia

Christianity began to spread in Vietnam during the nineteenth century. The ruling powers believed that Christianity posed a threat to their Confucian values, and outlawed Christianity. When Christianity continued to spread, the Vietnamese began to executing missionaries. France retaliated by taking Saigon and three other provinces in the south of Vietnam from 1859–1860. In 1884–1885, the French succeeded in conquering the rest of Vietnam. By 1887 **French Indochina** included Vietnam, Laos, and Cambodia. By that time, the only area of Southeast Asia that was not ruled by Europeans was **Siam (Thailand)**.

EUROPEAN IMPERIALISM IN THE PACIFIC

The Aboriginals of Australia

In 1770 **Captain James Cook** landed in Botany Bay, Australia. The voyages of Captain Cook opened up Australia to European colonization. In 1788, a group of migrants who were mostly convicted criminals founded the colony of New South Wales. The British argued that Australia was terra nullius, or land belonging to no one, that could be seized and used at will. By 1900 they had pushed the aboriginal population into reservations in regions that were largely desert.

The Maori of New Zealand

When Europeans colonized the New World during the Age of Exploration, they brought smallpox and other diseases that devastated the native populations. This was also true in New Zealand, where the native **Maori** population dropped from 200,000 to 45,000 within a century following the arrival of timber traders in New Zealand in 1790. European firearms also created more tension among the warlike Maori. The arrival of British farmers and herders in the mid-nineteenth century eventually culminated in a series of wars from 1860–1864, after which the British forced the Maori to reservations. Western education, however, gave some Maori the ability to fight for their rights, and the Maori continued to survive despite their near extermination.

Other Islands

The European powers that colonized Africa wasted no time in competing for the Pacific Islands. France had created colonial governments by 1880 in Tahiti and New Caledonia, while Britain took Fiji, and Germany took most of the Marshal Islands. The **Berlin Conference of 1884–1885** also divided up the Pacific Islands, with the United States and Germany dividing Samoa.

THE IMPACT OF EUROPEAN IMPERIALISM: COMPARATIVE PATTERNS IN AFRICA AND ASIA

Western colonization of Africa and Asia brought mixed results. In India, the availability of Western education created a new middle class of educated professionals, opening new job opportunities for native peoples. These professionals, however, were usually paid less than Europeans performing similar tasks in government or industry. Western ideas also provided a common foundation for those who were colonized. Since often there were many different ethnicities or tribal alliances that were in conflict before the Europeans came, Western education created a common framework. However, in places like Africa, Europeans often arbitrarily forced the warring peoples together into "tribes." After World War I, when Europeans began to lose their colonial empires, these forced alliances split apart with great force.

The newly educated class of colonized peoples in places like India often felt separated from those who still followed a traditional way of life. Western education had created in them a new mindset that distanced them from others not given such opportunities. Further, in India, those who received Western education were exactly those who later led rebellions against the British presence in India. Partly because of the difficulties in India and also largely due to racist assumptions about black Africans, colonizers in Africa did not provide as many opportunities for Africans to receive a Western-style education. In Africa, introduction to Western education was largely the work of Christian missionaries. Even here, however, few Africans were admitted to the priesthood of the Roman Catholic Church. As Europeans became more convinced of their racial supremacy in the late nineteenth century, the gulf between European colonizers and native peoples continued to widen.

European colonization also brought dramatic changes to daily lives of many native peoples. While Europeans brought with them consumer goods, in general, native peoples were used to produce raw materials or crops needed in Europe.

In the Belgian Congo, villagers who could not meet their expected production quota were beaten and, in some cases, killed. Taxes were imposed that could be paid in crops needed for transport to Europe. Uncultivated areas of land were now used to produce cocoa, hemp, rubber, and other items destined for export. Even fields that had been under cultivation for food crops were transformed into producers of export commodities. Unfortunately, while native peoples were used to work these lands, the profits went to European manufacturers and so did the manufactured goods. In Africa and India, especially, the economy was dependent on the global market for their resources, and this market was dominated and controlled by Europeans.

Imperialism in Africa and India and parts of Asia created a system whereby these continents were economically, politically, and socially subjugated to European powers. The long-term effects of Imperialism lingered even after the Western powers lost their colonies as a result of the total wars of the twentieth century.

THE UNITED STATES EMERGES AS AN IMPERIAL POWER

Although the United States historically had pursued a policy of isolationism going back to its founding fathers, in the nineteenth century it became a world power that intruded often into international affairs. **The Monroe Doctrine** in 1823 effectively put the Western Hemisphere under U.S. domination, as Monroe warned European nations against imperialist activity in the Western Hemisphere.

In 1867, the **purchase of Alaska** increased U.S. territory in North America, while in 1875 **Hawaii** became a U.S. protectorate. In 1893 a group of white planters overthrew the last queen, Lili'uokalani, with the help of the U.S. Minister to Hawaii, John Stevens, the U.S. Minister to Hawaii, and a contingent of marines from the warship U.S.S. *Boston*. Acting without the permission of the U.S. State Department, Stevens declared that Hawaii was now a U.S. protectorate. Most native Hawaiians opposed this action. Although the next president, Grover Cleveland, strongly criticized Stevens and the overthrow of Queen Lili'uokalani, Hawaii became a republic in 1894. When rebellion erupted, many natives were arrested along with Queen Lili'uokalani. The U.S. eventually annexed the islands in 1898.

Those who subscribed to the U.S. doctrine of **manifest destiny** (see Chapter 28) had always hinted at the desire to annex Cuba, one of the last remaining bastions of Spanish power. When the **U.S. battleship *Maine*** exploded in Havana harbor in 1898, the U.S. accused Spain of treachery and the **Spanish-American War** began. In 1899 the United States defeated Spain, taking Cuba and Puerto

Rico; soon thereafter, the U.S. took the Philippines and Guam from Spain. President William McKinley paid Spain $20 million for the Philippines, but the U.S. soon became involved in a bloody revolt led by Emilio Aguinaldo. The main thrust of the revolt ended in 1902, but it took a massive toll on human life and insurrections continued until 1906.

The acquisition of new territories of the United States required the construction of the **Panama Canal**, a way to more efficiently travel from the Atlantic to the Pacific Ocean without circumventing South America. President Theodore Roosevelt incited rebellion in Colombia to accomplish his goal, and helped the rebels establish a new state, Panama. Roosevelt's policy of the **"Big Stick"** also contributed to the further development of imperialistic aspirations and behavior.

THE RISE OF JAPAN AS AN IMPERIAL POWER

The industrial transformation of Japan during the Meiji period also inspired expansionist tendencies. Japan began to expand in the Pacific in the 1870s, when it encouraged Japanese settlers to live on Hokkaido and the Kurile Islands in an effort to block Russian expansion. By 1879, they had hegemony over Okinawa and the Ryukyu Islands, and now controlled the islands to the south and north of the four islands of Japan.

In 1876 they expanded control over Korean trade through an unequal treaty such as imposed on Asia by the Western powers after the Opium Wars. In 1894, the Koreans began a series of protests over foreign intrusion, leading the Chinese to send a force to restore order there and to reassert their authority. In August 1894 the Meiji government in Japan declared war on China. In a five-hour battle, the Japanese defeated the Qing (Ching) navy on the Yellow Sea and within only a few months took control of Korea. China recognized it as independent, and ceded Taiwan, the Pescadores Islands, and the Laiodong Peninsula to Japan. Japan also gained unequal rights in China that paralleled those of the United States and Europe following the Opium Wars.

These gains created tension with Russia, who had desires for much of the territory controlled by Japan, in particular Korea and the Liaodong Peninsula. Manchuria was also a common interest. The Japanese escalated their military buildup, and in 1904, the **Russo-Japanese War** broke out. The Russian Baltic fleet sailed halfway around the world to meet the Japanese, but the Japanese quickly routed them and won control of Sakhalin Island and a railroad in Manchuria. The Russo-Japanese War firmly established acceptance of Korea as a colonial territory of Japan.

Like the Europeans, the Japanese often justified their brutal imperialist regimes on the basis of their alleged racial superiority. Just as European imperialism has been condemned on this basis, so too, many scholars condemn the Japanese racist views that emerged as they became one of the major world imperial powers. The long-term effects of their quick rise to prominence culminated in World War II.

IMPERIALISM AND THE LABOR FORCE: CHANGING MIGRATION PATTERNS

In the nineteenth century, approximately 56 million Europeans left Europe and migrated to other areas in source of work. The poor of Southern and Eastern Europe migrated to the United States in the late nineteenth century, whereas earlier in the century, many from Britain, Ireland, Germany, and Scandinavia had gone to the United States. Their labor helped to support the U.S. move toward industrialization in the late nineteenth century, such as in the steel and railroad industries. Other migrants went to newly formed parts of the British Empire, such as Australia and New Zealand, where they often became herders or cultivators.

There was also a mass migration of Asians, Africans, and Pacific Islanders in the nineteenth century. Most of these migrants sold their services as indentured laborers. Many European powers had abolished slavery in the nineteenth century; when the trans-Atlantic trade in slaves ended, and plantation owners needed another labor force. Workers got free passage and food and shelter in exchange for their services. They pledged to work from five to seven years in most cases. Most indentured labor originated in India, but there were also laborers who came from China, Japan, Africa, the Pacific Islands, and Java. While the European migrants went to temperate climates, the indentured laborers went to tropical and subtropical areas in the Americas, Africa, the Caribbean, and Oceania. After the Opium Wars, Chinese migrants went to sugar plantations in Cuba and Hawaii, mines in various parts of the world, and railroad construction sites in the United States and other parts of the Americas.

The new migrations changed the makeup of the population in many parts of the world. As the ethnic makeup of various areas became more diverse and complex, tension often erupted. In the United States, for example, an effort was made to stop the flow of foreign migrations from certain areas, especially those from Central and Eastern Europe and Asia. The **Johnson-Reed Act** of 1924 **(the Permanent National Origins Quota Act)**, for example, implemented a quota system according to which countries could send legal immigrants to the United States in proportion to the percentage of the U.S. population (in 1924) who were of that particular nationality.

Review Questions

1. Which of the following is NOT a correct description of the European scramble for Africa?

    (A) Belgium ruthlessly grabbed land and abused its African subjects, forcing them to work.

    (B) The Afrikaners emerged victorious over Britain and stopped the British advance into the heart of Africa.

    (C) Africa and other underdeveloped areas provided raw materials and exported crops for European industrialists.

    (D) European colonizers brought Western education and transportation systems to the areas colonized.

2. Which of the following is NOT a correct description of Western Imperialism?

    (A) It prompted new waves of migration from Central and Eastern Europe and from Asia, Africa, and the South Pacific.

    (B) Europeans subjugated colonized peoples in part through lesser pay for professional work.

    (C) Europeans cultivated previously uncultivated lands in Africa.

    (D) Europeans focused on food crops in colonized areas and increased the food supply for their subjects.

3. Which nation was associated with indirect rule?

    (A) France

    (B) Japan

    (C) Britain

    (D) Belgium

4. Which of the following areas was NOT colonized by European powers in the nineteenth century?

    (A) India

    (B) Indochina

    (C) New Zealand

    (D) Thailand (Siam)

5. During the Opium Wars, the British defeated and earned trading rights from the

   (A) Ming Chinese.

   (B) Ching Chinese.

   (C) People's Republic of China.

   (D) Koreans.

6. Among the factors that prompted European Imperialism were

   (A) overpopulation.

   (B) industrialization and the need for raw materials.

   (C) poverty.

   (D) Both (A) and (B).

7. Which of the following does NOT describe the British contribution to India?

   (A) The British built railroads.

   (B) The British brought Western education to India.

   (C) The British improved communications.

   (D) The British strengthened the native Indian village industries.

8. The beginning of British rule in India followed

   (A) the Battle of Plassey and the defeat of the Nawab of Bengal.

   (B) the Sepoy Mutiny.

   (C) their conquest of the Deccan Plateau.

   (D) the fall of the Ottomans.

9. The theorist who suggested that European imperialism arose out of the desire for raw materials, advantageous markets, and desire to invest capital was

   (A) Rudyard Kipling.

   (B) J. A. Hobson.

   (C) Charles Darwin.

   (D) Herbert Spencer.

10. The theorist who argued that humans were divided into four racial types with different characteristics was

   (A) Rudyard Kipling.

   (B) J. A. Hobson.

(C) Charles Darwin.

(D) Count Joseph Arthur de Gobineau

11. What event began the "scramble for Africa"?

(A) The search for David Livingstone

(B) The exploitation of the Zambezi valley by Cecil Rhodes

(C) Stanley's claim to the Congo River for Belgium

(D) The French presence in Algeria

12. Which European power was most influential in West Africa?

(A) Belgium

(B) England

(C) Germany

(D) France

13. Which of the following was NOT true of the Boer War?

(A) It began over competition for diamonds and other resources between the British and Afrikaners.

(B) Black Africans became valued allies of the British and were given special favors for military assistance.

(C) The Union of South Africa was one result of the war.

(D) The British defeated the Afrikaners.

14. What is the language of trade in Mozambique and along the west coast of Africa?

(A) English

(B) French

(C) Portuguese

(D) Swahili

15. In what ways did European imperialism affect world trade?

(A) India became the leading producer of finished cotton cloth.

(B) Tea declined in value as an export commodity.

(C) The British began to produce more raw cotton for export.

(D) Britain exported textiles to India and undermined its native industries.

16. The Russo-Japanese War

   (A) was fought over control of Japan.

   (B) established Japanese control over Korea.

   (C) ceded Manchuria to the Russians.

   (D) ceded the Liaodong Peninsula to the Russians.

17. Which of the following is true of migration patterns in the Age of Imperialism?

   (A) Migration created ethnic tensions in many parts of the world as populations became more diverse.

   (B) Europeans migrated to subtropical areas.

   (C) Nations became less ethnically diverse and minorities left in search of other homelands.

   (D) Nations received migrants with open arms and used them for cheap labor.

Answers

1. (B)	6. (D)	11. (C)	16. (B)
2. (D)	7. (D)	12. (D)	17. (A)
3. (C)	8. (A)	13. (B)	
4. (D)	9. (B)	14. (C)	
5. (B)	10. (D)	15. (D)	

UNIT VII

A "Short Century?"
The World from World
War I Through the
Collapse of the Soviet
Union in 1991

Chapter 30

WORLD WAR I (1914–1918) AND ITS AFTERMATH

KEY TERMS

Total War	Ataturk
Mobilization	Zimmermann Telegram
Pan-Slavism	League of Nations
Serbs	Collective Security
Archduke Ferdinand	Short Century
Central Powers	Eric Hobsbawm
Allies	Freudian psychology
Schlieffen Plan	Heisenberg Uncertainty Principle
Belgian Neutrality	Isolationism
Trench Warfare	Return to normalcy
Western Front	Great Depression
Eastern Front	Black Thursday
Ottomans	John Maynard Keynes
Lawrence of Arabia	New Deal

OVERVIEW

World War I was the first war to encompass more than half the globe. It was also known as **The Great War** or "the war to end all wars," *at least before* World War II usurped that distinction. The term "world war" was first coined in the 1920s by Lieutenant Colonel à Court Repington in *The First World War 1914–18*. Some scholars have suggested that the First World War is more properly thought of as the first phase of a 30-year-long war that began with World War I and ended with the termination of hostilities in World War II in 1945.

In World War I 28 nations, the **Allies** and Associated Powers, fought four others nations or empires known as the **Central Powers**: Germany, Austria-Hungary, Bulgaria, and the Ottoman Empire. WWI was the first "total war" in history, as those involved used every resource available for the war effort. For the first time, people referred to the "home front," which referred to the mobilization at home of resources for the military front. Mobilization at home drained countries of their males who were old enough to fight, creating a vacuum in the workforce. Many women, particularly in Britain and the United States, went to work in factories making war products. The work was often very dangerous and women demanded more equal wages. In the wake of the war, women earned the right to vote in America, Great Britain, Germany, and Austria. The poor in America and Europe benefited from mobilization, as new work provided more funds than ever for basic needs.

During the war, European and American governments exerted more control over economies in an effort to generate needed supplies for war, and in Europe in particular, countries began to move toward **planned economies**.

The Great War brought about the end of the German Empire, the Ottoman Empire, the Russian Empire, and the Austro-Hungarian Empire. It created nine new nations. The First World War also brought about the end of the global supremacy Europe had enjoyed beginning in the Age of Discovery and reaching a high-point during its imperialist phase in the nineteenth century.

Nationalism

The rise of nationalist movements in the nineteenth century culminated in World War I. Independence movements erupted in the early nineteenth century and threatened the Ottoman world, when Greece won independence in 1830. At the Congress of Berlin, the Ottomans lost further territories, as the Austro-Hungarian Empire occupied Bosnia and Herzogovina. Serbia became independent.

Serbia was the center of many nationalistic aspirations. The Serbs wished to unite the various Slavic peoples within the Austro-Hungarian Empire. Poles, Czechs, Slovaks, and Croats bitterly struggled for independence. The Serb struggle was the most threatening to the Austro-Hungarian Empire and to peace in Europe. Tsarist Russia's support of Pan-Slavism furthered these rebellions in the hopes of eventually annexing them as part of the Russian Empire. In 1908 the Austro-Hungarian Empire had formally annexed Bosnia and Herzogovina, which had large populations of Serbs, Croats, and also Muslims, creating further tension between Serbia and Austria.

When Serbia, along with Greece and Bulgaria, fought the Ottoman Empire in the First Balkan War, Austria-Hungary attempted to control Serbian expansion. From 1912–1913, the Balkan states of Bulgaria, Greece, Montenegro, Serbia, and Romania fought two wars over territories held in Europe by the Ottomans.

Imperialism

The late-nineteenth-century colonial empires of Britain, France, Russia, and Germany had created conflict across the globe. Starting in 1905, a series of conflicts over colonial possessions erupted, laying a foundation for World War I. Although Germany was rather late in joining the imperialist colonization of Africa, for example, Germany often conflicted with Britain and France over its aspirations in Africa. In Morocco, the Germans supported the movement for independence against France. Britain had several disputes with other powers, such as France, as a result of its expanding presence as a colonial empire, leading to the creation of some of the treaties described below. While these treaties resolved some of the tensions in the nineteenth century, they created a system of alliances that quickly came into place during the early phases of World War I. European involvement in various parts of the globe during the late nineteenth century had created tensions that colored the more immediate events that gave rise to World War I.

Alliance Building

In the latter half of the nineteenth century, the nations of Europe participated in alliance building on a grand scale. The purpose was to form alliances for mutual defense, alliances to isolate potential enemies, and alliances to negate the potential of other nations to engage in wars that would threaten the security of one's own nation.

The great German statesman Bismarck led the way, making his Prussian-dominated Germany a great power in central Europe through treaties that, he hoped, would keep Germany's enemies weak and Germany's neighbors at peace.

Major Treaties that Created the System of Alliances

1873: Three Emperor's League: An alliance of Germany, Austria-Hungary, and Russia

1879–1918: Austrian-German Alliance (Dual Alliance)

1881–1887: Alliance of the Three Emperors: An Alliance of Germany, Austria-Hungary, and Russia

1882–1914: The Triple Alliance: An alliance of Germany, Austria-Hungary, and Italy

1887–1890: Russian-German Reinsurance Treaty, whereby Germany and Russia pledged neutrality in the event of an attack by a third party, provided Russia did not attack Austria or Germany attack France

1894: Franco-Russian Alliance

1902–1915: Anglo-Japanese Alliance

1904: Anglo-French Entente

1907: Anglo-Russian Entente

1907–1914: Triple Entente: An agreement between Russia, France, and Great Britain

These alliances, treaties, and agreements were intended to prevent war between the various nations of Europe. Instead, they formed an inescapable web so that what affected one, affected all.

By 1914, Europe's major powers were divided into two opposing camps: the **Triple Alliance** and the **Triple Entente**. The Triple Alliance became the Central Powers of World War I, and had grown out of the Dual Alliance of the treaty of 1879 formed for mutual protection against Russia. In 1882 Italy joined this alliance, creating the Triple Alliance. This alliance was tenuous at best, as Italy threatened German relations with the Ottomans and Austria-Hungary's possessions in the Balkans.

During the Franco-Prussian War of the nineteenth century, France had suffered a humiliating defeat. They were determined to contain the Germans. Russia feared the German-Austrian-Hungarian alliance, and Britain still feared events such as had happened in the Napoleonic Wars and tried to preserve the balance of power. Britain, France, and Russia, then, together formed the Triple Entente or the Allies of World War I. Between 1904 and 1914, Britain and France had signed a treaty (Anglo-French Entente) and so had Britain and Russia (Anglo-Russian Entente) over their colonial possessions.

The Event that Sparked a World War: The Assassination of Archduke Ferdinand and Sophie

On June 28, 1914, a Serbian revolutionary and member of the radical **Black Hand** group, Gavrilo Princip, assassinated **Archduke Franz Ferdinand** of Austria-Hungary and his wife Sophie in **Sarajevo**, which was the administrative center of Bosnia. The Black Hand wanted the unification of all Yugoslavs or South Slavs to form Serbia. Austria-Hungary was determined to punish the Serbs for this event. As a result of a treaty of alliance, Germany supported its neighbor Austria-Hungary while Russia supported its ethnic kinsmen the Serbs and their bid for independence, setting the stage for war in Eastern Europe. On July 23, the Austrians issued an ultimatum to Serbia, demanding the right to participate in the investigation of the assassination. The Serbs declined, and on July 28, the Austrians declared war on Serbia. In July, Austria-Hungary declared war on Russia, as Russia was mobilizing to defend the Serbs. In August, Germany responded by declaring war on Russia, followed by a declaration of war on France. Russia had been allied with France since the Dual Alliance between Russia and France in 1894, and in the Triple Entente, which included England. Therefore, Germany would have expected the French to join in the hostilities.

War Strategies

The alliances and plans for military mobilization based on projected points of conflict ensured that war could not be confined to one region. Austria moved against Belgrade, while Russia mobilized and prepared to attack both Austria and Germany.

The French based their maneuvers on **Plan XVII**, which relied on offensive attacks without concern for the opponent's strategy. French actions helped account for many of the massive casualties in the war.

The Germans wanted to avoid a war on two fronts, as this might mean that Germany would be surrounded. They relied on the **Schlieffen Plan** developed by Count Alfred von Schlieffen in 1905 that directed their first assaults on France and then focused on defending Germany from Russian attacks. Germany believed it would take a few weeks to mobilize the Russian forces, giving them the necessary time to knock the French out of the conflict.

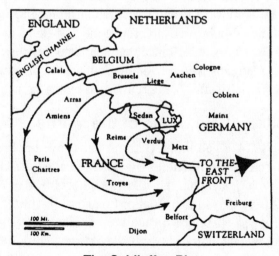

The Schlieffen Plan

German Advance

Germany, confident in its military, then marched west rather than east in their effort to knock France out of the war. Standing between Germany and its target of France was neutral Belgium. **Belgium's neutrality** in such conflicts had been recognized and supported by its more aggressive neighbors since 1839. Victory for Germany in France depended on its ability to invade swiftly. The German armies would have to enter France through Belgium. Belgium refused to grant Germany permission to pass its borders. Germany refused to be denied and attacked the neutral country in August 1914.

Germany failed to achieve the expected swift victory; its offensive stalled short of Paris. The two combatants flanked each other in a series of moves known as the "race to the sea." Paris was the objective of the German push. With the capture of Paris, France would fall and the Western Front of the war would be under German control. The German army drove hard into France, pushing the allied forces before it. The year ended with the two sides digging into a line of trenches marking the **Western Front**. The opposing armies engaged in the meat-grinder horrors of **trench warfare**. The majority of the action on the Western Front took place along a narrow line running from the coast of France to Alsace-Lorraine. Within this narrow area, the combatant forces pushed back and forth, gaining a few miles here and there only to lose it again, neither able to achieve the break-through victory it sought.

The German plan failed in part because Germany had expected Belgium to either allow the German army to pass or to offer minimal resistance. Instead the Belgian army fought well against the overwhelming superior German forces and withdrew in orderly fashion to the allies in France rather than breaking and running. Their efforts delayed the progress of the German army, allowing the British forces time to join with the French. German fear of a potential French invasion across the border between Germany and France had prompted them to leave behind some of their forces to protect the homeland, and so they sent a smaller number of troopers into France than mandated by the Schlieffen Plan. Consequently, the Germans were unable to counter the unexpected resistance of the Belgians, especially after being reinforced by the French.

Germans Halted at the Battle of the Marne

In September 1914, a gap in the German lines gave the French the opportunity to counterattack. The **Battle of the Marne** halted the German advance and forced the Germans back, but the allies were not able to mount an offensive strong enough to drive the Germans out of France.

The loss of life was on a scale difficult to imagine. In 1916 over 1,800,000 men were killed or wounded in just two battles; there were 1,100,000 combined casualties in the **Battle of the Somme** while there were 700,000 casualties in the longest battle of the war at **Verdun**. Those who did survive war on the Western Front were forever transformed by the carnage.

Battles of Verdun and the Somme

In 1916, the Germans attempted to break out of the trenches with an assault on **Verdun**, a fortress. The French were determined that "they shall not pass," and although they succeeded in stopping the Germans, the loss of life was frightening. At the **Battle of the Somme**, British forces attacked the Germans to help relieve pressure on Verdun. By November, the British had advanced only a few yards at tremendous cost of life. By 1916, neither side had managed to gain a strategic advantage.

The Eastern Front

The Eastern Front, with Germany and Austria-Hungary opposing Russia, was a different type of war. The Russian army mobilized and moved into eastern Germany where it faced stiff opposition from the German forces. The Germans were well commanded by Generals Paul von Hindenburg and Erich Ludendorff. The Battle of Tannenberg in August and the Battle of the Masurian Lakes in September 1914 drove the Russians back. They would not be able to mount another major offensive against Germany for the rest of the war.

In the Austro-Hungarian campaign, the Russians fared little better. Unable to make any progress against the Austro-Hungarian forces, they were soundly repulsed when the Germans were able to join the campaign. By 1915 the Russians had been driven back to their own territory, having suffered 2.5 million lost, captured, injured, or killed.

Other nations weighed in. In 1914, Italy had declared itself neutral only to reverse its position and join the Triple Entente of Great Britain, France, and Russia in 1915. Italy had not been able to resist the possibility of territorial gains at the expense of Austria. Bulgaria was neutral in 1914, but followed the Ottoman Empire in joining the Central Powers of Germany and Austria in 1915, lured by the possibility of defeating Serbia.

The Ottoman Empire

The entry of the Ottoman Empire into the war is significant because it broke the war from the confines of Europe and spread it to the Middle East. In 1915 **Winston Churchill**, who was then first lord of the admiralty, suggested a strike against Ottoman territories in an effort to distract the Germans. The British launched an attack in the **Dardanelles**, a strait through which supplies might be shipped to Russia. At **Gallipoli**, a heavy force of Ottomans defended the straits. The Allies dug their trenches and the result was a disaster. There were over

250,000 casualties at Gallipoli. Although the British led the campaign, many of its colonials actually fought. Following the war, the resentment of the Canadian, Australian, and New Zealander soldiers weakened the British Empire. The leader of the Turkish defense, **Mustafa Kemal**, formed the Turkish Republic and became known as **Ataturk**, "father of the Turks." **Lawrence of Arabia**, a British colonel, also took advantage of Ottoman weakness and aided the Arab revolt of **Ibn Ali Hussain**, sheriff of Mecca and king of the Hejaz, against the Ottoman Turks in 1917. The Ottoman Empire came to an end in 1918 as a result of defeat at the hands of the British, who employed troops drawn for the far reaches of the British Empire.

Conflicts Over Colonial Territories

The colonial territories of the warring European nations played significant parts in the war. British and French colonies remained loyal, providing food and supplies to the war effort and helping to take control of German colonies, thus removing Germany's ability to draw on its colonial resources. In Africa, the British and French gradually took the four colonies Germany held. Many Africans fought in the trenches of World War I in Europe and also provided a labor for the Allies. Meanwhile, the Japanese, allies of the British, moved against German possessions in the Pacific and in China. Japan captured the Shandong Peninsula and several islands possessed by Germany. The captured German island possessions later became the basis of Japan's line of defense in the Pacific during World War II. Japanese aggression also added to the tension existing between China and Japan.

United States Enters the War

In February 1917, the United States ambassador to the United Kingdom, Walter H. Page, obtained a copy of the **Zimmermann Telegram**, which helped to thrust the U.S. into the World War. In the telegram, which was sent by Germany to Mexico, the Germans offered to return the southwestern portion of the United States to Mexico if Mexico would declare war on the United States. The resumption of unrestricted submarine warfare also contributed to the U.S. decision to enter the war. The sinking of the passenger liner *Lusitania* in 1915 with 139 Americans on board had outraged the United States. Germany had quickly changed its policy for submarine warfare from one of total blockade in which any ship was a legitimate target to a more relaxed stance and so avoided war with the United States. By 1917, Germany felt the possibility of starving Britain was worth risking the enmity of the United States and had gone back to a policy of unrestricted warfare. U.S. President Woodrow Wilson declared Germany's new stance to be "warfare against mankind." The United States entered the war on the side of the Triple Alliance in April 1917.

Russia Makes Peace with Germany

The **Russian Revolution** crippled the already failing effort of the Russian army to combat Germany. In February 1918, Russia accepted Germany's peace terms, leaving Germany free to turn its attention back to the Western Front.

The Second Battle of the Marne

In the spring of 1918 Germany launched a new offensive in France, attempting once again to reach Paris. The Germans were stopped at the **Second Battle of the Marne** in July 1918. One-hundred-forty-thousand American troops joined the exhausted Allies in stopping the German advance. By August the Americans had committed two million men to the war effort.

This influx of the fresh Americans into the lines of the war-weary Allies proved to be the deciding factor in the war. By October 1918 the Allies had pushed the Germans back and the Germans were prepared to ask for peace terms.

Kaiser Wilhelm II Abdicates

The peace negotiations dragged on beyond the endurance of the German people. By November, mutiny and revolution were realities in Germany. Austria-Hungary surrendered, leaving Germany fighting on its own, but not for long. Before the end of November, Kaiser Wilhelm II abdicated, a German republic was declared, and Germany surrendered. By the end of the war, the Ottoman, Austria-Hungarian, German, and Russian Empires no longer existed.

The Treaty of Versailles

In 1919 the victorious powers met in Paris at the **Paris Peace Conference** to negotiate the fate of the nations. Woodrow Wilson went to Versailles with high hopes of crafting a lasting peace. He presented his **Fourteen Points**, advocating open treaties, free navigation of the seas, and equality of trading conditions. Chief among the Fourteen Points was his call for the creation of "a general association of nations," which became the **League of Nations**. Other Allies had other priorities, specifically the punishment of Germany. Clemenceau of France was particularly determined to see Germany punished and permanently crippled so that it could never again threaten France. Lloyd George of Britain was not as strident, but had to consider the opinion of the British people who, having had their lives forever changed by the war, were still angry and wanted retribution.

Wilson was able to deny France's most punishing demands with the support of the personally moderate Lloyd George. Clemenceau did not achieve the secure buffer zone he sought for France, but gained the promise from Britain and the United States that each would come to the aide of France should France be attacked again. Germany lost little territory within Europe, but all of its colonial holdings were divided among the victorious Allies.

Germany was allowed to maintain an army, but its size was limited to no more than 100,000. Germany was allowed to keep the Rhineland, but was not allowed to place military installations there. Germany returned Alsace-Lorraine to France. A part of northeastern Germany that was inhabited largely by Poles was given to the newly created **Poland**, an action in line with the national self-determination beliefs espoused by Wilson and others.

Wilson could not block the demand for **reparations**. The Allies insisted the fault for the war be laid squarely on Germany and Austria. Further, Germany would have to pay an undetermined amount of reparations for the destruction resulting from the war. Germany protested the terms of the treaty, but as it too suffered from the devastation wrought by the war, it had no choice but to sign the treaty on June 28, 1919.

The League of Nations

The **League of Nations** was the first permanent international security organization. Its purpose was to maintain world peace. It had two basic flaws in its structure. First, it had no means to enforce its decisions, and second, it relied on the notion of collective security to preserve the global peace. "Collective security" essentially meant that a threat to any one country was a threat to all, but since participation by the various powers was essential, the League could never attain its aims. Many important powers were, at one time or another, absent from the League. Wilson had been the driving force for the formation of the League of Nations and for getting a treaty that would promise peace for Europe, but Wilson was unable to deliver American ratification of the treaty. The Senate had not been able to agree with the terms of the League of Nations, but the rejection of the treaty also meant that the United States was not bound by its promise to come to the defense of France. Britain then refused to ratify its defense agreement with France as well. France was left with no defensive buffer zone and no promise of aid in the case of German aggression. Germany left the League in 1933, as it believed it to be dominated by the Allies. The Soviet Union joined in 1934 and was expelled in 1940. The League utterly failed to stop World War II and so collapsed in 1940.

Interpreting World War I

World War I has been seen as the beginning of a coherent period in world history, from 1914–1991, when the Soviet Union fell. Eric Hobsbawm, in *The Age of Extremes: The Short Twentieth Century, 1914–1991*, published in 1994, argued that the period was a "short-century" dominated by the extremes of warfare on a global scale with unprecedented violence, genocide, the suffering of the peasantry and lower classes juxtaposed against the rapid technological advancement of the industrialized world. Hobsbawm's work has been criticized for its obvious pro-Communist stance as well as for his choices about dividing points in the "short century," but historians today still debate the extent to which World War I set in motion a tidal wave of events that are unified by common elements. For example, historians debate the role of industrialization and technology in the waging of both World Wars I and II, their global character, and German attempts to expand their power.

Many historians of World War II point out that to assume German aggression is the common factor in both world wars or that the events of 1914–1991 should be analyzed as a unified whole threatens to lessen the significance of the events of World War II, especially of the Holocaust. Many historians continue to see the events surrounding the rise of Nazi Germany as a significant breaking point in world history that cannot be adequately appreciated by including them within a larger set of events culminating in 1991.

Whatever one's interpretation of World War I, there is no doubt but that World War I set in motion a wave of nationalistic movements and that the terms of the Treaty of Versailles helped to fuel the rise of the Nazi party in Germany.

The Aftermath of War

One of the most important consequences of the World War was the beginning of the breakdown of the colonial empires of Europe.

Malaise in the Arts

The carnage of the First World War was the worst the world had ever experienced, and it left an indelible imprint on literature and other art forms. Gertrude Stein said that the postwar generation was a lost generation. Ernest Hemingway's *A Farewell to Arms* and Erich Maria Remarque's *All Quiet on the Western Front* expressed the malaise and disillusionment of the post-war era and captured the seemingly meaningless suffering of the Great War. The belief that there were objective measures of good and evil was rejected. Pablo Picasso was a leading exponent of cubism, according to which multiple perspectives on objects were displayed at the same time. Picasso and other artists also incorporated non-European influences into their work, such as from Africa. Salvador Dali and other artists and writers incorporated Freudian psychology into their works, often creating disturbing images of the world that matched the horrors of World War I.

Old Values Fall

Similarly, theologians reminded one that God's kingdom is not of this world, and Karl Barth's *Epistle to the Romans* questioned the belief that progress is the realization of God's purpose. The Russian orthodox writer Nikolai Berdiaev claimed that "man's existence had been one of steady failure," and claimed there was no evidence to suggest this would ever change.

Many scholars and political activists of the far right or far left questioned the value of democracy, while others questioned the power of the ordinary citizen to control a world of such chaos. Jose Ortega y Gasset, a Spanish philosopher, wrote the most famous argument to this effect in the *Revolt of the Masses*, where he warned that the masses may be unduly swayed by demagogues. He argued, too, that the masses have the power to destroy the greatest achievements of Western society, due to the attempt to impose a mass will on everyone and everything. Sigmund Freud, whose psychological theories first began to appear in 1896, created a new view of the self whereby much of one's inner life was relegated to the realm of the subconscious. While Descartes had earlier told one that the contents of one's mind were clear and distinct, now Freud wrote about the id: the seething, churning desires that are not conscious but that often dictate our behavior. For Freud, God was a mechanism of the superego, a projection of the moral authority of parents and other figures.

Relativism

Albert Einstein developed the **theory of relativity**, according to which space and time are relative to the person measuring them. Gone were all the absolutes of past ages, and reality or truth were merely mental constructs. **Werner Heisenberg** developed the **"uncertainty principle,"** according to which it is impossible to specify simultaneously the position and velocity of a subatomic particle. The more accurate is the statement of a particle's position, the less accurate can be the velocity. Heisenberg's theory suggested that one cannot accurately observe electrons, because the very act of observation interferes with them. One could not be objective, then, thus undermining some of the assumptions of the Age of Reason and its emphasis on observation.

Global Depression in the Wake of World War I

Under **President Warren Harding**, the United States reacted against the idealism of Woodrow Wilson, and the nation entered a period in which it sought to **"return to normalcy"** in the 1920s. His successor President Calvin Coolidge, known as Silent Cal, seemed to be a living expression of "normalcy," as he had a quiet and understated demeanor. One of the main planks of the return to normalcy was rejection of Wilson's belief in America's international role and a renewal of the former stance of **isolationism**. In fact, by the mid-1930s, a Senate committee chaired by North Dakota Republican Gerald Nye concluded that American involvement in World War I had been a mistake, contributing to American reluctance to enter World War II.

In the 1930s, however, the United States and the rest of the world were caught in the **Great Depression**. The complex system of reparation demanded by the Treaty of Versailles was the basis for much of the economy in the 1920s, and Austria and Germany, for example, relied on U.S. loans to pay these debts. The French and British relied on reparation payments to pay their own loans from the United States during the war. By 1928, U.S. lenders had started to withdraw capital from Europe, straining the financial system.

People crowd the Darmstaedter and National Bank after the bank—one of the five largest in the country, with capital and reserves of about $30 million—suspended payments in Berlin, Germany, on July 13, 1991.

Other factors contributed, as the use of oil began to undermine the coal industry, and techniques for using reclaimed rubber, perfected during the war, hurt the rubber export industry of the Dutch East Indies, Ceylon, and Malaysia. In fact, overproduction contributed to the Global Depression. During the war, European agricultural production had fallen for obvious reasons. The U.S. and other parts of the world had expanded their production, and after the war, European production resumed. The result was a worldwide surplus. Demand declined and prices dropped. By 1929, the price of a bushel of wheat was at its lowest level in 400 years. This contributed to inability of farmers to purchase manufactured goods, leading businesses to cut jobs.

The Stock Market Crash of 1929

On **Black Thursday**, October 24, 1929, investors across the world pulled out of the market. Stocks plummeted. Many lost their life's savings, and banks began to call in loans. President **Herbert Hoover's** response to the collapse of the American economy, of calling for increased volunteerism, proved ineffective.

By 1932 industrial production was at one-half the level of 1929, and the national income was also only one-half of what it had been. Almost half of the banks in the United States went out of business, and took with them the deposits of millions of people. Since so much of the world was dependent on the U.S. economy, the world economy collapsed as well. Germany and Japan, as well as Latin American, African, and Asian countries were hard hit. These were nations that relied on exports. In Germany, the unemployment rate reached 35 percent by 1932 and their production fell by 50 percent.

Economic difficulties forced Latin American nations to develop their internal economies. In Brazil, the dictator Getulia Dornelles Vargas created the Estado Novo or New State. Vargas ruled with the support of the military and created new industries, such as iron and steel, while also protecting workers with safety and health regulations, minimum wage laws, unemployment compensation, retirement plans, and limits on working hours.

Only China remained relatively unaffected by the global depression, although its exports of silk and tea dropped. China's economy, however, was not dependent on foreign trade for survival. Many parts of colonial Africa also escaped the ravages of the global slump.

World production declined by 38 percent in the three years following the crash of 1929. Trade dropped by over 60 percent, as nations imposed tariffs on imports in an attempt to become self-sufficient. The U.S., for example, enacted the **Smoot-Hawley Tariff** in 1930, raising duties on manufactured imported goods.

The author John Steinbeck described the suffering of the depression in such works as *The Grapes of Wrath*. In the 1930s, **President Franklin Delano**

Roosevelt responded to the plight of many Americans with his **New Deal**, a massive program of social reform legislation based on federal intervention in the economy. The government created new jobs through the Works Progress (Projects) Administration, the Civilian Conservation Corps, and other agencies. The government created **Social Security** and other measures for the relief of its beleaguered population.

New Economic Theories

The economist **John Maynard Keynes** put forth a new economic idea in 1936 rather like the New Deal in *General Theory of Employment, Interest and Money*. Keynes argued that the problem was lack of demand, and that governments should create more jobs and put more money into circulation, which he thought would lower interest rates and increase investment.

Review Questions

1. Which of the following was not a Central Power of World War I?

   (A) France

   (B) The Ottomans

   (C) Austria-Hungary

   (D) Germany

2. Which nation was the first to declare war in World War I?

   (A) Germany

   (B) Russia

   (C) Austria-Hungary

   (D) France

3. The term "total war" refers to

   (A) the involvement of every nation and part of the globe in the world war.

   (B) the mass mobilization of every sector of the economy and use of human and natural resources to wage war.

   (C) the total destruction of the war.

   (D) the refusal to seek peace rather than to wage war.

4. Which of the following was not a contributing factor to the Great Depression?

   (A) Overproduction of agricultural products by the United States to make up for the drop in production from Europe during the World War

   (B) The population decrease

   (C) Rising production of rubber during the war hurt the export industry from many colonial areas.

   (D) The complex system of reparations

5. Which of the following was not a consequence of World War I?

   (A) Strong belief in the possibility and reality of progress

   (B) Doubts concerning the possibility of objectivity

   (C) More complex theories about the nature of self-knowledge, according to which the self was no longer transparent

   (D) Awareness of multiple perspectives, reflected in cubism and other artistic styles

6. According to the Fourteen Points,

   (A) the complex system of often secret alliances that led to World War I was to be further supported.

   (B) navigation of the seas was to be divided among countries, which would be allowed to protect their interests through force.

   (C) trading conditions were to favor Britain and the United States.

   (D) there was to be "a general association of nations" created.

7. Among the criticisms of Eric Hobsbawm's thesis that the period from 1914-1991 represents a "short century" and a unified series of events are

   (A) the Holocaust is de-emphasized.

   (B) the pro-Marxist interpretation is universally valid and should have been applied in an even stronger manner than Hobsbawm does.

   (C) the period is artificial, as not all events shared precisely the same common elements and it could be moved further ahead or further back.

   (D) Both (A) and (C).

8. Which is the most correct statement about German aggression leading to the war?

   (A) It can be analyzed in precisely the same way as their aggression leading to World War II.

   (B) The complex nature of events, including the impending threat caused by Russia's mobilization, help to explain German aggression.

   (C) The complex nature of the alliances put great pressure on Germany to protect its interests against Russia and France.

   (D) Both (B) and (C).

Answers

1. (A)	3. (B)	5. (A)	7. (D)
2. (C)	4. (B)	6. (D)	8. (D)

Chapter 31

THE LEGACY OF WORLD WAR I: REBELLION AND REVOLUTION IN RUSSIA, AFRICA, THE MIDDLE EAST, AND SOUTH AND EAST ASIA

KEY TERMS

Sergei Witte
October Manifesto
Tsar Alexander II
Tsar Nicholas II
Lenin
Trotsky
Trans-Siberian Railroad
Alexander Kerensky
Provisional government
Duma
Bolsheviks
Treaty of Brest-Litovsk
Whites
Reds
New Economic Policy
Comintern
Stalin
Gosplan
Five Year Plans
Proletariat
Nationalist People's Party or
   Guomindang
May Fourth Movement

Sun Yat-sen
Mao Zedong
Jiang Jieshi (Chiang Kai-shek)
Northern Expedition
Long March
Taisho Democracy
Zaibatsu
Shidehara diplomacy
Manchukuo
Muslim League
Muhammad Ali Jinnah
Indian National Congress
Mohandas Gandhi
Non-Cooperation Movement
Civil Disobedience Movement
March to the Sea
Jawaharlal Nehru
Pakistan
Mustafa Kemal/Ataturk
Zionism
Balfour Declaration
Pan-Africanism
Oswald Spengler

CONSEQUENCES OF WORLD WAR I

World War I weakened and eventually destroyed the Ottoman Empire, leading to a republican revolution in Turkey and a wave of revolutionary activity in former Ottoman territories in the Middle East. World War I destroyed the colonial empire of Germany and weakened those of other European nations, leading to a wave of revolutions in Africa. Russia erupted in revolution during World War I, and the Russian revolution provided a model for communism in China. In South Asia, India moved towards independence from Britain. In East Asia, Japan's economy continued to grow and Japanese imperialism escalated.

THE RUSSIAN REVOLUTIONS OF 1905 AND 1917

The Industrialization of Russia in the Nineteenth Century

The **Crimean War** served as a motivating force for change in Russia and forced its leaders to realize that Russia was a barely industrialized, agricultural backwater compared to the rest of Europe. If Russia was to keep up with the world, great changes would have to be undertaken, and so, in the latter half of the nineteenth century, **Tsar Alexander II's** government embarked on a program of social reforms and modernization schemes.

In 1861, Alexander freed the serfs. No longer tied to the land, they were now allowed to own it. This was a major step forward for Russia, but it was not as revolutionary as it might have been, for while the serfs were now free to own the land, they could not own it outright as individuals. They had to own it as part of their local community or village. The serfs were free, but yet still bound if they could not buy their land. They remained in a state of "temporary obligation," but the tsar did implement legal reforms abolishing traditional punishments for serfs.

Reforms also implemented changes in local government, as zemstvoes or local councils regulated roads and made other decisions in the place of the aristocrats who formerly owned the serfs. However, the zemstvoes had no say in Russia's national policies and so political life in Russia remained largely unchanged. Alexander II had seen the need for reform, but the measures his government enacted did not go far enough to suit everyone. In 1881 he was assassinated when a bomb was tossed into his carriage.

Tsar Alexander III was naturally affected by his father's violent death and remained steadfastly opposed to political reforms. He was not blind to economic realities, however, and so it was in his reign in the 1890s that Russia truly joined in the industrial revolution.

In just 40 years Russia went from being a static, agricultural nation to being a world leader in the production of steel and oil. Missing from the newly industrialized Russia, however, was a middle class of professionals, such as developed in Western Europe following the Industrial Revolution there. Despite the reforms, Russia remained backwards in terms of agricultural techniques and, consequently, was still largely a peasant society. Also, foreign investments resulted in Russia becoming a debtor nation. Further, heavy taxes on imports had still not enabled Russia to export more products than it imported.

The October Revolution (1905)

The surging Russian economy, however, spurred an interest in imperialistic expansion, with the Far East as the target. Japan thwarted Russia's desires. In August 1905, imperial Japan defeated Russia. This defeat resulted in public protests. In January 1905, a peaceful protest occurred in St. Petersburg. A priest led the protestors as they sang songs and approached the **Winter Palace**, home of the tsar. **Tsar Nicholas II**, however, had already left St. Petersburg. Troops opened fire on the protestors. The resulting massacre turned the people against the tsar. Revolutionary political groups became openly active as the summer of 1905 dragged on and they organized revolts.

Tsar Nicholas II's Winter Palace

By October 1905 the opposition to the government had grown so great that a general strike was carried out, effectively shutting down the country. Tsar Nicholas responded with the **October Manifesto** that promised civil rights for the people, free elections for the Duma and more power to that body as well. It appeared the revolutionaries had won. In reality, the elections for the Duma did not constitute direct representative government. The tsar still chose and controlled his ministers and the ministers ran the government, not the Duma. The Duma did have the power to make laws, but the tsar had the power to veto any legislation the Duma passed. The tsar also held ultimate control over the Duma, being able to dismiss it as he pleased.

With the Duma failing to toe the line, the tsar dismissed it in 1906. New elections in 1907 brought in even more members opposed to the tsar's government. Again the tsar dissolved the Duma. The tsar's ministers then took steps to see to it that the tsar's supporters would gain the majority in the Duma by altering the election laws. They were successful and the next election, also held in 1907, yielded the results the tsar had sought.

All was not lost for the revolutionaries. The new leader of the Duma, **Peter Stolypin**, a supporter of the tsar, recognized the need for real reform. He rewrote agricultural policies to make it easier for the peasants to truly own the land they farmed. Although these and other reforms did much to modernize Russia, they failed to end the hardships that sparked revolution. Within a decade, Russia would be in flames.

The Revolutions of 1917

Long standing social unrest was brought to the boil by World War I in Russia. In 1914 Russia entered war with Germany with the same patriotic fervor that swept the rest of Europe. War seemed to be an opportunity for the various factions of Russian politics to make gains and so it had widespread support. But unlike Germany, Russia was ill-prepared for an all-out extended military campaign. The Russian army was ill-equipped and soon ran short of weapons and munitions. The Russian army suffered two million casualties in 1915 alone.

Tsar Nicholas II failed to provide effective leadership and failed to work with the Duma. By 1915 factions in the Duma were openly critical of the tsar and each other. Tsar Nicholas II, distrusting the Duma and dissatisfied with the progress of the war, dismissed the Duma and headed to the front, leaving his wife, Tsarina Alexandra, in charge in his absence.

The situation in Russia rapidly deteriorated and social unrest exploded into open revolt. Continued bad news from the front and shortages of food in the cities created an ugly mood among the people. Bread riots broke out in Petrograd (St. Petersburg) in March 1917. The tsar ordered his troops to restore order but they joined the revolt instead. The Duma declared a provisional government and the tsar abdicated, ending centuries of Romanov rule. **Alexander Kerensky**, a hero in the Duma, became the new leader of the Provisional Government.

The Russian Revolution was a revolt against the Russian monarchy and the Russian government as it then existed. The revolutionaries were diverse groups with differing goals, values, and ideals. Once their common goal of removing the tsar was achieved, they then turned against each other, each determined to see their vision for a new Russia realized.

The government formed after the abdication of the tsar was still pro-war, including Kerensky. They granted freedoms to the people, but did not engage in the social reforms the more radical revolutionary groups sought. Petrograd itself was in the control of the Petrograd Soviet, a collective of workers and soldiers that was determined to give power to the people. By the summer of 1917, Russia was in turmoil and the government faced a total breakdown.

Vladimir Ilyich Lenin (1870–1924) rose to prominence in the chaos of revolutionary Russia. Lenin had always been a revolutionary, but it was not until he became a law student that he found his revolutionary philosophy. In the work of Marx, Lenin found the theories that spoke to him. From Marx's Communist Manifesto, Lenin drew his first principle of revolution: that violent revolution was necessary to destroy capitalism. Lenin believed that revolution was necessary and possible even when a society such as Russia did not have a fully developed capitalistic economy. Further, he believed that a Marxist revolution was possible even without a well-developed bourgeoisie class. With adequate leadership, such as the **Bolsheviks** provided, he believed revolution would succeed in Russia. Only dedicated revolutionaries, with the intellect to fully understand the importance of revolution, could successfully lead a revolution. The **proletariats** (or working class) were necessary instruments of the revolution, as leaders would need an organized army of workers. It would be up to the leaders, however, to keep the revolution on course to take control of a nation.

Lenin had been living and plotting revolution in exile, but in 1917, Germany helped transport him back to Russia and even gave him financial aid, hoping that Lenin would destabilize the fragile provisional government. Lenin immediately took the lead of the Bolsheviks and refused to cooperate with other groups. He demanded an end to the war, land reforms, and power to the soviets. In July 1917, Kerensky ordered the arrest of the Bolsheviks, but he was unsuccessful in stopping their rise to power. When Kerensky's general, Kornilov, revolted and marched on Petrograd, Kerensky turned to the Bolsheviks for help, as they controlled the Red Guards and the Soviets. Lenin agreed to help defend Petrograd, but at the same time made a clear statement that he was not fighting for Kerensky. General Kornilov ultimately committed suicide, but now Kerensky was in deep trouble, as the Bolsheviks could clearly muster significant military forces against him. In October he ordered the arrest of the Military Revolutionary Committee and shut down the Bolshevik papers.

Leon Trotsky supported Lenin and urged him to overthrow the Provisional Government. He helped the Bolsheviks gain control of the Petrograd soviet and from there, control of Russia. On October 24, 1917, Lenin gave the order to take the railroad stations, and then for the Red Guards to march on the **Winter Palace**, the center of the Provisional Government. By October 26, 1917, Lenin's Bolsheviks had succeeded in their attempt to topple the government. The all-Russian Congress of Soviets officially handed over power to the Soviet Council of People's Commissars. They elected Lenin chairman and put Trotsky in charge of foreign affairs.

The Bolsheviks succeeded because by late 1917 the democratic dream of the Provisional Government was dead. Lenin and Trotsky were strong, charismatic leaders, and the Bolsheviks tried to appeal to the common people. Lenin moved quickly to solidify his position. He declared that the peasants had a right to seize land. He signed a treaty with Germany ending World War I for Russia. The terms were harsh. Russia gave up its western territories, areas that would eventually become Poland, Finland, Lithuania, and more with a loss of one-third of its population. Not everyone supported Lenin's surrender to Germany; even members of the Bolsheviks balked at the terms. But when the threat of invasion by Germany returned in 1918, the Russians quickly agreed to the **Treaty of Brest-Litovsk**. In 1918, the Bolshevik government executed Tsar Nicolas II, his wife Tsarina Alexandra, their children, and their servants.

Elections were held for the Constituent Assembly that was to be the new Russian government. The Bolsheviks, however, did not manage to take a controlling majority in the elections, so Lenin used his Bolshevik troops to dismiss the Assembly and take control. The Bolsheviks who became the Communists were referred to as the **"Reds."** The **"Whites"** represented the other revolutionary groups, groups that wanted a more democratic government for Russia. Once it became clear that Lenin intended to increase the power of the state and to control Russia as a dictator, the Whites revolted. The Whites were primarily conservative members of the Russian military. From 1918–1920 the armies of the Reds and Whites fought for control, and eventually the Reds defeated the Whites. Trotsky had managed to mold a formidable army for the Reds, while the Whites were never able to truly unite. Soviet Russia was born.

The Soviet Union from 1920–1927

By the 1920s the Bolshevik revolution in Russia was complete and Lenin could now devote his attention to controlling what remained of the country. Russia lay in ruins. Over half the people were starving due to famine brought on by drought combined with the devastation of war. The economy had been destroyed. The population, stretched to its limits, rioted once more. The Bolsheviks were still rebuilding Russian society when the global depression hit.

Lenin reacted quickly. In 1921 he issued the **New Economic Policy** or **NEP**, which allowed for some economic freedom by encouraging cottage industries and small farms to produce and trade. Major industries remained in the hands of the government. Lenin returned industries with less than 20 employees to the private sector. The NEP also allowed peasants to sell surpluses for free market prices. By 1926, the economy had rebounded to its pre-1913 levels.

Stalin

Lenin died in 1924, leaving the government scrambling to determine his successor. Trotsky was an obvious choice, having been so instrumental in the success of the revolution, but he was not alone. **Joseph Stalin's** star was rising as well. Stalin, born Joseph Dzhugashvili, was talented, daring, determined, but lacked the style of Trotsky. Still, Stalin was able to garner the support needed to become general secretary of the Central Committee, the most important committee in the government, and he used that position to gain even more power, influence, and supporters.

Trotsky believed that in order for the revolution in the Soviet Union to last, the revolution had to be taken to the rest of Europe. This position did not sit well with a nation of war-weary people just beginning to dig out of an economic grave. Stalin held the opposite position, believing that the Soviet Union could stand on its own as a socialist nation, a position far more appealing than Trotsky's to party members. Stalin achieved total power by 1927. He succeeded in having Trotsky exiled in 1929 and on August 20, 1940, had Trotsky assassinated. Stalin would ultimately be known as the gravedigger of the October Revolution, and his reign of terror in Russia would result in the death of millions of Russians.

Russian Response to the Post-War Period

While Lenin had attempted to spread the Russian Revolution abroad and supported this through the creation of **Comintern (Communist International or Third International)**, Stalin focused more on developing socialism in Russia. After Stalin took power, "the man of steel" quickly enacted several **Five Year Plans**, intended to promote rapid economic development. The first plan focused on heavy industry, which was to become centralized through the efforts of Gosplan, the central state-planning agency. Stalin created **collective farms** and subsumed all private land into these units. Members shared the profits. Peasants revolted, and many starved to death on their own lands when they were unable to meet production quotas set by the government. By 1931, when the plan ended, half the land in Russia was contained within collective farms.

As Russia focused on industry, consumer goods were virtually nonexistent. Rebellions emerged not only among those whose land was taken, but within the Communist party as well. Stalin embarked on a series of **purges**. Over two-thirds of the members of the 1934 Central Committee and one-half of the army's highest-ranking officers were removed, while three million citizens died and eight million were imprisoned.

As Stalin gained power in Russia, **fascism** and **National Socialism** took root in Italy and Germany, movements that would eventually bring the world to war again in World War II.

MARXISM SPREADS TO CHINA

The revolution that ended Qing rule and established **Sun Yat-sen** as president of the Chinese republic did not end China's problems. Many generals of the old imperial army became warlords in the provinces, and they preserved and supported the old opium trade. Although Sun Yat-sen's government controlled affairs in Beijing, China was not united as long as the warlords ran the provinces. Sun Yat-sen eventually relinquished the presidency to **Yuan Shikai**, a warlord who controlled the Beijing armies. Yuan Shikai, unfortunately, did nothing but reinvigorate aspects of imperial rule.

Mao Zedong and the Chinese Communist Party

The unequal treaties of the Opium Wars had resulted, too, in the influx of foreign trade in China. China had hoped that Wilson's Fourteen Points and the Treaty of Versailles might end foreign domination of China's trade and obliterate the unequal treaties, but they were bitterly disappointed when the United States actually helped Japan to increase its activities in China. Resentment boiled over in China in the **May Fourth Movement** (1919), led by intellectuals and students. They protested foreign imperialism and wanted the restoration of National Unity. As the U.S. had apparently abandoned its own principles, especially in the context of China, while the Russians advocated anti-imperialism, many turned to Communism. **Mao Zedong** was one of the most important members of the **Chinese Communist Party**, founded in 1921. He supported the equality of women, and fought against such practices as foot binding and arranged marriages, which had kept women from advancing. Although Sun Yat-sen also advocated the end of special privileges for foreigners and national reunification, he wanted a democratic republican government based on universal suffrage. Sun Yat-sen organized the **Nationalist People's Party** or **Guomindang** in 1912 and by 1926, Communists accounted for one-third of its membership. Soviet advisors lent aid to the process.

Jiang Jieshi (Chiang Kai-shek)

Sun Yat-sen fled to Japan during the tenure of Yuan Shikai, but returned in 1917 and in 1921, was elected president of what the Guomindang called the **Republic of China** in Guangzhou in southern China. He died in 1925, and **Jiang Jieshi (Chiang Kai-shek)** replaced him as leader of the Guomindang. Jiang Jieshi began a campaign to unite China and establish Guomindang rule through the land called the Northern Expedition. In 1926–1927, he defeated 39 warlords. He then moved on to Shanghai, where the Communists opposed his entry. He ordered a massacre of the Communists, and took control of the city. This convinced him that Sun Yat-sen's attempt to work with the Communists was dangerous, and he abandoned them by 1927. The Communists retreated to south China, while Jiang Jieshi marched on Beijing in 1928 and then established his headquarters in Nanjing. At this point he declared the Guomindang the official government of a united China.

The Long March

Despite rhetoric to the contrary, China was not united. Jiang Jieshi began a vicious battle to rid China of the Communist threat, and the Communists were forced to flee their retreat in southeastern Asia. In 1934 they began their historic **Long March** from their hideout in Jianxi, traveling 6, 215 miles north

Portrait of Mao Zedong

to Shaanxi province in northwestern China by October 1935. Thousands died along the treacherous march. They established headquarters in Yan'an, and they had attracted many new members as a result of what many Chinese perceived as heroism. Mao Zedong emerged as the leader of the Communists in China, and modified the teachings of Marx and Lenin about the revolutionary power of the urban, industrial proletariat to suit conditions in China. Among other things, he argued that the peasant was the foundation of revolution in China. The struggle between the Nationalists and Communists continued through World War II.

The Great Depression and China

The worldwide Great Depression after World War I affected China as demand for its traditional exports of silk and tea dropped. In the 1930s, most of China's industrial products were still from the craft industries.

Gender Issues in Post-World War I China

In the 1930s, most marriages continued to be arranged. However, women were demanding more freedoms, including the right to choose their own marriage partner. As Western education became more available in the late nineteenth century, Western ideas had entered Chinese culture. The New Culture Movement resulted in a challenge to the traditional Confucian structure of society along with its values.

JAPAN IN THE POST-WAR ERA

Japan's government continued to evolve, coming closer to democracy under Emperor Taisho in the 1920s. This period is known as the **Taisho Democracy**, and males were granted rights of universal suffrage. Women, however, were still not granted political rights, though they became increasingly active in social protest movements.

Democratization was undercut by the demands of rapid industrialization. The economy of Japan continued to grow at a rapid rate in the early twentieth century as a result of the Meiji reforms of the late nineteenth century. In the 30 years from 1900–1930, production of raw materials nearly tripled, leading to increased exports. Industries, which had received generous subsidies from the Meiji government, began to form conglomerates known as **zaibatsu**. By 1937, four of these zaibatsu controlled one-fifth of all banking enterprises, one-third of the shipbuilding industry, and 38 percent of commercial shipping.

The population in Japan increased from 43 million in 1900 to 73 million in just over 40 years. Subsequent food shortages led to rice riots after World War I. The contrast between the industrial elite and the peasant farmers was enormous, and even by the 1940s, half of all farmers were still tenant farmers.

Japan joined the League of Nations and became one of the big five powers. In 1922, as a result of growing concerns about Japanese imperialism in Manchuria, for example, the United States hosted the Washington Conference and pushed through a treaty signed by nine powers recognizing the Open Door

Policy in China. In 1928 Japan signed the **Kellogg-Briand Pact**, renouncing war as an instrument of national policy.

Consequently, Japan turned to Shidehara diplomacy in order to seek out the natural resources demanded by its expanding industrialization. "Shidehara" was the name of Japan's foreign minister and later prime minister.

Shidehara was unable to obtain enough resources through diplomacy to pacify the industrialists, and Japan eventually invaded Manchuria in 1931. Instability in China made the invasion feasible, while the Japanese military presence there to maintain the Manchurian railroad created a jumping off point. On September 18, 1931, Japanese troops blew up a portion of the South Manchuria Railroad that the Japanese had built. They blamed the Chinese, creating the pretext for war. This act of treachery became known as the Mukden Incident. By 1932 the Japanese had set up a puppet state called Manchukuo. The Chinese protested to the League of Nations, who eventually called for the withdrawal of Japan, but since the League lacked the power to take action, Japan went unpunished. The conquest of Manchuria set the stage for future aggression, as Japan feared the growing power of Chiang Kai-shek and worried that he might threaten their presence in Manchuria. In 1937 the Japanese invaded China, pursuing Chiang Kai-shek up the Yangtze River. Japan's aggressive actions ultimately culminated in their involvement in World War II as a member of the Axis.

SOUTH ASIA AFTER WORLD WAR I

India

Beginning in the 1850s, the British ruled India. World War I weakened the empire, leading to, among other things, a movement for Indian independence. The **Indian National Congress** was founded in 1885, and after World War I the congress increasingly turned against the British. The **Muslim League**, founded in 1906, feared that Hindu domination would replace the British, and considerable conflict arose between Hindus and Muslims that continues today. Wilson's Fourteen Points encouraged self-determination, and the Indian population eagerly embraced the ideal. The British responded with more repressive measures, creating a wave of rebellions and violence across the subcontinent of India.

Mohandas Gandhi emerged as an important leader. He was a Hindu who had been educated in law in London and had spent 25 years in South Africa, another British colony. While in South Africa, he had organized resistance within the Indian community to racial segregation. There he also developed his philosophy of **ahimsa**, or nonviolence and tolerance, and **satyagrha**, meaning "truth and firmness" but referring to his method of passive resistance. He renounced worldly pleasures, including sex, and, although he was a member of the merchant caste, he lived a life of simplicity. Gandhi returned to India in

1915, and became active in the Indian National Congress. He helped to launch the **Non-Cooperation Movement** of 1920-1922 and the **Civil Disobedience Movement** of 1930. These were mass movements that boycotted British goods and British institutions. Gandhi urged the people to wear Indian spun cloth as opposed to British manufactured clothing. Women, therefore, played a role in Gandhi's movement, as they spun the thread and made the cloth. In general Gandhi opposed Western-style industrialization in India. Although Gandhi advocated nonviolence, the movements inevitably did result in violence, and the British arrested the offenders. In 1919 in **Amritsar in the Punjab**, colonial troops dispersed an unarmed crowd with rifles and killed 379 demonstrators.

Gandhi

In 1921, the British government gave in and enacted the **Government of India Act**, which gave India the institutions for a self-governing state. However, it also passed legislation limiting the production of salt to the British. In response, Gandhi led followers on a 230-mile march to the sea in 1930. He picked up salt from the shores and urged his supporters to refuse to follow the British law. Gandhi, only recently released from prison from previous protests, was arrested again. While Gandhi opposed industrialization as immoral, **Jawaharlal Nehru** did not and he supported the creation of an independent nation-state in India. Nehru was a Brahmin educated in Western traditions. He would eventually serve as prime minister in India following the creation of an independent government.

The Muslim League, led by **Muhammad Ali Jinnah**, however, rejected this compromise, as it feared Hindu domination. Jinnah advocated the formation of separate states, one for Hindus in India and another for Muslims in **Pakistan**, which would be the "land of the pure." Following World War II, the British would partition India and Jinnah's dream would become a reality.

THE MIDDLE EAST AFTER WORLD WAR I

Ataturk

A group of liberal nationalists who favored Western-style governments, called the "Young Turks," led the revolution against the Ottoman Young Turk regime. Their leader, Mustafa Kemal, wished to modernize and Westernize Turkey. He is known today as **Ataturk**, or "Father of the Turks." Ataturk was president of Turkey from 1922 to 1928, and during this period he introduced a series of legislative reforms adopting European legal systems and civil codes. In so doing, he overthrew the Islamic law of the Shari'ah and also the Ottoman laws, the kanun. He implemented European-style Roman writing and secularized the state by eliminating the Arabic call to prayer, the caliphate or the Muslim civil and religious leadership of an Islamic state, and the mystical Sufi orders of Islam. His radical reforms survived and the Turkish Republic remains an independent and secular Islamic state.

Ibn Ali Hussain and the Hejaz (Saudi Arabian Peninsula)

As Ottoman power weakened, **Ibn Ali Hussain**, sheriff of Mecca and king of the Hejaz along the eastern shores of the Red Sea, revolted against the Ottoman Turks in 1917. Hussain was a descendent of Muhammad who collaborated with Lawrence of Arabia in war against the Turks. The Treaty of Versailles rewarded the revolt of Hussain by recognizing Hejaz as an independent kingdom. Hussain's son Faisal attended the conference at Versailles hoping to achieve independence for the Arab world, but his efforts were thwarted by the competing interests of the British and French, who had secretly signed the **Sykes-Picot Agreement** in 1916. According to this agreement, the British were to receive Palestine, Iraq, and Jordan, while the French were to govern Lebanon, Syria, and large portions of Turkey. This secret agreement was in open opposition to pledges made after World War I came to an end, and created great resentment among the Arabs.

THE CREATION OF ISRAEL AND THE PROBLEM OF PALESTINE

Zionism

Since the 1890s, **Zionism** had been an important movement in Europe. Zionists fought against anti-Semitism and sought to create a homeland for Jews, an idea first suggested by Theodore Hertzl, a Hungarian Jew, in Der Judenstaat (1896). Hertzl organized the first Zionist World Congress (1897), which created the World Zionist Organization.

At first, their interests were not in Palestine, as they planned the creation of a Jewish state in Africa, but various factions within the movement returned to biblical teachings developed after the return of the Jews from the Babylonian Captivity. At this time in antiquity, biblical Scriptures reflected a growing emphasis on Jerusalem, first established by King David and the capital of the southern Hebrew Kingdom of Judah. Gradually, the focus of Zionism became Palestine. Some Jews continued to believe that the Jewish nation would return to their homeland only with the coming of the messiah, and these Jews opposed the radical Zionist movement.

Balfour Declaration

The **Balfour Declaration** (1917) promised to establish a secure homeland for Jews in Palestine, and this declaration was supported at the Paris Peace talks following World War I. After World War I, the League of Nations established in 1922 a British mandate in Palestine. A mandate was a territory surrendered by Turkey or Germany to the victorious allies in World War I and governed by a European power. Arabs resented both the British and the Jewish settlers and rioting erupted in the 1920s and 1930s.

Syria

The Syrian National Congress attempted to proclaim Syria independent, governed by Hussain's son Faisal. However, the French moved an army from Lebanon into Damascus in 1920, driving Faisal from power. After World War I, the League of Nations created a French mandate in Syria.

Iraq

During World War I, the British took Basra in southern Iraq (1914) and Baghdad (1917). After World War I, the League of Nations created a British mandate in Iraq and carved Iraq from Ottoman territories. Britain installed the brother of the king of Jordan, Emir Faisal ibn Husayn, as leader there. In 1921 the Iraqis later elected and proclaimed him king. The discovery of huge oil fields near Kirkirk helped Iraq considerably, though the British-dominated firm, the Iraqi Petroleum Company, had the rights to develop the fields. The British mandate in Iraq ended in 1932.

Persia (Called Iran after 1935)

In 1906, Persia underwent a series of nationalistic reforms and had created a national assembly called the Majlis. However, foreign intervention thwarted the movement. Britian, France, and Russia squabbled over Iran before the Russian Revolution took Russia out of the picture. In 1919 Britain attempted to essentially take over Iran through a treaty installing British officers in every level of the government. The Majlis stood firm and would not ratify the treaty, strengthening anti-British sentiment throughout Iran. **Reza Shah Pahlavi** came to power as shah in 1925. He attempted to free Iran of foreign influences, but to create a modern industrialized nation-state, which often conflicted with the antisecular religious factions in Iran. Though he built railroads and stimulated the ecomony, his brutal methods alienated many.

Afghanistan

Afghanistan became independent in 1919, after a wave of rebellions against the British in India. Amir Amanullah attempted to modernize Afghanistan, but strong tribal and Islamic current prohibited him from achieving success.

AFRICA AFTER WORLD WAR I

Many Africans fought alongside the allies in World War I, often as a result of force. The war caused many disruptions in the economy on a global basis, and in Africa, these shortages were acutely felt. Following the war, memory of these hardships created greater discontent when the European colonizers failed to reward their colonists for their sacrifices. Further, Western-style education brought by European colonizers had exposed Africans to revolutionary ideas, which erupted in Afro-centric agitation in the years following The Great War. **Pan-African movements** attracted followers, but many of the Pan-African organizations were led by people, many of whom were African-Americans, whose interests were different from those of Africans. **Marcus Garvey** and **W.E.B. Dubois**, who were African-Americans, were influential in inspiring Pan-Africanism. Just as Pan-Africanism failed to develop as its leaders envisioned, so too, Pan-Colonial associations, intended to address issues across many African colonies, failed when most colonial associations instead began to focus on issues related to individual colonies. African independence movements would not succeed until the period following World War II. Pan-Africanism, however, never succeeded in creating a united Africa, and ethnic conflict continues to disrupt Africa even in the twenty-first century.

"THE DECLINE OF THE WEST"

Early in the twentieth century the historian **Oswald Spengler** wrote an important book, ***The Decline of the West***. He predicted the eventual collapse of Western culture, but argued that the seeds of decline were already becoming visible. In the wake of World War I, many historians believed that Spengler's approach had been generally validated, even if they disagreed about the extent of the decline or the mechanism of it. As we have seen, Europeans experienced difficulties in their colonial empires in Africa and India, while the Middle East began to assert its desire for independence as well. Further, throughout the remainder of the twentieth century, the rate of population growth fell in Western European nations. During the rest of the twentieth century, there would be years of economic troubles, as in the 1930s during the Great Depression. While there is no doubt that Western civilization experienced challenges in the years following World War I, it nevertheless managed to survive. The rise of fascism and Nazism and the coming of World War II, however, posed new threats to stability and added another layer of chaos to a world that had never fully recovered from The Great War.

Review Questions

1. The Long March refers to

   (A) the flight of the Nationalist Chinese Communists to Taiwan.

   (B) the flight of the Chinese Communists from southern China to Shaanxi province in the north.

   (C) the Japanese invasion of Manchuria.

   (D) the German march into Russia during World War II.

2. The man who was the head of the Provisional Government in Russia following the first revolution in 1917 was

   (A) Lenin.

   (B) Trotsky.

   (C) Kerensky.

   (D) Stalin.

3. Which document pledged to create a secure homeland for Jews?

   (A) Treaty of Tilsit

   (B) Dayton Agreement

   (C) Balfour Declaration

   (D) Unequal treaties

4. "Non-violence is the greatest force at the disposal of mankind. It is mightier than the mightiest weapon of destruction devised by the ingenuity of man … Non-cooperation is directed not against men but against measures. It is not directed against the Governors, but against the system they administer. The roots of non-cooperation lie not in hatred but in justice, if not in love." Which figure most likely said this?

   (A) Nehru

   (B) Jinnah

   (C) Mohandas Gandhi

   (D) Mao Zedong

5. Which Communist leader most believed in the importance of spreading revolution abroad?

   (A) Stalin

   (B) Kerensky

(C) Stolypin

(D) Lenin

6. Which is the most correct description of Ataturk?

    (A) He moved Turkey closer to the traditional values of Islam.

    (B) He abolished the Shari'ah and secularized the Turkish state.

    (C) He favored the Sufis.

    (D) He preserved the call to prayer while abolishing all other Islamic traditions.

Answers

1. (B)	3. (C)	5. (D)
2. (C)	4. (C)	6. (B)

Chapter 32

EUROPE IN THE 1920s AND 1930s: THE RISE OF NAZISM AND FASCISM

KEY TERMS

Fascism	Gestapo
Socialism	Kristallnacht
Communism	Rhineland
Hitler	Appeasement
Nazis	Anti-Semitism
German Worker's Party	Mussolini
Führer	Socialist Party
Enabling Act	Blackshirts
The SA	Hannah Arendt
The SS	Ethiopia

THE RISE OF HITLER

At the end of World War I, the Allies, particularly France, demanded severe reparations from Germany. The purpose was two-fold: first, to repay France for the damage caused by the war and, second, to punish Germany so harshly that it would never again be a threat to the peace in Europe and the security of France.

The harsh terms of the treaty that ended Word War I had the unintended, but not altogether unpredictable, effect of galvanizing a nationalistic feeling in the hearts of the German people. The very measures designed to keep Germany down had in fact primed it to rise to the call of a strong leader.

Adolf Hitler was an Austrian. His father died while Hitler was young. Hitler had difficulty in finding a direction for his life. He went to Vienna, intent

Adolf Hitler

on entering the Academy of Fine Arts and becoming an artist, but his application was rejected. With no particular place to go and no plans, Hitler stayed in Vienna. His time there was critical to his development.

It was in Vienna that Hitler was first exposed to the ideas that would later be the foundations of his Nazi doctrine. Among the ideas that floated around Europe were the interest in German nationalism and a belief in the natural superiority of the Germanic peoples; following from these ideas was belief in the natural inferiority of the Semitic and Slavic peoples, and alleged evil conspiracies of Semites to undermine German nationhood and destroy German culture. Hitler also saw capitalism and liberalism as threats to German unity. Hitler watched, listened, and absorbed the radical, somewhat irrational ideas swirling among the Austro-German nationalists. He believed what he learned there and found the road to his ultimate destiny.

In 1913 Hitler moved to Munich, Germany, to avoid service in the Austrian army. Soon World War I broke out and Hitler found himself in the German army. Hitler found a home in the army and a purpose in life. In the army, although a lowly enlisted man, Hitler was proud to be serving the cause of German nationalism. He was really doing something for the first time in his life that he felt had any real meaning. When the war ended with the defeat of Germany in 1918, Hitler was devastated. He was not prepared to give up the fight and move on. The defeat of Germany by the combined forces of the Allies convinced Hitler that all he had learned in Vienna was true. Hitler began preaching what he believed. In the grim aftermath of World War I, he found Germans willing to listen.

In 1919 Hitler found himself once again in Munich. He became a member of the **German Worker's Party**. The German Worker's Party was small in size, radical in outlook. It was anti-Semitic, anti-Marxist, anti-democratic, anti-capitalistic. It was for **"national socialism,"** for building Germany into one large community of Germanic, and only Germanic, people.

The party grew, and Hitler's power within the party grew as well. In 1921 he took control. Honing the skills and ideas he first learned in Vienna, Hitler kept the party moving forward and growing with radical propaganda and mass meetings at which he delivered mesmerizing speeches railing against his usual targets and the government of Germany, the **Weimar Republic** itself. Hitler had transformed from a youth without direction into a charismatic leader with a dangerous message.

By 1923 the Weimar Republic was clearly becoming unstable. Hitler seized the opportunity to launch a revolt in Munich. Hitler's revolt failed and he was arrested. Hitler turned this defeat into something of a victory. He used his trial as a platform to expound on his ideals, gaining increased notoriety and exposure. He served less than a year in prison, just long enough to become a near-martyr to his supporters and to write *Mein Kampf*, which articulated the fundamental ideas of the Nazis. This defeat and imprisonment also gave Hitler time to rethink his tactics. He decided that rather than attempt to overthrow the Weimar Republic by open rebellion, he would do better to use his ever-growing base of support to take over the government by political means.

His party, now the **National Socialist German Workers' Party** or **Nazi Party** continued its growth, reaching a membership of 100,000 by 1928. These members were dedicated, disciplined, and devoted to the Nazi cause. Hitler continued to build the party and broadened its appeal by targeting Bolshevism as a menace to be fought while lessening his protests against capitalism. This made the party more appealing to the middle-class Germans.

The Nazis were still just a small part of the total German political system, but in the elections of 1928 they did manage to win twelve seats in the **Reichstag**. This represented only 2.6 percent of the total vote, but it was enough of a start for the Nazis to begin their attack on the Weimar Republic from the inside.

In 1929 the Great Depression gripped Germany as it did the rest of the industrialized world. As the economy of Germany entered a severe downswing, it gave the Nazis the opening they needed to find an issue to appeal to the masses. By 1932 43 percent of German workers were unemployed. The government could not contain the economic crisis and in desperation they enacted emergency measures. The president, **General Hindenburg**, agreed to Chancellor Bruning's suggestion of rule by decree. This was a legitimate move under the constitution, but an unpopular one with the lower and middle classes. Bruning was attempting to arrest the economic slide by cutting government spending and driving down prices and wages. His well-intentioned attempt failed to do anything other than increase popular support for Hitler's ideas. In 1932 Hindenburg forced Bruning to resign, but the situation did not improve.

Hitler seized his opportunity. He altered his speeches to appeal directly to those most effected by the failing economy. The middle and lower classes had traditionally supported the conservatives and moderates. In the face of economic disaster, the Communist party was rising in power. Reacting to the threat of Communism, the danger of personal financial ruin, and the promise of Hitler that the Nazi party, if given the chance, would turn the economy around and stamp out Communism as well, the middle- and lower-class voters turned their support to the Nazis.

Meanwhile, Hitler sought the support of big business by promising to help them bring back their profits, even sacrificing worker's wages if need be. To the army leadership he promised that if given the opportunity, he would overturn the Treaty of Versailles with its punitive conditions and rearm the German military. To the youth of Germany he promised a purpose for living a chance to make a difference, to build a better Germany and to be a leader in the new Germany. German nationalism appealed to the young. They flocked to the Nazi party in droves. Almost 40 percent of the party was under the age of 30 in 1931. No other political party in Germany could compete with the Nazis for their appeal to German youth.

In 1932 the work of Hitler and his party paid off. They won 14.5 million votes and took control of the Reichstag as the largest single party represented there. If the other two major parties, the Social Democrats and the Communists, had been able to cooperate, they would have had enough votes to block the Nazis. But the two parties had been enemies too long to be allies now. Still, the Social Democrats tried, even going so far as to appeal to the Soviet Embassy, but to no avail. Hitler now had his chance to put his ideas into practice.

Hitler Becomes German Chancellor and then Führer

Hitler demanded to join the government as the chancellor. The conservatives believed that as they held the majority of government posts, they could control Hitler, even if he were the chancellor. They agreed to his demand and on January 30, 1933, President Hindenburg appointed Hitler as chancellor of Germany. Hitler immediately called for new elections. In the violence surrounding the campaign, part of the Reichstag was burned. Hitler blamed the Communists and convinced President Hindenburg to grant him emergency powers. The new election gave the Nazis an even greater number of seats in the Reichstag. With his support in the Reichstag and the streets growing, Hitler was able to outlaw the Communist party and arrest its Reichstag representatives. In March he pushed the **Enabling Act** through the Reichstag, which made Hitler absolute dictator for a year. The act gave Hitler power to enact legislation without the approval of the Reichstag or Hindenburg.

Hitler moved quickly with his new power to end opposition to the Nazi party. He kept his opponents divided until he could remove them as threats to his Nazi party. The Nazi party became the only party in Germany. Elections continued, but served no real purpose as the only candidates were Nazi party members. After the death of Hindenburg in 1934, Hitler abolished the presidency and became **Führer**. Hitler did not dismantle the government; he simply replaced non-Nazi officeholders with Nazi party members.

Hitler banned strikes and established the Nazi Labor Front to replace the labor unions. Professional organizations were also with Nazi organizations. No independent organizations were allowed in Germany. Only those related to the Nazis could exist. Books and art that did not fit the Nazi mold were banned. Anything that did not fit the Nazi mold was banned. The Nazis controlled virtually every aspect of German public life by 1934.

Hitler took control of the army by winning the loyalty of its officers. The SA, the brown shirts who had supported Hitler in the beginning and who were known for their thuggish ways, had become a powerful group of three million.

They expected to be rewarded for their loyalty, but as a group, they were powerful enough to threaten Hitler and they were powerful enough to create problems in other areas as well. They wanted to take control of the army. Hitler decided the best course of action was to remove the SA leadership. He had a thousand of them executed. To do this, he used the **SS (Schutzstaffel)**, the Nazi elite and Hitler's most trusted guards. The army responded by swearing allegiance to Hitler. The SS grew in power and with the **Gestapo** became a dreaded organization with few limits on its power.

Anti-Semitism

The Nazi's attitude towards the Jews had never been a secret as **anti-Semitism** was a founding principle of the party. Once Hitler took control of Germany, life for the Jews became increasingly difficult. Jews found themselves unemployed, barred from working. In 1935, the **Nuremburg Laws** were passed. These laws declared that anyone with at least one Jewish grandparent was themselves Jewish and as such could not be German citizens. By 1938 a quarter of all the Jews in Germany had left the country. They were the lucky ones.

Kristallnacht

In the latter half of 1938, the situation for the Jews grew suddenly worse when on November 9–10, **Kristallnacht**, or night of shattered glass, organized attacks against the Jews began. Their homes, property, and synagogues were damaged and destroyed, and the Jews themselves were forced to pay for the damage. At the same time, they were no longer as free to leave Germany as they had once been. They were now trapped by a government that viewed them as the enemy within.

While Hitler's persecution of the Jews increased, along with the other groups Nazis viewed as inferior or deviant, he also enacted policies that improved the situation for the average German. Hitler introduced work programs, and the improved economic opportunities for the masses helped maintain the popularity of his government. Similarly, his rearmament program, started in 1936, generated public support. It helped quiet those who might criticize his persecution of the Jews. Those who would not be quiet in their opposition were imprisoned or executed.

German Expansion

As Hitler had made clear in 1924 in *Mein Kampf*, he believed in the superiority of the German race and, due to its superiority, its right to take whatever space it needed to fulfill its destiny. Nazi German had the right, even the duty, to expand. Those nations opposed to such expansion did not know how to handle Hitler. They tried appeasement and failed, and did not understand that Hitler's ambitions for expansion would not be limited to what other nations were willing to give up.

Still, Hitler felt that if he moved carefully, he would be able to gain much before the other nations offered any real resistance. In 1933 Germany withdrew from the League of Nations. Austrian Nazis assassinated the Austrian chancellor in 1934, acting on the goal of joining Austria and Germany into one united Germanic nation. **Benito Mussolini**, sensing the danger in a German-Austria union, blocked the move with his troops at the Brenner Pass. Hitler was stopped, but not for long.

In 1935 Hitler issued a general draft and fulfilled his promise to the army by declaring that Germany would no longer be bound by the Treaty of Versailles. Hitler announced his intention to rearm Germany in violation of the treaty. Italy, France, and Great Britain protested, but the protest was weak and an alliance of the three nations failed to form.

Germany Takes the Rhineland

Instead, Britain tried **appeasement**, first with the Anglo-German naval agreement, then in other ways. In 1936 the German army occupied the Rhineland in direct violation of the Treaty of Versailles. France had specifically demanded the Rhineland be a de-militarized buffer zone as a defensive area to protect France from German aggression. Now Hitler was ignoring the treaty and putting troops in the Rhineland and no one but France seemed alarmed. German troops occupying German territory did not seem to be such a terrible thing to the British. The French were afraid to do anything alone and so did nothing.

There were several reasons why the British tried appeasement. First, the memory of the overwhelming loss of life in World War I was still fresh in the minds of the British. They did not want to enter another devastating war. Also, the British felt that Germany had been harshly punished for World War I, and so could understand some of Hitler's demands, such as rebuilding the army and moving into the Rhineland. Further, Russia and the emergence of Stalin's brand of Communism had been the foremost threat in the minds of the British. They did not believe that Hitler was as dangerous as Stalin. Hitler was something of a champion against the spread of Communism, as he had stamped it out in Germany. This made Hitler at least somewhat sympathetic in the eyes of the British. As long as Hitler did not do anything that could not be excused or ignored, the British were not going to move against him. Without the British, the French would do nothing as well unless forced to act in the defense of France.

THE RISE OF MUSSOLINI

Before World War I, Italy had been a largely rural society. Most people were poor, the country was controlled by a small middle and upper class, the Church had power but was often at odds with the government, and the head of the government was a constitutional monarch who was ineffective. As far as European governments of the time went, Italy was fairly liberal. The people had civil rights and universal male suffrage. Still, the difference between the classes was large and the poverty most people experienced spawned social movements. The **Socialist party** in Italy was opposed to any involvement in World War I, but was unable to keep Italy out of the war.

Italy had joined the war on the side of the Allies believing that if the Allies won, Italy would be able to gain territory for itself. They were wrong. The Italians left Versailles practically empty handed. Worse, the government had made promises of reforms to the working classes during the war and now that the war was over, failed to deliver. The situation was ripe for revolt.

In 1920 revolutionary socialist elements in Italy were on the move. They seized factories and land. These seizures made no real gains for the socialists, but caused the property owners to become more active themselves. At the same time a Catholic party was gaining strength and conservatives were flexing their muscles as well. These groups were all very different from each other, but all united in their opposition to the current Italian government.

Benito Mussolini began life in an Italian village. His mother was a school teacher, his father a blacksmith. As a young man, Mussolini became a Socialist and worked on a newspaper. In 1914, Mussolini urged Italy to join the Allies in World

War I, which was the opposite of his party's stand on the subject. But Mussolini did not restrict himself to following his party's policies. In this instance, he was listening to anti-democratic groups. The Socialists threw him out of the party. Mussolini joined the army and was wounded at the front in 1917. Upon his return to Italy, Mussolini began organizing war veterans into a new group, the **Fascists**.

Benito Mussolini

His early ideology was a blend of nationalism and socialism. He wanted territorial expansion and land reform, both of which had been promised by the Italian government but never delivered. He also wanted benefits for the working class. Since many of his ideas were also the ideas of the Socialists, Mussolini had difficulty in attracting people to his party. By 1920 Mussolini had discovered that by attacking the Socialists he could draw Conservatives to his cause. He had found a winning formula and his party grew.

His **Blackshirt** supporters were sometimes violent. They would attack Socialists, usually at night. They pushed them out of the northern Italian city governments. Although they usually stopped short of killing, their tactics were enough to intimidate their Socialist opponents.

In 1922 the government of Italy broke down, due in part to the activities of Mussolini's supporters. Mussolini stepped to the fore. He demanded the resignation of the current government and that he be appointed by the king to form a new government. His supporters marched on Rome to make their demands clear. The king, **Victor Emmanuel III**, agreed. Mussolini was made dictator for a year.

Mussolini changed the election laws so that in 1924 his party was able to gain a clear majority in the government. Then the Socialist leader, Giacomo Matteotti, was kidnapped and murdered by Mussolini supporters, creating his first political crisis as opposing parties demanded Mussolini disband his Black Shirts. Mussolini responded with force. He declared that Italy would be a Fascist nation. He enacted restrictive laws, abolished independent unions, abolished freedom of the press, put the schools under the control of fascists, and created fascist unions, organizations, and a youth movement. Mussolini summed it up in 1926, "Everything in the state, nothing outside the state, nothing against the state."

THE PATH TO WORLD WAR II

Mussolini Attacks Ethiopia

Germany was not alone in looking to flex its muscles in 1935. Mussolini decided to attack Ethiopia. Ethiopia was an independent African nation on the east coast of Africa. Italy had colonies in East Africa and used these to launch the attack. The reason for the attack really had nothing to do with Ethiopia, beyond its convenience as a target. Mussolini, like Hitler, felt that expansion was an important part of his doctrine. While he could not expand in Europe without engaging in a war he could not win, Africa provided opportunities for colonial expansion with little risk of all-out war. Publicly Hitler supported Mussolini; privately he supplied arms to Ethiopia.

Haile Selassie

Ethiopian Emperor **Haile Selassie** personally led his troops into battle, but was eventually forced to flee. The League of Nations condemned Mussolini's actions, but otherwise did nothing to help Selassie. Only in 1941, with the help of the British, did Selassie regain his throne.

The Rome-Berlin Axis Agreement

Thankful for Hitler's public support, and apparently unaware of his private dealings with Ethiopia, Mussolini signed the **Rome-Berlin Axis Agreement** with Hitler. By 1940 Japan would also join the Axis.

The Spanish Civil War

Meanwhile the **Spanish Civil War** raged. Both Hitler and Mussolini gave support to the fascist forces of **General Francisco Franco**, who eventually was the victor in the war.

Hitler Invades Austria

In 1938 Hitler, by threatening invasion, convinced the Austrian chancellor to give control of the government to the Nazis. Hitler then invaded anyway and divided Austria into two provinces, absorbing both into Germany.

Hitler Invades the Sudetenland and Czechoslovakia

Hitler demanded that the **Sudetenland**, an area of Czechoslovakia with some German-speaking citizens, be given to Germany. This was a more difficult problem than the Austrian situation. Czechoslovakia did not want to cooperate. Their position was strengthened by their alliance with France and by France's agreement with the Soviet Union. If Germany attacked Czechoslovakia, France was obligated to declare war on Germany and the Soviet Union was pledged to come to the defense of France.

Neville Chamberlain, prime minister of Great Britain, negotiated feverishly with Hitler to avert the almost certain war. Chamberlain and France agreed to Germany's immediate annexation of the Sudetenland. Czechoslovakians had no choice, being unable to stand alone in the face of the German army. The Sudetenland went to Hitler. Chamberlain proclaimed that he had achieved "peace with honor" and "peace for our time." Seeing this betrayal of Czechoslovakia as a sign of weakness, Hitler then used his army to occupy the remainder of Czechoslovakia in 1939. The British and French finally realized that appeasement would not work.

Review Questions

1. What is true of fascism and communism?

   (A) Both share all the same assumptions.

   (B) Both are characterized by an emphasis on the state as an end unto itself.

   (C) Both emphasize class struggles as driving history.

   (D) Fascism emphasizes the role of the state as an end, while socialism advocates class struggles to advance history through a dictatorship of the proletariat.

2. What is Kristallnacht?

   (A) Hitler's shattering invasion of Czechoslovakia.

   (B) Hitler's invasion of the Rhineland, which violated the Treaty of Versailles.

   (C) Mussolini's invasion of Ethiopia.

   (D) Hitler's organized attacks on Jews that began in 1938.

Answers

1. (D)   2. (D)

Chapter 33

WORLD WAR II

KEY TERMS

Non-aggression pact

Blitzkrieg

Dunkirk

Vichy government

Battle of Britain

Luftwaffe

Two-front war

The Final Solution

Arsenal of Democracy

Island-hopping

The Manhattan Project

Nagasaki

Hiroshima

D-Day

VE Day

VJ Day

The WAVES

During the late 1930s, Western powers had sought appeasement with Hitler, but by 1939 it was evident that their strategy would not work. Hitler would have to be stopped, which became even more apparent as he turned his attention to Poland.

HITLER INVADES POLAND

The pretext for Hitler's interest in Poland was that its free port of Danzig had been taken from Germany by the Treaty of Versailles and there were still Germans in Danzig. Chamberlain promised that this time there would be no appeasement. If Germany moved into Poland, Britain and France would rise to defend her. Hitler did not believe that Britain and France would take action, as they had never made a stand before. Hitler felt certain that he could continue to push, and the British and French would continue to give.

Germany's Non-Aggression Pact with Stalin

Hitler did not move until he secured a **non-aggression pact** with Stalin in August 1939. Germany and the Soviet Union each pledged to remain neutral if the other country became involved in a war. The agreement included a secret plan for the division of Eastern Europe between Germany and the Soviet Union. Britain and France had hoped to make Stalin their ally and trap Germany into a potential two-front war. Stalin never trusted the West and while he did not trust Hitler either, an alliance with Hitler offered territorial gains, while one with the Allies did not.

Britain and France Declare War on Germany

On September 1, 1939, Hitler invaded Poland. Contrary to Hitler's expectations, Britain and France did not back down and declared war on Germany. **World War II** had officially begun. Poland was able to fight against the German invasion for just four weeks. The German military used its blitzkrieg ("lightning war") tactic of hitting hard and fast in an attempt to so overwhelm the enemy that they could not form a significant defense. After Hitler occupied Poland, he honored his agreement with Stalin. The Soviets took eastern Poland, Lithuania, Estonia, and Latvia.

WAR IN EUROPE

Dunkirk

Germany turned its attention west, launching another blitzkrieg through Denmark, Norway and Holland, then moving through Belgium, the

Netherlands, and finally into France. The French and British forces dug in to defend France, but Hitler's surprising movements through Luxemburg and the Ardennes forest divided the British from the French and trapped the British on the coast at **Dunkirk**. In a famous rescue effort, the British employed practically anything that would float, be it military or civilian, to save its army. The soldiers were brought home, but the loss of equipment and supplies was enormous.

The Vichy Government in France

German forces then took France, something they had not been able to do during the four years of World War I. **Marshal Henri-Philippe Pétain** of France, who had once been a hero in World War I, formed the **Vichy government** and accepted defeat. With the defeat of France, Germany occupied most of continental Europe and the rest was in the hands of nations friendly to Germany. In 1940 Hitler controlled northern Europe from the Atlantic to eastern Poland. Italy was firmly in the hands of Mussolini; Spain was in

Seated from left, Winston Churchill, Franklin Roosevelt, and Joseph Stalin

the hands of Franco's fascists; and the Soviets were pleasantly neutral. The only European power opposed to Hitler lay across the English Channel. Chamberlain was out of office and now the prime minister of Britain was **Winston Churchill**, a man who would prove an implacable enemy to Hitler's Germany.

The Battle of Britain

Britain refused to surrender to the German assaults. Hitler was savvy enough to realize that an invasion of Britain across the British Channel would fail if the British could attack the Germans from the air. Germany, then, launched an air attack with the **Luftwaffe** in what became known as the **Battle of Britain**. German forces hoped to cripple Britain's ability to defend itself or to launch a counterattack through massive air assaults on British military targets. Britain would then be unable to interfere with Germans forces on the continent. Both sides sustained heavy losses, but the British held on. Hitler then made the mistake of ordering the attack to strike civilian targets as well as military ones. He hoped to break the morale of the British people. Instead, this change of tactics steeled the British against the German aggressors. The people pitched in and pulled together. Factories increased production. British pilots flew as if their world depended on them, which it did. By October 1940 German losses in the air outnumbered British losses three to one. The East End of London became a symbol of British defiance, and that defiance became a source of national pride. The air war against Britain had failed.

The Germans Begin the Two-Front War

Instead of trying another means to soften up Britain for invasion, Hitler turned his armies east, to the Soviet Union. Hitler believed that support from the Soviets enabled the British to stay in the war. The attack on Russia that began in 1941 was a dangerous move that ultimately put Germany into a two-front war. Britain had survived the German air onslaught and was steadily building up its forces. Its supply lines had not been cut. The Soviet Union was not as susceptible to the strategy of blitzkrieg as was the rest of Europe. The logistics of launching such an attack successfully over the vast distances required to be effective against the Soviet forces made it a long shot at best.

After protecting himself in the Balkans and taking Greece and Yugoslavia, Hitler launched an attack against the Soviet Union in June 1941 along a front that was 1,800 miles long. At first the momentum was with the Germans, and within five months they were threatening Leningrad and Moscow and had taken much of the Ukraine. The Soviets held on, and the winter caught the Germans unprepared. The unforgiving Russian winter punished the Germans and stopped them in their tracks.

THE WAR IN THE PACIFIC AND THE U.S. DECLARATION OF WAR

Japan

Hitler's string of victories in 1940 had prompted the Japanese to join the Axis, especially as it had hopes of taking advantage of European colonial empires in Southeast Asia. Soon after joining the Axis, Japan invaded French Indochina. The Japanese invasion sent a dangerous signal to the United States, which immediately demanded that Japan withdraw from China, where since 1937 it had moved up the Yangtze River Valley in pursuit of Jiang Jieshi (Chiang Kai-shek). The Japanese had long been worried that Jiang Jieshi would unite China and threaten their presence in Manchuria, established in the 1905 victory over Russia. Consequently, the Japanese had invaded Manchuria in 1931 and established a regime there using ousted Chinese emperor Pu Yi as a puppet figure. In fact, many historians have argued that Japanese aggression in Asia began earlier than German aggression in Europe, the latter of which has traditionally been credited with having begun World War II. At any rate, Japanese imperialism had been a concern among Western powers since the Japanese defeated the Russians in 1905, and one can argue that evidence of imperialist expansion dates back to the Sino-Japanese War in the late nineteenth century.

While fear of public opinion against involvement had kept President Roosevelt from acting strongly when Japan initially invaded China, he was now determined to no longer tolerate the situation in China and to act quickly against the latest wave of Japanese aggression in Southeast Asia. The United States imposed a quarantine, cutting off its sales of rubber, iron, oil, and aviation fuel to Japan. On December 7, 1941, Japan replied with the devastating attack on the U.S. fleet at anchor in **Pearl Harbor**. The Japanese attack practically destroyed the naval base. The ships that had been in the harbor were all damaged or destroyed, including the *Arizona*, which was left where it sank in Pearl Harbor as a memorial to the servicemen who lost their lives in that fateful attack. **President Franklin D. Roosevelt** called December 7, 1941, a "date which will live in infamy."

The Japanese navy had planned on destroying the U.S. Pacific fleet, especially its aircraft carriers, but the carriers were not in the harbor at the time. Although the blow Japan struck that day was a heavy one, it was not the crippling stroke they had hoped it would be. The Japanese had hoped to knock the United States out of the war before the United States really had a chance to enter. Instead, the attack, seen by the American people as an unprovoked, unannounced, sneak attack, galvanized support for President Roosevelt and instantly gave him the ability to bring the United States openly into World War II on the side of Britain. The U.S. had been feeding supplies to Britain all along,

Attack on Pearl Harbor

but public opinion did not support joining the war. The attack on Pearl Harbor changed the face of the war in an instant.

Hitler declared war on the United States in support of Japan, which largely sealed the fate of his troops in Russia. Japanese forces moved quickly to conquer more territory in Southeast Asia, from deep in Manchuria in the north to New Guinea in the south, to Burma in the west, to an area beyond Wake Island in the east. In February 1942, the British surrendered Singapore, a symbol of European power in Asia, to the Japanese. The area was too large, with too much ocean and too many islands to be easily defended.

The United States reacted by rounding up over 120,000 Japanese-Americans in the United States and sending them to camps without charges or trials. Many argue this event represents the most serious civil rights violation in the history of the United States.

Hitler's Racism

Although Hitler's army was stalled on the Eastern Front, Britain was pulling itself together in the west, and the U.S. war machine was now being pushed into war-time production mode, Hitler went ahead with his plans for a German-dominated Europe as if victory was assured. This "New Order" meant that the superior peoples, Germans and their closest kin, the Scandinavians, were treated as privileged people. Slavic peoples were among those considered most inferior, as little better than pack animals, and the Germans treated them accordingly. Those who fell into Nazi hands were treated as disposable slave labor and were worked to death. The French were considered to be better than Slavs, but still definitely inferior to the Germans. They were not treated particularly harshly, but did have to suffer the indignity of paying taxes to fund the German war effort.

The Jews were considered to be so low as to warrant extermination as rapidly as possible, along with Gypsies, Jehovah's Witnesses, and Communists. Their rights had been taken away before the war began. The Jews who did not make it out of Germany or the areas conquered by Germany found themselves herded into ghettos, treated as sub-humans, and forced to wear the Star of David to identify themselves as Jews. Then in 1941 Germany enacted its **"Final Solution."** German forces executed some Jews in the villages where they lived. Nazis shipped others off to the concentration camps where the weak were sent straight to the gas chambers. The Nazis worked the stronger ones until they became weak and died. Some became test subjects in medical experiments. Once dead, the Germans pulled their gold fillings from their teeth and used them to fund the war effort. Germans cremated their bodies in ovens that belched black smoke into the skies day and night over the camps. An estimated six million Jews died at the hands of the Nazis.

Allied Strategy

Britain, the United States, and the Soviet Union now found themselves bound together as allies by their common enemy, the Axis Powers. The United States agreed to join with Britain and the Soviet Union in fighting Germany first, with Japan remaining as the secondary target. The United States became the "arsenal of democracy," giving roughly $50 billion in military aide to its allies. Britain continued to stand firm, and soon U.S. troops and equipment were pouring into the country as Britain and the U.S. prepared to push against Hitler's Western Front.

On the Eastern Front, the Soviets had regrouped from Germany's initial push into Soviet territory. The Nazi invasion helped spark a nationalistic fire in the hearts of the Russian people. They responded to the call of their country with great determination and personal sacrifice. The supply lines to the Red Army kept up a steady flow and, unlike the Germans suffering in the cold, the Soviets were in better shape with each passing day.

There was resistance to Hitler both within the German-occupied territories and within Germany itself. An underground resistance network was formed. Governments in exile from those countries now under German control operated in London, bringing together information to aid the Allied forces.

Nevertheless, Hitler continued to make progress. In 1942, Hitler captured the Crimea, while his General Rommel made advances in North Africa.

The Battle of Stalingrad

Moreover, the standstill on the Eastern Front ended in July 1942 as the Germans mounted a major offensive against Stalingrad. The Germans managed to take part of the city, the first time during the war they had managed to actually enter a major Soviet city, and occupied it for a month of intense combat.

War in North Africa

War raged in North Africa as well, but the tide was turning against the Germans. At the **Battle of El Alamein** (1942), the British defeated the German and Italian desert forces. The British also launched attacks in Egypt, and the British and Americans landed in Morocco and Algeria. These were French possessions in Africa and they went willingly over to the Allied side. By spring 1943, the Axis powers were out of Africa.

The Surrender of the German Sixth Army

As the Allies were fighting their way to victory in Africa, in November 1942 the Soviets were launching their first major offensive of the war, a counter-attack against Germany. Facing Romanian and Italian troops, the Soviets dealt with them and quickly positioned themselves to trap the German Sixth Army. When the Sixth finally surrendered in January 1943, only 123,000 of its original 300,000 troops were left standing. The Soviets had been able to successfully encircle the German Sixth Army because Hitler had refused to allow the army to retreat. The defeat was a hard blow to the Germans. The Soviets now had the momentum and were on the offensive. They defeated the Germans at the Battle of Kursk in 1943, and then moved on to retake the Ukraine. Soon thereafter, the Soviets managed to free Leningrad.

Fall of Mussolini

With the Axis out of Africa, the Allies could now concentrate on Europe. They launched an invasion through Sicily in 1943 and deposed Mussolini. The new Italian government surrendered unconditionally in September 1943. The Allied victory was short-lived. The Germans launched a counteroffensive, rescued Mussolini, captured Rome and northern Italy, and continued the fighting in 1944, when the Allies entered Rome. In the end Italians killed Mussolini.

D-Day

On June 6, 1944, the Allies launched a massive invasion of **Normandy**, France, known as **D-Day**. This offensive, launched from Britain, was the beginning of the liberation of France and Western Europe. American and British forces hit the beaches and marched inland. The Allies pushed the Germans slowly back. American **General Dwight D. Eisenhower** served as supreme commander of the Americans and British. His plan was not to run straight for Berlin, but rather to roll the Germans back all along the front, liberating Europe with the Allied progress. His forces crossed the Rhine in March 1945. As the Allies moved forward, the Soviets entered Warsaw and then turned south, clearing the Germans from Romania, Hungary, and Yugoslavia.

The Surrender of Germany

The British firebombing raid on **Dresden** in February 1945 was the culmination of two years of bombing of German industrial targets. Meanwhile, the Soviets had continued their offensive on the Eastern Front. Then, in January 1945, they turned for Germany once more. The Soviets and Americans met at the Elbe River, and the Soviets broke into Berlin in 1945. Hitler was not captured, but chose to commit suicide only two days after Italians had murdered Mussolini. His aides burned his body to ash. The Germans surrendered on May 7, 1945. May 8, 1945, is celebrated as **VE day**, or "victory over Europe" day.

The Battle for the Pacific

Although Germany had surrendered, the war in the Pacific continued. While the Allies were fighting the Axis Powers in North African and Europe, other events were taking place in the Pacific, where the Americans had a fleet able to sail again. The U.S. stopped the Japanese advance at the fiercely fought **Battle of the Coral Sea** in May 1942. In the **Battle of Midway** on June 4, 1942, the Japanese navy suffered a devastating blow. The U.S. had managed to break the Japanese code in an operation known as Magic, and knew of Japanese plans to attack Midway. All four of the Japanese aircraft carriers involved in the battle were sunk. The United States, rather than Japan, now had the superior navy in the Pacific. Midway marked the turning point in the war in the Pacific. In August 1942, land troops finally entered the war in the Pacific. American Marines landed on **Guadalcanal** in one of the most famous and hard fought battles of the war. The Americans and their Australian allies pushed on and forced Japan into fighting a defensive war, using the strategy of "island-hopping," or taking one island at a time. Midway had been the last island in the Pacific controlled by the U.S., but the United States fought bitter battles closer to Japan on **Iwo Jima** and **Okinawa**.

Fighting continued on Okinawa for two months, and the Japanese introduced for the first time **kamikaze** pilots, who flew their planes loaded with just enough fuel to reach Allied ships and then made suicide dives right into them. The Japanese flew over 1,900 kamikaze suicide missions and many Okinawans also died in the battle, convincing the United States that victory over Japan

Raising the Flag on Iwo Jima

would not come quickly or easily. Saipan fell in July 1944, thus bringing the islands of Japan closer to the reach of U.S. bombers. U.S. bombers unleashed a wave of napalm firebombs over Tokyo in March 1945, destroying 25 percent of the city's buildings and killing over 100,000 people.

The Atomic Bomb

The war in the Pacific did not look promising. The Allies were making progress, one island at a time, but there was so much territory to re-take from the Japanese and the Japanese put up a determined fight. U.S. **President Harry Truman** felt the circumstances justified drastic measures. A crucial consideration was to prevent greater loss of life through months or even years of continued fighting, though some historians have made the controversial suggestion that Truman wished to test the atomic bomb, developed through the efforts of the **Manhattan Project**. At any rate, he authorized its use, and in August 1945 the first bomb fell on **Hiroshima**, Japan. Japan did not surrender. Three days after the Hiroshima bombing, the United Stated dropped a second atomic bomb on **Nagasaki**, Japan. The world had never seen bombs with the destructive force of these. The cities of Hiroshima and Nagasaki were blown from the face of the earth in an instant. One hundred thousand people were killed in the blink of an eye, and others suffered horrible injuries. Over fifty percent of the population of Hiroshima and Nagasaki in 1945 either died in the attack itself or were dead from thermal and nuclear radiation exposure by 1950. The magnitude of the devastation was shocking, even in comparison to the two days of firebombing of Tokyo in March 1945. One hundred thousand people died in the firebombing of Tokyo, but it took two days and hundreds of tons of bombs to accomplish what two bombs did in a split second. Japan finally surrendered on August 14, 1945, ending World War II. The war formally ended on September 2, 1945, when Japan signed the terms of surrender aboard the battleship *Missouri*. This date is now celebrated as VJ day, or "victory over Japan" day.

Hiroshima after dropping of the Atomic Bomb

AFTERMATH

Approximately sixty million people died in World War II. The U.S.S.R. lost over twenty million people, only one-third of whom were soldiers. China lost fifteen million people, who were primarily civilians. Germany lost four million, while Japan lost two million. Great Britain lost 400,000 and the United States lost 300,000. The Poles suffered the loss of six million inhabitants. Six million

European Jews died. Scholars estimate that Nazi persecutions also resulted in the deaths of one million other people from minority groups, including gypsies, homosexuals, Serbs, anti-Nazi political dissidents, and those with mental illnesses. Over 3.3 million Soviet prisoners of war died in Nazi camps, and six million Soviet citizens died.

World War II left virtually no one untouched. The war devastated Europe and left it in need of reconstruction. Millions of refugees from devastated areas migrated across Europe, and over thirteen million of them settled in post-World War II Germany. The Germans lost territory to Poland, and the Soviet border expanded to the west. Germany was divided into three occupation zones controlled by the United States, Britain, and the Soviet Union. The agreements made by the Allies during and after the war concerning the fate of Europe eventually led to the **Cold War** and the creation of a bipolar world split between the world's democratic superpowers and the world's Communist superpowers. While western European nations, such as France, Italy, and West Germany, recovered from the war and re-established republics, Eastern Europe came progressively under Soviet influence and control. Independence movements also swept through the Middle East and Africa as Western imperialism was weakened during and after the war. To review these events, consult the later chapters on these topics.

Review Questions

1. Which of the following was not a member of the Axis powers in World War II?

   (A) Germany

   (B) Russia

   (C) Italy

   (D) Japan

2. Germany's invasion of which country prompted the British and French to declare war, starting World War II?

   (A) The Rhineland

   (B) Poland

   (C) Sudetenland

   (D) Austria

3. Which of the following statements best describes the Japanese motivation for attacking Pearl Harbor?

   (A) The United States had invaded Indochina during World War II, provoking the Japanese to protect their possessions.

   (B) The United States had put a quarantine on Japan following its invasion of Indochina.

   (C) The United States had put a quarantine on Japan immediately following its invasion of China.

   (D) The United States had sent troops to Manchuria to remove the Japanese puppet regime.

4. The first time that Germans managed to enter a major Soviet city during the conflict on the Eastern Front was the battle of

   (A) Moscow.

   (B) Stalingrad.

   (C) Leningrad.

   (D) the Dresden.

5. Following the dropping of the atomic bomb on Hiroshima, Japan

   (A) surrendered.

   (B) evacuated the Pacific islands.

(C) continued to fight.

(D) evacuated the Japanese island where Hiroshima was located.

6. Hitler committed suicide following

(A) the D-Day invasion of Normandy.

(B) the firebombing of Dresden.

(C) the Soviet advance into Russia.

(D) Both (A) and (B).

7. Among those who were persecuted during World War II were

(A) Japanese-Americans.

(B) French children.

(C) Gypsies.

(D) Both (A) and (C).

	Answers		
1. (B)	3. (C)	5. (C)	7. (D)
2. (B)	4. (B)	6. (D)	

Chapter 34

THE COLD WAR

KEY TERMS

The Cold War
Yalta
Potsdam
Truman Doctrine
Marshall Plan
Containment
East and West Berlin
Berlin Airlift
Korean War
38th parallel
Vietnam War
Domino Theory
Viet Cong
Gulf of Tonkin Resolution
Tet Offensive
Richard Nixon
Lyndon Baines Johnson
Khmer Rouge
NATO
Warsaw Pact
Organization of European Economic
    Cooperation (OEEC)
Council of Europe
Common Market
Demilitarized zone (DMZ)
Marshall Tito
Charles de Gaulle
Cuban Missile Crisis
Bay of Pigs Invasion
John F. Kennedy

Nikita Khrushchev
"De-Stalinization"
Peaceful co-existence
Leonid Brezhnev
Brezhnev Doctrine
"De-Krushchevization"
"Re-Stalinization"
Berlin Wall
Velvet Revolution
The Prague Spring
Charter 77
Alexander Dubček
Imre Nagy
Afghanistan
Benigno and Corazon Aquino
Ferdinand Marcos
Ronald Reagan
Mikhail Gorbachev
Glasnost
Perestroika
COMECON
Mujahideen
Taliban
Solidarity
Lech Walesa
Pope John Paul II
Helmut Kohl
Vladimir Putin
Eric Hobsbawm

OVERVIEW

The **Cold War** refers to the ideological conflict between the Communist nations of Eastern Europe, led by the Soviet Union, and the Western democracies, led by the United States. Although the U.S. and the Soviet Union were allies during Word War II and united to fight Nazi Germany, the two nations had opposing ideologies and a deep-seated mistrust of each other. During the Cold War the United States sought to contain the spread of Communism, while Soviet leaders often sought to spread Communism to other countries, particularly those of Eastern Europe.

Yalta

In 1943 in Tehran, Soviet, American, and British leaders had agreed on the strategy that eventually defeated Hitler. According to this strategy, however, the Soviets were to liberate Eastern Europe. In 1945, the Big Three, as Soviet, America, and British leaders came to be known, met again at **Yalta**, which was located in southern Russia. By that time, Soviet forces controlled Poland, Bulgaria, Hungary, Romania, as well as parts of Czechoslovakia, Yugoslavia, and Germany, while the forces of Britain and the U.S. were still struggling to get out of France. At Yalta the parties agreed that when victory came, they would divide Germany into zones under the control of the Big Three, and Germany would pay reparations to Russia. Free elections for all the Eastern European countries under Soviet control were guaranteed, but those countries had to remain friendly to the Soviet Union. In return, Stalin promised to declare war on Japan after the defeat of Germany.

Potsdam

The agreement did not hold up for long, and in many Eastern European nations, important positions were going to the Soviets without the elections promised at Yalta. Moreover, Roosevelt died, and he had been the key figure in trying to work with Stalin to preserve the alliance. When the Big Three met at **Potsdam** in July 1945, a new president, Harry Truman, represented the United States. President Truman had recently learned that the atomic bomb had been tested and that it was functional, and this may have encouraged him to take a tough stance. Truman insisted that Stalin allow the promised free elections. Stalin refused, as he believed that such elections would result in anti-Soviet governments in the Eastern countries. One reason why Stalin wanted pro-Soviet countries along his western border was that they would serve as a buffer against future German aggression, something Stalin greatly feared after the German invasion of Russia in World War II.

Truman and Churchill were in no position to force Stalin to comply. At the same time, they could not simply ignore the situation. Truman cut off U.S. aid to Russia and declared that the U.S. would not recognize any government that was not freely elected. The **"Cold War"** era had begun.

THE COLD WAR

Why is the conflict referred to as the **"Cold War"**? Although armed conflict would erupt around the world between Soviet- and U.S.-backed factions and the leaders of these two nations would engage in tough talk, these two "super-powers" managed to avoid engaging in direct military conflict with each other. Thus, the war was "cold."

However, during the Cold War in both the Soviet Union and the United States, a considerable amount of resources went into the military and the world lived with the constant threat that the conflict might become "hot." In the Soviet Union, more resources were channeled into the military than into any other sector of the economy. The Soviets became a super power during the Cold War, developing atomic and hydrogen bombs. After World War II, the Soviets had the most powerful forces in Eastern Europe, whose countries had largely been devastated by Nazi occupations and military actions. The Soviet alliance with the Communists in Vietnam provided it with bases for its naval fleets, while it also established an alliance with North Korea and briefly with China. Soviet influence also spread to other parts of the world including Cuba.

The Iron Curtain

Elections in Britain ousted Churchill from office, but he remained adamant in his opposition to Stalin. In one of his most famous speeches, he coined the phrase, the **"Iron Curtain"** to describe the division of Europe into free democracies and states under Communist control.

The Truman Doctrine

Truman developed the **Truman Doctrine**, which was a pledge of financial aid to countries threatened by the spread of Communism through force. Although the Truman Doctrine was initially directed towards Greece and Turkey, Truman's Secretary of State George C. Marshall then offered economic aid under the **Marshall Plan** to European nations recovering from World War II. Truman believed that Soviet expansion was made possible partly through economic chaos in recovering nations, and wanted to foster the economic recovery of Europe. The Marshall Plan mandated cooperation among recipients on tariff policies and other economic matters. The United States also created a Defense Department, the Central Intelligence Agency, and Strategic Air Command, and increased military spending.

Meanwhile, the Soviets thought the Marshall Plan was nothing less than imperialism in disguise. Stalin refused aide for the Eastern bloc nations. Stalin then solidified his control over them by removing all noncommunists from governmental positions. Such was the case in Soviet-occupied Czechoslavakia, which had attempted to restore a democratic-style government following the war. Stalin opposed any form of democratic government and insisted that the Czechs refuse aid under the Marshall Plan. In 1948 members of the Cabinet who were not Communists resigned, hoping to force a new round of elections. Jan Masaryk, the foreign minister, was the only remaining opposition leader. Two weeks after the coup, he fell from a window. Although his own secretary believed that he committed suicide, many have accused Soviet sympathizers of orchestrating the event. The new Czech government then deposed the president, Edvard Benes, and replaced him with the leader of the Czech Communist party, Klement Gottwald. The government also imprisoned many advocates of democracy.

Stalin then blocked access to Berlin. The Big Three had divided Germany into four zones, each zone controlled by a different nation. Berlin was situated in the zone controlled by the Soviet Union, but the city itself was also divided into zones. When the three powers that occupied West Germany worked toward economic unity and the formation of a West German government, Stalin blocked all movements through the Soviet zone of Germany to Berlin, and the U. S. and its allies launched the **Berlin Airlift** to bring supplies to West Berlin despite the Soviet blockade. The airlift succeeded. The Soviet blockade of Berlin combined with the successful Communist revolution in China prompted the U.S. to change its foreign policy into one of **containment** of Communism, after the ideas of George F. Kennan in a well-known article in *Foreign Affairs*.

NATO

In 1949 the United States and its allies formed **NATO**, the **North Atlantic Treaty Organization**. Its main purpose was to thwart the advance of Communism in Europe. One of the aims of NATO was to combat the spread of Communism by rearming West Germany. Stalin answered by strengthening his control over Eastern Europe in what would ultimately become known as the **Warsaw Pact** of Eastern European nations and the Soviet Union.

Western European Economic Organizations

Many post-World War II European countries sought to prevent another conflict through economic organizations designed to promote European unity. Europeans created the **Organization of European Economic Cooperation (OEEC)** and the **Council of Europe**. These organizations paved the way for the creation of the **Common Market**, wherein tariffs on goods traded between the members (West Germany, France, Italy, Belgium, Luxemburg, and the Netherlands) were reduced, creating a single market for goods that rivaled the United States in size. European economies not only recovered, but boomed in the post-World War II era. Consumer goods were more readily available, and as more and more people owned cars, for example, travel and tourism increased exponentially. The Common Market evolved into the **European Union**, which by 1992 abolished trade barriers between member nations and then established a common currency, the euro, in 2001. The European Union has more member states than did the Common Market.

Economic Recovery in Europe

The economy boomed in post-World War II Western Europe, partly due to economic cooperation in the Common Market and aid from the Marshall Plan. Many European governments enacted reforms that helped the working class, from national healthcare to government grants for poor families. Many Western European nations become welfare states, and economic growth was a consequence of these developments. The gross national products of European nations experienced their largest surge since the Industrial Revolution. Incomes rose, food production increased, and industries churned out more and more consumer goods. The standard of living rose while unemployment rates were low. By the 1980s some Western European countries, such as Scandinavia and the Federal Republic of Germany, had a higher standard of living than the United States.

Changing Class Structures in Europe

As the economies of Western European nations rebounded, class structure underwent radical changes. As corporations grew, a new middle class arose. Whereas the old middle class prior to the war had been composed of independent business owners or those in the professions, such as law, now the new members of the middle class were experts needed for corporate business. The new positions worked against old hereditary structures, and members of the salaried class of experts came from all levels of society. Meanwhile, those living in rural areas flocked to cities in increasing numbers. Class structure was more democratic, a benefit of welfare reforms that helped the working class. The economic prosperity of the post-World War II continued until a series of crises in the 1970s created a new set of challenges.

Social and Economic Changes in the Soviet Satellites

Although the Marxist ideal of a classless society was never truly achieved, nevertheless, the old ruling aristocracy lost its former status while those of the lower class gained in terms of educational levels and economic status. A much lower percentage of the population in Eastern Europe made their living through agriculture by the late twentieth century. Eastern European nations, along with the Soviet Union, changed from being predominantly agricultural societies and entered the industrial era. Educational levels increased, as many Communist states mandated education and insisted on quotas that allowed for the education of the peasantry and working classes. The more industrialized the nations became, the more they emphasized education in more specialized professions. As the need for specialists grew, many countries dropped their quota system and a new elite class of party members and professionals arose. Women were an important part of the labor force in Eastern Europe, but as in the West, they continued to be paid less and did not achieve the same standing as men. Birth rates also fell in Eastern Europe. Rising alcoholism rates also contributed to social problems.

The Soviet Union rapidly industrialized between the 1920s and 1950s. However, industry was focused on the production of heavy goods rather than consumer goods, and unlike Western Europe, the inhabitants of the Soviet Union never quite entered the age of consumer culture during the Cold War era.

The Korean War (1950–1953)

The Marshall Plan ultimately failed to stop the spread of Communism and, during the period from 1946–1950, the United States had formulated a new policy of **"containment"** in response to the continuing spread of Communism. The revolution in China resulted in a Communist government for that country, and the United States eventually decided to prevent a Communist takeover of Taiwan.

Events in Korea created further alarm. Following the 1905 war between Russia and Japan, Korea was occupied by the Japanese until the end of World War II. The country was divided into two occupation zones after the war, and the Soviets occupied North Korea. Independent elections were to establish a unified government, but the Cold War escalated and two governments resulted, a Communist one in the north and an anti-Communist government in the south.

With the support of Russia, North Korea invaded South Korea in 1950. Truman responded with military aid, including troops of fifteen members of the United Nations countries. **General Douglas MacArthur** led the United Nations forces. When he drove the North Koreans back past the 38th parallel and threatened the Chinese border at the Yalu River, Communist China entered on the side of North Korea. Russia provided aid, but did not directly enter the conflict and the United States chose not to confront them openly in order to avoid a direct conflict. On October 19, 1950, the Chinese assault began under the command of General Peng Dehuai. Some 380,000 People's Liberation Army troops pushed the United Nations' troops back to the 38th parallel. The Communist Chinese and North Korean forces captured Seoul on January 4, 1951, and defeated U.N. troops at the **Battle of Chosin Reservoir**. After MacArthur suggested the possible use of atomic weapons, Truman removed him from command in 1951. That same year peace negotiations started in Kaesong and parties agreed to a ceasefire. A **demilitarized zone (DMZ)** was created around the 38th parallel, which is still in existence today and defended by North Korean troops on one side and South Korean and American troops on the other. No peace treaty was ever signed; the conflict was officially a **police action** rather than a war.

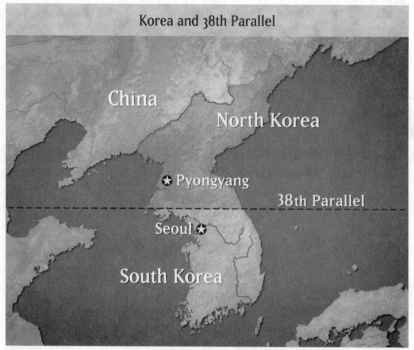

Map Showing the 38ᵗʰ Parallel Separating North and South Korea

The impact of the Korean War on China was profound. China's intervention in the war resulted in greater determination to keep the Chinese out of Taiwan. Truman sent a fleet to Taiwan to block Chinese expansion, but the Chinese actions had also cut them off from other Western powers and the economic and other assistance they might have provided. China, then, was left to turn to Russia for assistance.

CHALLENGES TO THE SUPERPOWERS IN EUROPE

France

The Cold War, which polarized the world in a standoff between Communism and Democracy, renewed desires in France to assert itself. Under **President**

Charles de Gaulle, France resisted the attempts by Americans to dominate Europe. They feared that American protection would be insufficient against the threat of a nuclear attack by Russia, and also wished to regain the status they had enjoyed before the world wars. The French wanted independence from NATO, and in 1963 refused to sign a treaty banning the testing on nuclear weapons. In 1964 they detonated their first atomic bomb in the Sahara desert. Over the next four years the French created a *force de frappe* or nuclear strike force, which they hoped would encourage other European nations to disengage from NATO and American domination.

REBELLIONS IN EASTERN EUROPE

Yugoslavia

Meanwhile, the Soviet Union's influence was also challenged. In Yugoslavia, **Marshal Tito (Joseph Broz)** ruled from 1945 until 1980 and fought for Yugoslavian independence from Soviet control. In 1948 Stalin ousted Yugoslavia from the Soviet Bloc.

Rise of Khrushchev and de-Stalinization

Stalin died in 1953 and, after a brief transitional period, **Nikita Khrushchev** took control of the Soviet Union and embarked on a policy of "de-Stalinization." He ended Stalin's reign of terror and freed many prisoners from Siberian camps, such as Alexander Solzhenitsyn, who in 1970 won the Nobel Prize for his literary works that depicted the horrors of Stalin's prison camps. Khrushchev channeled resources into the production of consumer goods and the improvement of agriculture through cultivating new lands in Kazakhstan. To those who worked the lands, he promised profits as an incentive. Although agricultural production did not grow as much as Krushchev had hoped, his reforms benefitted the people as a whole by raising the standard of living. Krushchev also embarked on a policy of "peaceful coexistence" with capitalist countries, a policy that created tensions with China. The Chinese wanted Soviet help to defeat Chiang Kai-shek on Taiwan, but Krushchev refused to become involved. Krushchev's policies also stimulated rebellions against the Soviets and Communism began to crumble in the Eastern Bloc.

Rebellion in Poland

In 1956 unrest in Poland over Communist economic policies and infringements on freedom of religion led the party leader to resign in favor on **Wladysalw Gomulka**, a more popular leader among the people who allowed those within the Catholic Church greater freedoms. The Church became an important symbol of Polish independence from Soviet influence. Gomulka also addressed economic unrest by stopping collectivization of farms and allowing for peasants to own property. Gomulka, however, agreed to stay in the Warsaw Pact and maintain loyalty to Moscow.

Hungary

Events in Poland inspired rebellion against the Communist government of Hungary, whose leader Matyas Rakosi had acquired a reputation as the "little Stalin" for his brutality. Although scholars dispute the character and ultimate aims of the **Hungarian Uprising**, often termed a "revolution," freedom of speech, religion, greater autonomy in the workplace, and ability of the peasants to own land were among the demands. Massive rebellions ensued, started by students and later aided by workers. The Hungarian Security Police (AVO) attempted to quell the uprising by opening fire on the protestors. The rebellions grew more intense, and the Soviet army became involved at the request of the Hungarian Communist Party.

Castro in Cuba

Krushchev's leadership was further challenged by events that unfolded in Cuba. In 1958 **Fidel Castro** led his supporters to a successful revolution in Cuba, establishing a Communist country within striking distance of the U.S. coastline. Tensions remained high for decades, culminating in the **Bay of Pigs** invasion in April 1961. **President John F. Kennedy** authorized the invasion by armed Cuban exiles to overthrow the Castro government. The fighting lasted only two days, as the exiles did not receive the support of their fellow Cubans nor of the Americans in the air or on the ground. Castro imprisoned several, but 20 months later he released them in exchange for $53 million worth of food and medical supplies.

The Cuban Missile Crisis

Tension continued to mount, culminating in the **Cuban Missile Crisis**. Khrushchev sent 60 ships to Cuba in May 1962, many carrying military material. The Soviets wanted to shift the advantage in the nuclear arena from the United States and place missiles in Cuba. A U–2 flight of October 14 photographed an SS–4 site under construction near San Cristobal. By October 19 surveillance photographs showed four sites operational. While the Soviets had made no special attempt to keep secret their placement of missiles in Turkey, for example, they had not informed Washington of missiles in Cuba. This alarmed the administration, as not only was Cuba well within easy striking distance of the United States, but the United States could not be sure of Khrushchev's motives.

Kennedy addressed the nation on October 22 and announced a naval quarantine or blockade within 500 miles around the Cuban coast. On October 25, Adlai Stevenson brought the case to an emergency session of the United Nations. The Soviets at first denied the charges, but later made two offers of settlement, offering to withdraw their missiles for an American promise not to invade Cuba. In addition, the U.S. was to withdraw missiles from Turkey. On October 27, a U–2 was shot down over Cuba, while Russians almost intercepted another U–2 flying over Russia. After several tense days, Kennedy accepted both offers of the Soviets, and the crisis was over. Khrushchev never recovered politically, since he had not only backed down in the face of U.S. threats, but also initiated the crisis in the first place. In 1964 the Politburo removed him from power, and he died under house arrest in Moscow seven years later.

As for Kennedy, some of his advisors saw his handling of the situation as weak, and had advocated an invasion of Cuba. Given the proximity of nuclear warheads and the fact that the Soviets had given authorization to the Cubans to use them when deemed necessary, many of Kennedy's advisors believed his response to the crisis was too weak to guarantee national safety. The crisis was clearly the closest that the United States and the Soviets came to nuclear war in the Cold War era and Kennedy's choice of diplomacy over a military response kept an invasion and conflict from happening. The Cuban Missile Crisis also prompted the two superpowers to seek a better means of communication. They established a "hot line" between Washington and Moscow and developed a policy of **détente** (**relaxation** or **loosening**).

The Brezhnev Doctrine

Krushchev's blunders during the Cuban Missile Crisis increased opposition to him at home, which was compounded by the growing tensions in the Eastern Bloc countries as a result of his de-Stalinization program. **Leonid Brezhnev** replaced him in 1964 and put an end to de-Stalinization. Brezhnev also began the process of "de-Krushchevization." He attempted to reunite the apparatus of the Communist party and give it responsibility for planning. The more the government controlled industry through quotas, the more production stagnated. Lack of incentives for workers or competition to produce goods derailed the Soviet economy. Brezhnev also renewed the persecution of dissidents and regulated the content of newspapers. He also retreated from Krushchev's policy of peaceful coexistence. In 1968, Brezhnev articulated a new policy known as the Brezhnev Doctrine, which pledged opposition to antisocialist forces. More funds were channeled into the military than into any other sector of the Soviet economy under Brezhnev.

Czechoslovakia and the Prague Spring

Despite Brezhnev's attempt to move away from Krushchev's policies, de-Stalinization had resulted in movement away from the Soviets in the Eastern Bloc. In Czechoslovakia **Alexander Dubček** led reforms in 1968 known as the Prague Spring. These ended when the Soviet Union invaded Prague and took Dubček to Moscow to force him to accept Soviet demands. **Gustav Husak** eventually replaced Dubček and was a dedicated Stalinist.

Re-Stalinization in Russia

The events in Czechoslovakia prompted Soviet leaders to "re-Stalinize" at home by clamping down on protest movements. However, during this period a massive shift of the population in Russia was occurring as more and more people moved to cities. There, they were educated, and the class of professional grew. As educational levels increased, however, protest also increased.

The Berlin Wall

Rebellion brewed in East Germany as well. The Soviets crushed a workers' protest movement in 1953, and many sought refuge in West Germany. Most of the workers who fled to West Germany were highly skilled laborers, which

Adding height to the Berlin Wall

created economic problems in East Germany. In 1961 the government attempted to block the steady stream of refugees by erecting the **Berlin Wall**, as most attempted to enter West Germany through Berlin. East Germany was firmly in the Soviet camp throughout the Cold War Era, especially under such leaders as **Erich Honecker**.

THE SUPERPOWERS IN THE MIDDLE EAST AND ASIA DURING THE COLD WAR

The Vietnam War (1964–1975)

Both the Soviet Union and the United States had interests in Asia. The conflict in Vietnam was also an outgrowth of the Cold War, and in the U.S. belief that once Communism was allowed to flourish in South Vietnam, all of the other governments in southeastern Asia, such as those of Thailand, Laos, Cambodia, Malaysia, and Indonesia, would fall to Communism. This idea was known as the **"domino theory."** The United States, the Republic of Vietnam or South Vietnam, Australia, and South Korea fought against the Democratic Republic of Vietnam or North Vietnam and the National Liberation Front, a South Vietnamese guerrilla movement led by Communists. While Krushchev's policy of peaceful coexistence had resulted in the Soviets discouraging North Vietnamese aggression in the south, Brezhnev did not share the same views. Not only did the Soviets not attempt to end the war, but actively supplied arms to the North Vietnamese. As in the Korean conflict, however, they did not directly participate in hostilities. China watched with great interest, but did not want to become directly involved either. While the Chinese verbally supported their fellow Communists, they quietly promised the United States that they would not enter the conflict unless the U.S. military actions threatened their southern border. Moreover, they refused to allow the Soviets to transport goods to the North Vietnamese through Chinese territory, further deepening the divisions between China and the Soviet Union.

The First Indochina War

The origins of the war go back to French struggle in the First Indochina War against Communist party leader **Ho Chi Minh**, who led a movement for independence of the colony from France. The Vietnamese Communist forces, or Viet Minh, defeated the French army at the Battle of Dien Bien Phu in 1954. Following this event, the French granted the colony independence. At a settlement reached in Geneva, Vietnam was divided into a Communist North and a non-Communist South, with hopes that the South would be a democracy.

Elections in 1956 were intended to unify the two Vietnams, but the southern President Diem and the American President Eisenhower worried about a possible victory for Ho Chi Minh and the elections were never held.

The Viet Cong

The Communists in the north launched a guerilla movement against the south known as the **National Liberation Front**. This movement was also known in the U.S. and in South Vietnam as the *Viet Cong*, from *Viet Nam Cong San*, meaning "Vietnamese Communist." The United States began sending support to the south, while the U.S.S.R. and the North Vietnamese Communists provided arms, advisors, and military to the Viet Cong along the Ho Chi Minh trail.

The Gulf of Tonkin Resolution

The United States never declared war in Vietnam. In 1964 the Senate approved the **Gulf of Tonkin Resolution**, which authorized the use of armed forces in support of freedom in Southeast Asia. On March 8, 1965, President Lyndon Baines Johnson sent 3,500 marines to South Vietnam, which escalated to over 500,000 troops by 1968. The commander of the U.S. forces was General William Westmoreland.

The Nixon Doctrine

By 1968 President Johnson was in political trouble, and eventually announced he would not seek reelection. Robert Kennedy, who might have drawn on the mystique of his bother, the former president, ran for the nomination, but his bid was cut short when he was assassinated by Sirhan Sirhan. **Richard Nixon**, a Republican, won the presidency, and initiated the Nixon Doctrine, according to which South Vietnam would be enabled to fight on its own. Although he gradually withdrew troops from Vietnam, Nixon continued air raids and more U.S. servicemen eventually died during his presidency than during Johnson's tenure in office.

In 1970, Nixon ordered a strike in Cambodia against the Viet Cong. Protests against U.S. involvement in Vietnam had been escalating since 1966, but the events at Kent State in 1970 horrified many Americans, who were having increasing difficulties understanding the goals of the conflict and Washington's justification of its decisions. When several students on the campus of Kent State University protested the war, the National Guard was called in and several students were literally shot down.

The conflict further escalated in 1971, when South Vietnam invaded Laos with the help of the United States. Although George McGovern ran as an anti-war candidate against Nixon in 1972, Nixon triumphed and ended heavy bombing in North Vietnam that same year. Also in 1972, tensions between the Soviets and China were increasing, and Nixon played his trump card. He traveled to China on a goodwill tour. Some scholars believe this visit contributed to the willingness of the North Vietnamese to enter peace talks, as they came to believe their fellow Communists in China might no longer support their military actions. In 1973 the **Paris Peace Accords** officially ended U.S. involvement in Vietnam and in 1975, Congress made the end more official when it refused further aid to South Vietnam.

The North Vietnamese invaded South Vietnam in 1975, captured Saigon, and formed the Socialist Republic of Vietnam in 1976. Saigon became Ho Chi Minh City, a painful reminder of the failure of the United States in Vietnam to stop the spread of Communism.

Meanwhile, the Communist Khmer Rouge seized power in Cambodia in 1975, beginning the infamous reign of terror of Pol Pot, who tried to return Cambodia to its ancient agricultural ways and to wipe out its religion. By the end of his regime, he had exterminated a sizeable proportion of Cambodia's population in the infamous killing fields.

Détente

The many difficulties faced by the superpowers during the Cold War eventually led them to agree to détente, or a reduction in hostilities, in the 1960s. In 1973–1974, the Soviet and U.S. leaders began to agree to a number of treaties, the most important being the **SALT** treaties, growing out of the Strategic Arms Limitation Talks. By the end of the 1970s, however, détente was weakening. The U.S. established full diplomatic relations with the People's Republic of China in 1979 and announced the sale of weapons to the Chinese military in 1980. The diplomatic relationship between China and the United States was directed largely against efforts of the Soviets to expand their power in Asia. These new developments between the U.S. and China created hostility among the Soviets, who were themselves ignoring pledges they had made to respect human rights in the Helsinki Conference (1975).

American **President Ronald Reagan** (1980–1988) contributed heavily to the deterioration of Soviet-U.S. relations through his description of the U.S.S.R. as the "evil empire." He supported a massive military budget and the creation of the **Strategic Defense Initiative**, or **Star Wars**, a system that allegedly would have provided protection from nuclear attack.

Soviet military intervention in Afghanistan also contributed to the decline of détente, as America once again came to believe in the need for a policy of containment.

The Soviets in Afghanistan

In December 1979, the Soviets invaded Afghanistan, further creating renewed tension with the United States. In 1978 a pro-Soviet faction of Muslims took power as the People's Democratic Party of Afghanistan (PDPA). The PDPA implemented radical reforms, leading to massive protests from Islamic leaders. By 1979, the rebellions had become so intense that the Soviets intervened and installed Babrak Karmal as president. He was a confirmed Marxist. The United States supplied ground-to-air missiles to the **mujahideen**, the Islamic resistance in the countryside. In 1986 the Soviets replaced Karmal, who had not succeeding in pacifying the revolt, with Muhammad Najibullah, who had been head of the Afghan Secret Police and who had a close working relationship with the Soviets. This move was not successful either, and so in 1988, the Soviets agreed to a ceasefire in the United Nations and in 1989 withdrew their forces. The mujahideen, however, disintegrated into tribal and ethnic factions who warred against one another. In 1996 the **Taliban**, an army of religious students, took Kabul and executed Najibullah. So was born the Islamic State of Afghanistan. In 2003, the United States toppled the regime, accusing it of harboring the terrorists of the radical **al-Qaeda** organization responsible for the terrorist actions in the United States on September 11, 2001. The al-Qaeda evolved out of the mujahideen, and ironically, the U.S. helped to train and provided weapons for many of their terrorists.

The Philippines

American President Ronald Reagan, who had funneled arms to the Contras in Nicaragua in an effort to halt what he perceived as Sandinista support of Communism, supported the regime of **Ferdinand Marcos**, one of the world's most hated and notorious dictators. Marcos was elected president in 1965 and became the first president to be reelected in 1969. He implemented educational and agricultural reforms and earned the support of the United States as a result of his anti-Communist rhetoric. In 1972, he declared martial law and dissolved the democratic political institutions of the Philippines. The regime also did not respect human rights. The Communist New People's Army and the Muslim Moro National Liberation Front led fierce resistance to Marcos, and in 1981 he declared an end to martial law and began to restore "democratic" reforms. His problems increased when **Benigno Aquino** was assassinated at the Manila airport in August 1983. In 1986, Aquino's wife, **Corazon**, won election as the new president of the Philippines. President Reagan asked Mrs. Aquino to attempt to reconcile with Marcos, since he respected Marcos for his fight against Communism, but the people of the Philippines had the final say.

GORBACHEV AND THE SOVIET UNION FROM 1982–1991

After the death of Brezhnev in 1982, power passed quickly through the hands of Yuri Andropov and Konstantin Chernenko before **Mikhail Gorbachev** came to power. Gorbachev was caught between those who wanted to end Communism and those who wanted to take a hard line and crack down on dissent. In 1986 Gorbachev initiated a radical period of reform, instituting *Glasnost*, or "openness," and *Perestroika*, or "restructuring." *Perestroika* allowed for freer prices and even for the creation of enterprises for profit. According to the new spirit of *Glasnost*, free elections were held in Russia for the first time since the Revolution of 1917. *Glasnost* also allowed for free criticism of Soviet policies. In 1988 Gorbachev abandoned the Brezhnev Doctrine and allowed the Eastern Bloc countries to move away from Communism and even to adopt democracy.

Solidarity in Poland

The realities of Communist society had never matched its ideals in Poland and by the 1980s economic problems sparked public unrest. Poland had been the first to experience rebellion against Soviet-style Communism in 1956 following Krushchev's de-Stalinization. However, Poland's dreams of autonomy did not materialize until the rise of Solidarity beginning in 1980. Solidarity was a workers' union that had transformed itself into a political party led by **Lech Walesa**. The election of the Polish Archbishop Karol Wojtyla as **Pope John Paul II** further fueled demands for reform, and Pope John Paul II was a staunch opponent of Communism. Although the government banned Solidarity in 1981, *Glasnost* made further demands for reform possible. In 1989, free elections were held in Poland, and Solidarity won all of the available seats and soon thereafter elected a non-Communist leader.

Czechoslovakia's Velvet Revolution

Another response in 1989 to Gorbachev's new policy of openness was the **Velvet Revolution**, a peaceful movement that resulted in the overthrow of the Communist government in Czechoslovakia. **Václav Havel**, who had long protested human rights violations along with other members of a group of dissidents known as Charter 77, ousted Husak and became the new leader of Czechoslovakia. Democratic elections were held, and in 1993 Czechoslovakia split into the **Czech Republic** and **Slovakia**.

Romania

Romania experienced revolution as well, but the Romanian military violently resisted the attempt to overthrow the Communist government of **Nicolae**

Ceausescu. Thousands of people were slaughtered in the fighting, but eventually anti-Communist forces won and arrested and executed Ceausescu.

Hungary Responds to Glasnost

Gorbachev's new policy of openness in the late 1980s also resulted in reform in Hungary. In 1989 the Communist government initiated reforms that led to a multiparty system and competitive elections in 1990.

The Fall of the Berlin Wall

The fall of Communism in Hungary opened once again the border between Hungary and Austria. Hungary allowed East Germans to come over the border to Austria and to freedom in the West. Back in East Berlin, resistance to the Communist government grew, and in 1989 the Berlin Wall fell. Free elections were held, toppling the Communist government. Skillful leadership from West German Chancellor **Helmut Kohl** succeeded in creating once again in 1990 a united country for the first time since the end of World War II. Kohl pledged not to develop nuclear or other weapons of mass destruction, reassuring Western powers that a united Germany would pose no threat to European stability. Despite this achievement, there was widespread unemployment in Germany, with greater suffering in the east than in the west. Women in eastern Germany actually lost ground as they were increasingly pressured to stay at home rather than to continue to work.

The End of the Cold War: The Fall of the Soviet Union

Although Mikhail Gorbachev received the Nobel Peace prize in 1990 and was elected as the first executive president of the Soviet Union, his detractors worried that he was leaning towards ending Communism. Gorbachev was surprised when ethnic tensions erupted as a result of *Glasnost*. Lithuania responded to *Glasnost* by declaring independence from the Soviet Union. Although the Soviet Congress of People's Deputies nullified the declaration of independence, ethnic movements were spiraling out of Gorbachev's control. In 1991 a force of Communist hardliners kidnapped him and detained him in the Crimea. **Boris Yeltsin**, elected president of Russia in 1991, rushed to the White House in Moscow and convinced some of the armed forces to switch sides. He sent rescue forces to Gorbachev, who returned and arrested the Gang of Eight that had attempted to oust him.

Nevertheless, Gorbachev never fully regained control. Yeltsin, who had urged Gorbachev to more reform, outlawed Communism in Russia. In 1991, the Ukraine voted for independence, and soon thereafter the presidents of Russia, the Ukraine, and Belarus created the Commonwealth of Independent States. As

Russia had in fact been the very heart of the Soviet Union, its declaration of independence was the death blow for the U.S.S.R. By 1991 the Soviet Union no longer existed and Gorbachev resigned. Boris Yeltsin served as president of Russia until December 31, 1999, and Russia took the place of the U.S.S.R. in the United Nations. Yeltsin vigorously opposed resistance to his economic reforms and his attempt to impose a political system that allowed for divergent political viewpoints. Yeltsin's efforts to create a free market system in Russia, however, had disastrous results for industry, whose output dropped by 30 percent or more. Unemployment was rampant.

Today, most of the former Soviet republics are now part of the **Commonwealth of Independent States**. With the fall of the stronghold of Communism, the Cold War ended. It is ironic that although Yeltsin fought for the independence of Russia, he bitterly repressed the revolts in **Chechnya**, whose population is largely made up of Sunni Muslims who declared independence from Russia in 1991. The situation there has reached genocidal proportions under **Vladimir Putin**, who succeeded Yeltsin as president. Putin opposed the expansion of NATO into Eastern Europe and opened negotiations for renewed cooperation with former Soviet republics.

Review Questions

1. The Velvet Revolution marked the fall of Communism in

    (A) Hungary.

    (B) Czechoslovakia.

    (C) Poland.

    (D) Yugoslavia.

2. The Soviet leader whose policies of *Glasnost* and *Perestroika* encouraged the fall of Communism in the Eastern bloc was

    (A) Brezhnev.

    (B) Khrushchev.

    (C) Stalin.

    (D) Gorbachev.

3. The doctrine that would allow South Vietnam to fight on its own while American forces withdrew was called the

    (A) Nixon Doctrine.

    (B) Marshall Plan.

    (C) Truman Doctrine.

    (D) Monroe Doctrine.

4. Which country did Stalin oust from the Soviet bloc in 1948?

    (A) Romania

    (B) Yugoslavia

    (C) Czechoslovakia

    (D) Lithuania

5. Which of the following was most responsible for the defeat of the Soviets in Afghanistan?

    (A) United States

    (B) Iraq

    (C) Pakistan

    (D) The Taliban

6. The brutal Cambodian regime that exterminated thousands of citizens was

 (A) the Khmer Rouge.
 (B) Viet Cong.
 (C) the Laotian Liberation Front.
 (D) the Kampuchean Democratic Republic.

7. The Gulf of Tonkin Resolution

 (A) mandated an end to hostilities in Vietnam.
 (B) was an official declaration of war against North Vietnam.
 (C) condemned the My Lai massacre.
 (D) authorized the use of military force by the United States in Vietnam.

8. Communists were not in control of which of the following governments in the post-World War II era?

 (A) North Vietnam
 (B) North Korea
 (C) Cuba
 (D) South Vietnam

Answers			
1. (B)	3. (A)	5. (D)	7. (D)
2. (D)	4. (B)	6. (A)	8. (D)

Chapter 35

ASIA AFTER WORLD WAR II

KEY TERMS

Mao Zedong

Jiang Jieshi (Chiang Kai-shek)

Taiwan

People's Republic of China

Great Leap Forward

Great Proletariat Revolution

Deng Xiaoping

The Four Modernizations

Tiananmen Square

Hong Kong

Macao

World Trade Organization

Little Tigers

General Chung Hee Park

Keiritsu

Chaebol

Muhammad Ali Jinnah

Great Calcutta Killing

Mohandas Gandhi

Jawaharlal Nehru

Policy of Non-Alignment

Bandung Conference

Bangladesh

Kashmir

Indira Gandhi

Sikhs

THE IMPACT OF COLONIALISM:
THE MIDDLE EAST, AFRICA, AND ASIA
IN CRISIS FOLLOWING WORLD WAR II

A new world order began to emerge in the post-World War II period, as colonial empires were broken apart and nationalistic movements dotted the landscape. Colonialism had a profound impact on many regions of the world, especially in Africa, parts of Asia, and the Middle East. Western imperialists had often created arbitrary boundaries in places where they colonized; these arbitrary divisions often attempted to unite groups of people who had long been torn by ethnic and other rivalries. When the European colonizers departed, these ethnic rivalries erupted into many violent clashes in Africa, the Middle East, and India. The conflict between India and Pakistan is one example of these clashes, as are the many ethnic conflicts in Africa, such as those of the Hutus and the Tutsis.

Although the Cold War broke the world into two opposing camps for many years after World War II, the bipolar world of the Cold War eventually broke down too. The world entered a global age of unprecedented change in the decades following World War II.

CHINA

Japanese aggression in China had been a major factor in the events leading to World War II in Asia. The Japanese occupation of China had a pronounced effect on internal politics in China as well. Some historians suggest that the Japanese presence helped to solidify the forces supporting Mao Zedong and the Communists. In response to the Japanese advance into China in 1938, Jiang Jieshi (Chiang Kai-shek) and the Nationalists moved to Chongqing (Chungking), a location deep in the interior of China. Mao, on the other hand, preferred to use tactics of guerilla warfare in the countryside and in so doing, managed to build support among the peasantry. When Japan finally surrendered in 1945 after the bombings of Hiroshima and Nagasaki, the Nationalists and Communists no longer had a common enemy to fight and now competed for control of China. Fighting erupted in Manchuria in 1946, but by 1949, however, the Communists had defeated the Nationalists in several engagements and the People's Liberation Army, or the Communist forces, controlled most of the Chinese mainland. The Nationalists, still led by Jiang Jieshe (Chiang Kai-shek) fled to **Taiwan**, and proclaimed his government there the legitimate government of China as the **Republic of China**. Most of the country's gold resources went with him.

The People's Republic of China

On October 1, 1949, Mao Zedong established the **People's Republic of China**, led by the Chinese Communist Party. Chairman Mao reformed Chinese society, using Soviet Russia as his model. Mao referred to this phase of China's history as the New Democracy, and he sought to encourage support of his program among the population. The close relationship between the Soviets and the Communist Chinese resulted in Soviet support for the removal of Taiwan from the Security Council of the United Nations. Approximately one-half of Chinese exports went to the U.S.S.R. and the Soviets further supported the development of Communism in China with loans. Later, the Chinese argued that the Soviets had not helped with enough aid, especially in their quest to reassert authority in Tibet. The Soviets remained neutral in this conflict and even made loans to India, whom the Chinese believed helped to encourage the rebellion of Tibetans. Although the relationship between China and the Soviet Union broke down in the 1960s, the Soviet model profoundly influenced Mao's programs in China.

Purges

As in the U.S.S.R., the Communist party in China controlled the nation through its Central Committee and Politburo, but the constitution did create, at least on paper, a national assembly to be chosen through popular election. Just as Stalin had purged all those who opposed him, Mao and his followers purged China of Nationalist supporters and others who opposed their policies. In 1951, for example, he executed thousands of Chinese and thrust many more into labor camps. Between 1949 and 1954, Mao claimed to have eliminated over 800,000 "class enemies" in the purges.

Land Reform

Mao introduced his own version of the Five Year Plan in 1955. Like Stalin, Mao wanted to transform China into an industrial nation that was self-sufficient. The policies of the first plan mimicked those of Stalin, by focusing on heavy industry to the detriment of the production of consumer goods. Like Stalin as well, he attempted to equalize land holdings in the countryside. Mao took the land of the largest ten percent of the landholders, who together owned a shocking 70 to 80 percent of the land. He redistributed the land to over 300 million peasants. Each peasant received an equal amount of land, and these allotments are still visible in today's rural villages.

The Great Leap Forward

Mao's **Great Leap Forward** (1958–1961) moved the country further on the road to industrialization. He abolished private farms, and collective farms were created. Through small-scale industrial production on the farms, Mao hoped to bring China firmly into the industrial age. On the collective farms, families ate with other families in communal dining halls and Communist propaganda worked against the traditional emphasis on family bonds. Individualism was discouraged. Mao emerged as even more radical than the Soviets in his effort to implement true Communism and to spread the Communist revolution abroad.

Just as Stalin's attempt to collectivize the farms of Russia resulted in disaster, however, so did Mao's "Great Leap Forward" result in a "great leap backward." Production fell as the peasants could not meet quotas, and a series of bad harvests doomed the program. Mao refused to accept responsibility and blamed the failures on the eating habits of sparrows, which he called "counterrevolutionaries." When he ordered sparrows killed, he left the way open for insects to devour the remaining crops. By 1962, the "Great Leap Forward" had resulted in the deaths by starvation of twenty million Chinese.

The Great Proletarian Cultural Revolution

Mao's **Great Proletarian Cultural Revolution** (1966–1976) was another attempt to weed out opposition to his reforms. He had accused the Soviets by this time of being "revisionists," a term that was very offensive within the Communist world. Now he found revisionists throughout China, and targeted the intellectuals, professionals, and others associated with foreign influences or bourgeois values. The so-called Revolution set China back many years as it stripped China of its educated population and sent thousands to jails, rural labor camps, or to their deaths.

Deng Xiaoping

Chairman Mao died in 1976, having brought China to its knees. **Deng Xiaoping** took power in 1981, and condemned to life in prison or executed the **Gang of Four**, which included Mao's widow, Jiang Qing. One of the most controversial aspects of Deng Xiaoping's rule was the institution of the one-child policy in 1979. China's population had exploded by the 1970s despite a series of famines and other problems. From 1949 to 1970 the population increased by 270 million people. The effect of those people having children at previous rates would have been disastrous. The one-child policy applied to people living in cities and only to the Han Chinese. Ethnic minorities were exempt. Although many people skirt the policy by abandoning their female children to orphanages, having abortions, or simply not reporting the births, the policy continues to be in effect.

More successful were a series of reforms known as "Deng's revolution." Deng emphasized the "four modernizations," in agriculture, industry, national defense, and technology. In agriculture, Deng Xiaoping allowed collectives to lease land to peasants. Whatever they were able to produce above the rent payment could be sold on the market. Industries rather like cottage industries were also tolerated in the countryside to provide an outlet for excess labor. By the 1980s, the average farm income doubled. Many peasants now valued production of cash crops that might further their economic position, and so inadvertently, the new agricultural policies detracted from the production of staple crops like rice. Further, rural families were more willing to violate the one-child policy and pay the required fine in order to boost their farm's productivity. Nevertheless, the overall effect of the policies was to significantly elevate the standard of living in China. Per capita income dramatically increased. By the 1990s, the private sector in China produced ten percent of the gross domestic product, China had an affluent middle class, and the government began to shut down state-run industries.

The more the standard of living was raised, however, the more the younger generation was attracted to protest. When Deng Xiaoping reversed the isolationism of Mao Zedong and allowed foreign capitalist investments in China, he allowed many Chinese students to study at foreign universities. The exposure to new views, such as democracy, that came from the end of isolationism brought unintended consequences. In 1989 students staged a sit-down protest at **Tiananmen Square** in Beijing in front of the Forbidden Palace, once home to the emperors of China. Deng Xiaoping had himself been persecuted and condemned to labor during the Mao era, and he feared revolutionary movements of any kind. He responded with vicious force to the students in Tiananmen, mowing them down with tanks and guns. Many students died, while reporters filmed the events and showed them to a worldwide audience.

Unknown protester blocks tanks in Tiananmen Square in 1989. Hundreds perished after the government repressed student-led pro-democracy demonstrations.

Return of Hong Kong and Macao

When Deng died in 1997, China was changing rapidly. The British abided by earlier treaties and returned Hong Kong to Chinese rule. Deng promised a "one country, two systems" style of rule, according to which the Chinese socialist system will not be implemented in Hong Kong. The Portuguese soon thereafter followed by returning Macao in 1999 to the Chinese. Deng had allowed China to enter the worldwide economy, and the return of its possessions from the European colonizers forced him to address issues for which there were no precedents, especially in the wake of Mao's isolationism. China continued to progress toward global superpower economic status, and in 2001, China joined the **World Trade Organization**.

Economic Problems in Contemporary China

While the economy of China has increased rapidly over the last two decades, there are also signs of significant problems in China. The rapid increase of the population has meant a decrease in the amount of land available to cultivate. A grain surplus has caused difficulties for farmers, as has China's membership in the World Trade Organization, which has brought competition from foreign imports. There is presently a mass exodus from the rural areas to urban areas such as Shanghai, where many remain without work. The closing of many state-run factories has further increased unemployment, and often women are the ones to suffer the most, with many being forced into prostitution.

JAPAN

Asia experienced an "economic miracle" after World War II, especially in Japan. The transformation of Japan made it one of the technological giants of the world. Japan currently holds the record as the world's largest exporter, and its gross domestic product exceeds that of Great Britain and France combined, an amount equal to about one-half that of the United States. In 1950, Japan's gross domestic product was only about one-third that of France and Great Britain combined. Agricultural reforms fostered by the U.S. occupation also broke up large landed estates with absentee landlords and spurred the growth of a class of yeoman farmers.

This transformation is remarkable, especially in light of the fact that the industrial base developed during the Meiji era was almost completely destroyed in World War II. The Allies, in fact, also tried to break up the *zaibatsu* conglomerates in the years following World War II, out of the belief that the Meiji's centralization of industry contributed to the militaristic ethos of Japan. Nevertheless, part of the *zaibatsu* structure was preserved under a new system of "interlocking arrangement," called the **keiritsu**. As the Allies worried about the spread of Communism in Asia, they looked to Japan to help them, and became more willing to tolerate economic conglomerates.

Among the other reasons often cited for Japan's transformation after World War II are the fact that it was occupied and under the protection of the United States and, therefore, had to channel little of its wealth into its own defense. In fact, the total destruction of its Meiji industrial plants actually promoted faster development, as development in other countries was often hindered by older machinery and plant structures. Other historians point to the Confucianism of Japanese society as a reason for its remarkable recovery and growth after World War II. Confucianism contributes to higher rates of education, and Japanese workers are among the most skilled in the world. Further, Japanese society is oriented toward the common good, as opposed to individual advancement, a fact that contributes to the success of its industries. Further, the Japanese government continued to be heavily involved in promoting industry. The Ministry of International Trade and Industry controlled imports, while flooding foreign markets with goods priced below cost.

In the 1990s, however, these policies backfired as the Japanese economy ran into difficulties. When the value of the yen rose, it was more difficult to export goods. As the economic crisis hit, the tradition of employing workers for life was a tremendous strain on the resources of manufacturers. As workers were laid off, women tended to suffer the most. Moreover, Japanese began to criticize the quality of their goods, leading the government to accept more foreign competition at home.

THE LITTLE TIGERS

The **"Little Tigers"** of Hong Kong, South Korea, Singapore, and Taiwan also experienced phenomenal growth. By the 1980s, the Little Tigers were a force to be reckoned with on the international scene. Among the factors that contributed to the rise of the Little Tigers are significant foreign capital and also autocratic governments led by an elite group of people interested in modernization that promoted industry and restricted opposition.

In South Korea the economic transformation was the work of **General Chung Hee Park**, who instituted a series of five-year plans to develop the private sector, whose growth had been limited while under Japanese rule. Per capita income increased and the economic growth rate also increased. The creation of massive conglomerates called **chaebol**, such as Hyundai and Samsung, was spurred in part by low wages. The *chaebol* contributed, though, to corruption, as they often bribed officials for favors. However, Chung Hee Park was a very autocratic ruler, who was eventually assassinated. **Kim Young Sam**, who was elected president in 1992, attempted to end corruption associated with the *chaebol*. Nevertheless, the economy continued to be troubled, as the trade deficit increased while the growth rate declined. Unemployment rose.

Taiwan's growth was spurred by a security treaty signed with the United States in 1954, protecting it from a possible invasion from the mainland Chinese. The government of Taiwan calls itself the Republic of China. As in Japan, the government of Taiwan supported important industries. Taiwan also encouraged foreign investment and enacted land reform provisions. The government purchased large tracts of land over three acres and then sold them to the tenant farmers. Private enterprise was encouraged as well. Political tensions, however, have grown in Taiwan, especially following the death of Chiang Kai-shek in 1975. The Democratic Progressive Party has grown in opposition to the Nationalists, and in 2000, one of their leaders, Chen Shuibian, was elected president. The Democratic Progressive Party favors an independent Taiwan, something China has pledged never to allow.

Singapore gained independence from Britain in 1965. Under Prime Minister Lee Kuan-yew, Singapore has become the hub of the banking industry in Malaysia and beyond. The government also promoted industries here. The most successful industries are shipbuilding, tourism, electronics, and oil. Singapore, as is the case in other Asian states, was ruled by an autocratic regime that contributed to its economic development. Recent leadership, such as that of Goh Chok Tong, has retreated from harsh policies.

Hong Kong was returned to the People's Republic of China in 1997 by the British, and its economy has benefited from tourism and cheap labor. Unlike other Little Tigers, Hong Kong had a system of free enterprise that continues to function even after its return to Chinese rule.

Asia was rocked by a severe financial crisis in 1997, however, whose impact was felt in the West. The crisis began when foreign investors began to pull out of Thailand. The Thai stock market dropped by 75 percent, and the crisis spread to Malaysia, Indonesia, South Korea, and the Philippines. In an earlier era, the crisis would not have spread so quickly, but globalism has created a vast economic worldwide network.

SOUTH ASIA AFTER WORLD WAR II: INDIA

World Wars I and II unleashed a tidal wave of colonial revolts, which resulted in the end of British rule in India after World War II. The Indian National Congress had failed to coalesce into a unified front, as Muslims disagreed with Hindus over the fate of India. The British made few attempts to reconcile the two groups, and in the end, made decisions that ensured a permanent split.

The Great Calcutta Killing

The leader of the Muslim League, Muhammad Ali Jinnah, advocated a Day of Direct Action in 1946, and as rioting erupted, approximately 6,000 people died in the Great Calcutta Killing. Jinnah took a hard-line stance on the issue of Indian independence, rejecting any possibility that Hindus and Muslims might live and work together to build a new and united India. According to him, the only solution was to create a separate state for Muslims, Pakistan.

Partition of India

Other Indian leaders, such as Mohandas Gandhi and Jawaharlal Nehru, did not want to see India partitioned. On August 15, 1947, however, Britain partitioned India into two separate regions, creating an independent Pakistan for Muslims. Gandhi called the event a **vivisection**, the cutting up of a living body. By 1948, ten million Muslims or Hindus had migrated to either India or Pakistan, amidst tremendous violence. Gandhi went on hunger strikes to persuade Indians to protest Western imperialism and to use only Indian-made goods. His method was that of *ahimsa* or nonviolence, which he referred to as "soul-power." Gandhi rejected all forms of Western culture as material, and believed that the Western notion of progress was bankrupt. He advocated a return to the simple agricultural life of India before the arrival of the British. In the end he fell victim to an assassins bullet.

Nehru

Nehru, devastated at the death of Gandhi, then pursued a policy of **nonalignment** with the superpowers of the Cold War, which he articulated most clearly at the Bandung Conference in April 1955. At the **Bandung Conference**, twenty-three Asian and six African leaders met to formulate a "third path," or an alternative to alliance with either of the superpowers of the Cold War.

Unlike Gandhi, however, Nehru believed in the development of the economy along Western industrial lines. Nehru believed India could not succeed without a firm industrial base and a vibrant economy. Nehru took control of major industries but allowed private enterprise to continue on the local level. While in general he discouraged foreign investments, he did accept economic help from the Soviets, which often gave rise to questions about his policy of nonalignment.

Unfortunately, Nehru could not stop the violence between Hindus and Muslims, and war erupted between India and Pakistan over the province of **Kashmir** in 1947. Pakistan lost its bid to annex the province, and then turned to the United States for help. Nehru accepted help from the Soviets, but continued to pursue his policy of neutrality. Tensions within Pakistan continued to increase, and in 1971 East Pakistan seceded with the help of troops from India and became the separate nation of **Bangladesh**.

Indira Gandhi

Nehru's daughter **Indira Gandhi** became prime minister in 1966 and twice served in that capacity. She attempted to revive Indian agriculture through the "Green Revolution," but her policies created further misery among the poor. Overpopulation contributed to the problem. Following a series of charges that her party committed fraud in the 1971 elections, in 1975 she declared a state of national emergency and assumed dictatorial powers. Her methods during the next two years were repressive, as her son Sanjay forced millions of poor people to undergo involuntary sterilization to deal with serious overpopulation problems. In 1977, elections ousted her from office. She returned in 1980, but now faced growing rebellion from the Sikhs. She ordered an attack on the Sikh temple in Amristar and, as a result, two of her Sikh bodyguards assassinated her in 1984. Her son **Rajiv Gandhi** attempted to resolve the Shik situation, but he was assassinated in 1991.

Review Questions

1. Which of the following was NOT a factor that contributed to the economic miracle in Japan following World War II?

   (A) High education levels due to Confucian influence

   (B) The preservation of industrial plants from before the war despite the devastation caused by bombings

   (C) Agricultural reform that broke up large landed estates

   (D) The need to spend little on defense

2. Which conditions were common among the Little Tigers and helped to create strong economies following World War II?

   (A) Strong regimes that promoted industry

   (B) Land reform packages

   (C) Free enterprise

   (D) Both (A) and (B)

3. China was opened to foreign investment by

   (A) Mao Zedong.

   (B) Deng Xiaoping.

   (C) the revolts in Tiananmen Square.

   (D) the Great Proletarian Cultural Revolution.

4. Among the factors that caused the student protest movement in Tiananmen Square in 1989 was

   (A) exposure to Western ideas.

   (B) the increasing economic strength of China brought by the four modernizations.

   (C) the declining economic security caused by the failure of the four modernizations.

   (D) Both (A) and (B).

5. Among the consequences of the four modernizations of Deng Xiaoping was

   (A) rising per capita income.

   (B) rigid state control of all agricultural production in the rural areas.

(C) farmers turned to cash crops to take advantage of the new right to sell products on the open market.

(D) Both (A) and (C).

6. The predominant religion of Pakistan is

(A) Hinduism.

(B) Christianity.

(C) Islam.

(D) Buddhism.

7. The leader of India who attempted to reform agriculture and to implement laws to control the population was

(A) Mohandas Gandhi.

(B) Jawaharlal Nehru.

(C) Muhammad Ali Jinnah.

(D) Indira Gandhi.

8. Among the problems faced in post-World War II India is

(A) population decline.

(B) poverty.

(C) religious disputes over territory.

(D) Both (B) and (C).

Answers

1. (B)	3. (B)	5. (D)	7. (D)
2. (D)	4. (D)	6. (C)	8. (D)

Chapter 36

THE MIDDLE EAST AFTER WORLD WAR II

KEY TERMS

Balfour Declaration

Haganah

Jerusalem

East Jerusalem

West Bank

Palestine

Gaza Strip

Six-Day War

Intifadas

Anwar Sadat

Yom Kippur War

Camp David Peace Accords

Menahem Begin

Palestinian Liberation Organization

Yasser Arafat

Yitzhak Rabin

Oslo Accords

Gamul Abdel Nasser

Operation Litani

Hezbollah

War of the Camps

Amal Militia

Ta'if Agreement

Operation Grapes of Wrath

The League of Nation Mandates
    in the Middle East

Ba'ath party

Saddam Hussein

Operation Desert Storm

Operation Iraqi Freedom

Ayatollah Khomeni

Mohammad Reza Pahlavi

OVERVIEW

Following World War II, many Middle Eastern countries won their independence from the European mandates established by the League of Nations following World War I. Among these was **Jordan**, which gained independence from Britain in 1946. **King Hussein** ruled Jordan until he died in 1999. King Hussein was a member of the Hashemite monarchy, whose origins date back to Muhammad's great grandfather, Hashim. Similarly, the fall of France in 1940 during World War II led to its evacuation of Syria. In 1946, Syria's republican government, formed during the French mandate period, took control of the new country. The history of the Middle East, however, was further complicated by the creation of Israel.

THE CREATION OF ISRAEL
AND THE PROBLEM OF PALESTINE

The **Balfour Declaration** (1917) had promised to establish a secure homeland for Jews in Palestine. As World War II progressed and Hitler's Final Solution threatened the very existence of European Jewry, Jews flocked in increasing numbers to Palestine. Simultaneously, rising Arab nationalism in the wake of the formation of Arab states after World War II contributed to the hostility. The British tried to allay Arab fears by limiting Jewish immigration. Leon Uris's fictionalized account, *Exodus*, of the many Jews forced to enter Palestine illegally due to British blockades portrays the Catch-22 that entrapped all parties. In 1945 Jewish resistance to British rule began in earnest, led by the **Haganah**, an underground military organization founded to protect Jewish settlers and refugees. By 1947, the British announced their intention to withdraw and allow the United Nations to decide the matter.

Creation of Israel

The U.N. proposed to divide the area into a Jewish and Palestine state and, before the Arab outcry could even be heard and the matter further debated, Jews took matters into their own hands and announced in May 1948 the creation of the state of Israel.

Arab-Israeli Wars

Arab states mobilized in support of the Palestinians, and Egypt, Syria, Jordan, and Iraq declared war on Israel. The **Arab-Israeli** wars had begun. Nevertheless, in 1949, the U.N. forged a truce and partitioned Palestine. Significantly, Jerusalem was partitioned between Israel and Jordan, with Jordan in control of East Jerusalem. The West Bank went to Jordan, while the Gaza Strip went to Egypt.

Israel controlled the coastal areas of Palestine and the Negev desert to the Red Sea. Many Palestinians fled their homelands and sought refuge in other Arab lands.

EGYPT

Nasser

Led by **Gamul Abdel Nasser**, the Egyptians deposed **King Farouk** in 1952. Nasser wanted to unite and lead the Arab world against the Israelis. Nasser also refused to become allied with any of the superpowers of the Cold War, and terminated British rights to the Suez Canal in 1954. In 1956 he nationalized the Canal, resulting in the combined attack of British, French, and Israeli forces. The United States condemned the military invasion of Egypt, and so did the Soviets. The forces withdrew, and Nasser became the acknowledged moral leader of the Arab world. Nevertheless, Israel had not been toppled, and both the U.S. and the U.S.S.R. supported its right to exist. Nasser continued to promote Pan-Arabism, and united with Syria in 1958 as the United Arab Republic. The union dissolved when Syrian leaders were toppled in a coup in 1961.

The Six-Day and Yom Kippur Wars

In 1967 Israel defeated Egypt and Syria in the **Six-Day War**, and created further tension when it occupied the Gaza Strip, Golan Heights, the West Bank, (formerly a territory of Jordan), and the Sinai Peninsula. For Egypt, the loss of the Sinai meant loss of access to the Suez Canal. Nasser's ambitions for Pan-Arabism had failed to stop the advance of Israel. Egypt lost again to the Israelis in the 1973 **Yom Kippur War**, and its attack on Israel on Yom Kippur, an important holy day for Jews, brought tremendous condemnation. It had, however, managed to regain a portion of the Sinai Peninsula. As a result of a 1979 peace treaty, Israel withdrew from the Sinai entirely by 1981.

Anwar Sadat

During the presidency of **Anwar Sadat**, who followed Nasser, U.S. **President Jimmy Carter** initiated the Camp David talks, which resulted in the **Camp David Peace Accords** with Israel, led by **Prime Minister Menachem Begin**. Sadat was assassinated, however, in 1981, and many planks of the peace accords were never enacted. In retaliation, the Arab states and the **Palestinian Liberation Organization (PLO)** attempted to isolate Egypt.

The Intifada of 1987

Palestinians have launched several uprisings, or **intifadas** ("shaking offs") against Israeli occupation of the West Bank and the Gaza Strip. In 1987, a massive rebellion began on the Gaza Strip as a result of the stabbing of an Israeli

Presidents Anwar Sadat and Jimmy Carter along with Prime Minister Menachem Begin celebrate the Camp David Peace Accords.

while shopping in Gaza. One day later, four residents of the Jabalya refugee camp in Gaza died in a traffic accident. Rumors spread that Israelis had killed them. While the violence was at first spontaneous, it later became more organized, as protestors bombarded the Israeli troops with Molotov cocktails and other devices. The Intifada dissipated by 1990, but it created a new center of resistance independent of the PLO.

PLO and Israeli Peace Treaties

In 1993 and 1994, however, the leader of the **Palestinian Liberation Organization**, **Yasser Arafat**, was willing to negotiate. **Yitzhak Rabin**, the prime minister of Israel, and Arafat secretly negotiated a peace agreement, the **Oslo Accords**, whereby there would be limited Palestinian self-rule in territories occupied by Israel. This led to the creation in 1994 of the **Palestinian National Authority** (PNA) to administer the West Bank and Gaza Strip, and plans were that eventually the PNA would become an independent Palestinian State. Transfer of power and territory was to occur in stages, but an interim period of self-government was proclaimed. Many Jews were outraged by Rabin's attempts to make peace, as they believed it threatened Israel's security and also meant the loss of numerous Israeli settlements in those areas.

In 1995, a Jewish extremist assassinated Rabin. The peace process seemed hopelessly stalled when the Israelis sent occupation forces in 2002 into the Palestinian National Authority.

The peace plan had failed, and although efforts to achieve peace between Israel and the Palestinians continued, no agreements have been reached. Israeli **Prime Minister Benjamin Netanyahu** attempted to galvanize the U.S. and other powers against terrorism, further aggravating Palestinian and Israeli peace talks. When the Palestinians elected a new prime minister, **Mahmud Abbas**, hopes were that the peace process would accelerate. However, the current prime minister of Israel, **Ariel Sharon**, has often expressed the belief that peace is impossible between Arabs and Jews. Sharon has authorized the construction of a barrier to separate the Israelis from the PNA and also the Gaza Strip. Palestinians and human rights activists throughout the world have criticized this action as a serious threat to the peace process.

LEBANON

Lebanon became a French mandate following World War I. Lebanon declared independence in 1943, and the French withdrew after World War II in 1946. Tension between various groups has always been present in Lebanon. In 1958, U.S. Marines were sent to help the Lebanese put down an insurrection, and the arrival of Palestinian refugees from the 1967 Arab-Israeli war further complicated the situation.

The Palestinian Liberation Organization

Yasser Arafat was one of those who fled to Lebanon, and eventually his Palestinian Liberation Organization (PLO) established headquarters in Beirut (Lebanon) and Damascus (Syria). The PLO was founded in 1964, and joined the Arab League in 1976. It launched a wave of terrorist activity that resulted in several Israeli campaigns into Lebanon. However, its agitation for Palestinian autonomy ultimately led to the creation of the Palestinian National Authority in 1994. Today the headquarters of the Palestinian National Authority are in **Ramallah** on the West Bank.

Civil War

Tension between Christians and Muslims increased and erupted in 1975 in civil war. Various Muslim factions fought against the predominantly Christian Lebanese army. An Arab Deterrent Force headed by Syria arrived to help calm the situation, but when the Palestinian Liberation Organization blew up a bus in Israel, the Israelis launched Operation Litani and invaded in 1978. During the operation, Israelis massacred civilian inhabitants of three villages at Abbasieh, Khiam, Kawnin. The United Nations issued a resolution calling for Israel to withdraw, which it did. However, it left an ally, the South Lebanon Army, to protect a buffer zone between Lebanon and Israel.

PLO Occupies South Lebanon

In 1981, the PLO occupied South Lebanon and escalated terrorist attacks against Israel. The PLO and other factions virtually tore Lebanon to shreds and it had no effective government. Although the U.S. negotiated a cease-fire in 1981, the PLO continued to shell Israel.

Operation Peace for Galilee

In 1982, Israel launched Operation Peace for Galilee against the PLO. Within six months the Israelis withdrew, again leaving the South Lebanon Army in charge of a smaller buffer zone. In 1982, the U.S. again attempted to intervene and established a multinational force, including U.S. Marines, in Lebanon. Syrian and PLO forces withdrew from Beruit.

Two Governments in Lebanon

Lebanon elected a candidate supported by the Israeli president, but he was soon assassinated, and the Israelis entered West Beirut. The Israeli army took no action as the Lebanese Christian militias massacred almost 800 Palestinian civilians in the Sabra and Shatila refugee camps. Ariel Sharon, the Israeli minister of defense, was indirectly blamed for the incident and was forced to resign.

Terrorism on the Rise in 1983–1984

During this period, significant terrorist attacks occurred against the United States, including a suicide bombing at the U.S. Embassy in West Beirut.

Hezbollah

The terrorist organization **Hezbollah** also emerged during this period, from militant Shi'ite groups who were opposed to intervention from the United States and Israel, and they bitterly resented perceived advantages of this foreign aid for the Christian population of Lebanon. Syria and Iran supported the Hezbollah.

The Amal Militia

To further complicate affairs, an Iranian Shi'ite founded the **Amal militia** to protect Shi'ite interests in Lebanon. "Amal" is the word for "hope" in Arabic.

It is also the acronym for Afwaj al Muquwamah al Lubnaiyyah, which means "Lebanese Resistance Detachment." The Amal, a moderate faction, clashed with Arafat and the PLO. The Amal militia captured West Beirut in 1984, and the U.S. Marines withdrew in 1984.

The Hizballah and Amal militias fought one another bitterly in the **War of the Camps** (1985–1986) and conflict erupted again in Beirut in 1988. In 1988, Lebanon was further divided as a Christian government was formed in East Beirut to compete with a Muslim government in West Beirut.

The Ta'if Agreement

A committee appointed by the Arab League negotiated the Ta'if Agreement of 1989, which finally brought the civil war to an end. The Lebanese ratified the accord in November and elected Rene Mouawad as president. The new president was assassinated in a car bombing only a few days later, and Elias Hrawi succeeded him, serving until 1998.

End of Lebanese Civil War

Muslims have been given a greater voice in Lebanon since the civil war, but the government has since fought Sunni rebels in the north and Hizballah still retains its weapons. Branches of the al-Qaeda terrorist organization have also been linked to Lebanon. In 1996, Israel launched "Operation Grapes of Wrath" in response to Hizballah bombings of northern Israeli villages. During the operation, Israel was accused of killing through bombing attacks 106 civilians who had taken refuge in a United Nations shelter in Cana. Another 110 civilians were injured. In April, Israel and the Hizballah agreed to the "April Understanding" according to which the combatants were to avoid civilian targets. On May 23, 2000, the Israelis withdrew their armies from the south and the Bekaa Valley. Hizballah forces have continued to launch periodic attacks on Israel.

Syria maintained troops in Lebanon until it announced its withdrawal in 2005.

IRAN

In 1953, the United States Central Intelligence Agency, with help from the British, put **Mohammad Reza Pahlavi** in power as the Shah of Iran and supported his controversial regime. The shah was an abusive dictator at home who did not respect civil liberties. Under his regime, Iranians were tortured and there were numerous other human rights violations. Eventually, Iranians rebelled and overthrew the regime in 1979. The **Ayatollah Khomeni** took power and established a strict Shi'ite state, the Islamic Republic of Iran. In

1979 resentment of U.S. support of the shah led to the capture of the U.S. embassy in Tehran. For two years, Shi'ite militants held U.S. hostages. President Jimmy Carter's covert attempt to rescue the hostages was a disaster, and combined with economic and other difficulties at home, the Iranian hostage crisis helped to usher him out of office. The hostages finally returned home during the early presidency of Ronald Reagan. After Khomeni's death in 1989, Iran relaxed some of its conservative tendencies. Since the fall of **Saddam Hussein**, however, the Shi'ite population of Iran has attempted to influence the largely Shi'ite population of southern Iraq.

IRAQ

After World War I, the League of Nations created a British mandate in Iraq and carved Iraq from Ottoman territories. The British mandate in Iraq ended in 1932 and in 1945, Iraq joined the United Nations and helped to found the Arab League. In 1958 a coup d'etat overthrew the monarch in Iraq and established the Republic of Iraq led by Abdul-Karim Qassem, who was known as "il-Za`im."

Kuwait and Iraq

In 1961 Kuwait gained independence from Britain, but the Iraqis attempted to annex it. The British sent forces and in 1963, Iraq was forced to recognize the sovereignty of Kuwait. In 1963, the Ba'ath party overthrew Qassem's government following his assassination. Nine months later the Ba'ath were overthrown as well, but in 1968 they retook the government. Ahmed Hasan al Bakr led the government, and in 1979, the United States supported **Saddam Hussein**, who succeeded al Bakr as president and chairman of the Revolutionary Command Council. Hussein fought a bitter war with Iran (1980–1988), and became the strongest military power in the Persian Gulf. Hussein repressed the nation's Shi'ite population in the south and created a secular government.

Invasion of Kuwait

In 1990 Iraq invaded Kuwait, accusing it of not respecting Iraq's borders. The United Nations condemned the invasion, delivered an ultimatum, and authorized a complete embargo on trade with Iraq. Hussein failed to be moved, and in 1991, the United States launched **Operation Desert Storm**, which pushed Iraq out of Kuwait in just over a month. On the way out of Kuwait, Iraqi troops set fire to several hundred oil wells and fields, creating one of the worst ecological disasters of the century.

The United Nations continued to impose strict embargoes on Iraq through resolution 661. Hussein's brutal use of chemical weapons on the Kurds in the north led the United States to declare "air exclusion zones." The development of chemical and biological weapons continued to worry the United States, finally culminating in the 2003 invasion.

In 1993, an assassination attempt failed against former President George H. W. Bush, and President Clinton bombed the Iraqi Intelligence Headquarters in Baghdad. Hussein's rule became more brutal when his two sons, **Uday** and **Qusay**, were given vice-presidential authority in 1995. They ruthlessly purged all dissidents and others who had offended the family in any way. In 2003 the administration of President George W. Bush argued that Hussein had continued to develop weapons of mass destruction in violation of the United Nations Resolution. The U.S. decision to invade Iraq in 2003 without the sanction of the United Nations Security Council remains one of the most controversial military actions of the recent past. The Security Council was deeply divided on the issue of the invasion of Iraq, and while the Bush administration maintained that Iraq posed a serious threat, various intelligence sources contradicted the Bush administration, arguing that the regime had not continued to develop weapons of mass destruction and that Hussein posed no imminent threat. Further, several high-ranking officials in the U.S. government as well as numerous reporters accused President George W. Bush of erroneously claiming in his State of the Union address in 2003 that the Hussein regime had sought supplies for nuclear weapons in Africa.

Operation Iraqi Freedom

Hussein's brutal regime controlled Iraq until the United States and Great Britain, along with help from Australia and a few other minor forces, defeated him in **Operation Iraqi Freedom** in 2003. As of October 2003, no credible evidence of the existence of weapons of mass destruction has been found and the United States is still attempting to establish order in Iraq. There have been as many as 9,000 civilians casualties in Iraq since the United States began the invasion. On July 22, 2003, a United States occupation force in Iraq killed Uday and Qusay Hussein after an informant turned them in for a reward. Saddam Hussein was captured in 2003.

In June 2004, the United States turned power over to an interim government in Iraq. The Iraqis continue to attempt to form a new government in the wake of the U.S. invasion.

Review Questions

1. The strongest military power in the Persian Gulf after 1980 was

   (A) Kuwait.

   (B) Jordon.

   (C) Iran.

   (D) Iraq.

2. A conservative religious revolution established a strong Shi'ite government in

   (A) Iraq.

   (B) Iran.

   (C) Lebanon.

   (D) Saudi Arabia.

3. Nasser's Pan-Arabism resulted in the

   (A) nationalization of the Suez Canal.

   (B) defeat of the Israeli's in several battles.

   (C) strong and lasting unification of all the Arab states.

   (D) the Camp David Peace Accords.

4. Which of the following was NOT a campaign launched by the Israelis in response to acts of the Palestinian Liberation Organization?

   (A) The War of the Camps

   (B) Operation Peace for Galilee

   (C) Operation Grapes of Wrath

   (D) Both (A) and (C).

5. Which of the organizations emerged primarily to support Shi'ite interests?

   (A) The Hamas

   (B) The Hizballah

   (C) The Amal Militia

   (D) Both (B) and (C).

Answers

1. (D)	3. (A)	5. (D)
2. (B)	4. (D)	

Chapter 37

LATIN AMERICA IN THE POST-WORLD WAR II ERA

KEY TERMS

Raul Prebisch

Getúlio Vargas

Lázaro Cárdenas

Juan and Eva Perón

The Dirty War

Falkland Islands (or the Malvinas Islands)

Military Junta

Augusto José Ramón Pinochet Ugarte

Miracle of Chile

President Jacobo Arbenz Guzmán

United Fruit Company

Colonel Carlos Castillo Armas

Genocide

Mayan Indians

Sandanista Liberation Front

Samoza

Sandino

Contras

Panama Canal Treaty

Ronald Reagan

Jimmy Carter

Iran-Contra Scandal

NAFTA

Institutional Revolutionary Party (PRI)

Banana republics

Favela

Liberation Theology

Zapatistas

OVERVIEW

Latin America had been dominated by European powers since the Age of Exploration, and it had to deal with constant U.S. intervention as the United States became more and more imperialistic. The Argentine economist Raul Prebisch argued that Latin American economies, in fact, were damaged by their dependence on industrial nations, especially those of North America and Europe. Prebisch divided these nations into two groups, the "center" and the "periphery." In his opinion, Latin American nations on the periphery of international trade needed to diversify their domestic trade and to promote their own industrial growth. In the wake of World War II, many Latin American countries fought vigorously against U.S. and other foreign influences, and especially against U.S. intervention in their politics and economies. Despite the warnings of Prebisch and others, Latin American countries had enormous foreign debts. During the recession of the 1970s and 1980s, the debt problem became worse.

Despite the movements to separate Latin America from U.S. interference, economic issues continued to force many Latin American areas to accept aid and so also to accept U.S. terms. For example, U.S. investments in industries resulted in American control over the copper mining industry in Chile and Peru through the Anaconda and Kennecott companies, the oil industry in Mexico, Peru, and Bolivia, and the fruit industry through the United Fruit Company in Guatemala. Further U.S. involvement came as a result of the growing influence of Marxism in Latin America, with the U.S. supporting rebellions against many governments. The governments supported by the U.S. that were largely dependant on exports are known as banana republics.

BRAZIL

Brazil attempted to create a nationalized economy. Under the leadership of **Getúlio Vargas** (1930–1945), industrialization occurred rapidly, supported with high tariffs on imports. President **Juscelino Kubitschek** continued the policy of economic nationalism, and through heavy borrowing from international powers, Kubitschek attempted to achieve "Fifty Years' Progress in Five." In the 1960s, President **João Goulart** attempted to promote greater social equality by breaking up large estates and allowing those of lower classes, even those who were illiterate, to vote. The result was a conservative backlash in Brazil. The military took over in 1964. Brazil was another "economic miracle" after 1968, partly due to farming in the Amazon basin. The exploitation of the Amazon destroyed significant portions of the rain forests, which remains today a pressing issue for global concern. As economic growth continued, the upper classes benefited more than the lower. The gap between the wealthy and the poor increased in Brazil. Huge inflation rates and an enormous foreign debt prompted the advent of democracy in 1985. Democratic leaders such as **Fernando Collor de Mello** attempted to curb inflation through wage and price controls and reductions in government spending.

MEXICO

A movement to oust foreign control in Mexico predated World War II, and in fact followed Mexico's loss of territory to the United States in the nineteenth century. In 1910, a revolution occurred against foreign interests, and a new constitution was created in 1917. The revolution reached a high point in the presidency of **Lázaro Cárdenas** (1934–1940), who stripped foreign investors of control in Mexican oil wells, nationalized the petroleum industry, and then returned over forty-five million acres of land to peasants. Cuauhtemoc Cárdenas, the son of the president, fought conservative backlash groups for years after Cárdenas left office in 1940. Peasant revolts against the succeeding conservative governments and the Institutional Revolutionary Party in Chiapas disrupted stability in Mexico.

During the 1950s and 1960s, Mexico was dominated by the **Institutional Revolutionary Party (PRI)**. Under their leadership, Mexico experienced economic growth. Despite the economic prosperity, the one-party system had its disadvantages. Protest movements, such as a demonstration by students in Tlaltelolco Square in 1968, resulted in brutal retaliation by police. Later presidents attempted to enact greater civil liberties, but economic difficulties disrupted their efforts. Mexico discovered new reserves of oil in the 1970s, and became more dependent on oil exports for income. When the price of oil dropped in the 1980s, Mexico defaulted on its interest payments for its foreign debt. In 1994, the **Zapatistas** movement arose in Chiapas in defense of the oppressed poor, and took seven towns. The growing gulf between classes combined with the move toward **NAFTA** (North American Free Trade Agreement) aroused the anger of the peasantry. NAFTA, among other things, resulted in the influx of cheaper goods, particularly corn, which negatively impacted the peasantry. By 2000, people were ready for a change, and **Vincente Fox** defeated the Institutional Revolutionary Party and became president of Mexico.

ARGENTINA

Like Mexico, Argentina also fought against U.S. intervention and foreign control in Latin America. Argentina has avoided U.S. intervention and **Juan Perón** eventually won the presidency in 1946 on the basis of his opposition to foreign, and especially U.S., intervention. Perón was the culmination of the increasing power of the military in Argentina's politics. His wife, **Eva**, was herself from the lower classes and personally implemented aspects of his program of assistance to the poor by seeing long lines of people at their house, the Casa Rosada (the "Pink House"). Perón also advocated industrialization and protection of workers. Under Perón, the government controlled the banking, railroad, shipping, and other industries, and was in many ways an authoritarian leader. While the couple was very popular with the lower classes of Argentina, others saw them as opportunistic and believed that they sympathized with fascism. The military overthrew Perón in 1955 and he went into exile in Spain. He returned to power in 1973, only to die one year later.

After Perón, Argentina was controlled by a series of brutal military dictators. During the 1970s and 1980s, these dictators persecuted opponents in a "dirty war" that ultimately took the lives of over 23,000 people. A new wave of democratic movements swept through Peru, Ecuador, and Bolivia in the 1980s, and democratic urges began to infiltrate Argentina. When in 1982, Argentina took the Falkland Islands (or the Malvinas Islands) from Britain and was subsequently defeated, the government had no choice but to hold democratic elections.

CHILE

Chile was another example of U.S. interference. Chile suffered from serious economic difficulties, including the decline of the copper industry, which provided the bulk of the exports in Chile. In 1970 **Salvador Allende** was elected president. He nationalized the copper industry, largely owned by Americans, and socialized other industries. In response, President Richard Nixon cut off United States aid to Chile. Acting on Marxist ideology, Allende also broke up large estates. As in so many other Latin American countries, a conservative backlash followed. Strikes were organized with American support from the C.I.A. Allende managed to control the strikes and even to increase his bloc in the elections of 1973.

However, the military junta of **Augusto José Ramón Pinochet Ugarte** took power in a U.S. supported coup d'etat. Allende, along with thousands of supporters, was killed. Pinochet would lead Chile through massive economic reforms called the Miracle of Chile before open elections removed him as president in 1990. He remained commander-in-chief of the army until 1998. Pinochet's regime was one of the most brutal in history. Thousands fled to avoid torture and other abuses, while thousands more simply disappeared. Although he was arrested for human rights abuses in London in 1998, the British refused to extradite him to Spain, where his trial was to be held. The Chileans eventually dropped the charges against him. Some see him as saving Chile from Communism, and his brutality as necessary in the face of increasingly violent resistance. However, Pinochet was one of the most brutal rulers in Chile's history. U.S. support of such figures is indicative of policy in this period, which sought to obtain political and other benefits for the U.S. while often overlooking the miseries of the various populations governed by U.S.-supported governments abroad.

GUATEMALA

Similarly, Guatemala also fought U.S. intrusion into its internal affairs. Foreign investors virtually controlled Guatemala's economy after World War II. The economy was heavily dependent on exports of coffee and bananas. In 1953, **President Jacobo Arbenz Guzmán** began a program of economic nationalism, and took control of transportation and the electrical network. Arbenz then attempted to take unused lands from large estates, including a sizeable amount of property from the United Fruit Company, which was controlled by U.S. investors. Land was to be redistributed to peasants. Although he offered compensation for the land, U.S. President Dwight Eisenhower reacted by ordering the CIA to overthrow the government. Eisenhower believed that Communist influences were at work behind the nationalization of the United Fruit Company land, and the U.S. trained non-Communist forces under **Colonel Carlos Castillo Armas** to combat the government. Armas toppled the government in 1954 and returned the land taken from the United Fruit Company. He also ruled as a military dictator, killing and torturing opponents. Under Armas, the deaths and disappearance of over 200,000 people have been reported. These events are being investigated by various agencies as acts of **genocide** against the Mayan Indians. His brutality resulted in intense rebel activity and his assassination in 1957. Guatemala fought a civil war until the 1990s.

NICARAGUA

While the U.S. engineered the coup d'etat in Guatemala, it also provided arms to Nicaragua and Honduras, both of which bordered Guatemala. Nicaraguans such as Augusto Caesar Sandino had also fought U.S. influence, but members of the Nicaraguan National Guard, led by **Anastacio Somoza Garcia Sandino**, assassinated Augusto Caesar Sandino. Somoza strongly supported U.S. policies, and later outlawed the Communist party in Nicaragua. He and his sons controlled Nicaragua for over 40 years. Protests erupted in Nicaragua over U.S. influence as well as over the corruption of the Somozas. The **Sandanista Liberation Front** was founded in honor of Sandino, and the Marxist organization took power in 1979. President Jimmy Carter refused to aid the Samozas in their fight for survival. In 1990, however, free elections were held and, while the Sandanistas remained the strongest party, they were defeated by a coalition led by **Violeta Barrios de Chamorro**.

Panama Canal

PANAMA

Carter also signed the **Panama Canal Treaty** in 1979 giving Panama control over the Canal and all its territory, effective in 1999. President Carter generally did not support Cold War anti-Communist policies or rhetoric, nor U.S. imperialist activity. Unfortunately, he was relatively alone in the political arena and was strongly criticized for focusing on human rights abroad rather than on issues many Americans felt required more immediate attention at home, such as the economy issues. Coupled with his failure to resolve the **Iran Hostage Crisis**, Americans turned to new leadership and elected Ronald Reagan in 1981.

THE IRAN-CONTRA SCANDAL

President Reagan reacted strongly to the Sandanistas and to their Marxist ideology. Reagan believed the Sandanistas were supporting Communist insurrections in Latin American countries, and his fierce anti-Communist rhetoric renewed with vigor the Cold War. He cut off aid to Nicaragua, instituted an economic boycott, and began to support a rival movement, the **Contras**. The Contras led terrorist attacks on Sandinista strongholds, and the C.I.A. helped to train them. In 1984 Congress banned aid to the Contras, but Reagan was undeterred. He secretly sold arms to Iran and funneled the money to the Contras. The most shocking aspect of Reagan's flaunting of a Congressional act was the fact that he had made a deal with Iran, who had held American hostages in Tehran during 1979–1980 and was then under an embargo. The sale of arms to Iran had also been made in exchange for hostages in Lebanon. The scandal exploded in 1986. Reagan later admitted that the arms sale was, in part, to resolve the hostage crisis in the Middle East, but the idea of selling arms to a power that was then hostile to America never sat well with the American public nor with the Congress. In 1989 the United Nations stepped in to help resolve the civil war in Nicaragua. Elections held in the 1990s brought about more democratic policies.

GENDER ISSUES

Women gained the right to vote for the first time in Latin America in Ecuador in 1929. Other nations eventually also implemented women's suffrage. In Argentina the struggle was rather difficult, and passed in 1945 only after fifteen bills had been introduced to the senate. Women were a strong foundation of Juan Perón's support. During World War I, women entered the workforce in large numbers, making up as much as 80 percent of the workforce in the textile industry. By the 1990s, women had achieved impressive gains in Latin America, coming close to the rights of women in North America and Europe, especially in political office-holding.

POPULATION PATTERNS

The population of Latin America has increased dramatically, from 165 million in 1950 to over 400 million in 1985. Rising birth rates accounted for the growth, as well as a decline in mortality rates. While the birth rates have declined since the 1990s, population continues to be a problem.

MIGRATION PATTERNS

Migration between areas of the Americas dominates this period, such as from Mexico to the United States or from Colombia to Venezuela. Most migrants are poor workers in search of jobs. Political repression has also been an important factor, with refugees seeking greater freedoms elsewhere. Migration patterns also show movement from rural areas into urban areas, creating several very large cities in Latin America. Further, the rate of population growth in the cities exceeds that of the rural areas, leading to mass unemployment. Many poor live in slums, such as the favela of Brazil.

LIBERATION THEOLOGY

The increasing disparity between the wealthy and the poor in Latin America, combined with the existence of brutal regimes before the implementation of democracies, resulted in the development of **Liberation Theology**. Liberation Theology was developed by Roman Catholic priests in Latin America as a response to the needs of their flocks. According to Liberation Theology, Christ did not mean for the poor to suffer injustice and it is the duty of the Church to liberate them from oppression. Clergy such as **Archbishop Oscar Romero** advocated human rights and the need for reform. Romero was assassinated, and even the Roman Catholic Church was uneasy about the combination of Marxist ideology and Catholic doctrine.

LATIN AMERICA AT THE END OF THE 1980S

After decades of military rule, most Latin American countries had instituted democratic-style governments by the end of the 1980s. Renewed freedoms at home also brought an end to economic nationalism. Free trade arose again with neighboring countries. In 1994, The United States, Mexico, and Canada created **NAFTA (North American Free Trade Agreement)**. In that same year 34 countries in the Americas reached an agreement on an even more comprehensive free trade policy. Nevertheless, the problems caused by migration patterns and the increase in population remain.

Review Questions

1. Which statement best describes changes in Latin America since World War II?

    (A) Women have lost rights and power.

    (B) The population has increased, but so have jobs.

    (C) Latin American countries relied heavily on foreign investments and on exports.

    (D) Latin Americans welcomed the presence of the U.S. and other foreign powers in their industries and politics.

2. Which statement best describes the policy of economic nationalism followed by Latin American countries following World War II?

    (A) The attempt to rely upon foreign investments and guidance to build native industries

    (B) Coordinated policies within countries of nationalization of industry and development of agriculture through land reform bills

    (C) Policies designed to benefit the poor while applying heavy taxes to the wealthy

    (D) The attempt to implement a central treasury system through taxation

3. Which of the following leaders supported U.S. policies and/or gained power through U.S. aid?

    (A) Sandino

    (B) Samoza

    (C) Armas

    (D) Both (B) and (C).

4. Which of the following movements arose in support of the interests of the poor or in rebellion to policies that negatively affected the poor?

    (A) Zapatistas

    (B) Liberation Theology

    (C) Junta of Pinochet

    (D) Both (A) and (B).

Answers

1. (C)	3. (D)
2. (B)	4. (D)

Chapter 38

EMERGING GLOBAL TRENDS

KEY TERMS

Globalism
International Monetary Fund
European Union
ASEAN
NAFTA
Global and multinational
  corporations
Mass epidemics
AIDS
SARS
Population growth
The Club of Rome
Infant mortality rates
Global inequities
Slobodan Miloševicñ

Bosnia
Serbia
Herzegovina
Dayton Agreement
Kosovo
Religious Fundamentalism
Al-Qaeda
Osama bin Laden
Terrorism
Hamas
Ethnic conflicts
The Internet
McDonaldization
Samuel Huntingdon

GLOBALISM

The foundation of the United Nations in 1945 was a response to the world wars and the role of nationalism in the origins and events of those wars. The U.N. was founded to preserve international peace and foster international cooperation in solving the world's economic, political, and other problems. Although the member nations of the Security Council of the United Nations have often acted more out of their own self-interest than for the common good, the United Nations has been an important force in world politics since 1945.

The foundation of the **International Monetary Fund** in 1944 at the Bretton Woods Conference helped to initiate a new era of global cooperation, as the fund encourages free trade and high growth rates. Free trade across borders was one of the most important issues that affected the post-World War II era. The 1947 General Agreement on Tariffs and Trade, supported by the U.S., helped to establish the **World Trade Organization**, which took the agreement's place in 1995. The end of the Cold War also created greater opportunities for trade, as China and the members of the former Soviet Union now entered international trade.

The new age of global economy was evident in the severe financial crisis in 1997 in Asia, whose impact was felt the West. The crisis began when foreign investors began to pull out of Thailand. The Thai stock market dropped by 75 percent, and the crisis spread to Malaysia, Indonesia, South Korea, and the Philippines. In an earlier era, the crisis would not have spread so quickly, but the new global economy has created a system whereby the world is linked through a vast economic network.

Global corporations now dominate the business world. In the last 20 years, perhaps as many as 50,000 such corporations have been created. Whereas earlier forms of international business took the form of a multinational corporation, operating under the restrictions of a particular country but doing business abroad, global corporations are operated from offices across the globe. One of the motivating factors of the global corporation is the search for cheap labor and places that offer few restrictions, thus lowering operating costs. Many global corporations manage to escape local tax laws, leading to a depletion of resources from tax revenues in various parts of the world. In fact, United States corporations are among the leaders of this trend. Japanese corporations also lead, with many of its industries conducting some manufacturing in the United States. In 1989, for example, Japanese industries invested more in their branches in the U.S. than U.S. corporations invested in their Japanese branches. Global corporations often farm their labor out across many national borders or pull up locations in one place in favor of another with cheaper labor. Further, some corporations located in one region "outsource" jobs to another, where labor is cheaper. This often results in loss of jobs at home.

Old alliances, however, are not easily undone, and various nations have formed trading blocks to protect their interests in the global market. The European Economic Community was first formed in 1957, and in 1993, the **Maastricht Treaty** established the **European Union** of 15 nations. In 1999 11 members implemented a system of common currency, and members of the union today are attempting to write a constitution. **OPEC**, or the Organization of Petroleum Exporting Countries, was established in 1990. The Association of Southeast Asian Nations, **ASEAN**, was established in 1967. Meanwhile, the United States, Canada, and Mexico established **NAFTA**, or the North American Free Trade Agreement, in 1993. These associations have tremendous power, as demonstrated by OPEC's embargo on oil shipments to the United States in 1973 in retaliation for its support for Israel. The cost of a barrel of oil increased by four-fold, triggering a global recession.

The rise of new technologies have contributed to globalism. Television, radio, telephones, and other communication devices have made it easier than ever to communicate. The rise of the Internet since its development in 1990 as a global means of instant communication has furthered the interconnections among world societies. English has become an important language of communication, arising out of the long-lasting legacy of British colonial rule.

Globalism has heightened inequities between areas of the world, many of which were evident in the Industrial Revolution. One-fifth of the population of the world is clustered in industrialized nations, yet this same percentage of the population consumes four-fifths of the world's products. Belgium, for example, had a gross domestic product that equaled the sum total of 40 nations in sub-Saharan Africa. The new globalism has inspired many protest movements, such as those of 1999 in Seattle. Many of these protests are against the use of cheap labor by global corporations and the increasing inequality between wealthy nations and poorer ones.

The Population Explosion

In 1798 Thomas Malthus published a paper on "The Principles of Population," in which he asserted that population increases geometrically, far outstripping the supply of food, which only increases arithmetically. He argued that disease and famine were nature's ways of controlling the population. Although Malthus has often been criticized, not the least for his mathematics, his predictions about the potential rapid growth of population in future generations have been confirmed.

The population of the world has rapidly increased due to better health care. Malthus was mistaken in one respect, however, as increased supplies of food in various parts of the world have also contributed to growth. The United Nations has estimated that the population of planet earth will reach 11.6 billion by 2200 and become more stable, but in the last three hundred years it has increased by five times what it was in the seventeenth century. In 1972 a group of scholars known as the Club of Rome warned that the planet's resources are finite and in danger of being exhausted by continued growth in population. Their predictions that natural resources would be exhausted have not yet materialized, but their message about the dangers of overpopulation continues to resonate.

Population growth has had a dramatic effect on the environment in places such as sub-Saharan Africa. Over population led to increased attempts to cultivate land, eventually destroying it and further increasing the extent of the Sahara desert. Lack of land to cultivate combined with droughts has promoted devastating famines. Africa had the fastest rate of population growth in 1985 at around 3.2 percent a year. By 1994, the rate had fallen, with women having an average of six as opposed to eight children each. Similarly, the birth rate began to fall as well in other areas of the world, particularly in the industrialized areas, which had the lowest rates of population growth. Latin American countries also witnessed a large decline in birth rates, as did East Asia and other poorer areas of the world.

With the overall rise in population, however, there has also been a rise in mass epidemics in the twentieth century, such as **AIDS** (aquired immuno-deficiency syndrome), that particularly threaten underdeveloped regions such as Africa. The Center for Disease Control in Atlanta, Georgia, reports that in 2003 there are 42 million people living with HIV infections or full-blown AIDS. A large percentage of these cases are in sub-Saharan Africa. Experts predict that deaths among women, who make up the largest percentage of victims, will lead to a drop in population of 70 million by 2010. Two of three children are orphans due to the ravages of AIDS in some parts of Africa, and experts have suggested that the deaths of so many young adults will lead to a rise in child labor.

Many experts believe that AIDS began in Africa, as the virus that causes the disease, HIV, has the most mutations there. Similarly, Africa has also seen outbreaks of the Ebola virus and other frightening hemorrhagic diseases. In 2003, **SARS** (sudden acute respiratory syndrome) circled the globe, beginning in Asia and makings its way to the Americas. Although preventative vaccines helped to eradicate smallpox and diphtheria in the twentieth century, epidemic diseases still threaten the globe. Our increased interconnectivity helps to make us more vulnerable than ever to killer diseases that now can circle the globe within days or weeks.

POVERTY

Despite advances in agriculture and technology, poverty remains a significant issue in the world today. According to the World Bank, poverty is defined as between $1 and $2 per day in 1993 Purchasing Power Parity (PPP), which measures the relative purchasing power of currencies across countries. In 1999 an estimated 1.2 billion people worldwide had consumption levels below $1 a day, which represents 23 percent of the population of the developing world. An estimated 2.8 billion people survived on less than $2 a day. Although every nation of the world has a significant population of those who live in poverty, the vast majority of the world's impoverished are in Europe, Central Asia, and sub-Saharan Africa. Asia has by far the largest population of those living in poverty, estimated at about 490 million people. Although the number of impoverished people has declined in the last two decades in Asia, the AIDS crisis in Africa threatens to dramatically raise the level of poverty there.

Poverty is related to infant mortality rates. In Africa, an average of 151 of every 1,000 children die before reaching the age of five. Worldwide, infant mortality rates have dropped to around 59 per 1,000 in 1999 and life expectancy has dramatically increased by an average of four months per year since 1970. Unfortunately, these gains do not eliminate the pressing need to address the world's impoverished.

Poverty brings with it other social problems, such as illiteracy. Although the worldwide level of adult literacy has risen from 53 percent in 1970 to 74 percent in 1998, illiteracy still remains a major problem in Africa and the Middle East, the two geographic areas that have not reported gains in the number of children enrolled in primary schools. Across the world, over 110 million primary-school-age children in developing countries are not in school and 60 percent, or 66 million, of these children are female. In 1998, 879 million adults in developing countries, representing one in four adults, were illiterate. Most of these were women, representing 64 percent of the total figure. In South Asia only 40 percent of women are literate, while 65 percent of men are literate. In Afghanistan only about 20 percent of women are literate. While the overall rate of illiteracy in the world has fallen since 1970, the population explosion has resulted in an additional 41 million illiterate adults. This decrease was most dramatic in East Asia. Since 1990, however, illiteracy increased in South Asia, the Middle East, North Africa, and sub-Saharan Africa.

These statistics on poverty reflect continuing inequities throughout the world between industrialized nations and underdeveloped nations, and between men and women. Most of the world's women continue to live in poverty and to be uneducated and, despite gains in employment in certain parts of the world, much still needs to be done to address these serious global issues.

MIGRATION

Population growth in areas such as Latin America, Asia, and Africa led to increased migration to Europe and the United States. In France, for example, ten percent of the population is now Muslim. In the United States, fully one-quarter of the population do not speak English as a first language. New patterns of migration have contributed to the growth of ethnic and religious tensions. One important form of protest to globalization has been based on national interests and a desire to maintain traditional cultural values.

ETHNIC CONFLICTS

Despite the increasing globalization of the world, it is still not quite a "world without borders," as various ethnic clashes continue to rip at the fabric of unity.

Bosnia and Herzegovina declared sovereignty in 1991 and independence from Yugoslavia in 1992 and has since fought a series of ethnic wars between Catholic and Orthodox Christians and Muslims. Serbian nationalism led Serb minorities in Bosnia and Croatia to attempt to secede, prompting furious fighting. In 1995 a U.N. force went to Bosnia to help implement the **Dayton Agreement** to ceasefire. The force still remains, and so does hostility between Christians and Muslims. Similarly, the situation in **Kosovo** erupted into war in 1999 when Albanians protested Serbian rule. Kosovo was declared an autonomous region of Serbia following World War II, and its boundaries were redrawn to form an Albanian majority. During the Kosovo War of 1999, many Serbs left, and **Slobodan Miloševic**, leader of Serbia, was later prosecuted by the United Nations for war crimes, including genocide in Bosnia and war crimes in Kosovo and Croatia. Serbian nationalists continue to resent Miloševic for the Dayton Agreement.

Other ethnic conflicts occurred in Rwanda between the Tutsis and the Hutus, between Palestinians and Israelis, and in many other parts of the world.

Such simmering ethnic clashes, along with poverty, continued inequities for women, underdeveloped peoples, and classes in the world's societies, suggest that the world has far to go before truly becoming a "world without boundaries."

Religious Fundamentalism

The clash between Muslims and Christians in Bosnia and Croatia highlights the role played by religion in many modern conflicts. The rise of fundamentalist religious sects in many parts of the world is in part due to their rejection of the tendency of globalization to produce a common identity, where the religious groups wish to retain their traditional identities. Further, globalization has promoted mass consumerism, which often conflicts with the values of religious fundamentalists. Fundamentalism can be found among Hindus in India, Muslims in various parts of the world, and Christians who are members of Protestant fundamentalist sects, especially in Latin America, but also in other parts of the world.

Samuel Huntingdon, in *The Clash of Civilizations* and *The Remaking of the World Order*, argues that ethnic and religious conflicts will dominate the twenty-first century. For Huntingdon, common cultural values as opposed to the old national boundaries will create several new interest blocs in world affairs, and these values will clash with one another, negating the tendency towards globalization of the post-World War II era.

Terrorism

Terrorism can be seen in parts of the world as an outgrowth of movements related to nationalism or to ethnic and religious identity; it can also be seen as a response to increasing globalization. Members of the al-Qaeda ("the base") organization, for example, have strong feelings of resentment for increasing American military presence in the Middle East. Many terrorist organizations in the Middle East fight for Palestinian autonomy against the Israeli occupation of Palestinian territories. The Hamas, formed in 1987 during the Palestinian uprising against Israel, is just one of literally hundreds of terrorist groups in existence today.

While the current population explosion and modern diseases can often lead to deep fears about the future, the rise of terrorist organizations have created an even deeper feeling of insecurity. This is especially true for Americans, who felt relatively immune from terrorism. Americans watched the PLO launch innumerable terrorist attacks against Israel and Presidents Clinton and George H. W. Bush even lifted a ban on funding the PLO found in the 1987 anti-terrorism act. Americans also watched the Irish Republican Army lead attacks against Britain, and Protestant terrorists lead attacks against Irish Catholics; but it was not until September 11, 2001, that Americans recognized that their own daily security might be an issue. American embassies were bombed in the 1990s in Africa, for example, but nothing on such a large scale had ever occurred within U.S. borders. **Osama bin Laden's** al-Qaeda organization reflects the new global culture of the twenty-first century, as it has spawned operations across the globe from Indonesia, to America, to the Middle East and Africa. Bin Laden rose to prominence as an American-funded mujahideen in Afghanistan, and fled there after the attacks of 9/11. The U.S. pursued him there and toppled the Taliban regime. President George H. W. Bush's subsequent "war on terrorism" has not yet achieved the goal of finding bin Laden or of stopping continued al-Qaeda attacks.

IMPACT OF GLOBALISM

Globalism has reduced the role of governments in shaping the economy. Critics argue that global corporations have contributed to environmental problems. Some argue that indigenous cultures and diversity are threatened as a more

**President George W. Bush and First Lady Laura Bush observe a moment
of silence after the 9/11 terrorist attacks.**

homogenous global culture emerges. The spread of American culture throughout
the world has disturbed many, as McDonald's and other corporations can even
be found now on the streets of China. One of the most potent symbols of the
"McDonaldization" of the world is, oddly enough, the Barbie doll. Barbie has
been exported to many parts of the world, and to women in the countries of the
Middle East and other non-Western countries, Barbie represents a stereotype
of the modern American woman, a woman whose values often clash with those

of the Islamic and Asian worlds. Barbie's svelte body revealed under skimpy clothing, her flashy makeup, and her various hair styles clash with the insistence in many parts of the Muslim world that the woman's body be covered, sometimes from head to toe, and that she rarely be seen alone or outside of the home. Conservative Muslims and Asians see the Barbie doll as a dangerous symbol of Western permissiveness. Nevertheless, the new globalism may be a valuable tool in the face of such worldwide problems as global warming and the destruction of natural habitats.

A View of Planet Earth from Space

The space race has opened up even newer frontiers for the world's nations. The race into space, a product of the Cold War conflicts between the U.S.S.R. and the United States, began with the Soviet launch of *Sputnik* on October 4, 1957. Americans were the first to put a man on the moon in 1969, and Neil

Armstrong put it well when he remarked, "That's one small step for [a] man; one giant leap for mankind." Armstrong and the Apollo 11 team landed on the Sea of Tranquility. A picture of the earth taken by the *Voyager* spacecraft has shown us what a tiny speck of the universe the earth represents. As globalism ties together the world's communities through trade, communication, and other avenues, we may need to find new ways to cooperate as we explore the vast, uncharted regions of space. Although we have not yet managed to defeat the problems of sectarianism, poverty, disease, global warming, and other issues, our collective memory of Armstrong's walk in the Sea of Tranquility and the possibilities of what humankind can achieve may yet inspire the creation of a "world without boundaries."

Review Questions

1. Examples of globalization include all of the following EXCEPT

   (A) multinational corporations.

   (B) the United Nations.

   (C) the International Monetary Fund.

   (D) ethnic attempts to preserve traditional national or cultural interests.

2. Which of the following is true of the rate of birth rates in the years since World War II?

   (A) They have risen in industrialized nations.

   (B) They have fallen in Africa.

   (C) They have decreased in industrialized nations of the world.

   (D) Both (B) and (C).

3. Which of the following is true of world literacy rates?

   (A) They have risen since the 1970s.

   (B) Women are most affected by illiteracy in all areas of the world.

   (C) Illiteracy has dropped in Africa and the Middle East.

   (D) Both (A) and (B).

4. Globalization

   (A) has created a greater sense of inequality among the nations of the world, as industrialized nations benefit more than underdeveloped nations.

   (B) has resulted in the creation of a homogeneous culture across the world.

   (C) has been challenged by increasing attempts to preserve ethnic and cultural interests.

   (D) Both (A) and (C).

Answers

1. (D)	3. (D)
2. (D)	4. (D)

▼

PRACTICE TEST 1
AP World History

This test is also on CD-ROM in our special interactive AP World History TEST*ware*®. It is highly recommended that you first take this exam on computer. You will then have the additional study features and benefits of enforced timed conditions and instant, accurate scoring. See page xix for guidance on how to get the most out of our AP World History software.

AP WORLD HISTORY

PRACTICE TEST 1

SECTION I

TIME: 55 minutes
70 multiple-choice questions

DIRECTIONS: Each of the questions or incomplete statements below is followed by five suggested answers or completions. Select the one that is best in each case.

1. Which of the following statements best describes global trends in the 1990s?

   (A) Globalization has decreased ethnic conflicts as a more homogenous culture is created.

   (B) Infant mortality rates have increased throughout the world.

   (C) Global corporations contribute to the "McDonaldization" of the world.

   (D) Poverty continues to rise in Asia, while it has dropped in Africa.

   (E) Illiteracy rates continue to decrease in every region of the globe.

2. Which represents the most correct statement about the Soviet bloc before 1948?

   (A) Nikita Khrushchev successfully led Russia through a period of "de-Stalinization."

   (B) Yugoslavia's Marshal Tito failed to cooperate with Russia and Russia ousted Yugoslavia from the Soviet bloc.

(C)   Czechoslovakia experienced massive reforms under Alexander Dubček and Russia ousted the Czechs from the Soviet bloc.

(D)   Poland experienced reforms under Wladysalw Gomulka and Russia ousted Poland from the Soviet bloc.

(E)   Imre Nagy successfully led Hungary through a revolution that freed Hungary from the Soviet bloc.

3.   Which of the following statements best describes events in the Communist countries of Asia and Europe during the Cold War?

(A)   China provided overt and copious aid to the North Vietnamese during the Vietnam War.

(B)   Russia and China were firmly allied with one another and on good diplomatic terms throughout the Cold War era.

(C)   Mao Zedong saw the workers as the heart of a Communist revolution, while Lenin believed the peasants would lead Russia through a revolution.

(D)   Early in the Cold War, Nikita Khrushchev moved away from Stalin's policies while later in the Cold War, Deng Xiaoping in China also moved away from the isolationism of his predecessors.

(E)   Russian leaders such as Nikita Khrushchev focused on exporting the revolution abroad, while leaders such as Mao Zedong focused on developing the revolution at home.

4.   Which of the following statements best describes the foreign policy of the United States during the Cold War?

(A)   The United States had a policy of noninvolvement in Latin America.

(B)   The United States supported coups against the governments of Iran and Guatemala in this period.

(C)   The United States had few investments in Latin America during this period.

(D)   The United States refused to support abusive regimes in Latin America, the Middle East, and the Philippines, even if their leaders were not aligned with Communism.

(E)   United States President Ronald Reagan actively avoided involvement in Latin American politics, while President Jimmy Carter actively interfered with Latin American politics.

5.   Which of the following statements best describes Asia, the Middle East, and Africa following World War II?

(A)   Nationalism, based on ethnic, religious, and tribal interests, played little role in Africa, but played a strong role in the separation of Pakistan from India and in the Palestinian Liberation Organization's activities.

(B)   Nationalism, based on ethnic, religious, and tribal interests, was the foundation of Nasser's Pan-Arabism and the Pan-African movement, but it played little role in Indian politics prior to the 1980s.

(C)   Japan experienced rapid economic growth, while the Little Tigers, the Middle East, and Africa did not.

(D)   Africa and Japan experienced rapid economic gains, while China and the Middle East did not experience gains before the 1990s.

(E)   Japan, the Little Tigers and, to a lesser extent, China, experienced rapid economic gains until the 1990s; African countries generally lagged behind the developed parts of the world, while poverty and illiteracy continued to be significant problems in the Middle East, Africa, and Asia.

6.   Which of the following areas was NOT assigned to Spain as a result of the Treaty of Tordesillas?

(A)   Mexico

(B)   North America

(C)   Peru

(D)   Brazil

(E)   Both B and C

7.   The United States most succeeding in dominating policy in Latin America under which leader?

(A)   Peron

(B)   Somoza

(C)   Sandino

(D)   Guzmán

(E)   Cárdenas

8.   The darkly shaded area in the map below reflects the boundaries of which empire in the early thirteenth century?

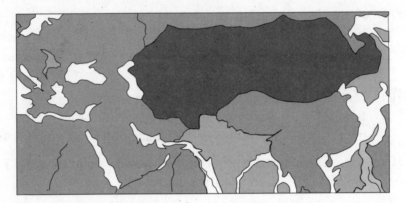

(A)   Abbasid Caliphate

(B)   Safavid Persians

(C)   Ottoman Turks

(D)   Mongol

(E)   Mughals

9.   Which of the following statements does NOT represent a general trend during the Italian Renaissance?

(A)   Humanism had a positive impact on the rights and status of women and slaves.

(B)   Neo-Platonists combined elements of pagan philosophy with Christian teaching.

(C)   The Guttenberg printing press made books more expensive and less easily obtainable.

(D)   As conflicts between city states ceased, civic humanism became an important trend.

(E)   Church affairs were separate from the political dealings of powerful families such as the Medici and Borgia.

10.   Which of the following areas were NOT colonized by European powers in the nineteenth century?

(A)   South Africa

(B)   Liberia

(C)   New Zealand, Indochina, and Australia

(D)   (Siam) Thailand

(E)   Both (B) and (D)

11.   Which of the following areas is NOT included in the Palestinian National Authority?

(A)   The West Bank

(B)   The Gaza Strip

(C)   Jerusalem

(D)   The Sinai Peninsula

(E)   Both (C) and (D)

12.   Which of the following statements is NOT true of political changes during the Renaissance?

(A)   Machiavelli separated politics from morality.

(B)   The Borgia controlled the Papal States.

(C)   The Medici patronized the arts, developed a powerful banking empire, and even gained control of the papacy.

(D)   Byzantium continued to flourish.

(E)   Spanish power grew as wealth flowed in from the New World.

13.   The desire of Serbs to unite as a nation led to conflict in

(A)   Bosnia and Herzogovina

(B)   World War I

(C)   Romania

(D)   (A) and (C)

(E)   (A) and (B)

14.   "Non-violence is the greatest force at the disposal of mankind. It is mightier than the mightiest weapon of destruction devised by the ingenuity of man … Non-cooperation is directed not against men but against measures. It is not directed against the Governors, but against the system they administer. The roots of non-cooperation lie not in hatred but in justice, if not in love."

Which figure most likely said this?

(A)   Aurangzeb

(B)   Jinnah

(C)   Mohandas Gandhi

(D)   Abbas I

(E)   Akhbar

15.   Which of the following factors does NOT explain the reasons why Asia experienced an economic decline in the 1990s?

(A)   Thailand's prosperity as a Little Tiger negatively impacted other Asian countries.

(B)   Deng Xiaoping's policies in rural China contributed to a shortage of staple crops and also to unemployment as the government closed its state-run factories.

(C)   The rising value of the yen created problems for Japan, which was dependent on its export industries.

(D)   New competition from foreign imports created problems for China.

(E)   China had an over abundance of grain products that created problems for China.

16.   "The Mass is the greatest blasphemy of God, and the highest idolatry upon earth, an abomination the like of which has never been in Christendom since the time of the Apostles."

Who said this?

(A)   Calvin

(B)   Luther

(C)   Zwingli

(D)   Melancthon

(E)   Henry VIII

17.   Which of the following most correctly describes the enlightened *philosophes?*

I.   They adhered to old values, especially the teachings of the Roman Catholic Church.

II.   They rejected institutionalized religion as superstition.

III. They advocated for reform of government based on "natural laws."

(A)   I only

(B)   II only

(C)   III only

(D)   I and II only

(E)   II and III only

18.   Which of the following statements best describes conditions in Africa before the European Age of Exploration?

(A)   African cultures did not have the capacity to make iron before the first century C.E.

(B)   African cultures developed iron-making without influence from other cultures.

(C)   Axum participated in the Indian Ocean trade, which ceased when it was conquered by Muslims.

(D)   Ghana was central to the trans-Saharan trade in gold and salt.

(E)   Zimbabwe flourished when the Arab trading ports along the east coast of Africa declined.

19.   "The program of the world's peace, therefore, is our program; and that program, the only possible program, as we see it, is this: Open covenants of peace, openly arrived at, after which there shall be no private international understandings of any kind but diplomacy shall proceed always frankly and in the public view. Absolute freedom of navigation upon the seas, outside territorial waters, alike in peace and in war, except as the seas may be closed in whole or in part by international action for the enforcement of international covenants."

The quotation above represents the process of peace

(A)   envisioned at Yalta and Potsdam in World War II

(B)   envisioned by the United States following the war of 1812

(C)   at the end of World War I envisioned by Woodrow Wilson in the Fourteen Points

(D)   envisioned by the Congress of Vienna following the Napoleonic Wars

(E)   envisioned by the Monroe Doctrine

20.   The religion that most influenced the development of sub-Saharan Africa before the Age of Exploration was

(A)   Christianity

(B)   Hinduism

(C)   Judaism

(D)   Islam

(E)   Buddhism

21.   Which of the following statements does NOT accurately describe independence movements following the French Revolution?

(A)   The revolution in Saint Domingue gave rights to the *gens de couleur.*

(B)   Francois Dominique Toussaint led a slave revolt and officially declared independence from France.

(C)   Creoles remained powerful in Mexico even despite the reforms of Juárez.

(D)   European monarchies were abolished throughout Latin America.

(E)   Independence movements in Latin America resulted in more political rights for women.

22.   Which statement best describes the leadership of the United States and the Soviet Union during the Cold War?

(A)   U.S. President Jimmy Carter's rhetoric increased tension between the United States and the Soviet Union, while Nikita Khrushchev's efforts to de-Stalinize had contributed to greater stability.

(B)   U.S. President Ronald Reagan's anti-Communist stance increased tension between the United States and the Soviet Union, just as Brezhnev's re-Stalinization policies had earlier increased tension.

(C)   Gorbachev's aggressive expansionism threatened the peace efforts of U.S. President Ronald Reagan.

(D)   U.S. President John F. Kennedy's invasion of the Bay of Pigs and the subsequent Cuban Missile Crisis enabled Nikita Khrushchev to strengthen his power base in Russia.

(E)   U.S. President Ronald Reagan's noninvolvement position in Latin America contributed to détente.

23.   Which statement does NOT describe nineteenth-century imperialism?

(A)   The need to control the interests in the Suez Canal drove Britain to put down a revolt in Egypt and then to fight against another revolt in the Sudan.

(B)   The need to connect new territories drove the United States to support a revolution in Panama and to construct the Panama Canal.

(C)   Japan had no imperialistic interests during the Meiji era.

(D)   Competition between Britain and France resulted in further expansion of their empires in Asia.

(E)   Western education provided in the colonized areas fueled rebellions in later times.

24.   Which of the following countries or regions in Africa escaped European domination during the nineteenth century?

(A)   South Africa

(B)   The Congo

(C)   Rhodesia

(D)   Liberia

(E)   Both (A) and (C)

25.

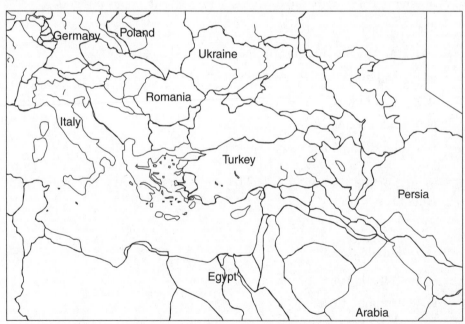

This map reflects the Middle Eastern world after

(A)   World War II ended in 1945

(B)   World War I

(C)   1935

(D)   1950

(E)   1890

26. "If the people be led by laws, and uniformity sought to be given them by punishments, they will try to avoid the punishment, but have no sense of shame. If they be led by virtue, and uniformity sought to be given them by the Rules of Propriety, they will have the sense of shame, and moreover will become good."

    Which figure most likely said this?

    (A) Lao Tzu

    (B) Han Fei

    (C) Wu Ti

    (D) Confucius

    (E) Shi Huang Ti

27. "Thus this person when embraced by the intelligent self, knows nothing that is without, nothing that is within…then a father is not a father, a mother is not a mother, the worlds not worlds, the gods not gods."

    The statement above reflects

    (A) the Muslim doctrine of jihad or struggle against evil

    (B) the Hindu doctrine of *moksha*

    (C) the Chinese view of ancestor worship

    (D) Sufi mysticism

    (E) the Hindu doctrine of samsara

28. Which of the following is NOT a location primarily associated with Buddhism?

    (A) Magao

    (B) Poltala palace

    (C) Angkor Wat

    (D) Drepung Loseling

    (E) Both (B) and (C)

29. In the post-World War II era,

    (A) North Vietnam and North Korea remained free from Communist influence

    (B) India was unable to free itself from American influence

    (C) Cuba remained free from Soviet or U.S. influence

(D)   Chile remained free from U.S. influence

(E)   Argentina and Mexico fought against foreign influence

30.   In the seventeenth and early eighteenth centuries, what was true of France and Russia?

    I.   Their attempts to rigidly control trade and impose heavy internal tarrifs led to the development of the absolutist monarchies.

    II.   Constant warfare for protection or expansion drove the formation of absolutist monarchies.

    III.   Their monarchs had experienced the dangers of a strong nobility during their childhoods, which motivated the creation of the absolutist monarchies.

(A)   I only   (D)   II and III only

(B)   II only   (E)   I and II only

(C)   III only

31.   Which of the following statements best describes China and Europe during the seventeenth and eighteenth centuries?

(A)   Europe industrialized at a slower pace than did China, where Confucianism promoted the development of industry.

(B)   The development of absolutism in Europe helped to create a strong merchant class and economy, while in China, the strength of the Ming Emperors also created a strong, centralized economy.

(C)   The Ming never industrialized to any extent or developed a monetary economy, whereas the Europeans did.

(D)   While the Ming had the rudimentary beginnings of industry and a monetary economy, poor management by the Hongwu emperor and Confucian values repressed the development of capitalistic enterprise; in Europe, centralized monarchies developed strong economies and supported industry, and industrialization proceeded rapidly, beginning in Britain.

(E)   China was very isolationist following the voyages of Zheng He and did not engage in overseas trade, while Europeans engaged in capitalistic expansion abroad.

32.   "If the spring of popular government in time of peace is virtue, the springs of popular government in revolution are at once *virtue and terror* ... Subdue by terror the enemies of liberty, and you will be right, as founders

of the Republic. The government of the revolution is liberty's despotism against tyranny."

In what period of the European history does this quotation originate?

(A) The Thermidorian Reaction

(B) The Directorate

(C) The Reign of Terror

(D) Louis XIV

(E) The Rump Parliament

33. Which of the following statements best represents the message of this political cartoon?

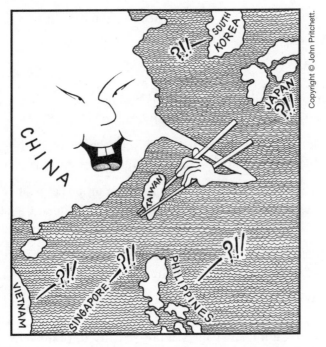

(A) China has attempted to dominate many countries in her area, but poses the most immediate threat to Taiwan.

(B) China and Taiwan are close allies while other nearby countries resist Chinese domination.

(C) China and Taiwan are enemies, but the status of other nearby nations is in question.

(D) Taiwan's status is threatened by China, who has never accepted Taiwan as an independent country.

(E) Both (A) and (D).

34. Which of the following areas was NOT influenced by Greek culture as a result of Alexander the Great's conquests?

   (A) Egypt

   (B) Mesopotamia

   (C) China

   (D) Persia

   (E) Asia Minor

35. The legal systems of Mesopotamia and the Hebrews

   (A) Discriminated against people on the basis of social standing and wealth

   (B) Did not permit debt slavery

   (C) Did not protect a master against an injury to his slave or a slave against an injury from his master

   (D) Permitted a man to divorce a woman without cause

   (E) Were both based on the principle of "an eye for eye," but they applied the principle differently

36. Which statement is NOT correct about women's social status in ancient Rome and China?

   (A) Women were subordinated to their fathers and husbands.

   (B) Christianity had little impact of the social roles for Roman women, while in China, Buddhism transformed the social roles of women.

   (C) Some women in the Roman world played important roles in protest movements leading to social reform, while women in China were subject to Confucian ideals of obedience.

   (D) Roman and Chinese women were expected to be industrious in the home.

   (E) A Roman *materfamilias* might have considerable power in the home, while a Chinese woman was subject even to her sons, especially the eldest son.

37. Which of the following statements best represents conditions within Han China and the Roman Empire?

   (A) People living within the Roman world spoke and wrote the same language, while those in Han China did not.

   (B) Roman created a far more centralized and strong monarchy than did China.

(C) There were many different customs and cultures represented by those the Romans ruled and the Romans never managed to thoroughly unite them; those ruled by the Chinese, on the other hand, adopted Chinese customs and greater unity was achieved.

(D) Romans built roads but the Chinese lacked a system of roads.

(E) The Chinese traded with India but the Romans did not.

38. Which of the following statements does NOT describe changes in trade after the decline of the Roman Republic and the transformation of Rome into an imperial power?

(A) Production of glass and ceramic wares in Italy continued to flourish compared to other regions of the western Roman world.

(B) Roman expansion created new sources for copper and tin for the Italian bronze working industry.

(C) Mines in conquered areas produced gold and silver for Roman coins.

(D) Provincial merchants with access to the sea undercut the ability of inland farmers in Italy to sell their goods.

(E) Romans traded more coins with Indian merchants than they traded goods, creating a trade imbalance that led to massive economic difficulties in the imperial period.

39. Which of the following was a major motivating factor behind Roman expansion?

(A) The desire for peace with the Latins, Sabines, Etruscans and other conquered peoples

(B) Italy, which controlled the grain distribution for Rome, could not produce enough grain to feed its expanding population

(C) The Romans were threatened by the conquests of the Han Chinese

(D) The Romans were afraid of losing their supremacy in the Indian Ocean trade

(E) The Romans needed access to the sea

40. Which of the following statements is true of slavery in the Greek and Roman worlds?

(A) Slavery produced a vibrant, continually growing economy.

(B) Slaves were difficult to find, particularly after the conquests of Alexander the Great.

(C)   Slavery contributed to the failure to increase production and develop thriving industries.

(D)   Slavery promoted more civil relations between peoples.

(E)   Slaves were often treated as part of the family in the Roman world, while in Athens, for example, they were treated as outcasts.

41.   Which of the following was NOT a consequence of the British defeat of the Chinese in the Opium Wars?

(A)   Confucianism declined.

(B)   Women's roles improved as more education was provided for them and foot binding was less commonly practiced.

(C)   The Chinese had failed to develop their internal transportation networks and so became dependent on the European-controlled coastal areas.

(D)   Europeans brought new technologies and means of production into China, which some historians credit with modernizing China.

(E)   Europeans enabled the Chinese to progress towards capitalism and did not interfere with the future evolution of China.

42.   What does the following table illustrate?

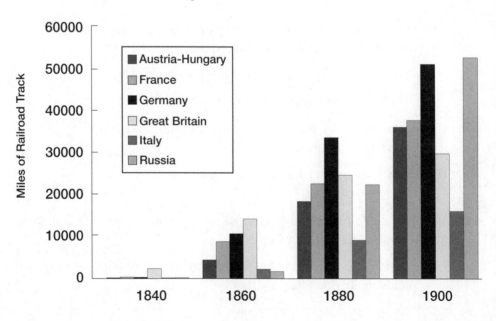

(A) Germany had the greatest number of railroads prior to 1860.

(B) Britain clearly held the lead in industrialization after 1860.

(C) Russia lagged behind Britain in industrialization, when measured by railroad lines, after 1880.

(D) Russia and Germany eclipsed Britain in miles of railroad created after 1880.

(E) Germany held the lead in railroad production throughout the period charted.

43. Which of the following statements reflects conditions in Athens and Sparta during antiquity?

(A) Both developed democracies.

(B) Both were dominated by an aristocratic elite.

(C) Sparta had slavery while Athens did not.

(D) Athens depended on her sea empire but never compromised her fundamental view of democracy at home applying it equally to its allies abroad; Sparta allowed all inhabitants of the city state a great role in decision making and refused such a role to outsiders.

(E) Women were confined to the home.

44. During the Crusades,

(A) Europe benefited from aspects of the Islamic culture, such as medical practices, introduced by returning knights.

(B) Europeans refused to interact with pagan infidels.

(C) Muslims were treated with great compassion by the Crusaders.

(D) Muslims and Christians developed lasting understanding of their respective cultures.

(E) Italy was lost to Islamic invaders.

45. Which of the following best describes the economy of Western Europe in the eleventh and twelfth centuries?

(A) Agriculture was stagnant, limited by the cultivation of only two fields in the open field system.

(B) There was no money economy.

(C) The moldboard was an ineffective plow.

(D) The development of the horse collar significantly revolutionized agriculture, leading to increased production.

(E) The development of the open field system in the twelfth century revolutionized production.

46. Which of the following statements best describes the medieval monarchies?

(A) The Frankish monarchy was very stable and the custom of passing the king's territories intact to his eldest son strengthened it.

(B) The rise of the Norman monarchy in England threatened the holdings and security of the Capetian monarchy in France.

(C) The Normans dismantled the native government of England and replaced it with a weak feudal bureaucracy.

(D) The German monarchy accepted the primacy of the Roman Catholic Church and allowed its bishops to appoint secular lords to important lay positions.

(E) The early Frankish monarchy was built by an alliance with the Byzantine church.

47. Which of the following statements is true of the Black Death that cycled throughout Europe starting in the fourteenth century?

(A) It originated in India.

(B) Rats were linked with the plague in every region of Europe.

(C) It first appeared in Europe in France.

(D) It caused mass labor shortages, demands for higher wages, and strong governmental responses leading to the Peasants' Revolt in England and the Revolt of the Jacquerie in France.

(E) Art became more realistic and it attempted to portray an ideal world rather than the sorrow people experienced during the plague.

48. In the fourteenth and early fifteenth centuries,

(A) the English Parliament was weakened through the Hundred Years' War

(B) the French monarchy was also weakened during the Hundred Years' War

(C)   the Roman Catholic Church remained a powerful force in European politics and it was able to withstand attempts by the medieval monarchs to control it

(D)   the papacy developed Rome as an even stronger power base

(E)   Joan of Arc led the French to a number of victories over the English but they ultimately lost the Hundred Years' War

49.   Which of the following statements does NOT describe the impact if Western Imperialism on Africa and Asia?

(A)   It brought western education and consequently, later rebellions against European control.

(B)   It effectively kept Africa from industrializing, as Africa was used to grow crops to export and produce raw resources for European industry.

(C)   It had a dramatic effect on India's cottage industries, as India was used to produce raw resources for English manufacturing.

(D)   It created a new class of professionals who were educated in the western style and paid on an equal scale as the European elite.

(E)   Europeans in Africa often abused their native workers.

50.   Which of the following statements correctly describes the causes of World War I?

(A)   Unprovoked German aggression, similar to that in World War II.

(B)   An alliance between Britain and Germany that provoked the Russians and Italians into a war of self-protection.

(C)   Serbian nationalism, which led to the assassination of Archduke Ferdinand and an Austrian declaration of war, which set in motion a series of declarations of war based on a complex chain of alliances.

(D)   Germany's quick strike on France through the Schlieffen plan.

(E)   Russia's declaration of war on Germany for its role in the assassination of the Archduke Ferdinand.

51.   Which of the following was NOT a consequence of World War I?

(A)   The Ottoman Empire was strengthened and remained a threatening force in the Middle East.

(B)   Intellectuals questioned the possibility of progress.

(C) Intellectuals questioned the possibility of objectivity.

(D) Rising production of rubber during the war hurt the export industry from many colonial areas.

(E) The complex system of reparations helped to fuel the Great Depression.

52. Which of the following is NOT a correct description of World War II?

(A) Independence movements arose in the Middle East after World War II.

(B) Japanese imperialism in Asia provoked the United States to impose a quarantine on Japan, leading the Japanese to attack Pearl Harbor.

(C) Italian imperialism in Africa was a precursor to World War II.

(D) The German invasion of Czechoslovakia provoked an allied response.

(E) Independence movements arose in Africa following World War II.

53. Which of the following best describes the impact of the development of colonies in the New World on slavery?

(A) The trade in slaves decreased, as more slaves were available at home.

(B) More women than men were enslaved, leaving an overabundance of men in Africa.

(C) The trans-Sahara trade in slaves controlled by Arabs produced more slaves than the trans-Atlantic slave trade.

(D) Large portions of Africa became overpopulated as Africans attempted to create a stronger base for slavery.

(E) The gun and slave cycle created powerful slave trading kingdoms in Africa, such as Dahomey and the Ashante kingdoms.

54. Which is the most correct description of the Crusades?

(A) The Crusaders were often united and fought together for common goals.

(B) The Crusaders originally went to the Holy Land to convert Muslims to Christianity.

(C) The Crusaders established long-lasting kingdoms in the Orient that lasted until 1453 C.E.

(D)   The Crusaders never successfully captured Jerusalem.

(E)   The first Crusade succeeded in capturing Jerusalem and Edessa, but these locations were all soon prompting another series of Crusades that resulted in the loss of all possessions in the Holy Land by 1291 C.E.

55.   What is NOT true about the spread of Christianity?

(A)   It arrived in Britain through the missionary efforts of St. Augustine of Canterbury.

(B)   It arrived in amongst the Saxons through the missionary efforts of monks.

(C)   Boniface and Leoba carried Christianity from Anglo-Saxon England to the Germans.

(D)   Russia was forcibly converted to Christianity following the marriage of its prince Vladimir to a Byzantine princess.

(E)   Irish monks helped to spread Christianity in Northumbia during the Anglo-Saxon period.

56.   Which of the following statements most correctly describes attempts in Asia to limit overpopulation?

(A)   The one-child policy in China has been an overwhelming success, reducing the rate of population growth.

(B)   Indira Gandhi's policy of forced sterilization successful reduced the population of India.

(C)   The one-child policy in China applies to all Chinese.

(D)   The one-child policy in China applies only to those living in the country.

(E)   The one-child policy in China applies only to Han Chinese living in cities.

57.   Which of the following statements most correctly describes Native American societies before Columbus?

(A)   Many cultures in Mesoamerica began as egalitarian societies and later evolved into hierarchical ones.

(B)   The North American cultures had a more sophisticated social structure than native American cultures in Mesoamerica.

(C)   There were no urban centers in the Americas before Columbus.

(D)   The earliest urban center in the Americas was Teotihuacán.

(E)   In contrast to the Aztecs, the Maya were not warlike.

58.   Which of the following statements is NOT a correct description of medieval monasticism?

(A)   The Benedictine philosophy of *ora et labora* helped to revitalize barren lands along the frontiers of Germany and in the northern reaches of England.

(B)   *Ora et labora* also inspired the copying and preservation of ancient manuscripts.

(C)   Nuns were not instrumental in the spread of Christianity.

(D)   Anglo-Saxon abbesses were very powerful.

(E)   European monks and nuns often lived according to mixed rules prior to the reforms of Benedict of Aniane.

59.   The United States supported dictatorial regimes in all the following places EXCEPT

(A)   Zaire

(B)   Chile

(C)   Guatemala

(D)   Nicaragua

(E)   Egypt

60.   The discovery of the New World had all of the consequences EXCEPT:

(A)   The Ming Chinese instituted the Single Whip Reform following the influx of silver from the New World, but so much silver entered China its value eventually dropped by two-thirds.

(B)   Silver flooded the European markets, creating a Price Revolution and a global depression.

(C)   Europeans discovered sweet potatoes and maize in the New World, which ultimately revolutionized the diets of the Chinese.

(D)   Smallpox traveled from Europe to the New World, devastating the Native American population.

(E)   Europeans brought cattle and coffee to the New World.

61. Which of the following statements does NOT describe the feudal societies of both Japan in the Tokugawa period and Europe in the Western Middle Ages?

(A) The samurai were paid in rice while European knights received grants of land.

(B) Samurai fought one-on-one combat while knights fought in groups.

(C) Daimyo often lived on their *shoen*, while European knights generally did not reside on their manorial estates.

(D) Both knights and samurai lived by a code of warfare and behavior.

(E) Both knights and samurai were considered aristocrats in their respective societies.

62. Which of the following statements is most correct regarding Western European Imperialism in the nineteenth century and Mongol expansion?

(A) Mongol civilization was "superior" to those regions it conquered in the twelfth century, just as Western European civilization brought advances to those regions colonized.

(B) The Mongols were engaged in capitalistic enterprise, as were the western Europeans.

(C) The Mongol civilization was rooted in capitalism, as were the European imperialists of the nineteenth century.

(D) The Mongols were not interested in spreading their intellectual ideals of their culture to regions conquered, whereas European imperialists were.

(E) The regions conquered by the Mongols, such as China and the Abbasid Caliphate, were underdeveloped, in the same way as Africa and India were when the Europeans arrived.

63. Which of the following statements most correctly describes the influence of India and China on Southeast Asia, South Asia, and East Asia from 500–1500 C.E.?

(A) India influenced North Vietnam, while Chinese influence was felt throughout the area.

(B) China influenced North Vietnam, Koryo, and Japan while India was the most prominent influence in Southeast Asia.

(C) Indian influence was spread through warfare with Southeast Asian countries.

(D)   Angkor was primarily influenced by China.

(E)   The Pagan Dynasty was primarily influenced by China.

64.   Which statement does NOT describe changes in Latin America since World War II?

(A)   Women made gains in rights and power.

(B)   The population increased.

(C)   Latin American countries relied heavily on foreign investments and exports.

(D)   Latin Americans welcomed the presence of the U.S. and other foreign powers in their industries and politics.

(E)   People migrated from rural to urban areas.

65.   Which of the following statements best describes India during the reign of Akbar as compared to China during the late Ming Dynasty?

(A)   China had a capitalistic economy, while India did not.

(B)   India had only a modest trading network while the Chinese had an enormous external trading network.

(C)   Women of both societies participated in businesses and received education.

(D)   Women during Akbar's reign were visible in business and some were educated, but most Indian women remained in arranged marriages and were uneducated; the status of women in Ming China declined, as they were restricted by the Confucian Rules of Propriety and most were illiterate.

(E)   Both were intolerant of outside traditions and religions.

66.   Which of the following statements best describes conditions in Latin America and Africa following World War II?

(A)   Totalitarian dictatorships were present in Latin America but not in Africa in the early decades following World War II.

(B)   Democracies were established in Africa, but not in Latin America by the 1990s.

(C)   Democracies were established in Latin America by the end of the 1980s, and began to take root in sub-Saharan Africa in the 1990s.

(D) Women in Africa have made impressive gains and have been freed from traditional roles and arranged marriages, while women in Latin America still remain without political rights.

(E) Foreign investment was prominent in Latin America, but not in Africa.

67. Which of the following statements does NOT describe the Middle East after World War II?

(A) Iraq was the strongest power in the Persian Gulf after 1980.

(B) A Shi'ite government was established in Iran.

(C) Shi'ite groups, such as the Amal Militia and Hizballah, have been involved in terrorism during the struggles for independence in the region.

(D) The Israelis were defeated by the Egyptians in the Six Day War and their territories greatly restricted.

(E) Lebanon fought a bitter civil war following World War II, during which the Israelis invaded several times and Christian militias fought against various factions of Muslims.

68. Which of the following statements does NOT accurately represent the civilizations in ancient Egypt and China before the first millennium of the common era?

(A) Both were ruled by powerful emperors or pharaohs who united the civilizations.

(B) Egypt failed to develop a powerful empire outside of the Nile River Valley, while China developed a large empire during the Han period, conquering Vietnam, Korea, and other areas.

(C) There were powerful women rulers in Egypt, but women in China were restricted to the home and fields.

(D) Both were agricultural societies.

(E) Both believed that the ruler served as an intermediary between the heavens and life on earth.

69. Which of the following statements does NOT describe the expansion of Islam during the seventh and eighth centuries?

(A) According to the Shari'a, the jihad was a communal duty that must be carried out perpetually until the world was converted, and Caliphs waged at least one jihad annually.

(B) The Byzantine and Persian empires were at war, and they were unprepared for the Arab assaults.

(C) After the riddah, or apostate tribes, were subdued, Islamic leaders turned their attention elsewhere in order to keep the tribes from fighting one another.

(D) According to the fifth pillar of Islam, Muslims are required to convert infidels.

(E) The Umayyads built heavily fortified garrison cities to protect their conquests.

70. Which of the following is NOT a true statement about the Islamic world prior to 1500 C.E.?

(A) Following the collapse of the Abbasid Caliphate, Egypt became a center of trade in the Islamic world.

(B) Islam was successful in converting large numbers of inhabitants of inland Southeast Asia.

(C) The Abbasid Caliphate and T'ang China provided the stability needed for trade along the Silk Road.

(D) Arabs conquered India to protect trading routes.

(E) Islam arrived in Southeast Asia via trading ports.

STOP
This is the end of Section I.
If time still remains, you may check your work only in this section.
Do not begin Section II until instructed to do so.

Section II

Part A – Document-based Essay

TIME: Reading Period – 10 Minutes
Writing Period – 40 Minutes

DIRECTIONS: The following question is based on accompanying Documents 1–6. Read the documents and write an essay that:

- Has a relevant thesis and supports that thesis with evidence from the documents
- Uses all the documents
- Analyzes the documents
- Accounts for the sources of the documents and analyzes the author's point of view
- Explains the need for additional documentation

You may refer to relevant historical information not mentioned in the documents

---

1. Drawing on the following documents, discuss the causes of the conflicts in Vietnam against the French and then against the U.S. Include information not provided in the documents below.

Historical background: Two global themes emerged soon after the Second World War ended: (1) The Cold War; (2) anti-colonial movements.

Document 1

Source: The Atlantic Charter devised by U.S. President Franklin D. Roosevelt and British Prime Minister Winston Churchill, August 1941, in Richard Hofstadter, *Great Issues in American History* vol. III (1982).

The President of the United States of America and the Prime Minister, Mr. Churchill, representing His Majesty's Government of the United Kingdom, being met together, deem it right to make known certain common principles in the national policies of their respective countries on which they base their hopes for a better future for the world.

FIRST, their countries seek no aggrandizement, territorial or other;

SECOND, they desire to see no territorial changes that do no accord with the freely expressed wishes of the peoples concerned;

THIRD, they respect the right of all peoples to choose the form of government under which they will live; and they wish to see sovereign rights and self-government restored to those who have been forcibly deprived of them...

Document 2

Source: Communist Vietnamese leader Ho Chi Minh, telegram to President Harry S. Truman.

HANOI   FEBRUARY 28 1946

TELEGRAM

PRESIDENT HOCHIMINH VIETNAM DEMOCRATIC REPUBLIC HANOI

TO THE PRESIDENT OF THE UNITED STATES OF AMERICA WASHINGTON D.C.

ON BEHALF OF VIETNAM GOVERNMENT AND PEOPLE I BEG TO INFORM YOU THAT IN COURSE OF CONVERSATIONS BETWEEN VIETNAM GOVERNMENT AND FRENCH REPRESENTATIVES THE LATTER REQUIRE THE SECESSION OF COCHINICHINA AND THE RETURN OF FRENCH TROOPS IN HANOI [.] MEANWHILE FRENCH POPULATION AND TROOPS ARE MAKING ACTIVE PREPARATIONS FOR A COUP DE MAIN IN HANOI AND FOR MILITARY AGGRESSION [.] I THEREFORE MOST EARNESTLY APPEAL TO YOU PERSONALLY AND TO THE AMERICAN PEOPLE TO INTERFERE URGENTLY IN SUPPORT OF OUR INDEPENDENCE AND HELP MAKING THE NEGOTIATIONS MORE IN KEEPING WITH THE PRINCIPLES OF THE ATLANTIC AND SAN FRANCISCO CHARTERS.

RESPECTFULLY

HO CHI MINH

Document 3
Source: The Final Declaration of the Geneva Convention, July 21, 1954.

The Conference declares that, so far as Viet-Nam is concerned, the settlement of political problems, effected on the basis of respect for the principles of independence, unity, and territorial integrity, shall permit the Vietnamese people to enjoy the fundamental freedoms, guaranteed by democratic institutions established as a result of free general elections by secret ballot.

In order to insure that sufficient progress in the restoration of peace has been made, and that all the necessary conditions obtain for free expression of the national will, general elections shall be held in July 1956, under the supervision of an international commission composed of representatives of the member states of the International Supervisory Commission referred to in the agreement on the cessation of hostilities. Consultations will be held on this subject between the competent representative authorities of the two zones from April 20, 1955, onwards.

Document 4

Source: Statement from Ngo Dinh Diem, non-communist leader of South Vietnam, 1954, in Marilyn B. Young et al., *The Vietnam War: A History in Documents* (2002).

Dear Compatriots,

You know the facts: a cease-fire concluded at Geneva without the concurrence of the Vietnamese delegation has surrendered to the Communists all the north and more than four provinces of the central part of our country.

The national Government, constituted less than two weeks ago, in spite of its profound attachment to peace, has lodged the most solemn protest against that injustice. Our delegation at Geneva has not signed that agreement, for we cannot recognize the seizure by Soviet China—through its satellite the Viet Minh—of over half of our national territory. We can neither concur in the enslavement of millions of compatriots faithful to the nationalist ideal, nor to the complete destitution of those who, thanks to our efforts, will have succeeded in joining the zone left to us.

Document 5

Source: Historian Justus M. Van Der Kroef in an article "Marxism in Southeast Asia," published in the magazine *Current History*, November 1954.

Communism has been an enduring ally of nationalism. With the exception of the kingdom of Thailand, all countries of Southeast Asia have experienced a period of prolonged colonial control, either by France, England, the Netherlands, Spain or the United States, the very powers which today find themselves in varying degrees united against communism....

The solutions to the problems of Southeast Asia advanced by the Communist spokesmen are invariably attuned to the new dynamic and revolutionary temper of the area: all relics of the past are to be swept away, be they outmoded land tenure systems, Western enterprises of colonial origin, diversity of language and alphabets, grinding poverty and ill health, illiteracy, tax gouging or nepotism.

Document 6

Source: Historian Thomas E. Ennis, in an article "The French Empire I: In Asia," published in the magazine *Current History*, May 1955.

French educational aims [in Vietnam] were limited. After a century of French mastery, 80 per cent of the people were illiterate. Civil liberties were restricted with a vigor leading to a hatred of all things French....

France and her friends wait for the elections of 1956, hearing the voice of Ho Chi-minh lifted over the free world:

We gained a great victory at the Geneva Conference with the full assistance of the Soviet Union and China. We must continue our utmost efforts during the peace to win the unification, independence and democracy of the whole nation.

Part B — Change-Over-Time Essay

TIME: 40 minutes (5 minutes suggested for planning and outlining answer)

DIRECTIONS: Write an essay that answers the following question. Your essay should include:

- A relevant thesis and support for that thesis with appropriate historical evidence
- Answers for all parts of the question
- Use of world historical context to show changes over time
- An analysis of the process of change over time

---

2. Cultural mixing and cultural clashes are among the most common themes in human history. Focusing on the period 1300 to 1600, discuss the cultural mixing and cultural clashes involving one of the groupings below.

Protestants, Catholics, and Jews in Western Europe
Muslims and Hindus in India
Spaniards, Africans, and Aztecs in Mexico

Part C — Comparative Essay

TIME: 40 minutes (5 minutes suggested for planning and outlining answer)

<u>DIRECTIONS:</u> Write an essay that answers the following question. Your essay should include:

- A relevant thesis and support for that thesis with appropriate historical evidence
- Answers for all parts of the question
- Direct, relevant comparisons
- An analysis of relevant reasons for similarities and differences

---

3. Compare and contrast the basic features of the religions given in one of the following groupings:

Hinduism and Judaism
Confucianism and Christianity
Islam and Buddhism

AP WORLD HISTORY

PRACTICE TEST 1

ANSWER KEY

1. (C)	19. (C)	37. (C)	55. (B)
2. (B)	20. (D)	38. (A)	56. (E)
3. (D)	21. (C)	39. (B)	57. (A)
4. (B)	22. (B)	40. (C)	58. (C)
5. (E)	23. (C)	41. (E)	59. (E)
6. (D)	24. (D)	42. (D)	60. (B)
7. (B)	25. (B)	43. (B)	61. (C)
8. (D)	26. (D)	44. (A)	62. (D)
9. (B)	27. (B)	45. (D)	63. (B)
10. (E)	28. (C)	46. (B)	64. (D)
11. (E)	29. (E)	47. (D)	65. (D)
12. (E)	30. (E)	48. (A)	66. (C)
13. (E)	31. (D)	49. (D)	67. (D)
14. (C)	32. (C)	50. (C)	68. (D)
15. (A)	33. (E)	51. (A)	69. (D)
16. (B)	34. (C)	52. (C)	70. (B)
17. (E)	35. (E)	53. (E)	
18. (D)	36. (B)	54. (D)	

DETAILED EXPLANATIONS OF ANSWERS

TEST 1

SECTION I

1.   **(C)**

The United States, and other nations, export their culture as their businesses develop global bases of operation. Ethnic contrasts have increased in response to globalization, and some areas of the world continue to experience poverty and illiteracy. Africa is one of the most impoverished continents of the world, and illiteracy has actually increased in sub-Saharan Africa, South Asia, and the Middle East.

2.   **(B)**

Marshal Tito openly disagreed with Soviet policies, resulting in a split with Stalin and the Soviets.

3.   **(D)**

In fact, Mao Zedong broke with Russia over the belief that Russia had lost its revolutionary fervor for exporting revolution, and he also believed peasants were the key to a successful revolution. Russia and China did not maintain positive diplomatic relations throughout the period, and China refused to allow the Soviets to transport goods or other forms of support through China to North Vietnam.

4.   **(B)**

The United States supported the revolution that placed Reza Pahlavi in power as Shah of Iran; he proved to be an abusive ruler. The U.S. also supported the revolution of Armas in Guatemala, and he ruled as a dictator; Ronald Reagan supported the Marcos regime in the Philippines. U.S. investments in Latin America prompted involvement in Guatemala and other countries.

5. **(E)**

Ethnic, tribal, and religious interests played a strong role in Pan-African and Pan-Arabic movements following World War II and in the separation of Pakistan from India, and of Bangladesh from Pakistan, along with continuing disputes over Kashmir. Japan and the Little Tigers experienced phenomenal growth, while under Deng Xiaoping, China also experienced growth. Economic difficulties arose for many parts of Asia in the 1990s. Asia, Africa, and the Middle East are among the areas with the highest rates of poverty and illiteracy.

6. **(D)**

Brazil became Portuguese territory, and Portuguese is still the language spoken in Brazil today.

7. **(B)**

Somoza's support of U.S. policies in Nicaragua incited rebellions, including those of the Sandinistas.

8. **(D)**

These are the boundaries following the death of Genghis Khan in 1226. The empire would expand further by the end of the thirteenth century.

9. **(B)**

The emphasis on pagan philosophies and ideals during the Italian Renaissance by many Neo-Platonists created a new worldview that was not thoroughly orthodox in its assumptions. Humanism did not profoundly affect the subordinate status of women, nor did it result in the end of slavery. Civic humanism was developed partly as a result of the constant conflicts among city states, and the church was involved in these conflicts, especially when Medici and the Borgia family gained control of the papacy.

10. **(E)**

Thailand is the only Southeast Asian country never to have been colonized by Europeans, while South Africa was colonized by the British and, before them, the Dutch Afrikaners. At the turn of the twentieth century, Liberia was one of only two areas in Africa not colonized by Europeans.

11. **(E)**

Neither Jerusalem nor the Sinai Peninsula is currently included in the PNA.

12.   (E)

The Seljuk Turks captured Byzantium in 1453 after a long period of decline.

13.   (E)

Following the declaration of independence of Bosnia and Herzogovina in 1991, ethnic Serbs attempted to secede from Bosnia and Herzogovina and were aided in their struggle by Serbia. World War I began when a Serb assassinated the Archduke Ferdinand.

14.   (C)

Gandhi was disturbed by talk of the partition of India and attempted to unite Muslims and Hindus as well as other factions in their bid for independence from the British through a program of nonviolent resistance.

15.   (A)

In fact, an economic crisis hit Thailand in 1997, which quickly spread throughout many parts of Asia.

16.   (B)

Luther's language was often vehement and inflammatory. By 1520 he regarded Catholic theology as the instrument of the anti-Christ.

17.   (E)

Enlightened thinkers viewed religion as superstition and emphasized reason and natural law.

18.   (D)

Gold from Ghana was the basis of Mediterranean trade with the east. Iron-making arose in Africa as early as the first millennium B.C.E. and gradually spread throughout sub-Saharan Africa, but most scholars believe that Phoenicians introduced iron-making to Africa. Axum participated in the Indian Ocean trade, but it was never conquered by Muslims.

19.   (C)

The quotation represents two of Wilson's famous Fourteen Points.

20.   (D)

Islam spread in Africa starting in the seventh century, and influenced the cultures of Ghana, Mali, and other African states. Although Axum was Christian and North Africa was influenced by Christian culture during the late Roman period, sub-Saharan Africa was primarily influenced by Islam.

21.   **(C)**

The revolution in Saint Domingue did not grant rights to the *gens de cou-leur*, but Haiti was not proclaimed an independent republic until after the death of Toussaint. In general, creoles remained in power in the Latin American countries, and women did not immediately benefit from the independence movements.

22.   **(B)**

Reagan sold arms to Iran to fund the Contras in Nicaragua against the enactments of the U.S. Senate, and supported other anti-Communist movements. His Star Wars initiative further contributed to deteriorating relations. In the Soviet Union, Brezhnev's re-Stalinization efforts further separated the U.S. from the Soviet Union, and the era of "peaceful coexistence" under Khrushchev was over.

23.   **(C)**

In fact, rapid industrialization during the Meiji period prompted a need for foreign outlets for Japanese goods. Japan began a series of wars and a wave of expansion that culminated in its invasion of China in the years leading to World War II.

24.   **(D)**

Only Liberia and Abyssinia escaped colonization by Europeans.

25.   **(B)**

The map reflects the new Turkish Republic and the partition of the Ottoman Empire. Since it refers to Persia, it is a map of this area before 1935, when Persia became Iran. Israel does not yet exist on the map, again pointing to the period before 1948, when Israel proclaimed its existence.

26.   **(D)**

Confucius believed in the development of virtue through example and the leadership of virtuous rulers. Virtue would create an ordered society, rather than law and punishments.

27.   **(B)**

The Hindu tradition teaches that ultimate enlightenment is loss of self and unity with the Absolute, called *moksha*.

28.   **(C)**

Angkor Wat is predominantly a Hindu complex built by the Khmer of Cambodia.

29.   **(E)**

Communists were in control of North Vietnam and North Korea, while the United States supported the revolution that put Pinochet in power in Chile. India remained nonaligned with either the United States or with the Soviets, but did accept Soviet aid for its struggle against Pakistan. Many Latin America countries, including Argentina and Mexico, sought to free themselves from foreign domination.

30.   **(E)**

Both Louis XIV and Peter the Great were in danger from the nobility as children, and both later sought to create a strong state in order to protect their kingdoms from the threats of other countries. Louis XIV fought a series of wars that took on a global character, while Peter the Great fought wars in search of a warm water port. In France, Colbert created the Five Great Farms, the largest tariff-free area in Europe, while Peter the Great westernized Russia to make it competitive.

31.   **(D)**

Chinese Confucianism discouraged capitalistic enterprise. Despite the fact that the Chinese did have a monetary economy, it was badly managed by the Hongwu emperor. The Chinese never completely turned inward and continued to have a thriving trade with Southeast Asia following the voyages of Zheng He, but China never succeeded in industrializing like the west in part due to lack of centralized control over their economy. Europe, on the other hand, benefited from the development of absolutism. In France, mercantilism contributed to the development of trade and industry.

32.   **(C)**

Maximilian Robespierre led France during the Reign of Terror, and ruthlessly attempted to exterminate counter-revolutionary movements.

33.   **(E)**

Taiwan declared itself the Republic of China following the flight of the Nationalists there after World War II. The government on Taiwan regards itself as the legitimate government of China, while the mainland Chinese, known as the People's Republic of China, regard themselves as the legitimate government. Due to its miraculous economic transformation following World War II, Taiwan is known as the Little Tiger of the Pacific. Some leaders of Taiwan today are agitating for a declaration of independence from China, which China threatens to punish. The cartoon also points out the threat China may pose to other areas.

34.　　**(C)**

Alexander's armies conquered the Persian Empire, including Mesopotamia, Asia Minor, and Egypt. They never reached China.

35.　　**(E)**

Mesopotamians did discriminate between people on the basis of social standing and wealth, while Hebrews generally did not. Both permitted debt slavery, and both provided some protection for slaves. Neither permitted women to be divorced without cause. While they both relied upon the principle of "an eye for an eye," it was applied only to two people of the same social class in Mesopotamia.

36.　　**(B)**

Christianity had a profound effect on the social roles for women in its early history, as it freed women from traditional roles in marriage. However, as the religion evolved, marriage and divorce laws in the late Roman world tended to reconfirm traditional values. While there were some women in the Roman world who were able to influence protest movements, women in China rarely played such roles in antiquity. A Chinese woman was subject to the will of her father, then her husband, and finally her son, while a Roman *materfamilias* might be very influential behind the scenes as the mistress of her household.

37.　　**(C)**

People in the Roman world spoke a variety of language and used a variety of writing styles; they were very diverse culturally, and the Roman practice of offering citizenship to only Romans failed to firmly unite these diverse peoples. In China, on the other hand, the Chinese after Shi Huang Ti firmly united a tremendously diverse group of people, who used 5 styles of calligraphy. Both Romans and Chinese had a system of roads, and both traded with India.

38.　　**(A)**

As Rome expanded, provincial manufacturers in Gaul and in the Germanic areas supplanted Italy as the center of glass and ceramic production.

39.　　**(B)**

Romans could pay taxes in grain and they also paid soldiers in grain. Slavery alone could not generate the grain needed to supply the army and feed Romans.

40.   **(C)**

Economic historians argue that slavery provided no incentive to increase production in the ancient world and, therefore, both the Greek and Roman worlds failed to develop the sort of economies that might be expected. Slavery also promoted warfare, particularly between Greek city states, as people went in search of slaves. Following the conquests of Alexander the Great, slaves were in great abundance, further limiting the growth of the economy. Slaves were, however, often treated well in Roman families and were also well treated in Athens.

41.   **(E)**

Marxist historians argue that Europeans interfered with the natural path of China's development, and prohibited China from developing capitalism on her own. However, other historians insist that the arrival of the Europeans benefited China through introducing western modes of production and capitalistic enterprise.

42.   **(D)**

In the Second Industrial Revolution, Germany took the lead over Britain. This is evident in terms of sheer miles of railroad produced. Russia also began to rapidly industrialize and this is revealed by the miles of railroads created in this period.

43.   **(B)**

Athens was a democracy, but those who produced 500 bushels of wheat or other crops, the so-called 500 measure men, had greater privileges in terms of office holding than those who produced less. Sparta was more properly an oligarchy, and texts such as the *rhetra* make it clear that the initiators of legislation were the kings and ephors, who could also veto the will of the people. Only males who held a *kleros* participated in this process.

44.   **(A)**

The Crusades created a great deal of ill will between Muslims and Christians. Christian knights brutally slaughtered Muslims and Jews during the course of the Crusades. While Islamic forces invaded Spain and eventually France in the early Middle Ages, during the Crusades, Italy herself was safe.

45.   **(D)**

The open field system was in use well before the ninth century, when it was extended to include three fields. The moldboard was in fact a very useful device. In the Central Middle Ages there was a monetary economy.

46.   **(B)**

The Frankish monarchy was strengthened by the marriage of Clovis to a Roman Catholic, but no Frankish ruler was able to pass his inheritance on intact since all possessions were divided between the ruler's sons. Franks were beset by civil war throughout most of their early history. Later French rulers in the Middle Ages had to contend with their powerful Norman vassals, who became the kings of England starting in 1066. The Norman kings of England eventually had holdings along the western coast of the continent known as the Angevin kingdom and power more extensive than that of their French overlords until King John began to lose these territories to King Philip II of France. The German monarchy was involved in a long-running dispute with the papacy over investiture, the custom of investing a cleric with lands and the symbols of his priestly office. The church fought to free itself from the influence of the state.

47.   **(D)**

Scholars today dispute the origins of the plague, which was once thought to have come from China. Events in China that can be associated with the plague are separated from later events in India by several years, leading scholars to question the connections once universally assumed to be true. Scholars now question, too, the exact nature of the plague, and since rat bones are not found in parts of Europe in the north, some scientists have questioned whether *yersinia pestis* was responsible for all the deaths reported and have suggested other possible diseases. Art was preoccupied with death in some European locations such as Sienna, and it reverted to earlier, more rigid styles.

48.   **(A)**

The French monarchy was actually strengthened through its control of the *taille*. The Church was beset by a number of difficulties with the French monarchy, culminating in the move of the papacy to Avignon, where it remained under the control of the French throughout most of the fourteenth century. The Great Schism further fragmented the Church. Joan of Arc in fact helped lay the foundation for a French victory in the Hundred Years' War.

49.   **(D)**

Newly educated professionals were paid less than European colonizers, creating resentment.

50.   **(C)**

Though Germany did use the Schlieffen plan, it was a war strategy and not the cause of the war. Germany declared war on Russia as a result of its alliance with Austro-Hungary and Russia's support of the Serbs. German involvement in the war was the result of the complex system of alliances in place before World War I and its treaties with the Austro-Hungarians.

51.　　(A)

The Ottoman Empire was dismembered following World War I and a system of European mandates was carved from its former frontiers in the Middle East.

52.　　(C)

It was the invasion of Poland that provoked an allied response.

53.　　(E)

More men than women were enslaved, the Arab trade across the Sahara was weakened, and large portions of Africa were depopulated as a result of the slave trade. Although the trans-Sahara trade in slaves continued to flourish in the Age of Exploration, the trans-Atlantic trade produced far more slaves.

54.　　(D)

The Crusaders often fought with one another, especially during the First and Third Crusades. The First Crusade was launched with the intent of recapturing the Holy Land, but the intent was to exterminate and not convert the "infidels." The First Crusade was the most "successful" of all Crusades, in that western knights captured Jerusalem, Antioch, and Edessa, while the Byzantines re-captured Nicaea following a siege by the Crusaders. Edessa fell to Zengi in 1144, prompting the Second Crusade, while Jerusalem fell to Saladin in the late twelfth century, prompting the Third Crusade. By 1191 c.e., the Crusaders had lost all their territory in Outremer, or the Latin domains in the Holy Land.

55.　　(B)

Charlemagne forcibly converted the Saxons through several war campaigns against the Saxons, who repeatedly attempted to return to their pagan ways.

56.　　(E)

Neither China's policy nor Indira Gandhi's policy of forced sterilization can be called an unequivocal success. Both generated waves of protest and resentment toward the governments who implemented them and in both places, the population continues to grow.

57.　　(A)

The structures of the Mesoamerican and South American cultures were more complex than those in the North. There were many urban centers in the Americas before Columbus, but the earliest was at Caral in modern Peru.

58.   **(C)**

Leoba was a famous nun who accompanied Boniface on his mission to Germany along with several of her nuns.

59.   **(E)**

The U.S. funded coups in all of the places listed except for Egypt, which established leaders who rule as dictators.

60.   **(B)**

The influx of silver from the Americas brought about inflation in Europe.

61.   **(C)**

The Daimyo often did not live on the *shoen*.

62.   **(D)**

The Mongols were not capitalists and were not superior to the technologically advanced civilizations of China and the Abbasids when they began their wave of expansion. In these respects, the comparison to European imperialism breaks down.

63.   **(B)**

North Vietnam was one of the few areas of Southeast Asia influenced by China, while Indian influence was felt throughout the area, including Angkor and the Pagan Dynasty.

64.   **(D)**

Although Latin American countries were forced to rely upon foreign investment, following World War II many countries attempted to free themselves from foreign domination.

65.   **(D)**

India had a thriving capitalistic economy and an enormous internal and external trading network, while the Ming had not yet developed a capitalistic economy and, after the voyages of Zheng came to an end, maintained their trading network primarily with Southeast Asia. Akbar was very tolerant of other religions and stopped taxes for non-Muslims. The Chinese, on the other hand, were suspicious of religions such as Christianity, and their experience with the Jesuits created a good deal of mistrust of foreigners.

66.   **(C)**

Both Latin America and Africa saw the rise of many dictatorships in the years following World War II, but both have established democracies. In sub-Saharan Africa, democracy is still in its early stages, but new forms of government have not brought new rights and roles for women. In Latin America, women have made impressive gains. Foreign investment was an issue in both regions of the world.

67.   **(D)**

In fact, the Israelis won the Six Day War and occupied the Sinai Peninsula, Gaza Strip, Golan Heights, and the West Bank.

68.   **(D)**

Egypt, in fact, conquered large portions of the eastern Mediterranean during the reign of Thutmosis III. Both societies had powerful rulers who united the kingdoms. In Egypt, the ruler was thought of as the living Horus and the Osiris of the underworld, while in China, the ruler had the mandate of heaven.

69.   **(D)**

The fifth pillar is the hajj or pilgrimage to Mecca.

70.   **(B)**

Islam arrived in Southeast Asia via trading ports, and was generally unsuccessful in converting inhabitants not in the port cities. Inhabitants of Southeast Asia who lived inland were largely Buddhists and Hindus.

SECTION II

Sample Answer to Document-Based Essay

Before the Second World War, Vietnam (part of French Indochina) was colonized by the French. During WWII, it was occupied by the Japanese. After the war, Vietnam was returned the France. Soon after this, conflict broke out between anti-French Vietnamese and French forces with their own Vietnamese allies.

In 1954, France suffered a decisive loss at Dienbienphu. Fearing that Vietnam would become communist, the United States stepped in where France left off. Beginning in 1964, when the American Congress empowered the president to do whatever was necessary to defeat communism in Southeast Asia, the U.S. became deeply involved in Vietnam. In the view of many Vietnamese from the north and south of the country, these conflicts were wars of liberation from foreign occupation. For some in South Vietnam, and for the U.S. government, these were wars against communism. Thus, the Vietnam conflicts with the West that continued into the early 1970s can be seen within the contexts both of anti-colonial struggle and the global Cold War.

As we see in document #2, Ho Chi Minh, a French-educated communist leader in Vietnam, wanted the principles of the Atlantic Charter to apply to Vietnam. Among other things, the Atlantic Charter had called for peoples in the post-WWII world to be able to "choose the form of government under which they will live" (document #1). The United Nations Charter, formulated in San Francisco near the end of the war, used similar language. Since the U.S. President Franklin Roosevelt had been the key person behind the Atlantic Charter, Ho Chi Minh wrote to the U.S. president (in 1946, Harry Truman) asking for assistance against the French colonizers. After all, the U.S. government had never been fond of the French and British empires. Ho Chi Minh also knew that independence movements were alive throughout the world. India, for example, gained its independence from Britain in 1947.

In 1954, after the French had suffered a serious defeat at Dien Bien Phu, it seemed that the ideals of the Atlantic and San Francisco charters might go into effect in Vietnam. As we see in document #3, the Geneva Convention of that year called for elections in Vietnam that would allow for "free expression" of the Vietnamese peoples' "national will."

But the elections called for at Geneva never took place. This is mostly because the world had changed significantly since the Atlantic and San Francisco Charters. The most important change was the Cold War, which pitted non-communist countries (led by the U.S.) against communist countries (led primarily by the Soviet Union).

Immediately following the Second World War, the Soviet Union occupied Eastern Germany and most of Eastern Europe; civil war in Greece broke out between communists and non-communists; and China became communist in 1949. In every case, the U.S. had acted to stop the spread of communism—by assisting anti-communist Greeks and Chinese, and by preventing West Berlin from being grabbed by the Soviets. This was the context of American action in Vietnam. If elections were held in Vietnam, it was feared, the communists would win. This fear was probably based on a correct assumption. As the historians Van Der Kroef and Ennis made clear in their articles written in the mid-1950s (documents # 5 & 6), many Vietnamese saw communism as an alternative ideology to colonialism and its oppressive policies. Educated Vietnamese knew that the French Revolution had promoted "liberty, equality and fraternity," but many Vietnamese did not believe that the French had brought these ideals to Vietnam.

Some Vietnamese, especially in the southern part of the country, who had been pro-French—who spoke French and who had become Catholic—also feared that Vietnam would be come communist. Among these was Ngo Dihn Diem, who saw the Geneva agreement as a "surrender" to the mostly communist north (document # 4). Diem was by no means a democrat, but in the Cold War context, the most important thing to the U.S. was that he was anti-communist. So the U.S. supported Diem, believing (according to the "domino theory") that if Vietnam became communist, Laos, Cambodia, Thailand, Burma and India would follow. As Diem said in 1954, "Soviet China" was poised to take over Vietnam. Evidence that this might have been true came from Ho Chi Minh's own mouth: as we see in document # 6, he was grateful to the Soviet Union and China for their help at the Geneva talks.

In reality, Ho Chi Minh did like the Soviets or the Chinese; after the war with the U.S. ended, Vietnam experienced conflict with China. But in the Cold War context, they were the nations to rely on against the U.S., which many Vietnamese saw as just another foreign occupier. But because Ho Chi Minh was communist, and because he relied on the Soviets and China, the U.S. felt compelled to fight in Southeast Asia.

By 1975, the U.S. has lost 58,000 men killed. Vietnamese losses were perhaps ten times greater, though they did finally succeed in getting foreigners out of their country.

Discussion of Essay

This essay's thesis is stated in the last sentence of the second paragraph, following information that conveys important background information. Though the essay does not quote heavily from the documents, it does account for every one of them. The essay shows that the main points of each of the documents has been understood and properly contextualized. The essay also shows that the writer is able to distinguish different points of view expressed in the documents and is able to place these points of view in their proper context. Providing context for the documents required additional information to be added to the essay. The essay's final paragraph restates the thesis of the essay, while adding some new information.

Sample Answer to Change-Over-Time Essay

When Spaniards met Africans and purchased them as slaves from other Africans, and when the Spaniards and their slaves met Aztecs in present-day Mexico, violence and conquest were inevitable. But that conquest would lead to a new culture in the New World.

By 1500, Muslims who had occupied Iberia (Portugal and Spain) for centuries were pushed out. Also by that year, partly as a result of the Spanish Inquisition, Jews were being expelled from Spain. These experiences of conflict provide some context for the conquest of what would come to be called New Spain. At the same time, Europeans from France, Portugal and the Netherlands, as well as from Spain, were pursuing Asian wealth in the form of, for example, spices and silk. They also sought gold and glory for their monarchs, as well as souls to convert to Christianity. It was en route to Asia that the Portuguese and Spaniards came upon the New World—the West Indies, the Caribbean, North, Central and South America.

West Africans (from present-day Senegal to Nigeria) had enslaved one another for a long time before Europeans—at first, the Portuguese—capitalized on the slave trade. European traders provided commodities to tribal leaders in exchange for slaves. The Spaniards brought Africans to the New World with one generation of Columbus' landfall in the New World in 1492.

Unlike some indigenous peoples in the New World, the Aztecs were a sedentary people—that is, they established settlements and remained in them for long periods. The Aztecs employed sophisticated irrigation systems and used fertilizer to grow crops; they had highly organized political and religious structures; given the limits on their knowledge, they were capable astronomers; and the Pyramid of the Sun was the largest pyramid in the world. The Aztec capital, Tenochtitlan, was larger than the Spanish capital of Madrid.

Like the Spaniards and slave-selling African tribes, the Aztecs were conquerors. Just as the Spaniards had conquered Muslims and put great pressure on Jews, so the Aztecs had conquered and put great pressure on other Native groups. When the Spaniards and Aztecs met, conflict was inevitable.

The striking thing is that the Aztec empire, which had many thousands of fighters at its disposal, was toppled in a few years by a few hundred Spaniards. How was this possible? The most important weapon the Spaniards had was European disease, especially smallpox, which killed many more Aztecs than Spanish weapons did. The West Africans, who had contact with Europeans long before 1519 (the year the conquistador Hernan Cortes arrived in Mexico), were more able to survive European diseases. This is a major reason that Spaniards (and other Europeans) turned to African slave labor—the Aztecs and other Natives quickly died from disease.

Another thing the Spaniards had in their favor was advanced technology in the form of guns, cannon and swords. They also had ferocious dogs and horses, the latter of which the Aztecs had never seen before. These weapons contributed to an Aztec belief that the Spaniards had extraordinary spiritual power.

A third thing the Spaniards had on their side was the hatred of Native groups for the Aztecs. Like the Spaniards and Africans, the Aztecs enslaved conquered peoples, and some conquered people were used as human sacrifices in Aztec religious rituals. The Spaniards made use of the idea that "the enemy of my enemy is my friend" and convinced Native groups to help defeat the Aztecs. Of course, many of these Natives would soon die of disease.

After the conquest of the Aztec empire, a new culture began to emerge in present-day Mexico. Very few Spanish women accompanied the mostly young men who went to conquer and settle New Spain. This led to widespread intermarriage between Spanish men and indigenous women and to the creation of people who would be called *mestizos*, people of mixed ethnicity. Hundreds of Spanish words were absorbed by the language spoken by the Aztecs, Nahuatl, but that indigenous language did not die out; officials in New Spain often kept records in Nahuatl. The Spaniards' Catholicism became the religion of New Spain. This was made easier to accept by the Spaniards' practice of building churches on sites where Aztec gods had been honored before.

Since 1600, the descendents of the Spaniards, Africans, Aztecs (and other indigenous peoples) have forged unique Latin American cultures. Catholicism in Mexico today looks and feels different from Catholicism in the United States. This is largely because of indigenous influence.

Analysis of Essay

The thesis of the essay is clearly stated in its first sentence. It is re-stated, with additional information added, in the last paragraph. The least amount of information is provided about Africans, but the main reasons Africans went with the Spanish to the New World are given. Otherwise, the essay simply accomplished the required task. It describes how Spaniards, Africans and Aztecs came face to face; it provides some detail about the clash between the Spaniards and the Aztecs; and it provides information about the new culture that was created following the conquest of the Aztec empire.

Sample Answer to Comparative Essay

Buddhism and Islam are very complicated and, as I will show, they are very different, but they have some things in common. Buddhism and Islam both provide their adherents with comprehensive outlooks on life, they both address the big questions of human existence—such as "How can I live a good life?"—and they place at their centers individuals who acquired the truth and preached it to others. These individuals—Buddha Gotama and Mohammed—are essential to Buddhism and Islam, but they themselves are not worshipped. This is one difference these religions have with Christianity, whose central figure is Jesus Christ, whom Christians believe is God.

Compared to Buddhism, Islam is a new religion; it began in the late-sixth century Arabia. The Buddha Gotama (also called Siddhattha or Sidhartha), lived in India in the sixth century B.C.E. (According to tradition, twenty five Buddahs preceded him.) After standing up to significant temptation and after lengthy meditation, Buddha Gotama entered a transcendental realm. He could have stayed in that realm, but the decided instead to preach the Dhamma—that is, the truth about the world. Part of the Buddhist truth is that suffering is an illusion that is brought on by impermanent human desires.

According to Muslim tradition, in the late sixth century, near Mecca, Mohammed meditated through the night. He was disturbed by the polytheistic religious practice he saw in Arabia. At one point an angel told him to write down what the angel said, and these writings, became the Koran, which Muslims around the world are still encouraged to read in Arabic. According to Islam, Mohammad was the last and greatest of God's prophets on earth. He had been preceded by other important prophets such as Abraham, Moses, and Jesus, but none of these were as great as Mohammed. This is one important difference between Islam and Judaism, which do not recognize Mohammad as a great prophet. Also, Muslims are strictly monotheistic, and to them the Christian idea of the Trinity equals polytheism.

Islam spread quickly through Arabia, the rest of the Middle East, and North Africa, and it remains the dominant religion in those regions. Muslims occupied Spain beginning in the eight century, and they remained there for centuries. By the eleventh century, Muslims were moving into Afghanistan and India.

Islam spread primarily as a result of conquest, but also as a result of proselytism and of the conversion of local leaders. Buddhism, on the other hand, began in India, but it never was the dominant religion there (Hinduism and Islam gained more adherents). It became more dominant in other parts of Asia, such as Vietnam, Thailand and Cambodia.

Traditional Buddhists do not believe that individuals possess souls. Indeed, they believe that the idea of the "self" is an illusion. For Buddhists, the primary goal is achieve "awakening"—that is, freedom from the cares and concerns of this impermanent life. If a Buddhist achieves a desire-free life, then he or she has achieved nirvana, an eternal realm of selfless perfection. Traditional Muslims, on the other hand, believe in human souls, and they believe that people who do not submit to the will of Allah (i.e. God) will suffer in hell, about which the Koran (the Muslims' most important book) has a lot to say. People who do submit to the will of Allah will go to a paradise after this life. The word Islam means "submission," and the western concept of "free will" is not important to traditional Muslims.

Muslims are required to adhere to the "Five Pillars" of Islam. The first pillar is the Muslim's confession of faith—that there is only one God and that Mohammed is his prophet. The second pillar involves prayer five times a day, facing Mecca. The third pillar calls for alms to be given to assist the poor. The fourth pillar requires fasting from dawn to dusk during the month of Ramadan. The fifth pillar calls on all Muslims to make at least one pilgrimage to Mecca in their lifetimes, if they are able to do so.

Buddhists believe in the "middle way"—not going to extremes. This means, for example, that people should avoid both gluttony and extreme fasting. Buddhists call for meditation under the direction of an experienced practitioner, which leads to the elimination of earthly desire, and ethical behavior. Buddhists discourage clouding the mind with drugs and alcohol, sexual immorality and harming living things.

While Buddhism and Islam have some features in common, they comprise very different approaches to life.

Analysis of the response

Buddhism and Islam are very complicated topics and just about anything a person writes about them could be challenged. The first sentence of the essay points to this fact. This essay avoids controversial issues and focuses on major points. It provides some historical background, makes germane comparisons and focuses more on differences. The brief comparisons with Judaism and Christianity are not required, but they suggest to the reader that the writer possesses a broad understanding of two other major religions.

▼

PRACTICE TEST 2
AP World History

This test is also on CD-ROM in our special interactive AP World History TEST*ware*®. It is highly recommended that you first take this exam on computer. You will then have the additional study features and benefits of enforced timed conditions and instant, accurate scoring. See page xix for guidance on how to get the most out of our AP World History software.

AP World History

PRACTICE TEST 2

SECTION I

TIME: 55 minutes
70 multiple-choice questions

> **DIRECTIONS:** Each of the questions or incomplete statements below is followed by five suggested answers or completions. Select the one that is best in each case.

1. Which of the following statements best describes Asia's relations with Europe from 1500–1850 C.E.?

   (A) European powers colonized all of Asia, including Japan, during this period.

   (B) European powers colonized all of Southeast Asia, but not South and East Asia during this period.

   (C) European powers defeated China in the Opium Wars, colonized India and large parts of Southeast Asia but for Thailand, and Japan pursued a policy of isolationism during this period.

   (D) European powers colonized India and traded with Japan, but failed to develop colonies in Southeast Asia.

   (E) European powers colonized South and Southeast Asia, but failed to dominate either China or Japan during this period.

2. Which of the following statements does NOT describe both Islam and Judaism?

   (A) Both revere Moses and Abraham as prophets.

   (B) Both are monotheistic religions.

   (C) Both revere Jesus as a prophet.

(D) Both emphasize prayer, fasting, and charity towards others of the community.

(E) Both forbid the making of idolatrous images.

3. Which of the following statements best describes both Buddhism (as taught by Siddhartha in antiquity) and Hinduism?

(A) They originated in India.

(B) They both emphasize the importance of rituals.

(C) They both believe in the atman.

(D) They both believe in deities.

(E) They both believe that a person is born into the caste system as a result of karma from a past life or lives.

4. Which of the following statements best describes both Christianity and Buddhism ?

(A) Both had a tremendous impact on Southeast Asia.

(B) Both of their founders taught that they were divine.

(C) Both originated in South Asia.

(D) Both religions have continued to interpret their founders' teachings as they were in antiquity.

(E) Both religions grew after leaders of empires and kingdoms converted and helped to spread their teachings.

5. Which of the following statements is NOT true of *Homo erectus?*

(A) It likely overlapped in time with *Homo habilis.*

(B) It had the capacity to make fire.

(C) It depended on gathering for survival and also hunting or scavenging.

(D) It was the first hominid to leave Africa.

(E) The oldest fossils are found in Australia.

6. Which of the following statements best describes the development of agriculture in the Neolithic era?

(A) It first evolved in China and then spread to other areas.

(B) Wheat was grown in the Middle East.

(C)   It first evolved in the Americas and then spread to other areas.

(D)   Maize was cultivated in China.

(E)   Rice was the primary crop of the Indus River Valley.

7.   Which of the following statements best describes *Homo sapiens neander-thalensis?*

(A)   They were hunters and gatherers.

(B)   They became extinct in 85,000 B.C.E.

(C)   They painted art in caves.

(D)   They had no tools.

(E)   They had smaller brains than modern humans.

8.   Which of the following cultures fought with Mycenaeans over control of Asia Minor, and fought the Egyptians for control of the eastern Mediterranean?

(A)   The Babylonians

(B)   The Assyrians

(C)   The Hittites

(D)   The People of the Sea

(E)   The Persians

9.   Which of the following statements is NOT true of the relationship between the ancient Persians and the Greeks?

(A)   Both supported the growth of democracy.

(B)   They both had dualistic religions.

(C)   They both valued diversity in their societies and allowed people to practice a diversity of religions and other customs.

(D)   The Persians treated their emperor as divine and he ruled as a dictator, which repulsed the Greeks.

(E)   The Greeks believed that they had borrowed large portions of their culture from the Persians.

10.   Which of the following statements does NOT describe both Zoroastrianism and Christianity?

(A)   Both believe in forces of good and evil that are in combat with one another.

(B)   Both were never the religion of state in their respective areas.

(C)   Both believe in life after death.

(D)   Both believe in saviors who were incarnated as humans.

(E)   Both have a ritual meal.

11.   Which statement does NOT describe France during the reign of Louis XIV and England under the Stuart monarchy?

(A)   Both monarchies were based on the belief that their authority was from God.

(B)   Both allowed for freedom of religion.

(C)   Both were Catholic monarchies, though the Stuarts ruled a Protestant country.

(D)   Both successfully controlled their parliaments.

(E)   The Stuarts were allies of Louis XIV.

12.   Which of the following statements does NOT describe the Enlightened Despots?

(A)   Many were known for abolishing the death penalty and torture.

(B)   Some supported religious toleration.

(C)   Many passed their reforms through parliamentary means.

(D)   Many advocated freedom of the press.

(E)   Many built roads and otherwise improved their kingdoms.

13.   Which of the statements below best describes changes in the European Scientific Revolution and Chinese culture during the Ming Dynasty and the transition to the Qing Dynasty through the seventeenth century?

(A)   Empiricism was important, as illustrated by Francis Bacon's use of induction or Dai Zhen (Tai Chen)'s work on scientific reasoning.

(B)   The production of encyclopedias was a prominent feature of both cultures.

(C)   Math and science grew in importance in both cultures.

(D)   Textual and historical criticism grew in importance.

(E)   Europeans moved away from Christianity while the Chinese began to embrace it through Jesuit missions.

14. Which of the following statements is NOT a correct description of how gender roles have changed in Asia since 1500 c.e.?

    (A) The status of women improved during the Ming and Qing Dynasties.

    (B) The British defeat of China during the Opium Wars brought about an improvement in the rights of women.

    (C) After World War II, Communist leaders abolished forced marriages and foot binding in China.

    (D) In Japan, women were the hardest hit by the recession of the 1990s.

    (E) Women were typically repressed by Hindus and Muslims in India, but played an important role in Ghandi's movement for independence from Britain.

15. Who implemented the Great Leap Forward in China and a series of reforms based on the Soviet model?

    (A) Sun Yat-sen

    (B) Chiang Kai Shek

    (C) Mao Zedong

    (D) Deng Xiaoping

    (E) Pu Yi

16. Who was president of the Republic of China in 1911?

    (A) Sun Yat-sen

    (B) Chiang Kai Shek

    (C) Mao Zedong

    (D) Deng Xiaoping

    (E) Pu Yi

17. Who founded the government of Taiwan?

    (A) The Chinese Communists under Mao Zedong

    (B) The Nationalist Chinese under Chiang Kai Shek

    (C) The Qianlong emperor

(D)   The Kangzi emperor

(E)   Deng Xiaoping

18.   The Middle Eastern nation torn by civil war for sixteen years and occupied in the south by the Palestinian Liberation Organization and by Israeli forces was

(A)   Jordan

(B)   Lebanon

(C)   Syria

(D)   Israel

(E)   Iraq

19.   The twentieth-century Egyptian leader who nationalized the Suez Canal and who vowed to unite the Arab world in opposition to Israel was

(A)   Sadat

(B)   Nasser

(C)   Saladin

(D)   Netanyahu

(E)   Arafat

20.   The Israeli Prime Minister who attempted to make peace with Palestinians through the creation of the Palestinian National Authority was

(A)   Rabin

(B)   Begin

(C)   Netanyahu

(D)   Ariel Sharon

(E)   Shimon Peres

21.   The greatest Buddhist ruler of antiquity in India was

(A)   Chandragupta Maurya

(B)   Ashoka

(C) Aurangzeb

(D) Humayan

(E) Akbar

22. The center of the *Risorgimento* was in

(A) Naples

(B) The Kingdom of the Two Sicilies

(C) Rome

(D) Sardinia

(E) Venice

23. The leader of the Protestant Reformation in Zurich was

(A) Calvin

(B) Luther

(C) Zwingli

(D) Melancthon

(E) Charles VII

24. Who wrote the most famous account of court life during the Heian period?

(A) Lady Murasaki

(B) Prince Shotoku

(C) Hideyoshi

(D) Oda Nobunaga

(E) Sei Shonagun

25. Which Egyptian ruler created the Amarna revolution?

(A) Ramses II

(B) Pepi II

(C) Akhenaton

(D) Thutmose (Thutmosis) III

(E) Hatshepsut

26. The Byzantine ruler who attempted to reconquer lost western territories was

    (A) Sophia Paleologus

    (B) Justinian

    (C) Alexius Comnenus

    (D) Basil

    (E) Diocletian

27. This bronze head originated in

    (A) Ghana

    (B) Mali

    (C) Nok

    (D) Benin

    (E) Axum

28. The first successful permanent British colony in the Americas was

    (A) Maryland

    (B) Jamestown

    (C) Roanoke

    (D) Delaware

    (E) Plymouth

29. The final battle of the American Revolution was

    (A) Saratoga

    (B) Trenton

    (C) Yorktown

    (D) Bunker Hill

    (E) White Plains

30. The Spanish conquistador who discovered the Grand Canyon was

    (A) Ponce de Leon

    (B) Coronado

    (C) Cortes

(D)   Pizarro

(E)   Balboa

31.   Which U.S. President returned the Panama Canal to Panama?

(A)   Ronald Reagan

(B)   Harry Truman

(C)   Dwight Eisenhower

(D)   James Earl Carter

(E)   George H.W. Bush

32.

The image above is of a tablet written in

(A)   Egyptian hieroglyphics

(B)   Arabic

(C)   Cuneiform

(D)   Sanskrit

(E)   Hebrew

33.   Which of the following structures was built the earliest?

(A)   The pyramids in Mesoamerica

(B)   The Acropolis in Athens

(C)   The pyramids in Egypt

   (D)   The Gate of Ishtar in Babylon

   (E)   The lion gate in Mycenae

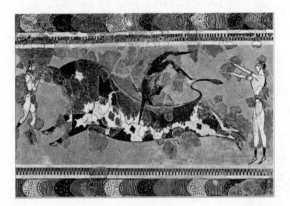

34.

The image above illustrates the

   (A)   Egyptian cult of Serapis

   (B)   Influence of Egypt on Minoan art

   (C)   Influence of China on Southeast Asian art

   (D)   Hindu worship of the Brahma bull

   (E)   The influence of Buddhism on the Indus River Valley

35.   Which of the following statements is true of Solon of Athens and Julius Caesar of Rome?

   (A)   They all attempted to equalize the rich and the poor.

   (B)   They attempted to transform their governments into autocracies.

   (C)   They attempted to address the needs of the wealthier members.

   (D)   They led coup d'etats to overthrow autocratic control.

   (E)   They gave citizenship to those previously denied citizenship.

36.   The decisions made by the Church at the Council of Nicaea reflected a

   (A)   concern over the theological unity of the Catholic Church

   (B)   desire to separate the Eastern Church from the heretical Western Church

   (C)   desire to give women greater status within the Catholic Church

   (D)   desire to clarify the human nature of Christ

   (E)   desire to establish papal supremacy

37. Which medieval ruler forcibly converted the Saxons?

   (A) Otto I

   (B) Charlemagne

   (C) Charles the Bald

   (D) Clovis

   (E) Dagobert

38. What do Popes Boniface VIII and Gregory VII have in common?

   (A) They were both dominated by secular rulers.

   (B) They both successfully dominated secular rulers.

   (C) They both launched crusades.

   (D) They both attempted to separate the Church from the control of monarchs

   (E) The both fought against the Protestant Reformation.

39. Look carefully at the following map. This map represents Africa

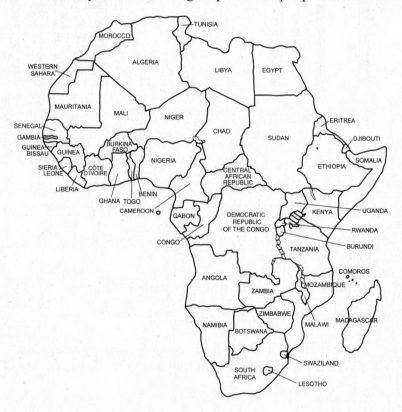

(A) after 1850

(B) before 1880

(C) in 1900

(D) after 1914

(E) post–1950

40. What can we conclude from the following chart?

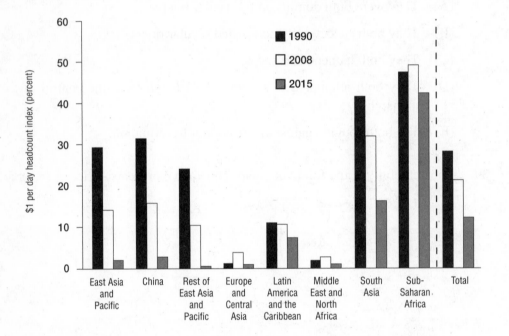

(A) Poverty rates are relatively equal throughout the world.

(B) There is more poverty in Latin America and the Caribbean than in Sub-Saharan Africa.

(C) Africa will make great strides in eradicating poverty by 2008.

(D) Poverty rates are falling in Europe.

(E) There are more impoverished people living in Asia (including South and East and the Pacific) than anywhere else in the world.

41. What does the following chart illustrate?

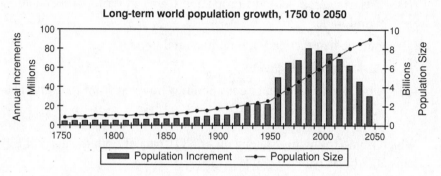

Long-term world population growth, 1750 to 2050

(A) The population of the world remains relatively stable.

(B) The rate of growth in world population has remained stable over the past fifty years.

(C) The rate of population growth is declining since 2000 while overall numbers continue to rise.

(D) The rate of population growth continues to increase as overall numbers remain stable.

(E) The rate of population growth decreased from 1750–1850 and overall numbers remained stable.

42. Which of the following does the map below NOT show about world trade in 1740?

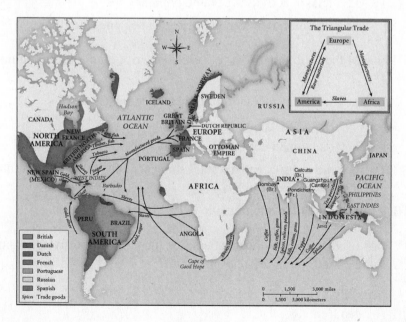

    (A)   Asian exchanged spices for slaves.

    (B)   Russia lagged behind Europe and China in terms of its position in world trade.

    (C)   Europe had the lead in manufactured goods.

    (D)   Africa supplied slaves.

    (E)   Gold, sugar, and other commodities traveled from the Americas to Europe.

43.   Which of the following statements is NOT true of both the ancient Egyptians and the Maya?

    (A)   Both built enormous pyramids.

    (B)   Both were agricultural societies.

    (C)   Both extended their influence over other cultures.

    (D)   Both had an elaborate system of writing.

    (E)   Both cultures had indigenous beasts of burden.

44.   Which of the following is NOT a social and economic change in Europe in the second half of the nineteenth century, during the Second Industrial Revolution?

    (A)   The illegitimacy rate rose.

    (B)   Marriages were formed out of love and not arranged by parents.

    (C)   Compulsory education became more common.

    (D)   Mass leisure activities became popular.

    (E)   The separation between gender roles became even wider.

45.   Which of the following is not a correct description of the Revolutions of 1848?

    (A)   They were unsuccessful in Italy and Hungary.

    (B)   They were led by social conservatives.

    (C)   They dampened enthusiasm for liberalism.

    (D)   They did not succeed in establishing socialist governments in many parts of Europe.

    (E)   In Prussia they attempted to get a liberal constitution.

46.   Which of these Communist leaders was the least supportive of exporting Communism through revolution abroad?

    (A)   Lenin

    (B)   Mao Zedong

    (C)   Leonid Brezhnev

    (D)   Nikita Krushchev

    (E)   Trotsky

47.   The following images relate to what trend in the world around 1989?

Events in Beijing, 1989

Events in Berlin, 1989

(A) The overthrow of Communism in China and in Germany.

(B) Growth of democratic movements in Central and Eastern Europe and in China.

(C) Growth of socialist movements in Central and Eastern Europe and in China.

(D) Growth of religious fundamentalism in Asia and Central and Eastern Europe.

(E) The overthrow of Communism in China and its revival in Czechoslovakia.

48. Both Luther and Calvin believed in

(A) consubstantiation

(B) transubstantiation

(C) the abolition of the celibate priesthood

(D) the preservation of the seven sacraments

(E) predestination

49. Which of the following statements does NOT describe Japan following World War I?

(A) Zaibatsu conglomerates gained control over large sectors of the economy.

(B) Production and exports increased dramatically.

(C) The population increased and food shortages were experienced.

(D) Japan formally renounced war as a national policy in the Kellogg-Briand pact but then later invaded Manchuria.

(E) Under the Taisho Democracy women gained political rights.

50. Which of the following statements does NOT describe the Middle East after World War I?

(A) Faisal of Hejaz attempted to create an independent Arab state in the Middle East in Hejaz and Syria but was thwarted by European powers.

(B) Europeans made a secret agreement to carve up the Middle East following World War I and Arabs attempted to revolt against it.

(C)   The representative body in Persia succeeded in keeping out foreign interests.

(D)   Afghanistan declared independence from Britain.

(E)   Palestine was a British mandate.

51.   Which of the following statements does NOT describe both the NEP of Lenin and Deng Xiaoping's four modernizations?

(A)   Both allowed for peasants to sell surplus crops on the free market.

(B)   Both maintained state control of some heavy industries but returned smaller ones to the free market

(C)   Both tolerated cottage industries.

(D)   Both sets of reforms created an economic revival.

(E)   Both sets of reforms created an affluent middle class.

52.   What is true of slavery in the Islamic world?

(A)   It was based on race and ethnicity.

(B)   Slaves worked on large plantations but did not fulfill other functions.

(C)   Islamic conquests produced a large and continuous supply of slaves.

(D)   Slaves did not serve in Islamic armies.

(E)   The Qur'an defined certain races as naturally suited to slavery.

53.   Which culture is associated with the most extensive capitalistic trading empire before the Age of Discovery?

(A)   China

(B)   Japan

(C)   India

(D)   Rome

(E)   The Islamic empires

54.   What is true of Islamic expansion following Muhammad?

(A)   Arab conquerors often freely mixed with those they conquered.

(B)   Non-Muslims were treated as equal citizens along with those of Arab descent.

(C) Expansion first began under Caliph Abu Bakr.

(D) Expansion first began under the Umayyads.

(E) Expansion was halted at the battle of Yarmuk.

55. Which of the following statements is true of the First and Second Industrial Revolutions?

(A) While Britain led the first Industrial Revolution, centered on steam power, Italy led the second, centered on the hydro-electric industry.

(B) While the first Industrial Revolution centered on the production of cotton and steam power, the most important aspect of the Second Industrial Revolution was hydroelectric power.

(C) While the first Industrial Revolution was spread throughout all parts of Europe equally, the second was centered in Germany.

(D) Inequities between Britain and the other European countries were evident in the first Industrial Revolution, while during the second Industrial Revolution, there were less clear differences between Germany and Italy, for example.

(E) Britain led the first Industrial Revolution, centered on the production of cotton cloth and the use of steam power, while Germany led the second, centered on the production of iron and steel for railroads.

56. Which of the following statements is true of the patterns of Industrialization in Russia and Japan starting in the nineteenth century?

(A) Both resulted in the creation of a class of western-educated professionals.

(B) Both encouraged foreign investments.

(C) Both were marked by rapid construction of railroads and government support of the railroad and other industries.

(D) Both countries saw the rise of exports in contrast to imports.

(E) Both were financed by agricultural taxes.

57. Which statement is NOT true of Christians in the Islamic world from Muhammad through around 1800 C.E.?

(A) Christian girls could enter the harem of the Ottoman emperors.

(B) Christian boys served as Janissaries during the Ottoman period and could rise to positions of great prominence.

(C)   Christians paid a poll tax in the Islamic world.

(D)   Christians were permitted to openly advertise symbols of their faith and seek converts.

(E)   Christians were forced to dress differently than their Arab conquerors.

58.   Which of the following statements is NOT true of the French and American Revolutions?

(A)   Both were based on rights they believed to be granted by natural law.

(B)   Both created a new system of equality among all inhabitants.

(C)   Both began over protests concerning taxation.

(D)   Both movements resulted in the end of monarchies.

(E)   During the early phases of each revolution, the parliaments or representative bodies in both areas refused to cooperate with the demands of their respective monarchs.

59.   Which of the following countries was the last to abolish slavery?

(A)   Britain

(B)   The United States

(C)   Russia

(D)   Brazil

(E)   Portugal

60.   What is NOT true of the Russian Revolution and the French Revolution?

(A)   Both had as an early result the end of their respective monarchies.

(B)   Both have often been interpreted by leading scholars as the culmination of class struggles.

(C)   Peasants played an important role in both revolutions.

(D)   Intellectuals played a leading role in both revolutions.

(E)   Both tried to create a representative government.

61. How did the French colonization of North America differ from that of the English?

    (A) The French primarily established trading colonies, whereas the English established settlement and plantation colonies.

    (B) The French colonized the eastern seaboard whereas the English primarily colonized in the northeast.

    (C) The French primarily established settlement and plantation colonies whereas the English established trading colonies.

    (D) The French colonized in the southeast whereas the English primarily colonized the northeast.

    (E) The French had hostile relations with Native Americans whereas the English had no major difficulties with them.

62. Which European country colonized the largest amount of land in Africa?

    (A) Germany

    (B) France

    (C) Belgium

    (D) Britain

    (E) Italy

63. Which of the following statements best describes the Vietnam War?

    (A) The Gulf of Tonkin Resolution was a declaration of war on Vietnam by the United States.

    (B) Following the negotiation of the Paris Peace Accords, North Vietnam invaded South Vietnam and captured Saigon.

    (C) Viet Cong from the south launched a guerilla war against the north.

    (D) According to the Nixon Doctrine, the United States would continue to send aid to Vietnam until hostilities ended.

    (E) South Vietnam invaded Laos with the help of the Soviet Union.

64. What is true of social changes in the Soviet Bloc during the Cold War?

    (A) The Soviet Union and the Eastern European nations remained primarily agricultural nations without an industrial base.

    (B) Birth rates rose.

(C) Educational levels remained the same.

(D) Women continued to be paid less than men.

(E) A new elite class of party members arose due to increased levels of education.

65. Women's roles in Europe changed during the Cold War era as compared to the changes following the Industrial Revolution in all of the following ways EXCEPT:

(A) Women agitated for equal roles not defined by gender.

(B) Women were present in the workforce in large numbers, whereas one result of the Industrial Revolution was that they were more confined to the household.

(C) Emphasis on the family increased during the Cold War.

(D) Working women were often married during the Cold War era, whereas following the Industrial Revolution, only lower class single women were often found in the workforce.

(E) Use of birth control measures increased.

66. Which of the following was considered the least successful Mughal ruler?

(A) Babur the Tiger

(B) Humayan

(C) Akbar

(D) Shah Jahan

(E) Jahangir

67. Which of the following kingdoms or empires was NOT part of the Islamic world?

(A) Axum

(B) The Mongols

(C) The Mughals

(D) The Safavid Persians

(E) Ghana

68. The leader who created the Miracle of Chile was

(A) Allende

(B) Pinochet

(C)   Somoza

(D)   Armas

(E)   Perón

69.   What important trends or events does the following map depict?

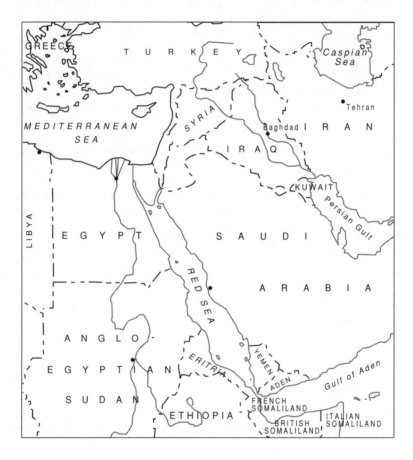

(A)   The Middle East in 1900.

(B)   The Middle East in 1850.

(C)   The Middle East before 1935.

(D)   The Middle East before 1948 but after 1935.

(E)   The Middle East after the end of the Cold War in 1991.

70.   What is true of Marxism and Fascism?

(A)   Both saw the state as an instrument of change to eventually bring about a classless communist society.

(B) Both advocated the proletariat as the revolutionary class and a dictatorship of the proletariat as the means to the realization of a fully communist society in which the state has withered away.

(C) Marxism and fascism are identical and have identical goals.

(D) Fascism is similar to socialism, which is only a means towards an end from a Marxist perspective.

(E) Marxism teaches that a dictatorship of the proletariat or a socialist state is an essential step along the path from capitalism to communism, whereas fascism rejects the Marxist view of progress and sees the state as an end to itself.

STOP
This is the end of Section I.
If time still remains, you may check your work only in this section.
Do not begin Section II until instructed to do so.

SECTION II

Part A — Document-Based Essay

TIME: Reading Period – 10 Minutes
Writing Period – 40 Minutes

DIRECTIONS: The following question is based on accompanying Documents 1–5. Read the documents and write an essay that:

- Has a relevant thesis and supports that thesis with evidence from the documents
- Uses all the documents
- Analyzes the documents
- Accounts for the sources of the documents and analyzes the author's point of view
- Explains the need for additional documentation

You may refer to relevant historical information not mentioned in the documents

---

Using documents 1–5, analyze the Mongol occupation of Russia.

Document 1

Source: John of Plano Carpini, "A History of the Mongols" (c. 1250), in David G. Rowley, *Exploring Russia's Past: Narrative, Sources, Images* vol. I (Upper Saddle River, NJ: Pearson/Prentice Hall, 2006)

Genghis Khan ordained that the army should be organized in such a way that over ten men should be set one man and he is what we call a captain of ten; over ten of these should be placed one, named a captain of a hundred; at thhe head of ten captains of a hundred is placed a soldier known as a captain of a thousand, and over ten captains of a thousand is one man....

When they are in battle, if one or two or three or even more out of a group of ten run away, all are put to death . . . In a word, unless they retreat in a body, all who take flight are put to death.

Document 2

Source: William of Rubruck, French ambassador (c. 1255), in Rowley, *Exploring Russia's Past.*

It is the duty of the [Mongol] women to drive the carts, to load the houses on to them, and to unload them, to milk the cows, to make butter and curd, to dress the skins and sew them... The men make bows and arrows, manufacture bits and make saddles; they build the houses and the carts, they look after the horses and milk the mares... and make skins in which [the mares' milk] is kept.... Both sexes look after the sheep and goats, and sometimes the men, sometimes the women, milk them.

Document 3

Source: *The Chronicle of Novgorod,* in Rowley, *Exploring Russia's Past.*

And when the lawless ones [the Mongols] had already come near and set up battering rams, and took the town and set it on fire ..., the Prince and Princess and Bishop, seeing that the town was on fire and that the people were already perishing, some by fire and others by sword, took refuge in the Church of the Holy Mother of God and shut themselves in the Sacristy. The pagans breaking down the doors, piled up wood and set fire to the sacred church, and slew all, thus they perished, giving up their souls to God....

And who, brothers, fathers, and children, seeing this, God's infliction on the whole Russian Land does not lament? God let the pagans on us for our sins. God brings foreigners on to the land in his wrath, and thus crushed by them they will be reminded of God.

Document 4

Source: "Mongol Charter of Immunity Granted to the Church" (1267) in Rowley, *Exploring Russia's Past.* [W]hatever legally belongs to the [Russian] Church and is duly registered in the records, should be neither occupied, expropriated, alienated or destroyed [byy Mongols]....

Priests who have received benefits from [the Mongols], and who pray for us [the Mongols] and bless us are to continue to enjoy their rights. Those, however, to fail to say prayers or who do not express their genuine feelings are hereby considered sinners and they will be punished accordingly. Finally, those individuals who are not priests, but who pray to God in our behalf, will also enjoy these benefits.

Document 5

Source: *Tver Chronicle* for the year 1237, in Rowley, *Exploring Russia's Past.*

The people, constantly hurt in their pride by thhe pagans [thhe Mongols], complained many times to the grand prince that he should defend them; but he, although he saw thhe injuries done to his people, could not defend them and ordered them to be patient; but the people...could not endure this and waited for a suitable moment.... [And] the people rose in tumult, and sounded the bells... and the entire city turned [against the Mongols].

And after he had heard this, the [Mongol khan] sent an army in winter into the Russian land....; and they killed many people, and took others captive, and put...all the towns to flame.

Part B — Change-Over-Time Essay

TIME: 40 minutes (5 minutes suggested for planning and outlining answer)

DIRECTIONS: Write an essay that answers the following question. Your essay should include:

- A relevant thesis and support for that thesis with appropriate historical evidence
- Answers for all parts of the question
- Use of world historical context to show changes over time
- An analysis of the process of change over time

2. Discuss the political, military, and economic effects of foreign relations on one of the three countries listed below in the nineteenth and twentieth centuries.

China
Japan
Korea

Part C — Comparative Essay

TIME: 40 minutes (5 minutes suggested for planning and outlining answer)

> **DIRECTIONS:** Write an essay that answers the following question. Your essay should include:
>
> - A relevant thesis and support for that thesis with appropriate historical evidence
> - Answers for all parts of the question
> - Direct, relevant comparisons
> - An analysis of relevant reasons for similarities and differences

3. Compare and contrast the geographical environment and the religious and political cultures of **two** of the following ancient societies:

The Egyptians
The Hebrews (or Israelites)
The Mesopotamians

AP WORLD HISTORY

PRACTICE TEST 2

ANSWER KEY

1. (C)	19. (B)	37. (B)	55. (E)
2. (C)	20. (A)	38. (D)	56. (C)
3. (A)	21. (B)	39. (E)	57. (D)
4. (E)	22. (D)	40. (C)	58. (B)
5. (E)	23. (C)	41. (C)	59. (D)
6. (B)	24. (A)	42. (A)	60. (C)
7. (A)	25. (C)	43. (E)	61. (A)
8. (C)	26. (B)	44. (A)	62. (D)
9. (D)	27. (D)	45. (B)	63. (B)
10. (B)	28. (B)	46. (D)	64. (E)
11. (D)	29. (C)	47. (B)	65. (C)
12. (C)	30. (B)	48. (C)	66. (B)
13. (E)	31. (D)	49. (E)	67. (A)
14. (A)	32. (C)	50. (C)	68. (B)
15. (C)	33. (C)	51. (E)	69. (D)
16. (A)	34. (B)	52. (C)	70. (E)
17. (B)	35. (E)	53. (E)	
18. (B)	36. (A)	54. (C)	

DETAILED EXPLANATIONS OF ANSWERS

TEST 2

SECTION I

1.   **(C)**

After the British defeat of China in the Opium Wars, Britain dominated trade in China. Britain colonized India, while France colonized Indonesia. Thailand remained free of European domination, and the Tokugawa expelled foreigners and pursued a policy of isolationism.

2.   **(C)**

Islam does revere Jesus as a human who was a prophet, but Judaism does not. Neither regard Jesus as God incarnate, which is the foundation of Ortho-dox Christianity.

3.   **(A)**

As Siddhartha taught Buddhism, rituals and deities were not important to one's salvation, while he also rejected the atman and the caste system. Hindus believed in numerous deities and worshipped them with rituals; Hindus also believed in the atman and the caste system.

4.   **(E)**

Buddhism has been very influential in Southeast Asia, while Christianity has had a more difficult time taking root in Asia. Christianity arose in the eastern Mediterranean while Buddhism arose in India. Both religions have undergone a profound evolution, characterized by the rise of many differ-ent sects with different interpretations of their founders' teachings. Ashoka converted to Buddhism and enabled its spread beyond the frontiers of India, while the conversion of Constantine legalized Christianity and by the end of the fourth century, Rome had adopted Christianity as the official religion of the Empire.

5.   **(E)**

The oldest hominid fossils are found in Africa.

6.   **(B)**

Agriculture first arose in the Middle East. Rice was the primary crop of China and wheat and barley were cultivated in the Indus River Valley.

7.   **(A)**

Neanderthal had larger brains, used tools, and became extinct around 35,000 years ago. Cro Magnon were known for painting caves.

8.   **(C)**

Many scholars believe the Trojan War resulted from a conflict between Hittites and Mycenaeans, while Ramses II fought the Hittites at Kadesh and negotiated a treaty with them after the battle, after which he married a Hittite princess.

9.   **(D)**

Herodotus analyzed the Persian wars as a clash of cultures between the imperialistic and monarchial Persians and the Greeks, who valued independent, self-rule. Greek religions were polytheistic, while the Persians developed a dualistic religion known as Zoroastrianism.

10.   **(B)**

Both religions were, in fact, the state religions following the conversion of the Persian monarchs and the Roman Emperor Constantine.

11.   **(D)**

Louis XIV controlled the French *parlements* and never summoned the Estates General, while the attempts of the Stuarts to control the Parliament repeatedly failed. Charles I, for example, was forced to summon the Long Parliament, which passed laws that, among other things, controlled the king's right to tax.

12.   **(C)**

The Enlightened Despots may have supported many freedoms, but they implemented their reforms through absolutist methods.

13.   **(E)**

The Chinese grew more suspicious of Christianity following the Jesuit missions, but the Jesuits did bring about a renewal of interest in mathematics, science, and other long-forgotten inventions in China.

14.   **(A)**

In fact, the status of women declined during the Ming and Qing period before the defeat by the British in the Opium Wars, after which women began to be educated and the practice of foot binding was gradually eradicated.

15.   **(C)**

Mao Zedong attempted to rapidly industrialize China, but his Great Leap Forward is often called a Great Leap Backward.

16.   **(A)**

Sun Yat-sen became the first president of the new Republic in 1911.

17.   **(B)**

The Communist Chinese defeated the nationalists and forced them to flee to Taiwan in 1949.

18.   **(B)**

Lebanon fought a civil war between Muslims and Christians. Syria lent support to the predominantly Christian Lebanese army while the PLO continued to launch terrorist attacks against Israel.

19.   **(B)**

Sadat attempted to negotiate a peace with Israel. Saladin is a medieval figure, and Netanyahu is an Israeli prime minister known for his stance against terrorism. Arafat was never leader of Egypt.

20.   **(A)**

Itzhak Rabin was assassinated in 1995 following the 1993 peace accords with the Palestinians.

21.   **(B)**

Ashoka spread Buddhism throughout India through the Rock Pillar Edicts, and eventually his influence led to the spread of Buddhism elsewhere.

22.   **(D)**

Victor of Emmanuel of Sardinia created a new constitution following the Revolutions of 1848, and Sardinia led the drive toward unity.

23.   **(C)**

Zwingli fought with the Swiss against Charles V and led them to reject Catholic customs such as the prohibition of meat during Lent.

24.   **(A)**

Lady Murasaki wrote the *Tale of Genji*, considered by many to be the world's first novel. She lived in the Heian court and her novel is our best account of Heian courtly rituals.

25.   **(C)**

Akhenaton instituted the worship of Aton, the creator god, as the sole god of Egypt and founded a new capital at a place known today as Tel el-Amarna. Akhenaton ruled during the New Kingdom period.

26.   **(B)**

Justinian's general Belisarius succeeded in reconquering much lost territory of the old Roman Empire in the sixth century, but following Justinian's death, much of this territory was later lost again.

27.   **(D)**

The artisans of Benin produced many thousands of heads of their obas during a renaissance of bronze casting in the fifteenth century.

28.   **(B)**

While Roanoke was the first British colony in the New World, it quickly disappeared. Jamestown was the first permanent British settlement in the New World.

29.   **(C)**

Cornwallis's surrender at Yorktown ended the Revolutionary War.

30.   **(B)**

Coronado explored the American southwest and was the first European to see the Grand Canyon.

31.   **(D)**

Carter cut off all aid to the Somozas in Nicaragua and returned the Panama Canal to Panama. The other presidents escalated the Cold War. Reagan supported the Contra in Iran and used inflammatory rhetoric against the Soviet Union; Eisenhower authorized a coup in Guatemala, President Truman's positions after WWII helped to create the Cold War.

32.   **(C)**

The first written records in world history are Cuneiform tablets.

33.   **(C)**

The pyramids were mostly built in the fourth dynasty of Egyptian antiquity, in approximately 3200 B.C.E. The pyramids of Mesoamerica were the last of the structures listed to be built.

34.   **(B)**

Minoan art shows the influence of Egypt but is very distinctive in its approach to color and nature.

35.   **(E)**

Although Solon ruled as sole archon, he did not attempt to establish an autocracy in Greece. By contrast, some historians argue that Caesar did attempt to establish a monarchy along eastern lines. While Caesar did lead a rebellion, Solon did not. Neither tried to equalize the poor and the wealthy, but both did offer citizenship to outsiders. Solon offered citizenship to foreign artisans, while Caesar offered it to non-Romans. Their reform policies were aimed at providing benefits to those who were not of the highest classes.

36.   **(A)**

The Council of Nicaea was held to combat the Arian heresy, one of many heresies that arose during the early Christian period.

37.   **(B)**

Charlemagne led several campaigns against the Saxons before succeeding in forcibly converting them.

38.   **(D)**

Both Gregory VII fought the German emperor Henry IV over lay investiture and Boniface VIII fought Philip IV over the issue of secular taxation of the Church. While neither can be said to have decisively won their battles with secular rulers, they were not dominated by them either.

39.   **(E)**

The map reflects countries that did not exist before the independence movements following World War II, such as the Democratic Republic of the Congo and Zimbabwe.

40.   **(C)**

If one combines all the columns representing areas of Asia, Asia has the greatest amount of poverty of any region in the world today. The chart reflects the global inequities that characterize the world today.

41.   **(C)**

While the birth and infant mortality rates have dropped worldwide, the average life expectancy has increased. The population of the world continues to grow.

42.   **(A)**

Note that the map does not indicate what goods Asia received in return for its spices, coffee, tea, and other goods.

43.   **(E)**

The Maya had no beasts of burden before the arrival of the Spaniards, and cattle, sheep, goats, and camels all arrived in Africa through the migrations of Asiatic peoples such as the Hyksos, who introduced the horse to Africa.

44.   **(A)**

As work outside the home became less available to women, more chose to enter marriages. The illegitimacy rate dropped.

45.   **(B)**

The revolutions of 1848 were led by liberals, and their failure significantly reduced support for liberalism.

46.   **(D)**

Krushchev's policy of "peaceful coexistence" backed away from revolutionary fervor and attracted the animosity of the Chinese Communists under Mao Zedong.

47.   **(B)**

As democratization began to take root across eastern Europe, the Soviet bloc started to unravel, and even China felt the effects of growing unrest. The chain of events included (1) Chinese students rallying for democratic reforms in Tiananmen Square (top photo) on June 3–4, 1989, before hundreds were killed under Deng Xiaoping's repressive regime, and (2) the fall of the Berlin Wall, which presaged East Germany's hard-line communists being forced from power in October 1989.

48.   **(C)**

Both Luther and Calvin believed in predestination and both denied the doctrine of transubstantiation as well as the Biblical basis of the Catholic seven sacraments. Luther, however, advocated for consubstantiation, while Zwingli taught that the Eucharist was primarily symbolic.

49.   **(E)**

Japan moved towards democracy, but never extended universal suffrage to women. The Taisho Democracy itself was undercut by the demands of increasing industrialization.

50.   **(C)**

The Majlis in Persia attempted to refuse to ratify a treaty putting British officers in positions of power and thus in control of Persia, but did not succeed.

51.   **(E)**

While the reforms of Lenin and Deng Xiaoping had some elements in common, economic prosperity following the four modernizations was greater in China than in Russia during the time of Lenin. Even during the post World War II era, Russian production centered on heavy goods and not consumer goods, while under Deng Xiaoping, China entered the age of mass consumer goods.

52.   **(C)**

Slaves fulfilled many functions in Islamic society, and even played a role in the Islamic armies. Slavery was not racially based and the Qur'an encouraged masters to treat their slaves fairly and even to release them.

53.   **(E)**

The extensive trading networks of the Islamic world interlocked cultures across a massive amount of territory from Spain, to Africa, to the Baghdad.

54.   **(C)**

Abu Bakr led a series of raids or *razzia*. Islamic expansion was stopped in Europe by the Franks at the Battle of Poitiers and by the Byzantines in the east in the eighth century. Earlier, however, the Muslims had defeated the Byzantines at Yarmuk.

55.   **(E)**

Inequities between Britain and other European nations were evident during the first Industrial Revolution, while during the second, Germany led the way but other countries, such as those of Southern and Eastern Europe, lagged behind.

56.   **(C)**

Japan discouraged foreign investments, while Russia encouraged them. Japan was successful in creating an economy that produced more for exportation than it took in from imports, while in Russia, exports never exceeded imports. Japan provided advanced western education in mathematics and the sciences creating a class of industrial professionals while Russia never succeeded in creating a middle class of professionals. Japan financed industrialization in the Meiji period with a tax on agriculture, while Russia primarily used foreign capital to finance industrialization.

57.   **(D)**

The *dhimma* of Umar, for example, makes it clear that Christians are not to be flagrantly open about the practice of their faith, nor are they to seek additional converts. In other parts of the Islamic world, such as in Islamic India, Muslim rulers were even less tolerant of faiths other than Islam and razed new Hindu temples to the ground.

58.   **(B)**

The French Declaration of the Rights of Man and Citizen distinguished between active and passive citizens and did not grant women the right of participation, while the American Revolution did not end the practice of slavery nor were women enfranchised.

59.   **(D)**

Britain was the first country to abolish slavery, followed by Russia, the United States, Portugal, and Brazil.

60.   **(C)**

While peasants were involved in many of the mass uprisings of the French revolution, it was the Third Estate that led the French Revolution, and many leaders of the Third Estate, according to modern scholars, had much in common with the class of capitalists Marxists referred to as the bourgeoisie. In Russia, it was primarily the proletariat class that initiated the Revolution.

61.   **(A)**

Because the French were more interested in trade, they tended to have positive relations with the Native Americans. The French colonized Canada and other areas while most English settlements were in the northeast and along the eastern seaboard. English colonies tended to be settlement and plantation colonies.

62.   **(D)**

Britain added 4.25 million square miles of territory to her empire.

63.   **(B)**

The United States never declared war on Vietnam, but opposed the Communist regime in North Vietnam. The Gulf of Tonkin resolution authorized the use of force against the North Vietnamese but did not declare war, which was always controversial especially among those who protested the war.

64.   **(E)**

Due to rapid industrialization, the Soviet Union and Eastern bloc nations changed from agricultural nations to industrialized ones. Education increased and, although women's roles in the workforce increased, their status remained below that of men. Better education created a new class of professionals and had an impact on party structure.

65.   **(C)**

As married women entered the workforce, their roles as mothers and wives were no longer emphasized to the extent they had been following the Industrial Revolution.

66.   **(B)**

Humayan lost much of Babur's territory in the early part of his reign and, although he later recovered much of it, he is considered the weakest of the Mughal rulers.

67.   **(A)**

Axum was a Christian kingdom of North Africa, and because it often took in Islamic refugees during the early period of Islam, Muslims never attempted to conquer it.

68.   **(B)**

Pinochet instituted a series of reforms that radically transformed the economy of Chile, but he was one of the most brutal dictators in history.

69.   **(D)**

The map reflects the Turkish Republic, placing it at least after World War I. It does not reflect modern Israel, which was declared a nation in 1948, but it does reflect Iran, the name taken by Persia in 1935. Note the references to European colonies still in Africa. By the 1960s, most African colonies had achieved independence from European powers.

70.   **(E)**

Marxism and fascism have significant differences, although some scholars maintain that those who espouse both views often rule as totalitarian dictators. However, their differences are equally as significant as their similarities.

SECTION II

Sample Answer to Document–Based Essay

The Mongol empire had very important long-term consequences. One major consequence is that this empire, which spread from East Asia into Eastern Europe, made it easier for goods, missionaries, merchants (such as Marco Polo), and adventures to travel the Silk Highway. This led to increased interest in Asia among Europeans and to a rising level of commercial exchange between Asia and Europe. This set the stage for the Age of Discovery, which would lead to the global empires of the French, Dutch, Portuguese, Spanish and British. In a sense, the Mongol empire begat several empires whose actions would, in turn, create many modern nations.

The documents above reveal many things about the Mongols and their occupation of Russia. For one thing, document #1 points to the order and discipline among the Mongol forces that account for their conquests. Chingiz Khan (also known as Genghis Khan), the greatest Mongol leader, established a clear chain of command among his forces and he instilled within them a sense of unity and discipline. He did this partly by promising loot to his conquering troops and, as we see in this document, partly by the threat of death for shirkers. Mongol soldiers were not paid; they relied on loot to make a living. That is one thing that attracted them to war. Fear of deadly punishment kept them fighting once battle began. Because the Mongols were a normadic people, Mongol fighters did not have the burden of being away from "home," a trial soldiers in their empires before and after the Mongols *did* have to live with.

In addition to being fierce and disciplined fighters, the Mongols employed weaponry and tactics that gave them advantages over their foes. As we see in document #2, Mongol men made bows and arrows and tended to horses. This reminds us that Mongols fought with powerful bows and arrows, and they fought mainly on horseback. Infantry were no match for them. Document #2 also suggests that Mongol women accompanied men during their campaigns, and Mongol men and women divided some tasks and shared others. As in the majority of the world's societies until modern times, Mongol men dominated in the public sphere and women cared primarily for homes and children.

In the western part of their empire, the Mongols remained in Russia the longest. Document #3 reveals how ruthless the Mongols could be, and how little they cared about sacred places when in battle. Document #3 also shows that, as was common before the modern period, the Russians interpreted the Mongols' ruthlessness as God's punishment for sin.

Following conquest, the Mongols usually allowed locals to run their own affairs, so long as they paid tribute and homage to the *khan*—the Mongol who ruled a region of the vast empire. Mongols would sometimes adopt the dominant religions of the regions they conquered. In China, many became Buddhist; further west, many became Muslim. In Russia, churches were exempt from paying taxes. This tolerance for local institutions is expressed in document #4, where we read that Russian church property "should be neither occupied, expropriated, alienated or destroyed [by Mongols]."

Of course, praying for and adhering to the rules of the Mongols required Russians to, at least, appear to have changed their opinions of the Golden Horde, as the Mongol occupiers were called. At first, the Mongols were seen as pagan, lawless, and godless scourges used by God to punish the people. Now Mongols had to be tolerated and prayed for. Sometimes, during the occupation, Russians would rise up against the Mongols, as we see in document #5. When this happened, Mongol ruthlessness returned: Russians were slaughtered and towns were burned.

The Mongol empire lasted into the sixteenth century, when it disintegrated as all empires eventually do.

Analysis of Essay

The first paragraph provides the reader with background and broad context. The first sentence of the second paragraph indicates that the writer intends to deal with each of the documents, and the essay does summarize and comment on the general themes of each of the documents. The essay also ties the documents together into a seamless narrative, adding useful information that is not included in the documents. The essay quotes from only one document, but the narrative makes it clear that the writer understands and is able to contextualize each of the documents.

Sample answer to Change-Over-Time Essay

In the ninety-nine years that passed between 1853 and 1952, Japan was fundamentally transformed, largely as a result of its interactions with Western powers. Through this period Japan admired Western technology while wanting to hold Western culture at bay. In this period Japan also became the dominant Asian military power.

Before 1853 Japan had little contact with the outside world, but in that year the American admiral Matthew Perry announced to the Japanese that he would return the next year and that the American government expected Japan to begin a trading relationship. Perry's display of American weaponry convinced the Japanese that they should agree with the Americans' demand. Before long, Japanese were being exposed to some of the wonders of Western industrialization—for example, the telegraph—and to American popular culture such as minstrel shows. The Japanese believed that Westerners were barbarians, but they also believed that they should learn about Western technology. In 1858 Japan and the United States exchanged diplomatic representatives.

In Japan there was considerable political debate about relations with foreigners; the shogunate (military command) was in favor of signing treaties with Western powers, the emperor was not. Relations with Westerners and the wealth and hardship this created led to power struggles between the shogunate and the daimyō (large land-holders). Some worried that Japan looked weak in a world where nations were competing for territory and resources, and others were concerned that Japan would be spoiled by Christianity. Some radical anti-Western Japanese called shishi attacked foreign sailors and merchants, and they tried to capture the monarch's palace in order to establish an anti-western monarchy. Japan experienced small-scale civil war between forces in favor of and opposed to relations with the Western powers. The shogunate was abolished in the late 1860s as a result, and Japan's political system theoretically united around the emperor.

Japanese loyalty to the emperor is one reason Emperor Hirohito was allowed to keep his position after World War II. While the victorious Allies did require Hirohito to deny that he was a god, they believed that removing the emperor would create political chaos in Japan.

By the end of the 1800s, Japan had adopted a written constitution that, in different parts, resembled the constitutions of Germany, Britain and the United States. In less than fifty years, Japan also became a world power. It defeated China in war in the 1890s, and Japan would dominate parts of China until the end of the Second World War. Japan also controlled Korea and defeated Russia in a short war in 1905. For a brief period (in the early 1940s, Japan occupied Indochina (Vietnam, Laos and Cambodia), Thailand, Burma, Indonesia, the Philippines and even the westernmost islands of Alaska. In December 1941, Japan delivered the largest surprise attack in American history to that time at Pearl Harbor in Hawaii, and, in terms of the number of men taken prisoner, Japan dealt Britain the greatest defeat of its history when Japan captured Singapore.

From the late 1800s up to the brink of World War II, Japan faced major challenges. One was that Japan could not provide for its own growing population. Consequently, many Japanese emigrated—for example to Hawaii and California. In the latter place Japanese faced discrimination and, as a result, there was some war talk between Japan and the U.S. in the first decade of the 1900s.

Another problem Japan had was that, being poor in natural resources, Japan could not feed the population that remained in Japan. This is one thing that drove Japan to acquire colonies in Asia. Until 1929, Japan made a great deal of money exporting silk and textiles, and with that money it purchased natural resources it needed. But the Great Depression led to a substantial reduction in Japanese exports.

A third problem was that Japan's growing military, especially its navy, needed steel and oil, but Japan could not produce nearly a sufficient amount of these goods on its own. When the U.S. placed an embargo of steel and oil on Japan because it had invaded and occupied China, Japan felt compelled to attack the U.S. fleet in Hawaii and to occupy the Dutch East Indies, which had oil resources.

The attack on Pearl Harbor triggered war between the U.S. and its Allies against Japan. The war in the Pacific was especially vicious, a "war without mercy." Partly because Japan's economy could not sustain itself, let alone a long war, Japan soon found itself on the defense, being pushed out of the territories it occupied and toward mainland Japan. The dropping of two atomic bombs on the Japanese cities of Nagasaki and Hiroshima in August of 1945 ended the Second World War.

Following the war, Japan was militarily occupied by the U.S. military. A U.S.-style constitution was imposed on the country and Japan was brought into the American sphere of influence. Japan's new constitution prohibited it from engaging in warfare except for purposes of defense. Japan benefited from not having to rebuild a large military and from trade relations with the U.S. and other countries. By the time the government of Japan was handed back to the Japanese in 1952, the country was in a position to become one of the great economic powers of the world.

Discussion of Essay

The last sentence of the first paragraph suggests why Japan was chosen for the essay, though the mention in the essay of Korea and China suggest to the reader that the essayist could have written on them as well. Obviously, the essay briefly touches on topics that could fill dozens of books, but it provides enough detail to suggest to the reader that, had the writer had more time, the essay would be longer. Assertions are supported with concrete details. The requirements of the essay left periodization up to the writer. In this case, the opening of Japan in 1853 and the end of American political control of the country in 1952 provided good beginning and end points.

Sample answer to Comparative Essay

The Mesopotamians and Egyptians had many things in common. Their cultures were built around great rivers, for example, and, with the exception of a brief period in Egypt, they were polytheists. They both developed written languages—cuneiform among the Mesopotamians, hieroglyphics among the Egyptians—and they engaged in trade with other peoples. They also build great monuments—ziggurats in Mesopotamia, pyramids in Egypt. But, as this essay will show, the Mesopotamians and Egyptians were also quite different.

Some of the key differences between the Mesopotamians and Egyptians appear as soon as one begins to compare their similarities. The Mesopotamian societies of Sumer, Akkadia and Babylon relied on the Tigris and Euphrates rivers; Egyptian civilization formed on the banks and delta of the Nile River. But where the Mesopotamians relied on elaborate canals, the Egyptians relied on the annual flooding of the Nile. And where the usually predictable patterns of the Nile's flooding led to a focus among Egyptians on orderliness in this world and in the afterlife, the unpredictability of the Tigris and Euphrates rivers contributed to the Mesopotamian worldview that included unpredictable gods who would inflict harm on people for no good reason. The importance of the rivers' dangerous flooding to the Mesopotamians is suggested by the story of the flood recounted in the Epic of Gilgamesh—a story about irrational, violent gods who have little concern for the well-being of people.

Politically, ancient Egypt was more united that Mesopotamia, which was dominated by city-states. There were important Mesopotamian empires, such as Sargon's in the third century B.C.E. and the dynasty of Ur III a little later, but compared to the Egyptians' society, these empires did not last long. The Babylonian king Hammurabi built an empire in the second century B.C.E., and he is most remembered for his elaborate written laws, which include the phrase "an eye for an eye."

Except for a period during the early third century B.C.E., Egyptian kings maintained unity based on their ability, through religious practice, to ensure the annual flooding of the Nile. Egyptians considered their kings, eventually called pharaohs, to be divine. As long as a king ruled according to the principles of Maat (the goddess of order and stability), all was well. The pyramids that still stand in Egypt were tombs for Egyptian kings. With them were buried things that would be useful, or would bring them pleasure, in the afterlife—such as jewelry and furniture.

One Egyptian pharaoh, Akhenaten, promoted a kind of monotheism—he believed that Aten—was the one and only true god. After his death, Egyptian religion returned to polytheism. The Book of the Dead instructed Egyptians on how to handle the trials and challenges they would face after this life. Generally speaking, Egyptians believed there was much to look forward to in the next world. Mesopotamians, on the other hand, believed that the afterlife was a dreary place of shadows, wandering, and mourning.

In both societies priests were important and prestigious. Both societies employed slaves. In Egypt women could own property, bring lawsuits, and conduct business affairs, but they could not serve in the government bureaucracy since they were barred from formal education. In Mesopotamia's cities, women controlled their homes and had authority over servants, while public affairs were left to men.

The greatest similarity and difference between ancient Mesopotamia and Egypt stems from their reliance on large rivers. The Nile River, being predictable and beneficial, helped to create a culture that was orderly, relatively peaceful and long-lasting. The Tigris and Euphrates rivers, being unpredictable and often deadly, helped to create cultures that were combative, of relatively short endurance, and that believed in gods who were out to get people—if they paid attention to people at all.

Analysis of Essay

The thesis of the essay is stated in the first paragraph. This paragraph suggests that the writer possesses some detailed knowledge about ancient Mesopotamia and Egypt. It also reveals that the writer understands that comparing and contrasting societies is a complicated process.

The focus on the importance of the Nile, Tigris and Euphrates rivers addresses geography; the discussion of different monarchs and the place of women in Mesopotamia and Egypt addresses politics. The religious cultures of Mesopotamia and Egypt get the most attention.

Answer Sheets

AP World History
PRACTICE TEST 1

ANSWER SHEET

1. Ⓐ Ⓑ Ⓒ Ⓓ Ⓔ
2. Ⓐ Ⓑ Ⓒ Ⓓ Ⓔ
3. Ⓐ Ⓑ Ⓒ Ⓓ Ⓔ
4. Ⓐ Ⓑ Ⓒ Ⓓ Ⓔ
5. Ⓐ Ⓑ Ⓒ Ⓓ Ⓔ
6. Ⓐ Ⓑ Ⓒ Ⓓ Ⓔ
7. Ⓐ Ⓑ Ⓒ Ⓓ Ⓔ
8. Ⓐ Ⓑ Ⓒ Ⓓ Ⓔ
9. Ⓐ Ⓑ Ⓒ Ⓓ Ⓔ
10. Ⓐ Ⓑ Ⓒ Ⓓ Ⓔ
11. Ⓐ Ⓑ Ⓒ Ⓓ Ⓔ
12. Ⓐ Ⓑ Ⓒ Ⓓ Ⓔ
13. Ⓐ Ⓑ Ⓒ Ⓓ Ⓔ
14. Ⓐ Ⓑ Ⓒ Ⓓ Ⓔ
15. Ⓐ Ⓑ Ⓒ Ⓓ Ⓔ
16. Ⓐ Ⓑ Ⓒ Ⓓ Ⓔ
17. Ⓐ Ⓑ Ⓒ Ⓓ Ⓔ
18. Ⓐ Ⓑ Ⓒ Ⓓ Ⓔ
19. Ⓐ Ⓑ Ⓒ Ⓓ Ⓔ
20. Ⓐ Ⓑ Ⓒ Ⓓ Ⓔ
21. Ⓐ Ⓑ Ⓒ Ⓓ Ⓔ
22. Ⓐ Ⓑ Ⓒ Ⓓ Ⓔ
23. Ⓐ Ⓑ Ⓒ Ⓓ Ⓔ
24. Ⓐ Ⓑ Ⓒ Ⓓ Ⓔ

25. Ⓐ Ⓑ Ⓒ Ⓓ Ⓔ
26. Ⓐ Ⓑ Ⓒ Ⓓ Ⓔ
27. Ⓐ Ⓑ Ⓒ Ⓓ Ⓔ
28. Ⓐ Ⓑ Ⓒ Ⓓ Ⓔ
29. Ⓐ Ⓑ Ⓒ Ⓓ Ⓔ
30. Ⓐ Ⓑ Ⓒ Ⓓ Ⓔ
31. Ⓐ Ⓑ Ⓒ Ⓓ Ⓔ
32. Ⓐ Ⓑ Ⓒ Ⓓ Ⓔ
33. Ⓐ Ⓑ Ⓒ Ⓓ Ⓔ
34. Ⓐ Ⓑ Ⓒ Ⓓ Ⓔ
35. Ⓐ Ⓑ Ⓒ Ⓓ Ⓔ
36. Ⓐ Ⓑ Ⓒ Ⓓ Ⓔ
37. Ⓐ Ⓑ Ⓒ Ⓓ Ⓔ
38. Ⓐ Ⓑ Ⓒ Ⓓ Ⓔ
39. Ⓐ Ⓑ Ⓒ Ⓓ Ⓔ
40. Ⓐ Ⓑ Ⓒ Ⓓ Ⓔ
41. Ⓐ Ⓑ Ⓒ Ⓓ Ⓔ
42. Ⓐ Ⓑ Ⓒ Ⓓ Ⓔ
43. Ⓐ Ⓑ Ⓒ Ⓓ Ⓔ
44. Ⓐ Ⓑ Ⓒ Ⓓ Ⓔ
45. Ⓐ Ⓑ Ⓒ Ⓓ Ⓔ
46. Ⓐ Ⓑ Ⓒ Ⓓ Ⓔ
47. Ⓐ Ⓑ Ⓒ Ⓓ Ⓔ
48. Ⓐ Ⓑ Ⓒ Ⓓ Ⓔ

49. Ⓐ Ⓑ Ⓒ Ⓓ Ⓔ
50. Ⓐ Ⓑ Ⓒ Ⓓ Ⓔ
51. Ⓐ Ⓑ Ⓒ Ⓓ Ⓔ
52. Ⓐ Ⓑ Ⓒ Ⓓ Ⓔ
53. Ⓐ Ⓑ Ⓒ Ⓓ Ⓔ
54. Ⓐ Ⓑ Ⓒ Ⓓ Ⓔ
55. Ⓐ Ⓑ Ⓒ Ⓓ Ⓔ
56. Ⓐ Ⓑ Ⓒ Ⓓ Ⓔ
57. Ⓐ Ⓑ Ⓒ Ⓓ Ⓔ
58. Ⓐ Ⓑ Ⓒ Ⓓ Ⓔ
59. Ⓐ Ⓑ Ⓒ Ⓓ Ⓔ
60. Ⓐ Ⓑ Ⓒ Ⓓ Ⓔ
61. Ⓐ Ⓑ Ⓒ Ⓓ Ⓔ
62. Ⓐ Ⓑ Ⓒ Ⓓ Ⓔ
63. Ⓐ Ⓑ Ⓒ Ⓓ Ⓔ
64. Ⓐ Ⓑ Ⓒ Ⓓ Ⓔ
65. Ⓐ Ⓑ Ⓒ Ⓓ Ⓔ
66. Ⓐ Ⓑ Ⓒ Ⓓ Ⓔ
67. Ⓐ Ⓑ Ⓒ Ⓓ Ⓔ
68. Ⓐ Ⓑ Ⓒ Ⓓ Ⓔ
69. Ⓐ Ⓑ Ⓒ Ⓓ Ⓔ
70. Ⓐ Ⓑ Ⓒ Ⓓ Ⓔ

AP World History
PRACTICE TEST 2

ANSWER SHEET

1. Ⓐ Ⓑ Ⓒ Ⓓ Ⓔ
2. Ⓐ Ⓑ Ⓒ Ⓓ Ⓔ
3. Ⓐ Ⓑ Ⓒ Ⓓ Ⓔ
4. Ⓐ Ⓑ Ⓒ Ⓓ Ⓔ
5. Ⓐ Ⓑ Ⓒ Ⓓ Ⓔ
6. Ⓐ Ⓑ Ⓒ Ⓓ Ⓔ
7. Ⓐ Ⓑ Ⓒ Ⓓ Ⓔ
8. Ⓐ Ⓑ Ⓒ Ⓓ Ⓔ
9. Ⓐ Ⓑ Ⓒ Ⓓ Ⓔ
10. Ⓐ Ⓑ Ⓒ Ⓓ Ⓔ
11. Ⓐ Ⓑ Ⓒ Ⓓ Ⓔ
12. Ⓐ Ⓑ Ⓒ Ⓓ Ⓔ
13. Ⓐ Ⓑ Ⓒ Ⓓ Ⓔ
14. Ⓐ Ⓑ Ⓒ Ⓓ Ⓔ
15. Ⓐ Ⓑ Ⓒ Ⓓ Ⓔ
16. Ⓐ Ⓑ Ⓒ Ⓓ Ⓔ
17. Ⓐ Ⓑ Ⓒ Ⓓ Ⓔ
18. Ⓐ Ⓑ Ⓒ Ⓓ Ⓔ
19. Ⓐ Ⓑ Ⓒ Ⓓ Ⓔ
20. Ⓐ Ⓑ Ⓒ Ⓓ Ⓔ
21. Ⓐ Ⓑ Ⓒ Ⓓ Ⓔ
22. Ⓐ Ⓑ Ⓒ Ⓓ Ⓔ
23. Ⓐ Ⓑ Ⓒ Ⓓ Ⓔ
24. Ⓐ Ⓑ Ⓒ Ⓓ Ⓔ

25. Ⓐ Ⓑ Ⓒ Ⓓ Ⓔ
26. Ⓐ Ⓑ Ⓒ Ⓓ Ⓔ
27. Ⓐ Ⓑ Ⓒ Ⓓ Ⓔ
28. Ⓐ Ⓑ Ⓒ Ⓓ Ⓔ
29. Ⓐ Ⓑ Ⓒ Ⓓ Ⓔ
30. Ⓐ Ⓑ Ⓒ Ⓓ Ⓔ
31. Ⓐ Ⓑ Ⓒ Ⓓ Ⓔ
32. Ⓐ Ⓑ Ⓒ Ⓓ Ⓔ
33. Ⓐ Ⓑ Ⓒ Ⓓ Ⓔ
34. Ⓐ Ⓑ Ⓒ Ⓓ Ⓔ
35. Ⓐ Ⓑ Ⓒ Ⓓ Ⓔ
36. Ⓐ Ⓑ Ⓒ Ⓓ Ⓔ
37. Ⓐ Ⓑ Ⓒ Ⓓ Ⓔ
38. Ⓐ Ⓑ Ⓒ Ⓓ Ⓔ
39. Ⓐ Ⓑ Ⓒ Ⓓ Ⓔ
40. Ⓐ Ⓑ Ⓒ Ⓓ Ⓔ
41. Ⓐ Ⓑ Ⓒ Ⓓ Ⓔ
42. Ⓐ Ⓑ Ⓒ Ⓓ Ⓔ
43. Ⓐ Ⓑ Ⓒ Ⓓ Ⓔ
44. Ⓐ Ⓑ Ⓒ Ⓓ Ⓔ
45. Ⓐ Ⓑ Ⓒ Ⓓ Ⓔ
46. Ⓐ Ⓑ Ⓒ Ⓓ Ⓔ
47. Ⓐ Ⓑ Ⓒ Ⓓ Ⓔ
48. Ⓐ Ⓑ Ⓒ Ⓓ Ⓔ

49. Ⓐ Ⓑ Ⓒ Ⓓ Ⓔ
50. Ⓐ Ⓑ Ⓒ Ⓓ Ⓔ
51. Ⓐ Ⓑ Ⓒ Ⓓ Ⓔ
52. Ⓐ Ⓑ Ⓒ Ⓓ Ⓔ
53. Ⓐ Ⓑ Ⓒ Ⓓ Ⓔ
54. Ⓐ Ⓑ Ⓒ Ⓓ Ⓔ
55. Ⓐ Ⓑ Ⓒ Ⓓ Ⓔ
56. Ⓐ Ⓑ Ⓒ Ⓓ Ⓔ
57. Ⓐ Ⓑ Ⓒ Ⓓ Ⓔ
58. Ⓐ Ⓑ Ⓒ Ⓓ Ⓔ
59. Ⓐ Ⓑ Ⓒ Ⓓ Ⓔ
60. Ⓐ Ⓑ Ⓒ Ⓓ Ⓔ
61. Ⓐ Ⓑ Ⓒ Ⓓ Ⓔ
62. Ⓐ Ⓑ Ⓒ Ⓓ Ⓔ
63. Ⓐ Ⓑ Ⓒ Ⓓ Ⓔ
64. Ⓐ Ⓑ Ⓒ Ⓓ Ⓔ
65. Ⓐ Ⓑ Ⓒ Ⓓ Ⓔ
66. Ⓐ Ⓑ Ⓒ Ⓓ Ⓔ
67. Ⓐ Ⓑ Ⓒ Ⓓ Ⓔ
68. Ⓐ Ⓑ Ⓒ Ⓓ Ⓔ
69. Ⓐ Ⓑ Ⓒ Ⓓ Ⓔ
70. Ⓐ Ⓑ Ⓒ Ⓓ Ⓔ

INDEX

Index

PHOTO CREDITS

INSTALLING REA's TEST*ware*®

SYSTEM REQUIREMENTS

Pentium 75 MHz (300 MHz recommended) or a higher or compatible processor; Microsoft Windows 98 or later; 64 MB available RAM; Internet Explorer 5.5 or higher

INSTALLATION

1. Insert the AP World History TEST*ware*® CD-ROM into the CD-ROM drive.
2. If the installation doesn't begin automatically, from the Start Menu choose the RUN command. When the RUN dialog box appears, type d:\setup (where D is the letter of your CD-ROM drive) at the prompt and click OK.
3. The installation process will begin. A dialog box proposing the directory "Program Files\REA\AP_WorldHistory" will appear. If the name and location are suitable, click OK. If you wish to specify a different name or location, type it in and click OK.
4. Start the AP World History TEST*ware*® application by double-clicking on the icon.

REA's AP World History TEST*ware*® is **EASY** to **LEARN AND USE**. To achieve maximum benefits, we recommend that you take a few minutes to go through the on-screen tutorial on your computer. The "screen buttons" are also explained here to familiarize you with the program.

TECHNICAL SUPPORT

REA's TEST*ware*® is backed by customer and technical support. For questions about **installation or operation of your software**, contact us at:

Research & Education Association
Phone: (732) 819-8880 (9 a.m. to 5 p.m. ET, Monday–Friday)
Fax: (732) 819-8808
Website: http://www.rea.com
E-mail: info@rea.com

Note to Windows XP Users: In order for the TEST*ware*® to function properly, please install and run the application under the same computer administrator-level user account. Installing the TEST*ware*® as one user and running it as another could cause file-access path conflicts.

NOTES

The ESSENTIALS®
of HISTORY

REA's **Essentials of History** series offers a new approach to the study of history that is different from what has been available previously. Compared with conventional history outlines, the **Essentials of History** offer far more detail, with fuller explanations and interpretations of historical events and developments. Compared with voluminous historical tomes and textbooks, the **Essentials of History** offer a far more concise, less ponderous overview of each of the periods they cover.

The **Essentials of History** provide quick access to needed information, and will serve as handy reference sources at all times. The **Essentials of History** are prepared with REA's customary concern for high professional quality and student needs.

UNITED STATES HISTORY
1500 to 1789 From Colony to Republic
1789 to 1841 The Developing Nation
1841 to 1877 Westward Expansion & the Civil War
1877 to 1912 Industrialism, Foreign Expansion & the Progressive Era
1912 to 1941 World War I, the Depression & the New Deal
America since 1941: Emergence as a World Power

WORLD HISTORY
Ancient History (4500 BCE to 500 CE)
The Emergence of Western Civilization
Medieval History (500 to 1450 CE)
The Middle Ages

EUROPEAN HISTORY
1450 to 1648 The Renaissance, Reformation & Wars of Religion
1648 to 1789 Bourbon, Baroque & the Enlightenment
1789 to 1848 Revolution & the New European Order
1848 to 1914 Realism & Materialism
1914 to 1935 World War I & Europe in Crisis
Europe since 1935: From World War II to the Demise of Communism

CANADIAN HISTORY
Pre-Colonization to 1867
The Beginning of a Nation
1867 to Present
The Post-Confederate Nation

If you would like more information about any of these books,
complete the coupon below and return it to us or visit your local bookstore.

Research & Education Association
61 Ethel Road W., Piscataway, NJ 08854
Phone: (732) 819-8880   **website: www.rea.com**

Please send me more information about your History Essentials® books.

Name _____

Address _____

City _____ State _____ Zip _____